Counterpoint and Compositional Process in the Time of Dufay

Perspectives from German Musicology

EDITED AND TRANSLATED BY
KEVIN N. MOLL

D0168987

GARLAND PUBLISHING, INC.
NEW YORK AND LONDON
1997

Library of Congress Cataloging-in-Publication Data

Counterpoint and compositional process in the time of Dufay : perspectives
    from German musicology / translated and edited by Kevin N. Moll.
        p.   cm. — (Garland reference library of the humanities ; vol.
    1982) (Criticism and analysis of early music ; vol. 2)
        Includes bibliographical references (p.   ) and index.
        ISBN 0-8153-2346-8 (alk. paper)
        1. Dufay, Guillaume, d. 1474—Criticism and interpretation.   I. Moll,
    Kevin N.   II. Series.   III. Series: Criticism and analysis of early music ; vol. 2.
    ML410.D83C68   1997
    782'.0092—dc21   97-25691
                                                                        CIP
                                                                        MN

Printed on acid-free, 250-year-life paper
Manufactured in the United States of America

Counterpoint and Compositional Process in the Time of Dufay

CRITICISM AND ANALYSIS OF EARLY MUSIC
VOLUME 2
GARLAND REFERENCE LIBRARY OF THE HUMANITIES
VOLUME 1982

CRITICISM AND ANALYSIS OF EARLY MUSIC

JESSIE ANN OWENS, *Series Editor*

TONAL STRUCTURES
IN EARLY MUSIC
edited by Christle Collins Judd

COUNTERPOINT AND
COMPOSITIONAL PROCESS
IN THE TIME OF DUFAY
*Perspectives from German
Musicology*
edited and translated by
Kevin N. Moll

To the spirit of

John Boronow

CONTENTS

SERIES EDITOR'S FOREWORD

Jessie Ann Owens

Brandeis University

Recent years have seen a critical reassessment of our approach to early music. Musicians, scholars, and critics have been searching for ways of talking about and reacting to the music that engage it not from the perspectives of later music but rather on its own terms. These new approaches would not be possible without the scholarship of the previous decades. The discovery and cataloguing of musical sources, the preparation of critical editions, and the investigation of archival documents have furnished important information about composers, performers, patrons, and institutions that supported the creation and performance of early music. Building on this work, the editors of these volumes now seek to develop and explore analytical methodologies for the discussion of early music as music.

Analytic methods are not easily found for early music. The theorists of the time had their own agendas, and they do not provide models that suit our purposes. As a consequence, many twentieth-century scholars have chosen approaches that reflect their own beliefs about early music and its relation to later music. While some continue to rely on common practice tonality as a prism through which to view early music, others have begun to explore methods that respect the integrity and self-sufficiency of the languages of early music.

We offer a forum for exploration of particular topics, from both a methodological and critical viewpoint. Our premise is that we can best develop new methodologies by encouraging debate. We will explore compositional procedures, tonal structures, musical borrowing, and other topics, focusing both on individual compositions and on theoretical systems. We seek to encourage critical writing about music that will be useful to performers, listeners, and scholars.

FOREWORD

Theodor Göllner

Director, *Institut für Musikwissenschaft,*

University of Munich

In the second half of the twentieth century, scholars in musicology have achieved impressive advances, especially in the cataloguing of sources, the editing of music, and lexicography. Less evident, and consequently either not mentioned at all in current methodological discussions or, more recently, sorely missed, are investigations into the nature of the music itself, its compositional techniques, that method known in German as *Satztechnik*. Since this involves the very substance of the music, we cannot attempt to place music in the context of the other arts or to culture as a whole without adequate knowledge of its principles. As a result the ever-more-pressing demands of recent years for a change in priorities within the discipline must be regarded as legitimate. In particular, the methodological discussions within the English-speaking countries have pursued this goal for more than a decade now, and these, in the company of other new theories, must be understood as a reaction against the older, once-dominant but still widely practiced, positivistic approach. As we know, this is generally identified with the "founding generation" of American musicology, consisting mainly of European emigré scholars.

The interest in *Satztechnik*, however, is not new. Almost fifty years ago Thrasybulos Georgiades, who replaced Heinrich Besseler at the University of Heidelberg after the war, insisted that his students pursue musicology primarily as *Satztechnik*, that is, that they acquaint themselves with the history of music from the inside, as it were, through the nature of the individual piece of music and of the work as composition. His intention was to form a counterpart to the normal method, which found its fulfillment in identifying sources, in learning methods of editing, or in setting up hypotheses more generally applicable to the cultural environment of the arts. "All of this only leads us away from the music—as tempting as it often seems; only the 'path of thorns' through the middle of the composition itself, not the 'high road' of grandiose historical perspectives, brings us to an understanding of the music and captures the music historian in its fascinations." With these and other similar words of warning, Georgiades strove to divert his students from false intellectualism and mere virtuosity or cultural generalizations. In addition to the methods of his own professor in Munich, Rudolf von Ficker, he urged his students to orient themselves on the contrapuntal studies of Knud Jeppesen, both scholars being from the school of Guido Adler in Vienna. The absolute necessity of proceeding from the inner nature of the music was particularly evident in the case of medieval music, a practice so far removed from our own experience that we can say nothing about it without acquiring a closer knowledge of its compositional techniques and the quality of its sound. The dissertations written under Georgiades in Heidelberg and later in Munich were therefore concentrated mainly around the music of the Middle Ages, approaching it both from theoretical writings and from the extant practical sources. These include among others the early investigations of Ernst Apfel into two- and three-voice writing of the later Middle Ages, studies which led to the articles included in the present volume. Within the curriculum at the University of Munich, questions of *Satztechnik* were further explored and complemented through experiments in performance, in an effort to attain as clear a picture as possible of this very different musical reality. The more formally oriented approaches from later theories of counterpoint and harmony were of no use here and had to be replaced by descriptions appropriate to the structure of early music.

Although known for some time, this method of musicological research has, however, within a discipline primarily devoted to other problems, received very little attention. The most recent awakening of interest in this approach is thus particularly welcome, an interest confirmed by the present publication within the series *Criticism and Analysis of Early Music*. Thanks are thus due to the general editor, Jessie Ann Owens, and especially to Kevin N. Moll, who has assembled an impressive number of essays pertinent to the topic by various German authors and has, through his translations, made them readily available to the English-speaking community of scholars.

Munich, December 1996

GENERAL PREFACE

The purpose of this book is to present, in English translation, a series of important musicological studies that appeared in German or international journals between the years 1948 and 1967.[1] Each of the twelve selections is introduced by a short editor's preface, whose purpose is to place it into the perspective of the whole, as well as to point out any notable idiosyncrasies.

Regarding the issue of translation a few preliminary observations are warranted. The German language offers great potential for economy of expression, but this very efficiency can lead to grammatical liberties resulting in exceedingly complex sentence constructions. Fortunately it is normally expedient to break up the longer sentences into shorter ones without altering the sense of a given passage, and I have tried to hold to the principle of keeping the prose flowing as smoothly as possible. On the one hand I have striven to render the original texts into idiomatic English, but on the other hand I feel it is desirable to preserve a sense of the distinctive German mode of expression, since otherwise one runs the risk of distorting the meaning imperceptibly. Certain phrases have been rendered somewhat freely in the translation, but when words not existing in the original German are inserted (often to clarify an antecedent expressed in the original as a gendered article or pronoun), these usually appear in square brackets.

Among the subtle points that arose in translating these studies was the question of how to render phrases that are accorded special emphasis by the author. Whereas English employs italics, boldface, or underlining to indicate such emphasis, German conventions dictate using expanded spacing between letters (s o t h a t t h e r e s u l t i n g t e x t l o o k s l i k e t h i s). I have adhered to standard italics to indicate special emphasis of single words or phrases, but these italics must then serve two purposes, since individual words or phrases in German or other modern foreign languages are also rendered in

---

[1] Each of the twelve numbered studies appeared in *Acta Musicologica*, *Archiv für Musikwissenschaft*, or *Die Musikforschung* during the period mentioned. Apart from my own contributions, Theodor Göllner's foreword, and Ernest Sanders's essay, all of the material in this book has been translated by me from texts originally written in German. Regarding the Sanders study, see the editor's preface to that selection.

italics. Extended quotations of foreign languages, however, are set in roman type, as are ubiquitous terms such as "fauxbourdon" and "contratenor."

Then there is the issue of the reportage subjunctive in the German language, which has no parallel in English grammar. In German, the verb form itself indicates unequivocally that the views being expressed are not necessarily those of the author. I indicate this method of distancing oneself from someone else's opinions by insertions that would be superfluous in the original. Thus, for example, when the statement "X is Y" in German uses the subjunctive verb "sei" rather than the indicative "ist," I usually render it as "X is allegedly Y," or by some equivalent expression.

Also requiring clarification is the use of parenthetical brackets. The translations in this book follow standard academic practice, wherein square brackets, as shown here: [ ], are used to indicate my editorial insertions or clarifications. In the relatively few cases when the original author uses square brackets, these have been replaced by pointed ones: { }, signifying that the editorial insertion existed as such in the journal article itself, i.e., as square brackets. At places where a particular term used by the original author is crucial to the argument or concept involved, and hence to the translation (for example, *Harmonieträger*), the German word is given in square brackets in the translation. This procedure allows the reader to monitor the actual terminology employed by the various authors at critical points. Such terms are always indicated in the nominative case (or in the infinitive for verbs), regardless of their original grammatical guise. Most of these specialized words are found in the appendix (glossary and concordance of terms) at the end of this book, which provides the English equivalent normally assigned to each and identifies the selections in which it can be found. The difficult issue of achieving terminological consistency is addressed below in the editor's introduction.

For anyone consulting the original articles in conjunction with the translations, it should be noted that certain studies renumber their footnotes on every page, whereas in my translations the notes are numbered consecutively throughout. In several selections I have liberally removed parenthetical documentation from the text itself and placed it as supplementary footnotes;[2] these notes, however, are indicated not by the standard consecutive numerals but by consecutive capital letters and thus are clearly differentiated as editorial emendations from the author's footnotes. In three of the studies, the original numbering of footnotes is slightly askew (particulars can be found in the

---

[2]Due to Professor Apfel's being available to provide corrections and approve changes, his articles have tended to undergo the most substantial editorial emendations of this sort.

respective prefaces to those selections). Otherwise, the footnote numbering in the translations conforms to their sequence in the journal articles.

The bibliography is comprehensive, comprising an aggregate of all the secondary sources cited in this volume. In order to bring the book up to date as far as modern editions of music and theory are concerned, I have augmented the list with quite a number of more recent publications.

Bibliographical citations and footnotes have been standardized throughout according to a format based on the *Chicago Manual of Style* (14th edition), even when this entailed providing supplementary information (e.g., publisher names). As a result of this standardization, footnotes have often been altered considerably. In general, I have taken liberties regarding free translation, omission of square brackets, and adding, juggling, or deleting information in footnotes such as I would never consider doing with the main texts. As noted above, I have in several articles removed as much documentary information as possible from the text proper and placed it as supplementary footnotes in order to make for easier reading. In rare instances it has not been possible to ascertain all information about a given source, in which case I have given as complete a citation as possible both in the footnote and in the bibliography.

One documentary convention found frequently in this volume is that the theoretical editions of Coussemaker and Gerbert are designated by the initials *CS* and *GS*, respectively, followed by the volume and column numbers.[3] These abbreviations have been retained in the translations. Another point also requiring explanation is that when citing volumes from the *Denkmähler der Tonkunst in Österreich* series (*DTÖ*), the authors usually give the *Jahrgang* instead of the volume number. Thus, for example, *DTÖ*, vol. 53, is referred to as *DTÖ* [*Jahrgang*] XXVII/1 or XXVII-1. This procedure I find unsatisfactory, and hence I have standardized all citations occurring after a first footnote so as to indicate the volume number only. The reader will need to keep this alteration in mind when referring to the original articles. I should emphasize that I have *not* typically expanded footnotes to give the fullest information possible regarding the availability of musical works and theoretical treatises in modern editions, although many are indeed to be found in the bibliography.

In the translations I have attempted to standardize all editorial procedures, especially when this results in improved readability. (For example, certain authors present lists of works or musical passages within a prose paragraph;

---

[3]Edmond de Coussemaker, *Scriptorum de musica medii aevi*, 4 vols. (Paris: Durand & Pedone-Lauriel, 1864–76); Martin Gerbert, *Scriptores ecclesiastici de musica sacra potissimum*, 3 vols. (1789; reprinted Milan: Bolletino bibliografico musicale, 1931).

wherever appropriate, I have reconfigured such lists into tables.) In many cases it has been necessary to augment the identification of pieces, as when they are referred to solely according to their placement in a modern edition. Also, the format of tables and musical examples, which varies to a greater or lesser extent in the original articles, has been standardized throughout this book: I have reengraved all musical and graphic examples, and in the graphic examples I have regularized the orthography of voice-part symbols, although this also means that the combination of symbols does not agree with any one article. The symbols adopted (shown in the table below) are designed to reflect certain compositional techniques explained below in the editor's introduction.

Table of Systematized Voice-Part Symbols[4]

THREE-VOICE WRITING

	early 14th century		later 14th century		15th century
Vox 3:	● triplum	◐	[discantus]	◐	[discantus]
Vox 2:	● duplum (motetus)	◆	contratenor	◇	tenor
Vox 1:	◇ tenor	◇	tenor	◆	contratenor (bassus)
	klanglicher Satz	*freier Satz*		*klanglich-freier Satz*	

FOUR-VOICE WRITING

	early 14th century		later 14th century		15th century
Vox 4:	● quadruplum	●	triplum	◐	[discantus]
Vox 3:	● triplum	●	motetus	●	contratenor (altus)
Vox 2:	● duplum (motetus)	◆	contratenor	◇	tenor
Vox 1:	◇ tenor	◇	tenor	◆	contratenor (bassus)
	klanglicher Satz	*klanglicher Satz*		*freier & klanglich-freier Satz*	

Other specialized symbols are introduced as necessary in the applicable studies.

Wherever noted, errors in the original articles have been corrected, usually without comment. In this connection, and also regarding certain fine points of translation, I have received valuable advice from professors Ernst Apfel, Helga Meier, and James McJ. Robertson, and from Corinna Mori of Menlo Park. It is with gratitude that I acknowledge their assistance here. For any remaining mistakes or shortcomings, however, I assume full responsibility.

---

[4]Void symbols indicate the voice parts most typically acting as directors of contrapuntal progressions (referential voices). Diamond symbols indicate the voice parts that have the greatest potential to occupy the low note of sonorities (referential pitch). For explanations of these concepts and definitions of the German terms included here, see below, editor's introduction, Part II, Sections C-D.

ACKNOWLEDGMENTS

This volume is the culmination of a project that I have long felt would be a major pedagogical resource for graduate programs in musicology and in early music. Its theme has been a preoccupation of mine for over ten years. In the following I wish to express my gratitude to those who have contributed to it.

First and foremost, I owe thanks to those scholars whose work I am reproducing here in translation. Sadly, I can only thank a few personally since four of the seven writers are now deceased;[1] I can only hope they would have looked upon this undertaking with the same regard as have the living authors with whom I have been in communication.[2] Among the latter, it has been a particular privilege to work with Ernst Apfel. He is represented here by more articles than any other scholar, and this is entirely fitting, for of all modern musicologists he has achieved possibly the most comprehensive advancement of our understanding of compositional processes in early music. Moreover, he personally has furthered my grasp of the issues through innumerable letters and conversations, and has most generously provided me with any number of scarce source materials.

The other two authors whom I wish to acknowledge are Wolfgang Marggraf and Ernest Sanders, who have kindly given permission to reproduce in translation their important studies from 1966 and 1967, respectively.[3] Each of these contributions constitutes a notable strand of thinking on the subject

---

[1]Heinrich Besseler, Rudolf von Ficker, Bernhard Meier, and Günther Schmidt.

[2]In this connection I wish to acknowledge Helga Meier and Gerlinde Schmidt, who have kindly given permission to publish their husbands' articles in translation. Frau Dr. Meier, herself an accomplished musicologist, has indeed been extremely helpful and supportive, to the extent of providing a list of errata from Bernhard Meier's original article, proofreading my translation, and offering several valuable suggestions. Similarly, I wish to thank Professor Rudolf Flotzinger, current editor of *Acta Musicologica*, for giving permission to publish the articles of Rudolf von Ficker (d. 1954) and Heinrich Besseler (d. 1969), which originally appeared in that journal.

[3]These two articles stem from their authors' respective dissertations: Wolfgang Marggraf, "Tonalität und Harmonik in der französischen Chanson vom Tode Machauts bis zum frühen Dufay" (University of Leipzig, 1964); Ernest H. Sanders, "Medieval English Polyphony and Its Significance for the Continent" (Columbia University, 1963).

of compositional priorities in the time of Dufay; their inclusion makes for an expansive and balanced representation of viewpoints reflected in this volume. Special thanks are also due to Theodor Göllner, director of the *Institut für Musikwissenschaft* at the University of Munich, who acted as advisor during my Fulbright Graduate Fellowship there in 1992–93. Professor Göllner has generously taken the time to contribute a foreword to this book. His remarks carry the authority of firsthand acquaintance with many key figures in German musicology, and they also demonstrate his concern for certain fundamental philosophical issues confronting the discipline.[4]

In producing this book it has been especially pleasurable to work with the staff of Garland Publishing. In particular, I would like to express my gratitude to vice-president Leo Balk, to senior editor Phyllis Korper, and also to Tania Bissell, Laurel Stegina, Chuck Bartelt, and Elizabeth Manus, for the estimable help and courtesy extended to me throughout the process of publication.

As great as is my appreciation to all those mentioned above, I should emphasize that the initial impetus for publishing this volume was due to the series editor, Jessie Ann Owens. I am thus indebted to her belief in the value of the enterprise, and no less to her astute editorial recommendations, which without exception have resulted in improvements to the book.

During the course of conceiving and realizing this project, it has been most gratifying to observe the extent to which my interests have been shared by various individuals with whom I have studied, conversed, or corresponded. Unfortunately there are far too many to acknowledge singly, but I would like to thank all for helping to awaken and cultivate those interests. I would surely be remiss, however, if I failed to thank Professors William Mahrt, Albert Cohen, and Karol Berger of Stanford University, and Richard L. Crocker of the University of California at Berkeley, for their assistance and guidance.

Lastly, it would be impossible to underestimate the debt I owe to my wife Melanie, who has supported my work in innumerable ways, and to our two sons, Alexander and Andrew, who have brought such great joy into our lives.

The dedication on page *v* is to my high-school German teacher, John Boronow, now deceased. At the time I studied with him I was in a position to appreciate the depth neither of his wisdom nor of his insight, but I have never forgotten his example.

---

[4]Professor Göllner has recently published an article devoted to exploring these issues as they have been viewed by important scholars associated with the Universities of Vienna and Munich; see "Guido Adler, Rudolf von Ficker und Thrasybulos Georgiades," *Anuario Musical* 51 (1996): 5-10. I am grateful to the author for providing me with an advance copy of that study.

COUNTERPOINT AND COMPOSITIONAL PROCESS IN THE TIME OF DUFAY

EDITOR'S INTRODUCTION

Toward a Comprehensive View
of Compositional Priorities in the Music of Dufay
and his Contemporaries

Kevin N. Moll

As a focus for this volume, which presents translations of venerable studies by authors who often address diverging themes, the figure of Guillaume Dufay is well chosen. In the first place, Dufay is the subject of the earliest article represented here, Heinrich Besseler's "Dufay Schöpfer des Fauxbourdons" (1948), and he is also named in the only other study whose title mentions actual composers: Wolfgang Marggraf's "Tonalität und Harmonik in der französischen Chanson zwischen Machaut und Dufay." Secondly, some 90 percent of the works discussed below fall within the period encompassing the lifetimes of Machaut (d. 1377) and Dufay (d. 1474), and of these two preeminent figures, it is Dufay who, along with his contemporaries, stands at the center of attention. Thirdly, Dufay must probably be acknowledged as the premier composer of the fifteenth century in terms of productive output and influence—a point affirmed by his pivotal place in the literature.[1]

A prime benefit of this kind of disparate compilation of essays is precisely that it reflects the opinions of several different commentators. The polemics one encounters in these selections make for fascinating—one might even say entertaining—reading, but more importantly, they frame a dialectic that is useful for testing our own hypotheses.[2] While the articles comprising

---

[1]Dufay is comparable to Haydn in that both composers took a leading part in stabilizing the formal devices of their respective eras, and each contributed materially to forging a musical language that arguably represents a "classical" phase of development.

[2]For this reason it is especially desirable that the studies be presented in their original configuration (i.e., as complete translations and not merely in the form of a predigested critical commentary) so that each author's methodology is clearly represented.

this volume can hardly be expected to have remained current in every respect, many topics discussed in them retain a surprising degree of vitality, and some of their findings have never been superseded. Indeed, it is difficult to account for the lack of recognition accorded certain of these ideas or to explain why they are so consistently unacknowledged in English-language monographs and histories. For it is not the case that they have been thoroughly tested and rejected—quite to the contrary, only relatively rarely have they even been mentioned. In perusing the Anglo-American scholarship of the past three decades, one would be hard put to discern several key concepts that are routinely discussed in the German literature. This is not to depreciate the indubitable value of many studies that have appeared during that time; nevertheless, the present collection even now is probably the closest approximation to a textbook on counterpoint and compositional process in the fourteenth and fifteenth centuries.

The continued undervaluation of these essays is, in fact, the primary justification for publishing them now. If one acknowledges a place in Anglo-American musicology for a translation of Carl Dahlhaus's *Über die Entstehung der harmonischen Tonalität* (1968), or of Bernhard Meier's *Die Tonarten der klassischen Vokalpolyphonie* (1974),[3] then the selections offered here are certainly no less worthy of publication in English, especially since they focus on an earlier period than do the Dahlhaus and Meier texts.[4]

My task in this introduction is to review the main strands of hypotheses regarding compositional priorities in late medieval polyphony, to evaluate them critically, and finally to forge a more systematic interpretation. The discussion is divided into two parts: Part I comprises a general historiography from the mid-nineteenth century through the end of the period encompassed by the journal articles presented below, that is, roughly 1970. Although focusing primarily on Austro-German scholarship, my purview is not limited strictly to German-language contributions. Part II is devoted to a detailed analysis of the conceptual axioms, terminology, and arguments arrayed by the authors of the respective studies included below. Most significantly, it identifies some subtle terminological discontinuities existing within the set of contributions, and as a means of achieving common ground, suggests an alternate set of general terms. Thus, by leveling the conceptual playing field, Part II attempts to establish a stable foundation upon which further discussion can be framed.

---

[3]Carl Dahlhaus, *Studies on the Origin of Harmonic Tonality*, trans. Robert O. Gjerdingen (Princeton: Princeton University Press, 1990); Bernhard Meier, *The Modes of Classical Vocal Polyphony*, trans. Ellen S. Beebe (New York: Broude Brothers, 1988).

[4]Note that a seminal study by Meier himself from 1952 is presented below.

PART I. Historiography of Literature to c. 1970

The requirements and tasks of early-music scholarship have quite naturally changed over the course of time. Successive generations of scholars, responding to the achievements of the past and needs of the present, have directed musicology into ever more refined, subtle, and demanding channels of inquiry. In the evolving process of the discipline, the assumptions of earlier writers have been, and continue to be, reexamined. This is as it should be, but the desire to be "progressive" in one's thinking runs the risk of devaluing insights of previous scholars (which may have been offered long ago), or worse, of repeating mistakes that have already been made and since forgotten. Hence, it would be useful to identify the seminal research in the field of compositional process, paying particular attention to studies addressing the period from approximately 1300 to 1475. My purpose in doing so is to point out certain important conceptual changes that have occurred since the inception of modern musicology as well as to indicate the progressive sharpening of focus and refinement of methodology.

In pointing out certain questionable premises from which many of the pioneering musicologists proceeded, my purpose is more to clarify than to censure. The progressive piecing together of an analytical vocabulary appropriate to the period has required several generations of dedicated scholarly effort and is, indeed, still underway. To criticize superannuated efforts for their axioms or methods, which may seem to us misguided through the benefit of hindsight, would in most cases be unfruitful. Moreover, such judgments in no way affect the unquestioned contributions made by many of these scholars in paleographical, theoretical, biographical, and archival studies.

A. Early Studies: c. 1850–1930

The awakening of active historical interest in the music of previous eras is a phenomenon of the late eighteenth and early nineteenth centuries.[5] While it would be pointless to try to fix a precise date for the genesis of modern research into late-medieval music, the year 1852 may be taken as a convenient

---

[5] See Walter Wiora, ed., *Die Ausbreitung des Historismus über die Musik, Studien zur Musikgeschichte des 19. Jahrhunderts* 14 (Regensburg: Bosse, 1969). The inclusion of transcriptions of mensural music in the histories of the eighteenth and nineteenth centuries is traced by Rudolf Bockholdt, "Französische und niederländische Musik des 14. und 15. Jahrhunderts," *Musikalische Edition im Wandel des historischen Bewusstseins*, ed. Thrasybulos Georgiades (Kassel: Bärenreiter, 1971), 148-54.

starting point, for it was this year that saw the appearance of Edmond de Coussemaker's *Histoire de l'harmonie au moyen âge*.[6] While this book was not without forebears,[7] it was highly significant to the future of early-music scholarship, for it largely defined the scope of subsequent research. The work comprises three main sections: I) History, II) Documents, and III) Monuments (i.e., transcriptions of music). The first section consists of three parts, of which the first is entitled "Harmonie"—which represents perhaps the earliest instance in the secondary literature of the vertical aspect of pre-Baroque music being treated in a systematic way. The other two parts of the book's first section are devoted to rhythm in measured music and notation, and both of these topics became major foci of research in the coming decades. While the book contains no "analyses" of works in the sense of a critical explication of musical structure, its general descriptions of selected compositions pointed the way to a more intensive scrutiny of individual works. Especially intriguing is Heinrich Besseler's report of a subsequent book by Coussemaker entitled *L'Art harmonique du XIVe siècle*, which was reportedly listed as being "at the printers" in 1869 but of which there unfortunately remains no trace.[8]

Another landmark among nineteenth-century studies was August Ambros's *Geschichte der Musik*,[9] a formidable and highly astute attempt at a comprehensive interpretation of music history but one that, typically for the period, concentrates largely on the twin questions of biography and music theory at the expense of musical exegesis.

Since musicology remained in these early years an incipient discipline (although even then a variegated one), the subsequent research into medieval music up through the 1920s was principally devoted to describing and cataloguing manuscript sources,[10] collecting biographical and historical data

---

[6]Edmond de Coussemaker, *Histoire de l'harmonie au moyen âge* (Paris: Didron, 1852).

[7]See, for example, the histories of Charles Burney, John Hawkins, François-Joseph Fétis, and Raphael Kiesewetter. All of these, however, were general overviews that did not focus on the late medieval period. One exception, dedicated to secular song, is Kiesewetter's *Schicksal und Beschaffenheit des weltlichen Gesanges* (Leipzig: Breitkopf & Härtel, 1841).

[8]Heinrich Besseler, "Studien zur Musik des Mittelalters [Part] I: Neue Quellen des 14. und beginnenden 15. Jahrhunderts," *Archiv für Musikwissenschaft* 7 (1925): 167. Besseler mentions Coussemaker's short bioraphical tract, entitled *Les harmonistes du XIVe siècle* (Lille: Lefevre-Ducrocq, 1869), as having been a preliminary sketch for the study cited.

[9]August Ambros, *Geschichte der Musik*, 5 vols. (Leipzig: Leuckart, 1880–91). The medieval period is discussed in vol. II (1880).

[10]For present purposes, the most important of these studies was Heinrich Besseler, "Studien zur Musik des Mittelalters [Part] I" (see above, note 8): 167-252; and its addendum: "Nachtrag zu Studie I," *Archiv für Musikwissenschaft* 8 (1926): 233-58.

through archival study,[11] classifying the various repertories,[12] clarifying notational problems,[13] and with the first attempts at establishing authoritative editions of music and theory.[14] Also at this time, Hugo Riemann completed his monumental *Geschichte der Musiktheorie*,[15] the first volume of which constitutes a bold attempt at a comprehensive interpretation of the medieval music treatises then known.

While much progress was made in the aforementioned areas during these early decades of modern musicology, the issue of compositional process in the late medieval period (or indeed, in early music generally) remained in great measure unexplored. The single major exception was Guido Adler's *Studie zur Geschichte der Harmonie* (1881),[16] dedicated to elucidating the phenomenon of fauxbourdon as described by the theorist Guillielmus Monachus.[17] This was the first substantial monograph to focus on contrapuntal issues in music before the Baroque era. Moreover, the intense interest that was later lavished

---

[11]Particularly relevant to the present inquiry is the foundation-laying article of Franz X. Haberl, "Wilhelm du Fay: Monographische Studie uber dessen Leben und Werke," *Vierteljahrsschrift für Musikwissenschaft* 1 (1885): 397-530.

[12]Perhaps the most significant repertorial study from this time was Friedrich Ludwig's classic study on the Notre-Dame corpus: *Repertorium Organorum Recentioris et Motetorum Vetusissimi Stili* (Halle: Niemeyer, 1910), left incomplete at the author's death. See also Ludwig's "Die mehrstimmige Musik des 14. Jahrhunderts," *Sammelbände der internationalen Musikgesellschaft* 4 (1902): 16-69, which constitutes a noteworthy attempt at sorting out the corpus of surviving fourteenth-century polyphony on the basis of the sources known at the time. The first effort made to place the polyphonic mass within the historical context of the sung liturgy was Peter Wagner's *Geschichte der Messe* (Leipzig: Breitkopf & Härtel, 1913).

[13]An especially noteworthy study is Johannes Wolf's *Geschichte der Mensural–Notation*, 2 vols. (Leipzig: Breitkopf & Härtel, 1904), which long remained the premier textbook on notation. Moreover, it proved of equal value for its transcriptions of many pieces that for years were otherwise unavailable in modern editions.

[14]Edmond de Coussemaker's *Scriptorum de musica medii aevi*, 4 vols. (Paris: Durand & Pedone-Lauriel, 1864-76) serves as the best example of the latter pursuit (although even earlier precedents exist, most notably the editions of Gerbert and La Fage). The *Denkmähler der Tonkunst in Österreich* series of music editions (begun in 1894) is the most impressive representative of the former task.

[15]Hugo Riemann, *Geschichte der Musiktheorie*, vols. I-II (Berlin: Max Hesse, 1898; 2nd ed. 1920). English translation as *History of Music Theory*, trans. Raymond Haggh (Lincoln: University of Nebraska Press, 1962).

[16]This was Adler's *Habilitationsschrift* at the University of Vienna, 1882. It was published in the series *Sitzungsberichte der kaiserlichen Akademie der Wissenschaften, philosophisch-historische Classe* 98 (Vienna: Carl Gerold's Sohn, 1881): 781-830.

[17]Latin text edited in Coussemaker *CS* 3, 273-307, see particularly chapters 5-13, 288 ff.

on fauxbourdon (discussed below) and on the treatise of Guillielmus in particular, stemmed to a large degree from questions generated by Adler.

Early in the twentieth century, two books appeared that took the music of the early fifteenth century as a frame of reference. The first was Victor Lederer's *Über Heimat und Ursprung der mehrstimmigen Tonkunst*,[18] in which the author emphasized the contribution of English music to the development of polyphony and, indeed, to the tonal coherence of Western music in general. The other study was *Studien zur Musikgeschichte der Frührenaissance*, published in 1914 by Arnold Schering. While mainly dedicated to illustrating the participation of instruments—particularly the organ—in late medieval music, this book also made a groundbreaking observation regarding conceptual categories of counterpoint.[19] Schering later recast the material of the book into one of the earliest studies devoted to the question of performance practice in early music.[20]

Subsequent studies tended to follow the precedent of Adler, Lederer, Schering, and others in taking the early fifteenth century as a point of focus. Werner Korte's book published in 1929, whose title translates as *The Harmonic System of the Early Fifteenth Century and Its Connection to Formal Techniques*,[21] takes up several issues that are specifically discussed in articles translated below, yet the author evidently did not feel it necessary to ground his arguments in the music and theory of the fourteenth century, even though a consideration of the latter would seem to have been a prerequisite for investigating compositional procedures that had undergone no fundamental change.[22] This reluctance to come to grips with the music of the fourteenth century appears to be rooted in a conviction that the roots of modern harmony

---

[18]Victor Lederer, *Über Heimat und Ursprung der mehrstimmigen Tonkunst*, 2 vols. (Leipzig: Siegel, 1906).

[19]Arnold Schering, *Studien zur Musikgeschichte der Frührenaissance* (Leipzig: Kahnt, 1914). A related contribution of Schering's was "Das kolorierte Orgelmadrigal des Trecento," *Sammelbände der internationalen Musikgesellschaft* 13 (1911–12): 172-90. The "groundbreaking observation" just referred to is introduced below (see note 48).

[20]Arnold Schering, *Aufführungspraxis alter Musik* (1931, reprint Wilhelmshaven: Heinrichshofen, 1975).

[21]Werner Korte, *Die Harmonik des frühen 15. Jahrhunderts in ihrem Zusammenhang mit der Formtechnik* (Münster: Suhrbier & Bröcker, 1929).

[22]This point of view is argued in Richard L. Crocker, *A History of Musical Style* (1966; reprinted New York: Dover, 1986), 153, see also 223-4. It has been substantiated by my own research into compositional techniques in fourteenth-century France; see Kevin N. Moll, "Structural Determinants in Polyphony for the Mass Ordinary from French and Related Sources (ca. 1320–1410)" (Ph.D. dissertation, Stanford University, 1994), 343 and elsewhere.

are to be found in the music of the early fifteenth century (beginning around 1420) and in the corollary belief that the music of the fourteenth century is harmonically undeveloped and therefore not amenable to analysis:

> The word "chord" derives from the conceptions of our functional system [of harmony] and presumes a certain particular order in the simultaneous sounding of tones, as well as in the progression of chords originating in this way. These chords exist in and of themselves, without having their origin in melodic complexes. But this is not true for the music of the Middle Ages through the time of the *Ars nova*. [At this time,] a way of ordering sonorities is not at hand, but only a gradually waning [tradition of] interval teaching, which absolutely did not exist in the sense of a tonal system, but which rather at any given time remained linked to the [linear] progress of several polyphonic voices. [Thus, the] two systems, fundamentally foreign to each other, stand as polar opposites.[23]

Almost all these early studies express—either implicitly or explicitly—the sentiment that the fifteenth century represents the beginning of "real" counterpoint, i.e., of voice-leading techniques whose rules proceed in direct lineage to the revered contrapuntists and harmonic theorists of the eighteenth and nineteenth centuries. Perhaps the classic expression of this viewpoint is in Lederer's history,[24] where, following a discussion of a numerical vertical shorthand found in certain theoretical sources, the author concludes:

> From this it is evident that in the first half of the fifteenth century, not only were the following things known: [1] triadic harmony, [2] the basing of the compositional treatises upon a harmonic teaching consisting of a fauxbourdon and its completion through a ground bass, [3] the fundamental significance of harmony, out of which the melody proceeds, [4] the conception of the scale in the sense of harmonies, [5] the word and concept

---

[23]Korte, *Die Harmonik des frühen 15. Jahrhunderts*, 4. Original: "Das Wort 'Klang' entstammt dem Begriffsgebiet unseres funktionalen Systems und setzt eine phänomenal deutliche Ordnung im Zusammenklingen von Tönen, wie im Nacheinander der so entstandenen Klänge voraus, die, ohne aus melodischen Komplexen entstanden zu sein, für sich bestehen bleibt. Das trifft für die Musik des Mittelalters bis in die Zeit der ars nova aber nicht zu. Eine Klangordnung ist nicht vorhanden, lediglich eine graduell nach der abnehmenden Konsonanz geordnete Intervallenlehre, die absolut nicht existiert im Sinne eines Klangsystems, sondern jeweils sinngemäß an den Ablauf mehrerer polyphoner Stimmen gebunden bleibt. Zwei wesensfremde Systeme der Mehrstimmigkeit stehen sich polar gegenüber."

[24]Lederer, *Über Heimat und Ursprung*, 274 (entire passage emphasized in the original).

of the modern "major" and "minor," but also that [6] even the phenomenon later known as figured bass notation already lay at hand.[25]

There did exist, however, a few exceptional cases even among the early studies, where late medieval music was interpreted in a less prejudicial way. Among these may be named Alwin Elling's dissertation on the central Apt manuscript,[26] which addresses a range of compositional issues in analyzing a specific body of fourteenth-century works. As a result, Elling clarified many aspects of the mass settings in Apt (such as the extent of use of isorhythm) and drew attention for the first time to many of their musical interconnections.

The beginning of a new and more specialized phase of research was heralded in the 1920s by the appearance of two essays by Rudolf von Ficker and Jacques Handschin, respectively.[27] Both of these articles investigate the structural use of preexistent voices in medieval polyphony. In expounding a procedure of "structural embellishment" (*Kolorierungstechnik*) of the cantus firmus in mass settings from the Trent Codices, Ficker restricted his discussion to a fairly narrow time span—the early fifteenth century. Handschin, on the other hand, in tracing the use of "melodic paraphrase" in the Middle Ages, strove to encompass a large portion of early polyphony from the twelfth through the end of the fourteenth century.

At this same time, Ficker also attempted to widen the discussion of general principles of order in the music of the later Middle Ages. In two articles from 1925 and 1929, respectively, Ficker insisted that a distinction be made between harmonic conceptions of the polyphonic era and those of the period of so-called "triadic tonality," although in neither case were the

---

[25]Ibid., 274-5. Original: "Es ergibt sich somit, daß in der ersten Hälfte des 15. Jahrhunderts nicht nur die Harmonie des Dreiklangs, die Basierung der Kompositionslehre auf einer im Faulxbourdon und dessen Erweiterung durch den Grundbaß enthaltenen Harmonielehre, die fundamentale Bedeutung der Harmonie, aus welcher die Melodie hervorgeht, die Deutung der Skala im Sinne von Harmonien, Wort und Begriff des modernen 'Dur' und 'Moll' bekannt sind, sondern daß sogar die nachmals sogenannte Generalbaßschrift bereits vorliegt."

[26]Alwin Elling, "Die Messen, Hymnen und Motetten der Handschrift von Apt" (dissertation, University of Göttingen, 1924).

[27]Rudolf von Ficker, "Die Kolorierungstechnik der Trienter Messen," *Studien zur Musikgeschichte* 7 (1920): 5-47; Jacques Handschin, "Zur Frage der melodischen Paraphrasierung im Mittelalter," *Zeitschrift für Musikwissenschaft* 10 (1928): 513-59.

ramifications yet fully worked out.[28] Another Ficker study from 1925,[29] aptly dedicated to Guido Adler, includes a concise explanation of the philosophy behind this wider point of view:

> Our musical sensitivity since the close of the Middle Ages has in fact been altered to such an extent that we today consider the preceding manifestations of medieval music as completely foreign and incomprehensible, and we are only too inclined to speak here [regarding music], in contrast to the other arts, of primitive stages of development. The insight that this view is not accurate has begun to dawn only in the last [few] years, and with it the recognition that we must completely retrain [ourselves] in a musical connection, as well as in an aesthetic, if we wish to approach more closely the meaning and individuality of the medieval (as well as any other kind of) musical phenomenon that is foreign to us.[30]

---

[28]See Rudolf von Ficker, "Formprobleme der mittelalterlichen Musik," *Zeitschrift für Musikwissenschaft* 7 (1925): 195-213, and by the same author, "Primäre Klangformen," *Jahrbuch der Musikbibliothek Peters* 36 (1929): 21-34. In emphasizing the sonorous [*klanglich*] element in early polyphony, the latter study exerted a decisive influence on later scholars.

[29]Rudolf von Ficker, "Die Musik des Mittelalters und ihre Beziehungen zum Geistesleben," *Deutsche Vierteljahrsschrift für Literaturwissenschaft und Geistesgeschichte* 3 (1925): 501-35.

[30]Ibid., 502. Original: "Unser musikalisches Empfinden ist in der Tat seit dem Ausgange des Mittelalters derart umgestaltet, daß wir den vorangehenden Erscheinungsformen mittelalterlicher Musik heute noch vollkommen fremd und fassungslos gegenüberstehen und nur allzusehr geneigt sind, im Gegensatze zu den übrigen Künsten hier von primitiven Entwicklungsstadien zu sprechen. Daß diese Ansicht nicht richtig ist, diese Einsicht beginnt erst seit den letzten Jahren aufzudämmern, zugleich aber auch die Erkenntnis, das wir sowohl in musikalischer, als auch in ästhetischer Beziehung vollständig umlernen müssen, falls wir der Bedeutung und Eigenart des mittelalterlichen, sowie eines jeden anderen, uns fremden Musikgeschehens nahekommen wollen."

B. Sharpening of Focus: c. 1930–1970

The names mentioned above demonstrate that it was in the German-language scholarship that exploration of the difficult question of the technical bases of musical organization in medieval polyphony was pioneered. During the National-Socialist era (1933–45), research in this field in Germany and Austria was substantially curtailed, resulting in a relative dearth of publications.[31]

From just after the Second World War through about 1970, musicological literature on compositional process tended to divide itself into two distinct schools of thought. This bifurcation was precipitated by a debate over the origins of fauxbourdon, although both sides of the argument had their antecedents in the pre-war German literature.[32] While both persuasions were established within the German academic sphere, it should be emphasized that each has had international adherents.

The first school, whose philosophical antecedents are reflected in the work of Hugo Riemann, takes the position that the driving force in the history of Western music before 1600 is an evolution towards functional triadic

---

[31] The two seminal dissertations of Manfred Bukofzer and Thrasybulos Georgiades, both completed in 1935, are introduced below (see notes 37 and 54, respectively). Other significant studies produced in German-speaking lands during this period include the following: 1) Götz Dietrich Sasse, *Die Mehrstimmigkeit der Ars antiqua in Theorie und Praxis* (Leipzig: Noske, 1940). 2) Assen Kresteff, "Die mehrstimmigen Messkompositionen des Codex Ivrea" (dissertation, University of Munich, 1942); this study, written under Rudolf von Ficker's supervision, was destroyed in the bombing of 1944–45 and now exists only as a six-page summary dated 1947. 3) Rolf Hoffmann, "Form und Gestalt in der frühen Kunstmusik, Beiträge zur ästhetischen Wertung der gotischen Musik in Form von Analysen ausgewählter Beispiele der Epoche Leonin bis Machaut" (dissertation, University of Marburg, 1943); as a historical document this study is especially noteworthy, since Jewish authors (e.g., Adler) are specifically identified in the bibliography. 4) Ernst Rohloff, *Der Musiktraktat des Johannes de Grocheo* (Leipzig: Reinecke, 1943). 5) Jacques Handschin, "Aus der alten Musiktheorie," in 5 parts, *Acta Musicologica* 14-17 (1942–45). Handschin was based in Switzerland at this time.

[32] A concise outline of the fauxbourdon dispute of the 1950s is given by Brian Trowell in "Faburden and Fauxbourdon," *Musica Disciplina* 13 (1959): 44-6. However, the role of earlier commentators, such as Guido Adler, as catalyst should not be overlooked. Regarding the more essential aspects of composition that these views entail, several of the main arguments are explained in greater depth along with a critical assessment of their respective merit, in Chapters I and III of my M.M. thesis: Kevin N. Moll, "Analyzing Four-Voice Vertical Sonorities in Fifteenth-Century Sacred Polyphony" (New England Conservatory, 1988; UMI version 1995, with minor revisions and altered pagination, No. 1376627), 8-26 and 39-71, respectively. The discussion below will merely amplify certain aspects of that history.

tonality.[33] Heinrich Besseler has been a vociferous proponent of this point of view, expressed most forcefully in his well-known book, *Bourdon und Fauxbourdon*, that the early fifteenth century witnessed the self-conscious "discovery" of triadic relationships:

> That which is thrust into light here is a new feeling for harmony, a strength and security of triadic connection, which surpasses all previous example. The chords no longer stand next to each other as individual colors, but rather, [in] coming into motion, they fashion an inner cohesion, flooded with the power of sensitivity, which instantly becomes intelligible to us as harmonic "tonality."[34]

This position—which appears not quite so revolutionary in light of Korte's and Lederer's comments quoted above—is tightly bound up with Besseler's arguments concerning: 1) the genesis, nature, and historical significance of fauxbourdon technique; 2) the existence of a hypothetical *bourdon* voice, or "director of harmony" (*Harmonieträger*); 3) his suggested opposition of an Italian predilection for "tonal harmony" with an English attribute of "full sonority"; and 4) his identification of Dufay's alleged manifold achievements as musical genius.[35] A number of the same general

---

[33]For example, Riemann says that with the admittance of thirds and sixths into the realm of consonances, "the darkness of those minds which are still concerned with the antique theories of consonance is suddenly illuminated" (*History of Music Theory*, 92). See also Bernhard Meier's introduction to *The Modes of Classical Vocal Polyphony* (13-19), which places the phenomenon within the perspective of general currents of intellectual history.

[34]Heinrich Besseler, *Bourdon und Fauxbourdon* (1st edition 1950, 2nd edition, ed. Peter Gülke, Leipzig: Breitkopf und Härtel, 1974); 38. (N.B.: all page references to this source are cited from the first edition, since the second, posthumous edition cannot be considered as definitively stemming from the author; in any case the page numbers from the first edition are provided in the margins of the second edition.) Original: "Was hier ans Licht drängt, ist ein neues Harmoniegefühl, eine Kraft und Sicherheit der Dreiklangsverbindungen, die alles bisher Gewohnte übertrifft. Die Klänge stehen nicht mehr als Einzelfarben nebeneinander, sondern geraten in Bewegung, bilden einen von Gefühlskraft durchströmten inneren Zusammenhang, der uns als harmonische 'Tonalität' sogleich einleuchtet."

[35]Many of these suggested accomplishments are discussed in the Besseler articles translated below, but they are fully detailed only in the book cited in note 34. According to Besseler, Dufay acted as the instrumental agent in bringing about the following musical innovations of the time (page numbers in parentheses are citations from *Bourdon und Fauxbourdon*): 1) creation of fauxbourdon technique, whose earliest manifestation Besseler traces to the Postcommunio of the *Missa Sancti Jacobi* (14); 2) creation of the so-called "double-octave" form of cadence (36), which entailed a "decisive contrapuntal recognition of the foundational bass" (91); 3) creation of the "true 'six-line contratenor'" acting as a "ground-voice," i.e., *Bourdonkontratenor* (47-8); 4) extension of the usable tonal space to D below the bass clef

theses were subsequently advocated by Manfred Bukofzer and Wolfgang Marggraf (both of whom at different times were students of Besseler).[36] Bukofzer's dissertation research, which was initiated under Besseler's guidance, in fact contributed materially to some of the latter's theses advanced in *Bourdon und Fauxbourdon*.[37] Thirty years after the publication of Bukofzer's dissertation, Marggraf condensed his own dissertation results into an article entitled "Tonality and Harmony in the French Chanson between Machaut and

---

through use of the slide-trumpet (50, based on testimony of contemporary theorist Adam of Fulda); 5) the "creative achievement" of effecting a "breakthrough" in the employment of "tonal harmony" in chanson composition (56); 6) development of "a dominant tonality with variable quality of the third" (57/99); 7) manifestation for the first time of "the 'natural' system of tonality in its essential elements in the system of Bourdon harmony" (66-7); 8) adoption of a "melodic style... flooded with a new harmonic feeling and already dominated to a great extent by an encroaching tonality" (98); 9) "decisive participation" in the creation of the "new flowing rhythm [*Stromrhythmus*]" and its associated quality of "cantabile melody" (137); 10) development of a new format for manuscripts in the form of "Folio-choirbooks" (144); 11) creation of "probably... the earliest surviving [musically unified] mass cycle of the fifteenth century," i.e., nos. 9-10-12-14-15 in the codex Bologna Q15 (148), demonstrating "Dufay [as] the founder of the new form of the mass" (154); 12) composition of the *Missa Sancti Jacobi*, an "epoch-making work" (150), containing "all sonorous resources of the time, up through fauxbourdon" (149); 13) development of the "third phase" in the creation of the unified tenor mass cycle: the four-voice mass with cantus-firmus tenor in a middle position and a lower contratenor, which "served [to effect] the [musical attributes of] full sonority and harmony," as an example of which Besseler adduces Dufay's *Missa Se la face ay pale* (155); 14) placement of the two upper voices in a four-voice motet texture at a fifth's spacing, as indicated through cleffing, which "surfaces in 1433 for the first time in the ceremonial music *Supremum est*" (161), thus indicating a "transition from the Ars nova discant duet to the new discantus-altus ordering in motet composition" (171); 15) achievement in the tenor motet of the 1430s of a "decisive synthesis" of "[Italian tonal] harmony and [English] full sonority, bourdon and fauxbourdon, into a unity" (175/207); 16) participation in the "important process" of the "vocalization of the contratenor" (176), and also of the tenor, i.e., their transformation from instrumental into sung parts, which Besseler assesses as constituting "an early form of the Netherlandish choral sonority" (186).

[36] Hence Bukofzer can criticize "Besseler's pointed antithesis of 'bourdon' and 'fauxbourdon,'" as "a speculative terminological construction lacking a solid historical foundation," yet "this does not mean that his stylistic observations are not valid—on the contrary, they retain their value independently of his theory." See Manfred Bukofzer, "Fauxbourdon Revisited," *Musical Quarterly* 38 (1952): 28.

[37] See Manfred Bukofzer, *Geschichte des englischen Diskants und des Fauxbourdons nach den theoretischen Quellen*, Sammlung musikwissenschaftlicher Abhandlungen 21 (Strasbourg: Heitz, 1936). The dissertation, begun at Heidelberg under Besseler, was completed at the University of Basle under Handschin in 1935. For an example of Bukofzer's influence on Besseler's positions, see "Dufay Schöpfer des Fauxbourdons," *Acta Musicologica* 20 (1948): 26, note 4 (see 66 below).

Dufay," a study which upholds Besseler's findings, while also contributing some original ideas regarding tonal coherence in the repertory named.[38]

A French proponent of this teleological point of view was Armand Machabey, whose 1955 book is entitled *The Genesis of Classical Musical Tonality from Its Origins to the Fifteenth Century.*[39] In a manner reminiscent of Riemann, this work takes a somewhat different tack from Besseler: instead of arguing that triadic tonality was invented essentially in a flash of "enlightenment," Machabey claims that it was the result of a long, steady, inexorable process:

> The perfect [i.e., V–I] cadence is hence the product of the musical intuition of the West, that is to say, [a product] of experience, of a long series of essays, echoes and strivings with a view to discovering a universal formula responding to all needs. And we have found the same thing in comprehending its forms [as being at first] scarcely perceptible, then subsequently rudimentary, in the course of the preceding centuries. [Thus,] by considering the most characteristic works of the fourteenth and fifteenth centuries, we are going to attempt to follow the progressive refinement of its design and of its structure, until the form [of the perfect cadence] is achieved.[40]

Arguments similar to those above have occasionally been made in the pages of American publications. Ernest Sanders, for example, argues assiduously that principles of "tonality" are manifest in English music even as early as the thirteenth century,[41] and indeed even credits Victor Lederer as

---

[38]The germinal study of Marggraf was his dissertation, also written under Besseler's supervision: "Tonalität und Harmonik in der französischen Chanson vom Tode Machauts bis zum frühen Dufay" (University of Leipzig, 1964). The article referred to above is Wolfgang Marggraf, "Tonalität und Harmonik in der französischen Chanson zwischen Machaut und Dufay," *Archiv für Musikwissenschaft* 23 (1966): 11-31 (translated in this volume).

[39]Armand Machabey, *Genèse de la tonalité musicale classique des origines au XVe siècle* (Paris: Masse, 1955). Machabey also published specifically in the field of late medieval music, including an edition of Machaut's mass.

[40]Ibid., 220. Original: "La cadence parfaite est donc le produit de l'intuition musicale en Occident, c'est-à-dire d'une expérience, d'une longue série d'essais, d'échecs et de réussites en vue de découvrir une formule assez universelle pour répondre à tous les besoins. Et de même que nous avons cherché à saisir ses formes à peine perceptibles, puis rudimentaires, au cours des siècles précédents, nous allons tenter de suivre à travers les œuvres les plus caractéristiques des XIVe et XVe siècles la précision progressive de son dessin et de sa structure jusqu'à sa forme achevée."

[41]Ernest Sanders, "Tonal Aspects of 13th Century English Polyphony," *Acta Musicologica* 37 (1965): 19-34.

being the first scholar to reach this conclusion.[42] Also, Sanders, like Machabey, points to the evolutionary significance of the V–I cadence, whose appearance, "no matter in what guise, indicates a change."[43] An even stronger proponent of this thesis is Edward Lowinsky (another student of Besseler's), who has asserted in several publications that the roots of triadic harmony are directly traceable to the fifteenth century[44]—a view upheld by Don Randel in a widely cited article from 1971, and more recently by Bonnie J. Blackburn.[45]

The other school of interpretation centers around various scholars associated with the aforementioned Rudolf von Ficker, and Thrasybulos Georgiades, his student at the University of Munich. This group argues that the vertical component of counterpoint in late medieval music is based on a hierarchy of two-voice intervals, with the corollary position, developed subsequently, that sonorities occurring in medieval music in more than two parts are related only indirectly to principles of later triadic harmony.

In a 1951 article that rather polemically attacks Besseler's ideas, Ficker accounts for voice functions in the fifteenth century (which also apply to the late fourteenth century) and credits Knud Jeppesen with first mentioning their significance in print.[46] The original passage is found in the introduction to Jeppesen's edition of the *Copenhagen Chansonnier*, where he states that:

> ... the Franco-Burgundian chanson of the fifteenth century is, musically speaking, an unusually interesting object for observation. Each of the three voices: superius, tenor, and contratenor, has an individual task and a character that is so individual that possibilities for a richly contrasting

---

[42]See Ernest Sanders, "Die Rolle der englischen Mehrstimmigkeit des Mittelalters in der Entwicklung von Cantus-firmus-Satz und Tonalitätsstruktur," *Archiv für Musikwissenschaft* 24 (1967) : 24-53 (translated in this volume). The Lederer reference is at the end of the article.

[43]Ibid., 36.

[44]The strongest case for this is put forth in Edward Lowinsky, "Canon Technique and Simultaneous Conception in Fifteenth-Century Music: A Comparison of North and South," *Essays on the Music of J.S. Bach and other Divers Subjects: A Tribute to Gerard Herz*, ed. Robert L. Weaver (Louisville: University of Louisville Press, 1981): 181-222.

[45]Don Randel, "Emerging Triadic Tonality in the Fifteenth Century," *Musical Quarterly* 58 (1971): 73-86; Bonnie J. Blackburn, "On Compositional Process in the Fifteenth Century," *Journal of the American Musicological Society* 40 (1987): 210-84.

[46]Rudolf von Ficker, "Zur Schöpfungsgeschichte des Fauxbourdon," *Acta Musicologica* 23 (1951): 93-123 (translated in this volume); the Jeppesen citation is made in note 77 of that study. It should also be noted that Ficker credits music theorist Ernst Kurth with certain "fundamental findings ... regarding harmony and its usefulness for the recognition of historical development" (ibid., see note 35 and its accompanying discussion). Besseler's immediate replies to Ficker can be found in "Tonalharmonik und Vollklang" (cited above in note 37).

interplay are at hand, and are frequently exploited with brilliant intellectual energy.[47]

Jeppesen used the above quotation as a point of departure to illustrate that the chansons belonging to the repertory of the manuscript upon which his edition is based can be performed as duets, without the contratenor. But in fact this idea of a two-part contrapuntal foundation is considerably older even than Ficker suggests. As early as 1914, Arnold Schering had maintained that in Western polyphony around 1400 there were two basic contrapuntal procedures. The first is characterized by "a perfect two-voice entity," to which "a sonority-enhancing contrapuntal voice is added."[48] In a composition resulting from such principles "the discant and tenor stand in the relationship of a *bicinium* constructed according to all the rules of counterpoint," whereas the third part— "contratenor (formerly called triplum)"—is a contrapuntal afterthought.[49] The second procedure Schering identifies as being in evidence when "the composition is from the beginning exclusively conceived for three voices."[50]

As a matter of fact, specific references to a two-voice framework can be traced in earlier writings of Ludwig (1902),[51] Ambros (1880),[52] and allegedly even Raphael Kiesewetter (1834),[53] a fact which only underlines the historical significance of these pathfinders of musicology. Nevertheless, the decisive applicability of the two-part foundation as a basis for codifying medieval procedures of counterpoint was neither recognized nor exploited at that time.

---

[47]Knud Jeppesen, *Der Kopenhagener Chansonnier* (Copenhagen: Levin & Munksgaard, 1927, XLV). Original: "... die franco-burgundische Chanson des 15. Jahrhunderts [ist] musikalisch gesehen ein ungemein interessantes Beobachtungsobjekt. Jede der drei Simmen: Superius, Tenor und Kontratenor hat eine selbständige Aufgabe und eine so individuelle Physiognomie, dass Möglichkeiten für ein sich reich kontrastiert entfaltendes Zusammenspiel vorhanden sind und auch oft mit glänzender geistiger Energie ausgenutzt werden."

[48]Schering, *Studien zur Musikgeschichte der Frührenaissance*, 123.

[49]Ibid.

[50]Ibid. These two contrapuntal categories are very close to types 2 and 3 as identified by Ernst Apfel in "Der klangliche Satz und der freie Diskantsatz im 15. Jahrhundert," *Archiv für Musikwissenschaft* 12 (1955): 297-313 (translated in this volume), and in this article Apfel indeed remarks upon the significance of the Schering passages just quoted. For an extended discussion of contrapuntal types, see below, Part II, Section D.

[51]In connection to Machaut's chansons, Ludwig had proposed the possibility of performance as two-voice pieces; see "Die mehrstimmige Musik des 14. Jahrhunderts," 36.

[52]Ambros, *Geschichte der Musik*, vol. II, 350.

[53]Both Kiesewetter and another ninteenth-century figure, Stephen Morelot, are mentioned by Ambros in the passage just cited, but unfortunately without any indication of source.

If interpreted more broadly, however, the dyadic concept attains validity as a general organizing principle behind the "harmony" of medieval polyphony. This maxim holds that vertical sonorities are best comprehended as concatenations of discrete two-voice intervals, and Thrasybulos Georgiades must be cited as the researcher who first identified its theoretical foundations.

In his 1935 dissertation, Georgiades presented the original texts of a number of English discant treatises dating from approximately 1400, along with an extensive commentary upon them.[54] He was able to show that even though the theoretical discussions were always framed in terms of two voices only, certain treatises actually describe possibilities for multi-voice polyphony (i.e., in three and four voices) as well:

> [The fact] that only two-voice examples are encountered throughout in all treatises, is likewise to be traced to this condition [i.e., that the upper voices of a composition are not readily distinguishable from each other]; they are thus valid as a direction for the making of any counter-voice, since all [parts] are governed by the same rules. It would accordingly be mistaken to try to connect the [teachings of the] treatises simply to two-voice compositions.[55]

Georgiades correspondingly asserted that "the essence of the technique" described by Leonel Power and other English theorists "consists in the construction of closed complexes of [two-voice] intervals, which are realized predominantly through the individual components in contrary motion."[56]

The observations just quoted were made by Georgiades in connection with English discant theory, but the author emphasizes that these treatises stand essentially in the same vein as the contemporary Continental ones.[57] Thus, if one accepts the view that "discant in England is in all essentials the same as

---

[54]Thrasybulos Georgiades, *Englische Diskanttraktate aus der ersten Hälfte des XV. Jahrhunderts, Schriftenreihe des Musikwissenschaftlichen Seminars der Universität München* 3, ed. Rudolf von Ficker (Munich: Musikwissenschaftliches Seminar der Universität München, 1937). The dissertation was completed at the University of Munich two years previously under Ficker's supervision.

[55]Ibid., 56-7. Original: "Daß bei allen Traktaten durchwegs nur zweistimmige Beispiele anzutreffen sind, ist ebenfalls auf diesen Umstand zurückzuführen; sie gelten nämlich als Anweisung zur Bildung irgend einer Gegenstimme, da alle gleichen Regeln unterliegen. Es wäre daher fehlerhaft, sie nur auf zweistimmige Kompositionen beziehen zu wollen."

[56]Ibid., 38. Georgiades follows Ficker in emphasizing the element of sonority as opposed to melodic line (ibid., 67; see above, note 28).

[57]Ibid., 55-66, especially 65.

discant anywhere else,"[58] the concept of multi-voice composition in the late medieval era as concatenations of two-voice intervals must be equally valid for music on the Continent.

Another early contribution advocating dyadic analysis of early vocal polyphony was Bernhard Meier's 1952 article whose title translates as "Harmony in the Cantus-Firmus Compositions of the Fifteenth Century."[59] In his very first paragraph, Meier seems to be responding specifically to Besseler (although the latter is not mentioned), when he advocates "a decisive abandonment of all current methods that proceed from conditions of the late sixteenth century and aim to connect the sonorities built over a bass tone to a tonal center."[60] Instead, Meier argues that tonal coherence in the period "is solely identifiable with the tenor as preexistent monophonic melody, to which the remaining voices are joined as an embellishing but always-dependent adornment."[61] In his concluding paragraphs, Meier emphasizes that "the compositional teachings of Cochlaeus [1507] still designate the choice and preparation of the tenor as the first requirement of a polyphonic composition," whereupon composition "proceed[s] from the two-voice discant-tenor foundation," leading to cadences that "are still considered only according to [dyadic] intervals and stereotypical voice leading [procedures]."[62]

The idea of multi-voice counterpoint as an extension of simple discant procedures, which had been espoused by Georgiades and Ficker and seconded by Meier,[63] was significantly expanded and developed by Ernst Apfel in a series of articles and books.[64] In his 1953 Heidelberg dissertation, written under the tutelage of Georgiades and entitled "The Discant in the Music Theory of the Twelfth through the Fifteenth Centuries,"[65] Apfel identified

---

[58]Richard L. Crocker, "Discant, Counterpoint, and Harmony," *Journal of the American Musicological Society* 15 (1962): 2. See also Sylvia Kenney, "English Discant and Discant in England," *Musical Quarterly* 45 (1959): 31.

[59]Bernhard Meier, "Die Harmonik im cantus-firmus-haltigen Satz des 15. Jahrhunderts," *Archiv für Musikwissenschaft* 9 (1952): 27-44 (translated in this volume).

[60]Ibid., 27 (149 below). Meier subsequently does cite Besseler's *Bourdon und Fauxbourdon* (30, note 1; note 5 of the translation below) and so obviously was aware of its theses.

[61]Ibid.

[62]Ibid., 43. For a citation of the treatise Meier is referring to, see below, 149, note 1.

[63]Interestingly, Meier's article mentions neither Ficker nor Georgiades.

[64]For a complete account of the author's publications, see the "Postscript" to this volume.

[65]Ernst Apfel, "Der Diskant in der Musiktheorie des 12.–15. Jahrhunderts" (dissertation, University of Heidelberg, 1953), available as a reprint through the Musikwissenschaftliches Institut der Universität des Saarlandes (Saarbrücken: Selbstverlag Ernst Apfel, 1981). A revised version of the dissertation, unfortunately with many printing errors, was published as *Diskant*

certain basic contrapuntal types and traced their roots in contemporary theory. Subsequently the author elaborated upon these ideas in various studies, culminating in a comprehensive historical sketch of compositional resources in a book whose title can be rendered as *Foundations of a History of Compositional Technique* [Part I:] *From the Thirteenth to the Sixteenth Century*.[66] In this text, Apfel classifies all the major genres of polyphony during the period and shows how distinct compositional categories can be differentiated by identifying characteristic ways of expanding two-part into multi-part counterpoint—each associated with certain standards of voice function and dissonance treatment, and often correlated with other musical elements.[67]

In 1960 appeared Rudolf Bockholdt's Munich dissertation on the early mass settings of Dufay.[68] This study, also completed under Georgiades's supervision,[69] represents another seminal contribution to the scholarship on compositional process in the early fifteenth century and, in a general sense, reflects the ideas introduced in the paragraphs above. Bockholdt proceeds from the findings of previous scholars regarding "compositional characteristics in the narrow sense"[70] and seeks to ascertain "how these suppositions are

und Kontrapunkt in der Musiktheorie des 12. bis 15. Jahrhunderts, Taschenbücher zur Musikwissenschaft 82, ed. Richard Schaal (Wilhelmshaven: Heinrichshofen, 1982). Subsequently, a third revised and expanded version was brought out under the latter title (Saarbrücken: Universitätsbibliothek der Universität des Saarlandes, 1994).

[66]Ernst Apfel, *Grundlagen einer Geschichte der Satztechnik* [Teil I:] *vom 13. bis zum 16. Jahrhundert* (Saarbrücken: Musikwissenschaftliches Institut der Universität des Saarlandes, 1974, reprinted 1988 with minor corrections). This book is a thorough revision of the author's previous *Beiträge zu einer Geschichte der Satztechnik von der frühen Motette bis Bach* (Munich: Eidos, 1964), which is itself a reworking of several previous articles.

[67]The basic categories just referred to are explained and enumerated in Apfel, "Der klangliche Satz" (see citation above, note 50); certain refinements are introduced in later studies of that author. A unique and almost entirely overlooked perspective on certain aspects of these theories is provided in Günther Schmidt's thought-provoking article, "Zur Frage des Cantus firmus im 14. und beginnenden 15. Jahrhundert," *Archiv für Musikwissenschaft* 15 (1958): see particularly 247-8 (215-6 below).

[68]Published as Rudolf Bockholdt, *Die frühen Messenkompositionen von Guillaume Dufay, Münchner Veröffentlichungen zur Musikgeschichte* 5, ed. Thrasybulos Georgiades (Tutzing: Hans Schneider, 1960).

[69]Georgiades had since assumed the directorship of the musicology faculty at the University of Munich.

[70]Bockholdt, *Die frühen Messenkompositionen von Guillaume Dufay*, 13. Scholars explicitly mentioned here as contributing "specialist research" into the music of Dufay are Rudolf von Ficker and Heinrich Besseler (ibid., 12). In addition to these, Bockholdt mentions Manfred Bukofzer, Thrasybulos Georgiades, and Ernst Apfel as contributing intensively to research into

realized, sometimes innovatively, in the individual particular work."[71] The study traces the interaction of rhythmic and motivic elements, dissonance treatment, and cantus-firmus usage, all within the framework of overall mensural practice.[72] The author's theme can be seen as a reaction to, and a continuation of, the research into Dufay's music hitherto published.

Hellmut Kühn, at one time Ernst Apfel's student at the University of the Saarland, made a substantial and important contribution to the literature on compositional process in the fourteenth century with his book, *Die Harmonik der Ars Nova*.[73] In putting forth the hypothesis that "a tonal system, analogous to the systems that are subsumed under the term 'harmony,' prevails in the music of the Ars nova,"[74] Kühn directly contradicted the view that hitherto had prevailed among musicologists, thereby inaugurating a new phase of research into the elements of harmonic order in fourteenth-century polyphony. Subsequent research has sought to expand upon this theme.[75]

Among the contributions of English-language musicologists to the dialogue on compositional process in polyphony, Richard Crocker's "Discant,

---

"the music of the first half of the fifteenth century as a whole," and he notes further that "in Besseler's contributions, Dufay stands in the center of the inquiry" (ibid.).

[71]Ibid.

[72]Chapters I and VI–VII serve as introductory and concluding sections, respectively. Chapter II discusses extensively a single Gloria (Et in terra "De Quaremiaux"). The remaining chapters (III–V, comprising about two-thirds of the book) are each named after a specific mensuration and devoted to works reflecting it.

[73]Hellmut Kühn, *Die Harmonik der Ars Nova*, Berliner musikwissenschaftliche Arbeiten 5, eds. Carl Dahlhaus and Rudolf Stephan (Munich: Emil Katzbichler, 1973), comprising a revision of his dissertation, "Das Problem der Harmonik in der Musik der Ars nova," (1969). The book contains an illuminating account of "previous interpretations" of harmony (12–29), which advocates much the same viewpoint as the present inquiry and discusses topics largely paralleling those treated here.

[74]Ibid., 5. Original: "... in der Musik der Ars nova ein Klangsystem herrscht, das mit den Systemen, die unter dem Begriff Harmonik subsumiert werden, vergleichbar ist."

[75]Kühn's work portended an entire sub-genre of writings on "sonority" in late medieval polyphony, of which the most signal representatives are probably the following: Ramón Pelinski, "Zusammenklang und Aufbau in den Motetten Machauts," *Die Musikforschung* 28 (1975): 62–71; Friedemann Otterbach, *Kadenzierung und Tonalität im Kantilenensatz Dufays*, *Freiburger Schriften zur Musikwissenschaft* 7, ed. Hans Heinrich Eggebrecht (Munich–Salzburg: Emil Katzbichler, 1975); Sarah Fuller, "On Sonority in Fourteenth-Century Polyphony: Some Preliminary Reflections," *Journal of Music Theory* 30 (1986): 35–70; Dolores Pesce, "A Case for Coherent Pitch Organization in the Thirteenth-Century Double Motet," *Music Analysis* 9 (1990): 287–318; Sarah Fuller, "Tendencies and Resolutions: The Directed Progression in *Ars Nova* Music," *Journal of Music Theory* 36 (1992): 229–58. See also Kevin N. Moll, "Voice Leading, Sonority, and Contrapuntal Referentiality in Late-Medieval Polyphony," forthcoming.

Counterpoint, and Harmony" (1962) has exerted perhaps the strongest influence on subsequent scholarship.[76] Taking the arguments of the Ficker-Georgiades school as a starting point, Crocker argues that functions between two-note entities constitute the functional element of medieval counterpoint, and that "the logic of such progressions is distinct on the one hand from melodic, 'linear,' logic, and on the other from the logic of triads."[77]

Although standing somewhat aside from the two poles I have been discussing, David Hughes's unpublished 1956 dissertation has only recently garnered some of the attention it perhaps always had deserved.[78] In retrospect, this study can be seen as an early and significant attempt to systematize the study of counterpoint in Western Europe according to concepts justified from the writings of the theorists active during the period. Hughes considers a large number of Italian, French, and English compositions in seeking to identify aspects of national style on the basis of musical characteristics. Hence, the study represents a breakthrough of sorts in thinking on the subject even though its immediate influence was negligible.[79]

Gilbert Reaney is an imposing figure in the scholarship of the *Ars nova*. A significant component of his research is a series of articles systematically investigating germane issues of textual, harmonic, and melodic organization in the secular oeuvre of Machaut.[80] These analytical writings are indebted to neither of the intellectual branches outlined above, and evince a curious

---

[76]Cited above, note 58.

[77]Crocker, "Discant, Counterpoint, and Harmony," 2, where the author specifically acknowledges Georgiades's importance.

[78]David Hughes, "A View of the Passing of Gothic Music: Line and Counterpoint 1380-1430," Ph.D. dissertation, Harvard University, 1956. For latter-day acknowledgment of this study's value, see Daniel Leech-Wilkinson, "Machaut's *Rose, lis* and Early Music Analysis," *Music Analysis* 3 (1984): 28, note 31; also Howard M. Brown, "A Ballade for Mathieu de Foix: Style and Structure in a Composition by Trebor," *Musica Disciplina* 41 (1987): 77, note 6.

[79]Leech-Wilkinson (in the citation mentioned in the above note) avers that "had it been more widely known, early music analysis might by now have progressed further."

[80]Among others, the following studies by Gilbert Reaney suggest themselves: "Fourteenth Century Harmony and the Ballades, Rondeaux and Virelais of Guillaume de Machaut," *Musica Disciplina* 7 (1953): 129-46; "The Ballades, Rondeaux and Virelais of Guillaume de Machaut: Melody, Rhythm and Form," *Acta Musicologica* 27 (1955): 40-58; "Notes on the Harmonic Technique of Guillaume de Machaut," *Essays in Musicology: A Birthday Offering for Willi Apel*, ed. Hans Tischler (Bloomington: Indiana University Press, 1968), 63-8; "Modes in the Fourteenth Century, in particular in the Music of Guillaume de Machaut," *Organices Voces: Festschrift Joseph Smits van Waesberghe*, ed. Pieter Fischer (Amsterdam: I.M.M. Institut, 1963): 137-43; and "Transposition and 'Key' Signatures in Late Medieval Music," *Musica Disciplina* 33 (1979): 27-41.

mixture of sophisticated and anachronistic ways of framing the discussions. For example, in his 1953 study on Machaut's "harmony," Reaney demonstrates an awareness of the significance of contemporary theory and is generally careful in his use of terminology, yet many of his observations imply that the composer consciously recognized and exploited modern harmonic functions.[81] When addressing the issue of tonal coherence, Reaney proceeds from doubly anachronistic premises when asserting that "the secular music of Guillaume de Machaut proves that the Ionian mode was very popular in his day."[82] Elsewhere, he claims that "the modes of Guillaume de Machaut may be summed up almost without exception as two in number, one a near major and the other a nearer minor."[83] The foregoing comments seem excessively self-assured, considering that many specialists have since disputed the connection of ecclesiastical modes to fourteenth-century polyphony.[84] Another of Reaney's doctrines, namely that "the principle of successive counterpoint is paramount in all fourteenth-century music"[85] has also come to be viewed with increasing skepticism in recent years.[86]

Toward the end of the period with which we have been concerned, the seminal study of Carl Dahlhaus concerning the "genesis of harmonic tonality" appeared.[87] This book has been very widely cited in the subsequent literature on compositional process and "harmony" in early music, but in fact it discusses only tangentially or superficially several of the crucial issues that are treated in depth by the scholars introduced above. In one point, however, he is

---

[81]For example: "conjunct motion is so much favoured that the relations between dominant and tonic are only sporadically observed" ("Fourteenth Century Harmony," 146).

[82]Reaney, "Modes in the Fourteenth Century, in Particular in the Music of Guillaume de Machaut," 139. The quotation is doubly anachronistic in that: 1) not only is the concept of mode exceedingly problematic in its application to the polyphony of the time, but even if it were fully justified, 2) the Ionian mode is demonstrably a conception of the sixteenth century, not the fourteenth. Thus, Reaney's use of the term "Ionian" in the context of Machaut's works is useful only in the most narrow descriptive sense but is devoid of historical meaning or justification.

[83]Ibid., 143. Both this and the above citation are quoted by Jehoash Hirshberg, "Hexachordal and Modal Structure in Machaut's Polyphonic Chansons," *Studies in Musicology in Honor of Otto E. Albrecht*, ed. John Walter Hill (Kassel: Bärenreiter, 1980): 20.

[84]For example, Hirshberg's conclusion is that modes are "of little use for the analysis of fourteenth-century secular polyphony...." (ibid., 19). The issue is still being vigorously debated.

[85]Reaney, "Notes on the Harmonic Technique of Guillaume de Machaut," 63.

[86]See, among others, Leech-Wilkinson, "Machaut's *Rose, Lis* and the Problem of Early Music Analysis," 9-11. For a specific consideration of the issue of "simultaneous vs. successive composition," see Moll, "Structural Determinants," 184-5.

[87]Carl Dahlhaus, *Studies on the Origin of Harmonic Tonality*, trans. Robert O. Gjerdingen (cited above in note 3).

quite definite: he rejects Besseler's opinion that principles of "tonal harmony" are evident in the works of Dufay.[88] Moreover, he recognizes the significance of the two-voice framework as a compositional basis in Dufay's songs.[89]

*   *   *

As is obvious from the above sketch, the aggregate of musicological scholarship appearing through about 1970 concerning compositional process in fourteenth- and fifteenth-century polyphony was important more for its stimulative effect upon analytical thinking than for producing any one unified point of view. Indeed, no such agreement has ever really been achieved. Rather, the various schools of thought have tended to attract adherents who have continued to argue the respective cases, sometimes doing so merely in the process of developing some other topic. Nevertheless, in recent years, the ideas initially developed by Georgiades and Ficker have managed to achieve currency in the English-language literature, to the point where the idea of late medieval polyphony being based on some kind of two-voice framework is now normally accepted as self-evident.[90] At the same time, however, the rather wide acceptance of such concepts has not precluded the continued use of triadic terminology in describing vertical sonorities in fourteenth- and fifteenth-century music.[91] Thus it can be seen that in certain respects, the Besseler–Ficker controversy has still not been unequivocally resolved.

---

[88]Ibid., 85. See below, note 162.

[89]Ibid., 341 (Chapter 2, endnote 11); regarding contemporary theorists' descriptions of this procedure, see 96.

[90]For a recent example, see the discussion of chanson styles in David F. Wilson, *Music of the Middle Ages: Style and Structure* (New York: Schirmer, 1990), 338 ff. This recognition doubtless stems to some extent from Richard L. Crocker's publications, especially "Discant, Counterpoint, and Harmony" and *A History of Musical Style* (cited above in note 22). Yet other scholars appear to have "reinvented" similar theories independently, insofar as they do not cite previous literature on the subject; see Andrew Hughes, "Some Notes on the Early Fifteenth Century Contratenor," *Music and Letters* 50 (1969): 376-82. On the other hand, there have been prominent exceptions even quite recently, as witness Bonnie J. Blackburn's attempt to contradict "a current view of fifteenth-century music as purely intervallic counterpoint founded on a superius-tenor framework"; see "On Compositional Process in the Fifteenth Century," 283.

[91]See, for example, Reinhard Strohm's discussion of Ockeghem's *Missa Caput*, in *The Rise of European Music, 1380–1500* (Cambridge: Cambridge University Press, 1993), 422. Strohm does, however, put his triadic chord labels within quotation marks, as though to emphasize their questionable applicability.

PART II. Evaluation of Concepts and Terminology

Having sketched out the most significant work done through about 1970 regarding compositional issues in late-medieval polyphony, I propose now to inquire more systematically into the methods and terminology applied in the respective articles translated below to certain crucial issues of compositional process. This kind of critical evaluation is necessary if a full understanding of the findings registered in the various studies—and more importantly, their relationship to each other—is to be achieved.

Throughout the following discussion, the reader may wish to consult the appendix below—a glossary and concordance of terms used by the various authors. This list compares terminology employed in the respective selections and includes citations of specific terms occurring in the original articles.

A. Roots of the Basic Conceptual Disagreement

In any number of respects, the influence of Heinrich Besseler's *Bourdon und Fauxbourdon* (initially published in 1950)[92] can scarcely be underrated, since that book constitutes the point of departure for a great deal of what is discussed in the selections translated in this volume.[93] As might be expected, both of the Besseler studies represented below proceed directly from ideas espoused in *Bourdon und Fauxbourdon*, and the first of them is nothing less than an expanded version of the book's first chapter. Furthermore, Besseler's book acted as a direct stimulus to the two divergent articles of Rudolf von Ficker and Wolfgang Marggraf. The overarching significance of *Bourdon und Fauxbourdon* is underscored by the fact that it is cited in all but one of the essays included in this volume.[94]

As is related above in Part I, the theories advanced by Besseler in *Bourdon und Fauxbourdon* and in a series of his other writings were subjected to the intense criticism of Rudolf von Ficker in "Zur Schöpfungsgeschichte des

---

[92]For bibliographical information, see above, note 34.

[93]Since the achievements of Guillaume Dufay play such a large role in *Bourdon und Fauxbourdon*, it would not be amiss to report here that Besseler acted as editor of the sole comprehensive publication of Dufay's works in modern format: Heinrich Besseler, ed., *Guilielmus Dufay: Opera Omnia*, 6 vols., *Corpus Mensurabilis Musicae* 1 (Rome: American Institute of Musicology, 1951–66).

[94]The sole exception is Ernst Apfel's "Spätmittelalterliche Klangstruktur und Dur-Moll Tonalität," *Die Musikforschung* 16 (1963): 153-6, which is merely an addendum to an article that appeared in the same journal the previous year. See below, essays 9 and 10.

Fauxbourdon." Ficker's main purpose in this article was to point out that the technique of fauxbourdon was not likely to have been Dufay's invention but rather was probably a long-standing (and indeed rather primitive) improvisatory device stemming from England. He argued that fauxbourdon was a relatively trivial and simple technique compared to the thoroughgoing method of writing polyphony—what he referred to as "English discant"—that was concurrently being practiced, which exerted a far more decisive influence on the future.[95]

It is noteworthy that Besseler seemingly reversed his own position on the significance of fauxbourdon without acknowledging it. In the first of his two studies translated below he claims that Dufay's "invention" of the technique in the Postcommunio *Vos qui secuti* was "the creative act of a master," whose effect "cannot be characterized as primitive," and he also makes reference to the "hugely penetrating power of fauxbourdon."[96] Four years later, however, in the wake of Ficker's criticisms, Besseler had changed his views considerably: now he characterizes fauxbourdon uniformly as "rigid and mechanistic"—as a technique "strangely conspicuous by its primitivism," and he even argues that it received its name (allegedly by Dufay) only as a "mocking self-criticism."[97]

As fascinating as the questions of fauxbourdon (considered with or without its English analogue, faburden) may be in any number of respects, they cannot be a focus of the present inquiry,[98] for the mechanical device of

---

[95] According to Ficker, the phenomenon of English discant "is fundamentally more significant from the standpoint of evolutionary history" than fauxbourdon. See "Zur Schöpfungsgeschichte des Fauxbourdon," 94 (93 below).

[96] Heinrich Besseler, "Dufay Schöpfer des Fauxbourdons," *Acta Musicologica* 20 (1948): 31, 39 (72, 81 below). Besseler's initially tentative assignment of Dufay's Postcommunio as the earliest fauxbourdon composition in the first chapter of *Bourdon und Fauxbourdon* (13-4) is symptomatic of the author's methodology, since by the second chapter the work is already considered "without doubt the earliest transmitted work [of fauxbourdon]" (27). Hence, a position initially stated as a possibility, unproved, is subsequently asserted as a fact, which then is used to buttress other, dependent arguments. Curiously, Ficker's own methodology regarding the issue of "discant embellishment" was itself subjected by Edgar Sparks to this same criticism, although that reproach has no bearing on the question of the discantus-tenor framework. See Sparks's assessment of Ficker's theories in *Cantus Firmus in Mass and Motet: 1420-1520* (Berkeley and Los Angeles: University of California Press, 1963), 404.

[97] Heinrich Besseler, "Tonalharmonik und Vollklang," 143, 145 (145-7 below). The self-contradictions just pointed out are adumbrated even within the first article itself (Besseler speaks of the "deficiencies" of the technique in "Dufay Schöpfer des Fauxbourdons," 45, see 89 below). See also the varying assessments in *Bourdon und Fauxbourdon* (22-3 and 222-3).

[98] The philological aspects of this problem were rather conclusively treated by Hermann M. Flasdieck in an article entitled "Elisab. *Faburden* 'Fauxbourdon' and NE. *Burden* 'Refrain.'"

fauxbourdon becomes a secondary issue of compositional process in all of the articles subsequent to Besseler's 1948 study (even including Besseler's own 1952 contribution, as is shown above).[99] The lasting significance of the Besseler–Ficker polemic thus lies not in its initial focus on fauxbourdon and faburden, but rather in its engendering of serious consideration of the respective functions of the three or four independent parts in multi-voice discant composition during the fourteenth and fifteenth centuries. These are the kinds of issues that prevail in the articles translated below, and accordingly they comprise the substance of the remaining sections of this introduction.

B. *Gerüstsatz* versus *Bourdon-Tiefstimme*

Notwithstanding certain later refinements, the issue of contrapuntal priorities in the fourteenth and fifteenth centuries as it has generally been approached by subsequent scholars was already fully framed in the respective premises of Ficker and Besseler. In certain important respects these two viewpoints are mutually exclusive. On the one hand, Ficker hypothesizes a "primary core counterpoint" (*primärer Kernsatz*) as the irreducible manifestation of contrapuntal integrity in a given piece, regardless of whether or not another voice lies below it.[100] On the other hand, Besseler posits the existence of a "bourdon low-voice" (*Bourdon-Tiefstimme*), whose appearance signifies the beginnings of a foundational bass line, which then is treated in such a manner as to create a feeling of "dominant tonality," and he further asserts that this

---

Anglia 74 (1956): 188-238. Other useful discussions include: Brian Trowell, "Faburden and Fauxbourdon" (cited above in note 32); Ernest Trumble, "Authentic and Spurious Faburden," *Revue Belge de Musicologie* 14 (1960): 3-29; Ernst Apfel, "Nochmals zum Fauxbourdon (Faburden) bei Guillelmus Monachus," *Die Musikforschung* 19 (1966): 284-8; Dagmar Hoffmann-Axthelm, "Tenor/Contratenor und Bourdon/Fauxbourdon" (dissertation, University of Freiburg im Breisgau, 1970); and Anne Besser Scott, "The Beginnings of Fauxbourdon: A New Interpretation," *Journal of the American Musicological Society* 24 (1971): 345-63.

[99]See above, note 97. It is hard to take seriously Besseler's 1952 claim that the fauxbourdon issue "comprises only a small part of my book, and never once the most important" ("Tonalharmonik und Vollklang," 131), since the topic comprises the very point of departure of *Bourdon und Fauxbourdon* (see Introduction and Chapter 1, 1-26), not to mention its centrality to his subsequent arguments regarding the presumed existence of an earlier *bourdon* technique from which it supposedly derived its name (ibid., 69), and to Besseler's postulated adoption on the Continent of the English quality of *Vollklang*, alleged to have been mediated by Dufay through his "invention" of fauxbourdon (ibid., 101).

[100]Ficker, "Zur Schöpfungsgeschichte des Fauxbourdon," 115 (118-9 below). This concept is perhaps more typically represented in the literature as the "[basic] contrapuntal framework" (*Gerüstsatz*).

low line is responsible for delineating "tonal harmony" (*Tonalharmonik*) in Franco-Flemish polyphony after about 1400.[101]

The two positions are irreconcilable insofar as Ficker claims that the low voice in any given composition around 1400 is not necessarily integral to the counterpoint, whereas Besseler claims that it is, and especially in those works manifesting a *Bourdon-Tiefstimme*. The essence of the debate can be reformulated as two basic questions: 1) what is the driving element of contrapuntal (or more loosely, "harmonic") function in polyphony after 1400, and 2) does this function manifest itself as an expression of "triadic tonal harmony" in polyphonic works from the period?[102]

In order to clarify the positions of both sides with respect to these questions, let us look more closely at some specific arguments that have been advanced by important participants in the dialogue.[103]

The controversy may be said to have begun in earnest with Besseler's "Dufay Schöpfer des Fauxbourdons." This article was brought out even before *Bourdon und Fauxbourdon*, and thus represents the first appearance in print of his novel interpretation. The crux of Besseler's account is his postulation of a voice-archetype he refers to as *Harmoniefundament, Grundstimme, Bourdon-Tiefstimme, Harmonieträger*, etc., which he claims is decisive to contrapuntal continuity and which heralds the origins of modern tonal harmony:

> The "six-line contratenor" proves in the event to be a typical harmonic foundation [*Harmoniefundament*] with fifth-fourth-octave leaps. But most importantly, this new ground-voice [*Grundstimme*], in numerous cadences—and above all at the main close of the work—remained low as a bass, whereas the tenor was thrust into the middle position. If one examines the general cadential relationships of the fifteenth century, then the decisive revolutionary change is brought to light. *While before the tenor was the main voice and as such supported the final chord in all works, henceforth the harmony-supporting contratenor assumed its place.* [This did

---

[101]Documentation for these and other assertions is presented above in note 34. According to Besseler, this "tonal harmony," native to Italy, was adopted by northerners, including Guillaume Dufay, who played a major, if not *the* major, role in consolidating these developments.

[102]Besseler does not always make it obvious in his arguments that triads are an essential component of his theory of *Tonalharmonik*, but comments such as those cited above in note 34 indicate that they are.

[103]N.B.: due to the extent of material quoted in the following discussion, and also since the original studies should be readily available in any university library, I am not presenting the German texts in a footnote as was done above in Part I. Instead, the quoted passages are given in translation only, omitting any footnotes in the source. Page citations to articles translated in this volume are given first to the original journal, then to the page number below.

not happen] everywhere and immediately, and also not without resistance and regressions. But the groundbreaking inventions around 1430 achieved a cadence formula with Dufay's "double-octave cadence" that belonged to the future. In this [cadence], the recognition of the system of harmony [*Harmonik*] found a convincing expression.[104]

On the other side of the argument, Rudolf von Ficker takes exception to Besseler's interpretation of what constitutes "harmonic function" in the period concerned:

> Here, however, is where Besseler fails to recognize a hitherto little-noticed principle of construction, fundamental to medieval polyphony: In the structure of three-part writing, the tenor and contratenor are differentiated not in terms of their particular voice range but rather through their wholly divergent duties or functions, to which they must conform in the process of creating the counterpoint. Specifically, the upper voice and the tenor together always comprise the *primary structural framework* [*primärer Kernsatz*], which exists as a fully closed and independent entity and which can stand alone in and of itself throughout, musically speaking. Hence, it would be completely impossible on voice-leading grounds that the tenor could ever have made a cadence with the upper voice at the fourth below; its cadence tone had to be, as a rule, an octave below. *To this musically complete, two-voice core counterpoint, the contratenor then entered the picture as a decidedly secondary filling voice*, allocated to the fifth above the *finalis* of the tenor (with the upper voice an octave above), thus completing the customary 8-5 cadence sonority.[105]

In his 1952 study, Bernhard Meier emphasizes the preeminence of the cantus firmus in the compositions he analyzes (which stem from the late—not the early—fifteenth century), but he nevertheless assigns contrapuntal priority even in the latter half of the century to the "discantus-tenor voice pair" in both theory and practice,[106] and so adheres to Ficker's essential formulation:

---

[104]Besseler, "Dufay Schöpfer des Fauxbourdons," 43, emphasis added (86-7 below).

[105]Ficker, "Zur Schöpfungsgeschichte des Fauxbourdon," 115. Note: in line 7 of the quotation, the emphasis is in the original; in lines 12-14, the emphasis is added (118 below). I should also mention here that Georgiades's much earlier (1935) valuation of the contratenor actually corresponds in its essentials to Besseler's position, not Ficker's; see *Englische Diskanttraktate aus der ersten Hälfte des XV. Jahrhunderts*, 109-10. This circumstance seems to indicate that Georgiades had not worked out the ramifications of his own theories at that time.

[106]Meier, "Die Harmonik im cantus-firmus-haltigen Satz," 31.This priority is based on the fact that those voices make the major-sixth-to-octave cadence.

The concords arising in such a composition between the structural voices (tenor and discantus), and the contratenor (bassus), are comprehensible throughout according to the rules of Cochlaeus, which stipulate the position of the third voice by proceeding from the tenor and the interval between it and the discantus. The concord prevailing at any time thus stands in and of itself and is not linked through a direct functional connection of the bass tones to the following concord, independent of an intervallic reference to the tenor.[107]

Three years later, Ernst Apfel invoked the functional authority of discantus and tenor as one cornerstone of his theory of compositional types in the mid-fifteenth century, positing the following attributes as characteristic of a contrapuntal technique he labels *freier Diskantsatz*:

> ... when this type (which now is designated as being in "discant-" or "chanson-" or "cantilena-style") came to be cultivated principally as a three-voice piece, it was always conceived as proceeding from the two-voice structure of free discant (i.e., from the structural unity of the discantus-tenor framework), just as is evident from the rules of the theorists. The primary voice was the tenor, and the contratenor had to concord with it. Moreover, whatever consonance the contratenor held was dependent upon the interval of the discantus (superius) with the tenor and the position of these two voices. Where the tenor occupied a high position, and thus found the discantus only slightly above it, the contratenor was placed at a consonant interval below the tenor. Where the tenor occupied a low position so that the discant voice proceeded at a larger distance above, the contratenor acted to fill the space between them.... It is of particular significance that whenever the contratenor occupied a position below the tenor, it was subordinate to the position of the discantus. In this manner conspicuous dissonances between the two voices were avoided, just as when the contratenor was positioned above the tenor.[108]

The above description is as definitive an exposition of Ficker's discant-tenor *Gerüstsatz* as one will find in the musicological literature of the time, and it is diametrically opposed to Besseler's idea of the functional authority of the so-called *Bourdon-Tiefstimme*. Also significant is Apfel's comment that

---

[107]Ibid., 42-3 (168 below).
[108]Apfel, "Der klangliche Satz," 304-5 (180-1 below).

the existence of this compositional technique is borne out in the writings of contemporary theorists.[109]

Regarding the somewhat later sacred repertory of Obrecht and his contemporaries, Meier notes that the voice-leading archetypes of tenor and discantus by this time could be transferred to other voice parts, while still retaining their contrapuntal identity and function:

> ... it is necessary to keep in mind that the cadential structure portrayed in the foregoing remains strictly intact, but the structural voice-leading framework of the tenor and discantus does not remain restricted to the association of the original voices; rather, it is variable within the complex of voices, according to the wish of the composer, to the extent that if a discant cadence is made with some other voice [besides the discantus], it requires placing the corresponding tenor cadence in another voice (and vice versa), whereas a rather great freedom is afforded the remaining voices, [acting] as contratenors.[110]

In opposition to Ficker's criticisms in "Zur Schöpfungsgeschichte des Fauxbourdon," Besseler, in the second of the two articles presented below, enters more closely into the genesis of his hypothesized *Harmonieträger*:

> Ciconia's director of harmony [*Harmonieträger*] comprises a typical example of exactly this [kind of prototype]: around 1400, the new voice type makes its appearance; it becomes widespread in the upper-Italian motet, and is soon taken up even by musicians from the north.... This is attested to above all by the youthful works of Dufay from the 1420s, which I have discussed. The impetus to further development lay in the fact that the Netherlandish musicians around Dufay generally held to the tenor as fundamental voice, both for the motet and the chanson. For this reason, after the 1420s the old-fashioned cantus-tenor framework now stepped to the fore again in Italian lands. But the voice type [acting as] "director of harmony" in no way disappeared. Now it was combined with the cantus-tenor framework under the designation *contratenor*, shifted downwards and took over the lowest ground-tone in the newly created double-octave cadence. Exactly the same thing happened in the four-voice tenor motet. There the cantus firmus remained in the tenor (which Ciconia had cast aside) untouched, and likewise the duet of the two vocal parts, triplum and motetus. In order to furnish a harmonic foundation, however, Dufay added to

---

[109]For a catalogue of contemporary theoretical descriptions of the *freier Satz*, see Ernst Apfel, *Die Lehre vom Organum, Diskant, Kontrapunkt und von der Komposition bis um 1480* (4th ed., Saarbrücken: Universitätsbibliothek der Universität des Saarlandes, 1993), 396-406.

[110]Meier, "Die Harmonik im cantus-firmus-haltigen Satz," 32 (156 below).

this superstructure at first a *tenor secundus*, [and] later a *contratenor*, which is nothing other than a "director of harmony." This is still true even in the four-voice tenor masses of his mature period. One can recognize without effort in their *contratenor bassus* the Ciconia model, that is, in the characteristic melodic framework tonic-fifth-octave....[111]

As is clear from the above quotation, Besseler does not deny the existence of a "cantus-tenor framework"—he only denies its priority as a director of the counterpoint, a role he unequivocally assigns to the *Harmonieträger* contratenor. As evidence for the significance of this *Harmonieträger*, the author emphasizes the role of the "double-octave cadence," in which the contra comes to lie an octave below the tenor (as opposed to the fifth above). As Besseler himself admits, this progression initially comprised only a small fraction of cadences, but "because its share grew to as much as 42% after a generation, it was apparently the cadence form that belonged to the future."[112]

Besseler's point of view was adopted in its essentials by his student Wolfgang Marggraf, who emphasizes the role assumed by Dufay in pioneering a "system of dominant harmony" (*Dominantik*)[113] in Western music:

> Taken together, Dufay's chansons present a picture not fundamentally different from the one developed by his predecessors and contemporaries. However, [these chansons] possess certain features pointing to [Dufay's] more secure recognition of the driving forces of historical development. The large role played by the fifth scale degree and the system of dominant harmony, the fluency in utilization of cadence forms, the renunciation of absolute progression effects [*Absolute Fortschreitungswirkungen*]—all these things in no way represent a break with tradition but rather result as their natural consequence. Those works incorporating six-line and deep-clef contratenors go even further in this direction [to the extent that] the multifarious potentialities found in Dufay's other works, as generally in his time, are reformulated to a principle. Even if the foundational role of the contratenor in certain respects had already been explored, it is nevertheless certain that the thoroughgoing employment of a low voice acting as a

---

[111]Besseler, "Tonalharmonik und Vollklang," 139-40 (140 below). Elsewhere the author specifically acknowledges the discantus-tenor framework as an integral facet of Franco-Flemish song during the period; see *Bourdon und Fauxbourdon*, 88-9.

[112]Ibid., 138.

[113]See the Appendix below for a complete list of this and related words, of which the most universal term is *dominantische Tonalität*.

director of sonorities [*klangtragende Tiefstimme*] was an innovation of surpassing import.[114]

The next year (1967) Ernest Sanders offered a relatively non-sectarian opinion in "Die Rolle der englischen Mehrstimmigkeit des Mittelalters in der Entwicklung von Cantus-firmus-Satz und Tonalitätsstruktur." In expounding his individualistic viewpoint, Sanders sees fit to disagree with Besseler on several issues. Nonetheless, his arguments regarding the relative value of voice parts in polyphony uphold those of Besseler and Marggraf, while attempting to refute the theses advanced by Ficker, Apfel, and Richard L. Crocker.[115]

> The impression created by Apfel is that the contratenor is never essential and hence dispensable.... And so he concludes that the music of 1400 to 1440 cannot be called "harmonic." But discant treatises were manuals for the techniques of counterpoint, as are harmony books for techniques of chord progression. In both cases the rules they contain are notoriously poor tools for analysis. Quite obviously, the composers of the first half of the fifteenth century adapted new concepts to traditional techniques, which were becoming atavistic; to lead the tenor 2–1 in a V–I cadence of a chanson is no more (or less) meaningful that Schönberg's failure to replace the convention of sharps and flats with a new system of "panchromatic" notation. Some of the old functions and tendencies occasionally seem to lead a sort of ghost existence, but they are no longer essential. *Besseler's rebuttal of Ficker clearly has the better of the argument; it faces the facts: in such a piece "no voice is dispensable any longer, since otherwise the character of the composition would be destroyed."* Ficker's and Apfel's denial of the musical realities is the more surprising when it is realized that V–I cadences already appear in a number of Machaut's chansons. Moreover, both authors fail to explain why the double-leading-tone cadence did not retain its prominence. It is particularly strange to see their position adopted by Crocker, since he repeatedly emphasized the importance of the ear....[116]

---

[114]Marggraf, "Tonalität und Harmonik in der französischen Chanson," 29-30 (324 below). Marggraf's *klangtragende Tiefstimme* (see last sentence of the quotation) is equivalent to Besseler's *Harmonieträger*.

[115]Crocker's positions are not presented here but are cogently expressed in "Discant, Counterpoint, and Harmony," 13-5.

[116]Sanders, "Die Rolle der englischen Mehrstimmigkeit," 34-5 (339-40 below), emphasis added. The passage is also contained in an earlier study of the author; see Ernest Sanders, "Medieval English Polyphony and its Significance for the Continent" (Ph.D. dissertation, Columbia University, 1963), 371-2. The Besseler reference can be found in "Tonalharmonik und Vollklang," 141.

Sanders emphasizes a provocative aspect of the debate in the italicized passage, where he quotes Besseler's argument against the dispensability of voice parts and supports the former's view that all voices are essential to forming "the character of a composition" during the period in question.[117]

At the time Besseler and Ficker were engaging in their controversy, the conceptual impasse between them was not yet recognized as being partly terminological. Ficker tends simply to employ Besseler's terms, even when criticizing the concepts they represent.[118] Only later does the issue of *Klang* versus *Harmonie* arise.[119] This dichotomy is embodied in the words *Harmonieträger* and *Klangträger*, used by Besseler and Apfel, respectively.[120] These two terms can stand as symbols for the respective positions.

---

[117]These issues are entertained further in Section E below.

[118]See, for example, Ficker's discussion of the contratenor acting as a *Harmonieträger*, "Zur Schöpfungsgeschichte des Fauxbourdon," 115 (119 below). Ficker does, however, question the "intelligibility" of Besseler's concept of *dominantische Tonalität* (ibid., note 20).

[119]The most neutral translation of the word *Klang* as it is normally employed in the studies translated below would be "simultaneity of multiple tones." However, the word has been rendered rather consistently in this book by the simpler term "sonority" (for an exception, see the text and translation cited above in note 23). Generally, only the German *Harmonie* has been translated as "harmony." This is a case where the German usage historically has had an advantage over the English, since the latter for many years dictated that vertical organization in polyphony be referred to as "harmony," even though that term has been inextricably linked with triadic concepts. The German language, on the other hand, with its two terms *Klang* and *Harmonie*, even from the earliest days of musicology was potentially freed from the propensity to equate vertical aggregations of tones with "functional triadic harmony," although it should be emphasized that this potential has not always been realized. Indeed, the purpose of authors such as Korte and Besseler was precisely to connect the music of the early fifteenth century with so-called "common-practice" harmony. See also the Ficker citations above in notes 29 and 30.

[120]*Träger* literally means "bearer," or "carrier," but I have consistently translated it as "director," for reasons that will become clear presently (see below, note 131). Apfel prefers always to use the word *Klangträger*, even when responding specifically to Besseler's arguments regarding the *Harmonieträger*; see "Der klangliche Satz," 300, note 1 (174-5 below, note 6). Thanks to Professor Apfel, I am in possession of copies of private correspondence between him and Besseler from the year 1957, in which Besseler makes it clear that the latter term, which "for [him] is a voice archetype," should be used in researching "the harmonic processes of Ciconia and Dufay." He further asserts in these communications that the two terms are not identical and that "the word *Klangträger* ... does not occur anywhere in my book." In truth, it does occur occasionally in *Bourdon and Fauxbourdon*: 84, 87, 199 (Thesis 10), and elsewhere.

C. Contrapuntal Referentiality as a Conceptual Key

How, then, is one to assess critically the foregoing arguments regarding compositional priorities? Is it even possible to evaluate more objectively the significance of Ficker's "discantus-tenor *Gerüstsatz*" versus Besseler's "*Bourdon-Tiefstimme / Harmonieträger*"?

As is intimated in the last paragraph of the section above, a chief symptom of the problem is that the German participants in the debate not only failed to agree on their concepts but also on their terminology. Even more significantly, the full extent of this lack of consensus has never been specifically acknowledged by any of the participants in the dialogue even in later years,[121] a circumstance which led these authors (as well as more recent commentators) to argue their respective cases without ever having achieved common ground. If, however, we translate all the applicable terms used by the various authors according to certain concepts introduced below, then it becomes possible to compare the arguments more directly.[122]

By definition, Besseler's *Harmonieträger* is always the low voice, acting "as a bass,"[123] in the works to which his theory applies (predominantly those in the so-called chanson style, with discantus, tenor, and contratenor parts). Furthermore, this low line is clearly valued by Besseler as the functional basis of harmony, at least in those pieces he suggests as being progressive.

On the other hand, the term *Klangträger*, as used by Apfel, is in some cases used specifically to represent the voice directing the sonorities in a sense that is principally linear and which need not necessarily entail the lowest pitch in a given sonority:

> This "contratenor" of the three-voice free discant composition had a greater ambitus than its counterpart in tonal discant and had a completely different function than the latter: it was a completing voice, but one that did not amplify the tenor, i.e., it was not a director of sonorities [*Klangträger*].[124]

In the above passage, the tenor clearly is being identified as *Klangträger* in a horizontal (or more accurately, a contrapuntal) sense, since Apfel is here speaking of a contratenor that often descends below the tenor, thus taking the

---

[121]Some important aspects of this problem were pointed out by Kühn in 1973, but the author did not identify a common denominator between Besseler's and Ficker's theories; see *Die Harmonik der Ars Nova* 21-4.

[122]This is a main objective of the appendix presented below.

[123]See the quotation cited above in note 104.

[124]Apfel, "Der klangliche Satz," 304 (179-80 below).

low pitch in the polyphony. Even more decisively, Apfel makes the following observation about the tenor in this compositional technique:

> Even though the contratenor was often placed under the tenor, [the former] was still dependent upon the [position of the] discantus, so that the tenor did not "support" [*tragen*] the sonorities but rather "constrained" [*halten*] them. It became, so to speak, a "proprietor of sonorities" [*Klanghalter*].[125]

A historical perspective for this problem of the potentially multifaceted nature of tonal directorship in medieval counterpoint is sketched out in Günther Schmidt's important study on cantus-firmus techniques:

> With the introduction of a [more] "artistic" conception of composition within early polyphony, the c. f. [cantus firmus] undergoes a deep-rooted change in its significance. Its melodic unfolding is reassessed to [that of] a potential director of sonorities [*Klangträger*]. The c.f. is looked upon solely as an aggregation of individual tones, which are rendered usable for the purpose of building vertical sonorities. The c.f. henceforth conducts itself in a manner diametrically opposed to its originally intended purpose. This process is fittingly characterized in [contemporary] theory by its framing of the rules of consonance progression. The theorists were interested only in the vertical progression to which the individual tones of the c.f. were ordered, not, however, in what occurred in its intervening distance. Here the c.f. still acts only as an intellectual and constructive acknowledgment of legitimacy with respect to the liturgy. In this function, the c.f. becomes a foundation or root voice and is generally identified simply with the "tenor." In the original definition as "chant," and the [subsequent] identification with "tenor," the polarity of the c.f. problem is embodied.[126]

The above series of quotations evinces three different compositional elements potentially inherent in a polyphonic complex, all of which can fall under the umbrella term of *Klangträger*:[127]

---

[125]Ibid., 304, note 2 (180 below, note 13). This passage clearly indicates that Apfel was aware of two separate functions often falling to the tenor: 1) to support the vertical sonorities as a low pitch, and 2) to direct the contrapuntal progressions as a leading melodic voice (often a cantus firmus or *cantus prius factus*).

[126]Schmidt, "Zur Frage des Cantus firmus," 231, paragraphs elided (195 below).

[127]Rudolf Bockholdt occasionally employs the term *Klangträger* in yet a fourth sense: to denote the shortest rhythmic unit (semibreve, minim, etc.) capable of defining a stable sonority. This meaning is immaterial to the context now being considered. See Bockholdt, *Die frühen Messenkompositionen von Guillaume Dufay*, 40.

1) the lowest referential tone, crucial to the integrity of individual vertical sonorities;
2) the linear proprietor of progressions, expressed variously as the *Harmonieträger*, i.e., delineator of "tonal harmony" (Besseler), or as the self-sufficiency of the *Gerüstsatz* (Ficker);
3) the cantus firmus.

Of these three elements, it is the first two that embody the problem of interpreting the German literature, since the third element is not always present, although when it is, it is normally equivalent to the second element, which in turn may or may not be equivalent to the first element. This third element serves only to confuse the issue further in that the terms "tenor" and "cantus firmus," which in compositions of the fourteenth and fifteenth centuries are anything but identical, are sometimes used by modern musicologists and theorists as though they were synonymous.[128]

Besseler explicitly identifies his *Harmonieträger* only as the first element, yet a clear consequence of his theory is that the low line acts as both the vertical referential tone (element one) and as the linear proprietor of progressions (element two).[129] Ficker's theory, on the other hand, stipulates that a clear distinction be made between the two.[130] Unfortunately, any possibility of evaluating this disagreement adequately was vitiated by the fact that neither Besseler nor Ficker ever pointed out the abstract principles that serve to differentiate the first two elements listed above, and few subsequent commentators have made any progress towards alleviating the situation.[131]

---

[128]See the quotation cited above in note 126. The source of this confusion is probably the fact that contemporary theorists almost always explain composition as being based on a tenor cantus firmus. On the other hand, there is little congruence between the cantus firmus and the *Bourdon–Tiefstimme*, a fact illustrative of the subtle distinctions that must be drawn between Besseler's *Harmonieträger* and Apfel's *Klangträger*.

[129]See the italicized passage in note 104 above. The linear aspect is manifest in terms such as *Harmonieträgerlinie*, which Besseler often employs.

[130]In fact, Ficker unequivocally uses the term *Harmonieträger* in the sense of "[linear] director of harmony" in the following quotation from "Zur Schöpfungsgeschichte des Fauxbourdon" (note 86): "Here also [in the anonymous motet *Anima mea*] the self-contained discant-tenor framework remains unaltered. The original contratenor is replaced in the later, four-voice version with a contratenor altus and a contratenor bassus. Only this contratenor bassus is now unmistakably a lowest voice, which now, together with the higher contratenor, brings about a new type of harmonic realization. But the development process shows clearly here that even this true low voice is a secondary completing part and accordingly cannot be the primary director of harmony [*Harmonieträger*]."

[131]Were it not for this consistent lack of differentiation in the German-language scholarship, I would translate *Klangträger* in its vertical sense as "foundation of sonority" and in its linear

As a key to evaluating these vexatious issues of terminology, I have developed the concept of "contrapuntal referentiality."[132] Since this theory is explained in detail elsewhere,[133] I shall confine my remarks here strictly to essentials.

The lowest tone of any given sonority I define as the "referential pitch"; this quantity is a controlling element of the polyphonic complex in that the intervals of all upper parts must conform to it. Its low position in a given sonority guarantees that it will be heard as a sonorous platform—a foundation for the tones placed above it. This referential pitch relates principally to the *vertical* aspect of composition and is distinct from another component, which I refer to as the "referential voice." The latter is a specifically *contrapuntal* quantity, i.e., one serving to connect adjacent sonorities. I define the referential voice as the one in an intervallic progression whose linear progress is conceptually anterior to the other parts—the one to which the others must "react." In the absence of any demonstrable preexistent voice, it is typically recognizable as the part against which the largest number of voices move in contrary motion. The cantus firmus (or other type of *cantus prius factus* such as an isorhythmic tenor) comes into play here in that whenever it exists, it is likely to be treated as a referential voice.

The crucial aspect of referentiality, then, is that in a given piece, the referential pitch and the referential voice may be distinct throughout, they may

---

sense as "conveyor of sonority" (and similarly with the term *Harmonieträger*). Given the subtle confusion that pervades the literature, however, I feel it is necessary to render both linear and vertical connotations in English with exactly the same word. Therefore I decided to employ a single translation for the term *Träger* ("director")—one which fits both senses adequately, albeit one not normally associated with it. In the former context this translation of *Klangträger* denotes a "director [i.e., authorizer] of [vertical] sonority," whereas in the latter context it denotes a "director [i.e., proprietor] of sonority [progression]." For one of the very few explicit indications of this dichotomy in the literature, see the quotation cited above in note 125.

[132]The neologism "referentiality" can be defined as "the quality of being referential." It is useful as an abstract resource for assessing conceptual priorities in Western polyphony, wherein tones are referenced to each other both in a purely vertical sense and in the linking of adjacent sonorities (see above note). Some musicologists have used the term "referential" in connection with extramusical associations, but my usage does not have that connotation.

[133]See Moll, "Structural Determinants," especially 234-8, where these concepts were first suggested. They are presented in a more definitive manner in my subsequent article entitled "Voice Leading, Sonority, and Contrapuntal Referentiality in Late-Medieval Polyphony," forthcoming.

be identical throughout, or they may be in some places distinct and in other places identical.[134]

The concepts of referentiality prove to be useful in evaluating several of the arguments in the Besseler–Ficker debate. Perhaps the most important of these, and the one which I feel is of decisive importance, is the issue of Besseler's so-called *Bourdon-Kontratenor* versus Ficker's conception of the contra as a "completing voice" (*Ergänzungsstimme*). Besseler plainly argues that his *Bourdon-Kontratenor* is the primary component of the counterpoint: "while before the tenor was the main voice and as such supported the final chord in all works, henceforth the harmony-supporting contratenor assumed its place."[135] Yet Ficker maintains the exact opposite, claiming that the discantus-tenor *Gerüstsatz* is the conceptual basis of the composition and that "to this musically complete, two-voice core counterpoint, the contratenor then entered the picture as a decidedly secondary filling voice."[136]

Looking at the situation depicted above from the standpoint of referentiality, one sees that while the contratenor often—perhaps in some pieces even exclusively—assumes the referential pitch, the referential-voice continuity in such a composition is manifest through the discantus-tenor framework, not through the contra. And this is precisely what Ficker argues in challenging Besseler's analysis of the Dufay chanson *Helas, ma dame* when he assesses the contratenor of that work as a "substitute" voice.[137] The same argument (i.e., one based on the phenomenon of contrapuntal dispensability) is invoked by Dahlhaus, who asserts that the contra in *Helas, ma dame* is "the last voice to be composed."[138] The comments of both authors may well be overstatements as far as practical composition is concerned; nevertheless, it cannot be denied that the contra is always the last voice added in the contemporary teachings of discant.[139]

Perhaps the most persuasive evidence in favor of the contrapuntal priority of the *Gerüstsatz* in surviving compositions of the type described above is that

---

[134]For a comprehensive assessment of contrapuntal techniques in a substantial polyphonic repertory according to the principles of referentiality, see ibid., 341-3.

[135]Cited above in note 104 (see italicized passage in quotation).

[136]Cited above in note 105 (see italicized passage in quotation).

[137]Ficker, "Zur Schöpfungsgeschichte des Fauxbourdon," note 86. Besseler's analysis of the chanson, expressed thoroughly in terms of functional triadic harmony, can be found in *Bourdon und Fauxbourdon*, 41. Ficker's criticisms are supported, although not compellingly, by Schmidt, "Zur Frage des Cantus firmus," 247 (215 below).

[138]Dahlhaus, *Studies on the Origin of Harmonic Tonality* (trans. Robert O. Gjerdingen), 85.

[139]See Apfel, "Zur Entstehung des realen vierstimmigen Satzes in England," *Archiv für Musikwissenschaft* 17 (1960): 93 (235 below).

in the course of manuscript transmission, contratenors are frequently subject to interchangeability or recomposition, whereas one seldom finds this phenomenon occurring with voices belonging to the basic contrapuntal framework. Of 106 complete works belonging to the corpus of French and related mass settings from the *Ars nova* through the first decade of the fifteenth century, there are nine pieces transmitted with alternative contratenors (some recomposed in multiple versions), whereas there is only one example of an alternative tenor (simplified, not recomposed), and one example of an added triplum expanding a three-voice work into one for four voices.[140] In acknowledging this paleographical fact, Apfel makes the extremely pertinent point that "an exchangeable part ... cannot be the decisive voice of the composition."[141]

It should be emphasized that in three-voice polyphony (including both sacred settings and chansons such as *Helas, ma dame*) based on a discantus-tenor framework, both those parts act as referential voices relative to the contratenor, since it is to the resulting self-contained duo that the contra is added. This contrapuntal hierarchy holds equally in works incorporating a cantus firmus and in freely composed pieces. In the latter it may not be possible to assign the role of referential voice consistently to either the tenor or the discantus, but whichever of these two parts was not a primary referential voice would still be a secondary one, as opposed to the contra, which remains of tertiary referential significance from the standpoint of voice leading, notwithstanding its potential status as occupier of the referential pitch.[142]

---

[140]Moll, "Structural Determinants," Appendix II, 392-497 (on each page, see under the heading of "Alternative Voices"). This list disregards *solus tenor* parts and voices evincing slight variations between manuscript versions. For an accounting of alternative parts in secular music through the early fifteenth century, see Hans-Otto Korth, *Studien zum Kantilenensatz im frühen 15. Jahrhundert, Berliner Musikwissenschaftliche Arbeiten* 29, eds. Carl Dahlhaus and Rudolf Stephan (Munich–Salzburg: Emil Katzbichler, 1986), 16-36. Here the author notes that after about 1400, every piece manifesting alternative parts includes "not less than one interchangeable contratenor or an interchangeable voice that lies [in a range] comparable to the contratenor" (ibid., 23).

[141]Ernst Apfel, "H. Besseler, Bourdon und Fauxbourdon und die Tonalität," *Aufsätze und Vorträge zur Musikgeschichte und historische Musiktheorie* (Saarbrücken: Selbstverlag Ernst Apfel, 1977), 114.

[142]For general evidence regarding compositional primacy of the tenor in the fourteenth century, see Moll, "Structural Determinants," 186-7. Still, there is no compelling reason why the discantus in a chanson-style composition could not assume the role of primary referential voice at times or even throughout. This is particularly true of liturgical works setting the cantus firmus in the discantus and also in the chanson repertory itself, where preexistent tenors are all but

Yet consider the point of view articulated in the following passage of Don Randel from 1971:

Another objection to applying the expression "V–I" to our fifteenth-century cadence concerns the question of root progression. This objection asserts that the contratenor in fifteenth-century cadences, with its leap of a fourth or fifth, is only a supplementary voice (*Zusatzstimme*) instead of a true harmonic foundation (*Harmonieträger*).... Hence, the inquiry becomes, once again, a search for the composer's own view of the music or a search for his compositional method. This often amounts to asking which voice the composer wrote down first. And this in turn often leads to attempts to distinguish linear thinking from vertical or harmonic thinking.[143]

Here, Randel greatly oversimplifies the objections of Ficker and Apfel as constituting merely a vague (and ostensibly ignoble) attempt "to distinguish linear thinking from vertical or harmonic thinking," whereas in reality their purpose is to *identify the primary element of contrapuntal function*, which they see (I think rightly) as deriving from the dyadic voice-leading principles of discant and not from the anachronistic concept of "root progressions" allegedly constituting a "true harmonic foundation." Hence, Randel's "historically justified interpretation" of the V–I cadence as being in evidence in the fifteenth century is rendered dubious in that contemporary evidence accounts for the phenomenon perfectly well without requiring "the historian ... to adopt a different view" of the principles at work: Apfel's account of contrapuntal priorities (derived from analyses of actual works) concurs exactly with the prescriptions of Coussemaker's Anonymous XI, Cochlaeus, Aron, and many other theorists of the fifteenth and sixteenth centuries, wherein the discantus-tenor interval is invariably considered first, upon which the voice or voices labeled *contratenor* are added in turn. In very many cases this process precludes "root motion" from playing a primary role in the progression.[144]

---

nonexistent. See Marggraf, "Tonalität und Harmonik in der französischen Chanson," note 36 and its accompanying text; also Bockholdt, *Die frühen Messenkompositionen von Guillaume Dufay*, 59, and Schmidt, "Zur Frage des Cantus Firmus," 248 (216 below).

[143]Randel, "Emerging Triadic Tonality in the Fifteenth Century," 80.

[144]Additional quotations ibid., 76-7. As an illustration of my point, see Apfel, "Der klangliche Satz," 306 (182 below); then compare Cochlaeus's rules of four-voice counterpoint as given by Meier, "Die Harmonik im cantus-firmus-haltigen Satz," 41-2 (167 below). See also my previous discussions of this issue: "Analyzing Four-Voice Vertical Sonorities" (UMI version), 32-7 and 45-55; and "Structural Determinants" 199, note 37 and its accompanying text. Marggraf and Sanders, on the other hand, argue that concepts expressed in these counterpoint treatises do not necessarily reflect the compositional priorities of contemporaneous

As a result of their undervaluation of the applicability of discant theory, and their collateral overvaluation of the low-pitch sequence and the general presence of "triads" in music of the time in question, Besseler and his followers misconstrue the central aspect of the issue, which consists precisely in the dynamic relationship between referential voice and referential pitch.[145] Besseler, Marggraf, Sanders, and Randel all characterize the double-octave cadence as heralding the origins of "dominant tonality" (or "the V–I cadence"), but the only solid grounding for this argument is the presence of referential pitch motion from scale degree 5 to scale degree 1 at the point of closure:[146]

Example 1: Referentiality in "Double-Octave" Cadence

10	—>	15	Discantus	=	open oval
5	—>	8	Tenor	=	open diamond
D	—	G	Contratenor	=	filled diamond

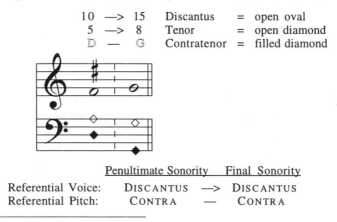

	Penultimate Sonority		Final Sonority
Referential Voice:	DISCANTUS	—>	DISCANTUS
Referential Pitch:	CONTRA	—	CONTRA

practice, which they view as manifesting principles of triadic or dominant tonality. See Marggraf, "Tonalität und Harmonik in der französischen Chanson," 12 (302 below); Sanders, "Die Rolle der englischen Mehrstimmigkeit" (see the passage cited above in note 116).

[145]While I believe strongly that sonorities in the fifteenth century are not codifiable as triadic entities in a functional sense (see below, note 158), one is perhaps justified in associating the concept of referentiality with the concept of chord inversion. On the one hand, the referential pitch is purely identifiable with the bass note of a given chord (not necessarily the root); on the other hand, the referential voice, when not identical with the referential pitch, is analogous to—but not necessarily identifiable with—the root of a chord in inversion.

[146]See Besseler, *Bourdon und Fauxbourdon*, 31-8; Marggraf, "Tonalität und Harmonik in der französischen Chanson," 28-9 (322-3 below); Sanders, "Die Rolle der englischen Mehrstimmigkeit," 33-6 (338-42 below); Randel, "Emerging Triadic Tonality in the Fifteenth Century," 78. It should be noted that Marggraf and Randel (13 and 78-9, respectively) ascribe dominant function even to the earlier "octave-leap" progression, in which the 5-1 "root motion" is expressed merely as a composite of pitches taken by the contra and tenor, respectively. To some degree this is merely a question of terminological convenience, and I would not quibble with anyone who chooses to employ the expression "V–I cadence" colloquially for an octave-leap or double-octave progression, but I think such a usage does tend to obscure, rather than clarify, the "harmonic" continuities between fifteenth- and, say, eighteenth-century music.

Let us assume that the above example represents a final cadence, so that there is no doubt whatever as to the degree of closure intended. Here, no one would argue that the task of providing a sonorous foundation belongs to the contra: to use the vocabulary of referentiality, it occupies the referential pitch in both the penultimate and final sonorities. Analyzing the cadence according to principles of discant, however, reveals that the referential basis of voice leading (i.e., the syntactic element defining the first sonority as penultimate and the second as cadential) is the stepwise contrary motion of discantus and tenor proceeding from the major sixth to the octave—the nearest available perfect consonance.[147] This principle of stepwise resolution of adjacent sonorities (Georgiades's *Nachbarschaftsverhältnis der Klänge*) constitutes the prototypical agent of function in contrapuntal closure from around 1300 until 1500 at the very earliest.[148] Thus, Besseler's invoking of the "dominant leading tone" (*Dominantleitton*)[149] as an indication of *Tonalharmonik* in such a progression is groundless, since discant theory would stipulate equally raising the F in the discantus to F-sharp. Note also that the contra can be removed entirely from the above progression without lessening the cadential signification of the remaining parts, but the same cannot be said of either the tenor or the discantus: the removal of the former would yield a relatively weak ("relaxed") interval progression leading to an empty fifteenth; the latter's removal would result in a progression consisting entirely of perfect intervals proceeding in similar motion.

In failing to recognize the difference between the concepts signified by the referential pitch and the referential voice, Besseler and his adherents are led to

---

[147]In the above example, I have identified the discantus as referential voice, since it moves in contrary motion with both other parts (although not stepwise against the contra). However, if the piece were based on a tenor *cantus prius factus*, that part would most likely be assessed as the referential voice. In any case, both tenor and discantus act as referential voices with respect to the contra (see above, note 142).

[148]This formulation reflects the "strict" rule of intervallic progression; regarding "relaxed" rules, which do not require stepwise resolution (but which are less common in cadences of this period), see Moll, "Structural Determinants," 208-9. These terms were coined by Karol Berger, *Musica ficta* (Cambridge: Cambridge University Press, 1987), 123 ff. A historical overview of theoretical accounts of both phenomena is given by Klaus-Jürgen Sachs, *Der Contrapunctus im 14. und 15. Jahrhundert, Beihefte zum Archiv für Musikwissenschaft* 13, ed. Hans Heinrich Eggebrecht (Wiesbaden: Franz Steiner, 1974), 103-11. For another thoughtful treatment of these issues, see Sarah Fuller, "On Sonority in Fourteenth-Century Polyphony" (cited above in note 75), especially 45 ff. Interestingly, neither Georgiades himself (*Englische Diskanttraktate aus der ersten Hälfte des XV. Jahrhunderts*, 109-10), nor Randel ("Emerging Triadic Tonality," 78), ascribes the requisite functional significance to this phenomenon in music after c. 1420.

[149]Besseler, *Bourdon und Fauxbourdon*, 41.

attribute the sole constitutive element of counterpoint as being the former—or better, they unconsciously treat the two modes of referentiality as being synonymous and identifiable with the former, whereas in fact they are *least equivalent* in the polyphony of the very period these scholars choose to emphasize—the early fifteenth century.[150] Accordingly, their identification of the double-octave cadence as signifying the origins of the "dominant cadence" is unjustified historically. In response to the arguments presented above,[151] I would argue that "V–I" motion in the "bass" (referential pitch) is merely one facet of a potentially complex referential hierarchy and that in fifteenth-century polyphony, what we would now call "root motion down a fifth" is in the vast majority of instances outweighed functionally by the stepwise resolution of an imperfect consonance to a perfect one in contrary motion between two principal voices—most often tenor and discantus.[152] The statistical preponderance of such dyadic motion in cadences signifies not a mere continued "ghost existence," as Sanders maintains, but rather constitutes strong evidence that these "old functions and tendencies" continued to exert a direct functional influence in polyphony until well into the sixteenth century, despite the encroachment of "triadic" sonorities.[153] Or to put it another way: it is the stepwise resolution of imperfect intervals to perfect ones, not the

---

[150]It is worth reiterating an observation I initially made in 1988, that the multi-voice polyphony of the late-medieval period "appears to have been the only time in the history of Western part music where ... the bottom voice was not necessarily a primary determinant of the sonorous direction of a given piece." See Moll, "Analyzing Four-Voice Vertical Sonorities" (UMI version), 120.

[151]See above, notes 116 and 143.

[152]It is revealing that a "strict" form of discant closure is observed without exception in the crucial textual articulations in Dufay's *Helas, ma dame*, which Besseler offers as a paradigm of "tonal harmony" in the fifteenth century; see Besseler's edition (Beispiel 9 in *Bourdon und Fauxbourdon*, mm. 5, 10, 15, 20, 31—i.e., at the end of the textless prelude and at every significant phrase ending). Note that in the two least significant articulations (mm. 10 and 20), this closure is effected between tenor and contra. Further statistical evidence, derived from liturgical pieces spanning the entire fourteenth century, is presented in Moll, "Structural Determinants," see Examples 7–10 and 8–4 for taxonomies of major cadences in three- and four-voice works, respectively. While the practice from later periods has yet to be tabulated, there can be little doubt that some two voices describe a "strict" intervallic progression in an overwhelming percentage of main cadences in Franco-Flemish polyphony through 1500.

[153]See the passage cited above, note 116. For a valuation of triadic sonorities in fourteenth- and early fifteenth-century cadences, see Moll, "Structural Determinants," 256. A general corroboration of my point is made by Crocker, *A History of Musical Style*, 207; further support can be found in Kühn, *Die Harmonik der Ars Nova*, 78-84, Otterbach, *Kadenzierung und Tonalität im Kantilensatz Dufays* (cited above in note 75), 76, and Berger, *Musica ficta*, 130.

"dominant relation," that constitutes the *sine qua non* of contrapuntal closure in both the theory and the practice of late medieval polyphony.[154]

The point introduced above regarding the triadic component of vocal polyphony brings us to the second of the two topics mentioned at the beginning of Part II, namely the issue of whether the music we have been discussing can be said to manifest the beginnings of functional triadic tonality. Besseler, of course, holds that modern harmony was "invented" by Dufay, in his fusion of the native Italian element of "tonal harmony" [*Tonalharmonik*] with the native English attribute of "full sonority" [*Vollklang*].[155]

Besseler's invoking of *Vollklang* strongly implies that triads are central to his theory of the origins of tonal harmony. Yet when he comes to speak of the issue, discussion of precisely how triadic connections are realized functionally is conspicuously absent.[156] Instead, apart from its connection with fauxbourdon, Besseler's definition of *Vollklang* is exceedingly vague. Technically, the term should be applicable to any sonority having two imperfect intervals, and hence it has no necessary connection to triadic progressions as understood in later music.[157] If one acknowledges the conceptual basis of polyphony as being *dyadic*, however, the presence of "triads" in fifteenth-century music is revealed as a mere byproduct of a harmony conceived as concatenations of perfect and imperfect consonances. Such dyadic combinations necessarily yield a large proportion of triadic

---

[154]Note that all of Randel's musical examples ("Emerging Triadic Tonality in the Fifteenth Century," 78-9) proceed from a discant progression of major sixth to octave between two of the voices. This, indeed, represents the defining element of functional continuity in such cadences, and it is not overridden by the presence of another, lower, part. A capsule history of the phenomenon is presented in Ernst Apfel, *Grundlagen einer Geschichte der Satztechnik, Teil II: Polyphonie und Monodie, Voraussetzungen und Folgen des Wandels um 1600* (Saarbrücken: Selbstverlag Ernst Apfel, 1974), 96-7. Even more decisive is Bernhard Meier's evidence that the phenomenon just described constitutes the functional basis of cadences even in the sixteenth century; see *The Modes of Classical Vocal Polyphony* (trans. Ellen S. Beebe), 90-1.

[155]Besseler, "Tonalharmonik und Vollklang," 136 (135 below).

[156]The notion of *Terzfreiheit* ("variable quality of the third") is as close as Besseler comes to assessing the functional significance of triads in the music he analyzes (ibid., 137). This and other incongruities inherent in Besseler's analyses of fifteenth-century works according to principles of triadic tonality are pointed out by Otterbach; see *Kadenzierung und Tonalität im Kantilenensatz Dufays*, 5.

[157]Besseler actually acknowledges this point when he says that the sonorous result of fauxbourdon "amounts to each tone of the melody being accompanied by its own tonic triad [in inversion]." See "Dufay Schöpfer des Fauxbourdons," 45 (89 below).

sonorities, without entailing any inevitable sense of their construction—or connection—as unified entities.[158]

Moreover, triads in practical composition are only exceptionally found as goal sonorities in final cadences until the late fifteenth century, or even somewhat later.[159] This point was not lost on Meier, who asserted that:

> Precisely this substantiation [i.e., that perfect sonorities were deemed most suitable as cadential goals], so inimical to modern conceptions, shows clearly how a thinking of vertical sonorities [in terms of] tonal functions is lacking or in its rudiments is still not suited to explicit, independent formulation.[160]

Marggraf chooses to ignore the triadic component of harmonic tonality when he defines *dominantische Tonalität* as "a form of central tonality in which, along with the tonic scale degree, the fifth scale degree plays a dominant role in the construction of the piece."[161] In my view, this formulation is too loose to be viable; furthermore, it does not include any discussion of cadences per se, even though Marggraf continually refers to "dominant progressions" (*dominantische Klangfortschreitungen*) and similar terms (see appendix below). Rather, the signification of the dominant in a functional sense requires more than consistent employment of a referential pitch on the fifth degree of a given scale in which the first degree is defined as the referential pitch of the final sonority. While the establishment of "dominant tonality" may not require the resolution of the tritone of the dominant seventh chord, one could well argue that it does at least necessitate using chords with thirds in both the penultimate and final sonorities, a condition which, as is intimated above, is found only atypically in fifteenth-

---

[158]Sachs, *Der Contrapunctus im 14. und 15. Jahrhundert*, 126; also Moll, "Analyzing Four-Voice Vertical Sonorities" (UMI version), 57-8. Randel argues that "the concept 'triad' ... adds nothing except a kind of shorthand" to the discussion of contrapuntal principles ("Emerging Triadic Tonality in the Fifteenth Century," 79). On the contrary: it presupposes an entire system of codifying vertical sonorities as integral entities consisting of a third and a fifth above a specific referential pitch (which then can be inverted without losing its identity), whereas the codification of triads as discrete entities is precisely what is lacking in both the theory and the practice of polyphony in the late Middle Ages. See also the sources cited above in note 153.

[159]Moll, "Analyzing Four-Voice Vertical Sonorities" (UMI version), 66-70. Regarding Dufay's use of thirds in interior cadences, see Otterbach, *Kadenzierung und Tonalität im Kantilenensatz Dufays*, 28, 38. Further evidence supporting this view is found in Berger, *Musica ficta*, 138-9.

[160]Meier, "Die Harmonik im cantus-firmus-haltigen Satz," 31-2.

[161]Marggraf, "Tonalität und Harmonik in der französischen Chanson," 13.

century works. Conversely, Marggraf's and Besseler's arguments depend upon one's accepting the referential pitch as being solely definitive for establishing tonal coherence in any given passage of polyphony. As I have already demonstrated, that presupposition is fallacious, and accordingly I must agree with Dahlhaus that the Besseler–Marggraf argument regarding the cadential force of the dominant relation in the fifteenth century is based on insufficient premises.[162] To accept this latter interpretation, however, is not to deny the influence of the referential pitch as a controlling agent in individual sonorities and, in a general way, for the piece as a whole.[163]

As a conclusion to the above discussion, I submit that the interpretation offered by Georgiades, Ficker, and Apfel accurately reflects the contrapuntal resources, priorities, and propensities described by fifteenth-century theorists and exploited by composers. Marggraf and others have specifically challenged that judgment, of course, and it is clear that one's point of view is largely a question of what compositional elements one chooses to emphasize. However, one cannot explain away the sovereignty of the two-voice framework in works of the type described above simply because at some point they ceased to be transmitted in two voices only (without the contratenor),[164] or because a low contratenor describes a "tonic-fifth-octave [melodic] framework,"[165] or because a sequence of referential pitches progresses down a fifth (or up a fourth) at a cadence. Such arguments are ultimately unsuccessful for three reasons: 1) they

---

[162]Dahlhaus's criticism of Besseler's—and by extension Marggraf's—theories of the genesis of harmonic tonality after about 1400 runs as follows (*Studies on the Origin of Harmonic Tonality*, 85):

> [Besseler's concept of] "music composed strictly voice by voice on a chordal-harmonic foundation" [*Bourdon und Fauxbourdon*, 42] is indeed possible. But it presupposes that the notion of chords has become a foregone conclusion. Only when tonal chord combinations have stabilized as conventional formulas can they constitute the basis or guide for the successive composition of voice parts. The evolution from manifestly "chordal-harmonic" composition to works based on a latent "foundation" cannot be reversed.

I do not second Dahlhaus's apparent acceptance of Besseler's blanket implication that this music was composed in a strictly successive manner, but this criticism does not affect the validity of the former's requirement for "conventional formulas" underlying "the notion of chords." Subsequent to the above quotation, Dahlhaus argued that Dufay realizes "neither the concept of a chord nor the system of functions" and thus that "the thesis that Dufay established tonal harmony must be set aside" (ibid., 86).

[163]This issue is discussed below in Section E.

[164]See Marggraf, "Tonalität und Harmonik in der französischen Chanson," 19.

[165]Besseler, "Tonalharmonik und Vollklang," 135 (136 below).

cannot displace the *Gerüstsatz* as the primary vehicle of contrapuntal function and voice-leading continuity in the period concerned; 2) they overvalue the significance of the referential-pitch sequence at the expense of the concept of the referential voice; and 3) they do not make a convincing case that triads were being treated as unified entities—a condition whose establishment is prerequisite to any convincing explanation of the origins of "tonal harmony" as exemplified in the theory of Rameau.[166]

On the other hand, the preceding points do not invalidate Besseler's (and related) positions in every respect. Rather, certain judicious aspects of these arguments lead to an acknowledgment that: 1) one must make yet a further distinction between the purely *contrapuntal* aspects of composition and other musical elements, which I have discussed elsewhere under the rubric of *musical texture*;[167] and 2) the referential pitch is still potentially an authoritative component of polyphony, even when it is distinct from, or subordinate to, the concept of the referential voice. As is shown below in Section E, this latter point has ramifications for assessing tonal coherence in works of the period with which we are concerned.

D. Ernst Apfel's Basic Contrapuntal Types

A major impediment to a ready comprehension of Ernst Apfel's long series of publications on late medieval polyphony is that the categories he suggests as fundamental contrapuntal classifications have remained essentially stable, but the terminology he has used to describe them has varied.[168]

Disregarding for the moment these variations in nomenclature, my research into the French mass repertory of the fourteenth century has substantiated Apfel's distinction between two basic contrapuntal techniques in

---

[166]Ironically, it was left to Apfel himself to trace systematically the disintegration of the discantus-tenor framework, and the concomitant rise of instrumentalization and of the bass and the triad as integral components of harmony, during the sixteenth and seventeenth centuries. See, in particular, Ernst Apfel, "Zur Entstehungsgeschichte des Palestrinasatzes," *Archiv für Musikwissenschaft* 14 (1957): 30-45; also "Wandlungen des Gerüstsatzes vom 16. zum 17. Jahrhundert," *Archiv für Musikwissenschaft* 26 (1969): Part I, 81-104; Part II, 209-35. The existence of an entirely separate technique of counterpoint, *not* based on a single two-part framework, does not nullify the above statements, since this method was cultivated to an increasingly lesser extent in the fifteenth century (see below, Section D).

[167]See particularly Moll, "Structural Determinants," 126-35. These issues are introduced below in Section E.

[168]For a schematic representation of the main terms introduced in the following discussion and their English equivalents, see Example 2 below.

evidence at that time.[169] In his earliest article devoted to the subject, Apfel illustrates how the voice part usually designated "contratenor" can be of "decisive significance" in differentiating the two procedures.[170]

The first of these two contrapuntal types is the so-called *klanglicher Satz*. Elsewhere, I have identified this technique consistently as "multiple two-voice counterpoint"—a rendering of Apfel's later term, *mehrfach-zweistimmiger Satz*, which first appears in the literature in 1959.[171] In the Apfel articles presented below, however, it is almost invariably translated as "tonal [discant] counterpoint," since I am attempting to represent clearly the distinction between two concepts developed over a period of several years.[172] According to Apfel's 1955 definition, the essential characteristic of the *klanglicher Satz* is that the contratenor "complement[s] only the tenor, whereby the other voices are directed by whichever voice (contratenor or tenor) is lowest at any given time."[173] The author subsequently characterized his revised term, *mehrfach-zweistimmiger Satz*, as a type of composition wherein "two or three voices, varied in register and rather independent from each other" are added to a lower voice or to the sequence of low pitches resulting from two lower voices (*solus tenor*) such that "each of these [upper] parts comprises its own counterpoint with the low voice (or *solus tenor*)."[174]

Apfel originally referred to his second basic contrapuntal type as *freier Diskantsatz*. This I translate consistently in the articles below as "free discant

---

[169]This material has already been discussed at length in my dissertation and in an article currently submitted for publication (these studies are cited above in notes 22 and 75, respectively). Consequently, the following is restricted to a general account.

[170]Apfel, "Der klangliche Satz," 301-2 (177 below). Sometimes the author employs yet other names, such as *vielstimmiger Verdoppelungsdiskant* ("multi-part discant based on voice doubling"), for this technique.

[171]See Ernst Apfel, *Studien zur Satztechnik der mittelalterlichen englischen Musik*, 2 vols., *Abhandlungen der Heidelberger Akademie der Wissenschaft, Philosophisch-historische Klasse 5, Jahrgang 1959* (Heidelberg: Carl Winter, 1959), vol. 1, 104. See appendix below.

[172]The potential conceptual difficulties of translating *klanglicher Satz* as "tonal counterpoint" I have addressed elsewhere ("Structural Determinants," 196, note 17), but it is justifiable in that one of the signal characteristics of this contrapuntal type is that the sequence of low pitches is decisive for the tonal direction of a given piece. Another possible rendering of *klanglicher Satz* is "sonorous counterpoint," but neither translation characterizes the basic compositional principles as well as does "multiple two-voice counterpoint." I am eschewing the latter only because the equivalent German term had not yet been coined.

[173]Apfel, "Der klangliche Satz," 302 (177 below).

[174]Apfel, *Studien zur Satztechnik der mittelalterlichen englischen Musik*, vol. 1, 104. This concept clearly proceeds from Georgiades's comments cited above in note 55 and represents the other technique I referred to above at the end of note 166.

counterpoint." Again, he later coined a revised term, *erweiterter Satz*, which does not occur in the earlier studies (my normal English equivalent for this is "expanded two-voice counterpoint," to emphasize the parallel with "multiple two-voice counterpoint"). Apfel identifies the role of the contratenor in this technique as "expand[ing] a given self-sufficient two-voice framework to one of three voices,"[175] and hence it is identifiable with the one described by Ficker in "Zur Schöpfungsgeschichte des Fauxbourdon." This technique is characteristic of the vast majority of chansons, as well as many sacred works, stemming from the late fourteenth and early fifteenth centuries.

Out of this second basic procedure, the *freier Diskantsatz*, Apfel identifies two subsequent, derivative techniques, both of which he refers to as *klanglich-freier Satz*, or "tonal-free counterpoint."[176] He claims that the first variant of this compositional type is characterized by a contratenor that "belong[s] as an essential extension of a two-voice framework, which indeed is no longer self-sufficient, but neither is the contra fully assimilated into the three-part counterpoint."[177] Apfel assesses the contratenor's specific role as follows:

> ... the contratenor is not really a director of sonorities; rather, it merely legitimizes irregular vertical intervals existing between the voices above it, but the latter do not altogether lose their significance [as the structural basis of the composition]. [Instead,] they find themselves in mutual interaction with the contratenor.[178]

Contrapuntally speaking, the second variant of the *klanglich-freier Satz* is equivalent to the first, except that in this other procedure the contra and the tenor essentially exchange functions, so that "the tenor brings forth a cantus firmus in long notes, while the contra comprises a two-voice entity with the

---

[175]Ibid. For a comprehensive description, see the quotation cited above in note 108.

[176]In later writings, Apfel intimates that the *klanglich-freier Satz* is not strictly derivative from the *freier Satz* but rather evolved as an independent technique in England at a time when Continental composers were pursuing predominantly the *freier Satz*. Also, Apfel never proposed an alternative name for the *klanglich-freier Satz* as he did for the other two; therefore I am offering no second English equivalent here. In order to emulate Apfel's gradual abandonment of the terms *klanglicher Satz* and *freier Satz*, however, I have elsewhere rendered the concept of the *klanglich-freier Satz* as "consolidated discant counterpoint," a term which I believe well reflects the interdependent, yet still dyadic, nature of the various voice relationships. Regarding certain dispositions of texting that Apfel has claimed are related to the existence of this technique, see below, note 201, and its accompanying discussion.

[177]Apfel, "Der klangliche Satz," 302 (177 below).

[178]Ibid., 309, note 1 (note 27 of the translation below).

top voice."[179] According to Apfel, such "compositions thus approximate those of the [first] tonal-free type, and differ from the latter only in that the tenor proceeds more slowly and that the contra assumes the tenor's place and vice versa."[180] By employing this same principle of identifying the archetypal voice functions of tenor and discantus and illustrating how they could be reassigned *ad libitum* to other voice parts, Bernhard Meier in 1952 had, in fact, already succeeded in recognizing an extension of the principles of the *klanglich-freier Satz* in practical compositions of the late fifteenth century.[181]

In reading Sections B and C above—indeed, in considering the vast majority of musicological descriptions of compositional practice in fourteenth- and fifteenth-century music—one might be led to conclude that the pure discantus-tenor framework with added triplum or contratenor(s) was the sole means of conceiving counterpoint in the late Middle Ages.[182] As is clear from the above discussion, such a contention would be hopelessly simplistic. Yet an extraordinary fact of modern scholarship is that of Apfel's three basic contrapuntal types, only one, the *freier Diskantsatz*, is typically identified by other authors, who rarely evince a comprehension of the precepts—or even the existence—of the other categories.[183] This curious situation in the literature

---

[179]Ibid., 310. This technique may have originated as an improvisatory procedure wherein one voice consistently "counters" below the plainsong; see Trowell, "Faburdon and Fauxbourdon," 52-3.

[180]Ibid. For further refinements of the *klanglich-freier Satz* in cantus-firmus compositions, see Apfel, *Studien zur Satztechnik der mittelalterlichen englischen Musik*, vol. 1, 91.

[181]See the quotation cited above in note 110. Another such instance is Dahlhaus's discussion of primary voice pairs in the frottola (*Studies on the Origin of Harmonic Tonality*, 284-7).

[182]A few relevant exceptions should be mentioned here. As was just shown, in 1952 (i.e., previous to any of Apfel's publications) Bernhard Meier had already identified traits characteristic of the *klanglich-freier Satz*, thus evincing a high degree of understanding of the contrapuntal precepts governing late-fifteenth century polyphony—a corpus in which the strict *freier Satz* was essentially *passé*. Also in 1952, Besseler pointed out a compositional archetype characterized by "a duet of two imitative sopranos and an instrumental bass." With this observation, Besseler had identified one manifestation of the *mehrfach-zweistimmiger Satz*. Rather than pursuing the theoretical and compositional significance of the phenomenon, however, he merely used it to support his theory of the *Harmonieträger*; see "Tonalharmonik und Vollklang," 139 (139-40 below). Another exception among the studies presented below occurs in Schmidt's "Zur Frage des Cantus firmus," note 79. Here the author makes some pertinent observations in connection with the *klanglich-freier Satz*, "the evolutionary development of which," he notes, "has still not been investigated."

[183]The sole specific reference of which I am aware in an English-language publication illustrating the full range of Apfel's contrapuntal categories as outlined above is to be found in Sylvia Kenney, *Walter Frye and the* Contenance Angloise (New Haven and London: Yale University Press, 1964), 121.

seems attributable in some measure to an inclination on the part of scholars towards researching the chanson, a corpus of polyphony which in the period from about 1350 to 1450 is predominantly three-voiced and in which the discantus-tenor *Gerüst* is particularly evident. But my research has indicated that before about 1340 the *freier Diskantsatz* does not appear to exist at all, and in the period after about 1450 it evidently had been replaced as a four-voice technique on the Continent by various forms of the *klanglich-freier Satz*. Hence, the pure discantus-tenor framework as represented by the *freier Diskantsatz*—a technique that lasted as a primary means of conceiving three-voice counterpoint for perhaps 100 years but which was probably cultivated seriously in four-voices for only some 30 years (c. 1420–1450)[184]—is discussed in the literature with very few exceptions as if no circumscribed alternatives existed.

Given the lack of attention Apfel's categories have received (particularly in English-language scholarship), Example 2 is offered to depict more clearly the terms for the basic techniques, along with their associated translations:

Example 2: Equivalent Terms for Apfel's Categories

Type*	Apfel's Initial Term	=	Translation	—>	Apfel's Revised Term	=	Translation
1	*Klanglicher (Diskant)Satz*		"Tonal (discant) counterpoint"		*Mehrfach- zweistimmiger Satz*		"Multiple two-voice counterpoint"
2	*Freier (Diskant)Satz*		"Free (discant) counterpoint"		*Erweiterter Satz*		"Expanded two-voice counterpoint"
3	*Klanglich- freier Satz*		"Tonal-free counterpoint"		None		†"Consolidated discant counterpoint"

*As enumerated in the passage cited above in note 170.   †See note 176.

---

[184]My research results indicate that the three-voice *freier Diskantsatz* probably began to be cultivated on the Continent around the middle of the fourteenth century but that the technique does not appear in four-voice composition in Franco-Flemish sources of liturgical polyphony until around 1420; see Moll, "Structural Determinants," 199-202 and 297 (three-voice composition), and 224-6 (four-voice composition). Regarding four-voice works conceived as *freie Diskantsätze*, see also Apfel, "Der klangliche Satz," 298 (173 below), where the author says of the four-voice Ockeghem masses:

> There are not many four-voice compositions in the old style of the *Missa Sine nomine* [i.e., *freier Diskantsatz*], in which two further voices are added to a self-sufficient two-part framework. In Ockeghem's works published to date we find none of these types. His four-voice works are all composed in the technique of the *Missa Quinti toni* [i.e., *klanglich-freier Satz*].

According to Apfel, a critical distinction between the first two contrapuntal techniques, as opposed to the third, is that the voice-leading principles of the former two are "not really a question of three- or four-voice counterpoint" since in the *klanglicher Satz* and the *freier Satz* "the contrapuntal interplay of the voices is lacking,"[185] whereas the latter technique (*klanglich-freier Satz*) is "conceived from the beginning as being [three- or] four-voiced" (i.e., depending on the total number of parts in the composition).[186]

The above observations are offered for the benefit of anyone attempting to come to grips with the complex nature and evolution of Apfel's writings. Now I shall proceed with a few revisionary comments regarding his theories. These remarks are suggested merely as a series of queries or refinements, some of which must be regarded as provisional and subject to further investigation. None of the following points affects the fundamental soundness of his system of classification, which I believe is likely to stand up well to posterity.

I will begin by suggesting a revision of Apfel's characterization of the *klanglicher Satz* and the *freier Satz* as not being "true" three- and four-voice compositions, which I think overstates the case. Simply because two upper parts are added quasi-independently to a sequence of referential pitches (*klanglicher Satz*), or because the contratenor is contrapuntally subordinate to the discantus-tenor framework (*freier Satz*), it does not necessarily follow that any voice part in these techniques can be singled out as being entirely irrelevant or superfluous.[187] Nor does it necessarily mean that "contrapuntal interplay between the voices" is lacking, even in cases where supplementary voices have been added (in the course of a work's manuscript transmission) to a previously existing two- or three-voice entity. Rather, it simply means that three- and four-voice pieces realized in these techniques are subject to certain limitations based on contrapuntal independence of upper parts or on a hierarchy of dyadic values. That both the *klanglicher Satz* and *freier Satz* are technically reducible to dyadic combinations does not diminish the potential entitlement of the added voice(s) as an integral part of the resulting polyphonic

---

[185]Apfel, *Studien zur Satztechnik der mittelalterlichen englischen Musik*, vol. 1, 104.

[186]Apfel, "Zur Entstehung des realen vierstimmigen Satzes," 82.

[187]The general validity of this position is best established through other attributes of polyphony, existing apart from the realm of counterpoint (see the quotation cited below in note 205 and the following discussion). However, it is observable in contrapuntal treatment as well: the two articulations in Dufay's *Helas, ma dame* where the contra and tenor effect a discant cadence demonstrate how the former can contribute to achieving contrapuntal clarity while still being technically a dispensable part (see above, note 152).

texture, and the fact that such procedures are more "successive" in their approach to fitting voices together than is the case in the *klanglich-freier Satz* does not invalidate them as potential "true" three- or four-voice compositions. Indeed, an element of successivity enters into the *klanglich-freier Satz* as well, since it is still based essentially on a discantus-tenor framework.[188] One might, therefore, describe the *klanglicher Satz* and the *freier Satz* as "additive dyadic counterpoint" and the *klanglich-freier Satz* as "integral dyadic counterpoint."

In his seminal publication outlining three distinct contrapuntal types, Apfel intimates that the *klanglicher Diskantsatz* (equivalent to *mehrfach-zweistimmiger Satz*) was conceived as a four-voice technique,[189] and in a subsequent article he argues that it was native to England.[190] However, my research indicates that this assessment is inconsistent with the apparent developmental history of the technique, such that it would be untenable to hold that multiple two-voice counterpoint was native solely to England or that it was ever restricted to four-voice works (except in the latest stages of its existence).[191] On the contrary: as far as I can now discern, multiple two-voice counterpoint appears to have been the standard way of realizing three-part polyphony throughout Europe until around the middle of the fourteenth century (albeit in at least two forms) and was the sole procedure of four-part composition on the Continent until about the second decade of the fifteenth century.[192] Apfel himself obviously recognized this point when he noted that Continental theorists such as Franco appear to be discussing a variant of the multiple two-voice technique.[193] In the three-part Franco-Flemish mass

---

[188]Apfel affirms this point in the quotation cited above in note 178.

[189]Apfel, "Der klangliche Satz," 308 (184 below).

[190]See Apfel, "Zur Entstehung des realen vierstimmigen Satzes," 83-4 (222-3 below), where the author makes the following points:

> The process of adding equivalent upper voices at specific distances from a low-lying tenor (c.f.)—which are independent of each other to the extent that a true four-voice piece does not actually ensue, but rather, merely a multiple two-voice piece—is actually described only by the English theorists of the fifteenth century. In contrast to this, the theorists on the Continent either deal with a two-voice discant [procedure] based solely on octave consonance, or else their rules for three and (seldom) four voices proceed from those for two voices. This fact confirms that the so-called "tonal counterpoint" was truly native to England.

[191]See Moll, "Structural Determinants," 238-9 and 369-70.

[192]This judgment requires a further examination taking full account of thirteenth-century polyphony and the English corpus through 1420. Regarding four-voice writing, see ibid., 224-5.

[193]See my discussion of this topic, ibid., 197-8.

settings of the fourteenth century, the evidence suggests that expanded two-voice counterpoint was in its incipient stages about mid-century, whereas the multiple two-voice technique is most evident in sources such as the Tournai and Ivrea manuscripts, which reflect the earliest layers of the corpus.[194]

A related point involves Apfel's description of Montpellier motets as "expanded two-voice compositions" (*erweiterte zweistimmige Sätze*).[195] Such a characterization elicits the obverse side of the criticism just suggested, since (if my surmises in the preceding paragraph are valid) these works are not "expanded" compositions in the same sense as is the fourteenth-century chanson based on the technique of the *freier Diskantsatz*. It is not sufficient simply to point to both phenomena as "three-voice works ... based on two-voice pieces," since the integrity of the resulting composition in the respective contrapuntal techniques differs fundamentally: in the motets of Montpellier there is no single two-voice framework, based upon structural nodes at the interval of an octave, which can be identified as forming a clear contrapuntal basis for the composition. Rather, the added triplum simply comprises an alternate counterpoint against the tenor (or against the sequence of low pitches if the duplum occasionally descends below the tenor—but in most cases the resulting composite line would still be predominantly identifiable with the tenor). The triplum would thus be nominally independent of the duplum, although further adjustments could certainly have been made in the course of composition (or recomposition). On the other hand, the added contratenor in chanson-style composition after about 1350 is not written solely against the tenor (or *solus tenor*) but rather against the dual contrapuntal entity of discantus *and* tenor. Thus, as I define the respective terms, the Montpellier motets are multiple two-voice pieces, whereas the fourteenth-century chansons (and their counterparts in the sacred realm) are expanded two-voice pieces. Accordingly, I would advocate referring to the phenomenon in Montpellier as resulting in "augmented," not "expanded,"

---

[194]Ibid., 338-44. Apfel mentions at one point that "against the other hypothesis advanced [by the author], that the so-called 'tonal discant counterpoint' must have originated in England, [it remains evident] that this type of counterpoint in England appears in the teachings of the theorists only in the fifteenth century, yet on the Continent it is recognizable already in the mass of Machaut"; see "Zur Entstehung des realen vierstimmigen Satzes," 81-2 (220 below).

[195]Apfel, "Zur Entstehung des realen vierstimmigen Satzes," note 34 and its accompanying discussion. Richard L. Crocker seems to be saying the same thing when he asserts that "the fourteenth-century song texture" was generated "directly out of the tenor-duplum pair"; see "French Polyphony of the Thirteenth Century," *The New Oxford History of Music*, Vol. II, *The Early Middle Ages to 1300* [Revised Edition], eds. Richard L. Crocker and David Hiley (Oxford: Oxford University Press, 1990), 675.

works, with the understanding that the latter is the more organic process. Also, paleographical evidence would seem to suggest that two-voice performance of a polyphonic work existing in three parts was a much more viable alternative in the thirteenth century than in the fifteenth, by which time the *Gerüstsatz* represents merely a conceptual point of departure for a piece that in all probability was considered musically insufficient without some form of contratenor.[196]

Another refinement I would suggest involves Apfel's claim that "by the middle of the fifteenth century,... the technique of free discant counterpoint was modified according to the paradigm of the tonal discant technique,"[197] or in other words, that the *klanglicher Satz* exerted an influence on the *freier Satz* in producing the compositional principle of the *klanglich-freier Satz*. On the face of things this hypothesis certainly seems plausible. However, the process is perhaps better explained as a renewed manifestation of the acoustical phenomenon of the referential pitch (as a generator of overtones and as a legitimizer of vertical sonorities) asserting itself more strongly rather than as a conscious reintegration of a contrapuntal procedure that must have been considered very old-fashioned by 1440.[198] This tendency of the referential pitch towards asserting itself as an indispensable component of polyphony—the essence of the progressive element of the *klanglich-freier Satz*—seems to me to be a basic driving force in Western multi-part music of all historical periods.[199] It is, indeed, the basis of the *klanglicher Satz* too, but we should not confuse the exclusively referential-pitch orientation of the *klanglicher Satz* with the predominantly referential-voice orientation of the *klanglich-freier Satz*, which proceeds from the discantus-tenor framework of the *freier Satz*, not from the multiple two-voice concept of the *klanglicher Satz*.[200]

---

[196]This issue is elaborated upon in Section E below.

[197]Apfel, "Der klangliche Satz," 313 (192 below).

[198]See Moll, "Analyzing Four-Voice Vertical Sonorities" (UMI version), 61-4, especially note 42. In a private communication, Peter Urquhart has also questioned the idea of a strict influence from the less-sophisticated *klanglicher Satz* upon the *freier Satz*.

[199]See above, note 150.

[200]In other words, in the *klanglicher Satz* the sequence of referential pitches by definition comprises the referential voice, whereas in the *klanglich-freier Satz* both referential-voice functions (discantus and tenor) exist quite independently of the referential pitch, although the last-named takes on a greater contrapuntal significance than it had in the *freier Satz*, since the low voice (normally the contratenor bassus) now acts to legitimize impermissible dissonance between those parts acting as structural voices, and can itself take over the tenor function.

My final comment on Apfel's theories again relates to the *klanglich-freier Satz*, whose attributes (as outlined above) were later recharacterized by the author in connection with a series of four-voice English works:

> When all of the voices added to the tenor (c.f.) are located above it, one may refer to the piece as being in the style of "tonal counterpoint".... When one of the voices added to the tenor (c.f.) comes to lie underneath it, or moves continuously underneath it, then it is in a general sense indispensable to the counterpoint, since it functions as a director of sonorities and must therefore be the first voice added to the tenor (c.f.), because the consonances taken by the upper voices are subordinate to its consonance with the tenor. The voice that acts as director of sonorities [in place of the tenor c.f.]—either partially or during the entire composition—can be either with or without text. When it is textless, one can speak of the piece as being "tonal counterpoint"; when it is texted, then we are considering a piece written as "tonal-free counterpoint." The textless sonority-directing voice in tonal counterpoint is rhythmically more akin to a tenor (c.f.), [whereas] the texted low voice in tonal-free counterpoint acts more like the [other] texted voices of the composition.[201]

This quotation suggests that voice texting comprises a key criterion for identifying works conceived as *klanglich-freie Sätze*. While such correlations may indeed exist, text disposition is not likely to prove a reliable indicator of compositional technique in the period concerned, since it is voice function that most decisively differentiates a contra in "tonal-free counterpoint" from one in "tonal counterpoint" and also because text disposition and underlay in manuscript sources from the period can be exceedingly capricious.[202] If one can specify a consistent two-voice framework (or series of two-voice frameworks) as forming a contrapuntal basis for the composition, then the work is going to be identifiable as a *freier Diskantsatz* or a *klanglich-freier Satz*;[203] if not, then it must in all probability be assessed as a *klanglicher Satz*. Hence it is essentially immaterial whether text disposition constitutes a viable criterion for identifying contrapuntal types except insofar as this would facilitate quick visual differentiation of works belonging to various categories.

---

[201] Apfel, "Zur Entstehung des realen vierstimmigen Satzes," 82-3 (paragraphs elided).

[202] This statement applies both to the extent and accuracy of text underlay of individual voices in a single source and to the consistency of text disposition among the various voices when concordant versions of a given work are compared.

[203] The particulars of differentiating these techniques are explained above. However, further research into both is warranted, particularly regarding the developmental process of the *klanglich-freier Satz* in England and on the Continent, respectively.

The above remarks are offered in order to illustrate some ways in which Apfel's three main contrapuntal types are susceptible of further clarification. I should reiterate, however, that none of these criticisms controverts the applicability of the voice-leading principles serving to distinguish them.

E. Referentiality, Musical Texture, and Tonal Coherence

In Section D above I observed that in the *freie Diskantsätze* from around 1400, the *Gerüstsatz* comprised merely a conceptual point of departure for a piece that in all probability was not considered musically complete without some form of contratenor. This recalls Ernest Sanders's comments also quoted above, wherein he invokes Besseler's argument regarding three-voice works of Dufay's time to the effect that "in such a piece 'no voice is dispensable any longer, since otherwise the character of the composition would be destroyed.'"[204] Although I have attempted in this essay to confute certain theories advanced by Besseler and others regarding the contrapuntal significance of the contratenor in that repertory, it nevertheless remains that their positions do in fact hold some merit *vis-à-vis* the opinions of Ficker's school. Most notable is their argument affirming the contratenor's entitlement as an integral member of the composition. Regarding the *Bourdon-Tiefstimme* contratenor, Besseler's argument entails that such entitlement *is* contrapuntal, but Marggraf asserts that the contra's indispensability is more generally "musical":

> In the latticework of voices, generally quite complex, of these late [i.e., *Ars subtilior*] works, the omission of the contratenor would be most palpably apparent. If one were to leave it out, a [bare contrapuntal] framework would result—one which would suffice as far as the rules of the theorists were concerned but which musically would be insufficient.[205]

This observation leads in the direction of that phenomenon which I have elsewhere characterized as "musical texture," comprising namely the interrelationships between voice-part ambitus, rhythmic coordination, and timbre.[206] The first two of these components are essentially precompositional, and the third is conditioned by performance alternatives. The presence of these attributes as signal elements of a polyphonic work

---

[204]See the italicized passage of Sanders in note 116 above. The passage cited occurs in Besseler, "Tonalharmonik und Vollklang," 141 (for my translation, see 141—sic—below).

[205]Marggraf, "Tonalität und Harmonik in der französischen Chanson," 19 (312 below).

[206]Moll, "Structural Determinants," particularly 126-35 and 318-24.

signifies that contrapuntal integrity is not the absolute arbiter of what is and is not essential to a composition. To acknowledge this conception, however, is not to invalidate Ficker's interpretation of the compositional priority of the discantus-tenor framework in works manifesting that technique, nor does it preclude the contra being a voice of secondary contrapuntal importance, in the same way that the alto's voice leading may be secondary to that of the outer voices in a Bach chorale. Rather, it simply means that *contrapuntal* dispensability does not equate to *musical* dispensability, since the element of texture can play an equally essential role in defining the degree of "completeness" of a polyphonic composition.[207]

As is shown above (Section B), commentators tend not to dispute the existence of a two-voice framework in chanson-style pieces—especially Continental ones—stemming from the period encompassing several decades either side of 1400. The question of the compositional significance of this *Gerüstsatz* as opposed to the contratenor has been discussed exhaustively above. Another side to the debate, however, involves the question of whether the tenor or the discantus is the primary component of that voice pair.[208] Disputing Apfel's claim that the tenor is the most important part even in compositions without a cantus firmus, Marggraf emphasizes the priority of the top voice in chansons, saying that "the songlike cantus,... is always the first [voice] conceived."[209]

The disparity just outlined between Apfel's and Marggraf's views opens up the further issue of whether the discantus line can have a primary effect upon the tonal coherence of a given piece.[210] In a much more recent study, Peter Lefferts strongly emphasizes the primacy of the discantus-tenor framework as "a coherent and self-sufficient duet," to which any additional parts (triplum or contratenor) "are inessential harmonically."[211] Subsequently

---

[207] See also the discussion above, note 187, and its accompanying text.

[208] This issue has already been raised above; see note 142.

[209] See particularly Apfel, "Der Diskant in der Musiktheorie des 12.–15. Jahrhunderts" (cited above in note 65), where the author states that "in the fifteenth century... the entirety [of voice leading] proceeded from the tenor" (2); also Marggraf, "Tonalität und Harmonik in der französischen Chanson," 25 (319 below), where the author adduces a contemporary theoretical statement supporting his opposite claim (note 36).

[210] See Marggraf, "Tonalität und Harmonik in der französischen Chanson," 14 (305 below). Elsewhere, the author claims that the forms of sacred music were not conducive to hierarchical differentiation of cadences (30), but this is untrue, especially of Kyrie, Sanctus, and Agnus movements. See Moll, "Structural Determinants," 263-6, 271-5, 324-31.

[211] Peter M. Lefferts, "Signature-systems and Tonal Types in the fourteenth-century French Chanson," *Plainsong and Medieval Music* 4 (1995): 119.

he echoes Marggraf's claim regarding the conceptual priority the discantus had over the tenor in the chanson, and remarks upon the difficulties this circumstance poses to the modern theorist: "We cannot yet grant modal primacy to the tenor, or give analytical priority to the lowest note of the final sonority if it is different from the cantus and tenor."[212]

Accordingly, Lefferts categorizes all of the chansons he analyzes (congruent with the earlier works considered by Marggraf) strictly according to the behavior of the discantus and tenor parts. Moreover, he analyzes pieces according to the principle that "a piece cadencing to cantus G over tenor C needs to be reckoned 'on G,' not 'on C,'" since "it is the cantus final with which other features of tonal behaviour correlate."[213] Here the author is essentially ascribing to the discantus the role of referential voice in the song repertory, and this point may well be valid for certain groups of works.[214]

As I have already indicated, however, it is an overstatement of the case to assert that added parts are "inessential harmonically," even though the voice added to the two-part framework of the *freier Diskantsatz* is clearly subordinate as far as voice-leading is concerned.[215] When it comes to occupy the lowermost tone of a cadential sonority—and especially if this is a major cadence—this referential pitch cannot simply be explained away as an irrelevant appendage: it will inevitably be experienced as a sonorous foundation or platform, notwithstanding the voice-leading priority of the discantus and tenor.[216] (The same thing can, of course, be said of the tenor in its relationship to the discantus.) This fundamental acoustical phenomenon

---

[212]Ibid. The very question of "mode" in fourteenth-century polyphony is, of course, problematic. Lefferts attempts to frame his discussion in "more neutral language" so as "to avoid modal terminology" (142). Conversely, an interpretation of mode and hexachord as unified determining factors in late fourteenth-century chansons has recently been offered by Christian Berger in *Hexachord, Mensur und Textstruktur, Beihefte zum Archiv für Musikwissenschaft* 35 (Stuttgart: Franz Steiner, 1992), but these theories have not been received well. Sarah Fuller criticized the author's use of evidence in "Modal Discourse and Fourteenth-Century French Song" (paper read at the annual meeting of the American Musicological Society, New York, 3 November 1995). Other criticisms can be found in Wolf Frobenius's review, *Die Musikforschung* 48 (1995): 415-7, and in Moll, "Structural Determinants," 163-72.

[213]Ibid., 120.

[214]See above, note 142. However, there still may be some question of which voice acts as a leading element of tonal coherence even in chansons: William Mahrt remarks upon several ways in which the tenor acts as a "mode-determining voice" in Dufay's songs; see "Guillaume Dufay's Chansons in the Phrygian Mode," *Studies in Music from the University of Western Ontario* 5 (1980): 85; see also Berger, *Musica ficta*, 68.

[215]See note 187 above; also Marggraf's quotation cited in note 205.

[216]For theoretical evidence supporting this claim, see Moll, "Structural Determinants," 235.

comprises, in fact, the sole constitutive element of contrapuntal function in the *klanglicher Satz* and is a driving force in the *klanglich-freier Satz* as well.[217] Indeed, its crucial role in the system of functional triadic tonality is the very reason why Besseler and his adherents attached so much importance to the referential pitch even in the *freier Satz*.

In the sections above I have shown the pitfalls of undervaluing the voice-leading significance of the referential voice in certain contrapuntal techniques, but conversely there also exists the danger of undervaluing the sonorous significance of the referential pitch. Rather, these two qualities must be accounted for equally if one wants to analyze works as individual and complete entities. From the axiom that the discantus-tenor framework is the contrapuntal basis of a given piece, it does not follow that it *is* the piece or that one is justified in analyzing it as if it were. The existence of alternative contratenors and tripla does not invalidate this claim—in fact it strengthens the argument that the two-voice framework constitutes more a point of departure than a finished entity. This is especially true in the fifteenth century, since, as Marggraf points out, two-voice transmission of such pieces is not traceable after about 1400.[218] Furthermore, even if it can be shown unequivocally that the composer "worked 'from the top down' in making important choices about tonal behaviour" in the chanson,[219] this constitutes only one of several genres during the period, and the procedure cannot necessarily be assumed to be valid for motets, mass settings, etc., especially ones incorporating a tenor *cantus prius factus* or ones realized according to the technique of the *klanglicher Satz*.

If one accepts that the contra of the *freier Diskantsatz* is indeed indispensable to the composition in a larger textural sense, then its assuming the referential pitch must raise yet another issue, namely the relationship between sonority and tonal coherence in the fourteenth and fifteenth centuries. This question is separate from classifying works according to the pitch sets, linear behavior, and cadential goals of the primary voice parts (Leffert's primary objective), yet it is of equal significance in assessing individual works—indeed groups of works—as finished products, and in clarifying basic principles of contrapuntal practice. Regardless of whether the discantus constitutes a more coherent melody or is more stable in its tonal behavior

---

[217]See above, notes 199-200, and their accompanying discussion.

[218]See the citation above in note 164.

[219]Lefferts, "Signature-systems and tonal types," 119. Acknowledging the strict two-part framework that almost invariably characterizes chansons, the author accepts that "there might be some give and take between priorities that would occasionally favour the tenor" (note 4).

than the tenor or the contratenor, it is the referential pitch that will be heard as a sonorous foundation at main points of stability, and this sequence of tonal anchors (along with the intervallic quality of their sonorous superstructures) is a crucial component of a given work's overall sounding effect.[220]

An approach to tonal order derived from sonority treatment, and thus entirely different from those discussed above, is to be found in Friedemann Otterbach's book entitled *Cadence Procedures and Tonality in Dufay's Song Compositions.*[221] In this study the author attempts to deduce a "systematic representation of three-part sonorities" from the interval progression that characterizes the most typical cadence found in Dufay's three-voice chansons, that is, an 8-5 final sonority preceded by a 6-3 penultimate sonority and a parallel 6-3 antepenultimate sonority lying a step above the penultimate.[222] From the similarity between the antepenultimate and final sonorities (only the bottom notes differ), Otterbach derives a so-called "ultima-complex" of pitches, which—whether fortuitously or not—proves to be nothing other than a modern tonic triad. He further identifies a "penultimate-complex" of pitches, a triad built on the semitone below the final (i.e., a reversion of the 6-3 sonority to "root position"). Ultimately he proposes extending both complexes to "spheres" by adding notes a third above and below, claiming that the resulting scheme suffices to comprehend all sonorities in Dufay's chanson composition.[223] This system seems to be an attempt to create an analogy in late medieval polyphony to the primary tonic, dominant, and subdominant functions identified by Riemann for triadic tonal music, although in the case at hand there are only two basic functions, not three.[224] While novel and intriguing, Otterbach's methodology seems to be based on several arbitrary premises, not the least of which is the assumption that the antepenultimate and ultimate sonorities represent variations of a single codifiable entity.

The foregoing points do not purport to be anything like a definitive examination of tonal coherence in early music (another topic that has experienced a long and lively history of debate).[225] As a final thought,

---

[220]See Moll, "Structural Determinants," 267 ff.

[221]*Kadenzierung und Tonalität im Kantilenensatz Dufays,* cited above in note 75.

[222]Ibid., 56-7.

[223]Ibid., 63.

[224]A concise explanation of Riemann's theory is provided by Robert O. Gjerdingen in the introduction to his translation of Dahlhaus's *Origins of Harmonic Tonality,* xi ff.

[225]"Tonality" is a recurring theme in the selections presented below. In this connection I would draw particular attention to the article of Ernest Sanders, translated below as "The Effect

however, I would like to suggest a basic principle applicable to the polyphony of the period, which can serve as a point of departure for joining the discussion of counterpoint with that of tonal integrity. This principle proceeds from concepts developed above in relation to the intervallic disposition of the final sonority.[226] It stipulates that in three-part works, the 15-8 sonority represents a thoroughgoing expression of one final in all parts, notwithstanding variations of pitch set among the individual voices attributable to partial signatures, primary pentachord-tetrachord combinations (if discernible), or accidental inflections. This also applies to the 8-8 and the 8-1, both of which are rather rare as terminal sonorities. The 8-5 sonority exists as an octave frame with a subordinate intervening fifth, and represents the prototypical expression of closure in three-voice works of the period before about 1440; the related 12-8 sonority exists as an octave frame with a subordinate upper fifth. The 12-5 sonority (also rare) represents either a foundational pitch with two subordinate upper fifths an octave apart from each other, or an octave frame with a subordinate lower fifth.[227] Subordinate fifths typically are assigned to the contratenor or triplum (the contrapuntally dispensable voices in the *freier Satz*), or to either of the two nominally independent upper parts (in the *klanglicher Satz*). In the *klanglich-freier Satz* it becomes possible to place subordinate fifths—and eventually even thirds—in any voice part. According to the scheme just laid out, broad relationships based on the disposition of the final sonority have the potential to be expressed as follows: when the referential pitch of the final sonority coincides with the referential voice, then one can speak of a "foundational tonality"; if the referential pitch and the referential voice differ by an octave (or much less likely, two octaves), then one can speak of an "octave-related tonality"; if the referential pitch and the referential voice differ by a fifth or a twelfth, then one can speak of a "fifth-related tonality."[228] These exhaust the normative

---

of Medieval English Polyphony upon the Development of Continental Cantus-Firmus Techniques and Tonal Structure" (essay 12), which enters closely into the question of definition.

[226] It is certainly arguable that "the final cadence is the single most important tonal feature of the cantus-tenor chanson" (Lefferts, "Signature-systems and tonal types," 120). On the other hand, one must keep in mind that the final does not always prove to be the most decisive criterion of tonal behavior in a given part or piece as far as classification is concerned. This point was acknowledged as early as Leo Treitler's study, "Tone System in the Secular Works of Guillaume Dufay," *Journal of the American Musicological Society* 18 (1965): 165.

[227] The former condition would apply to works conceived as *klangliche Sätze*, and the latter would apply to works realized as *freie Sätze* or *klanglich-freie Sätze*.

[228] In four-part writing of the later fifteenth century, the bassus often takes the fifth below the tenor. I think that Tinctoris, in his famous statement attributing modal priority to the tenor,

possibilities found in the corpus of polyphony considered in this book, and constitute a useful sonorous rudiment for assessing tonal coherence in late medieval music.

*   *   *

The above discussions represent an attempt to shed new light on a series of intractable and often neglected issues. I have not treated—or even addressed—all questions of compositional process raised in the studies translated in this volume, and indeed many germane topics have been to a greater or lesser extent ignored. My main purpose has been to illustrate the manifold ramifications flowing from an acknowledgment that dyadic principles of counterpoint, derived from contemporary discant theory, are paramount in Western polyphony through the early sixteenth century, and that this dyadic conception is manifest through two fundamental paradigms of counterpoint: multiple two-voice and expanded two-voice—both of which are susceptible of considerable modification. The abstract principle of contrapuntal referentiality serves to unify and also to differentiate the techniques. I believe that proceeding from these precepts in the analytical and critical exegesis of musical texts is likely to shed more light on other aspects of polyphony (such as cantus-firmus treatment, tonal coherence, problems of text underlay, or improvisational practices) than information gained about those other aspects will ever shed on basic procedures of contrapuntal treatment.

In the articles translated below, and equally in my commentaries above, the music of Guillaume Dufay assumes a central position. Yet in many ways we still stand close to the beginning of an evaluation of his artistic production, and few questions regarding his significance to music history can be regarded as having been conclusively settled.[229] Dufay undeniably does occupy a position of prominence in the pantheon of Western composers of the fifteenth century, but whatever status as a compositional innovator is accorded him by musicologists over the next several decades will likely be very different from that ascribed to him in *Bourdon und Fauxbourdon*.

---

was simply distinguishing the normative referential voice. For the original text of the passage, see Johannes Tinctoris, *De Natura et Proprietate Tonorum*, *Opera Theoretica* 1, ed. Albert Seay, *Corpus Scriptorum Musicae* 22 (Rome: American Institute of Musicology, 1975), 85-6.

[229] In his comprehensive overview of the composer's life and oeuvre, David Fallows remarks upon "how little we still know about the nature and styles of music in the fifteenth century and how little we understand about the range of style and techniques within Dufay's work"; *Dufay* (New York: Vintage, 1988), 189.

Dufay—Creator of Fauxbourdon[1]

Heinrich Besseler

EDITOR'S PREFACE: *In the article translated below, Besseler applies his extensive knowledge of the manuscript sources of early fifteenth-century music to the task of establishing a chronology of fauxbourdon pieces, and singles out the Postcommunio movement of Dufay's* Missa Sancti Jacobi *as the earliest surviving fauxbourdon piece. On the strength of this identification, Besseler claims that fauxbourdon was a Continental innovation, one that "began its life as the creation of a leading master [Dufay] shortly before 1430." Subsequently Besseler offers a theory for the derivation of the term "fauxbourdon" by positing the existence of "a genuine or true 'bourdon,'" which "presumably ... was a contratenor with the character of a low voice." The suggested compositional importance of this "bourdon–low voice" fits into the author's more general arguments regarding the genesis of so-called "tonal-dominant harmony" in the compositions of the early fifteenth century, which, according to Besseler, was also pioneered by Dufay.*

The [re-]discovery of early music [that has taken place] since the eighteenth century has brought to light a singular practice, which lived on in the Roman tradition: the *falsibordoni* of the chapel of pope Sixtus. According to A.W. Ambros, this type of singing possesses "something undeniably solemn and plainly dignified" and is "even in our day not completely extinct."[2] This name, often discussed but remaining enigmatic, is also found in writers such as Adam von Fulda and Gafurius in its French form: *fauxbourdon*. Thus one

---

[1] The present study comprises an expanded version of the first chapter of a book, *Bourdon und Fauxbourdon: Studien zur Klangtechnik des 15. Jahrhunderts*, whose appearance has been delayed at the present time due to publication difficulties. [Editor's note: the subtitle of the book as it was actually published in 1950 had been altered to *Studien zum Ursprung der niederländischen Musik*.] A short communication for the Congress of the *Gesellschaft für Musikforschung* in Rothenburg (May 1948) appears in volume 2 of the journal *Die Musikforschung* [1948]: 106-12, under the title "Der Ursprung des Fauxbourdons."

[2] August Ambros, *Geschichte der Musik*, Vol. II (Leipzig: Breitkopf & Härtel, 1864), 315.

may presume that the Italian term is a vestige of some venerable prehistory, a mystery from the days when the polyphonic art was first arising and developing. Only belatedly, with Guido Adler's *Habilitationsschrift* of 1881, did musicology begin to uncover the mystery.[3] From this has sprung a rather extensive literature on fauxbourdon, but the fundamental questions are as disputed today as ever, and a convincing explanation of the name still eludes us. Two contemporaneous studies from 1936 and 1937 were devoted to the theoretical sources, but they reached contradictory conclusions. Manfred Bukofzer traced a homogeneous tradition of the so-called "English discant," and separated it sharply from the "Continental fauxbourdon."[4] Thrasybulos Georgiades considers both phenomena as a unity and fauxbourdon as merely a derivative of the English practice on the Continent.[5]

It is a decidedly unsatisfactory state of affairs that no consensus can have been achieved on such an elementary question and that not once has it been possible to clarify the actual process of the creation [of fauxbourdon] and coining [of the term]. If two foundation-laying studies such as those named above can draw diametrically opposed conclusions from the same material, then the very basis of the inquiry itself must be reexamined. [This basis] consists in both cases of the theoretical writings, which moreover can be considered as a closed, thoroughly examined entity. In addition, Bukofzer has taken practical musical sources into consideration.[6] From a methodological standpoint, however, these [musical sources] deserve not only consideration but even the lion's share of attention, since they stand closer to the [contemporary] events and survive in greater quantities. For this reason it is attempted here, through the help of the *musical* sources, to solve the enigma of the genesis of fauxbourdon and to explain its name. Theoretical stipulations will be invoked only as a secondary recourse as long as the real [musical] antecedents can be recognized with certainty.

In researching the genesis of fauxbourdon from the basis of the musical sources, the first requirement is for a definition. The designation *faux bourdon* occurs in the musical manuscripts only when the following two conditions are present:

---

[3]Guido Adler, *Studie zur Geschichte der Harmonie, Sitzungsberichte der Wiener Akademie, phil.-hist. Klasse*, Vol. 98 (Vienna: Carl Gerold's Sohn, 1881), 781-830.

[4]Manfred Bukofzer, *Geschichte des englischen Diskants und des Fauxbourdons nach den theoretischen Quellen* (dissertation, University of Basle; published Strasbourg: Heitz, 1936).

[5]Thrasybulos Georgiades, *Englische Diskanttraktate aus der ersten Hälfte des 15. Jahrhunderts* (Munich: Musikwissenschaftliches Institut der Universität München, 1937).

[6]Bukofzer, *Geschichte des englischen Diskants*, Chapter VI, 121 ff.

1) The work must be notated in two voices, for discantus and tenor, while the contratenor must be provided [through improvisation].

2) The sole consonances allowed are sixth chords and 8-5 sonorities.

In the modern literature, the word "fauxbourdon" is used for the most part in a general sense. This is taken to mean simply progressions of sixth chords over a specified section, even when the piece is composed out in three parts or when such chord progressions only occur occasionally and immediately make way for another method of voice leading. This imprecise terminology is not grounded in the manuscripts; it indicates a modern shift of conceptual meaning and a generalization, which neither the musical nor the theoretical sources justify. In the interests of clarity, a distinction must be made between the old technical term "fauxbourdon" and the modern stylistic concept "fauxbourdon manner." In order to forestall any possible misunderstanding regarding fifteenth-century music, we will thus speak of a "fauxbourdon piece," understood as a three-voice composition which, either throughout or in a clearly demarcated section, corresponds to both of the above-named conditions.

Regarding the genesis of the fauxbourdon piece the surviving sources do not give any unambiguous information, but they do give indications sufficient to allow for an evaluation. In this connection it is necessary to consider the manuscripts and their constituent parts in as precise a chronological order as possible in order to gain a perspective for dating. A preliminary overview of the sources for the time of Dufay was previously published by the present author. The catalogues and sigla given there may be consulted to make the following more comprehensible.[7] A more precise examination of the fifteenth-century sources will have to be reported in another context. Each piece discussed in this study is cited according to the oldest source in which it occurs, using the work's number in the manuscript.[8] As far as is necessary, the relevant manuscript fascicle or section also appears in parenthesis, e.g., *O* (2) 57, or [as] an indication of secondary entries, such as *BL(N)* 167. Works available in modern transcriptions are shown by asterisk (*).

---

[7]Heinrich Besseler, "Studien zur Musik des Mittelalters [Part] I: Neue Quellen des 14. und beginnenden 15. Jahrhunderts," *Archiv für Musikwissenschaft* 7 (1925): 209-45. An index of the sigla used is provided in that study, 245.

[8]For the manuscripts *O*, *BL*, *BU*, and *ModB*, a consecutive accounting of contents remains unpublished, even though it has already been much used in the literature, as by Charles van den Borren, *Polyphonia Sacra* (1932); Werner Korte, *Studie zur Geschichte der Musik in Italien* (1933); Erna Dannemann, *Die spätgotische Musiktradition in Frankreich und Burgund* (1936). For the sake of brevity, the same citations have been retained here, so that the user of the manuscripts can ascertain the pieces easily.

The oldest sacred or mixed collections of the fifteenth century, such as *Apt(4)*, *PadA*, *RB*, *ModA*, and *O*, do not yet contain any hint of fauxbourdon.[9] It is only with *BL* that the transmission [of fauxbourdon pieces] begins, although in approximately the same fashion and number as the main later sources up through after the middle of the century: *ModB*, *Ao*, *Tr 87*, *Tr 92*, *FM*, *Tr 90*, and *Em*.[10] These main sources each contain a group of around 10, 20, 30 fauxbourdon pieces; whose complete accounting would lead too far astray here. Individual examples exist in the fragment *MüL*, in *BU*, *Ca 32*, in the laude manuscript *Ven*, and in the treatise of Guilielmus Monachus. The total picture of the early transmission [of fauxbourdon] creates the impression that the new form sprang fully formed into life at a specific point in time, so that it found expression everywhere simultaneously. At any rate, codicology does not permit us to recognize an extended prehistory of fauxbourdon with rising numbers of works [in sources of increasingly late date]. It has already been established as a fundamental fact that the English manuscripts do not contain a single fauxbourdon piece.[11]

If one compares the composer names in the manuscripts mentioned above, it is unmistakable that Dufay must have taken an essential part in the forging of the fauxbourdon piece. Apart from the corpus in *Tr 90*, which is transmitted anonymously throughout, his is the sole name appearing in all manuscripts. Moreover, [his name occurs] in each case at a leading place, whereas the accompanying names change from case to case.[12] Whether an act of creation in the literal sense had taken place, or whether one must assume a gradual process of growth whose stages can no longer be traced, is a question that most likely can be decided with the help of the oldest manuscript, *BL*. *Tr 87* contains a collection that is in part contemporaneous, but it has later works mixed in, which were probably entered subsequently. If one proceeds

---

[9]At least the fourth fascicle of Apt belongs to the fifteenth century, since the name Jacobus Murrin occurs there. See Jacques Handschin, "Zur Geschichte von Notre-Dame," *Acta Musicologica* 4 (1932): 55. [Also, evidence for a late dating of the fourth fascicle is provided by the Gloria,] *Apt (4) 38 = BL 30, Baudet Cordier; see Heinrich Besseler, *Die Musik des Mittelalters* (Potsdam: Athenaion, 1931); Beispiel 100.

[10]*Em* is the codex (München mus. 3232 a) stemming from St. Emmeram in Regensburg, which became known in 1927; see Karl Dèzes, "Der Mensuralkodex des Benediktinerklosters Sancti Emmerami zu Regensburg" *Zeitschrift für Musikwissenschaft* 10 (1927/28): 65-105. *Ao* is the newly-discovered Italian manuscript in the Seminar of Aosta; see Guillaume de Van, "A Recently Discovered Source of Early Fifteenth Century Polyphonic Music," *Musica Disciplina* 2 (1948): 5-74.

[11]Bukofzer, *Geschichte des englischen Diskants*, 123-4.

[12]Specific cases are noted in the book cited above in note 1.

chronologically, then the source that was the earliest to be entirely completed, *BL*, must have priority. Among the 18 fauxbourdon pieces that are found there are the well-known hymns of Dufay, which display fauxbourdon composition in all its aspects. Does this give us a point of reference for separating the earlier and later pieces from [within] the total contents of *BL*?

Fortunately, the codex does provide such a device. The extensive utilitarian codex *BL*, stemming from Piacenza in upper Italy, was apparently laid out and enlarged in a painstaking fashion for a circle of musicians interested in the sacred repertoire.[13] The [original] corpus comprises about two thirds of the whole; the pieces are entered in a clearly recognizable order and are decorated with initials. The remainder of the works, something over a third of the whole, were then added in on empty pages and into fields in various places. They remain without initials and comprise a supplement [*Nachtrag*] to *BL* [individual works belonging to this supplement are indicated by Besseler as *BL(N)*]. Among the 18 fauxbourdon pieces, 16 stand in the supplement and only two in the corpus. These two command our first attention. If the oldest fauxbourdon pieces are separable at all according to paleographical evidence, then one must presume that this is such a case.[14] A dating would be possible if one were able to specify the chronological boundary between the corpus and the supplement. The earliest fauxbourdon pieces must be placeable shortly before this boundary, since the main repertory follows immediately in the supplement. Toward the end of the codex is a section containing hymns and Magnificats, which consists entirely of secondary entries, but some of the motets placed beforehand are also [secondary entries]. The earliest datable motets of the corpus stem from the 1420s: **BL* 214 *Plaude decus mundi* was composed for Venice in 1423, **BL* 236 *Apostolo glorioso* for Patras in 1426.[15] On the other hand, Dufay's ceremonial motet **BL(N)* 167 *Supremum est*, written on the occasion of the Peace of Viterbo in 1433, already belongs to the secondary entries.[16] The division thus lies between 1426 and 1433.

---

[13]Heinrich Besseler, "Studien zur Musik des Mittelalters [Part] I," 234-5.

[14]Particulars are given in the table below. The fauxbourdon pieces in the supplement to *BL* follow below in [Table II].

[15]*Plaude* was edited by Rudolf von Ficker, *Sieben Trienter Codices: Geistliche und weltliche Kompositionen des XIV. und XV. Jahrhunderts, Sechste Auswahl, DTÖ* 76 (*Jahrgang* XL) (Vienna: Universal-Edition, 1933), 6 and 99; *Apostolo* (undated) is contained in the same publication, 22 and 100. The evidence for the dating, "Patras 1426," will be presented [by the author] at another place.

[16]Edition in *DTÖ* 76 (cited above), 24 and 100.

[Table I:] Faux bourdon Pieces in the Corpus of *BL*

No.	Text incipit	Composer	Genre	Mensuration
BL 119	*Vos // qui secuti estis*	Dufay	Proper	ø
BL 198	*Regina celi letare*	Jo{hannes} de Lymburgia	Motet	C + ø

At this point a notational observation is warranted in order to narrow further the scope of discussion. The old means of notating the 6/8 rhythm with the help of *prolatio major* (C ♩♩♩ ♦), which gives the manuscripts of the early fifteenth century their characteristic appearance, was replaced after 1430 with the *tempus perfectum diminutum* (◗ ♦ ♦ ♦ ■). What this process signifies musically is explored elsewhere.[17] Dufay seems to have been the first of the Netherlandish musicians who carried out this change, so that the *prolatio* notation is as good as absent from even his middle-period output. In the five-voice motet *Tr 87:70 Ecclesie militantis*, written on the occasion of the election of Pope Eugene IV in March 1431, the new notational gambit is already being used.[18] It reappears in the ceremonial music from 1433 (mentioned above) and in later pieces, while previously, at corresponding places in the great isorhythmic tenor-motets, the *prolatio* dominates. Precisely in this time of transition, which must lie shortly before 1431, falls the boundary between the corpus and the secondary entries in *BL*. Three smaller motets of Dufay and several sections of his *Sancti Jacobi* Mass display already in the corpus the new *tempus perfectum diminutum*.[19] Conversely, in three sacred works representing supplementary entries, he still employs the old *prolatio* notation.[20] Therefore, one is justified in setting tentatively the boundary between the corpus and the secondary entries in *BL* around 1430. Accordingly, the first transmitted fauxbourdon pieces would have originated "shortly before 1430." In this assessment [of chronology,] the margin probably amounts to only a few years.

---

[17]See Besseler, *Bourdon und Fauxbourdon*, Chapter VII.

[18]Edition in *DTÖ* 76, 26 and 100. The transcription shows a shortened note form, although the same beginning rhythm exists as in *Supremum es*t (*DTÖ* 76, 24). In the original, the upper voices (except the contratenor) are notated in *tempus perfectum*. The sign of diminution to be applied to all voices stands at the beginning of the contratenor (m. 25 of the edition should be altered accordingly).

[19]The following works of Dufay begin in *tempus perfectum diminutum*: Introitus, Alleluja, and *Postcommunio* of the *Sancti Jacobi* Mass (*BL* 111, 114, 119) and the motets *Vergine bella*, *Flos florum*, and *Anima mea liquefacta est*, (*BL* 200, 233, 234).

[20]The four-voice *Et in terra* and *Patrem* of Dufay, *BL(N)* 107-108, as well as his motet *Balsamus*, *BL(N)* 168, begin in *prolatio major*.

An examination of the music confirms the source evidence in a surprising fashion. Of the two early works in the corpus of *BL* (introduced above), the first one, **BL* 119 *Vos qui secuti estis*, assumes a special position in every respect. Displaying the indication *post co(mmun)io*, it belongs as the final item to Dufay's *Missa Sancti Jacobi*—one of the oldest complete mass cycles, with five Ordinary and four Proper sections.[21] The *Postcommunio is an embellished discant treatment of the Gregorian Communio for the feast of the Apostles.[22] Besides the normal indication *faux bourdon* in the tenor, this is the sole fauxbourdon piece heretofore known that contains a specific canon instruction in the discantus in rhymed hexameters, the so-called Leonic verses:

> *Si trinum queras / a summo tolle figuras*
> *Et simul incipito / dyatesseron insubeundo*[23]

The missing middle voice is hence to be realized as a simultaneous canon at the lower fourth to the discantus. This indication itself denotes the piece as one of the first attempts at fauxbourdon from the time, since a firm practice did not yet exist. One also perceives as unusual the frequent cadence with the descending leap in the tenor (Example 1A), the effect of which is somewhat forced and is superseded in the mature fauxbourdons by the fluid tenor cadence with stepwise motion (Example 1B). We will have occasion to make further reference to these procedures.

Example 1: Tenor Cadences in Fauxbourdon Composition

A) Descending fourth-Leap cadence   B) Descending stepwise cadence

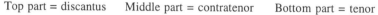

Top part = discantus   Middle part = contratenor   Bottom part = tenor

---

[21]See Heinrich Besseler, *Bourdon und Fauxbourdon*, Chapter VIII.

[22]An edition is included as an Appendix to the Congress Report listed above in note 1 (*Die Musikforschung* 1 (1948/49), volume 2).

[23][Translation: "if you seek each of three [parts] / take up the melody from the uppermost / and [take up] from the beginning simultaneously / at the fourth below."] The manuscript has *insubeondo*. Similar rhymed verses are also used by Jan van Eyck on the Gent Altarpiece, completed in 1432. The wording follows Hermann Beenken, *Hubert and Jan van Eyck* (Munich: 1941), 26, or Charles de Tolnay, *Le maître de Flémalle et les fréres van Eyck* (Brussels: Editions de la connaissance, 1939), 47.

In spite of this, the *Postcommunio cannot be designated [simply] as "primitive." On the contrary: the total effect is more exacting than that of the fauxbourdon pieces known to be later. Thus, above all the tenor is here in no way schematically dependent upon the tenor but rather has been fashioned into a self-sufficient voice. Its characteristic rhythm, which in mm. 2-3, 11-12, 14, and 20 demands hemiola coloration, betrays a painstaking configuration. If one comprehends the three-voice piece as a whole, the numerous syncopations, hemiolas, and suspensions point unmistakably to the artful polyphony of the 1420s. Melody and rhythm find their counterparts in early mass settings of Dufay or Arnold de Lantins.[24] On the basis of all these facts, Dufay's *Postcommunio must be considered as the oldest fauxbourdon piece now known to us. It provides the evidence that "fauxbourdon," in the sense of the old technical term, did not grow slowly and anonymously out of [contemporary] usage as a half-improvisatory utilitarian music but rather began its life as the creation of a leading master shortly before 1430. The fauxbourdon piece is revealed by its first appearance as a thoroughly crafted work of art. It is in keeping with the highest standards of the surviving Continental polyphony.

The most important and strangest thing to note in our context is the indication [of the third voice] as canon. Two parts are notated, while the third is derived from the first through a strict mechanistic process. This fact, heretofore unnoticed, provides a hint as to how one might imagine the genesis and artistic objective of the new form. Certainly the Burgundian-Netherlandish musicians were interested in somehow imitating or even surpassing the full sonorities of the English. However, in the Old Hall codex (now published), one searches in vain for such a prototype or counterpart to the Continental fauxbourdon. The name [fauxbourdon] does not occur [in Old Hall], and neither does any technique that could connect with the Continental one. If there had indeed existed a fauxbourdon form in England, then it would have had to be found in *OH*.[25] But even in this extensive collection one hears something that England alone had to offer—both before and after—in the free

---

[24]See the Ordinary cycle of Arnold de Lantins in Charles van den Borren, *Polyphonica Sacra* (London: Plainsong and Mediæval Music Society, 1932), 1 ff.

[25]Thrasybulos Georgiades justifiably maintains that the works in Old Hall correspond more or less to the general English technique (*Englische Diskanttraktate*, 102). The "fauxbourdon pieces" mentioned by him show only occasional chains of sixth chords and thus, strictly speaking, cannot be called by the old technical term as is set forth above.

motion of tones of the vocal conductus, which had long been cultivated.[26] It is fundamentally different from the schematic successions of sixth chords of fauxbourdon and cannot be considered as its origin. The opposition of paleographic appearance alone renders such a connection unlikely. While in England the stereotypical conductus notation in score remains also the rule for *OH* and dominates the voice format even in the later sources *OS* and Egerton 3307, a Continental fauxbourdon piece is notated only in individual voices.[27]

English music was known on the Continent before 1430, as the corpus of *BL* contains several [English] Ordinary settings and motets.[28] Even as early as around 1400, close cooperation between French and English musicians can be traced.[29] This cooperation assumed official form when, after the battle of Agincourt in 1415, King Henry V drove deep into [French] lands, in order to compel his marriage with Katherine of France in Troyes in 1420. After his [i.e., Henry V's] death in 1422, the Duke of Bedford as Regent of France maintained a chapel choir, in which Englishmen and Frenchmen operated together under Alain Kirketon.[30] Thus, it may be conjectured that a definite knowledge of English music was current in the northern areas [of France and Burgundy] not later than after 1420. Dufay's circle doubtless knew that the special quality [of English music] consisted mainly in the rich voice leading in thirds and sixths. Under such circumstances, it is not too daring to assume personal contacts of some kind [between English and French musicians]. Also, the improvisatory practice of "English discant" cannot have remained

---

[26]A decisive criterion for the division of the English conductus compositions in the fifteenth century is the writing down in score format, which stretches back in an unbroken tradition into the thirteenth century. In the edition (Alexander Ramsbotham, et al., eds., *The Old Hall Manuscript*, vols. 1-3 (Nashdom Abbey: The Plainsong and Mediæval Music Society, 1933–38), the works in score are recognizable by the fact that the text is placed only beneath the lower voice.

[27]*OS* contains, among 52 pieces, 44 conductus in score (see Besseler, "Studien zur Musik des Mittelalters [Part] I," 226). The newly surfaced codex Br. Mus. Egerton 3307 is particularly strong in evidence, since it stems from the royal chapel, just as does *OH*. Regarding score format in Egerton, see Bertram Schofield, "A Newly Discovered 15th-Century Manuscript of the English Chapel Royal [Egerton 3307]—Part I," *Musical Quarterly* 32 (1946): 515 and 521-2, with facsimile opposite page 512.

[28]Besseler, *Bourdon and Fauxbourdon*, Chapter VI.

[29]Handschin, "Zur Geschichte von Notre-Dame," 52.

[30]André Pirro, *La musique à Paris sous le règne de Charles VI* (Strasbourg: Heitz, 1930), 31 and 35-6. The latest conclusions [are found] in André Pirro, *Histoire de la musique de la fin du XIVe siècle à la fin du XVIe* (Paris: Renouard, 1940), 95 ff.

unknown, so that [Continental musicians] were probably conversant with its characteristic full sonority, based on parallel motion.[31]

To adopt such things, however, was forbidden to the Continental musicians by the fundamental law of their own counterpoint. It consisted in this: that in the construction of the work each voice was composed out by itself and possessed a specific role, clearly outlined, as cantus or tenor, triplum or motetus or contratenor. Extended parallel voice leading would have violated this [basic principle]: it would have coupled together two sharply defined single voices into a kind of voice pair—a concept impossible for the musicians schooled in the late-Gothic [styles]. In 1412, Prosdocimus de Beldemandis established the rule of forbidden parallels, saying that in such cases a voice would have the same melody as another: *quum idem cantaret unus quod alter*.[32] But that is not supposed to be the objective of counterpoint: *quod contrapuncti non est intentio / cum ejus intentio sit, quod illud quod ab uno cantatur, diversum sit ab illo quod ab altero pronuntiatur, et hoc per concordantias bonas et debite ordinatas*.[A] In this "diversity" of all voices lies the real reason why only short successions of imperfect consonances (practically speaking, thirds, sixths, and tenths) were allowed and why they had to be interrupted immediately by perfect [consonances], namely the unison or fifth or octave. The fourteenth century limited the count [of successive imperfect consonances] to two, three, or at most four.[33] In his fourth rule, Prosdocimus also expressly forbids extended (*continue*) counterpoint with imperfect consonances, since true "harmony" is lacking in such a progression.[34] There was thus only a single solution for the voice leading in parallels, that is, with the aid of the canon.

---

[31]Evidence of the theoretical and practical sources [is found] in Bukofzer, *Geschichte des englischen Diskants*, Chapters I, II, and V. Georgiades, in *Englische Diskanttraktate*, Chapter VI, emphasizes more strongly the connections with *Ars nova* theory, which applies to the art music but has no effect on the basic substratum of the indigenous [improvisatory] practice.

[32]Prosdocimus de Beldemandis, *Tractatus de contrapuncto* II, 2 (*CS* 3, 197).

[A][Translation: "... which is not the purpose of counterpoint; its purpose is that what is sung by one voice be different from what is pronounced by the other, and that this be done through concords that are good and properly ordered." Jan Herlinger, ed. and trans., *Prosdocimo de' Beldemandi: Contrapunctus* (Lincoln and London: University of Nebraska Press, 1984), 62-3.]

[33]See the *Ars contrapuncti secundum Johannes de Muris: due, tres vel quatuor imperfecte* (*CS* 3, 60a). Other similar citations include: *duas vel tres imperfectas ad plus* (*CS* 3, 61b) and *due vel tres vel quatuor tertie* (*CS* 3, 74a–b).

[34]*Quarta regula est hec, quod contrapunctare non debemus cum [vocum] combinationibus imperfecte concordantibus continue, nullam combinationem perfecte consonantem interponendo, quum* [or *quoniam*] *tunc ita durum esset hoc cantare, quod in ipso nulla penitus*

As is known, in the fifteenth century, [the word] *canon* denotes an "indication" of some sort, which is supposed to bring out from the written voice the sound really intended.[35] Thus, motet tenors often require a specific direction as to the number of repetitions and the various mensurations.[36] A written voice was to be doubled through canon whenever a second singer entered at a preappointed time interval.[37] It was equally meant to be doubled when one allowed the second singer to sing simultaneously at a specified pitch interval, such as a third. This "interval canon" now apparently offered the possibility to accept the parallel motion without violating the fundamental rule of counterpoint. It was not two different voices being led in parallel contrary to the rules but rather one single voice doubled through intervallic canon! That is the basic idea of fauxbourdon. It had as a consequence that the *voice doubling*, once chosen, had to remain in force unaltered throughout the entire piece. He who resorts to a canon subjects himself to its law. The task thus lay in finding the correct interval for such a fauxbourdon canon.

One might well assume that Dufay, in his first attempts, tested the interval canon in thirds and sixths but rejected them, since chains of thirds or sixths could only be connected to a third voice with difficulty. With parallel fourths on the other hand, the third voice could expand [sonorities] into sixth chords as well as 8-5s. Both possibilities are used alternatingly in the *Postcommunio, so that the sixth chords predominate only slightly. One recognizes Dufay's intention to break up the chains of sixth chords again and again with perfect consonances, namely octaves, as the law of counterpoint demands. The largest number of sixth chords he strings together is five (mm.

---

reperietur armonia, que armonia finis totalis musice existere videtur (*CS* 3, 197b). [Translation: "The fourth rule is this: that we ought not continually to make counterpoint with imperfectly concordant intervals without inserting any perfectly consonant intervals, because it would then be hard to sing; for no harmony whatever would be found in the counterpoint, and harmony seems to be the end of all music." Herlinger, ed. and trans., *Prosdocimo de' Beldemandi: Contrapunctus*, 62-3.]

[35] Johannes Tinctoris, *Diffinitorium* (about 1473): *Canon est regula voluntatem compositoris sub obscuritate quadam ostendens* (*CS* 4, 179b). ["A canon is a rule disclosing to some degree the purpose of the composer behind an obscuration."]

[36] See the realizations of *color* and *talea* in Heinrich Besseler, "Studien zur Musik des Mittelalters [Part] II: Die Motette von Franko von Köln bis Philippe von Vitry," *Archiv für Musikwissenschaft* 8 (1926): 211, and further examples from motets in Charles van den Borren, ed., *Polyphonia Sacra*, 159, 194, and 203.

[37] Regarding the Dufay period, Laurence Feininger reports about this canon in a narrow sense; see *Die Frühgeschichte des Kanons bis Josquin des Prez* (Emsdetten: Lechte, 1937), 18 ff.

5-6), which he does several times; otherwise two, three, or possibly four. Only in this manner are the frequent descending fourth leaps in the tenor explainable, that is, not only at cadences but also within individual sections: in mm. 3-4, 5, 9, 11, 14-15, 15-16, 17, and 21. It thus appears indisputable that the strange role of the fourth in fauxbourdon pieces—both as a sustained interval between the upper voices and as a frequent melodic interval in the tenor—can be traced solely to the contrapuntal considerations outlined above.

The discantus likewise evinces the difficulties with which the new harmonic technique had to contend. Numerous [instances of] suspensions, passing notes, and neighbor notes in the melody, in themselves typical and characteristic of the time, suddenly attain an abnormal emphasis through the doubling at the fourth. Only in places has Dufay thereby established the chord. At other places he makes do with double passing notes in the upper voices (mm. 2, 5, etc.) or with double suspensions (mm. 9, 11, 14, 19, 21). Short tenor organ-points are frequently used in order to support the play of fourths of the upper voices, and this gives rise to vertical sonorities that are both singular and bold (Example 2). The technique is thus free and avoids any schema apart from the self-imposed constraint of the doubling at the fourth. All [these] details mark the *Postcommunio as a prototypical work, with which the new full sonority [*Vollklang*] was tested. The piece provides evidence that Dufay literally "created" the technique of fauxbourdon and put it to use in a music that was in no way styled for it. In this respect, several things still needed to be improved, refined, and smoothed out. At first, the strongly emphasized construction in fourths created a general sonority whose brittleness constrains us today but at that time [this sonority] did not have a purview to the [developments of the] future.

Example 2:   Technique of Fourths in
             Dufay's *Postcommunio *BL* 119

The second of the two fauxbourdon pieces in the corpus of *BL*, the motet *Regina celi letare* of Johannes de Limburgia, seems to be a little later. Since the canon indication is missing, the procedure evidently was already taken for granted as common, stipulated by the notation *faulx bourdon*. Although this is a relatively extensive work, the characteristic descending fourth-leap cadence in the tenor (Example 1A) occurs only twice.[38] The well-known Marian antiphon is laid out in two contrasting sections, with discant embellishment; the first part is in *tempus imperfectum*, the second in *tempus perfectum diminutum*. No counterpart to this piece is known from the early period of fauxbourdon, since otherwise triple mensuration prevails everywhere.[39] Hence, *BL* 198 *Regina celi* assumes a special position and in any case still belongs to the oldest surviving fauxbourdon pieces. This fact is of significance insofar as Johannes de Limburgia most probably lived in Italy. There exist two motets by him, [one] for Padua and [one] for Vicenza.[40] His simple folklike strophic songs, whose style strikes one as thoroughly Italian, are also worthy of mention. Since his works occur almost solely in the codex *BL* stemming from Piacenza, the assignation of an extended sojourn in Italy for this Netherlander seems well founded.[41] If Johannes de Limburgia was indeed one of the very first fauxbourdon composers and a follower of Dufay's—a fact that is substantiated by *BL* 198 *Regina celi*—then for the early age [of fauxbourdon] one must turn one's gaze not only towards England but also towards Italy.

---

[38]The descending fourth leaps come in mm. 43-44 and 63. In addition, m. 36 in the first part has been transcribed in 3/4 time, the second part (m. 53 ff.) in 6/4 time.

[39]The table of the fauxbourdon pieces in *BL(N)* [see Table II below] shows without exception triple mensuration in column 4. Compositions in binary mensuration first appear only in the later manuscript *ModB*.

[40]*BL(N)* 287 Lymburgia, *Gaude felix Padua* (for St. Antonius) and *BL(N)* 185 Lymburgia, *Martires dei incliti*, (with the invocation of the two holies *pro hac urbe Vincencie*).

[41]Of the 46 pieces that are attributed to Johannes de Limburgia in *BL*, only two (*Tr 87*:100 and *Tr 92*:1530) recur [in later sources] The unpublished study of W.H. Rosen, "Die liturgischen Werke des Johannes von Lymburgia" (dissertation, University of Innsbruck, 1929) could not be consulted.

Example 3: *BL* 198 Jo(hannes) de Lymburgia, *Regina celi letare*[42]

Next to Dufay's *Postcommunio, the work appears unassuming, but [this very fact] does better justice to the essence of fauxbourdon as a sonorous art, since the composer in general restricts himself to setting the upper voice in simple chordal style. The [emphasis on] fourth-disposition recedes perceptibly, so as to give room to the full sixth chords. One can already sense here that the fauxbourdon [style of] composition was taken up sympathetically in Italy, because it made concessions to the propensity towards attractive harmony. It was only logical that Dufay also followed a similar course and simplified the construction. The next stage he reached, which stands out clearly from the early *Postcommunio, is characterized by eight self-sufficient fauxbourdon pieces in the supplement of *BL*. This group consists of a Kyrie and seven hymns.[43] Most importantly, the pieces comprise a closed group, in which the pervasive ternary rhythm of *tempus perfectum* assumes sole dominance. Accordingly, the melody of the upper voices now becomes more placid. The frequent occurrence of the dotted semibreve ligature with added minima:

(♩♩. ♪|♩♩. ♪)

---

[42]The indication in the lower voices reads: *Tenor letare faulx bourdon.* The tones of the chant (*Antiphonale Romanum* 1912, 56) are designated in the Example by asterisk (*).

[43]Table II below gives the pieces in their manuscript order as follows: *BL(N)* 123, 292, 294, 304, 307, 310, 311, and 313. The music of 294 recurs with another text in 305, and the music of 311 recurs as 315. The motet with fauxbourdon sections *BL(N)* 167 is discussed in another context.

betrays a fundamentally new character, which one could well refer to as "cantabile." This transformation, which here is noted only peripherally, is researched in another connection.[44] As an example Dufay's Kyrie *BL(N)* 123 will serve. This is the sole Ordinary composition in fauxbourdon in *BL* and is probably the oldest of its type. It is based on the [plainchant] *Kyrie Cunctipotens*, whose tones are again composed out in discant embellishment.

Example 4: *BL(N)* 123 Dufay, Kyrie[45]

This piece is altered not merely in the upper voices but also in its total effect. Dufay has apparently felt the descending fourth-leap cadence in the tenor as awkward, for it now occurs in only one solitary instance in the eight fauxbourdon pieces of the supplement of *BL*.[46] In their place finally appears the stepwise-descending cadence (Example 1B), and this goes hand in hand with a close, coordinated rhythmic-melodic cadence of discantus and tenor. The voice leading of the outer parts in parallel sixths becomes at this stage less dubious, more fluent, and convincing. The very simplicity of *BL(N)* 123 is a sign of mature experience. Only here does one encounter the true fauxbourdon composition, as it is generally known from Dufay's *hymns. The parallel voice leading of the middle part now allows the construction in fourths unmistakably to step to the fore, through suspensions, passing notes, and

---

[44]Besseler, *Bourdon und Fauxbourdon*, Chapter VII.

[45]Further sources: *BU*:62; *Tr 92*:1387 Dufay; *Em*:56; *Tr 93*:1672; The chant tones (*Graduale Romanum*, p. 16**) are marked with an asterisk (*). Measure 8 is without a ligature in *BL*.

[46]In *BL(N)* 310 *Exultet celum laudibus*, measures 10-11 (Gerber No. 18a).

changing tones. This characteristic fauxbourdon color, however, merges more and more into the flowing full sonority, which the parallel sixths of the outer voices generate. Thus it seems that the thrilling impression of the new sonorous art soon led [composers] to alter the transmitted rules of counterpoint also, whenever they contradicted the [judgment of the] ear. The fourth rule of Prosdocimus, with its proscription of imperfect consonance progressions, is for all intents and purposes rendered powerless even by 1430, as the fauxbourdon pieces in the supplement to *BL* demonstrate.[47]

[Table II:] Fauxbourdon Pieces in Supplement of *BL*

No.	Text incipit	Composer	Mensuration	Edition[1]
123	Kyrie[2]	Dufay	O	Beg. see Ex. 4
167	*Supremum est mortalibus*	Dufay	Ø	*DTÖ* 76, 24
281	*Magne dies leticie*[3]	Lymburgia	O	—
292	*Conditor alme siderum*	Dufay	O	Gerber No. 1
294	*Criste redemptor omnium*	Dufay	O	Gerber No. 2
296	*Ad cenam agni providi*[4]	Lymburgia	O	—
300	*Lucis creator optime*	Feraguti	O	—
304	*Ave maris stella*[5]	(Dufay)	O	Gerber No. 15
305	*Criste redemptor omnium*	Dufay	O	(as 294)
307	*Tibi Criste splendor patris*	Dufay	O	—
310	*Exultet celum laudibus*[6]	Dufay	O	Gerber No. 18
311	*Deus tuorum militum*	Dufay	O	Gerber No. 19
313	*Iste confessor domini*	Dufay	O	Gerber No. 21
314	*Virginis proles opifexque*	Lymburgia	O	—
315	*Jhesu corona virginum*[7]	(Dufay)	O	(as 311)
319	*Magnificat de secundo tono*	Lymburgia	Ø	—
320	*Magnificat de sexto tono*[8]	Lymburgia	O	—
324	*Et exultavit*	Feragut	O	—

[Notes to Table II]

[1] For Dufay's hymns reference is made to Rudolf Gerber's edition: *Guillaume Dufay, Sämtliche Hymnen zu 3 und 4 Stimmen, Das Chorwerk* 49 (Wolfenbüttel: Möseler, 1937).

[2] A true contratenor exists for the last Kyrie.

[3] Contains a *Tenor au faulx bourdon si placet* and a contratenor *sine faulx bourdon.*

[4] Three-voiced at beginning; the third strophe *Protecti pasce vespere* is in fauxbourdon.

[5] A choice exists between performing in fauxbourdon or with a written-out contratenor *sine faulx bourdon.*

[6] A choice exists between performing in fauxbourdon or with a written-out contratenor.

[7] The piece exists in *BL* without composer indication.

[8] The piece exists without fauxbourdon indication. Since the tenor is glued over and is hardly readable, the fauxbourdon disposition cannot be ascertained with certainty.

---

[47] See citation above in note 34.

If one considers these connections, then the [technique of] fauxbourdon, which is often somewhat looked down upon, is revealed for what it really is: the creative act of a master. To coax such an enriched sonority out of a two-voice piece through doubling [one part] at the fourth was a new and unheard-of achievement. This is tantamount to [Dufay's] surpassing the English on their own ground, for it was precisely the systemization and consequence of the procedure that eluded them. One finds in England here and there individual chains of sixth chords but never a fauxbourdon piece. The unification of the whole through the fourth-canon, which moreover had as a consequence the restriction to sixth chords and 8-5 sonorities, was the new principle, and it was not English. Upon this was based the self-sufficiency of the Continental practice of fauxbourdon. Judging from the surviving sources, the English made no use of this technique in the realm of the *res facta*.[48] The procedure seems to have been usable to them only through improvisation, and there it mingled with the ancient indigenous custom of improvisatory faburdon, whose trace appears as late as [the treatise of] Guilielmus Monachus, when he contrasts the characteristic Continental practice *apud nos* with the *modus Anglicorum*.[49]

If it really was Dufay who called the new harmonic technique into life, then the French designation "fauxbourdon" must indicate a real historical significance wherever it occurs. Hence, the anglicized name *faburdon* must also be linked somehow to Dufay's creation. [The name faburdon] itself, however, without doubt originated from the special preconditions of the Continent, where the deeply rooted contrapuntal conception of the intervallic canon at the fourth led. This stroke of genius gave currency on the Continent, shortly before 1430, to the English method of sonorous enrichment. Thus was polyphony placed upon the foundation of full sonority, and [these] profound influences opened up the gate to the future. It is only in this manner that the hugely penetrating power of fauxbourdon is explainable: its sweeping effects were so consequential that the creator was soon forgotten.

In one essential point, the previous conception [of fauxbourdon] appears to require revision. It was customary to regard fauxbourdon as a loose extempore improvisatory practice and, accordingly, to consider the missing

---

[48]See above, note 11. The earlier formulation of the author (Heinrich Besseler, "Von Dufay bis Josquin," *Zeitschrift für Musikwissenschaft* 11 (1928/29): 7) that one may consider the rise of fauxbourdon parts precisely as an argument *against* English provenance, now proves its true essence, since the unified, through-composed "fauxbourdon piece" does not exist among the English.

[49]See Besseler, *Bourdon und Fauxbourdon*, Chapter VI.

middle voice as being freely added. Actually, however, it is a strict form corresponding to the canon, and this explains the relatively small total corpus of approximately 100-150 surviving fauxbourdon pieces.[50] The true exploitation of the new full sonority presumably took place in the tremendous preponderance of free three-voice compositions. To what extent one might speak of "fauxbourdon style" in these works and what their characteristics might be is examined elsewhere.[51] Where both [a fauxbourdon stipulation and a composed-out contratenor] occur contiguously or stand as equal choices, it is in any case the three-voice piece with contratenor that is the free form, whereas the fauxbourdon is the *strict* one. The missing middle voice thus is not to be provided through some supposed [process of] improvisation but rather is realized canonically as a doubling of the discantus at the fourth below. On the Continent, fauxbourdon was a *res facta*, which only subsequently and partially succeeded within the province of improvisation.[52]

The confirmation of the above statements lies in the fact that all Continental [theoretical] writers discuss fauxbourdon in connection with the fourth. Only the English proceed differently, and thereby they betray their unique position.[53] On the other hand, when Guilielmus Monachus, who wrote in Italy, reports on the practice there, he confirms in his description of the contratenor the canonic dictum in Dufay's *Postcommunio: Contra vero dicitur sicut supranus accipiendo quartam subtus supranum.*[54] Tinctoris explains in his counterpoint treatise of 1477: *per totum discursum cantus quem fau bourdon vocant, quarta sola admittitur.*[55] Indeed, the parallel fourths, which faithfully participate in every discant figuration, appear as late as 1496 in Gafurius as a distinguishing characteristic of fauxbourdon: *medius ipse*

---

[50]In addition, some two-voice works are taken into consideration here, which are presumably lacking the fauxbourdon stipulation. This issue is discussed further in the Introduction to *Bourdon und Fauxbourdon*.

[51]See Besseler, *Bourdon und Fauxbourdon*, Chapter IX.

[52]Almost all the previous assumptions about fauxbourdon in *DTÖ*, in Gerber's hymn edition, and also in the present author's *Musik des Mittelalters*, Example 139, would seem after this recognition to require revision. Bukofzer interprets the example of Guilielmus Monachus correctly but without drawing [any] conclusions from it (*Geschichte des englischen Diskants*, 78 and Appendix, No. 14).

[53]Besseler, *Bourdon und Fauxbourdon*, Chapter VI.

[54]*CS* 3, 293b. [Translation: "In truth, the contra is said to be just like the superius, taking the fourth below it."] Dufay's canonic indication is given above (see text accompanying note 23).

[55]Johannes Tinctoris, *Liber de arte contrapuncti*, Book I, 5 (*CS* 4, 85a). [Translation: "through the whole discussion of songs that are called fau bourdon, *only* the fourth is admitted." The emphasis is Besseler's.]

contratenor saepius notulas cantus subsequitur, diatessaronica sub ipsis depressione procedens.[56] It was in this sense that Heinrich Isaac inserted the fourths—doubtless with [specific] intention—in the famous second version of the Innsbruck Lied.[57] Now it is possible to recognize the reason for the Continental musician's tenacious hold on the construction in fourths. This basic contrapuntal concept of fauxbourdon had not only made the new full sonority possible technically but also likewise justified it in a fashion both amazing and enlightening. It was a stroke of genius—the dawn of a new era [*Ei des Columbus*]!

How, now, can the name "fauxbourdon" be accounted for? The previous assumptions were mostly aimed at clarifying the tenor as a "false bass," since it was not supposed to have been a cantus-firmus voice. Most recently reference has been made to the [tenor's] singular sixth-relationship with the discantus, which is not a bass-like function, and this doubtless comes closer to the truth.[58] In order to gain some firm ground, the source evidence must first be elucidated. The testimony of *BL* is here of particular weight, since this codex stands closest to the beginnings of fauxbourdon and seems in general to be trustworthy. The pieces belonging to the corpus (*BL* 119, 198—discussed above), and the secondary Kyrie entry *BL(N)* 123, entered in by the same scribe on the empty part of a page early in the mass section of the manuscript, have only the indication *fau(l)x bourdon* beneath the first system of the tenor. However, in that part of the supplement that was completed later—the large hymn and Magnificat collection beginning with Dufay's Advent hymn **BL(N)* 292 *Conditor alme siderum*, the 16 indications display a new and unified form.[59] Only in one solitary instance, namely *BL(N)* 315 *Jesu corona virginum* of Dufay, does the indication read: *Tenor a faulx bourdon*. This represents the wording so common in the later sources, which probably

---

[56]Gafurius, *Practica musica*, Book III, 5 (citation in Bukofzer, *Geschichte des englishen Diskants*, 83). [Translation: "This contratenor, enclosed in the middle, accompanies the melody of the cantus, proceeding at a fourth below it."]

[57]See Theodor Kroyer, "Die threnodische Bedeutung der Quart in der Mensuralmusik," *Bericht über den musikwissenschaftlichen Kongreß in Basel* [1924] (Leipzig, Breitkopf & Härtel, 1925), 231 ff.

[58]Jacques Handschin, "Zur Ambrosianischen Mehrstimmigkeit," *Acta Musicologica* 15 (1943): 14.

[59]Among the 16 pieces in *BL(N)* mentioned above, the Magnificat 320 exists without indication, the Kyrie 123 is here disregarded for the same reasons. Added to these are hymns 305 and 315, whose music represents only a repetition [of a piece with another text]. Particulars can be found above in Table II.

gradually took on the meaning of "in the fauxbourdon style."[60] It is, however, not the original [form of the fauxbourdon indication], [since] it does not otherwise occur in *BL* and [thus] could possibly be merely a scribal error in *BL(N)* 315.

All of the preceding and succeeding fauxbourdon pieces in the hymn and Magnificat section of *BL(N)* in fact have another indication, which in one case is placed in the discantus and in 14 cases stands in the tenor, reading as follows:

Tenor au fau(l)x bourdon.[61]

This cannot be translated as "in the fauxbourdon style" but rather means without qualification: "Tenor with false bourdon" or "Tenor to a false bourdon." The tenor itself is not the false bourdon; [that function] belongs instead to another voice, which carries this name. And thus [the name] can only apply to the unnotated voice in canon with the discantus, which Guilielmus Monachus and Gafurius refer to with the name *Contra(tenor)*.[62] "Fauxbourdon" was thus at first a designation for the *contratenor*. This conclusion is astounding but nevertheless cannot be dismissed in the face of the source evidence. It can hardly be an accident that the expression *au faux bourdon* appears precisely in the supplement to *BL*, where for the first time a repertory showing the characteristics of mature fauxbourdon composition was ascertainable.[63] If, in the oldest collection of this type that is transmitted to us, a conspicuous grammatical form of the fauxbourdon stipulation is so regularly used, then one must ascribe a special significance to it.

The results of the source research is confirmed in the fact that the fauxbourdon indication is by no means restricted to the tenor or is bound to it as has up to now been tacitly assumed.[64] Even Dufay himself repeatedly places the indication in the discantus, not in the tenor. The most telling piece of evidence is his motet *BL(N)* 167 *Supremum est* from the year 1433 (already mentioned several times), which in all five manuscripts carries the

---

[60]Already in *BU* this wording exists in all three fauxbourdon pieces and [it] remains the rule in the even later source *ModB*.

[61]In the first three fauxbourdon pieces in this section, the text incipit is also added after the word "Tenor": *BL(N)* 281, 292, and 294.

[62]The citations are given above in notes 54 and 56.

[63]See the discussion above in connection with Examples 3 and 4.

[64]See the most recent terminological explanations in Bukofzer, *Geschichte des englischen Diskants*, 10 and 68, Georgiades, *Englische Diskanttraktate*, 95, and Handschin, "Zur Ambrosianischen Mehrstimmigkeit," *Acta* 15 (1943): 14.

indication only in the upper voice and in *BL(N)* at the beginning has the wording *au faulx bourdon*.[65] It is thus clear that Dufay in no way understood the term "fauxbourdon" as referring to the tenor. Also, his motets *MüL* 13 *Juvenis qui puellam*[66] and his Kyrie *BL(N)* 123 have the indication in the discantus in their identical concordances in *BU*.[67] The attitude of Dufay's contemporaries and the younger generation is another question, but first the original meaning must here be clarified. As Dufay certainly invented fauxbourdon, his use of the name requires particular consideration. If one wants to explain the designation "fauxbourdon," one will in any case have to turn one's attention in the first place to the contratenor.

The origin of the word "bourdon" does not need to be dealt with in a modern context, since as a technical term of music, possibly stemming from the medieval Latin *burdones*, it was already customary in the thirteenth century.[68] Hieronymous of Moravia uses the medieval Latin *bordunus* in the second half of the century for the *bordun* string of the vielle.[69] Anonymous 4, after 1272, speaks in a figurative sense of a *bordunus organorum*, according to which the long-held notes of the tenor are to be understood.[70] As a designation of an organ register, the French *bourdon* is traceable from the fourteenth century.[71] How the word was used in the fifteenth century, that is to say, in Dufay's proximity, is shown by an instrumental treatise of Henricus Arnaut of Zwolle, which originated around 1440 at the Burgundian court.[72] Here, the various octaves of keyboard instruments are referred to as follows:

---

[65]The edition is cited above in note 16.

[66]Edition in Johannes Wolf, *Geschichte der Mensural-Notation*, vol. 2-3 (Leipzig: Breitkopf & Härtel, 1904), No. 36, where the words *faulx bourdon* occur twice in the discantus.

[67]*BL(N)* 123 has *faulx bourdon* in the tenor; *BU* 62 has *a faulx bourdon* written twice in the discantus.

[68]Regarding its origin and elucidation, see Curt Sachs, *Reallexikon der Musikinstrumente* (Berlin: Bard, 1913), 56, under *Bordun*.

[69]Hieronymus de Moravia, "Petri Picardi: *Musica mensurabilis*," Chapter 28 (*CS* 1, 153). A new edition has been prepared by Simon M. Cserba (Regensburg: Pustet, 1935), 290-1.

[70]Anonymous 4, *De mensuris et discantu*, Chapter 5 (*CS* 1, 359a). Further passages in the theorists can be found in Heinrich Sowa, *Ein anonymer glossierter Mensuraltraktat 1279* (Kassel: Bärenreiter, 1930), XXXVI-XXXVII.

[71]Amédée Gastoué, *L'Orgue en France de l'antiquité au début de la périod classique* (Paris: Au Bureau d'edition de la 'Schola,' 1921), 40 (Rouen 1380), and in Norbert Dufoureq, *Documents inédits relatifs à l'orgue français*, vol. 1 (Paris: Droz, 1932), 25 (Rouen 1383).

[72]See the edition by Georges Le Cerf and Edmond-Renée Labande, *Instrumente de musique du XVe siècle* (Paris: A. Picard, 1932), 13 and 19.

barduni	=	H — b
naturales	=	h — b'
supernaturales	=	h' — h''

Accordingly, the French *bourdon* was without doubt used with the general meaning of "lowest register" or "low voice." If a voice in a middle register, such as a fauxbourdon contratenor, was designated as a "false bourdon," then logic compels us to assume that at that same time a genuine or true "bourdon" must also have existed. Presumably this was a contratenor with the character of a low voice.

The genesis of fauxbourdon thus seems to be connected with the problem of the contratenor, whose importance for the time of Dufay has already been emphasized. On the other hand, some researchers have stressed the role of the English, laying a claim to precedence in this arena for them.[73] In order to achieve clarity and to treat the fauxbourdon question on more secure foundations, further questions must be asked. With its enigmatic name, fauxbourdon seemingly hides a mystery. This mystery can be revealed if the circumstances under which Dufay's creation sprang into life are precisely examined. The connection [of fauxbourdon] with England is not the real problem; rather, it is its development out of the special position of Continental art. The first thing to be clarified would be what the period really understood "bourdon" to be. The term has hitherto been encountered neither in musical sources nor in [the writings of] the theorists. But the term must at least have been used in spoken fashion, for otherwise the name fauxbourdon would not have originated.

Thus the second part of the inquiry begins, which [upon investigation] was thrown into relief as considerably more extensive and deeply layered. Here, several main points can only be reported briefly. It was to be expected that the *bourdon* must have some connection with those strange ground-voices notated on six lines, which one encounters many times in the middle period of Dufay's output.[74] The "six-line contratenor" proves in the event to be a

---

[73]Georgiades, *Englische Diskanttraktate*, 110. The "Treatise B" mentioned there (Br. Mus. Lansdowne 763, fols. 113v–116v) uses the word *faburdon* right in the introductory paragraph and can thus only have originated subsequent to Dufay's creation of fauxbourdon. (The treatise is published in Georgiades, 23 ff. and in Bukofzer, *Geschichte des englischen Diskants*, 146 ff.)

[74]Besseler, *Bourdon und Fauxbourdon*, Chapters I-III. In previous editions the following six-line pieces can be found: *O(3):114 *Se la face ay pale* (John F.R. Stainer and C. Stainer, eds., *Dufay and His Contemporaries* (London: Novello, 1898), 140); *Tr 87:95 *Donnez l'assault* (Guido Adler and Oswald Koller eds., *Sechs Trienter Codices: Geistliche und weltliche Kompositionen des XV. Jahrhunderts, Zweite Auswahl, DTÖ 22 (Jahrgang XI/1)* (Vienna:

typical harmonic foundation [*Harmoniefundament*] with fifth-fourth-octave leaps. But most importantly, this new ground-voice [*Grundstimme*], in numerous cadences—and above all at the main close of the work—remained low as a bass, whereas the tenor was thrust into the middle position. If one examines the general cadential relationships of the fifteenth century, then the decisive revolutionary change is brought to light. While before the tenor was the main voice and as such supported the final chord in all works, henceforth the harmony-supporting contratenor assumed its place. [This did not happen] everywhere and immediately and also not without resistance and regressions. But the groundbreaking inventions around 1430 achieved a cadence formula with Dufay's "double-octave cadence" that belonged to the future. In this [cadence], the recognition of the system of harmony [*Harmonik*] found a convincing expression.[75]

The six-line contratenor of Dufay, described above, was an early form of the later *contratenor bassus*. Besides this, it served in three-voice composition also as a filling voice and so remained simultaneously a *contratenor altus*. This double role led to its abnormally wide ambitus and to its being notated on six lines. It is now revealed that the problem of the harmony fundament in general arose in the context of these extraordinary voices, which one could most likely bring into connection with the word "bourdon," and this comprised the central core of artistic endeavor. Hence, [composers] explored the "low-cleffed contratenor," which [even] on a five-line system was distinguished from the tenor in ambitus, or sought to couple the typical equal-cleffed lower voices in such a manner that linked the "combination bass" with tenor and contratenor, which likewise did justice to the new harmonic demands.[76] As a comparison of the works teaches, the leadership was provided by Dufay, who entered the picture around 1430 as a decisive figure. He was the main creator of the new harmonic art. One can compile the complete system of a "bourdon harmony" from his works, and this commands a place in

---

Universal-Edition, 1904), 82); *Tr 92:1383 *Ave virgo* (Rudolf von Ficker and Alfred Orel, eds., *Sechs Trienter Codices: Geistliche und weltliche Kompositionen des XV. Jahrhunderts, Vierte Auswahl, DTÖ* 53 (Jahrgang XXVII/1) (Vienna: Universal-Edition, 1920), 22); *Tr 92:1532 *Alma redemptoris mater* (*DTÖ* 53, 19) and Heinrich Besseler, *Guillaume Dufay: Zwölf geistliche und weltliche Werke, Das Chorwork* 19 (Wolfenbüttel: Möseler, 1932), No. 3.

[75]Compare the main cadences of the works cited above in note 74. Another typical example is the *Contratenor trompette* in the manuscript *Esc.* Pierre Aubry, "Iter Hispanicum: Notices et extraits de manuscrits de musique ancienne conservés dans les bibliothèques d'Espagne [Part] II: Deux chansonniers français à la Bibliotheque de l'Escorial," *Sammelbände der internationalen Musikgesellschaft* 8 (1906–07), 526 ff.

[76]Besseler, *Bourdon und Fauxbourdon,* Chapters III and V.

history as a unique early form of dominant tonality. The harmonic novelties of the fifteenth century, which are traceable everywhere, may be said to have their center here.

Italy offered a background of traditions for such attempts. Not only the tonal ordering of ground-tones but also particulars such as the instrumental harmonic fundament stem at their latest from the art of the Trecento, in which the *caccia* comprises the point of departure. Evidently Dufay was influenced particularly by his Netherlandish predecessor, Ciconia. In any case, one observes in him [i.e., Dufay] in the 1420s a multifarious attention to harmony, which probably can only be explained by his long sojourn in Italy. Through these attempts, Dufay came to shift the harmonic fundament (which had already been transformed by Ciconia) down to an even lower position, because he wanted to keep the tenor in the middle of the texture as the primary voice. In this manner the bourdon/low voice originated, even before 1430, out of a design to fuse a definitely Italian harmony into the music, while still retaining the traditional northern attribute of having the tenor as leading voice. Here the appropriation of the foreign—similarly to the adoption of fauxbourdon—went hand in hand with a determined defense of the foundations of native art traditions.

Now the name "fauxbourdon" becomes more understandable. As Dufay composed the first pieces shortly before 1430 so as to seize upon the full sonority of the English for [his] sacred music, he eschewed a thorough realization of the tonal harmony that had been so essential to him in his previous works. A contratenor as a doubling of the discantus at the lower fourth remained shackled in the middle stratum and could never be used as a combination-bass of tenor and contratenor, not to mention as a bourdon-type low voice. [Such a contratenor] is, in fact, [literally] a "false bourdon." Whoever does not consider the arguments advanced above in favor of the contratenor as convincing but rather wants to understand the tenor as [being the] *faux bourdon* will find similar circumstances:[77] the tenor [of a fauxbourdon piece] is bound to the discantus in sixths and octaves and is no more in a position to provide a harmonic foundation [than is the contratenor]. The end result is the same. The name "fauxbourdon," for so long a conundrum, is applied not in conjunction with the cantus firmus and its position but refers to the lack of a harmonic foundation. This unusual word can only have been coined within a circle of musicians who were coming to

---

[77]The contratenor issue is discussed above; see notes 61-64 and their accompanying discussion.

terms with questions of the new harmony and configuration of a bass [voice]. Since Dufay was the one who invented the fauxbourdon technique, one is justified in assuming that the name as well can be traced to him or to his closest environs. In the negative [connotation of the] designation, one can thus detect a certain criticism by the creator of his own work. It concerns exactly that which today also is perceived as a shortcoming: the harmonic insufficiency of successions of sixth chords. The procedure amounts to each tone of the melody being accompanied by its own tonic triad. Harmonically speaking, fauxbourdon was without doubt a step backwards [for the time] around 1430 or, to put it better: a conscious renunciation. For what Dufay the master had to say about harmony at that time is testified by the freely composed works, especially those with the six-line contratenor. But why did he embrace a technique whose deficiencies he well knew, and how was it possible for fauxbourdon nevertheless [to become] such a huge success among his contemporaries?

In order to answer this question, the different styles and origins of the basic musical currents, which coexisted at that time, must be taken into consideration. The [attribute of] dominant tonality, which in Dufay reached a first summit, had its roots in Italy, whereas the [attribute of] full sonority, conditioned by thirds and sixths, had its home in England. Neither current was amenable to unification without a further factor, so that at first, bourdon composition with rich harmony stands apart from the fully sonorous but harmonically primitive fauxbourdon pieces. To effect an equalization in this respect and, above all, to carry out the leading demands of counterpoint was a central task of the Netherlandish musicians who entered the arena around 1430 as exponents of a new creative mandate. Thus, the inquiry of the individual questions of bourdon and fauxbourdon flows into a larger context, which seems to have had consequences for the interpretation of [the music of] the fifteenth century.

2

Toward a History of the Genesis of Fauxbourdon

Rudolf von Ficker

EDITOR'S PREFACE: *This article comprises a review and a critique of some of the main ideas developed by Besseler in his influential text,* Bourdon und Fauxbourdon. *The point of departure for Ficker's arguments is that Besseler had not only overrated the capacity of the surviving sources to trace the genesis of fauxbourdon on the Continent but that he had greatly overvalued the historical significance of the technique itself. The bibliographical abbreviations of studies authored by Besseler (B I, B II, B III), constantly cited throughout the article, are identified in note 1. As originally published, Ficker's article incorporates a supplementary double note (18-19), placed at the end of the text. In the translation, these notes have been repositioned to their correct location within the body of the article, with the numbering of footnotes kept consistent by offsetting notes 18 and 19 slightly within the same sentence.*

In the history of art, it is most particularly Josef Strzygowski who has demanded that the historian pay attention to the "lacunae" in artistic transmission and ground these in the context of what he advocates as "research into evolution." For scientific conclusions, when drawn solely from surviving artistic monuments whose survival is sometimes due only to special circumstances, often can be thoroughly problematic and misleading if these conclusions are not rendered in connection with a corresponding mention of the known lacunae in a given body of artistic works.

As in the realm of art history, such a demand must likewise be valid in the area of early music history, since here the lacunae assume a particularly wide scope. This is the case both for the transmission of manuscripts in which important intermediate sources are often missing and, in particular, with respect to those [musical] phenomena (often highly significant in an evolutionary sense) resulting from certain routine practices that were at various times improvised and not committed to written form and accordingly are considered by the latter-day researcher as never having existed.

There are, however, two possibilities whereby an improvisatory practice would take on the status of a *res facta* and thereby become a "work of art": 1) if it is undertaken as an individual artistic enrichment and a fully formed entity, which comes out of definite norms of the conventional improvisatory practices; or 2) if is taken over from a foreign artistic environment and imitated, although in this case most of the preconditions for a long developmental period of spontaneous improvisation are not present. Hence, that which was originally pure improvisation is here suddenly revealed as a graphically visible *res facta*, with the [corresponding] demands of an "artwork." However, the historian who judges only according to the surviving corpus of written sources and does not take lacunae into consideration will tend in such cases to appraise the adopted sphere as the original.

The hypotheses regarding the origin and significance of fauxbourdon, which Heinrich Besseler has recently formulated,[1] seem to me to be founded in large measure upon just such a failure to observe such [source] lacunae, although the latter are not particularly difficult to recognize. It may therefore be permitted—particularly in view of the judgments [of Besseler] in their latest formulation, presented in the form of unshakable "theses"—to make the following contrary observations.

As points of departure for his presentation of evidence, Besseler cites the two relevant studies of Manfred Bukofzer[2] and Thrasybulos Georgiades,[3] from which it is maintained that they arrive at contradictory findings.[4] Nevertheless, if one disregards their differences and the scope of their respective methodological approaches, such a generalization does not hold true. Actually, both authors revise—in rare unanimity—the previous opinions about fauxbourdon which, due to the sometimes incomplete and sometimes flawed interpretations of the pertinent theorists, had hitherto prevailed. Both studies adduce evidence showing that within the scope of the English teachings (wherein [the technique of] "discant" stands unilaterally in the foreground), fauxbourdon is either never discussed or is only treated late and incidentally as a phenomenon of secondary importance. The prestige that had earlier been

---

[1] See the following studies [of Besseler], which in their essentials are in agreement. [Each is preceded by its bibliographical abbreviation as used below]: (B I), "Der Ursprung des Fauxbourdons," *Die Musikforschung* 1 (1948): 106-12; (B II), "Dufay Schöpfer des Fauxbourdons," *Acta Musicologica* 20 (1948): 26-45 [translated above, see essay 1]; (B III), *Bourdon und Fauxbourdon* (Leipzig: Breitkopf & Härtel, 1950).

[2] Manfred Bukofzer, *Geschichte des englischen Diskants und des Fauxbourdon nach den theoretischen Quellen* (Strasbourg: Heitz, 1936), (abbreviation: Bu).

[3] Thrasybulos Georgiades, *Englische Diskanttraktate aus der ersten Hälfte des 15. Jahrhunderts* (Munich: Musikwissenschaftliches Seminar der Universität München, 1937), (abbreviation: Ge).

[4] B I, 106; B II, 26; B III, 1.

accorded to fauxbourdon ever since Guido Adler's work on the subject[5] must after these findings appear utterly pale compared to the later phenomenon of "English discant,"[6] whose emergence is fundamentally more significant from the standpoint of evolutionary history.

Bukofzer's sole divergence from the formulation of Georgiades (who also does not wish to dispense with the genetic connection of the fauxbourdon technique with England) lies in the sharp division of English discant from "Continental" fauxbourdon which Bukofzer—at least at the beginning of his study—takes up.

Hence, it is only in connection to this difference in opinion that Besseler's observation [introduced above] can apply, but that is quite easy to challenge, since Bukofzer supports his Continental hypothesis above all in the erroneous view that the [procedure of] discant embellishment, so significant for the evolution of style in the fifteenth century, stems not from England but from the Continent. In making this argument, Bukofzer cites the pertinent passages of Besseler's, which, however, can only be regarded as conjectures ungrounded in proof.[A] Bukofzer further maintains that—in contrast to English practice, which placed the c.f. in the tenor—the c.f. on the Continent generally lay in the upper voice.[B] Since this latter [condition] is also the case for fauxbourdon, it follows according to Bukofzer's thinking that fauxbourdon can only have arisen on the Continent.

In response to this, the following points should be noted: As early as 1920 and 1924, respectively, I had pointed out that the practice of discant embellishment [*Diskantkolorierung*] was already known in England at the beginning of the [fifteenth] century.[C] I had even shown, for example, that the premier composer of the Old Hall manuscript (*OH*), Leonel [Power], had cultivated a unique "constructive" style of embellishment,[7] which forms a

---

[5]Besseler, too, still sees in fauxbourdon the "genesis of the harmonic element in our music" (B I, 106), and "a vestige from venerable prehistory, a mystery out of the origin and growth stages of the art of polyphony" (B II, 26; B III, 1).

[6]For examples, see Bu, 11.

[A]Heinrich Besseler, "Von Dufay bis Josquin," *Zeitschrift für Musikwissenschaft* 11 (1929): see 4 ff.

[B]Bu, 10.

[C]See Rudolf von Ficker, "Die Kolorierungstechnik der Trienter Messen," *Studien zur Musikwissenschaft* 7 (1920): 24; also Rudolf von Ficker, "Die frühen Messenkompositionen der Trienter Codices," *Studien zur Musikwissenschaft* 11 (1924): 39 ff.

[7]The presumption of this as an old practice seems in this connection to be confirmed in the *Quatuor principalia* of Tunstede (*CS* 4, 294 ff.). See also Ge, 85 and 93.

fully new and independent melodic process out of the c.f. This technique was subsequently developed further by the English into those complex configurations about which I reported at length in connection with the mass settings published in *DTÖ* 61.[D]

On the other hand, at this time the new technique of constructive [discant] embellishment was still totally unknown on the Continent. In the very infrequent Continental instances where the chant appears in the upper voice, such as in the hymns from Apt,[8] its melodic qualities remain almost unaltered. The chant undergoes only a simple mensural rhythmicization and structuring. In this manner it acquires an almost songlike bearing, which proceeds very clearly within the simple structure of these hymns.

The early Netherlanders, including the young Dufay, also employed the chant in this new, continuous, songlike form,[9] not in the discantus but rather in the tenor, according to the customary practice. Hence, its conception was fundamentally different from the constructivist, unmelodic fragmentation of the older motet tenors. The c.f., framed by the animated motion of the other voices, already was anticipating the structure of the German Lied tenors of the sixteenth century. It proceeds either in a continuous row of measure-length breves[10] or in a smoothly moving, mostly trochaic rhythmicization. From the oldest part of *BL*, a couple of movements should be emphasized: the Kyrie, fol. 15v of Dufay, and especially his Sanctus, fol. 19v, since this represents a three-voice paraphrase of the four-voice *Sanctus vineus secundum Loqueville*, which follows in the manuscript. Dufay here adopts the trochaic, songlike tenor unchanged from the work of his teacher,[11] but he then proceeds to

---

[D]See Ficker, "Die frühen Messenkompositionen der Trienter Codices" (cited above); the edition referred to is Rudolf von Ficker, ed., *Sieben Trienter Codices: Geistliche und weltliche Kompositionen des XV. Jahrhunderts, Fünfte Auswahl, DTÖ* 61 (*Jahrgang* XXXI) (Vienna: Universal-Edition, 1924).

[8]Amédée Gastoué, *Le manuscrit de musique du trésor d'Apt* (Paris: Droz, 1936), 57-64.

[9]"Songlike" is to be understood as closely associated with a simple rhythmic organization and also with a rigorous periodic structure in connection to that of the text, which hitherto had already displayed a clear quadruple meter. For examples, see *BU*: No. 43, *Gaude flore*; No. 69, *Ave regina*; No. 65, *Ave fuit*, etc.

[10]As an example, sections of a chant tenor mass by Arnoldus de Lantins can be referred to (*BL* [fols.] 1r, 2v, 6v–8r) and, further, the *Salve santa parens* and Kyrie of Johannes de Lymburgia (*BL* [fols.] 179v–180v). In conformity with historic–diplomatic usage, these citations are given according to the folio of the manuscript and not according to the work's numbering, which usually varies greatly even in the catalogues heretofore published.

[11]The trochaic patterns may be of Italian origin. They are particularly noticeable in the anonymous small sacred forms in *BU*. The mass settings in Ivrea and Apt only rarely utilize a chant cantus firmus, and this tradition is carried on by the early Netherlanders. In contrast, the

construct the other voices as completely new and independent parts. Here it can probably be assumed that Dufay's paraphrase probably originated not long after his time of study with Loqueville, who died in 1418. This would seem to confirm the supposition that this songlike conception of the tenor, which then again receded, is characteristic of the c.f. technique of the Netherlanders before the advent of English influence. Also, this procedure heralds the attempt of that time to gain new melodic resources for the chant [c.f.], which subsequently was realized in another and far-reaching way through the [technique of] embellishment. However, the sources do not provide a basis for assuming that [discant] embellishment might have been simultaneously familiar on the Continent along with the technique just mentioned.[12]

In light of the above points, Bukofzer's essential arguments for the Continental hypothesis cease to be applicable, and he himself, at the end of his study, comes to concede for the English a significant share in the genesis of fauxbourdon.[E] His definition that "fauxbourdon arose out of the English chordal technique and the Continental style of discant embellishment" would, according to the corresponding correction, affirm even a full English share!

Besseler, it might be added, does not return to the question of the origins of discant embellishment. One can probably conclude from this that he no longer shares the viewpoint of Bukofzer, which he had originally incited.[13] Rather, he attempts at least to place on secure ground the [question of] Continental provenance for fauxbourdon. The arguments that Besseler marshals for this seem on the face of things to be consistent, and they tend to be convincing to the reader only dimly acquainted with the unfolding of this still-murky transition period, that the earlier assumption regarding the English origin of fauxbourdon, (which was, indeed, more intuitive than grounded in hard facts), is incorrect. Above all, he bases this contention upon the existing sources, which yield the well-known, and at first blush astounding, fact that not a single piece in fauxbourdon style can be found among the [works of the] English masters. [Besseler also adduces evidence] that the French designation "fauxbourdon" in the early sources occurs only in connection with Burgundian

---

use of a chant [c.f.] continued in England during this time without interruption.

[12]A strange juxtaposition of the two techniques is seen in the Introit *Michi autem* from the *Missa Sancta Jacobi* of Dufay (*BL* No. 111, fols. 121r–122r). The first statement places the chant in the tenor, in a broad, if at times also somewhat free treatment. Then follows a section designated *repetitio*, with the embellished chant in the upper voice. This represents the new, modern style, and may have been added at a later date.

[E]Bu, 126-7.

[13]Only in B III, 107, is there a return to the topic of "Dufay's discant embellishment."

composers, and he concludes on the basis of the sources that Dufay should be considered the creator of fauxbourdon.[14]

To be sure, Besseler is careful to restrict the concept of fauxbourdon to the express designation "fauxbourdon piece." He separates this "genuine" fauxbourdon from its later, more widely dispersed manifestations, which, in their preferred use of thirds and sixths, obey the same harmonic principle, but whose rather free and frequent alternation of sonority types renders them fundamentally distinct from the rigid sixth-chord parallelism of fauxbourdon. It is acknowledged that researchers were always accustomed to speak in such cases of "fauxbourdon manner," or "fauxbourdon style."[15] Besseler at first rejects such terminology, as he rejects the designation "fauxbourdon" to describe short stretches of [parallel] sixth chords.[16] But in chapter IX of *Bourdon*, which presumably was written later, Besseler again finds it necessary to introduce the term "fauxbourdon style" in connection with the freer manifestations mentioned above,[17] which according to Besseler's reckoning are only found after 1430. In this manner, Besseler reconnects himself with the terminology previously employed,[18] but [actually,] none of these designations is appropriate.[19]

---

[14]B I, 106 ff.; B II, 28 ff.; B III, 11 ff.

[15]See Hugo Riemann, *Handbuch der Musikgeschichte*, vol. II/1 (Leipzig: Breitkopf & Härtel, 1919), 95; Alfred Orel, "Einige Grundformen der Motettkomposition im XV. Jahrhundert," *Studien zur Musikwissenschaft* 7 (1920): 73, 88; also Alfred Orel, "Die mehrstimmige geistliche (katholische) Musik von 1430–1600," *Handbuch der Musikgeschichte*, vol. I, ed. Guido Adler (Berlin: Keller, 1930), 299 ff.

[16]See B II, 27; B III, 2.

[17]The cases mentioned in B III, 159 ff. as being in "free fauxbourdon style" all fall under the realm of "discants."

[18]Fauxbourdon is neither a style, nor is it a form, as both Besseler and Bukofzer claim. Rather, it is a stereotypical harmonic technique, which can be employed equally in whole pieces as well as in shorter or longer phrases and which, in both cases, is always designated expressly as "fauxbourdon." A prerequisite for the designation is that at least one voice is not notated and hence needs to be provided [through improvisation]. When, however, this same technique is employed in fully notated works, it renders superfluous the term "fauxbourdon," since none of the parts needs to be completed. See in this connection, among others, *In exitu Israel* of Binchois (see below, note 56), which even Besseler has to admit is a fauxbourdon (B III, 163). Further, see the fauxbourdon passages mentioned by Besseler from Dufay's *O proles* and Dunstable's *Quam pulchra* (B III, 115 and 169). However, this technique of manipulating sonorities is widely discernible in England before its use on the Continent (see below).

[19]Hence, the formulation of the concept "fauxbourdon piece" can in no way be justified, since the transference of a purely technical concept to a concept of form (which fauxbourdon never was during the time in question) leads to an arbitrary limitation, which is both unusable and deceptive as an assumption for adducing evidence regarding provenance and significance

Thanks to the two studies of Bukofzer and Georgiades, we know today that the compositional practice of decisive evolutionary significance—as opposed to the rigid and primitive fauxbourdon—is seen in the practical artistic application of the voice-leading technique of "English discant" as set forth in the numerous English treatises. It is this latter technique which, as Bukofzer has expressly remarked, was enthusiastically taken up by the Continental composers, with Dufay at their head.[20]

The opinion subsequently expressed by Bukofzer that English discant experienced a fundamental transformation on the Continent due to the fact that here the c.f. was allegedly put into the upper voice for the first time, is not accurate, as was already demonstrated above. This erroneous assumption proved disastrous not merely in connection with clarifying the provenance of fauxbourdon—it also hindered Bukofzer from assessing in full measure the influence of English discant upon the Continental practice. Besides this, Bukofzer did not understood that for the theorists it is merely a question of demonstrating the voice-leading rules of the new discant, which remain exactly the same and are independent of whether the c.f. in its practical use is placed in the tenor, the upper, or the middle voice—all three possibilities occur as early as *OH!*—or even whether no c.f. is used at all.

Hence, if one inserts the correct term "discant" in the place of "fauxbourdon manner," or "fauxbourdon style," this appearance of the designation [fauxbourdon]—confirmed in the sources—is explained. But it nevertheless remains of consequence that this English discant up to now has always been referred to as "fauxbourdon manner" or "fauxbourdon style." This suggests the conclusion that close relationships exist between discant and fauxbourdon as has previously been taken for granted.

---

of this harmonic technique.

[20]Bu, 126. Without further elaboration, it should simply be added here that the harmonic attainments of the Trecento in Italy at this time had developed another style of discant, to which an essential impetus in the work of the early Netherlanders is indebted. With regard to Besseler's statements (B III, 102, note 1) the following should be remarked: As early as 1925 I had pointed out for the first time, in "Formprobleme der mitteralterlichen Musik," *Zeitschrift für Musikwissenschaft* 7 (1924–25): 209, that the principle of tonality or tonal harmony is first realized in the music of the Trecento. My study "Primäre Klangformen," in *Jahrbuch Peters* (1929), is not associated with this discovery, nor does it explore further the thoughts of Guido Adler's *Studien zur Geschichte der Harmonie, Sitzungsberichte der Wiener Akademie, Phil.-hist. Klasse* 98 (Vienna: Carl Gerold's Sohn, 1881), 781-830, with appended musical examples, pages I-XXXI. The Trecento art has in no way just been discovered; on the contrary, a "tonality independent of chords" is as unintelligible to me as the concept of a "dominant tonality" emphasized by Besseler.

Clearly, when evaluating a specific phase of evolution, it is not so much a question of the [notational] representation, to which this [evolution] is in some places and at some times joined, nor [it is a question] of the manner of craftlike stylization, which it at times experiences. Rather, it is above all [a question] of determining the primary concrete musical qualities that are available [at a given time] in each sphere of creation and of [ascertaining] their origin. But when Besseler points to Dufay as creator of fauxbourdon, when he proclaims this creation as a stroke of genius, or even as the dawn of a new era,[21] then this deed, in a musical sense, must represent something so fundamentally new and revolutionary that every idea [of doubt] seems out of the question, but [in fact,] fauxbourdon could only represent some kind of concurrent or partial manifestation of a fundamentally more far-reaching process of development, which is phenomenologically dissimilar from—and more significant [than—fauxbourdon].

Besseler is not able to disregard fully [the possibility] that one cannot consider fauxbourdon as an isolated phenomenon. [This is evidenced by] his emphasis upon the following attributes of English music (or English discant, as the case may be):[22] 1) voice leading in thirds and sixths; 2) practices of improvisation; and 3) characteristic "full sonority founded on parallel motion." The foregoing attributes are in their essentials identical with fauxbourdon; only the term "full sonority" [*Vollklang*] appears [here] as something new, yet its primary effect is one of vagueness, since it invites the supposition that along with it there must also have been an "empty sonority" [*Leerklang*].[23] This latter quality, then, is presumably to be imputed to the Continental music posture since, according to Besseler's view, it was only through Dufay that the English "enrichment of sonority" [*Klangfülle*] was facilitated on the Continent.[24]

From [Besseler's] later writings, however, it is made unequivocal that the term "full sonority" is to be understood as the employment in English music of "full" triads, or sixth chords, in a close position.[25] This, together with the

---

[21]B III, 111; B II, 40; B I, 23. [Besseler's phrase is *Ei des Columbus*.]

[22]B II, 32 ff.; B III, 15.

[23]This "empty sonority" is, in fact, mentioned as the 8-5, i.e., without the third (B III, 40).

[24]With respect to this "sonority enrichment," the English tripla and quadrupla must as early as about 1200 have attained at least an equal measure of "full sonority." For even here the tones of the three (or four) voices are at times compressed into the space of an octave [i.e., including imperfect sonorities].

[25]When he speaks of "greater fullness of sound," Gustave Reese interprets the facts in an exactly opposite fashion, [emphasizing] namely the wide range of the triadic texture sometimes

concomitant employment of parallel voice leading in England, would signify that all elements of fauxbourdon, including the placement of the c.f. in the top voice, were already familiar there. [Accordingly,] the creative achievement of Dufay, through which he "surpassed the English on their own ground," would [actually] have consisted merely in the act of reconciling to the English technique[s] the rigid procedure and colorlessness of a uniform fauxbourdon piece.[26] Thus, the accomplishment most probably would never have been perceived as being either creative or as a stroke of genius if Besseler had not latterly invested the genesis of fauxbourdon with the romantic glimmer of a legend.

Indeed, Besseler is of the opinion that it would have been impossible for the Continental musicians, considering the basic rules applying to their characteristic counterpoint, to adapt these to the "English full sonority founded on parallel motion."[27] Although the Continental masters around the turn of the century, including the young Dufay, did not trouble themselves overly with contrapuntal rules and deliberations—just as their English colleagues did not[28]—Besseler holds that Dufay, in the creation of fauxbourdon, must have had serious reservations about his culpability in not avoiding prohibited parallel fourths between superius and contra as well as in his own contrapuntal scruples [or lack thereof] with respect to the unbreakable rules of the theorists.

According to Besseler's view, however, Dufay found a way out of this dilemma, namely, that the parallel fourths were not to be interpreted as parallels but rather as a canon at the interval of a fourth. That is, [they were] not [to be regarded] as a normal intervallic canon, in which the second voice follows the first at a specific distance of time and interval, but rather [as one] in which both voices are introduced simultaneously. Following this chain of reasoning once again, in reverse, according to this interpretation, yields the following result: a canon, which is not a canon but rather parallel fourths, which, however, in consequence of their derivation from contrapuntal canon technique, are not to be grasped as parallels but rather as the "basic

---

encountered; see *Music in the Middle Ages* (New York: Norton, 1940), 403.

[26]B II, 39; B III, 20.

[27]B I, 108; B II, 33; B III, 16.

[28]The French works of around 1400 display—particularly in the conception of their lower voices (for example the notorious leaping contratenors, discussed below)—a technique which above all was dictated by concerns of simple filling out of the sonority and which cannot be described as contrapuntal in the accepted sense. Besseler, on the contrary, cites the leaping contra as evidence of an "all-encompassing contrapuntal thought."

contrapuntal concept" [*kontrapunktische Kerngedanke*] in fauxbourdon.[F]

This fairy tale, through which the adoption of English "full sonority" was allegedly made possible, would have not indeed even been necessary, since this "full sonority" [itself] can hardly be spoken of as a particular mark of English music of the time.[29] Besseler himself emphasizes that only here and there can one find sixth-chord progressions in English music.[30] And he mentions later that these [progressions] were also supposed to have been known for a long time on the Continent.[31] In addition, it happens that in the evaluation of English discant in the practical sources, this "full sonority" proves to be employed in hardly any great quantity, and this is also true in the Continental sources. But if the [theory of] English provenance of fauxbourdon is incorrect, then it is not easy to understand where in fact this "full sonority" in England is supposed to be secreted,[32] and why could it not have been derived from Continental practice? It is even less comprehensible why this "full sonority," which of course had to comprise an independent, closed phenomenon, should be founded on parallel motion—i.e., presumably upon several "full sonorities."

The creation of this imaginary "full sonority," as well as other terminological neologisms, seem better suited to obscure than to illuminate the issues now under investigation, which are not especially difficult to explain from a musical standpoint. This is just as true with respect to the strange explanation that interprets fauxbourdon as a putative end product in this process of development. In these [arguments,] Besseler gives prominence above all to the harmonic susceptibility of the sixth-chord progression, which supposedly leads back to the fact that the fauxbourdon technique amounted to each melody tone being accompanied by its own tonic triad.[33]

[F]B I, 111; B II, 40; B III, 23, 163

[29]A comparison of the hymns in Apt (Gastoué edition, Nos. XIX–XXVI) with similar works from *OH* shows indisputably that the contrast in the two techniques did not lie in [the presence or absence of] "full sonority," but rather in their respective characteristic means of sonority formation and of voice leading.

[30]B II, 39; B III, 20.

[31]See B III, 101. The motet *Clap, Clap* (Ivrea Codex, fol. 60v) already uses progressions of sixth chords. Also, open parallel triads in root position, as in Apt (see Gastoué edition, No. XXI, mm. 14, 16-17) must be assessed as particularly representative [examples of] "full sonorities."

[32]Also, Besseler's article "Ars nova" in the general encyclopedia *MGG*, vol. 1 (1949–51), col. 727, elucidates the concept of English "full sonority," but only emphasizes that it supposedly gave impetus to the genesis of Continental fauxbourdon technique, which assumed [the role of] a "primary force" in Netherlandish music.

[33]See B I, 112; B II, 45; B III, 101. Exactly this same definition is given by Werner Korte,

If this interpretation were tenable, it would not require an explanation of why the English practice of the time did not simply build a "tonic triad" in root position *over* each melody tone[34] rather than being obstinate about utilizing the "tonic triad" only as a sixth chord. Moreover, how can it be explained that even in fauxbourdon, the beginning and concluding sonorities, and even short phrases, are never set with such tonic sixth chords but rather are always set with an 8-5 sonority? What kind of harmonic function must these 8-5 sonorities have had, then, if the inner sixth chords exhibit themselves as a tonic? Should they perhaps be dominants? And it would also be difficult to understand why sixth chords—if they are supposed to be tonics—are never used as cadential sonorities, even in the fully formed harmony right through to today.

I believe that if the fundamental findings of Ernst Kurth (regarding harmony and its usefulness for the recognition of historical development)[35] had not been entirely ignored in the subsequent music research, then such an interpretation [as Besseler's] would scarcely have been possible. If this were the case, it would probably not have been the harmonic insufficiency of fauxbourdon that would have been especially emphasized.[36] For with the appreciation of the usability of thirds and sixths in harmonic progressions, and their recognition as "imperfect consonances," the history of harmony begins. [It was] the very tensions of the thirds and sixths (which the harmonically static sensitivities of ancient times regarded as dissonant) [that] first made possible in the harmonic realm that complex unity and highly charged dynamic [inherent] in a sequence of sonorities, which is completely analogous to the indivisible unfolding of a continuous moving line in the melodic

---

Die Harmonik des frühen 15. Jahrhunderts (Münster i. W.: Suhrbier & Bröcker, 1929), 12, and in Bu, 15. It can thus be said to comprise a common school of thought.

[34]The proof of open parallel triads demanded by Bukofzer (Bu, 5) I could easily have furnished. See above, note 31, further, as an English instance, see the example in Reese (403), etc. Also, hidden parallels, which are traceable up until the early Dufay period, belong to this class (see B III, 98, mm. 13-14). But here it is a case of typical transitionary phenomenon, in which the new harmonic elements are still employed in the old static dispositions of organum. The placement of the c.f. in the upper voice is not arbitrary. On the contrary, it should be considered a consequence of the new harmonic possibilities—at least, under the precondition that one does not detect tonic triads in sixth-chords. In this connection, see Ge, 81.

[35]Ernst Kurth, *Grundlagen des linearen Kontrapunktes* (Bern: Krompholz, 1917); [and the same author's] *Romantische Harmonik und ihre Krise in Wagners "Tristan"* (Berlin: Max Hesse, 1923).

[36]B I, 112; B II, 45; B III, 103.

realm.[37] The opposition between tense and relaxed harmonies comprises a harmonic unfolding of the type just described. Consequently, there can be no doubt as to which of the two categories the sixth chords of fauxbourdon belong and, on the other hand, to which the 8-5 sonorities belong.

With the help of parallel thirds and sixths or their simultaneous combination, the simplest and most natural kind of harmonic-polyphonic accompaniment of a melody is produced, and this is still demonstrated today in folk music. Its easy, harmonically pleasing effect can also be traced in art music, right up to Richard Strauss.

That this harmonic parallelism in thirds and sixths is a specifically English attribute that can be traced back at least to the thirteenth century through the comments of the theorists is recognized in the musicological literature and is also confirmed by Besseler.[38] As it continues to be today in folk-style polyphony, this practice also had the advantage that it was freely improvised and hence was not written down. Characteristic of this English [style of] improvisation, which was completely unknown on the Continent, is the technique of Sights,[39] which had been long handed down. It proceeded from a lone given voice, from which the remaining voices were improvised according to specific rules.

The improvisation [required] in fauxbourdon was especially simple, since it merely furnishes a melody with a sixth chord (or, for a cadence tone, an 8-5 sonority). Only the very least amount of clarification had to be provided [i.e., *Tenor au fauxbourdon*, etc.]. In England—where even the complicated discant technique (complicated, at least, in its written embodiments!) was still apprehended as improvisation—such a specification would have been perceived as completely senseless and superfluous. Hence, while there are no fauxbourdon pieces anywhere in the English manuscripts, this circumstance in no way proves that this simplest type of harmonic parallelism would not have been known as a transparently obvious improvisational practice. On the contrary, the fact that, in England, fauxbourdon pieces even in the late fifteenth century were exclusively improvised is particularly persuasive for the validity of the opposite assumption, not for the interpretation of Bukofzer[40]

---

[37]The [theorist] mentioned by Bukofzer (Bu, 86 and 158), Anonymous, British Museum, Add. 4911, speaks correctly of fauxbourdon as a "melodic way" of connecting sonorities ("melodius kynd of harmony").

[38]B III, 15. See also Riemann, *Geschichte der Musiktheorie*, 111 ff.; Ge, 63 ff.; Bu, 109-10.

[39]Discussed above.

[40]Bu, 9 and 121. Also, a report from [the year] 1484 is introduced here as evidence for the adoption of fauxbourdon from the Continent (Bu, 125). Bukofzer translates *extrinsecus* and

and Besseler[41] that the technique was taken over [in England] from the Continent. For it would be completely out of the question that a *res facta*, which fauxbourdon on the Continent always was, would, in its adoption into a foreign artistic environment suddenly become an improvisatory phenomenon, if [in this new environment] the capability for improvising the technique had not always been available and handed down.

But, even when one leaves out of account the fact that [written] fauxbourdon could never have turned up in the surviving old English sources, it must nevertheless have left occasional traces in those creative forms in which, due to their free and craftsmanlike conception, a notational record was deemed necessary. In the surviving English sources of the fourteenth and fifteenth centuries, this is abundantly the case. I will cite here as evidence only the examples from Worcester—and other fragments, as well as *OH*.[G] From *OH*, it would be instructive to reproduce the beginning (on page 1) of a Gloria fragment—one of countless similar examples:

Example 1

extranicus as "foreign" instead of as "not corresponding to convention." It only remains to be said that the means of delivery no longer was the accustomed, conventional one, [and that it] no longer agreed with the essence of fauxbourdon. Hence, the passage in question shows, in opposition to Bukofzer's assumption of a foreign importation, that fauxbourdon in England was a long accustomed practice, whose alteration by the new innovations being introduced at that time gave rise even to an attack by the church authorities.

[41]B III, 103 ff., with the chapter title: "England's Answer"!

[G]See Ge, 98 ff.; Bu, Appendix, 16 ff.; Reese, 399

One gets the impression from most of the English compositions of this type that the original framework consists of chains of sixth chords (with 8-5 sonorities at the cadence). [In these pieces,] the contrapuntal appearance of discant is only subsequently imparted, through occasional displacement of the structural tones into a wider intervallic distance, passing [tone] constructions, contrary motion, and similar devices. In this way, an essentially craftsmanlike and varied creation results in place of the oleaginous series of sixth chords, while still fully preserving the original effect of harmonic tautness. The same principle of restricting the commonplace improvised parallel 6-3s, in order to lend a more contrapuntally meaningful contour [to the piece], is then virtually equivalent to English discant as taught [in the treatises].

The preeminent evolutionary significance of this English discant, whose theoretical formulations are to be found in the treatises examined by Bukofzer and Georgiades, had been too little acknowledged, [precisely] because the technique of fauxbourdon—[which was actually an] insignificant [factor] in the following [technical] attainments—always stood in the foreground of consideration and was valued as the final stage in this phase of development. In truth, one is witnessing in these discant treatises the first methodical demonstration of a *system of harmony* [to be taken] in a completely new and modern sense. With respect to the pertinent sonority progressions, the rules and examples already correspond to the demands of classical harmonic voice leading.[42] It can probably be assumed rightfully that the author of the oldest treatise, Leonel Power, is identical with the composer Leonel (Leonellus), who must accordingly be regarded as a pioneer—even before Dunstable, who was younger—in the stylistic and technical concerns of discant embellishment and the new discant [procedures].[43] Indeed, the entire output of the later English masters is founded upon the rules of energized harmonic progressions, developed here for the first time in a systematic way by Leonel Power. The influence of discant upon the Continental practice was discussed above, but there can be no doubt—even if one leaves out of account the frequent sixth-chord progressions in older English works—that the future belonged not to the

---

[42]See the examples in Bukofzer's Appendix (1-11); also, Ge, 35. Without going further into Besseler's observations about cadence treatment (B III, 33 ff., 49 ff.), it should only be remarked that even at this early stage the leap of a fourth (or fifth) in the lowest voice warrants very special notice.

[43]However, the Leonel-Dunstable question seems still not to have been incontestably clarified. In consequence of the attribution of the Gloria from the *Missa Sine nomine* in Aosta [fols. 208v–210r] (*DTÖ* 61, 119-25) to the composer Bonnet (Benet?), the state of affairs has become even less clear.

primitive, improvised parallelism in thirds, sixths, or 6-3s; rather, [it belonged to] the considerably more exacting [technique of English] discant, which represents the more highly developed and above all more artistic principle.

Besseler mentions English discant only peripherally and sees in it only a subordinate practice of improvisation as opposed to the *res facta* of Continental fauxbourdon. Although the old Sight technique in the English treatises continued, as always, to be used for didactic demonstration of the contemporary voice leading, according to long-standing tradition, this does not in any way mean that a practical and artistic exploitation of the discant rules (which, after all, is their whole point) followed in the wake of improvisatory practice. In contrast to the unvarying and mechanical formalism of the fauxbourdon technique, discant exhibits so rich a multiplicity of possibilities in voice leading that its improvisation seems entirely out of the question, particularly in the three-voice discant works that were most frequently cultivated in the English practice of the time. Such improvisation would have been conceivable most likely in very simple, conductus-like pieces [performed by] seasoned singers, and such pieces are still contained in *OH*. But even here the sources confirm the qualities of *res facta*. Apart from the foregoing, Leonel Power emphasizes that the discant instructions are intended in equal measure for singers, *composers*, and teachers; thus, these rules also apply to [written] compositions worked out in advance.[44] This situation is also the case in exact reverse: fauxbourdon was and always remained an improvisatory practice in England.[45] Accordingly, it is no longer discernible today as an artistic legacy in the English sources. On the other hand, discant in England is always a *res facta*, even in its practical musical application.

This new and admittedly still unpretentious phenomenon at first occasioned hardly any notice at all on the Continent, since here the French *Ars nova* had developed highly mannered and complicated forms and techniques (particularly with respect to rhythm), over which the English music, locked in a rigid conservatism, had no claim. In the harmonic realm also, even in Machaut and some of his followers,[46] one encounters events of the most

---

[44]The original wording reads: "... by syngers or makers or techers." See Ge, 12, 31; Bu, 29, 132. [The emphasis above is Ficker's.]

[45]This observation is made even as early as Riemann, *Handbuch der Musikgeschichte*, II/1, 95.

[46]The young Dufay also belongs to this circle. The harmonic audacities that Besseler believes are to be identified with him should [actually] be comprehended entirely [as arising] from the harmonic outlook of the older generation. There are no grounds for assuming, as

striking sort, which seem especially modern to us today. But, in a fashion similar to that of the chromaticists of the sixteenth century, these [instances], despite their boldness, cannot be assessed as leading to the harmony of the mature fifteenth century. Rather, they must be appraised merely as exaggerations of a long-cultivated harmonic practice.

Around 1400, one can discern even in some centers of English music a strong influx of formal devices attained in the late *Ars nova*, which was stimulated by the presence of French music. And in Old Hall, the repertoire of the Chapel Royal, native composers were now making full use of the French motet techniques: hockets, isorhythm, and rhythmically complex constructions. But in unmitigated juxtaposition, they further emphasized their smooth discant counterpoint, rich in sixths and thirds, and now they also brought to the forefront as an independent development the melodically rich embellishment [technique], supported and conditioned by a new suave technique of harmonic progression.

It was just these unassuming creations appearing in England, disseminated everywhere as common musical practice, which then are said to have had a significant influence upon the Continental evolution. This influence was in effect shortly after the battle of Agincourt (1415). It reached its high point after the death of Henry V (an enthusiastic supporter of music), when the courtly music was nearing the end of its quick demise. Its nadir, under the rule of the weak Henry VI, is shown particularly in the MS Egerton 3307.[47] The compositions of this late repertoire of the royal chapel evince a regression into the simple discant style that had been developed even before the turn of the century and which had maintained itself almost unchanged in provincial areas. Nowhere can there be detected any influence of the higher art of a Leonel, Dunstable, or the other English masters. Thus, in the country of their origin, the resources demanded for the performance of their difficult-to-interpret works were probably now lacking. From this one must assume that, due to the emigration of the land's best musicians, the epicenter of English art music had for some time been displaced to the Continent. As early as 1417, Henry V had had the members of his court chapel brought over to Paris for the

---

Besseler does (B III, 55), that the ballade *Bonté bialté* of the older Cesaris was influenced by Dufay. Apart from that, the accidentals in the work [as contained] in the addendum of [MS] Florence Panciatichi 26 seem to be interpretive rather than stemming from the composer. Hence, they comprise a valuable bit of evidence for contemporary performance practice.

[47] See Bertram Schofield and Manfred Bukofzer, "A Newly Discovered 15th-Century Manuscript of the English Chapel Royal [Egerton 3307]—Part I," *Musical Quarterly* 32 (1946): 509-36; and Part II, *Musical Quarterly* 33 (1947): 38-51.

Christmas celebrations.[48] Here the Duke of Bedford, Regent of France, maintained a choir, to which—among other Englishmen—Dunstable belonged,[49] and the art-loving Duke of Suffolk, a patron of Binchois, was also staying in France.[50] Moreover, the English musicians were particularly valued at the Burgundian court.[51] On the other hand, however, the diverse artistic currents and traditions of the host country itself exerted a significant influence upon the emigrant English musicians, which only helped to facilitate the full development of their singular talents. Accordingly, their accomplishments comprised an important component in Continental music history far earlier than in that of England. This helps to explain why the musical output of the illustrious later English composers is almost exclusively transmitted in Continental manuscripts from the middle of the century, and further, why with their death, the creative power of England seems to have completely dried up, their art being taken over and furthered solely by the masters of their adopted land.

The clarification of these relationships is again made difficult by a significant gap [in transmission], which, when not acknowledged, makes it easy to draw erroneous conclusions. This gap now concerns the transmission of manuscripts. It is known—thanks not least to the outstanding source research of Besseler—that the central Burgundian manuscripts of the time in question have almost without exception been lost.[52] An elucidation of causes and manifestations in this process of development, which was fulfilled here in the north, can only in some measure be derived from the manuscripts which originated in north Italy around the middle of the century; these include Oxford [213], *BU*, *BL*, as well as *ModB*, and Trent 87 and 92. This means that we must reconstruct—from manuscripts distant as well as late—both the central Burgundian development, with Binchois as premier master, and also that of the English composers active on the Continent. The compiling of these manuscripts was conditioned, above all, by the outlook of the upper-Italian milieu. The two crucial Bolognese sources consist—outside of the few

---

[48]André Pirro, *La musique à Paris sous le règne de Charles VI* (Strasbourg: Heitz, 1930).

[49]Manfred Bukofzer, "Über Leben und Werke von Dunstable," *Acta Musicologica* 8 (1936): 102.

[50]Jeanne Marix, *Histoire de la musique et des musiciens de la Cour de Bourgogne sous le règne de Philippe le Bon (1420–67)* (Strasbourg: Heitz, 1939), 177 ff.

[51]Reported by Martin le Franc and cited in Victor Lederer, *Über Heimat und Ursprung der mehrstimmigen Tonkunst* (Leipzig: Siegel, 1906), 111.

[52]See Heinrich Besseler, "Studien zur Musik des Mittelalters [Part] I: Neue Quellen des 14. und beginnenden 15. Jahrhunderts," *Archiv für Musikwissenschaft* 7 (1925): 241 ff.

Italians, whose works hardly penetrated beyond the local area—almost exclusively of the Netherlanders active in Italy who, with Ciconia and Dufay at the head, were held here in high regard. In contrast, the masters of the Burgundian chapel and the English are represented here only exceedingly weakly and by few characteristic works. Thus, for example, a comparative count of *BL*, with its almost 330 compositions, yields the following results, whereby the numbers in parenthesis are later additions:

$$
\begin{array}{lcl}
\text{Binchois} & = & 2\,(+\,2) \\
\text{Dunstable} & = & 1\,(+\,3) \\
\text{Leonel} & = & 2\,(+\,2) \\
\text{Benet} & = & 2
\end{array}
$$

The manuscript evidence, then, demonstrates that the works of the central-Burgundian—and especially the English—composers remained practically unnoticed in Italy even as late as around 1440, at least with respect to the critical genres of the new motet and the mass. Only the Burgundian chanson, including works of Binchois, had by this time become generally accepted as the predominant secular art form, as can be concluded particularly [from the contents of] Oxford [213].

This observation is also of consequence to the question of fauxbourdon, since it is exactly here that Besseler, in spite of this source gap, considers the source distribution as decisive and draws the conclusion that the Postcommunio *Vos qui secuti* of Dufay from *BL* (mentioned by F.X. Haberl[53] and K. Dèzes[54]) represents the oldest example of a fauxbourdon piece and that, accordingly, Dufay is due the honor of being [acknowledged as] the "creator" of fauxbourdon.[55]

If there were any Burgundian manuscripts surviving from the period between 1420-40, the supposition would probably be demonstrated as correct that here in the north—where the contact with English music practice must have taken place earliest and also with most effect—fauxbourdon pieces probably would have made their appearance before those in the Italian manuscripts. Accordingly, it has to be considered daring to date the origin of, for example, the relatively numerous fauxbourdons of Binchois (which display

---

[53]Franz X. Haberl, "Wilhelm du Fay: Monographische Studie über dessen Leben und Werke." *Vierteljahrsschrift für Musikwissenschaft* 1 (1885): 477.

[54]Karl Dèzes, "Van den Borrens 'Dufay,'" *Zeitschrift für Musikwissenschaft* 9 (1926-27): 302-3.

[55]B I, 107; B II, 31; B III, 14.

the new technique in a particularly archetypal and clear form[56]) only *after* Dufay's creation of fauxbourdon, since, in consequence of the aforementioned gap in transmission, the latter appear only in later manuscripts, which evince a more universal viewpoint (particularly Trent). But if one wishes to construct an evolutionary chronology in a fashion more typical for art-historical research, i.e., not simply on the grounds of an uncertain source state (in the case at hand particularly so) but rather primarily with respect to the technical and stylistic characteristics—which here cannot be restricted exclusively to fauxbourdon, then one most probably would have to date the fauxbourdons of Binchois even earlier than Dufay's.

But even [with] a familiarity with the missing early Burgundian sources, [we] would probably only be able to answer the question of which Continental master should be accorded the primacy of fauxbourdon use, but it would hardly clarify the question of English origin of fauxbourdon technique. For such results would already indicate that, even at a later time, the significant English masters deliberately avoided availing themselves of the fauxbourdon technique. Thereby, they would have had precisely the opportunity to make extensive use, much earlier, of this allegedly Continental creation (which was fulfilled in its narrowest circle of activity) than it could have reached [in] the realm of the English homeland, which, according to Besseler's view, had sunk to the level of traditional utilitarian music. The total lack of acknowledgment of fauxbourdon on the part of the English composers allows only one conclusion: that it was definitely familiar from the homeland as a primitive, improvised technique[57] but that it must have seemed to them, particularly in its one-dimensional mechanistic formalism as a fauxbourdon piece, as completely unusable in an artistic sense compared to the fully developed discant technique.

---

[56]See the pages on fauxbourdon in Jeanne Marix, *Les musiciens de la Cour de Bourgogne au XVe Siècle (1420-1467)* (Paris: L'Oiseau-Lyre, 1937), 192 [No. 4], 218-226 [Nos. 13-15]. Also *In exitu Israel* (ibid., 196-208 [No. 8]) is a fauxbourdon piece. Its full three-voice repetition is occasioned exclusively by the freely handled cadence structures. From this it clearly follows that the rigid voice leading of the contratenor as a fourth-interval incarnation of the superius was recognized as musically unsatisfactory. Accordingly, the piece comprises the desired evidence for how the performance was done in practice, and, hence, these exceptional fauxbourdon sections correspond completely to the performance practice of the time. The blending of fauxbourdon with elements of the discant technique is shown particularly clearly in the three Magnificats of Binchois, contained in Marix (ibid.), 131-7, 144-7, 148-53.

[57]This is evidenced by the few measures of consecutive sixth chords in Dunstable's *Quam pulchra* (B III, 114), which, apart from *OH*, can be further augmented by similar examples from other English composers.

On the other hand, regarding the early effects of English practice of discant and of the embellishment [technique] upon the Continent, more thorough conclusions could probably have been reached from the lost manuscripts than are now possible on the basis of the late [and] peripheral sources alone. Accordingly, the zone of influence of fauxbourdon technique is, for the time being, probably to be sought less in the realm of art music than in the simple forms of service music—just as [was true] in England. This [surmise] is already supported by the fact that use of the technique remained restricted principally to the short, folk-style sacred forms, especially hymns. However, the documentary record, scanty though it is, also seems to confirm it.

As early as 1416, the German king Sigismund, on the occasion of his visit to Henry V of England, had articulated his admiration for the singularity of English music in these words: "Blessid Inglond, full of melody...."[58] One certainly should not feel at liberty to take such pronouncements very literally regarding the reality of underlying musical facts—especially when they stem from non-musicians, but it can probably be assumed that "full of melody" is to be understood as the melodically smooth method of energetic voice leading, rich in thirds and sixths, which had been spread widely through the English practices of improvisation and simple discant.[59] Certainly it cannot be a mere accident that Dufay later in his motet *Supremum est* (dated 1433) honoring Sigismund and Pope Eugene IV,[H] interpolated passages in fauxbourdon [right] next to [sections] restricted to the fluid three-voice discant counterpoint in the English style—a procedure that represents an unusual case among the contemporary large celebratory motets. In the face of the sublime conception of Dufay's motet *Ecclesiae militantis*, dedicated to Eugene IV,[60] the

---

[58]See Victor Lederer, *Über Heimat*, 111; André Pirro, *Histoire de la Musique* (Paris: Renouard, 1940), 96.

[59]Even in the Burgundian vocabulary of the time, the terms *mélodie, son mélodieux,* and others, were especially apt to be used in a general sense. See Marix, *Histoire,* 37, 40, 99, 183.

[H]Rudolf von Ficker, ed., *Sieben Trienter Codices: Geistliche und weltliche Kompositionen des XIV. und XV. Jahrhunderts, Sechste Auswahl, DTÖ* 76 *(Jahrgang* XL) (Vienna: Universal-Edition, 1933), 24-5.

[60]*DTÖ* 76, 26 ff. Besseler's dating of the work (3-11 March 1431; see B II, 30; B III, 12, note 5) is less than sound. It does not seem possible that this highly demanding composition would have been composed and rehearsed within a few days. Also, the textual context fits much better with the settlement of the dispute with Venice, as Haberl has already indicated (see citation above in note 53, 484). Hence, one can probably assume a date of composition no earlier than 1436. The shortening of note values, compared to *Supremum est,* in the edition mentioned above, which is censured by Besseler (B II, 30; B III, 12), was a result of the

unassuming *Supremum* can hardly be interpreted as an epoch-making work. Rather, it should be regarded only as a concession of the master to the king's musically simple tastes, taking pleasure in the *faberdon*, which even in Germany had early attained a general popularity among the people.[61]

When the English bishops traveled to the Council of Constance in 1416, the performances of the accompanying singers exerted a singular impression upon audiences both in the Cologne Cathedral and in Constance.[62] It cannot have been the singing achievements alone that elicited this enthusiasm, for in these affairs, the famous choirs of the Continental cathedrals, led by the leading masters of the time, would certainly not have balked at being compared with anyone. Rather, it can only have been a question of certain basic attributes of the musical language, which these singers, gathered from the remotest corners of the isle, employed in consequence of a long-tempered artistic heritage. It must have been precisely through its natural simplicity that this musical language engendered a spontaneous effect on its listeners here in the over-cultivated sphere of the late-Gothic music tradition.

Above all, the melodically and harmonically impressive polyphonic form of the English singers' conception of the chant must have been perceived as something thoroughly new and unfamiliar. For here the chant was no longer employed as a constructive base; rather, it was conceived again as melody,

---

completely different structure of the two works. The beginning rhythm of the duo in *Ecclesiae militantis* is not the decisive element, because the rhythmic construction is here dominated by the thrice-repeated contratenor with the richly associative text *Bella canunt gentes*, in which the musical structure absolutely demands a conception of two *tempus* for each double measure, which would be totally incoherent in *Supremum est*.

In *Bourdon*, 126, Besseler introduces the view that the changeover from *prolatio* to *tempus* notation had the result of [introducing] a slowing down of the overall tempo. It need only be said here that the motet *Ducalis sedes—Stirps* of Anthonius Romanus (see Arnold Schering, *Geschichte der Musik in Beispielen* (Leipzig: Breitkopf & Härtel, 1931), No. 30) exists in *BU* in *prolatio* notation and in *BL* in *tempus* notation. Thus, according to Besseler's assumption, the work as it appears in *BL* would have to be interpreted twice as slowly!

The prospects of evidence held out by Besseler for the dating of *Apostolo glorioso* (*DTÖ* 76, 22-3; see B II, 29; B III, 12, 73) are still not forthcoming. Pirro had already presumed (*Histoire*, 70) that the work had been intended for Pandolfo Malatesta, archbishop of Patras after 1424. The unusual use of the Italian language in this piece, as well as the text citation *Eligisti ... per sepulcro questo sancto speco* lead, however, to the conclusion that the motet was intended for Amalfi, where the gravesite of the holy Andreas had been located since 1208 (see *DTÖ*, 76, 100).

[61]Reported by Hanns Rosenplüt, 1447 (see Adler, *Studie zur Geschichte der Harmonie*, 788).

[62]Pirro, *Histoire*, 96.

elevated to a likewise newly simple [but] enchanting prominence through ternary rhythmicization and further through the equally definitive smooth accompanimental motion in thirds and sixths. It must have aroused especial astonishment that this practice of polyphonic chant setting was brought about by way of spontaneous improvisation, and one may assume thereby that these singers made only little use of an artistic reworking of the chant through embellishment and similar procedures.[63] The harmonic constructions in this improvisation probably were based less in the complicated English discant than on the long-standing tradition of sixth-chord technique, whose vestiges one encounters even in the worked-out compositions native to England (discussed above). In other words, these musicians were probably using the technique that we see on the Continent at that time as *res facta*, under the designation "fauxbourdon."

In central-Burgundian territory, the preconditions for the adoption and further development of such simple musical practices were especially propitious. Indeed, the plans of the Burgundian dukes were aimed—particularly in view of the low condition of France—at taking over and modifying the French patrimony not only in political but also in cultural affairs. This fundamental transformation was seen as being fulfilled also in the realm of music. Additionally, it can be recognized that the masters of the Burgundian court chapel had almost entirely avoided the artistic constructivism of the forms of the dying *Ars nova* in favor of a [more] natural tonal and formal language, whereas the other Netherlanders held on to the old traditions and developed them further.

The difference is demonstrated, for example, by a comparison of the chansons of the central-Burgundians' main representative, Binchois, with those of Dufay, who had been sojourning since early youth in Italy, and whose chansons transmitted in Oxford [213] can therefore be dated as originating before 1440.[64] In Binchois [one sees] a completely uncomplicated, songlike and clearly structured shaping of the dominant vocal [i.e., upper] voice, over a simple instrumental harmonic foundation. In Dufay, on the other hand, [one sees] a variegated, differentiated employment of the traditional technical practices, such as canon, imitation, [and] choral disposition of the voice parts, which apparently stem from the motet's stock of technical devices.

---

[63]This was completely dependent upon the technical and artistic abilities of the improvisers in question.

[64]See John F.R. Stainer and C. Stainer, *Dufay and his Contemporaries* (London: Novello, 1898).

This new, naturalistic principle of simple musical organization is also characteristic of the sacred works of the central-Burgundian masters.[65] Here the large celebratory motet had undergone little development,[66] and likewise the Franco-Netherlandish mass style with its rhythm of scanning declamation. But even if, in consequence of the discontinuity in the Burgundian sources, an unimpeded documentary record cannot be brought to bear, an examination of the complete source contents from the later manuscripts—especially those [containing works] of Binchois—establishes that here those techniques, which especially correspond to the aesthetic principles of a new musical naturalism (such as fauxbourdon, structural embellishment, and harmonically well-balanced discant counterpoint), became and remained the prevailing [style], likewise in unilateral use, as simple, clearly marked, and lasting [characteristics].[67]

It is well known that Binchois, since as early as 1424, stood in close contact in Paris and Hennegau with the Duke of Suffolk, who was himself a poet and composer.[68] Marix also considers it probable that the master [Binchois] also stayed for a time at the count's castle in Bedford. If this is true, Binchois must have been especially conversant with English music styles and their techniques even before his membership in the Burgundian court chapel, which is provable from 1430. Since he was a soldier in his youth and [thus] presumably came to music only in his mature years,[69] it is understandable that he must have seen in the uncomplicated, natural language of the utilitarian English music a model corresponding better to his artistic proclivities than the elaborate forms of his native traditions. Hence, one must

---

[65]Marix, *Histoire*, 218: "Le style est alerte, les developpements courts, les messes ont parfois le rhythme dansant d'une chanson."

[66]The sole isorhythmic motet of Binchois is *Nova cantum melodie* of 1430, published in Marix, *Les musiciens de la cour de Bourgogne*, 212-17.

[67]Contrary to Dufay, Binchois avoids the complex late style of Dunstable. The much-discussed Credo of Dunstable (published in Wolf, *Geschichte der Mensural Notation: 1250-1460*, II/III (Leipzig: Breitkopf & Härtel, 1904), No. 73) is just as little characteristic of his style as is *Quam pulchra* (B III, 113 ff.). The Credo is closer to the early Continental mass style and exhibits strong relationships with the Credo of Binchois that was published by Charles van den Borren, *Polyphonica Sacra* (London: Plainsong and Mediæval Music Society, 1932), No. 9. The pentatonic elements that Riemann has chosen to point to in Dunstable exist also in Binchois and other Continental composers. Accordingly, they have nothing to do with pentatonicism either in England or on the Continent (in this connection, see B III, 71, 112, and Thesis 19).

[68]Pirro, *Histoire*, 89; Marix, *Histoire*, 177-8.

[69]Ernest Closson, "L'origine de G. Binchois," *Revue de Musicologie* 5 (1924): 149-50; Marix, *Histoire*, 176. Nothing is known of Binchois's teachers.

assume that Binchois knew at first hand the English techniques of discant, fauxbourdon, and structural embellishment and probably made use of them earlier than Dufay, who was active primarily in Italy, only entering into close contact with the Burgundian court around 1440.

It seems to me that Besseler has fully misjudged the singular position of the plainchant-based song-mass of Reginaldus Liebert, which is a typical central-Burgundian creation.[70] A comparison with the *Missa Sancti Jacobi* of Dufay is, I should think, absolutely out of the question, since the individual sections of the latter work are completely ununified:[I] the Credo and especially the Gloria still exhibit the declamatory rhythm of the old French motet style, and in the other movements, the early Netherlandish tenor technique (discussed above) predominates. The more modern discant techniques of chant embellishment are employed only in the Kyrie, the repetition of the Introit, and in the Postcommunio.[71] On the other hand, the (presumed) Marian mass of Liebert,[72] while admittedly dispensing with intricate techniques, attains

---

[70]Rudolf von Ficker, ed., *Sechs Trienter Codices: Geistliche und weltliche Kompositionen des XV. Jahrhunderts, Vierte Auswahl, DTÖ* 53 *(Jahrgang* XXVII/1) (Vienna: Universal-Edition, 1920), 1-18. In *Bourdon*, 151, 162, the Liebert Mass is maligned on account of its lesser value and musical sterility. In this connection it should be remarked that judgments of aesthetic worth, which are made only on grounds of graphic note representations, are connected less to the quality of the art object [itself] than to its [abstract] contemplation. This is also true with respect to [Besseler's] opinion on the motet *O sidus Yspanie (DTÖ* 76, 75; see *Bourdon*, 169) that it can be identified with the composition of that name which is mentioned in Dufay's will. Evidence against this can be seen in the performance of the upper voice, sung alone by six boys, and, further, in the circumstance that there is no other work with the same text, and, finally, in the singular musical effect of the composition. Besseler's view that the statement in Dufay's will concerns *O proles—O sydus* (see "Nachtrag zu Studie zur Musik des Mittelalters [Part I]: Neue Quellen des 14. und beginnenden 15. Jahrhunderts," *Archiv für Musikwissenschaft* 8 (1926): 236) is erroneous in that this four-voice motet is expressly cited in the index to *ModB* as *O proles*, the text of the main voice. The underlaying of the second text to the leaping, unsingable trombone-contratenor cannot be musically justified and was probably only done later. Accordingly, one can understand that Dufay later had the urge to confer a more worthy musical treatment upon this text.

[I]B III, 150.

[71]Karl Dèzes (see citation above in note 54, 300) has already emphasized the pronounced mixture of styles in the *Sancti Jacobi* Mass of Dufay. It [actually] belongs entirely to the genre coined by Besseler as "pseudomass."

[72]According to the fact that Liebert was choirmaster at Cambrai in 1424 (see the present author's article "Die Kolorierungstechnik der Trienter Messen," *Studien zur Musikwissenschaft* 7 (1920): 6) and in view of the close link between the cathedral there and the Burgundian court, the supposition is apparently warranted that his is the work to be identified as the *Messe de Nostre Dame* that was performed at the celebrations of the Order of the Golden Fleece at Lille

nevertheless a stylistic unity and continuity through its songlike discant treatment of each movement's appropriate chant. This represents in its own way a completely valid implementation of the cyclic principle. Above all, the work confirms how significantly and definitely the practices of English service music such as structural embellishment, discant, and fauxbourdon technique had achieved currency in the central-Burgundian realm. The preference of these new songlike technical resources one may, no doubt, attribute primarily to a special partiality on the part of Duke Philip the Good and the Burgundian court, where the English musicians had also played a crucial role.

In contrast, the adoption of these simple and natural practices by the other Netherlanders, especially those active in Italy, seems to have been distinctly hesitant and [attempted] without abandonment of their traditional techniques. Similarly to the unusual second version of the Introit from the *Missa Sancti Jacobi*, the Postcommunio *Vos qui secuti* may also have been added only subsequently to allow for the new tastes taking root, especially in the north.

Besseler's view that the Postcommunio was Dufay's first attempt at the use of fauxbourdon technique is probably not to be doubted; however, this little piece is not a true fauxbourdon,[73] since in the course of the work one occasionally gets the distinct impression that the tenor is removed from the superstructure through a smooth, calm configuration. In this manner, isolated parallel fourths arise, fully detached from the tenor, acting as "false" passing sonorities, which now exhibit as a relic of the high Middle Ages the static effect of consonances led in parallel motion, but they in no way display the dynamic power of discant's voice leading in thirds and sixths, or of fauxbourdon. One can find only one explanation for this regression into a technique already wholly foreign to the time: that Dufay was at first only superficially acquainted with the new fauxbourdon technique, and the opinion was that only the voice leading in fourths was of primary importance here, independent of the construction of the tenor at any given time. Around 1430, a piece such as this Postcommunio could as a rule have been written neither in Italy nor in England. One would have to reckon it [as being] still at least as fitting to the harmonic resources of the fourteenth century as to those of fauxbourdon, but it also holds an exceptional position with respect to the later fauxbourdons of Dufay, which correspond far better to the harmonic exigencies

---

in 1431 (see also Marix, *Histoire*, 36, 151 ff.).

[73]See the transcription of the piece (B I, 109) and the instructive analyses (B III, 17). Also, the false fourths in Isaac's *Innsbrucklied* (B I, 111; B II, 40; B III, 23) above the text *im elend*(!) are here to be understood as conscious archaisms and might again today appear to be particularly daring. Regarding harmonic constructions in the fourteenth century, see Ge, 100.

of fauxbourdon.

The designation *faux bourdon* in the tenor of the piece certainly seems superfluous, since the completion of the contratenor (Ctr) at a fourth lower than the upper voice is already made known by the appended dictum (*dyatesseron in subeundo*). But one can conclude from this that the designation *faux bourdon* means the same thing as the canon, namely a performance specification for the unnotated filling part of the contratenor, which is to be performed as the upper voice, except at the fourth below. This thus represents an apparent influence on the part of the English Sight technique, and we shall return to this point below.

While this unfortunate first attempt at a fauxbourdon by Dufay was probably a result of a misunderstanding of the foreign practice, brought about by particular conditions (see below), his "correct" fauxbourdon pieces also show that the primitivism of the technique—[which had] now become popular and which he therefore could not avoid—was self-conscious. Accordingly, he went to the trouble in his later genuine fauxbourdon creations to differentiate the superstructure from the tenor (through syncopations and passing note constructions, suspensions, etc.) so as to give it a freer, contrapuntal appearance, in order to facilitate the impression of a more artistic creative possibility for the technique through its fashioning as a *res facta*.

But even this process could not disguise the problematic nature of the inartistic rigidity of the fauxbourdon principle to a master like Dufay. Hence, he preferred [to use] in his late fauxbourdons the simple and uncomplicated technique similar to that type that is most commonly found in Binchois. In this manner it may have been (along with his taking consideration of the Burgundian practice) above all the crucial recognition that fauxbourdon represented a less suitable object for the integration of artistic techniques. The pronounced difference between tenor and upper voice, along with the use of suspensions, neighbor-, and passing-notes in the superius must perforce have had as its result an increased emphasis upon the awkward open parallel fourths and hence a muddying of the harmonic relationships binding them to fauxbourdon, which was founded on a parallelism of *6-3 sonorities*, but *not*, however, upon [bare parallel] fourths.

Deliberations of this sort had most probably been instrumental in bringing Dufay and other composers to recompose finished fauxbourdon pieces subsequently into normal discant works. Here the notated structural counterpoint of upper voice and tenor remained unchanged, while the filling voice (contratenor) now was composed out into a real and self-sufficient voice—into a *contratenor sine* or *absque faulxbourdon*.[74] This procedure also provides evidence that the technique of fauxbourdon represents the primary, primitive process, whereas that of discant represents the developed artistic process (see above). Consequently, each fauxbourdon can directly be made into a discant piece through the requisite free composing-out of the contratenor, whereas a reversion to fauxbourdon is impossible without reconceiving both lower voices.

The numerical preponderance that Besseler ascertains in table form with regard to Dufay's fauxbourdon works, as opposed to the other composers of the epoch,[J] seems highly problematic in that the total number of surviving works of each composer—at least, of the applicable sacred works—would have to have been taken into consideration. In this case it would have been revealed that the percent of fauxbourdon pieces of some of the composers cited in the table is much higher than in Dufay's output. Moreover, those fauxbourdons which, as self-enclosed sections, are frequently inserted into expansive forms, such as motets and mass settings (also [those] by other masters), likewise would have had to have been cited.

The designation "fauxbourdon" has hitherto undergone extremely varied explanations in the literature. Besseler enlarges it into yet a new interpretation, which is hardly more convincing than the older ones. He is convinced that "fauxbourdon" is the designation of a [specific] voice, namely, the unnotated contratenor. This voice is thus supposed to be a "false bourdon," because here it is the middle voice and does not lie beneath the tenor as a low voice, director of harmony [*Harmonieträger*], or "bourdon," which, according to Besseler's view, are to be seen as the function[s] of the contratenor during the period.[75]

Besseler must in any event concede that the designation "bourdon" never occurs, neither in the theoretical nor in the practical sources, and that on the contrary, this alleged "bourdon" was always expressly named "contratenor."[76] Accordingly, if his interpretation were correct, the designation would more likely have to read something like *faux contrateneur*. Moreover, it is difficult to grasp why the composers, when they refashioned a fauxbourdon into a discant piece (as discussed above), would not have named this "real" contratenor simply as "bourdon" rather than using the convoluted and

---

[74]Dufay: *Ave maris* (*BL*, fol. 292v); *Exultet celum* (*BL*, fol. 295v); *Criste redemptor* (*ModB*, fol. 1v); Benoit: *Qui in mane* (*ModB*, fol. 16v), etc.

[J]B III, 7.

[75]B II, 42; B III, 24, 99, Thesis 26.

[76]B III, 68.

contradictory designation *contratenor sine faulxbourdon*. Indeed, one cannot discern even an intimation of proof that the designation "bourdon" would have been used at this time in the sense imputed to it by Besseler.

Furthermore, even the assumption that the contratenor, especially as early as around 1430, would in general have had the status of a low voice does not hold true, since it cannot possibly be admissible that the contratenor should have *previously* been a middle voice. Besseler believes it possible to conclude this from its position in the final cadence, which in by far the majority of cases actually does stand in the middle (a fifth above the tenor), and thus, according to his view (as generally expressed), the structure of the work should be characterized by the "special location" of the contratenor's voice leading.[K] Accordingly, this is supposed to establish for the contratenor in the era before Dufay the character of a middle voice.

Here, however, is where Besseler fails to recognize a hitherto little-noticed principle of construction, fundamental to medieval polyphony: In the structure of three-part writing, the tenor and contratenor are differentiated not in terms of their particular voice range but rather through their wholly divergent duties or functions, to which they must conform in the process of creating the counterpoint. Specifically, the upper voice and the tenor together always comprise the *primary structural framework* [*primärer Kernsatz*], which exists as a fully closed and independent entity and which can stand alone in and of itself throughout, musically speaking.[77] Hence, it would be completely impossible on voice-leading grounds that the tenor could ever have made a cadence with the upper voice at the fourth below; its cadence tone had to be, as a rule, an octave below.[78] To this musically complete, two-voice core counterpoint, the contratenor then entered the picture as a decidedly secondary filling voice, allocated to the fifth above the *finalis* of the tenor (with the top voice an octave above), thus completing the standard 8-5 cadence sonority.[79]

[K]B III, 31-2.

[77]It is particularly Knud Jeppesen who has drawn attention to these circumstances and has accordingly pointed out that the possibility always exists to simply leave out the contratenor, whereas this is not possible with the tenor. See *Der Kopenhagener Chansonnier* (Copenhagen: Munksgaard, 1927), XLVII-XLVIII.

[78]This procedure can be deduced from the numerous publications of contemporary three-voice compositions.

[79]Accordingly, it was not a [theoretical] requirement, nor a "contrapuntal hierarchy" (B III, 33) that assigned the contratenor to the middle position at the cadence sonorities but rather the simple fact that within the frame of the structural [two-voice] counterpoint, the fifth above the final was the only suitable location still available to accommodate the cadence tone of the contratenor. Also, the octave leap of the contratenor at the cadences, described by Besseler as

This disposition of the cadence tone, conditioned by the secondary creation of the contratenor is, however, not necessarily applicable to the part-leading for this voice thoughout the rest of the composition. Rather, the contratenor is only a purely completing part, filling in the sonority, lying sometimes under and sometimes over the tenor, and thereby taking on those characteristics of leapwise motion and unsingability, which have long been familiar (and held in bad repute) from the chanson literature around 1400 as the so-called "contra-style" of voice leading.[80]

Thus, the contratenor can have been neither the primary director of harmony nor the lowest voice. This applies even to those compositions with a six-line contratenor, which Besseler has judged as being particularly conclusive in support of his bourdon thesis.[81] In these instances we observe quite individualized and exceptional cases, in which performance of the completing voice, the contratenor, was realized on a trumpet-like instrument (trombone or slide trumpet),[82] thereby permitting the full advantage to be taken of the specific harmonic effects of low tones. But even here, this contratenor is by no means always the lowest voice; instead, it frequently lies higher than the tenor and, occasionally, even above the superius.[83]

The contratenor acts equally little as director of harmony, for the reason that the harmonic context is already clearly marked out in the structural counterpoint, so that the contratenor would be in this respect fully dispensable. Its function is primarily restricted to the subsequent completion and clarification of the already-closed tonal framework of the structural counterpoint. Only relatively seldom does it occur that the original harmonic context undergoes at some places an alteration caused by the supplementary contratenor, yet in many cases, this proves to be not at all in the best interests of harmonic clarity.[84] It might be added that it is indisputable that a voice

---

"ingenious" (B III, 33-4), was conditioned by this same external necessity.

[80]See the *Ars contratenoris* of Anonymous XI (*CS* 3, 465b): *Contratenor est ita gravis sicut tenor est, aliquando gravior* ["The contratenor is thus just as low as the tenor, and sometimes lower"]. The uncontrapuntal leapwise conception of the contratenor is, as Jeppesen observes (see citation above, note 77, XLIX) brought about "because it is necessary to lead [the voice] in this way in order to produce a full and complete sonority."

[81]B II, 43; B III, 28 ff., 45 ff.

[82]See B III, 50 ff.; see also Heinrich Besseler, "Die Entstehung der Posaune," *Acta Musicologica* 22 (1950): 8 ff.; and Jeppesen (see citation above, note 77, page L).

[83]This is true, for example, in Dufay's *O proles*. In none of the six-line pieces introduced by Besseler is the contratenor the lowest voice, even though performance by a trombone, with its wide lower range, would have been particularly suited to that kind of employment.

[84]This happens, for example, in the chanson *J'aime bien* of Pierre Fontaine, conspicuously

conception such as that evinced by the monstrous six-line contratenors, contrapuntally so heavy-handed, can scarcely be imputed to a true master such as Dufay. They were probably fabricated at various times by instrumentalists to demonstrate their proficiency and the technical and coloristic possibilities of their instrument.[85] As a so-called *concordantia*, the new contratenor served either: 1) as a substitute for the original or, 2) as an amplifying voice— frequently in a predominantly low range—of a complete polyphonic work.[86]

In all of these cases, however, the decisive thing is that even here the contratenor is always a secondary, supplementary voice, which can be unhesitatingly left out or replaced by another part. This clear musical fact, then, leaves it entirely out of the question that even a six-line contratenor of this sort—not to mention a regular contratenor of the type that comprises the vast majority— would ever have been designated as "bourdon," or that it ever in this period would have had the quality of a lowest voice or of a primary director of harmony.

Incidentally, Besseler's explanation already seems improbable in that its literal application implies that the particular harmonic structure of fauxbourdon (which, of course, constituted the essence of his theories) would not be in the least affected or circumscribed. Hence, every contemporary free contrapuntal discant work whose contratenor happened by chance to occupy a

---

mentioned by Besseler (B III, 50; "Entstehung der Posaune," 25 ff., 35) where, on account of the trumpet-contratenor (added later), the clear D minor [tonality] of the short piece is noticeably disturbed.

[85]The musical deformity of the foregoing chanson (see note 84), originally provided with an unobjectionable contratenor (in *BL*), is certainly not to be laid at Dufay's door (B III, 50; "Entstehung der Posaune," 30). Also, the empty octave cadences (mm. 3, 7, 12, 14, 17) show that this was no master conversant with harmonic clarity and fullness, but rather a musical hack, who merely had an ambition to flaunt the wide range of his instrument.

[86]As an example of the first—widely predominant—practice, one could point to *Helas, ma dame* (B III, 261), and for the second case, *Ma belle dame* (B III, 262, 73, 84), where a harmonically dispensable contratenor has been subsequently added as a sonorous supplement to a complete piece of three higher voices, yet the tones of the former even in this exceptional case frequently lie above those of [one or more of] the higher voices.

A particularly instructive example for the subsequent refashioning of a contratenor, from a somewhat later time, is offered by the two versions of the anonymous motet *Anima mea* (*DTÖ* 76, 86-8, 106). Here also the self-contained discant-tenor framework remains unaltered. The original contratenor is replaced in the later, four-voice version with a contratenor altus and a contratenor bassus. Only this contratenor bassus is now unmistakably a lowest voice, which now, together with the higher contratenor, brings about a new type of harmonic realization. But the development process shows clearly here that even this true low voice is a secondary completing part and accordingly cannot be the primary director of harmony [*Harmonieträger*].

middle position would have to have been a fauxbourdon.[87] In light of this [difficulty], it seems obvious to look for an explanation of the enigmatic name that corresponds to the musical facts and [that corresponds] above all to those things that would have to stand in conformity with the harmonic attributes of fauxbourdon as they are generally understood.

While the older researchers affirmed the English origin of fauxbourdon out of a healthy musical instinct, they were also of the opinion (as are their more recent followers) that the designation "fauxbourdon" was coined in France; only later was it supposed to have been taken over in England, Italy, and Germany under respective speech transliterations. Besseler[88] also considers the English term *ffaburdon*[89] only as an anglicization of "fauxbourdon," and he uses this contention to support his thesis of its Continental origin.

This generally accepted view nevertheless seems to me to be invalid, and to be one of the essential causes that heretofore have hindered a musically reasonable explanation both of the meaning of fauxbourdon and of its coining.

For [it seems that] out of fauxbourdon, a "false burdon" could have arisen in England—similar to the Italian *falso bourdon*—but never a *ffa-burdon*.[90] The English term must therefore have had another, self-sufficient meaning. This would correspond also to the circumstance already touched upon, that the interpretation of fauxbourdon in England was different than on the Continent, although in both places it referred to one and the same phenomenological process. Consequently, one must pay special attention to these distinctions between the two interpretations and ponder them mutually in order possibly to succeed in interpreting the concept coherently.

For the English reading, decisive importance is accorded, as always, to the anonymous treatise London, BM, Lansdowne 763 (previously ascribed falsely to Chilston).[91] Bukofzer places its origin only around 1470, but Besseler sees it as originating about 1430.[L] Georgiades eschews attempting to date the

---

[87]This same consideration makes it seem as out of the question that fauxbourdon could have had the qualities of a "false" bass, as Bukofzer also assumed (Bu, 10). But then in this case, every discant piece whatever having an embellished superius would likewise have to have been a fauxbourdon.

[88]B II, 39; B III, 105 ff.

[89]The double *f* is encountered frequently in English manuscripts of the period in words which stand at the beginning of sentences, after punctuation marks, and so forth. Here it is equivalent to a majuscule [i.e., capital] F. See Ge, 10.

[90]On the other hand, the German spelling *Faberdon* was doubtless adapted from the English term and pronunciation.

[91]Text in Bu, 152; Ge, 27.

[L]Bu, 71; BIII, 105.

treatise precisely but considers it to be an expanded continuation of the treatise by Leonel Power,[92] which deals with the developed discant technique and its rules of voice leading, with the usual limitation to two-voice counterpoint. The treatise of Pseudo-Chilston is closely connected to the account of Power's, but it expands upon the latter through a specialized treatment of the filling voice called the counter (Ctr), the gymel, and *ffaburdon*.

All of the English discant treatises display a wide-ranging agreement in their terminology. All of them use the long-handed-down technique of Sights (at that time still established only in England) for the demonstration of their respective subjects, and from this clearly results both the self-sufficiency of their representation as well as their independence from the Continental explications of fauxbourdon.

The excerpt in Pseudo-Chilston, which is fundamental for the recognition of the English conception of fauxbourdon, was misinterpreted by Bukofzer.[M] Instead of making a word-for-word exegesis [of the passage], he is satisfied simply to make an inexplicit description of the contents and consequently comes to the inaccurate conclusion that fauxbourdon as described here could only have been two-voiced.

In contrast, Georgiades gives an exact, word-for-word translation and critical interpretation of this important excerpt.[N] From this it clearly emerges that this represents an exposition of the familiar three-voice fauxbourdon phenomenon, but this explanation is of a special sort, which is articulated in English and is fundamentally different from the Continental [descriptions].

Taking no notice of these fully clarified circumstances, Besseler then speaks of the "unclarities of this all-too-brief description," which, as he says, "do not [need] to be considered in their particulars."[O] Such [a consideration], however, would certainly have been of advantage, for then Besseler would probably not have declared (as though the matter had not already been settled) whether it was a question of three- or only of two-voice counterpoint.

In agreement with Bukofzer, Besseler further maintains that the Sight practice employed here has nothing to do with fauxbourdon.[P] Actually, exactly the opposite is true, for nowhere is this Sight technique more natural and simpler than in fauxbourdon. That a Leonel Power did not expressly emphasize fauxbourdon (which in the English art music of the time was a

---

[92]Ge, 39; see also Bu, 132 ff.; Ge, 12 ff.

[M]Bu, 72 ff.

[N]Ge, 43 ff.

[O]B III, 104

[P] See Bu, 13; B III, 104.

neglected vulgar practice)[93] is completely understandable, since he concerns himself here with the much-further-developed practice of discant. In the latter, however, the employment of the Sight technique at this time must be judged as having been far too complex and no longer meeting its needs, for which reason only now, in the end stages of its evolution, did a specific didactic description become necessary. One has to assess its inclusion in the discant teachings as an attempt—as minute in detail as it was futile—to demonstrate the authority of the visual/imaginary method of the Sights (originally developed for the primitive harmonic procedures and long handed down in England) now also for the complex free contrapuntal style.

In spite of this, Power cannot fully keep from view certain basic harmonic procedures, as they are the same as those of fauxbourdon. This emerges clearly from his remarks at the beginning of the treatise and their accompanying examples.[94] The parallelism of sixths and thirds, which underlie the elements of fauxbourdon, comprise the point of departure and the basis for the following description of the broadly complex phenomenon of discant.[95] Although fauxbourdon is never the issue in these pages, pertinent examples regarding the actual musical process of fauxbourdon technique must be included and, indeed, also the practical specimens from an even older time (mentioned above).

What is new in the Pseudo-Chilston treatise can be seen above all in the fact that the vulgar practice of 6-3 parallelism, which in Power was merely touched upon as an unavoidable starting point, is here treated in a special fashion under the designation *ffaburdon*, as are also *gymel* and *counter*. Thus, it is not just the harmonic element of the two-voice structure that is considered here but also that of the respective filling voices. The treatise can

---

[93] It is termed even as late as Guilielmus Monachus (*CS* 2, 292a) a *modus communis*.

[94] See the musical examples in Bukofzer's Appendix (Bu, 2); see also Ge, 35 ff.

[95] Whereas Bukofzer assumes that the examples are intended [to be] for three voices (Bu, 31), Georgiades holds the view that they, exactly as the other discant examples, are only to be understood in two voices (Ge, 34). In this connection it should be remarked that here the two-voice character of the theoretical demonstrations outwardly [is] certainly correctly interpreted, but [it] is of a relative kind. Here, the [demonstration] concerns at first only the voice leading of the two-voice core counterpoint, which then undergoes an expansion through the addition of a counter or a fauxbourdon, as is the norm in practical employment [of these techniques]. The generally broad use of the designation: three-, four-voice, etc. in the sense of the concept of equality of the individual voices, [often considered to be] justified from the time of the advent of through-imitation, does not take into account the older principle of structural counterpoint. It easily leads one to false conclusions with respect to the process of voice conception, which in this study is conceived quite differently.

probably have originated around 1420 at the earliest, at the time that this common practice had become known on the Continent and there had become "qualified for courtly use" under the designation "fauxbourdon." There exist, at least, no records [indicating] that this term was used in England at an earlier time, especially since the phenomenon itself was always classified in direct connection with the more comprehensive concept of discant.[96]

Of particular significance is Pseudo-Chilston's explanation of the fauxbourdon phenomenon with the help of the Sight technique. As is well known, the purpose of this is [to facilitate] the polyphonic interpretation of a given monophonic cantus firmus (c.f.), whereby this [c.f.] is realized by singers simultaneously in various intervallic dispositions, interchanging [with each other] at various times. In this way, the singers are supposed to have the notion that they all are executing one and the same melody.[97]

The specifications for fauxbourdon yield the following results, repeated here: The c.f. is not sung in the notated range but rather an octave higher and thereby becomes the upper voice (treble). The middle voice (mene) is realized throughout at the fifth above the c.f.; the tenor, on the other hand, is realized both at the unison (at caesura tones) and also at the third (during the course of the piece) above the notated c.f. Hence, the lower voices sound as the fourth (mene), and as the octave or sixth (tenor) below the upper voice, respectively, so that the familiar rows of sixth chords, mingled with 8-5 sonorities, result as composite sonorities.

Thus, the technique of Sights concerns itself with the "imagination" or "seeing" of a single given melody in various normative positions such that— unself-consciously and without artistic reflection—a polyphonic event results. In his foundation-laying inquiry, Georgiades has pointed out that the English Sight technique comprises the last offshoot of the *situs* teachings stemming from as early as the *Musica enchiriadis*, which is of fundamental importance particularly for the musical understanding of organum.[Q]

That the Sight technique was still familiar and widely distributed in England even towards the end of the fifteenth century is demonstrated by the

---

[96]Accordingly, fauxbourdon is expressly designated at the end of the treatise as "degre of descant" (Bu, 153; Ge, 27).

[97]Thus, we see here in essence the same principle as still today can be observed in the polyphonic realization of folksongs: the accompanying voice follows the main melody, for example, tone for tone at the interval of a third or a sixth, and diverges from the contour of the main line only at caesura tones, at which, to reinforce a given cadence, it ends in a perfect consonance.

[Q]Ge, 67 ff.

Litanies from Lambeth Palace, M. 438,[R] in which the monophonic chant, notated by itself, carries the designation *ffaburdon*. From this [basis], a regular three-voice fauxbourdon piece could be realized without any particular difficulties according to the instructions for the reading of Sights given by Pseudo-Chilston. But it is absolutely self-evident that the method could be employed with any monophonic melody whatsoever, and—as the contemporary witnesses certainly substantiate—it was used in an extremely wide scope, without requiring any additional specific indications. Equally self-evident is the fact that, for the reasons mentioned above, there is no mention anywhere in the collective English sources of a fauxbourdon piece. This is not due, as Besseler and Bukofzer believe, to the lack of fauxbourdon pieces [in England] before Dufay, but rather because its notation in two (or even in three!) voices, as then became necessary on the Continent, would have been considered totally superfluous and pointless. Indeed, when in the treatise we have been considering it is expressly emphasized that fauxbourdon is supposed to be something "natural and circulated to the widest extent,"[98] then the technique of Sights—inseparably allied with fauxbourdon—must by all means have been long familiar even to the island realm's most remote church singers and must have been put to use virtually everywhere.

How different were the facts of the matter with respect to these issues on the Continent! For here, any connection with the old *situs* teachings had been severed since the thirteenth century, every memory of it erased. A three-voice piece from one single given part—which was to be realized not even once as notated!—to develop [a piece] only through the means of a purely imaginary change of interval—this kind of strange and unfamiliar procedure must have seemed completely incomprehensible and as good as unusable to the Continental musician, who in the practice of his art no longer knew anything except the ready written note of a *res facta*. If there had been, as one perhaps could assume,[99] an Englishman to explain the practice of fauxbourdon to a Continental musician, he might not have attempted to invoke the Sight technique described above, which was fully incomprehensible here [on the Continent]. Instead, he would have had to employ a means of description

---

[R]Mentioned in Bu, 123.

[98]See Bu, 152; Ge, 27. The same idea is expressed by the phrase *modus communis* (see above, note 93).

[99]Naturally, other suppositions could also be imaginable. They do not need to be introduced here since, while they could possibly alter the sequence of events, the events themselves are not susceptible to change. But among such possible scenarios, the hypothesis given here seems to me to be the most probable.

which was not based—as in England—upon the imagination-based subterfuge of a fictive visualization. Rather, he would have been in a position to interpret the actual intervallic relationship of each of the voices to the c.f. through a direct graphic representation, which was the only way to make it comprehensible on the Continent.

The elucidation of the interval relationships of the tenor (either sixth or octave) to the upper-voice cantus firmus cannot have met with much bewilderment on the Continent, since here one was simply presented with a diagrammatic representation of the voice leading, which could readily be acknowledged according to rules for structural counterpoint [that were] equally valid in France. In contrast to the English practice, the two structural voices in fauxbourdon were always notated here, so that no special performance indication was necessary.

On the other hand, the circumstances were quite different concerning the explanation and identification of the actual intervallic relationship of the counter (mene) to the upper-voice cantus firmus, which resulted in the awkward, prohibited parallel fourths. The method of indication and realization of the fauxbourdon contratenor, which was well known even on the Continent and never notated, could certainly have been most easily effected in imitation of the Sight technique. Indeed, even with respect to Continental fauxbourdon, it was simply a matter of deriving at least one voice—namely the contratenor—from a c.f. through a simple imaginary change of register. But the use of the term "Sight" would not have been comprehensible on the Continent; neither would it have corresponded to the actual occurrence of vertical sonorities, which there had to be unequivocally defined.[100] Hence, the word *burdon*, which is equivalent to "support,"[101] must have seemed far more suitable to specify the procedure, which at the same time offered the benefit of rendering "bourdon" understandable in the same sense in France as well.

In the theory and practice of the time, the syllable "fa," as is well known, signifies the interval of a fourth. Consequently, through the designation *fa-burdon*, the fourth relationship of the contratenor to be added to the upper-voice cantus firmus was clearly marked out.[102] Thus, *fa-burdon* indicates

---

[100]For the reason that the reading of the mene "in sight" results in a fifth from the c.f. in actual sounding pitch, as opposed to "in voice," which yields a fourth.

[101]Sir James A.H. Murray and Henry Bradley, et al., eds., "Burden and Faburdon," *A New English Dictionary on Historical Principles* (Oxford: Clarendon Press, 1895). "Burden" is here defined as "undersong," i.e., a song or voice that lies under another already at hand.

[102]Even in later times, the English way of writing [this word] is never "false burdon," as it would need to have been if it had been taken over from the French. Rather, it is always *fa*

nothing other than an instruction for how the unnotated contratenor should be realized, namely in the "fa," i.e., fourth interval to the upper voice, or as its fourth support. It is accordingly this same interpretation that is circumscribed for the performance of the contratenor in the canon phrase accompanying Dufay's Postcommunio.[S]

The term "faburdon" in England signified only a technical reminder or "ruse" for the way of realizing a counter, in which the composite sonority actually resulting was by no means intended to have been circumscribed. This indication resulted not in fourths, but (according to context) in 6-3 or 8-5 sonorities. Musicians in England were always fully clear on the distinction between visualization of intervals ("in sight") and the resulting acoustical-auditory interval ("in voice"). In this regard, it is conclusive that Guilelmus Monachus subsequently alludes to the Sight technique and its imagined intervals, but along with them, he names correctly the actual intervals, based this time on their correlation with the real sounding basis of the tenor.[T]

This distinction between a fictive-visual and a real-auditory conception of intervals was wholly unknown and incomprehensible on the Continent. Hence, it was unavoidable that here, the fourth-relationship of the contratenor to the upper-voice cantus firmus—indicated by the designation "faburdon"— was considered the *sole* definitive characteristic of fauxbourdon, whereas the special way of simultaneously deriving the tenor that was intimately bound up with it remained completely unacknowledged. In this connection it is illustrative that Continental theory held unswerving [allegiance] to this musically inaccurate definition,[103] which arose in consequence of the narrow and misconstrued interpretation of the English "fa-burdon," and they continued to do so even after—as the practical sources show—the true harmonic qualities of fauxbourdon had been long recognized. But yet the much-cited Postcommunio of Dufay is in fact a classic example of this misinterpretation, whereby the English way of indicating the practice was [falsely] received on

---

burdon, faburden, faburthon (1462), *fabourdoun* (1501), *fabourdon* (1590). Even as late as 1587, one encounters the following quotation: "When the descant sings in treble tunes above ... let fa burthen say below: I liv'd and did [sic] for love." The quotation is from Gascoigne, *Flowers Works*, cited in Murray-Bradley's article, "Burden and Faburdon" (see above note).

[S][See B II, 30 (translated above); B III, 13.]

[T] See *CS* 3, 288b; 292b

[103]See, for example, the theories of Guilielmus Monachus, drawn from various sources (*CS* 3, 293b); additionally, Tinctoris (*CS* 4, 85a) and Adam von Fulda (*GS* 3, 329, 353). Besseler (B I, 111; B II, 40; B III, 23, and elsewhere) even sees in the parallel fourths the "basic contrapuntal concept" of fauxbourdon.

the Continent, so that the bare parallel fourths between the upper voices of the piece contradict not only the harmonic requirements of fauxbourdon but all of the contemporary voice-leading rules as well.

Accordingly, the principle of an open parallelism of fourths, here allegedly circumscribed through the designation "faburdon," must [in truth] be considered as false and contrary to the rules. From this it would be evident that this contravention of rules—which has been erroneously laid at the door of the popular English practice—was emphasized in the very name ["fa-burdon"]. It could have happened that the rigid "fa," that is, fourth, interval of the upper voices moving in parallel was identified as a "false" intervallic relationship [i.e., contrary to the rules] from whence, out of the [original] "fa-burdon," musicians on the Continent derived a "faux bourdon."[104]

The foregoing explanation of the designation "fauxbourdon" seems to me to be as simple as it is intelligible and is one that—contrary to previous attempts—does justice both to its special type of harmony as well as to its differing theoretical interpretations on the Continent and in England.

In closing it should be indicated that, contrary to the opinions of Bukofzer and Besseler, both the technique of structural embellishment as well as the polyphonic technique of so-called fauxbourdon are of English origin.

---

[104]Adam von Fulda describes this process (*CS* 3, 352a) with the words: *musici gentium vocabulo faulxbourdon vocare coeperunt quia tetrum reddit sonum* ["musicians began to call faulxbourdon by that name, since it renders a sound in fourths"]. Whereas Adam had previously indicated that the fourth was a consonance only in connection with yet another interval (e.g., octave or sixth, as in fauxbourdon), he is revealed as the founder of the new term expressly [directed] at the practical musician, from which the singers of the contratenor must have had the impression that they should continually move in false or "hideous" parallel fourths. For contrary opinions, see Bu, 82; B III, 100, 105.

3

Tonal Harmony and Full Sonority

A Reply to Rudolf von Ficker

Heinrich Besseler

EDITOR'S PREFACE: *As its subtitle clearly indicates, this article represents Besseler's response to the criticisms expressed by Rudolf von Ficker in the translation presented above. The crux of the issue hinges on whether the technique of fauxbourdon was a long-standing (and rather primitive) improvisatory practice in England, which was taken over by Continental musicians as a* res facta, *as Ficker maintains, or whether the technique was a Continental innovation invented by Dufay, which subsequently was adopted in England as the so-called faburdon. In marshaling his counterarguments, Besseler brings both philological and stylistic arguments to bear. As philological evidence, the author alleges that the French word* fauxbourdon *chronologically precedes the English faburdon. Besseler's stylistic evidence concerns the genesis of what he refers to variously as "dominant tonality" or "tonal harmony" in Western music, which he claims stems from Italy, as opposed to the attribute of "full sonority," supposedly a signal characteristic of English music from this time. In this article, the parenthetical numbers are page citations to Ficker's "Schöpfungsgeschichte des Fauxbourdon."*

In an article [entitled] "Zur Schöpfungsgeschichte des Fauxbourdon," Rudolf von Ficker attempted to defend the traditional interpretation of this question [i.e., of the origins of the technique of fauxbourdon].[1] He disputes both the facts and the methodology of my inquiry [see the study cited below in note 2], which was aimed at explaining the style transformation in the fifteenth century otherwise than previously.

However, there can hardly be a question of a true opposition [between the respective arguments], since von Ficker restricts himself to the problem of fauxbourdon, [a topic that] comprises only a small part of my book, and not

---

[1]Rudolf von Ficker, "Zur Schöpfungsgeschichte des Fauxbourdon," *Acta Musicologica* 23 (1951): 93-123 [Translated above, see essay 2.]

once [is it] the most important [part].[2] The remaining issues are either glossed over by von Ficker or else are dispensed with in summary fashion. His thesis thus remains as before: that the genesis of the new is to be sought in England alone. According to von Ficker, fauxbourdon is supposed to have been a purely English attribute, even to the extent that the Continental musicians, with Dufay at their head, would at first have had to learn [from the English] like schoolboys. Only after misbegotten early attempts and misunderstandings are they supposed to have succeeded in imitating the English model (113). The traditional opinion had always explained the [historical] context in about the same terms, but from this von Ficker now undertakes a final step, which hitherto had still not been dared: he wishes to derive even the word "fauxbourdon" from [origins in] the English language.

His main argument is based on the orthographic form *faburdon*, which one regularly encounters in the sources. According to von Ficker, this denotes an independent meaning. If it had merely been taken over from the French word *fauxbourdon*, then, he argues, there would have to have been in English a *false burdon*, similarly to the Italian *falso bordone*. This hypothesis, however, is not confirmed in English philology. According to information kindly supplied by Dr. Gustav Kirchner, professor of English Studies at the University of Jena, it is an established fact that an *a* in English preceding labials follows from the French *au* since as early as the end of the thirteenth century. Thus, for example, the French *saufe* becomes the English *safe*. Since the *x* in the French *faux* was no longer pronounced in the fifteenth century, the French *fau (x) bourdon*, according to the same rule became the English *faburdon*. We thus have before us a thoroughly normal mutation. Hence, the hypothetical construction that von Ficker must erect to explain the alleged English concept (122-123) loses its foundation right from the beginning.

However, before such details can come into play, it should first be ascertained where to seek the true essence of the dispute between von Ficker and me. In this connection, the question of fauxbourdon comprises not [even] once the central point. For the historical facts—that England had an effect upon the Continent in the time of Dunstable and that fauxbourdon is traceable to English stimulus—are not disputed by anyone, not even by me. The question is merely the manner by which we must imagine the connection between the two traditions—the English and the Continental—taken individually. This, however, is more of a technical problem; for the historian

---

[2]Heinrich Besseler, *Bourdon und Fauxbourdon* (Leipzig: Breitkopf & Härtel, 1950). The title of this book is abbreviated below as *Bourdon*.

[it is] a question of the second order, so to speak. One can ponder *sine ira et studio* the arguments previously offered on this point, and, considering the relatively rich documentary materials, there probably are grounds for hope that a picture of the processes at work around 1420–30—so interesting and pregnant with consequences—can gradually be obtained.

Things comport themselves otherwise when a value judgment is rendered or [especially] when it tacitly becomes the basis of a historical interpretation. In such a case, any discussion would be pointless as long as the respective presuppositions are not clarified. In several places, von Ficker twists my judgments of the music into their exact opposite. Thus, for example, I had emphasized that, when considered as a melody line, the *Contratenor trompette* that was added later into a chanson of Pierre Fontaine evinces a high quality and must stem from a master of the first rank.[A] For von Ficker, this added voice is the work of a hack, who "merely had the ambition to show off the wide range of his instrument," and thus it represents a journeyman's product of no value. In justification, [von Ficker] points to the allegedly inferior harmony and to the occurrence of five empty octave cadences (116, note 85). This case is revealing of our respective modes of thinking, and therefore this [topic] should be dealt with forthwith.

I. Concerning the Essence of Linear Art

The empty-octave cadences in the *Contratenor trompette* censured [by von Ficker] belong as a rule to a "double-octave cadence," namely in measures 7, 12, 14, and 17. That this cadence form appears only around 1430 and that it represents an innovation of Dufay I believe I have demonstrated.[B] Any historian who observes such a chord again and again in the great master works must take it in earnest. He must seek an explanation for it while still taking the epoch itself seriously, leaving modern concepts aside and placing [the explanation] into the contemporary way of thinking. Whether the significance of the empty-octave cadence suggested by me represents the truth can be decided by those knowledgeable to do so.[C] In any case, I have striven to gain an understanding of the period, whereas von Ficker applies his own standards and pronounces censures accordingly. Empty-octave cadences are for him simply a deficiency, since in them he finds a lack of "harmonic fullness and

---

[A]Heinrich Besseler, "Die Entstehung der Posaune," *Acta Musicologica* 22 (1950): 25, 29. [See the translation of Ficker's article above, note 84.]

[B]Besseler, *Bourdon*, 34 ff., 91.

[C]See Besseler, *Bourdon*, 38.

clarity" (116, note 85). This is a modern concept, which possibly makes sense with respect to the nineteenth century. For the Dufay period I must reject it, just as I would reject the late-Romantic instrumentation for the Notre-Dame epoch, with which von Ficker has tried to modernize the organum *Sederunt*.[3]

That which applies to the empty octave closes of the double-octave cadence applies well and truly to the "monstrous" six-line contratenors, which von Ficker so thoroughly criticizes (116). Because this voice type occurs in master works of the first rank, I was careful here also to leave aside modern thinking and to find an explanation out of the epoch itself. Contrarily, von Ficker remains with the traditional prejudice against "contra-style" voice leading, which has "long been familiar (and held in bad repute) from the chanson literature around 1400" [115]. In consequence of this, he sees no other recourse than to dispute Dufay's authorship in all these cases. In his opinion such works would consist of a cantus-tenor contrapuntal framework [*Kernsatz*] and a contratenor "fabricated by some instrumentalist or other" [116]. Hence, that which is attributed under Dufay's name would be a bastard product of two genuine voices and one false one. So, for example, the motet *O proles Hispaniae* is transmitted identically in three sources, the ballade *Se la face* in as many as six different manuscripts—always in exactly the same form! A thesis that leads to such dubious consequences will likely find little approval among the specialists of the fifteenth century.[4]

Thus, the six-line contratenor cannot be disputed away from Dufay's work, and so there remains the task of explaining it. In making an unbiased examination, one fact came to light, of which von Ficker makes no mention. [In my research,] it became manifest that in such cases it is not an issue of a filling voice of little value but rather of a melodic-contrapuntal "line," which is trying to approximate the model of cantus and tenor. In this sense there is a natural distinction [that can be discerned] between good and bad. To be sure, von Ficker also differentiates the masters from the hacks, but in this judgment

---

[3]Perotinus, *Sederunt principes*, ed. Rudolf von Ficker (Vienna: Universal-Edition, 1930). Yvonne Rokseth and Heinrich Husmann have already argued against Ficker's modernization; see Heinrich Husmann, "Zur Rhythmik des Trouvèregesanges," *Die Musikforschung* 5 (1952): 120, footnote. Manfred Bukofzer takes exception to the exchange of choral and solo parts in Ficker's edition; see *Studies in Medieval and Renaissance Music* (New York: Norton, 1950), 176, footnote.

[4]*O proles* exists in Trent 87, Modena lat. 471, and Trent 88; *Se la face* is transmitted in the chansonniers at Rome (Vat. Urb. lat. 1411), Pavia, Wolfenbüttel, de Laborde, the collection Oxford Bodl. Can. 213, and in Coussemaker's copy of the lost Strasbourg manuscript. Only the later song collection Escorial IV.a.24 brings another contratenor in the middle position in place of the six-line one.

he uses a criterion such as "harmonic clarity and fullness," which was rejected [by me] on account of its modernity. In order to approach more closely the fifteenth-century way of thinking, I have put forth the term *linear value* [*Linienwert*]. It is intended to characterize the artistic [melodic] shaping of a voice. At that time, composition was founded on the individual voice part, and hence the modern analysis must also logically proceed from it. The melodic, rhythmic, and harmonic essence of a voice, as well as the coupling of these elements to a whole, constitute collectively its "linear value."[D]

This kind of a concept seems to me to be indispensable for [assessing] the old polyphony. It is the basis of all assertions in my book about the counterpoint of the fifteenth century. It only remains for the judgment of the experts to be passed as to whether, for example, my analyses of the ground-voice of Dufay's *Ma belle dame* or of Ciconia's *O felix templum* touch the essentials.[E] Still other such methods certainly will soon be discovered, but only in this direction will we attain the standards according to which works at that time were created and judged. Accordingly, a "melody textbook" of this type should today be a part of every inquiry.[5] It allows us criteria by which we can evaluate objectively a voice such as the *Contratenor trompette*—not according to the arbitrary personal taste of the beholder but rather in the sense of the contemporary times.[F]

The contratenor just described consists of a five-measure beginning in the tenor range, a contrasting middle section (measures 6-12) in the bass range, then a five-measure close, which finally utilizes the total ambitus of two octaves. The rising and falling of the melody is carefully balanced out, and this is best substantiated by the artistically shaped middle section (measures 6-12). Narrow intervals alternate with leaps, until the closing section switches over to broken chords in disappearing tempo, which are rhythmically and melodically homogenous. Measures 8:9 correspond to each other in their isorhythm as do measures 13-14:16-17, and since the 6/8 rhythm is, moreover, systematically broken up with 3/4 hemiolas, we have before us a well-thought-out artistic organism—a voice with a high "linear value." But now [von Ficker] considers the *Contratenor trompette* to be not freely composed but rather built into a complete composition of Pierre Fontaine,

---

[D]Besseler, *Bourdon*, 76.

[E]Ibid., 75, 79.

[5]The fact that a melodic textbook can be built on systematic foundations is shown for the sixteenth century by Knud Jeppesen in *Der Palastrinastil und die Dissonanz* (Leipzig: Breitkopf & Härtel, 1925).

[F] See the edition in Besseler, "Die Entstehung der Posaune," 35.

that is, by using the original contratenor, of which half the tones (indicated in the edition by *) have been retained! [Let us accord] all respect, then, to this "musical hack," to whom von Ficker credits such accomplishments. I prefer to speak here of a "master" even if he may have been an instrumentalist. At any rate he was a man who understood the linear art, in other words, [who understood] that which the Continent always valued highest, even at the time of this harmonic experimenting. Thus I remain as before with the presumption that the *Contratenor trompette* stems from Dufay [himself].[6]

It is unfortunate that von Ficker brings [to his argument] no understanding of this type of linear art, although earlier he had earned [such] merit through his authentication of the English technique of discant embellishment [*Kolorierungstechnik*]. As a consequence, everything that I detailed about the role of contrapuntal thought in the time of Dufay was either glossed over or misunderstood by him. His value judgments [of fifteenth-century music] seemingly are based on a feeling for harmony that is not suited to the essence of that art. Wherever these basic assumptions are lacking, the discussion can lead to no result. Moreover, and even more decisively, I reject that which von Ficker maintains about harmony and its place in the fifteenth century. Here lies the actual root of our disagreement.

II. Concerning the Essence of Tonality

The point of departure of my inquiry was the fact that in Dufay's masterworks of the 1430s, that is, in motets and chansons, a system of tonal harmony [*Tonalharmonik*] is at hand. [This system], of surprisingly modern character, is absolutely not comparable with the primitive chains of sixth chords of fauxbourdon.[7] How does one explain the concurrence of these two phenomena? If the same master in the same years utilizes such a mature

---

[6]Besides the empty-octave cadences, von Ficker also objects to the two cadences in F major of the *Contratenor trompette*, which disturb "noticeably the clear D minor of the short piece" ("Schöpfungsgeschichte," 116, notes 84-85). I have already indicated that the intention behind this must be [to achieve] contrast; see Heinrich Besseler, "Die Entstehung der Posaune," *Acta Musicologica* 22 (1950): 25. Fontaine almost always cadences in D minor, [but the] *Contratenor trompette* [cadences] twice in F major. Since contrast belongs to the essence of tonal harmony and since it is striven for everywhere in Dufay's songs, I maintain that the change to the parallel tonality, which happens twice, is not a "musical deformation" but rather is an improvement.

[7]It is not a question of these being youthful works as von Ficker wants to make believe ("Schöpfungsgeschichte," 104, note 46). The songs discussed here lie around and after 1430 and thus belong to the [composer's] first master period (*Bourdon*, 28).

harmony and, at the same time, the rigid and mechanistic [technique of] fauxbourdon, then the two must be fundamentally different. One cannot be derived out of the other. Tonal harmony is thus according to its essence something different from fauxbourdon [and its concomitant attribute of] full sonority [*Vollklang*].

An examination of the source materials confirms this state of affairs but shows also the way by which one can explain it. It was demonstrated that a unique tradition existed in Italian lands before the advent of Dufay and that this tradition was independent from England. Its most important representative is discernible as the Netherlander Johannes Ciconia, who migrated [to Italy] and who had effected a synthesis of the French *Ars nova* and the Italian Trecento as early as around 1400. The central phenomenon of this music is a "dominant tonality," which is based on the opposition of the two fundamental [harmonic] functions: tonic and dominant. The predominance in the bass of a tonic-fifth-octave [melodic] framework comprises its distinguishing characteristic; in the upper voice, [it is distinguished by] the emphasis of the fifth, often with the leading tone from above or below, and the tonic, typically with the leading tone from below. These facts will be further clarified below in Section III. Here, apparently, lies the genesis of the tonal harmony that Dufay develops so brilliantly in his masterworks.[8]

Since these trends described above play no role in English music (as is testified by the Old Hall manuscript), the [attribute of] full sonority (founded on parallel thirds and sixths), was thus something other than dominant tonality. Two different harmonic systems existed in England and Italy, and these must be differentiated [from each other] conceptually.[9] "Full sonority," stemming from England, belongs in the province of church music, whereas the dominant "tonality," which was developed in Italy, was associated with song forms. This classification holds not only for Dufay himself but also for his contemporaries and followers.

This fact seems to bear out the fact that England at that time cultivated only sacred music but [had] no independent tradition of [secular] song. Conversely, the French *Ars nova* and the Italian Trecento lay precisely in the latter area, whose legacy was consolidated by Ciconia. Thus, the historical

---

[8]Particulars can be found in the article by Heinrich Besseler, "Ciconia," *MGG*, vol. 2 (1952), cols. 1423-34.

[9]Against the designation "full sonority," von Ficker raises certain objections ("Schöpfungsgeschichte," 98-100), namely that if one considers the individual chord, the "fullness" of a triad containing a third or a sixth corresponds to the "emptiness" of an 8-5 sonority (i.e., without the third). This, however, is not intended.

events evince a polarity between *two fundamental currents*: full sonority affected Netherlandish polyphony from England, [while] tonal harmony exerted its effects from Italy. In this respect, sacred music and song art possessed at first a harmonic ordering of varied and even diametrically opposed character. Each generation of Netherlanders had to come to an understanding of the two trends and work them out individually. The advent of the epoch of Dufay, Ockeghem, and Josquin proceeded to place [the issue] in a new light.

How is it possible that von Ficker does not want to acknowledge these facts even though they are supported with many examples and pieces of evidence? According to his thesis, the "harmony of the mature fifteenth century" stems from England alone (105). He expects us to see in the English discant treatises the first demonstration of a harmonic system whose rules already correspond to "classic voice leading" (103). In truth, these tracts are dealing with a cantus firmus ground-voice, whose systematic treatment naturally involves, among other things, [the discussion of] fourth- and fifth-leaps of this cantus firmus. That, however, is completely different from Ciconia's method, where a free melody in the discantus is supported by a free director of harmony [*Harmonieträger*], with fifth-, fourth-, and octave-leaps in the bass. In the recent editions of English music [from this time], such a director of harmony is never to be found!

The reason is easy to divine. Even in Dunstable's time, musicians were brought up with the ground-voice cantus firmus just as before, as is depicted in the discant treatises. This evidence is provided by the three-voice tenor mass cycle created by Englishmen in the 1430s, which always sets the chant in the lower voice. This was a serious disadvantage for the harmony. When Dufay changed over from the three-voice to the four-voice tenor mass around 1440, his most important innovation consisted in the fact that he placed the cantus firmus in the tenor, whereas he added a free director of harmony as a fourth voice in the bass. In this way, harmonic voice leading [*Harmonieführung*], as it previously had applied to song composition, was now realized in the mass as well. Through this [change], the backwardness of English harmony was made evident to all the world. Thus, even during the lifetime of Dunstable, the leadership in mass composition now passed over to the Continent.[10]

Evidently von Ficker rejects the conceptual differentiation between tonality and sonority. According to him, not only is [the attribute of] full

---

[10]Heinrich Besseler's article "Bedingham," *MGG*, vol. 1 (1949–51), cols. 1493-94. For more specific information, see the "Vorwort" to the same author's edition, *Guilielmus Dufay: Opera Omnia*, vol. 3: *Missarum Pars Altera, Corpus Mensurabili Musicae* 1 (Rome: American Institute of Musicology, 1951), II ff.

sonority supposed to stem from England, but also the [attribute of] tonic-dominant harmony. He claims that in fauxbourdon the sixth chords acted as sonorities of motion, while the 8-5 sonorities served as points of repose [*Ruheklänge*]. This fact—that one perceives an imperfect interval as tension and a perfect interval as resolution—I do not deny. But I do challenge the conclusion that von Ficker draws from this. For the earlier times, say the thirteenth century, such an embryonic and vaguely formed representation of the basic harmonic functions might be adequate. The *Sumer* canon, for example, with its ostinato exchange of sonorities on the first and second scale degrees, was a progressive work for its time. The fifteenth century, however, had reached an entirely new stage. Already around 1400 one sees in Ciconia a clearly marked tonality, with a tonic-fifth-octave bass and leading-tone melody in the discantus. About 1430, Dufay had developed an elaborate system of "bourdon harmony" through incorporation of the neighboring scale degrees and expansion of the leading-tone principle to all the voices. The works sometimes have a major character, sometimes minor; predominantly they use a tonality with a "variable quality of the third" [*Terzfreiheit*].G Compared to this, the effect of fauxbourdon is downright backward and primitive. To see it [i.e., fauxbourdon] as the source of modern harmony is only possible on the basis of unclarified concepts. Possibly the solution to the puzzle lies in the fact that von Ficker himself says that the concept of "dominant tonality" is to him unintelligible (98, note 20).

Since the importance of the masterworks of Dufay that I have cited cannot be denied, von Ficker seeks a means of escape by which he represents them as backwards-oriented [and] as an exaggeration of the Trecento art, which did not open up a "road to the harmony of the mature fifteenth century" (105). Here the misunderstanding comes clearly to light. What von Ficker has in view is a harmonic variety [achieved] through the aid of *musica ficta*, similar to that of the chromaticists of the sixteenth century, whom he mentions. What I am talking about, however, is dominant tonality. It exists in ornate as well as in simple form; use of *musica ficta* has absolutely nothing to do with it. Dufay's *Alma redemptoris mater*, a typical example of tonal harmony from the 1430s that displays even the character of the modern major key and utilizes the dominant seventh, evinces not a single accidental in the original [source].[11]

GBesseler, *Bourdon*, 66-7.

[11] See Rudolf von Ficker and Alfred Orel, eds., *Sechs Trienter Codices: Geistliche und weltliche Kompositionen des XV. Jahrhunderts, Vierte Auswahl,* DTÖ 53 (*Jahrgang* XXVII/1) (Vienna: Universal–Edition, 1920), 19-20; see also Rudolf Gerber, *Guillaume Dufay: Sämtliche Hymnen, Das Chorwerk* 19 (Wolfenbüttel: Möseler, 1932), No. 3. In Modena lat. 471, the only

When von Ficker maintains that this harmony has had no effect on the mature fifteenth century, it is sufficient to take into hand the latest volume of the complete works of Dufay. It contains four four-voice tenor masses from the latest period of the master.[12] Particularly the masses *Se la face ay pale* (about 1450) and *Ave regina caelorum* (1464 or later) display a clearly marked dominant tonality with major-key character in by far the greater part of all sections. One is convinced [thereby] that the bass is carrying on [the function] of the harmony-directing model. Of course, it is melodically and harmonically enriched in order to adjust to the large dimensions of the mass cycle, but just as before, its essence consists of the same tonic-fifth-octave framework that can be observed in Ciconia (see below, Example 2).

Thus, the evidence is adduced that there existed beside fauxbourdon and its resulting manifestations also another harmonic system, which was independent from England. It was in effect throughout the entire fifteenth century, as its tradition proceeds from Ciconia to Dufay's maturity and, further, past these older works to Josquin and the Frottolists. The unique aspect of this harmony is indeed best characterized through the concept of dominant tonality.

III. What Was "Bourdon"?

Von Ficker counters my evidence of the importance of the director of harmony with the objection that such a voice never existed. [He claims that] if it ever did occur as an exceptional case, it would be without musical significance. For he alleges that the decisive [element] for the harmony of late medieval polyphony is solely the "primary contrapuntal framework" [*primärer Kernsatz*] of cantus and tenor. Conversely, the contratenor (even a six-line one) supposedly acts only as a secondary filling voice, which is allowed to be altered or even left out at one's discretion. Therefore, [von Ficker claims], it is out of the question that the designation "bourdon" would ever have been used [for a low contratenor voice] (115-7).

Lamentably, here again von Ficker presents my opinion falsely in this context. I have not maintained that the contratenor around 1430 had "the general character of a low voice" (114). On the contrary, I emphasized emphatically that the contratenor as director of harmony represents only a small minority of cases, and I even stated that the double-octave cadence—a

---

accidental is a B-flat in the contratenor in measure 90 (47), which is a reminder of the B-flat signature.

[12]Contained in Besseler, ed., *Guilielmus Dufay: Opera Omnia*, vol. 3.

decisive yardstick for this phenomenon—occurs around 1430 in only about two percent of all main cadences.[H] However, because its share grew to as much as 42% after a generation, it was apparently the cadence form that belonged to the future. Accordingly, I fixed my eyes especially upon them. This is not only the right but also the duty of a historian who wants to emphasize the truly motive forces from out of the plenitude of materials.

The six-line contratenor of Dufay, with which in the beginning the double-octave cadence is as a rule connected, proves to be an unusual voice type. The melodic framework of tonic-fifth-octave, the predominance of large interval [leaps] as well as the ambitus of at least one and a half octaves, all of these seem to have had no counterpart in the northern tradition. Surprisingly similar, however, were the ground–voices of the upper-Italian motets, which were designated as *Tenor*.[I] The oldest datable work, Ciconia's *O felix templum jubila*, makes the connection to the *caccia* clearly recognizable. Such a caccia-motet does not employ the customary [contrapuntal] framework of cantus and tenor but rather a duet of two imitative sopranos and an instrumental bass. That this represents a "director of harmony" under the designation *Tenor* even von Ficker does not dispute. Hence, besides the cantus-tenor paradigm (which von Ficker represents as the sole compositional type), there existed in truth yet another type: two equal melody voices in soprano range supported by an independent bass (Example 1).

E x a m p l e 1 : C i c o n i a, m o t e t *O f e l i x t e m p l u m j u b i l a*

Since the works of Ciconia are based on a tonal-dominant harmony, the most important characteristic of the director of harmony consists in the constantly returning melodic framework of the tonic-dominant-octave. It appears in major as well as in minor, mostly with the tonic *c*, *d*, or *f*. In this

---

[H]Besseler, *Bourdon*, 36-8.
[I]Ibid., 77-8.

melody of the director of harmony one recognizes a unique and sharply delineated "voice type," which is conspicuous even in the way it is notated and was soon taken up by contemporary [composers]. It is a well-known fact that the artists of that time were not accustomed to working freely in the modern sense but [worked] according to set standards. The histories of art and literature have drawn this conclusion and have acknowledged the necessity of [applying] research into prototypes for the Middle Ages. One might well consider it to be indispensable in musicology as well. Ciconia's director of harmony comprises a typical example of exactly this: around 1400, the new voice type makes its appearance; it becomes widespread in the upper-Italian motet and is soon taken up even by musicians from the north. This is demonstrated by the *Tuba-* or *Trompetta-*sections in [works of] Grossin, Franchois, and Arnold de Lantins, using techniques [involving] a director of harmony, which von Ficker cannot deny.[J] This is attested to above all by the youthful works of Dufay from the 1420s, which I have discussed.[13] The impetus to further development lay in the fact that the Netherlandish musicians around Dufay generally held to the tenor as fundamental voice, both for the motet and the chanson. For this reason, after the 1420s the old-fashioned cantus-tenor framework now stepped to the fore again in Italian lands. But the voice type [acting as] "director of harmony" in no way disappeared. Now it was combined with the cantus-tenor framework under the designation *contratenor*, shifted downwards, and took over the lowest ground-tone in the newly created double-octave cadence.[K] Exactly the same thing happened in the four-voice tenor motet. There the cantus firmus remained in the tenor (which Ciconia had cast aside) untouched, and likewise the duet of the two vocal parts, triplum and motetus. In order to furnish a harmonic foundation, however, Dufay added to this superstructure at first a *tenor secundus*, [and] later a *contratenor*, which is nothing other than a "director of harmony."[L] This is still true even in the four-voice tenor masses of his mature period. One can recognize without effort in their *contratenor bassus* the Ciconia model, that is, in the characteristic melodic framework tonic-fifth-octave (Example 2).

[J] Besseler, "Die Entstehung der Posaune," 12-22.

[13] In "Schöpfungsgeschichte" (116, note 86), von Ficker hypothesizes that the contratenor of *Ma belle dame* was subsequently added by a different hand. Since clearly this is a case of a director of harmony of the Ciconia type, there is no reason here to assign another composer [to this voice], as opposed to the other pieces of this sort, which von Ficker does not mention (see *Bourdon*, 84).

[K] Besseler, *Bourdon*, 88-91.

[L] Ibid., 173-5.

Example 2: Dufay, Kyrie of the mass *Se la face ay pale*

Thus, the director of harmony can be traced through many decades. It is the basis not only of the upper-Italian motets but also of courtly music with French text, sacred song-motets, and later even of tenor motets and tenor mass cycles. One finds it in experimental works and in masterworks of the first order. It was the indispensable aid to Dufay's work in the area of harmony. If von Ficker does not want to acknowledge the [existence of the] director of harmony, then this is the reason why he does not see the existence of such a "voice type" and its universal role. The final stage of this development— Dufay's four-voice motets around 1440—remains unmentioned by von Ficker, just as does its beginning stage, Ciconia's caccia-motet [stemming from] about 1400. Those things about which he remarks regarding three-voice counterpoint around 1430, however, miss the main point. The crux of the issue is not whether one can with greater relative ease omit the tenor or the contratenor (116). On the contrary, the decisive thing is that Dufay, during his experiments with the director of harmony, also transformed the old cantus-tenor framework of the north, that is, under the influence of Italy. [In the years] around 1430, the master was pressed into an "obbligato" three-voice texture, which was based on tonal harmony.

In this kind of composition, no voice could now be left out without destroying the character of the work. This holds even for the usual middle-voice contratenor such as [Dufay's] setting of Petrarch's *Vergine bella*.[M] One can readily convince oneself that [a contratenor] is used as an indispensable harmonic foundation in measures 5-6, 10, 17-21, 28-30, 35-37, 4-46, 71-75, and 81-82. If one looks at a [work with a] six-line contratenor, then its bass function is the rule throughout. Only exceptionally does [this kind of contratenor] serve, now and then, as a middle voice in the course of a work, [i.e.,] when the tenor moves in a lower position. If one examines Dufay's motet *Alma redemptoris mater*, the tenor comprises the harmonic foundation

---

[M]Ibid., 92-3.

in only three or four short places, but otherwise the contratenor [prevails in that role].[N] The melody of this contratenor, with its tonic-fifth-octave framework, admits of no doubt that here yet again a "director of harmony" is present. Thus, the clear major tonality of the work is obviously based on the ground-voice archetype, with which Dufay was thoroughly conversant throughout many years of work.

The existence of the director of harmony thus may be assumed to have been proven. The only thing left unclear is its designation, as Ciconia calls it *tenor*, Dufay *contratenor*, and other masters [call it] *tuba* or *trompetta*. Why it was never possible to achieve a consensus on this point has already been considered.[O] Presumably the expression "bourdon" has something to do with our inquiry, for at that time its meaning in the French and Latin forms was "low range" or "low tones." From this I came to the conclusion that the French "bourdon" designated either the director of harmony of the Ciconia type or else the lower-voice segments [from whichever voice] functioning as a bass, whereupon I left the final decision unsettled.[P]

If one reflects on the numerical proportion of the two things named above, then the decision is not difficult. The director of harmony manifested solely as a single ground-voice is only encountered exceptionally among the Netherlanders of Dufay's circle, and in Dufay himself, [one finds it] only in individual pieces without a tenor.[Q] As a rule, a director of harmony—typically just a normal contratenor—is coupled with a tenor, so that a "combination bass" [*Kombinationsbaß*] comprised of both [lower] voices, is crucial to the harmony. Already in the fourteenth century one observes the technique of four-voice motets, whereby the lowest tone at any given time is extracted in the form of a voice *ad libitum*, called *solus tenor*, which is given [in the source] along with the work. This procedure, which is reminiscent of the *basso seguente* of the thoroughbass era, was in force until the fifteenth century.[R] The musicians thus knew that all was dependent on the tones of the tenor and contratenor that at any given time were lowest [i.e., sequence of low pitches]. They were even accustomed to write out such a combined voice, containing the [tonal] foundation of the work, so that they could see it.

When in the 1420s masters such as Dufay, Grossin, Franchois, and Arnold de Lantins adopted the director of harmony, a settling of accounts with

---

[N]Ibid., 28, 62-4.
[O]Besseler, "Die Entstehung der Posaune," 22.
[P]Besseler, *Bourdon*, 231, Thesis 15.
[Q]Ibid., 84.
[R]Ibid., 93-5.

that which we call harmony was inevitable. At the time, such questions were doubtless debated. The kind of impression made by tonal harmony is shown by the ballade *Bonté biauté* of the somewhat older Johannes Cesaris, which falls totally outside the scope of this composer's other output.[14] The Netherlanders of Dufay's circle basically held to the tenor [as a low voice] but at the same time sought a sonorous foundation of the Italian type. In this manner resulted, in three-voice chanson composition, that "combination bass" of tenor and contratenor, which corresponds to the *solus tenor* of the motet.

The word "bourdon," therefore, points to those Netherlanders who had contact with Italy in the 1420s. Dufay's circle very probably understood the French *bourdon* as the sonorous foundation in chanson composition: the lowest tone at any given time of the lower voices—the analog of the *solus tenor* of the motet. For the most part, the bourdon was a combination bass consisting of tenor and contratenor; only seldom [was it] a single or double [i.e., composite] harmony director of the Ciconia type.

IV. Why "Fauxbourdon"?

That the expression "fauxbourdon" surfaces [as a new term] around 1430, occurring mainly in Continental sources but previously unknown in England, von Ficker cannot dispute. It is thus a matter of an innovation, in which [both] English and Continental musicians presumably took part. Whereas von Ficker considers the latter as simply students, to me it is a question of the point where the individuality [of the technique] and its particular characteristics betray themselves. What is the new and un-English principle of fauxbourdon? Without doubt [it is] the canon doubling the upper voice at the fourth. This is expressly demanded by Dufay but appears also in the three-voice written-out fauxbourdon of Binchois.[15] The music thus obtains a mechanistic formal sameness, for which I suggested the expression "unitary progression" [*Einheitsablauf*].[S] The word *fauxbourdon* appears in the sources only where such a progression is prescribed for an entire piece or for a closed section thereof [but] never for individual chains of sixth chords. Evidently the unique elements of the Continental practice lie in this point. My inquiry thus directed

---

[14]Von Ficker challenges my dating of the ballade, without taking into account its [stylistic] relationship with the other works of Cesaris (see "Schöpfungsgeschichte," 104, note 46). In this connection, see Heinrich Besseler, "Cesaris," *MGG*, vol. 2 (1952), cols. 983-9.

[15]The Introitus *Salve sancta parens* in Aosta, Trent 90, and Trent 93. In this connection, see Manfred Bukofzer, "Fauxbourdon Revisited," *Musical Quarterly* 38 (1952): 25.

[S]Besseler, *Bourdon*, 221.

itself upon the "fauxbourdon piece," to whose definition the characteristics [named above] belong. Since von Ficker rejects this concept, I must expressly correct him here with certain source evidence.[16]

The inflexibility of the fauxbourdon technique has a counterpart nowhere among the forms of music-making around 1430 and requires an explanation. Also one must realize that a rigid-mechanistic procedure was cultivated later to relieve [musical texture] but not vice versa. The mechanistic fauxbourdon canon thus certainly points to the Continent from the beginning, and only subsequently were modifications undertaken.[17] According to von Ficker, the explanation for the fauxbourdon canon is that [Continental musicians] had appropriated the improvisatory practice of English discant and had written it down as a *res facta* (113 and 121). This explanation, however, is not reconcilable with the facts.

In the improvisation of English discant, the cantus firmus lay without exception in the low voice. This is also true in the treatise of Leonel Power, whose examples von Ficker carefully states, correspond "with respect to the effective musical predecessors" to the fauxbourdon technique (119). Since fauxbourdon is mentioned for the first time [in the English treatises] by Pseudo-Chilston, it appears next to the long-standing practice of discant and is differentiated from it through the position of the cantus firmus in the upper voice. In this point the English themselves recognized the crucial characteristic, which von Ficker does not mention (119-20). Incidentally, how strong the effect of fauxbourdon was [in England] is demonstrated by the later manuscript London, Egerton 3307. Obvious fauxbourdon pieces can be observed there in many places, whereas [the technique] is still missing in the Old Hall codex, circa 1420-30.[18]

In order to explain the change of cantus-firmus voices, von Ficker points to the [technique of] discant embellishment, which [he claims] was used in England since the beginning of the fifteenth century (98 and 95). But there

---

[16]"Fauxbourdon piece" does not designate a form, as von Ficker maintains ("Schöpfungsgeschichte," 123, notes 18-19) but rather the unitary progression mentioned above. The assertion that the indication "fauxbourdon" is also employed in short phrases is likely based on Dufay's motet *Supremum est* (*Bourdon*, 173). Here the four fauxbourdon sections comprise preludes and interludes, which contrast in the same way with the main sections of the tenor. So, [the term] "unitary progression" is characteristic also for this work.

[17]Von Ficker speaks of this in connection with Binchois ("Schöpfungsgeschichte," 107). I had considered this question at the same time (*Bourdon*, 162-3). Regarding letter-perfect voice doubling in Binchois, see above, note 15.

[18]For information on Egerton 3307, see Bukofzer, *Studies in Medieval and Renaissance Music*, Chapter IV, 113 ff.

[fauxbourdon] was always a question of a *res facta*, not improvisation, and besides, as Old Hall evidences, [there were] only a few works standing opposed to the widely used placement of the cantus firmus in the middle or upper voice.[19] There is no indication that the upper-voice cantus firmus would have been used in improvisation; also, the treatise of Leonel Power says nothing [of this]. In other points, precisely the fact that [fauxbourdon] was written down shows that at that time the English absolutely did not direct their attention on improvisation but on completely other things, namely, on artistic technique and on raising the plateau [of art]. The musical works of the generation of Leonel-Dunstable show the same picture. Out of this background, the rigid and mechanistic [technique of] fauxbourdon is strangely conspicuous by its primitivism. It apparently employs English methods on un-English material.

Thus, it is certain that in the genesis of fauxbourdon the Continental musicians took part not only in a studentlike receptive capacity but also with their own deliberations. As long as no older testimony is discovered, von Ficker also considers the Postcommunio from Dufay's *Missa Sancti Jacobi* as the oldest [fauxbourdon] work (112). My dating "shortly before 1430" has in the meantime been focused more sharply: the St. Jacob Mass probably originated between 1426 and the end of 1428.[20] At that time, before his entry into the papal chapel, Dufay was permitted to go visit his homeland [and] met with English musicians. In order to adopt their sonorous but contrapuntally forbidden parallel voice leading, he gave [fauxbourdon] a permanent currency with the help of a *canon* indication. The purely mechanistic doubling of a voice at the interval of a fourth did not in fact fall under the rules of counterpoint, since [the canon rendered] it no longer an issue of free voice leading. The fauxbourdon piece was in the eyes of contemporaries not a three-voice piece but rather only a two-voice one: a cantus, mechanically doubled, with a free tenor. This explanation seems to me as ever to be the only one

---

[19]More precise particulars on the cantus firmus in Old Hall are found in Bukofzer, ibid., Chapter II, 45 ff.

[20]Heinrich Besseler, "Neue Dokumente zum Leben und Schaffen Dufays," *Archiv für Musikwissenschaft* 9 (1952): 160. The St. Jacob Mass does not belong to what I have called the "Pseudo-masses," as von Ficker holds ("Schöpfungsgeschichte," 112, note 71). On the contrary, it was created by one composer as a unity, and its pronounced [internal] contrasts reflect only a predilection in the sense of the ideals of "contrasting arrangement" current at the time. Against this, von Ficker extols the stylistic unity of the mass of Liebert (112). Such a unified creation was, however, still in no way the ideal that one perceives from the structure and contrast technique of the leading works.

that makes comprehensible Dufay's thought process and the decisive success of the new technique.[T]

With his comment that the parallel fourths of fauxbourdon were prompted by English discant, von Ficker may be said to have reached the truth. Also, the slow tempo of "flowing rhythm" [*Stromrhythmus*] and the "cantabile melody" that is associated with it (both discussed by me) stem most probably from England.[21] On the other hand, the transformation of improvised discant into a *res facta* and the introduction of the canon principle was a Continental concern, presumably that is, of the young Dufay. [The fact] that fauxbourdon originated at all can only be explained through the interest of Continental musicians, and likewise the placement of the cantus firmus in the upper voice must be considered their doing. This practice is found already about 1400 in the hymns of the Apt manuscript, which occasionally also have slight embellishment of the structural melody. Of course, in the following era, the English realized this [kind of] discant embellishment in a particularly artistic manner but hardly as an English monopoly, as von Ficker represents (95). On the Continent, where song composition with a leading upper voice had dominated the musical scene for generations, the soprano range of the cantus firmus corresponded to some extent to the natural [mode of] thinking and had, in fact, been known for a long time.[22] Therefore, nothing stands in the way of

---

[T] Besseler, *Bourdon*, 16-7, 101.

[21] The evidence that the Old Hall codex stems from the time of Henry V and [that it] was written about 1420-30, appeared only after my book was finished (*Bourdon*, 113). As a consequence, the relationship of Continental to English music was still not researched in detail (*Bourdon*, 138). This omission will be eliminated in an eventual new edition [of the book]. [Moreover,] I did not say that the changeover from *prolatio-* to *tempus*-notation "brought about" a rather slow process of change, as von Ficker formulates ("Schöpfungsgeschichte," 108, note 60). On the contrary, a cantabile melody with rather slow tempo came as a new [musical innovation], and composers sought a means by which to represent this slower movement in the notation (*Bourdon*, 132 and 154, note 7). Thus, von Ficker's conclusion with respect to the motet *Ducalis sedes—Stirps* is resolved (109, note 60 continuation).

[22] Around 1420, the Netherlanders preferred the melodicized cantus firmus in the tenor range, as von Ficker has depicted ("Schöpfungsgeschichte," 96). In the south, however, other conditions prevailed. There, when a chant was used, it lay in the discantus. Besides the Apt hymns, this [procedure] is evidenced above all by the Credo of Zacharias, who is traceable to [the service of] anti-pope John XXIII (1410-15) and pope Martin V in 1420. See the edition in Rudolf von Ficker, ed., *Sieben Trienter Codices: Geistliche und weltliche Kompositionen des XIV. und XV. Jahrhunderts, Fünfte Auswahl, DTÖ* 61 (*Jahrgang* XXXI) (Vienna: Universal-Edition, 1924), 16-9. Werner Korte, in *Studie zur Geschichte der Musik in Italien* (Kassel: Bärenreiter, 1933), 44, note 77, mentions that in this Credo a *cantus supra librum* technique is

ascribing likewise this characteristic innovation, which separates fauxbourdon from English discant, to the young Dufay.

If things around 1428 indeed played out as one is justified in presuming, then the elucidation of the word "fauxbourdon" also presents no difficulty. In this matter, von Ficker must resort to hypotheses that are concocted ad hoc and not vouched for in the sources (122-3). Even if one wanted to acknowledge the word *faburdon* as a solmization neologism, its transformation into the French *fauxbourdon* would still be unconvincing. But these hypotheses are unnecessary, because the form *faburdon*, as was established at the beginning of this article, represents the normal anglicization of the French *fau(x) bourdon*. The original word therefore was certainly French, as has heretofore always been assumed.

If one considers Dufay's position around 1428, it becomes clear how much the problem of harmony occupied him at that time. After several years' sojourn in Italy, he now saw his homeland again and had to come to terms with the foreign, new-style music of the English. His experiments with the director of harmony and with the sonorous foundation in song composition were by no means concluded but were in full swing. [These attempts] constituted precisely the middle period of his work, up through the mid-1430s. That he saw the new fauxbourdon technique in the context of this fundamental problem [i.e., of reconciling the English and Continental procedures] must be presumed from the beginning. For that which occupied him was the sonorous foundation, *bourdon*, which was dealt with above in Section III. Thus it is obvious that the new sonority-filling contratenor at a fourth [below the discantus], which can only be a middle voice and never a foundation, received the name *faux bourdon* as a mocking self-criticism.

Since no reports survive, such reflections lead basically to only a greater or lesser [degree of] probability. It may be taken as certain that fauxbourdon did have a connection to the English technique but at the same time brought something new [to it], since the English [theorist] Pseudo-Chilston also considers the soprano range of the cantus firmus as a criterion of differentiation from [English] discant. From whom this innovation stemmed now remains out of our ken. Since it is first discernible in the 1420s, and [since] it is connected with the name fauxbourdon, one should accordingly be in accord with the terminology [developed above].

---

probably at work. In any case, we can assume with good reason that Dufay was acquainted with the cantus firmus in the soprano range since his early years in Italy.

"English discant" is, as von Ficker reminds us, the correct name for the [contemporary] manifestations [of polyphony] in England itself (94-5). "Fauxbourdon" designates pieces with a unitary progression in Continental music, [and] "faburdon" [refers to] the corresponding improvisatory practice of the English. It seems perplexing to me, however, when von Ficker extends the discant concept even to the later Continental music (97, note 17). Considering the fact that [later Continental music] was characterized throughout by fauxbourdon, a term such as "fauxbourdon style" was coined, [since] corresponding to its nature, [the term fauxbourdon] cannot be used before 1430. For the earlier era, such phenomena fall under the concept of "discant."

The result of the discussion could be summarized in the following manner: The main question has to do with the genesis of the new style in the fifteenth century. According to von Ficker, all of the essential elements are supposed to stem from England—even tonic-dominant harmony. He sees the development "monistically." I claim that English music had a definite effect upon [that of] the Continent, but that there existed beside [this] another basic current, independent from England: the [technique of] dominant tonality in the south and the contrapuntal-linear thinking of the Netherlanders. The total picture is thus a "pluralistic" one.

When von Ficker emphasizes the role of the central-Burgundian masters, their relationship with England, and their inclination towards naturalism, one must agree with him (110). But this is only a part, not the whole. As early as around 1450, the cantus-firmus mass in four voices took over the leadership, so that it soon was considered as the quintessence of Netherlandish polyphony. Around 1480, the younger generation of composers who traveled to Italy took hold of the new [techniques] leading toward tonal harmony, which had already exerted a decisive influence in Italian lands around 1430. This general view of the fifteenth century was the actual theme of my book, and this follows from the [interpretation of] the essence and origin of the basic currents [of that time]. [Future] research will decide whether von Ficker's "England thesis" or my "pluralistic thesis" is better suited to the facts.

Harmony in the Cantus-Firmus Compositions of the Fifteenth Century

Bernhard Meier

EDITOR'S PREFACE: *Chronologically, the subject of this study is among the latest of the articles presented here. Hence, some of its concerns lie outside the scope of the other selections. Meier's treatment of certain issues, however, is extremely relevant and represents perhaps the earliest systematic assessment of a significant body of late medieval polyphony according to principles outlined in contemporary theory. The most consequential aspect of Meier's methodology is his conviction that vertical sonorities in vocal polyphony must be explained as proceeding from the tenor and not from the bass. Meier shows how this principle is reflected in the theory of Johannes Cochlaeus and how standardized progressions are used in the practical compositions of Jacob Obrecht and Jacob Barbireau. In the translation, a number of slight corrections, additions, and changes of orthography are due to the kind suggestions of the author's widow, Dr. Helga Meier.*

Just as in every fruitful and cogent analysis, one that concerns the harmony of cantus-firmus compositions must also derive its guiding direction and standards from the object itself. This means, to begin with, a decisive abandonment of all current methods that proceed from conditions of the late sixteenth century and aim to connect the sonorities built over a bass tone to a tonal center. Instead, the first requirement is to turn attention as energetically as possible to the music based on a tenor cantus firmus. Thus, Cochlaeus writes in *Musica activa*[1] (*De generalibus componendi preceptis*, beginning):

> Cantilenarum compositor imprimis tenorem cum suavi ac concinna melodia efformet. Siquidem a tenendo tenor dicitur, quod certe tonum teneat atque modulamina aliarum cantus partium. Nec ullo pacto tonorum regulas ac naturas ignorabit.[A]

---

[1]Johannes Cochlaeus, *Musica activa, pars tertia*: *De arte componendi et contrapunctus* (Cologne: Johannes Landen, 1507).

[A][Translation: "The composer of song-pieces fashions the tenor first with a suave and pretty melody. Inasmuch as the tenor is so called from its quality of sustaining, it thus sustains the mode

The boundary could not be sharper between the concept of a harmony based on bass progressions and the concept of a tonality consisting in the centralization of connected sonorities. [Tonal coherence among] the total complex of voices is not derived from the representation of a tonal space and a specific tonality; on the contrary, the *tonus* is solely identifiable with the tenor as preexistent monophonic melody, to which the remaining voices are joined as an embellishing but always-dependent adornment. Proceeding from these findings, the following attempts to ascertain—on the strength of manifold observations and substantiated through Cochlaeus's treatise—certain correlations within the cadences between the voice leading of the cantus firmus and the "tonal" consolidation of the composition, and in addition, to gain insight into the sonorous principles of the other passages [i.e., sections between cadences] of cantus-firmus compositions.

I. The Cadences

The importance [of cadences] is emphatically stressed by Cochlaeus:

> Agreeable cadence structures of the voices {*delectabiles vocum adinvicem clausule*} must be observed with no less care: multifarious, in order to delight [the listener] more, and well-sounding, in order to flatter the ear aurally. But whoever wants to be adroit in the composition of song-pieces {*cantilenae*} is well advised to impress such cadences deeply into his consciousness, so that when he first finishes fashioning a tenor, he will in no way leave pleasant sonorities of the voices {*placidas vocum convenientias*} out of account.

The various types of cadences are demonstrated through score examples on ten lines (comprehending Gamma-ut through d within the treble clef) and are also exercised by students in this manner, whereas practiced composers can write down the individual voices separately.[2] It must be well observed that these

---

securely as well as measuring the other parts of song. And [the tenor] should most carefully observe the rules and properties of the modes."]

[2]"Possunt autem omnes partes simul componi, et quelibet item primum ac seorsum. Frequentius tamen tenor ceteris prior poni solet. Etenim exercitatus cantilenarum compositor singulas partes seorsum facere potest, rudimenta vero addiscentes (quoniam vocum concordantie atque clausule animo nondum insident) per decem lineas omnes certe partes simul componere opere precium est."

[Translation: "However, it is possible to compose all the parts at the same time, and any voice can likewise [be placed] first and separately. Nevertheless, one is usually accustomed to place the tenor before the other voices. And indeed, the experienced composer of songs is able to fashion the single parts severally; but for those acquiring the basics [of composition]—since the

cadences be considered solely according to the progressions of the voices from the penultima to the ultima and according to the intervals between the voices; so, for example, [in] the three-voice octave-leap cadence:[3]

Ex ample 1

[Cochlaeus:] When we direct the imperfect consonances toward the perfect {*ex concordantia imperfecta perfectam petimus*} as in the close of a song-piece or one of its sections, then the penultima of the discantus must lie a sixth above the tenor, and both must progress in contrary motion {*contrariis motibus procedentes*}... to reach the interval of an octave. In addition, the penultima of the contratenor must be placed a fifth below the tenor... although its ultima can stand at a unison with the tenor or at the fifth above the tenor.

Thus, we still must conceive of the cadences completely in the sense of fixed voice leading, not as "cadences," i.e., as stereotypical sequences of sonorities conditioned by the progression of the bass tones. In this connection, the crucial [consideration]—independent of the voice leading of all parts subsequently added—is the motion of discantus and tenor that is described in the above quotation.

A. Leading-Tone Cadence

1) In three-voice counterpoint:

Ex ample 2   (and other forms)

---

consonances and closes of the voices are not yet settled in the mind— it is really worth the trouble to compose all the parts simultaneously by means of a ten-line staff."]

[3]The symbols for the various voice parts are as follows:

    O = discantus; **◆** = tenor; **◆** = contratenor.

The placing of a new upper voice above the two-part cadence at the penultima, voice-led to the third above the discant cadence at the ultima, is also very frequent.

Example 3   etc.   etc.

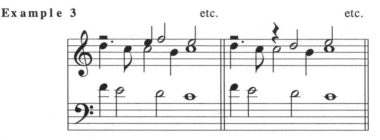

For this usage, the expression "superius third-cadence" will be employed.

2) In four-voice counterpoint:

In true four-voice composition of an entire cadence, the third-cadence appears in the way just demonstrated; this is also true of the assimilation of a newly composed upper voice into a three-voice piece. In this connection, one might well note the words of Cochlaeus (*De compositione quatuor partium contrapuncti,* {*septima regula*}):

> But if the tenor and bassus are separated by a sixth and move from here further into an octave's distance (*tendentes in octavam*), then the discantus very well can assume its place a fifth or a third above the tenor, and the altus is placed not clumsily a third above the bassus, as here:[4]

Example 4

B. Second Main Form of Cadence

These types of cadences incorporate a "low" contratenor, i.e., one lying below the tenor. Its various sub-types in three- and four-voice composition (octave-leap, fourth-leap, and double-octave cadence)[5] display in the voice leading of

---

[4]The symbols are as follows: ◐ = discantus; ● = altus; ◆ = tenor; ◆ = bassus. In place of "altus," Cochlaeus occasionally also uses the term "contratenor acutus," and instead of "bassus," he occasionally uses "contratenor," contratenor gravis," or "baritonans."

[5]These terms are derived from Heinrich Besseler, *Bourdon und Fauxbourdon* (Leipzig: Breitkopf & Härtel, 1950), 35, where the expression *Kadenz* is used [Meier's term is *Klausel*].

their contratenor (a fifth below the tenor at the penultima) the beginnings of the system of dominant harmony [*dominantische Harmonik*]. However, they are considered by Cochlaeus—as the example of the three-voice octave-leap cadence has already shown—likewise only according to voice leading and intervallic disposition of the voices. Even where the bassus remains the real lowest voice at the ultima, it is still not alienated from its origin as contratenor bassus. Examples of such cadences are universally known. It remains to point to the possibility of the bassus or tenor (not discantus) resting at the ultima of interior cadences. The ultima appears in many cases only after a pause, but now with a new melodic tendency leading away from the cadence; this means of composition is often bound up with a "deceptive" cadential structure in the bassus.

C. The Phrygian (Mi-) Cadence

The Phrygian cadence assumes a special position with respect to the cadence forms so far discussed. In order to understand the rule that Cochlaeus gives in this case, his stipulations for the composition of three-voice counterpoint must be recalled (*De compositione trium partium contrapuncti, quinta regula*):

> When tenor and discantus are separated from each other by an octave, the contratenor will sound well if it takes its place a third or a fifth above the tenor, or a third, a fifth, or an octave below the tenor.

The rules for the cadence on mi are as follows:

1) For three-voice counterpoint (*De cantilenarum conclusionibus tres partes complectentibus, secunda regula*):

> When the tenor closes on mi, the penultima of the contratenor must be brought in a third below the tenor, while the discantus persists in the sixth above the tenor, but the ultima of the contratenor must be placed a fifth below the tenor, by leaping down a fourth, sol–re.

Example 5

2) For four-voice counterpoint (*De quatuor partium conclusionibus, secunda regula*):

However, when three voices are ordered according to the prescription of the second rule, then the penultima of the fourth voice must be brought in a third above the tenor, but at the ultima [it must be] a fourth above the tenor, since the bassus lies a fifth under the tenor.

Example 6

Cochlaeus seems to consider this form of the mi-cadence to be equal in closing power to the one in which the bassus progresses from a fifth below the tenor into a unison with it or to an octave below it. This latter form is not mentioned at all, nor is the use of the two forms to differentiate between sectional cadences (bassus at the fifth below the tenor) and final cadences (bassus at a unison with the tenor or at the octave below it), although it is already plainly to be found in the [contrapuntal] rules of the sixteenth century, and also in [works of] Ockeghem and Obrecht in several places. (Ockeghem, *Missa Mi-mi*, Kyrie I; Obrecht, *Missa Sicut spina rosam*, Et resurrexit.)

D. Building the Superstructure of Cadences

The superimposition of a newly introduced superius upon a [previously composed] two- or three-voice leading-tone cadence has already been mentioned. In other instances it is found as the most frequent type of construction over a "deceptive cadence." Contrary to the first method of superimposition, here an alteration of the sonority succession appears, and this is essential for evaluating it according to the rules of modern harmony. But if one evaluates such "deceptive cadences" from the point of view of the teachings of the contemporary treatises, i.e., with respect to the voice leading occurring in them, it becomes evident that the motion of the counter-voices— remaining unaltered with respect to [the rules of the treatises]—is only of secondary significance compared to the [motion of the] discantus-tenor pair, even without [considering] the [latter's] crucial cadential motion [i.e., major sixth to octave]. This also is confirmed by Cochlaeus; as the first rule for making three-voice cadences he suggests that to the ultima of discantus and tenor (octave's distance), the contratenor could be placed a fifth above the tenor, at a unison with it, or also at the octave below it, thereupon moving ahead: "It can also be brought in a third below the tenor, so that it then makes a tenth with the discantus. But it cannot be voice-led in this way at the end of the entire piece (*in fine totius cantilene*), since perfect consonances (although not necessary at the beginnings of pieces) are the only ones fit to use at their ends (*namque perfectionem non principiis, sed terminationibus attribuere oportet*)."[6] Precisely this substantiation, so inimical to modern conceptions, shows clearly how a thinking of vertical sonorities [in terms of] tonal functions is lacking or in its rudiments is still not suited to explicit, independent formulation.

Superimpositions of this type occur very frequently through the introduction of a truly lowest voice underneath the penultima of the tenor:

Example 7

etc.

For the mi-cadence, the following forms can be ascertained:

Example 8   etc.   etc.

Finally, it remains to discuss the superstructure resulting from the insertion [of a previously resting voice] beneath the [parts having made a cadence at the] ultima. For this kind of construction, no modern designation is possible, but they are easily explainable from the beginning of Cochlaeus's

---

[6]Cochlaeus makes reference here to a previous passage in his treatise: "De specialibus contrapuncti mandatis. Prima regula est, quod principia cuiusvis cantilene sumantur per concordantias perfectas. Verum hoc primum mandatum non est necessarium, sed arbitrarium, nam et imperfectis concordantiis cantilenarum exordia plerique instituerunt."

rule cited from section C: precisely here there is no "logical" succession of sonorities from the penultima to ultima, but rather, the interval between discantus and tenor alone is considered crucial for the addition of the newly inserted voice(s); for example:

Example 9   etc.   etc.

E. The Compositional Application

For such an evaluation, it is necessary to keep in mind that the cadential structure portrayed in the foregoing remains strictly intact, but the structural voice-leading framework of the tenor and discantus does not remain restricted to the association of the original voices. Rather, it is variable within the complex of voices, according to the wish of the composer, to the extent that if a discant cadence is made with some other voice [besides the discantus], it requires placing the corresponding tenor cadence in another voice (and vice versa), whereas a rather great freedom is afforded the remaining voices, [acting] as contratenors. Cochlaeus adduces an example of this (*De quatuor partium conclusionibus, quinta regula*):

> When the tenor and discantus are at the distance of a sixth or octave at the penultima and have a sixth between them at the ultima, then the bassus will be placed at a third under the tenor at its penultima, and will reach the fifth [beneath] at the ultima. The altus, then, will quite agreeably assume the form of the discantus (*perpulcre tunc discantus formam assumet*), insofar as it takes its place the sixth above the bassus and a fourth above the tenor at the penultima, and appropriately at the octave above the bassus and a fourth above the tenor at the ultima.

Example 10

In the *Tetrachordum   musices* of Cochlaeus,[7] this same example is discussed even more clearly:

> Fifth rule. When the altus has taken on the form of the discantus, the bassus is brought in under it, progressing from sixth to octave. The tenor now takes the place of the altus (*tenor vero in locum alti subit*), so that it is at the third above the bassus at the penultima, and comes to rest at the fifth above [the bassus] at the ultima.

In view of this interchangeability of cadential voice leading within the polyphonic texture, it is possible to understand not only the caesura cadences but also at least a large part of even the episodic and transitory cadence formations, as stemming from the melody line of the cantus firmus. This [cantus firmus] exists for the composer as a monophonic *cantus prius factus*, whose [melodic] course encompasses interval progressions both by leap and by step, directed both upwards and downwards. Certain intervals allow for an interpretation as cadential voice leading—[this is true] of all voice-parts but particularly of contratenor voice leading—and are in fact often explained in this sense. The unique art of the composer seems, however, to consist in realizing the successive repetitions of a cantus firmus in varied sonorous guises each time it is stated, or in other words, in trying to find, out of one and the same melody, additional latent possibilities for being incorporated into cadential or other types of voice leadings at any given time. (A simple example of this is offered by Obrecht's *Missa Rose playsante*, Kyrie I, mm. 10-13, compared to its parallel passage at mm. 25-8.[8]) The occurrence and scale degree of at least many cadences are, accordingly, ordained directly and exclusively through the contour of the cantus-firmus voice as a monophonic melody line. The formation of cadences is a realization of the possibilities latent in the interval steps at any given time in the tenor, which are determined by the melodic interval and its constituent scale degrees. "Tonal coherence" (in the modern sense) of a rather extended section [of music] incorporating a cantus firmus is conditioned by tonal unequivocalness of the cantus-firmus melody line it is based on, whereby such tonality is to be conceived as in monophonic music, according to ambitus and the typical initial, mediant, and closing formulae and not by a "harmonization" related to a "tonality" (in the modern sense) imposed upon the tenor and existing outside

---

[7]Johannes Cochlaeus, *Tetrachordum musices* (Nuremburg: Johannes Weyßenbürger, 1511); the teachings of counterpoint and cadences in *Musica activa* are repeated here almost verbatim.

[8]Transmitted in the MS Segovia Cathedral. The Kyrie has been published in Albert Smijers, *Van Ockeghem tot Sweelinck* (Amsterdam: Alsbach, 1949–52), 58 ff.

of it. In this connection, one can consult (besides the [Obrecht] Kyrie mentioned above, mm. 27-8) the Patrem from Obrecht's *Missa Ave regina coelorum*,[9] mm. 42-3, where cadential formations—made possible and conditioned by the melodic progress of the tenor—suddenly appear, all of which apparently break through the closed "tonality" of the complete composition.

The voice register of a cantus firmus seems to be not immaterial for the interpretation of cadences: according to whether it lies in the superius, altus, tenor, or bassus, we find [the cantus firmus] interpreted in the sense of the characteristics of these voices (not exclusively, of course), [but certainly] in a considerable number of cases. This individuality is least emphasized in the altus and tenor range, since these voices, barely distinguished in their ambitus, move in frequent if not constant voice crossings; it is most pronounced when the cantus firmus lies in the bass register, particularly when the contratenor bassus is used to effect "deceptive cadences."

Examples from the masses of Obrecht:

1) Cantus firmus in the superius:

Expression as superius third-cadence [explained above]

Missa Malheur me bat	Et in terra	mm. 64, 66-67, 151-52, 168-69
	Patrem	mm. 45-46, 60-61, 108-09
	Et in spiritum	mm. 35-36, 38-39

2) Cantus firmus in the altus:

Missa Caput	Sanctus	mm. 34-35
	Benedictus	mm. 39-42, 49-50
Missa super Maria zart	Qui tollis	mm. 137-38, 153-54

3) Cantus firmus in the bassus:

Expression as low contratenor making "deceptive cadence"

| *Missa Caput* | Agnus I | mm. 22-23 |
| | Agnus II | mm. 11-12, 33-34, 26-27 (mi cadence) |

A comparison of the three-voice Benedictus and Agnus II sections of the *Missa Malheur me bat* is particularly revealing. Both are based on the chanson tenor, appearing in the original mensuration, laid out in the tenor in the Benedictus and in the bassus in the Agnus II. The disposition of the cadences in the Agnus II shows its idiosyncrasies as compared to the Benedictus, as they are characteristic for the expression of a cantus firmus placed in the bassus: the tenor cadences remain in general intact but not the discantus

---

[9]Johannes Wolf, ed., *Werken van Jacob Obrecht* (Amsterdam: Alsbach, 1908–21).

cadences (with the exception of mm. 27-28). New types of cadence formations, based on the fifth-leap e–A (mm. 16-17), are explainable above all as cadential in a "deceptive" sense, with progressions ascending stepwise and additional insertions, as in mm. 12, 39, 47-48, 49, and 55. Furthermore, reference can be made to Obrecht's so-called *Missa Schoen lief*, whose artistic challenge lies in the fact that discantus melodies consistently appear as cantus firmi in the bass.

A further possibility of cantus-firmus interpretation results when—as is indicated above—the ultima of the bassus or tenor is withheld. This can be realized as a cantus-firmus pitch with a rest immediately following:

1) As a bassus penultima with withheld ultima, when the c.f. is the real lowest voice at this place, as, for example, in [these works of] Obrecht:

Missa Je ne demande	Patrem	mm. 348-49, 383-84
Missa L'homme armé	Et incarnatus	mm. 30-31, 45-46

2) As a tenor penultima with withheld ultima, as in [the following passages of] Obrecht:

Missa Je ne demande	Patrem	mm. 78-79
	Sanctus	mm. 72-73, 92-93

II. The Passages Apart from the Cadences

Here, our concern is primarily the structure of the [melodic] sequences conditioned by the cantus firmus, whose great significance particularly for the cantus-firmus compositions of Obrecht is well known. Certainly these examples, cited many times, far from exhaust the widespread use of this compositional technique, which is present not merely when the sequence procedures are extended to all voices. It is also often detectable elsewhere as a compositional foundation involving only two voices, typically tenor and bassus, as in [the following works of] Obrecht:

Missa Je ne demande	Patrem	mm. 28-36	Tn, Bs
Missa Grecorum	Patrem	mm. 17-21	Tn, Bs
Missa Si dedero	Et in terra	mm. 65-84	Tn, Bs, Al
Missa de Sancto Martino	Et incarnatus	mm. 25-28	Tn, Bs
	Agnus I	mm. 22-24	Tn, Bs
Missa Sicut spina	Et in terra	mm. 28/29	Tn, Bs
Missa O quam suavis est	Patrem	mm. 18-20	Tn, Bs
	Sanctus	mm. 10-16, 20-24	Tn, Bs
Missa Petrus apostolus	Et iterum	mm. 22-30	Tn, Bs, Sp

[N.B.: Sp = superius; Al = altus; Tn = tenor; Bs = bassus]

In the mass just listed, the following places merit particular mention:

Qui tollis   mm. 4-13, 21-36,
                              43-60, 91-97   Tn, Bs

Schematic group construction within the bassus's discanting melody is avoided here, but the foundational sequencing structure becomes apparent when one focuses on the initial- and goal-tones of the bassus's melodic motion within each section whose sonority is conditioned by a held cantus-firmus pitch,[10] as, for example, in mm. 22-34:

Tenor: c' - - - - - - -   d' - - - - - - -   bb - - - - - - -   a
Bassus: f - - - - c   g - - - - d   eb - - - - Bb   d   etc.

This same thing is also found in the *Missa Virgo parens Christi* of Barbireau,[11] Kyrie I (mm. 1-5), Patrem (mm. 177-79), as well as in Barbireau's *Kyrie paschale* (mm. 18-24):

E x a m p l e   1 1   (◆ = ♩ ; original mensuration = C2)

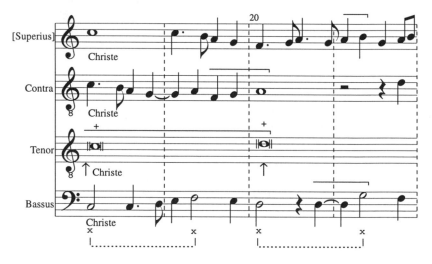

---

[10]The basic value as is transmitted in the source (dotted longs throughout) is meant here, but in Wolf it is divided up on account of the texting (the source gives only the incipit, "Qui tollis").

[11]The Kyrie I of this mass is published in André Pirro, *Histoire de la Musique de la fin du XIVe à la fin du XVIe siècle* (Paris: Renouard, 1940), 192-3; the complete Kyrie is contained in Johannes du Saar, *Het leven en de compositis van Jacobus Barbireau* (Utrecht: W. de Haan, 1946). The author has recently been entrusted with the complete edition of Barbireau's works in the series *Corpus Mensurabilis Musicae* [published as Bernhard Meier, ed., *Jacob Barbireau: Opera Omnia*, 2 vols., CMM 7 (Rome: American Institute of Musicology, 1954/57.)]

etc.

Finally, a particularly artistic employment of such sequencing not extended to all voices can be found in Obrecht's *Missa O quam suavis est*, Kyrie II (mm. 34-41) in superius and tenor. Here, Obrecht has created a possibility for bringing in a sequencing melody that is not evident in the cantus firmus without further [considerations], in that he conceives of certain tones (a–b-flat–a, f–g–f) as the core-tones of a sequencing tenor melody with the superius dependent upon this sequencing, but he has added the altus and bassus as obfuscating *vagans* parts, moving completely freely.

Within the realm of [melodic] sequencing conditioned by the cantus firmus, we also must make reference to the "repetition" of discanting formulae as they appear, for example, at the beginning of the Kyrie II of Obrecht's *Missa O quam suavis est*, or even more clearly at the beginning of the third Agnus of the same mass. To the tenor tones [listed below], a repetition occurs each time in the counter-voices, as follows:

Tenor tones: c' - - -, d' - - -, a - - -, b-flat - - -

to the tenor tone c', a repetition beginning on c in the bassus;
to the tenor tone d', a repetition beginning on f' in the superius;
to the tenor tone a, a repetition beginning on c' in the altus;
to the tenor tone b-flat, a repetition beginning on d in the superius.

A similar situation exists in the Kyrie II of the *Missa de Sancto Martino* as well as in Barbireau's *Kyrie paschale* (mm. 39-43), which could be represented as follows:

Example 12 (◆ = ♩ ; original mensuration = C2)

etc.

With respect to these sequencing techniques, reference should also be made to Alexander Agricola's *Missa paschalis*, Sanctus (mm. 55-68 and 169-77).

It is now necessary to comprehend those passages where the cantus firmus is neither fashioned into a cadencing voice nor is used as the foundational voice for sequence building. Imperfect consonance is the general basis of sonority in polyphonic composition in the late fifteenth century (perfect consonance is now only demanded at the final cadence, as we have seen from Cochlaeus). The sustained cantus firmus tone is explainable either as ground-tone ([or its] octave), third, or fifth. Thus, to the cantus-firmus tone c', the counter-voices can move within the sonorities C, a, or F, without implying in the change of these sonorities a preference for a "fifth-relationship" over a "third-relationship." (These conceptions lie beyond the awareness of the late fifteenth century, as also in the treatise of Cochlaeus the succession of sonorities is never at issue.) It would therefore be preferable to refer to such a treatment of sonorities with the expression "undifferentiated third-structure." With each successive cantus-firmus tone, the possibilities for the accompanying sonorities vary, and these [sonorities] at each "punctus" (segment) are independent from the preceding and the following sonorities alike. The possibilities are conditioned only by the allocation of the cantus-firmus tone into sonorities containing it as a ground-tone, a third, or a fifth. Examples of such sonorous treatment are too numerous to be accounted for completely; for example, in [works of] Obrecht:

Missa super Maria zart	Et in terra	mm. 22-25, 61-72
	Qui tollis	mm. 13 ff., 63/64, 83 ff., 122 ff.
	Patrem	mm. 28 ff., 88 ff., etc.
Missa Je ne demande	Et in terra	mm. 28-30
	Qui tollis	mm. 134 ff., 146 ff., 177 ff.
	Patrem	mm. 44 ff., 286 ff., 325 ff.
	Agnus I	mm. 40-45
In [the works of] Barbireau:		
Missa Virgo parens Christi	Kyrie	mm. 11-13, 24-31

Frequently encountered in Obrecht—and even more frequently in Barbireau—is also the solid sonorous foundation provided by the bassus for the cantus firmus. This vertically oriented approach to sonority must not, however, be approximated with a sonorous treatment based on [triadic] tonality: stepwise sonority progressions, successions of third-related sonorities, and successions of fifth-related sonorities have completely equal entitlement. Thus, for example, the foundation [provided by the bassus for] the beginning notes of the cantus firmus (c'–d'–c') [occurring] in various places of Barbireau's *Missa Virgo parens Christi*: [varies as follows]:

Et in terra	Tenor [c.f.]:	c' —	d' —	c'
	Bassus:	c —	g —	c
Patrem /Sanctus	Tenor [c.f.]:	c' —	d' —	c'
	Bassus:	c —	Bb—	c

The "tonal" [i.e., fifth-relation] realization [in the Et in terra] is thus definitely not preferred over the "non-tonal" one (stepwise progression). The usage shown below in Example 13 must also be regarded as this kind of ["non-tonal"] sonority progression, and it is clearly unjustified to impute a functional significance to it simply because it resembles a stereotypical formula [of triadic tonality].[12]

Example 13

NB.

Further evidence can be brought to bear in this connection from pieces whose bassus is clearly voice-led in the manner of a discanting part, but in which it often produces the impression of a figuration subsequently added to a basic [melodic] skeleton consisting of foundational tones [i.e., a bassus part that has been embellished through diminution]. This type of treatment can be found in Obrecht's *Missa de Sancto Martino*, Kyrie I, and in the *Missa L'homme armé*, Kyrie I and II. In order to illustrate the [underlying] structure, still visible through [the embellishments] that are apparent in the examples just adduced, Cochlaeus gives us the key: in his examples of three- and four-voice composition, he proceeds from a counterpoint *nota contra notam*, whereby the counter-voices are successively added to a structural framework of discantus and tenor. When the attempt is made in the following to reduce through radical simplification (particularly of the superius) the Kyrie I of the *Missa de Sancto Martino* to a counterpoint *nota contra notam*, this should not be taken to mean that some such schematic model really did precede [the composition as it exists in its finished form]. The long practice of composers perhaps made such a procedure superfluous. There also exist passages that are not reducible to this kind of [note-against-note] counterpoint ([such as] sequencing based on cantus firmus). Also, it would be equally dubious to

---

[12]Here also, the solely authoritative factor is the adherence to orthodox voice leading; the cadence formula of the tenor has simply been altered from that shown in Example N1-A to that shown in Example N1-B, which concurrently conditions the voice-leading alterations of the bassus as well.

Examples N1-A   N1-B

suggest as a certainty that all counter-voices were composed successively. The procedure of Cochlaeus, progressing from two-voice counterpoint to an expanded conception of voices, is conditioned by requirements as they are stated in a handbook; certain places in the examples chosen by us, however, provide evidence that, among the counter-voices, a simultaneous conception underlies at the very least the superius and bassus. Accordingly, this can be considered a mere experiment whose basic sonorous aspect (including the passages outside of the cadences and those conditioned by sequencing) cannot be understood precisely through concepts of our own time—[this conception of sonority can be comprehended] not from the outside but rather [only] with the aid of rules familiar to a composer of the late fifteenth century from youth onwards, corresponding to which the essence of his work is realized and thereby validated.

Since we are proceeding from three-voice composition, it is necessary to first reiterate the applicable rules as they are stated by Cochlaeus:

Concerning the composition of a three-voice piece (*De compositione trium partium contrapuncti*):

First Rule: Three-voice counterpoint is considered according to the following order: When the tenor and discantus stand at a unison, the contratenor will concord at a third, fifth, octave, or tenth below the tenor, as below in Example [14]-m.

Second Rule: But when the discantus is brought in a third above the tenor, the contratenor will concord very well and pleasantly at the third, octave, or tenth below the tenor, as below in Example [14]-n.

Third Rule: However, when the discantus has the pitch a fifth above the tenor, the contratenor can be brought in a third above the tenor or an octave below the tenor but not at a sixth underneath, since this usually sounds dissonant when in a low register, unless this sixth is voice-led in contrary motion [with the tenor] to an octave. See Example [14]-p.

Fourth Rule: When the discantus is at a sixth above the tenor, then the contratenor is brought in at a third, or better, at a fifth below the tenor, as below in Example [14]-q.

Fifth Rule: But when the discantus and tenor stand at an octave's distance to each other, the contratenor will take a very euphonious place a third or a fifth above the tenor, or at a third, fifth, or octave beneath the tenor, as below in Example [14]-r.

Sixth Rule: Finally, when the discantus is placed a tenth above the tenor, the contratenor will concord if brought in at a third, fifth, or octave above the tenor, or at a third or tenth below the tenor, as below in Example [14]-s.

Example 14   m   n   p   q   r   s

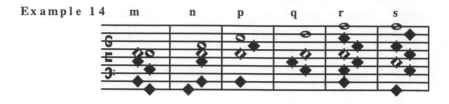

If we now adduce the schematic reduction of the Kyrie I of Obrecht's *Missa de Sancto Martino*, constructed so that it displays the concord at hand at the entrance of each new cantus-firmus tone, the following picture results:

Example 15

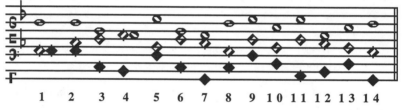

An examination of this piece shows that all of its concords are consistent with the rules cited above, that is:

Concord	1	according to Rule I	(*de specialibus contrapuncti mandatis*)
	2	according to Rule IV	
	3	according to Rule II	
	4	according to Rule I	
	5	according to Rule V	
	6	according to Rule II	
	7	according to Rule II	
	8	according to Rule V	
	9	according to Rule IV	(sequencing based on the cantus firmus)
	10	according to Rule IV	
	11	according to Rule IV	
	12	according to Rule II	
	13	according to Rule IV	
	14	according to Rule V	

The same thing applies to the Hosanna from Barbireau's *Missa Virgo parens Christi*, whose first eight measures are likewise given in reduction in the following:

Example 16

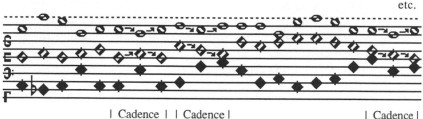

| Cadence | | Cadence | | Cadence |

Also, the ending passage in equal minims (which, indeed, is only one such passage composed in short note values) is especially to be interpreted in this way.

The rules for four-voice composition are as follows:

Concerning the composition of a four-voice piece:

First Rule: The composition of four consonant voices is arranged according to the following order: when tenor and discantus are at an octave's distance from each other, and the contratenor is brought in an octave below the tenor, then the higher contratenor (*contratenor acutus*) takes its place a third above the tenor, or a fifth above it (which sounds more pleasant), as is shown below in Example [17]-aa.

Second Rule: But when the baritonans is placed a fifth below the tenor, and the discantus stands a sixth or an octave above the tenor, then the altus concords at a third above the bassus or rises to an octave above it (since that is more pleasant), as in Example [17]-bb.

Third Rule: When the bassus has the tone an octave below the tenor, and the discantus lies a third above the tenor, then the altus is brought in a fifth above the bassus; it is thus a sixth below the discantus and is likewise a fourth lower than the tenor, as in Example [17]-cc.

Fourth Rule: But when the tenor and discantus are at a fifth from each other, and the bassus is placed an octave below the tenor, then the altus can take its place a third above the tenor or a fifth above the bassus, as in Example [17]-dd.

Fifth Rule: However, when the bassus has risen to the fifth above the tenor, while the discantus sounds the pitch an octave above the tenor, then the altus must be placed a third above the tenor, as in Example [17]-ee.

Sixth Rule: But when the discantus stands at a tenth above the tenor, then the bassus takes its place very euphoniously a fifth above the tenor, and the altus stands at best an octave above the tenor; or conversely,

the bassus will ascend to the pitch an octave above the tenor, and the altus will have the pitch a fifth above the tenor, as in Example [17]-ff.
[Seventh Rule:] Finally, when the tenor and bassus are at the distance of a sixth and progress further to the octave, then the discantus [in the penultima] will very well take its place a fifth or a third above the tenor, but the altus will not indelicately [take] the third above the bassus, as in Example [17]-gg.

Example 17   aa   bb   cc   dd   ee   ff   gg

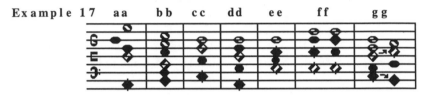

These rules are not as exhaustive as those for three-voice counterpoint, a point easily established through the example of the Kyrie adduced as a test case [see above, Example 15]. This is even more true of further parts attached to the four-voice texture, for whose addition Cochlaeus only provides the following general rules:

When one wants to join a fifth consonant voice to these four, it is advisable to adjust it reciprocally in various ways according to the rules and prescriptions of polyphonic composition.

As a result of our experiment, we can apprehend that whether or not the pieces adduced [above] manifested an underlying counterpoint *nota contra notam* as a [literal] sketch for the fully formed composition, this [contrapuntal reduction]—which can be laid bare without difficulty—certainly comprises the hidden foundation in these works, [which are] strongly oriented to the vertical-sonorous element. The concords arising in such a composition between the structural voices (tenor and discantus), and the contratenor (bassus), are comprehensible throughout according to the rules of Cochlaeus, which stipulate the position of the third voice by proceeding from the tenor and the interval between it and the discantus. The concord prevailing at any time thus stands in and of itself and is not linked to the following concord through a direct functional connection of the bass tones, independent of an intervallic reference to the tenor.

To conclude: Proceeding from the compositional methods of pieces incorporating a cantus firmus (as the embellishment of a *cantus prius factus* lying typically in the tenor with several discanting voices lying both in higher and in lower positions and moving around it), we sought to find an understanding of the sonorous processes within such pieces—[an understanding] whose conditions lie in the object itself, not in the principles of sonorous relationship applied from our time. Fundamentally, the cantus-firmus compositions of the late fifteenth century (predominantly those of Obrecht and his office predecessor in Antwerp, Barbireau) still evince the same structure that Johannes de Grocheo represents in such vivid pictures when he compares the tenor with the foundation of a house or with the skeleton, which lends stability but still acts as a sole foundation to all embellishing [elements of structure], whether they be obvious or obscure.[13] Like those of Grocheo, the compositional teachings of Cochlaeus still designate the choice and preparation of a tenor as the first requirement of a polyphonic composition. It is important to note that Cochlaeus does not waste a single word on that which we today call harmony. *Tonus* is used in the sense of monophonic melody and is identifiable with the tenor as a monophonic melody. Proceeding from this preexistent melody, the various intervallic placements and interval progressions in sonorities of two, three, and four voices are discussed successively. Following, [and] proceeding from the two-voice discantus-tenor foundation, the three- and four-voice forms of the cadences [are treated]; even these, in which the beginnings of dominant harmony lie, are still considered only according to [dyadic] intervals and stereotypical voice-leading [procedures].

From this standpoint, the sonority of cantus-firmus compositions can be represented thus:

1) as "undifferentiated third-structure," when [additional voices are] discanting to the successive held tones of the cantus firmus;
2) as a support of the cantus firmus through a firm foundation provided by the bass, but one that is not tonally bound in its sonority progression;
3) as a realization of specific interval progressions of the cantus firmus in the sense of stereotypical cadential voice-leading [procedures].

---

[13]Johannes de Grocheo: "Tenor autem est illa pars, supra quam omnes aliae fundantur quemadmodum partes domus vel aedificii super suum fundamentum, et eas regulat et eis quantitatem dat quemadmodum ossa partibus aliis." See Ernst Rohloff, *Studien zum Musiktraktat des Johannes de Grocheio* (Leipzig: Reinecke, 1930), 119. [Translation: "But the tenor is that part upon which all the others are founded, just as the parts of a house or building are built upon its foundation, and it [i.e., the tenor] regulates them and gives them quantity, just as the bones [do with respect to] the other parts [of the body]."]

   The goal of this inquiry has not been to deconstruct the artwork of polyphonic cantus-firmus composition into a plethora of cadences [or to represent] its activity in schematic construction. On the contrary: when one has identified [all] the craftsmanly ground rules and tutorials, which appear so barren, then one realizes with all the more wonder the mastery with which an almost unlimited modification of these rules is exercised by these composers. Above all, we marvel at the invention of widely spanned melodies, whose shape does not in any way suffer by the [cadential] crystallizations that appear episodically. The many-voiced wickerwork extends itself over the structural scaffolds, interweaving multifariously, without coming apart at any time; in doing so strictly according to the rules, it uplifts and transforms itself in each case into something singular.

5

The "Tonal Discant" and "Free Discant"
Techniques of Composition in the Fifteenth Century

Ernst Apfel

EDITOR'S PREFACE: *This study arguably represents the single most important contribution of the modern era to the analysis and interpretation of compositional styles in late medieval polyphony. For it is here that certain basic contrapuntal techniques of the fourteenth and fifteenth centuries were first defined in unambiguous terms and illustrated through actual surviving compositions. In the original article, specific musical works are often identified only by their page reference in one or another modern edition. In order to distinguish these pieces more precisely, I have broadened the citations considerably and provided titles or text incipits for them.*

The following inquiry will proceed from a comparison of the two three-voice masses—the mass No. 2 (*Sine nomine*) and No. 1 (*Quinti toni*)—from the *Collected Works* of Ockeghem.[1]

In the *Missa Sine nomine* the lower voices are labeled, from lower to upper, "contra" and "tenor"; in the *Missa Quinti toni* they are labeled "bassus" and "tenor." The uppermost voice is not designated in either mass; we follow the editor in labeling it "superius." In both masses, the superius begins individual movements and sections of movements either at the octave above the tenor or else at a unison with it; the superius and tenor are constantly returning to these consonances. Often the superius progresses in parallel thirds and sixths with the tenor.

In the *Missa Sine nomine* the superius has no fourths or diminished fifths with the tenor (in two-voice counterpoint, fourths and diminished fifths were classed as dissonances), apart from filling and embellishing figures, which essentially correspond to the suspension, passing tone, or anticipation

---

[1] Dragan Plamenac, ed., *Johannes Ockeghem, Collected Works* [2 vols.], *Publikationen älterer Musik*, ed. Theodor Kroyer (Leipzig: Breitkopf & Härtel, 1927), vol. 1, 15 ff. and 1 ff.). The following inquiry was materially furthered through conversations with my colleague and friend, Arnold Feil.

dissonance of classical vocal polyphony and which therefore can be so designated. Thus the superius and tenor could stand alone; they comprise a self-sufficient two-part entity. The contra is evidently only added to these two voices after the fact and extends the framework into a three-voice piece.

Things are differently conceived in the *Missa Quinti toni*. Here we do find fourths and diminished fifths between tenor and superius, which cannot be understood as suspensions or similar constructions. At such places the bassus takes the third, fifth, or sixth below the tenor and in this manner offsets, or legitimizes, the dissonance of the two other voices. In these instances the upper voices are thus subordinate to the bassus. On account of this, the bassus belongs to the counterpoint from the beginning and is of equal importance to the other two voices.[2] Therefore the tenor and superius do not comprise a contrapuntal entity unto themselves. [However,] since these two voices in general behave as do their counterparts in the *Missa Sine nomine*, one can assume that the compositional method of the *Missa Sine nomine* is the basis of that of the *Missa Quinti toni*. From being a part merely added on (as contratenor in the *Missa Sine nomine*), the lowest voice has become a part belonging to the composition in an essential sense and thereby equal (as bassus in the *Missa Quinti toni*). This process is associated with an alteration of the constructive aspects of counterpoint. What this alteration entails, and what significance is attached to it, will now be shown.

The cases in the *Missa Quinti toni* where the superius makes fourths or diminished fifths with the tenor can be divided into three types, whereby the first type occurs in the middle of a section, and the two others occur principally at major or interior cadences

1) The following places illustrate dissonances between tenor and superius, in which, through passing notes, suspensions, or other similar ornamental figures, one of the two voices arises from the other: Kyrie (mm. 9^{3-4}, 37^1); Gloria (mm. 27^2, 95^{1-3}; 108^1); Credo (mm. 6^3, 45^1, 146^1, 174^2, 184^1, 224^4, 228^4); Sanctus (mm. 44^4, 81^2, 82^2, 144^1, 166^1); and Agnus (m. 102^4).

2) In the Credo (mm. 42^4, 138^1, 185^4) and Sanctus (m. 42^2), the superius cadences with the tenor from a diminished fifth to a third, the bassus [moves] from a major sixth under the tenor to an octave.

---

[2]The bassus of the *Missa Quinti toni* remains always under the tenor at the cadences, during which it leaps from a fifth under the tenor as its penultimate note to the octave underneath at the cadence, whereas the contra of the *Missa Sine nomine* in each case returns to the middle position between tenor and superius and cadences at the fifth above the tenor (the conventional cadence of a motetus voice).

These two classes of fourths and diminished fifths do not yet provide sufficient evidence to assert that the mass corresponds to a different compositional principle than the *Missa Sine nomine*. However, there arise yet additional, decisive cases that fall under a third class.

3) In the Gloria (mm. 95-97) and in the Sanctus (mm. 146 and 164-166), we encounter fourths between superius and tenor, which cannot be explained as passing notes or analogous circumstances.[3]

There are not many four-voice compositions in the old style of the *Missa Sine nomine*, in which two further voices are added to a self-sufficient two-part framework. In Ockeghem's works published to date we find none of these types. His four-voice works are all composed in the technique of the *Missa Quinti toni*. [Thus,] in order to illustrate a work composed in the technique manifest by the *Missa Sine nomine*, the *Salve regina* of Dufay will be discussed.[4] The voices [in this work] are designated from low to high: "bassus," "tenor," and "contra"; the highest voice is not labeled. [Here,] the superius comprises a two-voice framework with the tenor, within which no fourths or diminished fifths occur and which therefore can stand complete in and of itself. The two voices move often in parallel thirds and sixths, and close at an octave's distance at interior cadences (mm. 5, 12, 20, 26, 30, 37, 40, 56, etc.). The bassus makes frequent leaps: at interior cadences it mostly takes a place a fifth above the tenor (octave-leap cadence), and in mm. 29-30, 81-82, and 183-84 at the octave below the tenor (seemingly because the sixth-to-octave cadence between superius and tenor lies in a high register). In mm. 36-37, 42-43, 46-47, 48-49, 57-58, 71-72, 95-96, 135-36, 146-47, 175-76, 191-92, 213-14, it proceeds to the third under the tenor and thus makes a close that looks similar to our deceptive cadence. We find noteworthy cadences at mm. 60-61 and 149-50. However, nowhere is the two-voice framework of the top voice with the tenor directed by the bassus; on the contrary: the bassus is subordinate to them. Solely the high contra, which in other similar compositions is usually designated "contra altus," is subordinate to the bassus, because it often has fourths in its relationship with the tenor, which require their legitimation through the bassus (mm. 3^3, 4^3, 11^{1-2-3}, etc.). The piece as a whole thus appears to be composed as follows:

---

[3]Only the most unambiguous cases are considered here.

[4]Guido Adler and Oswald Koller, eds., *Sechs Trienter Codices: Geistliche und weltliche Kompositionen des XV. Jahrhunderts, Erste Auswahl, DTÖ* 14-15 *(Jahrgang* VII) (Vienna: Universal-Edition, 1900), 178 ff. Dufay's authorship of this work is disputed by Karl Dèzes, "Das Dufay zugeschriebene Salve regina eine deutsche Komposition," *Zeitschrift für Musikwissenschaft* 10 (1927-28): 327-62.

Example 1

Explanation of diagram:

◆ = Tenor; ◯ = Superius; ● = Contratenor (Altus); ◆ = (Contratenor) Bassus

In examples without Altus (●): ◆ = Contra or Contratenor

In "tonal counterpoint" examples: ● = Motetus; ● = Triplum; ● = Quadruplum

To a pure two-voice framework a lower contratenor (bassus) was first added, and to the resulting three-voice counterpoint a higher contratenor was then added according to the consonance of the bassus with the tenor. The tenor and superius (the highest, unlabeled voice) are structural voices [*Gerüststimmen*] and in no case are dependent upon the bassus.

Things work differently in an anonymous *Salve regina*, which we now wish to consider.[A] The voices (from lower to upper) are designated: "contra 2," "tenor," "contra 1"; the highest voice (superius) is unlabeled. In mm. 32-33, 49-50, 78-79, 114-15, 134-35, 140-41, the superius closes at an octave (or unison) with the tenor,[5] proceeding beforehand in parallel sixths (or thirds). The contra 2 leaps at interior and major cadences from the fifth under the tenor at the penultimate note to either the fifth above the tenor, or to a unison with it, or to an octave below it; sometimes it proceeds to the third under the tenor. The contra 1 often takes the fourth above the tenor and thereby is subordinate to the contra 2. The work presently under consideration has these things in common with the *Salve regina* of Dufay. But in mm. 21, 30, 44, 46-48, 53, 75-77, 104, 105, 118, 121, and 137-38, fourths—and even parallel fourths and diminished fifths—occur between the superius and tenor. The two voices are thus at these places subordinate to the contra 2, which lies either a third, a fifth, or a sixth under the tenor. This corresponds to the situation already ascertained regarding the *Missa Quinti toni*.[6] However, at the

---

[A]Rudolf von Ficker and Alfred Orel, ed., *Sechs Trienter Codices: Geistliche und weltliche Kompositionen des XV. Jahrhunderts, Vierte Auswahl, DTÖ* 53 (*Jahrgang* XXVII/1) (Vienna: Universal-Edition, 1920), 55 ff.

[5]In mm. 136–37 the superius proceeds on immediately.

[6]In contrast to the bassus of the *Missa Quinti toni* (see above, note 2), the contra 2 of the work presently under consideration sometimes leaps to the fifth above the tenor (see above). This shows that the circumstance of the low voice remaining below the tenor, as is the case in the *Missa Quinti toni*, does not itself constitute a sufficient criterion to consider that it [i.e., the bassus] has become the directive voice. (But note Heinrich Besseler's argument to the contrary, *Bourdon und Fauxbourdon* (Leipzig: Breitkopf & Härtel, 1950), 32 ff. and elsewhere). Without

cadences (mm. 46-48, 75-77, 118-19, 121, 137-38) there occur between superius and tenor not only fourths, parallel fourths, and diminished fifths but also parallel perfect intervals, which at that time were forbidden in relationship with the tenor. These instances show, even more clearly than the fourths occurring between tenor and superius, that in this *Salve regina* the contra 2 was in places crucial to the counterpoint, since the [parallel perfect intervals] are neutralized [only] if one refers all [harmonic] events to it. At the above-mentioned places, the contra 2 describes the stepwise descending second that is otherwise made by the tenor, e.g., mm. 118-19 (Example 2), or in similar cases: mm. 47-48, 76-77, and 138 (the original form of Example 3 is embellished).

Examples   2   3

N.B.: Voice parts read from low to high: contra 2, tenor, contra 1, [superius]

In this piece the contra 2 indeed almost always lies under the tenor, but it is responsible for the integrity of the sonority only at the above-mentioned places. And to that extent it is indispensable to the composition, insofar as it legitimizes impermissible intervals between tenor and superius.

There exist, however, from the time of Machaut's mass until far into the fifteenth century, compositions in which the contratenor, wherever it comes to lie under the tenor, is indispensable. These compositions display the many fourths, parallel fourths, diminished fifths, and parallel perfect consonances

---

a doubt there exists a connection between the designation of the low voice in the *Missa Quinti toni* as bassus and the fact that this voice remains under the tenor at cadences. It is also no coincidence that the low voice of the anonymous *Salve regina* (*DTÖ* 53) resembles its counterpart in Ockeghem's *Missa Quinti toni*, that it frequently makes octave-leap cadences, and that it is called contra 2. The connection, however, does not concern the conception of tonal direction, nor does it concern compositional technique in a narrow sense; it is conditioned rather by performance practice. Only subsequently did a new conception of tonality emerge. Whenever different compositional techniques are not distinguished, there lies the danger of secondary events being assessed as primary. This danger is heightened when principles of harmonic theory are adduced as explanation (see Werner Korte, *Die Harmonik des frühen XV. Jahrhunderts in ihrem Zusammenhang mit der Formtechnik* (Münster: Suhrbier & Bröcker, 1928).

that appear between the upper voices and also [appear] in relationship with the tenor whenever it lies higher than the contratenor. As an example the anonymous *Elizabet Zacharie* will serve.[B] The lower voices are designated "tenor" and "contratenor"; the two upper voices are not labeled. In mm. 23, 28, 30, 33, 34, 38, 41, 43, 45, 49, 57, etc., the uppermost voice has fourths, and in mm. 118-19 parallel fourths with the tenor, and (without embellishment) in mm. 24-25, 36-37, 72-73, 78-79, 85-86, as well as in mm. 105-108, it proceeds in parallel perfect consonances with the tenor. At these places the contratenor always is found under the tenor. This suggests that here the contratenor, in place of the tenor, is essential for the integrity of the sonority and for the forward motion of the voices. Works such as these thus follow a compositional technique different from that in the *Missa Sine nomine* of Ockeghem and the *Salve regina* of Dufay, but also different from the *Missa Quinti toni* of Ockeghem and the anonymous *Salve regina* in *DTÖ* 53: [Here] the lowest voice is decisive, whether it be the tenor or, when it lies beneath the tenor, the contratenor. The upper parts stand in a position of equal importance with respect to the lowest voice. They must continually return to a perfect cadential consonance in contrary motion with the lowest part (the closest upper part a fifth above the fundamental voice, the next an octave above, and the highest a twelfth above), thus creating parallel [perfect consonances]. The contratenor thus becomes, wherever it lies below the tenor, the director of sonorities [*Klangträger*], and the tenor becomes an upper voice. On the one hand, in Ockeghem's *Missa Sine nomine*, the contratenor filled in or expanded [the sonority] of a two-voice framework, whereas in the *Missa Quinti toni* on the other hand, it completed [an otherwise not totally fulfilled sonority]. The basis of the technique of the works just mentioned was the treatment of one specific voice—the superius—relative to the tenor, so that no parallels occurred (compare the cadences in the *Missa Quinti toni* of Ockeghem with those of the anonymous *Salve regina* in *DTÖ* 53, see above).

Considering the surviving works, we recognize three contrapuntal types:

1) the counterpoint of the anonymous *Elizabet Zacharie* in *DTÖ* 76;
2) the counterpoint of the *Missa Sine nomine* of Ockeghem and the *Salve regina* of Dufay;
3) the counterpoint of the *Missa Quinti toni* of Ockeghem and the anonymous *Salve regina* in *DTÖ* 53.

[B]Rudolf von Ficker, ed., *Sieben Trienter Codices: Geistliche und weltliche Kompositionen des XIV und XV. Jahrhunderts, Sechste Auswahl, DTÖ* 76 *(Jahrgang* XL) (Vienna: Universal-Edition: 1933), 16 ff. Regarding similar pieces we will speak presently in more detail.

Type 1 and type 2 are fundamentally different, whereas the third type agrees with the second but has taken over elements of the first type.

In our [previous] inquiry, decisive significance was attributed to the contratenor (whether bassus or contra). In its role of making a piece complete, its function was essential. There arose only the following question: does it complement only the tenor, whereby the other voices are directed by whichever voice (contratenor or tenor) is lowest at any given time (Type 1); or does it expand a given self-sufficient two-voice framework to one of three voices (Type 2); or does it belong as an essential extension of a two-voice framework, which indeed is no longer self-sufficient, but neither is the contra fully assimilated into the three-part counterpoint (Type 3)? The designation "contratenor" allows us to surmise that the function it has in Type 1 was the original one.

What status now does the [interval of a] fourth assume in the description of the three contrapuntal types? In compositions of Type 1 there frequently occur fourths and diminished fifths between all upper voices but particularly in connection with the tenor, where it lies higher than the contratenor. This shows that the lowest voice was essential for the counterpoint. In compositions of Type 2 there never occur any [fourths or diminished fifths] between the uppermost voice (superius) and tenor. In compositions of Type 3, fourths and fifths between these same voices occur from time to time.

In a previous study,[7] taking the compositional treatises of the time as a point of departure,[8] I arrived at a differentiation of two different techniques of counterpoint in the fifteenth century: a "tonal" and a "free" discant technique, as they were named in that study.[9]

It would be appropriate to enter here briefly into this distinction, but for a full discussion of its foundations, the above-mentioned work must be

---

[7]Ernst Apfel, "Der Diskant in der Musiktheorie des 12.–15. Jahrhunderts" (dissertation, University of Heidelberg, 1953).

[8]Regarding techniques of composition, one obtains elucidation only by drawing upon the theorists, since the function of the individual note cannot be recognized from its graphic representation; see the Introduction to the author's dissertation (cited in above note).

[9]"Tonal" as in "tonal discant counterpoint" [*klanglicher Diskantsatz*] does not denote "harmonic tonality," as understood from the later art music. [The term] "free," as in "free discant counterpoint" [*freier Diskantsatz*] is [applied] in relation to the discantus (also called superius), which in this compositional style has a large ambitus and so has many options in its melodic treatment. In order to understand this distinction better one could also refer to free discant counterpoint as "contrapuntal composition." The tonal [discant] technique is at this point only demonstrable in the theory from English treatises of the fifteenth century. Regarding all these points, see the study cited above in note 7.

consulted. In the tonal discant counterpoint of the fifteenth century, which had its origins in England and which was described by English theorists, several voices were added simultaneously to the tenor;[10] these were called motetus, triplum, and quadruplum. The tonal discant composition was thus a multi-voiced work. The voices added to the tenor were placed above it. Each individual [voice] made with it a two-voiced entity, for which any of three to five consonances could be employed. The individual voices were not dependent upon each other; each was added to the tenor without consideration of any other voice, so that one can represent the voice relationships as in Example 4. As the lowest voice, the tenor was (apart from the fact that the entire construction of the counterpoint proceeded from it) the director of sonorities. Later, a "contratenor" ("voice against the tenor") was added to pieces conceived in such a manner, in which case the quadruplum was then omitted. This "special" tenor, the "contratenor," moved in the same realm as the nominal tenor, finding a place sometimes below and sometimes above it. Whenever it was under the tenor, it took over the latter's function as director of sonorities. This is recognizable by the fact that the other voices could now have fourths in their relationship with the tenor. Since the contratenor in such places was equally responsible for the building of sonorities, one must assume that it was fitted to the tenor before the other voices. It thus comprises a composite lower voice [*kombinierte Tiefstimme*] with the tenor; together they embrace both functions of the older tenor, namely, being [1] the predetermined voice of the entire composition and simultaneously [2] the director of sonorities. The upper voices were added to this combined lower voice without mutual consideration, exactly as they had been added to the earlier tenor (see Example 5). Since everything proceeded from the fundamental tones and since the fourteenth-century system of harmonic progression was still in operation, the

---

[10]The tenor was in the Middle Ages and even later the most important voice of a composition, regardless of whether it originated as a Gregorian chant or whether it was newly invented, [in other words, whether] it was a cantus firmus or a *cantus prius factus*, [respectively]. In the literature on composition in the fifteenth century, the question of the cantus firmus stands in the foreground of consideration, although it is of lesser interest. In tonal counterpoint the tenor of course always carried the cantus firmus, from which, moreover, the construction of the piece proceeded. In free discant counterpoint the cantus firmus could also be placed in the discantus (superius), yet this [fact] was only of significance to the two-voice structural framework. Indeed, the third voice, the "contra" ("contratenor bassus") had only to concord with the tenor but not with the discantus. The question of the structure of the counterpoint, as it is posed herein, seems to me to be more important than the question of the cantus firmus.

[principle of] neighbor-relationship of sonorities[11] prevailed in tonal counterpoint (particularly at cadences), as in the progressions illustrated in Example 6.

Examples
4   5   6-A   6-B   6-C

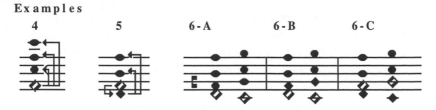

Frequent parallels arose between the voices added to the combined lower voice, but these were not viewed as incorrect, since they did not affect the progression with the lowest voice.

On the other hand, free discant counterpoint, as it circulated on the Continent, was originally a two-voice work of tenor and an added discant voice. As is manifest from the rules of the theorists and from the musical manuscripts, all consonances from unison up to twelfth above the cantus [firmus] were available to the single discant voice in contrast to the upper voices in tonal discant counterpoint.[12] From the two-voice [technique of] free discant counterpoint there originated now a three-voice composition, in which more and more frequently a third voice—also called "contratenor"—was added. This "contratenor" in three-voice free discant composition had a greater

---

[11] I am using this term [*Nachbarschaftsverhältnis der Klänge*] after Thrasybulos Georgiades, *Englische Diskanttraktate aus der ersten Hälfte des 15. Jahrhunderts; Untersuchungen zur Entwicklung der Mehrstimmigkeit im Mittelalter* (Munich: Musikwissenschaftliches Seminar der Universität München, 1937), referring to successive, similarly constructed sonorities moving stepwise—the decisive fundamental tones of the counterpoint. Georgiades has suggested that discant as taught by English theorists demonstrates more clearly than the teachings of Continental theorists the connection between the more modern polyphony and the doubling practice of the earlier Middle Ages.

Manfred Bukofzer's "English discant," [explained in] *Geschichte des englischen Diskants und des Fauxbourdons nach den theoretischen Quellen* (Strasbourg: Heitz, 1936), is to some extent identical with the tonal discant counterpoint of the present study. However, Bukofzer interprets the contratenor in English discant in the same manner as that of fauxbourdon: that it was first a filling voice and only later a bass (in a harmonic sense, that is, director of sonorities—see 89 ff.). It seems to me, however, that the contratenor in "English discant" was always the director of sonorities, whereas in fauxbourdon it was merely a filling or completing voice, completely dependent upon the framework of the structural voices, tenor and superius (also called supranus in fauxbourdon), which always behaved in the same manner.

[12] The fourth is counted as a dissonance in two-voice counterpoint.

ambitus than its counterpart in tonal discant and had a completely different function than the latter: it was a completing voice, but one that did not amplify the tenor, i.e., it was not a director of sonorities. Furthermore, when this type (which now is designated as being in "discant-" or "chanson-" or "cantilena-style") came to be cultivated principally as a three-voice piece, it was always conceived as proceeding from the two-voice structure of free discant (i.e., from the structural unity of the discantus-tenor framework), just as is evident from the rules of the theorists. The primary voice was the tenor,[13] and the contratenor had to concord with it.[14] Moreover, whatever consonance the contratenor held was dependent upon the interval of the discantus (superius) with the tenor and the position of these two voices. Where the tenor occupied a high position, and thus found the discantus only slightly above it, the contratenor was placed at a consonant interval below the tenor. Where the tenor occupied a low position so that the discant voice proceeded at a larger distance above, the contratenor acted to fill the space between them (see Example 12). It is of particular significance that whenever the contratenor occupied a position below the tenor, it was subordinate to the position of the discantus. In this manner conspicuous dissonances between the two voices were avoided, just as when the contratenor was positioned above

---

[13]Even though the contratenor was often placed under the tenor, [the former] was still dependent upon the [position of the] discantus, so that the tenor did not "support" [*tragen*] the sonorities but rather "constrained" [*halten*] them. It became, so to speak, a "proprietor of sonorities" [*Klanghalter*].

[14]For this reason the contratenor never took the fourth below or above the tenor (Example 7) and seldom took the sixth below the tenor (Example 8), even though both [of these possibilities] should have been unobjectionable from the point of view of the discantus. The contratenor was permitted to move with the discant voice—but not with the tenor—in parallel fifths. In cases where the tenor had crossed with the discantus (as in Example 9), the only question the theorists leave open is whether the contratenor was permitted to take the fourth above the tenor (Example 10). In the works of free discant discussed here, one seldom finds voice crossings between tenor and discantus. (The theorists do not consider this possibility at all; they presuppose that the discantus is placed above the cantus [firmus, i.e., tenor]). Also, the contratenor ascends above the discantus only in very few cases. Eventually the contrapuntal placement of the tenor will be at variance with a sonority where the contratenor makes a fourth with it. In the musical sources, when the discant and tenor cross, the contratenor always has a third (or a sixth) with the tenor (Example 11).

Examples   7   8   9   1 0   1 1

the tenor. Moreover, there are yet other special rules: 1) The voices added to the tenor should concord with each other to the degree that they could stand by themselves without the tenor (Example 13); and 2) the discantus and contratenor may not simultaneously take the fifth and a sixth above the tenor, since this results in the interval of a second between them (Example 14).

Examples   1 2   1 3   1 4

In this way a pure three-voice structure was preserved, in which no fourths occurred relative to the tenor, and almost none occurred between contratenor and discantus.[15] The discantus was continually voice-led back to the basic consonance of the two-voice structure, the octave, or in its place sometimes the unison. Preceding [such returns] the discantus accompanied the tenor mostly in parallel sixths or thirds. The contratenor had to leap constantly if parallel perfect consonances were to be avoided, especially at cadences, so that the following [types of] progression resulted:

Examples   1 5 - A   1 5 - B   1 5 - C

Such [situations] originated out of completely different circumstances and were based on completely different preconditions than our [modern] harmonic

---

[15]Between the discantus and the contratenor, however, there also arose striking fourths and diminished fifths corresponding to those occurring between discantus and altus (and also between altus and tenor) in four-voice works composed in free discant. In tonal-free discant counterpoint (Type 3) these vertical intervals also occurred between tenor and discantus. The observation that the contratenor in certain pieces could be left out (because the discantus comprises a self-sufficient framework with the tenor), I have found only in the writings of Arnold Schering: *Studien zur Musikgeschichte der Frührenaissance* (Leipzig: Kahnt, 1914), especially 123 and 176 ff., and of Wolfgang Stephan, *Die burgundisch-niederländische Motette zur Zeit Ockeghems* (Kassel: Bärenreiter, 1937), 26 ff., note 85. Stephan puts it this way: "without ... unsupported fourths originating." In neither of the two above studies, however, is the aforementioned fact brought into connection to the building of counterpoint. Rather, their theories are a result of only observing appearances or external circumstances, as Besseler [has done] in connection to the contratenor (*Bourdon and Fauxbourdon*, 300, note 1).

V–I cadence, and thus they stood beyond the scope of any [sense of functional triadic] tonality.[16]

In tonal discant counterpoint the tenor and contratenor were of paramount importance and acted as an enlargement of one voice. In free discant counterpoint, on the other hand, the tenor with the uppermost voice (discantus or superius) were preeminent. In both styles of composition, the voices had differing contrapuntal weight, and this is a significant point.

The free discant style of counterpoint [realized] in four voices consisted of the two-voice framework of tenor and discantus, a "contratenor bassus," and a "contratenor altus." The contratenor bassus was determined by the intervallic consonances of the structural framework, just as is the contratenor in three-voice free discant writing, the only difference being that in the former, it stayed more under the tenor than in the latter. The contratenor altus took mostly the fourth above the tenor, since the bassus predominantly occupied the fifth and the third beneath the tenor. The altus also sometimes took the third and, less often, the fifth [above the tenor].[17] In the free discant counterpoint that originated in this manner, there thus occurred fourths between the tenor and the contratenor altus, which required the [presence of a lower] contratenor bassus to legitimize them. Such fourths, of course, never occurred between the tenor and the uppermost voice (i.e., between the voices comprising the structural framework). The above discussion suffices for four-voice free discant counterpoint.

The altus of four-voice free discant and the motetus of four-voice tonal discant composition (with a contratenor instead of a quadruplum) both take predominantly the fourth [above] the tenor. Therefore motetus and altus are not essential to our distinction [of compositional techniques] but only the other voices, particularly the relationship between the uppermost voice— discantus (superius) or triplum, respectively, whose ambitus correspond to each other—to the tenor, and also the relationship of both of these voices to the contratenor (bassus). These [three] are the principal voices.

The distinction already encountered between tonal and free discant counterpoint we can now apply to the pieces of Ockeghem, Dufay, and the anonymous masters introduced above, since their characteristics—already noted

---

[16]This point is entertained further in the Introduction to the author's dissertation (see above, note 7).

[17]The four-voice free discant style of composition is taught in *Guilielmi Monachi de preceptis artis musice et practice compendiosus libellus*, [contained in] *CS* 3, 293 ff., and also in *Tractatus de musica figurata et de contrapuncto ab anonymo auctore*, [in] *CS* 4, 434 ff. In the treatise of Guillielmus Monachus, the structural voices only move in parallel sixths.

above—are the same as those just described. The anonymous *Elizabet Zacharie* (*DTÖ* 76) is a tonal discant piece (see the contrapuntal classification above, Type 1). The *Missa Sine nomine* of Ockeghem and the *Salve regina* of Dufay are free discant pieces (Type 2). The *Missa Quinti toni*, on the other hand, and the anonymous *Salve regina*, are pieces composed in the free discant style that also manifest characteristics of tonal counterpoint (Type 3). [The two last-named works have] fourths and diminished fifths with the tenor, and parallel perfect consonances between upper voices—including the tenor. These things demonstrate that the [technique of] tonal counterpoint had an influence upon the [technique of] free counterpoint. Even in the vocal polyphony of the sixteenth century, which was a later derivation of the free discant style of composition, we can still recognize elements of tonal counterpoint. The Palestrina style is, of course, a homogeneous one in which, to be sure, the relationship of all voices together is of decisive importance, but equally important is the relationship of each individual voice with the lowest (fourths and diminished fifths are permitted anywhere, except in connection with the bassus; parallel perfect consonances, however, are absolutely prohibited).

This "tonal-free" counterpoint [*klanglich-freier Satz*]—as we now can designate compositions of Type 3—we have encountered in the *Missa Quinti toni* of Ockeghem and in the anonymous *Salve regina* in *DTÖ* 53. Such pieces originated when the function of the contratenor in tonal counterpoint partially took over for the contratenor [function] in the free style, through which the possibility of placing fourths and diminished fifths between tenor and superius was preserved as long as the contratenor came to lie beneath the tenor. However, the contratenor (bassus) and superius had to be added to the tenor simultaneously, since they were mutually conditioned [to each other]: the superius had given up to the contratenor a part of its compositional importance—but only a part, since it was not completely dependent upon the contratenor. (One could well ask whether the tonal-free technique just discussed could have derived from the tonal style, but this is not possible.[18])

If one now considers the pieces from the Trent codices (published in *DTÖ*) from the standpoint of whether they are composed in the free or the

---

[18]As long as the imperfect consonances had to be resolved to their nearest perfect intervals, the kind of counterpoint that was determined by its lowest note [*durch Grundton bestimmter Satz*] was obliged to remain inflexible. Only after the classical phase of vocal polyphony, whose tonal principles had assumed a completely different quality (from the point of free discant counterpoint on), could a technique of free counterpoint founded upon the bass as the fundamental tone come into being.

tonal discant style, the following picture presents itself:[19] Compositions in pure tonal counterpoint one finds only infrequently; most of them are four-voiced.[20] This is in contrast to pieces written in the free discant style, which one often encounters.[21]

The tonal-free discant [technique of] counterpoint presently under consideration (Type 3), which is manifest in the Ockeghem's *Missa Quinti toni* and in the *Salve regina* from *DTÖ* 53, is likewise to be found in the Trent codices.[22] Moreover, [by considering such pieces] we can ascertain that tonal counterpoint is more strongly in evidence in the four-voice than in the three-voice works.[23] This fact suggests that the tonal counterpoint style (which continued to influence the free discant style that was based on it) was also cultivated in four voices from the very beginning.

We encounter yet other compositions (mostly four-voiced) of a mixed nature[24] in which no fourths exist between the highest voice and the tenor (even where it lies above the contratenor), and only very few [fourths] between

---

[19]The fifth selection in *DTÖ* 61 was not taken into consideration here. Out of the sixth selection (*DTÖ* 76, cited above in note B), the motets of Dunstable are discussed below.

[20]For example, *DTÖ* 76, 16 [the anonymous motet *Elizabet Zacharie*, discussed above]. Tonal counterpoint was for the most part merely improvised and achieved the most currency in England. In contradistinction, free discant counterpoint was typically a *res facta* composition, which had its origins on the Continent.

[21]Of these types, only the four-voice ones should be enumerated here, since the three-voice pieces from the Trent codices (outside of those discussed in notes 20 and 22) are all free discant compositions: *DTÖ* 14-15 (*Advenisti, desiderabilis, Venisti*, 83; *Tu ne quaesieris*, 89; Dufay, *Salve regina*, 178; Dufay, *Se la face ay pale* (à 4), 252; Hayne, *Amours*, 257; *Crist ist erstanden* (à 4), 260) and *DTÖ* 53 (*Christe redemptor* (No. 3), 83).

[22]For example, see Guido Adler and Oswald Koller, eds., *Sechs Trienter Codices: Geistliche und weltliche Kompositionen des XV. Jahrhunderts, Zweite Auswahl, DTÖ* 22 (*Jahrgang* XI/1) (Vienna: Universal-Edition, 1904), 13, where the various techniques blend with each other as compared with the following works: *DTÖ* 22 (Busnois, *Mon seul et sangle souvenir*, 74); *DTÖ* 76 (Johannes Verben, *O domina gloriosa*, 70; Forest, *Tota pulchra est*, 80), etc.

[23]*DTÖ* 14-15 (Compère, *Omnium bonorum*, 111; Dufay, *Missa Se la face ay pale*, 120); *DTÖ* 22 (*Missa O rosa bella* III, 28 both versions; *Heya, heya, nu wie sie grollen*, 118); Oswald Koller, et al., eds., *Sechs Trienter Codices: Geistliche und weltliche Kompositionen des XV. Jahrhunderts, Dritte Auswahl, DTÖ* 38 (*Jahrgang* XIX/1) (Vienna: Universal-Edition, 1912), Dufay, *Missa Caput*, 17; Ockeghem, *Missa Le serviteur*, 95; *DTÖ* 53 (*Salve regina* (No. 4), 50; *Salve regina* (No. 5), 52; *Salve regina* (No. 6), 55; *Ave maris stella* (No. 6), 80).

[24]*DTÖ* 14-15 (Brassart, *Ave Maria*, 95; Brassart, *Fortis cum quasvis actio*, 97; Leonel, *Ave regina coelorum*, 210; Velut, *Summe summi*, 221); *DTÖ* 53 (Dufay, *Basilissa ergo gaude*, 30; Touront, *Pange lingua*, 85); *DTÖ* 76 (De Monte, *Plaude decus mundi*, 6; *Maria mare—O Maria celi*, 12; Dufay, *Ecclesie militantis—Sanctorum arbitrio—Bella canunt*, 26; *Lamberte vir inclite*, 66; *Gaudeat ecclesia*, 72; *Gregatim grex audet*, 73; *O sidus yspanie*, 75; etc.).

the second-highest voice and the tenor. But such pieces differ from the tonal-free style, because in them the stepwise relationship of sonorities, bound up with [motion in] parallel perfect consonances, predominates. The contratenor is almost always placed above the tenor; it acts sometimes as a contratenor of tonal discant, and sometimes as one of a three-voice free discant piece. In the former it progresses by small intervals, and in the latter in leapwise motion. As the basic low voice, the tenor assumes the position corresponding to its function as director of sonorities. This [treatment of the voices] apparently is a characteristic of compositions in tonal counterpoint that also show traits of the free discant technique. We recognize in this a refinement of the principle of tonal counterpoint, which is probably connected with the working out of these pieces as a *res facta* and evidently represents a special stage of this compositional technique.

Besides the tonal and the free types of counterpoint as well as the mixed types, we also find yet other pieces that are composed unequivocally as free discant counterpoint, in which, however, there occasionally occur conspicuous fourths, tritones, and diminished fifths between the tenor and superius, while the contratenor lies below the structural voices.[25] The dissonances arise, for example, as passing tones of one of the structural voices against the other (see the above classification of dissonance treatment in the *Missa Quinti toni*, under No. 1). They are rendered inconsequential by the contratenor's holding or taking a tone underneath: the fourth is mitigated by [the presence of] a third or a fifth under the tenor (Example 16), the tritone by a third beneath (Example 17), and the diminished fifth by a sixth underneath (Example 18).

Examples   16   17   18   19

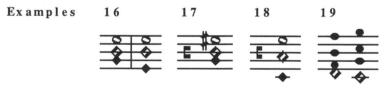

It is of particular importance that the contratenor in several cases expressly takes a new note under the tenor,[26] which mitigates the ornamental

---

[25]For example, *DTÖ* 14-15 (Dunstable-Leonel, *Salve regina*, 191, m. 68; Dunstable, *Sancta Maria*, 197, m. 55; Busnois, *Joye me fuit*, 247, m. 56; Dufay, *Je ne puis plus*, m. 11, and *Se la face ay pale*, m. 5, 251; Dunstable, *Puisque m'amour*, 254, mm. 3 and 20; Hermannus de Atrio, *Nouvellement*, 256, m. 55); *DTÖ* 22 (Binchois, *Je me recommande*, 71, m. 17), etc.

[26]For example, *DTÖ* 14-15 (Busnois, *Joye me fuit*, 247, m. 62; Dufay, *Craindre vous vueil*, 250, mm. 9 and 26; Hermannus de Atrio, *Nouvellement*, 256, m. 54; *Crist ist erstanden* (No. 3), 262, m. 21); *DTÖ* 22 (Bourgois, *Fortune*, 72, mm. 13 and 25).

dissonance of the structural voices. Such instances show that the contratenor has become strong enough to lend a new significance to impermissible intervals existing between the structural voices, i.e., to raise such intervals to the level of consonances. This became possible because the contratenor, in the process of compositional evolution, had been reworked from a dependent filling voice into one that had become concurrently decisive to the counterpoint.[27] As a result, the fourth [between the structural voices] was generally permitted by the theorists as long as another voice was placed under it, which ameliorated its dissonance.

We will now consider the cadence structures:

The most important and most frequent cadence in tonal discant was that described above (Example 19—[i.e., the triple-leading-tone cadence]). It was founded in the stepwise motion of the lowest voice (usually by descending second). It is recognizable by the stepwise relationship of [all voices in the progression of] sonorities.

The main cadences of free discant counterpoint were distinguishable in this: that the construction of the composition was defined by the structural voices of tenor and discantus (superius) and that all other voices, including any lying below, were subordinate to this condition. A similar extension of possibilities of counterpoint, as have been described above (the assimilation of fourth and tritone between the structural voices into the class of consonances,

---

[27]Besseler (*Bourdon und Fauxbourdon*, at the place cited above in note 6) says that the contratenor (in the works of Dufay) has become the director of sonorities. He derives this conclusion from the sole fact that the contratenor at times remains under the tenor at cadences, and from this circumstance he interprets the change in compositional style as happening at that time. However, as I have already demonstrated (see above, note 6), in order [to be able] to speak of the contratenor as director of sonorities, it is not enough that it [merely] remain below the tenor at cadences. Such a designation is only brought about when the contratenor simultaneously justifies an irregular progression in the structural voices. The [contratenor's] remaining under the tenor is to a certain extent merely an outward aspect, whereas [the question of] its indispensability affects the inmost nature of the counterpoint. This inner aspect is susceptible of investigation only to the extent that one attempts to relate the [writings of the] theorists to the structure of counterpoint [in surviving works]. These considerations lead to the conclusion that the stylistic shift is a product of Dunstable and not of Dufay (see below).

The designation "director of sonorities" [*Klangträger*], which Besseler applies to the contratenor when it remains under the tenor at cadences [the term Besseler usually uses is *Harmonieträger*], should actually be applied only to the contratenor of tonal discant and then only in conjunction with the tenor. Even in tonal-free discant composition the contratenor is not really a director of sonorities; rather, it merely legitimizes irregular vertical intervals existing between the voices above it, but the latter do not altogether lose their significance [as the basis of the composition]. [Instead,] they find themselves in mutual interaction with the contratenor.

under the condition that the contratenor take the fifth or the third beneath), now took place even at cadences: the theorists allowed the structural voices to cadence from diminished fifth to major third if the contratenor took the sixth below the tenor [at the penultimate] and progressed to an octave [with it].[28] In this manner the contratenor for the first time obtained genuine freedom to take the sixth under the tenor, through which the possibility of forming a diminished fifth was given to the structural voices. Here again, it is a question of the rational inclusion of what was originally a sonority occurring capriciously and of its incorporation into the free discant style of composition, whereby the tendency to place a contratenor tone under the [structural voices], not just at main sonorities but under any [given] vertical interval between the structural voices, contributed to the fashioning of a more active contratenor. In the cadence just described, the contratenor carries out the tenor's [nominal melodic] cadence, the descending step of a second, while the tenor closes with the [nominal] cadence of the discantus [i.e., the stepwise ascent]. This new potentiality of counterpoint signifies a further step in the evolution toward the Palestrina style, since the contratenor has a fresh possibility to proceed in a stepwise manner rather than in leaps and thus to fashion a melody.

[However,] we also find in the Trent codices compositions in which fourths occur particularly between the tenor and the uppermost voice, which cannot be understood as arising from incidental considerations, and [thus] retroactively rationalized. Rather, [the presence of such fourths] must be grounded in the distinctiveness of these pieces: the tenor brings forth a cantus firmus in long notes, while the contra comprises a two-voice entity with the top voice, as the tenor does with the superius in tonal-free discant composition (in which fourths occasionally occur).[29] These compositions

---

[28]See No. 2 of the three contrapuntal situations occurring in the *Missa Quinti toni*, introduced above in the fifth paragraph of this article. For a theoretical description, see Hugo Riemann, "Anonymi Introductorium musicae," *Monatshefte für Musikgeschichte* 30 (1898): 18, and, as an example, *DTÖ* 22 (Bedingham *Grant temps*, 70, m. 17). In the treatise just mentioned, several different cadences are described. One could add the following examples taken from contemporary works:

Ex a m p l e   2 0

(It should be noted that in the treatise, four-voice writing is not considered.)

[29]*DTÖ* 14-15 (Dufay, *Agnus papale*, 153; Dunstable, *Veni sancti spiritus* (No. 1), 201; Dunstable, *Veni sancti spiritus* (No. 2), 203). These pieces are discussed further below.

thus approximate those of the tonal-free type, and differ from the latter only in that the tenor proceeds more slowly and that the contra assumes the tenor's place and vice versa. Surely the fourths of the third type in the *Missa Quinti toni* of Ockeghem (see above) can only be due to a conception wherein the bassus was treated as the tenor and the tenor as a contra. The exchange of voice functions was made possible because the contratenor had become a voice of equal entitlement. The above-mentioned fourths in the *Missa Quinti toni* must thus stem from the same kind of counterpoint just discussed, which was cultivated especially by Dunstable (see below).

We thus hypothesize in the fifteenth century a refinement of the tonal style of counterpoint and a gradual alteration and disappearance of the free discant style, which is pervaded by [elements of] the tonal discant technique. As was already explained, tonal counterpoint could not be altered to such an extent that it could lead to the Palestrina style. Through [examination of] the structure of tonal counterpoint, it can be recognized that free discant counterpoint is the sole style that was susceptible of further development.

After the assimilation of the tonal principle into the free discant style, it was possible for the contratenor (or any lowest voice) to dictate and to direct [*tragen*] the cadences of all voice parts; the structural voices no longer had to be treated as a unity in the fashion of a free discant piece. The requirement now was that the lowest voice [make the] cadence, which now meant that it take the "ground-tone" [*Grundton*][30] (see Example 21). Thus, in works of the tonal-free style we again find cadences of the type previously described and also the parallel cadence, which now moves as is shown in Example 22. In the course of the alteration of free discant counterpoint by elements of the tonal technique, the fourth, the tritone, and the diminished fifth were gained as [elements of] musical awareness and musical composition. The voices accompanying the tenor were now composed simultaneously, and they now had an equal status. [Thus,] a three-voice discant counterpoint was produced from a tenor, discantus (superius), and bassus (or contra), in which the latter, to be sure, was dependent upon the structural voices, but these [structural voices] were also [themselves] subordinate to the contra whenever they were placed a fourth apart (Example 23).

---

[30]See the following places in the four-voice compositions in vol. 1 of the works of Ockeghem (see above, note 1): *Missa Au travail suis* (Kyrie, mm. 36-37); *Missa De plus en plus* (Credo, mm. 62-63, 234-35); *Missa Ecce ancilla domini* (Credo, mm. 92-93); *Missa L'homme armé* (Agnus, mm. 21-22); *Missa Ma maistresse* (Kyrie, mm. 13-14). This type of cadence is shown by the author in the study introduced above (note 7) as belonging to the tonal style of counterpoint, an opinion that should be confirmed here.

Examples   21   instead of   22

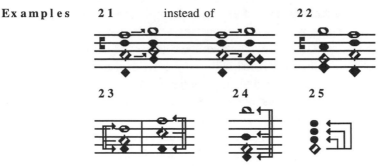

23   24   25

Just as the altus in four-voice pieces was previously allowed to have fourths in its relationship with the tenor, so now any kind of fourth was allowed to occur, except those occurring in connection with the lowest voice,[31] exactly as was the case in the multi-voice tonal discant style of composition. The difference, however, is that the voices are [now] mutually interdependent (Example 24), whereas [upper parts] in tonal counterpoint were merely placed [according] to the lowest voice without any [necessary] reference to each other (Example 25). The multifarious interdependency of the voices in tonal-free counterpoint is the principle of classical *a cappella* polyphony.

One can now ask whether the element of the tonal [discant technique] in pieces composed in the tonal-free style can still be discernible. This question is to be answered in the affirmative.

As an example, the *Missa Caput* of Ockeghem will serve.[C] [In this mass] the voices from low to high are designated tenor, tenor secundus, contra (contratenor in Codex [Trent] 88[D]); the uppermost voice is not labeled. The "tenor" (primus) moves almost throughout in long notes under the "tenor secundus." It behaves exactly as does a tenor in the refined tonal discant style: almost no fourths occur between it and the upper voices. But the same is true between tenor secundus and the upper voices. When considered from this perspective, the tenor secundus appears as a contratenor of a tonal discant composition. Upon closer inspection, however, it becomes evident that it

---

[31]Ever since this time the bass has [had] a certain priority above all other voices, since in connection to it (as lowest voice) the dissonance cannot be ameliorated. Only in a musical style that denies any differentiation between consonance and dissonance can the predominance of the bass in relation to vertical sonorities be taken away, thereby obtaining the freedom of an "absolute polyphony." (One thinks, for example, of the trends in composition during the 1920s.)

[C]Oswald Koller, et al., eds., *Sechs Trienter Codices, Dritte Auswahl, DTÖ* 38 (cited above), 59 ff.

[D]See the facsimile of the source, ibid., 49.

[also] acts as a tenor in tonal-free counterpoint, since it comports itself relative to the upper voice in the manner evinced by tenor and superius in Ockeghem's *Missa Quinti toni* (compare the cadences of tenor secundus and superius, and also [their behavior] within the individual movements). Thus, the tenor secundus is likewise a tenor—the tenor, so to speak, of a tonal-free discant piece, so that one must regard the nominal tenor [i.e., primus] in this work as the bassus of the entire composition. In this piece, then, are embodied simultaneously a refined four-voice tonal discant composition and one in the tonal-free discant technique. As a totality, however, it is a four-voice tonal-free composition, which is made evident particularly by the subordinate role of the tenor, since it pauses before the main cadences in order to allow the tenor secundus to effect its cadence with the other voices as in a three-voice free or tonal-free discant composition. In the course of the piece the following voice combinations cadence simultaneously: tenor and tenor secundus (Gloria, mm. 45-46); tenor and contra (Kyrie, m. 37); tenor and superius (Gloria, mm. 122-23); tenor secundus and contra (Kyrie, mm. 14-15); contra and superius (Gloria, m. 30)—all possible combinations thus occur. The interweaving of the whole and the parts demonstrates that two-voice discant relationships are in fact contained in three- and four-voice discant works. This is a composition in which the transformation of a free discant into a tonal-free discant structure is clearly recognizable.[32]

We find a similar composition in the motet No. VII, *Salve scema—Salve salus* of Dunstable.[33] With this work we come to the question of the position occupied by Dunstable in the history of musical style in the fifteenth century. The group of motets to which the above-mentioned work belongs might well symbolize the entire Trent codices. Of the 21 motets [of Dunstable], the first six (five three-voiced and one four-voiced) are free discant compositions of the type listed in note 29 above and described in the accompanying text. The three-voice motet No. XIII also belongs to this class. Nos. XV through XXI, on the other hand are three-voice works in free discant style as are Nos. IX and

---

[32]The fourths between the uppermost voice and the tenor are often suspensions (for example, 59, m. 21, fourth and fifth minims, and likewise 61, m. 30, etc.). At these places—through typical cadential leading of the upper voices in free discant—there result (I believe for the first time) six-four sonorities, which are related to the six-four chord of our harmonic cadence.

[33]Rudolf von Ficker, ed., *Sieben Trienter Codices, Sechste Auswahl, DTÖ* 76 [cited above in note B], No. VII, 43 ff.; also contained in Manfred Bukofzer, ed., *John Dunstable: Complete Works, Musica Britannica, A National Collection of Music*, vol. 8 (London: Stainer and Bell, 1953), No. 30, 81 ff.

X. The motets Nos. XI, XII, and XIV contain melismatic fourths in the structural voices, which are legitimized by the contratenor; these pieces thus belong to the group of works cited in notes 25 and 26 above. The motet No. VIII ultimately represents a refined tonal discant piece as it has been described above.[E]

In Dunstable's works we see everything in ferment. I would propose that he was a great stimulator and that he gave the impetus to the development discussed here in outline, since he was the oldest of the masters discussed above and since, on the one hand, that he as an Englishman was especially familiar with the style of tonal discant and, on the other, that he came into contact with the compositional styles of the Continent. The Netherlanders then evidently carried into full effect that which he had set into motion.

A moment ago we took a complete collection of motets into consideration. I would suggest that the development illustrated here was at its most advanced in the motet—[a genre] that stood between the categories of song (folk and secular music) and the mass. Thus, we find everything in flux also in the motets of Dufay. From the time of Dunstable, however, the mass also stepped to the forefront, above all in its unified cyclic form, so that from this point on we can trace the further development [of musical style] in this genre as well.

[E][See note 24 and its accompanying text. Full information on the modern editions of these works, presented in the order they are listed above, is given below. These listings show each work's number in *DTÖ* 76, with beginning page number in parenthesis, followed by the title of the motet, and then the corresponding work number and beginning page number from Bukofzer's edition, abbreviated *JD*:]

DTÖ	page	Title	JD	page	Remarks
XIII	(54)	*Specialis virgo*	31	(86)	
XV	(57)	*Salve regina mater mire*	63	(152)	Bukofzer doubts authorship
XVI	(58)	*Salve mater salvatoris*	62	(150)	Bukofzer doubts authorship
XVII	(60)	*Gaude virgo Katharine*	52	(129)	
XVIII	(61)	*Beata Dei genitrix*	41	(108)	
XIX	(63)	*Sancta Maria succurre*	49	(122)	
XX	(64)	*Speciosa facta es*	50	(124)	
XXI	(64)	*Gloria sanctorum*	43	(111)	
IX	(49)	*Regina celi*	38	(101)	
X	(50)	*Ave regina*	24	(62)	
XI	(51)	*Alma redemptoris*	40	(106)	
XII	(53)	*Ascendit Christus*	61	(148)	Bukofzer doubts authorship
XIV	(55)	*Sancta Dei genitrix*	47	(119)	
VIII	(46)	*Preco preheminencie*	29	(78)	

In summary: there exist clear intermediate forms between the tonal discant and the free discant techniques of counterpoint (the recognizable ones have been described above). However, the marked awareness of genre of the medieval musician, along with his constructive sense, always allow for a clear recognition of two basic techniques, so that one can separate cleanly the elements of a given work. Composition is a construction in which various techniques in all their individuality can be crafted simultaneously and with deliberate juxtaposition.[34]

By the middle of the fifteenth century, the cornerstone of the Palestrina style was laid, wherein the technique of free discant counterpoint was modified according to the paradigm of the tonal discant technique. The change consisted in this: that the fourth, tritone, and diminished fifth were incorporated as consonances into contrapuntal practice. This brought with it [the provision] that one no longer composed voices successively, as previously, but instead the several voices were added simultaneously to the tenor. The free discant technique that underwent alteration was already characterized by the interweaving of voices and by the progression of sonorities [moving from] the fifth to the first scale degree (V–I), which was conditioned by contrapuntal considerations. In this way the simultaneous conception of the voices could arise, and, hence, the style that one refers to as classical *a cappella* polyphony. At this point was reached the situation of musical composition that Tinctoris describes:[35]

... omnes partes rei factae sive tres, sive quattuor, sive plures sint, sibi mutuo obligentur, ita quod ordo lexque concordiantiarum cuiuslibet partis erga singulas et omnes observari debeat.[F]

---

[34]One could establish in each separate place cited in note 30 above, how old each is, and further, how it came to take its form.

[35]*Tractatus de musica*, CS 4, 129a. In the free and tonal-free discant styles of counterpoint there exist no chords and no chord progressions in our sense of the term, but only [two-voice] consonances and progressions of consonances, above all with respect to the tenor, but also between other voices, as appears from the music treatise of Cochlaeus around 1500. [Regarding this treatise,] see Bernhard Meier, "Die Harmonik im cantus-firmus-haltigen Satz des 15. Jahrhunderts," *Archiv für Musikwissenschaft* 9 (1952): 27-44 [translated above, see essay 4]. Meier's article deals with a somewhat later period [analyzing compositions of Obrecht, who died in 1505] and emphasizes the differentiation between the tonal structure of that time as opposed to that of later [art] music.

[F][Translation: "... all parts of written music, whether they be three, or four, or many, are mutually obligated to each other, and thus the order and rules of concords should be observed between any and all parts, just as for each individual part."]

6

The Cantus-Firmus Question
in the Fourteenth and Early Fifteenth Centuries

Günther Schmidt

EDITOR'S PREFACE: *Schmidt's is a prime example of a significant, yet neglected, study stemming from the German sphere. Citations of this article in English-language scholarship are rare, despite the fact that it is the most comprehensive overview of its subject ever written, and clearly outlines any number of potential avenues for further study. Many of these directions still remain unexplored after nearly forty years. The contrapuntal issues raised in the studies of Meier and Apfel (translated above) are deepened and placed into a highly interesting perspective by Schmidt in this article. Particularly illuminating is the author's consideration of the constructive aspects of the cantus firmus within the historical context of its symbolic and liturgical function.*

The problems to which questions regarding the cantus firmus (c.f.) lead are not new to musicological research. In general, the term c.f. is understood to be the use of a borrowed melody, sacred or secular, as the basis of a new composition.[1] The observations hitherto made regarding the c.f. can be largely classified as adhering to this definition. Questions have been asked about the origins of the c.f., about its voice disposition, [and] about its constructive function in the building of a musical composition.[2] Above all it has been the constructive significance of the c.f. that has been emphasized. Also, its symbolic importance has been pointed out. In truth, the c.f. corresponds to this conception in the polyphony of the central Middle Ages.[3] But is the essence of the c.f. as a factor of musical creation—[which is] the actual c.f.

---

[1] See Heinrich Husman's article, "Cantus Firmus," *MGG*, vol. 3 (1954), cols. 784-99.

[2] Manfred Bukofzer's chapters on cantus firmus treatment and "Caput" in *Studies in Medieval and Renaissance Music* (New York: Norton, 1950), do not essentially exceed this scope.

[3] See Rudolf von Ficker, "Die Musik des Mittelalters und ihre Beziehungen zum Geistesleben," *Deutsche Vierteljahrschrift für Literaturwissenschaft und Geistesgeschichte* 3 (1925): 501-35.

problem, the issue that led to a "problematic" of the c.f. [and] which stands as a driving force behind its history—comprehended with the "artistic" (constructive) and potentially symbolic conception of the connection between c.f. and new composition?

It is thought provoking that Heinrich Besseler,[4] for instance—to take a conspicuous example—could say about fauxbourdon, that "with it originated again in the realm of the liturgy, for the first time in a long time, a new form, which served the rite exclusively."[5] This sentence makes it perfectly clear that between c.f. and [any] new musical technique that is based upon it, a more basic genetic connection also comes into play. In fauxbourdon, a direct influence of the c.f. upon the musical structure is obvious, since the exceptional suitability of fauxbourdon for the liturgy and its virtually invariable limitation to this [realm] can scarcely be explained through [any] other set of circumstances.[6] It is the purpose of the present study to point out various phenomena that make recognizable the one unmediated influence the c.f. exerts on the composition that is built upon it. From that perspective the c.f. has a special significance for the fourteenth and fifteenth centuries. In order to comprehend this fully, one must be clear about the origins and historical development of the c.f.

In the Middle Ages, the term "cantus firmus"—generally referred to by the theorists simply as *cantus*—is at first identical simply with *cantus planus*: *cantus firmus sive planus, praecipue ecclesiasticus cantus.*[A] In its essence, cantus planus is exclusively a predetermined linear-melodic unfolding[7]—one that is presumably also rhythmically undifferentiated.[8] This character is almost strictly peculiar to the so-called Gregorian chant. The cantus planus is hence often simply identified with chant.[9] But what is decisive is that the cantus firmus, i.e., a cantus planus taken over for [purposes of] a polyphonic

---

[4]Heinrich Besseler, *Bourdon und Fauxbourdon* (Leipzig: Breitkopf & Härtel, 1950), 146.

[5]Fauxbourdon is not itself a form but rather a harmonic technique. On page 146 of the above mentioned book [note 4], Besseler says that fauxbourdon was used "as a compositional principle." On the contrary, the form of the composition was much more dependent upon what sort of c.f. procedures were followed.

[6]See Besseler, *Bourdon*, 21 and 45, with tables.

[A]*Discantus positio vulgaris, CS* 1, 89. [Translation: "fixed or plain song, principally ecclesiastical song"]

[7]Rudolf von Ficker, in "Die Musik des Mittelalters," [see above, note 3], 512, and "Die frühen Messenkompositionen der Trienter Codices," *Studien zur Musikwissenschaft* 11 (1924): 17 ff., has already indicated this line of thought.

[8]Husmann, "Cantus firmus," *MGG*, vol. 3, col. 786, considers rhythmic equality as a given.

[9]The theorists writing in English always use the term "plainsong."

composition, has as its point of departure the unfolding of a linear-melodic entity. This primary quality of the c.f. survives in the parallel (fifth-octave) organum transmitted in the *Musica enchiriadis*. The doubling of the cantus planus in exclusively perfect consonances, here [seen] for the first time as c.f. of a polyphonic complex, is only a secondary factor. The primary factor is the chant as such, sung simultaneously in different registers that are completely consonant with each other. [In such organa,] cantus firmus and planus are identical, even in their result. This holds true also for the so-called organum at the fourth, which is presumably somewhat later. Here, as is well known, the c.f. lies in the upper voice, [a circumstance] conditioned by the exigencies of ordering the fourths. The location of the c.f. thus results in a specific treatment of sonorities in the two types, respectively.

With the introduction of a [more] "artistic" conception of composition within early polyphony, the c.f. undergoes a deep-rooted change in its significance. Its melodic unfolding is reassessed to [that of] a potential director of sonorities [*Klangträger*]. The c.f. is looked upon solely as an aggregation of individual tones, which are rendered usable for the purpose of building vertical sonorities. The c.f. henceforth conducts itself in a manner diametrically opposed to its originally intended purpose.[10] This process is fittingly characterized in [contemporary] theory by its framing of the rules of consonance progression. The theorists were interested only in the vertical progression to which the individual tones of the c.f. were ordered, not, however, in what occurred in its intervening distance.[11]

Here the c.f. still acts only as an intellectual and constructive acknowledgment of legitimacy with respect to the liturgy. In this function, the c.f. becomes a foundation or root voice, and is generally identified simply with the "tenor." In the original definition as "chant," and the [subsequent] identification with "tenor," the polarity of the c.f. problem is embodied.

In the *Ars nova* the chant as c.f. has been very strongly estranged from its liturgical obligation through the incomplete—often only fragmentary— presentation of a framework. Such a state of affairs was, in the long run, not sustainable; also, it would not have been able to prevent an all-too pronounced penetration of incompatible elements into sacred music. The dismemberment of the chant in an isorhythmic c.f. must necessarily have also destroyed its

---

[10]Particulars of this development must be left out of consideration in this introductory overview.

[11]See Rudolf von Ficker, "Der Organumtraktat der Vatikanischen Bibliothek (Ottob. 3025)," *Kirchenmusikalisches Jahrbuch* 27 (1932): 73 ff.; Ernst Apfel, "Der Diskant in der Musiktheorie des 12.–15. Jahrhunderts" (dissertation, University of Heidelberg, 1953).

symbolic power, which hitherto had been thought of in constructive terms as well. This, in turn, had to lead to a conflict with the demands of the liturgy. References to this situation can be seen as early as the Second Council of Lyon in 1274, whose decrees of sacred music were recorded in the *Liber Sextus* of the canonic law (completed in 1298).[12] This situation is most clearly reflected in the well-known Bull, *Docta sanctorum*, of the reform pope John XXII from 1324-25—clear precisely because it reveals a detailed familiarity of the stylistic characteristics of the *Ars nova*: *Adeo ut interdum antiphonarii et gradualis fundamenta despiciant, ignorent super quo aedificant.*[13] This passage, as well as others, make it palpably evident that the main concern of the Bull was to address and reform the collapse of the chant in art music intended for the church. An excerpt such as the following cannot be aimed at ruling out artistic creation in sacred music, as it could have the appearance of doing:

> Per hoc autem non intendimus prohibere, quin interdum, diebus festis praecipue, sive sollemnibus in missis et praefatis divinis officiis aliquae consonantiae, quae melodiam sapiunt, puta octavae, quintae, quartae et huiusmodi supra *cantum ecclesiasticum* simplicem proferantur, sic tamen ut ipsius *cantus integritas* illibata permaneat.[B]

Rather, its purpose was directed towards the preservation of the chant, in whose polyphonic treatment, moreover, a component of individuality was not intended to remain forbidden. The stylistic principles of the *Ars nova*, and the previous ones of the *Ars antiqua*[14] were in not the common currency, artistically speaking, of musical cultivation in the West. On the contrary, they embrace a highly developed center of art that is limited to a specific area, namely the Isle de France and Champagne. Nor is it by mere chance that the

---

[12]See Otto Ursprung, *Die katholischen Kirchenmusik* (Potsdam: Athenaion, 1931).

[13]Published by Franz X. Haberl, "Die römische 'schola cantorum' und die päpstlichen Kapellsänger bis zur Mitte des 16. Jahrhunderts," *Vierteljahrsschrift für Musikwissenschaft* 3 (1887): 210 ff. [Translation: "When at times these [modern composers] disdain the foundational [melodies] of the Antiphonal and the Gradual, they are ignorant of that upon which they build."]

[B][Translation: "But by this we do not mean to prohibit—chiefly on certain feast days or for solemnities at mass or to introduce the divine Offices—the occasional superimposition of octaves, fifths, fourths and [intervals] of this kind (which are discerned [as an integral] melody) upon the *simple ecclesiastical song* [i.e., plainchant]; however, this must be done such that the *integrity of the chant* is preserved unimpaired." The emphasis is Schmidt's.]

[14]With respect to the two stylistic concepts, see the corresponding articles of Heinrich Besseler, *MGG*, vol. 1 (1949-51), cols. 679 ff. and 698 ff.

development of the typical conception for the Gothic cathedral was also concentrated in this region (Chartres, Paris, Reims, Amiens). Outside of this sphere, the practice of liturgical polyphony had hardly more than reached the status of a stylized organum of [the type described in] the *Musica enchiriadis*.[15] Conspicuous in this connection is the notation that one sometimes sees, scattered throughout the general liturgical manuscripts.[16] This circumstance strengthens the assumption that such a musical practice was cultivated widely as *Discantus ex improviso*.[17]

With the increasingly broad effects of the *Ars nova* began a perceptible, and to some extent more systematic, increase in the writing down of pieces acting to restore the liturgy.[18] This is to be interpreted as documentation of a conscious new liturgical tendency in the face of the *Ars nova*, since these tradition-bound compositions, which the fourteenth century transmits to us in great number, do not in any way renounce a further artistic stylization, but at the same time they plainly preserve the c.f. as chant.[19] This musical practice—a necessary step in developmental history—made it possible to give new stimulus to the equalization of these oppositions. However, seen in its totality, [an equalization] could not subsequently result, since the sonority remained here subordinate with respect to the chant. In this context, an equalization could only take place where the possibility was offered for a uniformity between the c.f. as a choral melody and the tonal realization of the composition.

In this connection, the testimony of the theorist Simon Tunstede is of some significance. In his *Quatuor principalia* (1351) he characterizes English discant as *alium modum discantandi* [the other method of discanting]:

---

[15]See Arnold Geering, *Die Organa und mehrstimmigen Conductus in den Handschriften des deutschen Sprachgebietes vom 13. bis 16. Jahrhunderts* (Bern: Haupt, 1952), 58 ff.

[16]See Geering, *Die Organa*, 6 ff.

[17]Anonymous 2, *CS* 1, 311. See Jacques Handschin, "Die Rolle der Nationen in der mittelalterlichen Musikgeschichte," *Schweizerisches Jahrbuch für Musikwissenschaft* V (1931): 1-42. In the twelfth and thirteenth centuries, organum was frequently looked upon as the French manner of singing. Documentary evidence points towards a direct adoption of French discant. What is more, a certain parallel between German, Spanish, and English sources is discernible. These facts, as well as [evidence from] the French manuscript London BM Add. 16 975 and Egerton 945, and further, the *Scientia artis musicae* (1274) of Elias Salomonis (*GS* 3, 16 ff.), point towards [the existence of] another center for the cultivation of organum, standing outside the Parisian school, [the location of] which today is hard to ascertain.

[18]See Geering, *Die Organa*, 8 ff.

[19]See Geering, *Die Organa*, 61.

In isto enim modo plures super planum cantum discantare apparebunt, cum tamen in rei veritate unus tantum discantabit, *alii vero planum cantum in diversis concordantibus* modulantibus....^C

Bukofzer has seen in these words the main argument that in English discant,[20] the lowest c.f. voice, i.e., the tenor is to be [understood] in the sense of a ground voice, and he has portrayed this as a fundamental principle.[21]

---

^CTunstede [attrib.], *Quatuor principalia*, chapter XLI, *CS* 4, 294. [Translation: "For in this method many seem to sing a discant above plainsong, but in truth only one is discanting, *the others actually* accompany *the cantus planus in various concords*"; the emphasis is Schmidt's.]

[20]Manfred Bukofzer, *Geschichte des englischen Diskants und des Fauxbourdons nach den theoretischen Quellen* (Strasbourg: Heitz, 1936), 20.

[21]However, in his article "Discantus," *MGG*, vol. 3 (1954), col. 573, Bukofzer aims to correct his opinion to the extent that Tunstede really was not describing the English discant but rather "an archaic improvisational practice, in which a decorated parallel organum of three voices is amalgamated with a fourth voice in thirds and sixths." However, Bukofzer does not discuss the specifics of how this improvisation was supposed to have been accomplished. It is not readily understandable how Tunstede could not have been referring to English discant when he contrasts "another type of discanting" with the typical Continental discant technique: "... *primus incipiet planum cantum in tenore, secundum ponet vocem suam in quinta voce; tertius vero in octava voce; et quartus,* si fuerit {i.e., only one further possibility!} *ponet vocem suam in duodecima voce.*" ["First, one begins with the plainsong in the tenor; secondly, one places a part to it at the fifth; thirdly, [one places a part] at the octave; and fourth, *if there is to be [another] part,* one places it at the twelfth [to the tenor.]"] Thus, the same assignation of a specific intervallic distance between the tenor and the individual voices exists here as is familiar in English discant. "*Is vero discantabit, vocem suam minime* {!} *ponet in concordantia perfecta, sed* tantummodo {!} *in concordantiis imperfectis, videlicet in tertia, et sexta et in decima....*" ["He who will discant truly will do so very little if he sets his voice in perfect consonance [with the tenor], but *only* [if he sets his voice] in imperfect consonances, for example in thirds, in sixths, and in tenths...."] Here, Bukofzer apparently is applying the phrase *is vero discantabit* only to one discanting voice. But even on the face of things, that is incomprehensible, since the names of the imperfect consonances correspond in analogous fashion to the interval distances of the discant voices as introduced at the beginning [of the treatise]. If Bukofzer were correct that the thirds and sixths were reserved for the fourth voice only, then it would not be understandable why the third and tenth are specified. It is out of the question that the fourth voice, which as expressly stipulated is supposed to begin at the twelfth, could take the third above the tenor. Bukofzer misinterprets discant theory as fundamentally differentiating only between c.f. (*planum cantum in tenore*) and discant voice[s], not, however, between the various discant voices among themselves. The possible part ranges of the discant voices are given in the very mention of their respective interval distances [from the tenor]. Correspondingly, the discussions of the consonance progressions also take into consideration only the various possibilities of part register. In discant there is no specified number of voices; rather, various part dispositions are possible—generally two to four. That the theory does not go into the interrelationship of the discant voices and does not treat them individually in a concrete

Georgiades points out the primary harmonic conception of English discant,[22] which is verified in the same citation, wherein the voices added to the c.f. are to be conceived in the sense of doublings. If one takes the essence and meaning of the c.f. also into consideration, the result is an enlargement of Georgiades's interpretation, that the discant voices were likewise thought of as *planus cantus in diversis concordantibus* ["plainsong in various concords"]. This conception is, no doubt, the decisive factor. The c.f. was thought of not just as the director of sonorities [*Klangträger*] (tenor). In its fundamental properties, the c.f. in English discant maintains its original significance as in the ancient parallel organum. On the other hand, the treatment of sonorities brings a new factor, in which the predominant (*tantummodo!*) use of imperfect intervals is called for. For this reason, possibilities completely different from those of the practice as it developed on the Continent were offered to the c.f. in English discant .

The fragment, Cambridge, Gonville and Caius College, MS 727/334 (CbC)[23] transmits on fol. IIa the fragment of an Introit (texts from the 70th and 30th Psalms, the latter still used today at Quinquagesima; Example 1).

---

fashion is grounded in the technique that it teaches: [this technique] does not depend on the consonant relationship between the discant voices; rather, they are only required to be consonant with the tenor (which is always identified in theory with the c.f.). As a consequence of this [approach], the musical examples offered by the theorists are always given in two voices. But that in no way means that discant composition was meant in principle to be [exclusively] two-voiced, since the examples also indicate the respective range possibilities in the realization of the rules of consonance progression—and this is analogous to the voice registers given as possible in stipulating a specific beginning interval with the tenor. The wording "but he who wishes to discant ..." cannot be interpreted in a literal translation as a limitation to one single discanting voice. This formulation is indeterminately prescribed, exactly as is the one referring to the number of voices. In other matters Bukofzer would have done well to follow again the opinion of Hugo Riemann, *Geschichte der Musiktheorie* (Leipzig: Breitkopf & Härtel, 1921), 122, which he had at first refuted convincingly.

[22]Thrasybulos Georgiades, *Englische Diskanttraktate aus der ersten Hälfte des 15. Jahrhunderts* (Munich: Musikwissenschaftliches Seminar der Universität München, 1937), 86 ff.

[23]See Henry Davey, *History of English Music*, 2nd ed. (London: Curwen, 1921), 27 ff. This source is also mentioned—with the abbreviated siglum CbC—by Heinrich Besseler, "Studien zur Musik des Mittelalters [Part] I," *Archiv für Musikwissenschaft* 7 (1925): 220.

Example 1: Introitus, CbC, fol. IIa (■ = ♩)

mi- se ri-cor-di-a tu- a   do- mi - ne su - per   nos,   qui ad modum spe- ra - vi - mus   in   te.

A rather unchallenging piece in itself, this can only be valued as simple liturgical currency of the time. On the other hand, the scheme of sonority formation is here particularly noteworthy. The tuba (*tonus currens*) of the psalm tone is exclusively supported by an 8-5 sonority, in a stereotypical manner. But at one cadence of the psalm tone (here appearing as the c.f.), a sequence of parallel 6-3 sonorities is formed. Thus, the melodic cadence proceeds in conformity with the harmonic cadence. The variation of vertical intervals is thus dependent upon the two melodic—or, to put it more exactly, melic—components of the c.f., namely the *tuba* and the cadence. It is significant that the impetus of melodic motion at the cadences is tied in with imperfect sonorities. The dissonant value of third and sixth in the Middle Ages was founded primarily in their tendencies of movement: *Praesertim imperfecta concordantia ab instabilitate sua merito denominatur, quae de loco movetur in locum et per se inter nullas certas invenitur proportiones....*[24] Whenever several imperfect intervals followed each other successively and in parallel motion, the anticipatory quality of movement was heightened due to the delayed resolution. In other words, as long as a melodic figure was not terminated, the vertical cadence could also be held in check—melody and sonority complemented each other with a combined effect that was new.

In the first section of the Introitus, the c.f. is located in the middle voice, a circumstance that points to its separation from [being] the root of sonorities. The second section brings a new c.f. (*Tedeum*) into the low voice (tenor). This section is rich in 6-3 sonorities, corresponding to the much more prominent melodic gestures of its new c.f.[25]

---

[24]Tunstede [attrib.], *CS* 4, 290b. [Translation: "Firstly, on account of their instability, they are called imperfect concords, which are moved from place to place and which in themselves prove to be of no definite proportions...."] Compare the similar characterization in Marchettus de Padua, *GS* 3, 83.

[25]This excerpt is published in Bukofzer, *Geschichte des englischen Diskants*, Example 18, and in the same author's article "Discantus," *MGG*, col. 573 ff., Example 7.

The fragment CbC belongs to the oldest English sources, which transmit discant compositions of an individual nature, diverging from Continental practice. Bukofzer[26] assigns this manuscript to the second half of the thirteenth century; Davey,[27] however, dates it around 1350. The two Sanctus on fol. I, to be discussed below, display the *longa-brevis* notation typical of the thirteenth century. The first section of the Introitus just mentioned is clearly notated at the breve-semibreve level, which, of course, is conditioned by the use of a c.f. from psalmody. Particular types of notation thus seem to be appropriate only as a basis for provisional dating. If one considers the style of all pieces surviving in fragmentary form—see above all Example 3—the manuscript [at hand] can hardly be fixed any earlier than 1300.

In the manuscript Oxford, Magdalen College, MS 267, there exist further pieces of this sort: fol. 90v, 91r, and 92r (*Canticum Simeonis*). The beginning sections of these pieces are always missing, but such omissions are not always due to missing leaves; above all, this cannot be advanced as a cause in the two *cantica* (see Example 2 below), since in these pieces the c.f. begins with the psalmodic *initium*. The beginning sections, accordingly, were presumably executed as chant; this kind of practice is frequently encountered in the fourteenth century. One speaks here in general of Lessons with polyphonic line-endings, which can also [be used to] expand entire sections. In connection with the Introitus in CbC, the three-voice Lesson *Cum natus est* from the manuscript Geneva, UB, Cod. lat. 38b, fol. 37r–40v is noteworthy. Here, the polyphonic line-endings correspond in their vertical treatment exactly to the cadences of the Introitus.[28] The Lesson of the Gospel text follows in chant, but [in the concluding polyphony] the c.f. wanders from the low voice (tenor) to the middle voice (contra) at the fifth [above], and subsequently to the upper voice (altus) at the octave, corresponding in each case to a given section of text. The concluding section is entirely set in three parts. In principle, this is only a variant of the practice in CbC.

This "homophonic recitation" [*Klangdeklamation*] again enters the foreground in the Italian *falsobordone* pieces of the late fifteenth century. These works are, however, not simply derivatives of fauxbourdon, rather, [they are] grounded in the type of homophonic declamation just discussed, with which they also have in common the distinctive affiliation with psalm

---

[26]Bukofzer, *Geschichte des englischen Diskants*, 115.

[27]Davey, *History of English Music*, 27.

[28]The beginning of this Lesson is contained in Geering, *Organa*, Example 1, which, moreover, draws attention to the pronounced 6—>8 cadences. Later, related examples of this recitation technique can be seen in Trent, nos. 111, 167, 169, 1059, 1166.

recitation. Judging from [works contained in] the considerable number of German sources of the fourteenth and fifteenth centuries,[29] these procedures would seem to represent a continually progressing practice within the liturgy. The only parallel in which the Italian designation *falsobordone* appears to be beholden to fauxbourdon is in their common stereotypical character.

Also belonging to this complex is the copy of a *Canticum Mariae* contained in the fragment Cambridge, UB MS Kk 1.6. (CbB),[30] fol. 247r–247v, contemporary with CbC but which assumes an exceptional place.

Example 2: *Canticum Mariae*, CbB, fol. 247r-v (■ = 𝅗𝅥)

qui - a   re spe- xit hu-mi- li- ta- tem   an - cil - la su - e   ec- ce

e-nim ex   hoc be- a- tamme di - cent om-nes ge-ne- ra - ti - o - nes.

The piece repeats four times the section given in Example 2. However, a new element is the replacement of the 8-5 sonority by the 5-3 sonority as support for the *tuba*. The c.f. here is also located in the middle voice. In Example 1, while the c.f. in the first section was no longer identical with the lowest pitch, its priority was disturbed only in a relatively weak manner due to [the stability provided by] the 8-5 sonority, whereas here the c.f. is clearly and markedly separated from the tenor by the deliberate application of the third. In this way it occurs that the parallel 6-3 progressions disappear, even at those places where the c.f. makes a melodic cadence. This circumstance stands out as a characteristic of all pieces that place the c.f. in the middle voice and which are constructed according to the principles of English discant. The

[29]See Geering, *Organa*, 31 ff. and 74 ff.

[30]This fragment, under the siglum CbB, is cursorily mentioned by Besseler, "Studien zur Musik des Mittelalters [Part] I," 220.

reasons for this will be discussed below. The sole exception can be observed in the final cadences, as in mm. 8, 15, and 17, whose special function lies [precisely] in their closing quality.

In previous research it has often been emphasized as a hard fact that in English discant the c.f. lay principally in the low voice (tenor).[31] One gained thereby an impression of the c.f. in the sense of a ground-voice [*Grundstimme*], i.e., a potential director of sonorities. Based on deliberations upon the inner structure of English discant, von Ficker had turned against this view,[32] as meanwhile the results of source studies also provided contradictory evidence. The manuscript CbC transmits on fol. Ib the fragment of a Sanctus with Benedictus, which unambiguously assigns the c.f. (*Graduale Romanum IV*) to the upper voice.

Example 3: Sanctus, CbC, fol. Ib (■ = ♩)

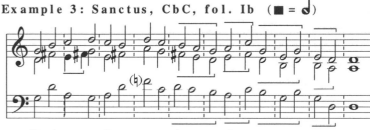

Ple-ni sunt ce-li et   ter-ra glo - ri - a   tu - a,   O -

san - na   in   ex - cel - - - - sis.

*This measure cannot be transcribed with certainty.

Bukofzer has already mentioned this piece, considering it as the oldest document of "choral discant," from which he judged it to be of English origin.[33] However, it is likely that the utilization of a c.f. in the upper voice is not specifically an English invention. In the older manuscripts of the fourteenth century (Maigrauge, Cod. 4, fol. 146, and Karlsruhe, Cod. St.

---

[31]See Bukofzer, "Discantus," *MGG*, vol. 3, col. 573 ff.

[32]Rudolf von Ficker, "Zur Schöpfungsgeschichte des Fauxbourdon," *Acta Musicologica* 23 (1951): 98. [Translated above, see essay 2.]

[33]Bukofzer, *Geschichte des englischen Diskants*, 115.

Peter, perg. 29a, fol. 37–38) exist Kyrie compositions that assign the c.f. (*Graduale Romanum* V) to the upper voice. The Benedicamus trope *Nova laude terra plaude* in the manuscript Geneva, UB, Cod. lat. 30a, fol. 159v— which stems from the thirteenth century—divides the c.f. (first Vespers) sectionally between the lower and upper voices. Thus it may on the contrary be assumed that the various possibilities for the c.f. with respect to part range were a matter of common usage, as was established [even] in the two basic types of organum of the *Musica enchiriadis*.[34] The external appearance of the c.f. in a specific part register does not render it valid to consider cadential progressions as events with developmental consequence as long as the mutual prerequisites of c.f. and counterpoint are not in contact [with each other]. The position of the c.f. at any given time was dependent upon which aspect of the c.f. the composition was based on. The Sanctus in CbC is significant in an evolutionary sense, not so much because of its having a c.f. in the upper voice; rather, its interest is due much more to the way in which the progression of sonorities is related to the c.f. In this context, Bukofzer's observation must remain incomprehensible, that the piece is "not, however, [structured] with preference for 6-3 accompaniment, but rather in the standard three-voice counterpoint."[35] In spite of several poorly discernible notes, this Sanctus is not difficult to transcribe, yet already in the manuscript there occurs almost stereotypical voice leading in fourths between the upper and middle voice, which of course must create 6-3 progressions. The piece thus conforms to the simplest form of English discant as it is known from the theory.

The valuation of the c.f. as fundamental voice [*Fundamentstimme*] in English discant has resulted in the all-too-literal exegesis of the theoretical

---

[34]In the fourteenth century there are yet further examples of c.f. in the upper voices. Geering (*Die Organa*, 44) is of the definite opinion that the upper-voice c.f. was probably specified earlier in the Ballade-style compositions than in the *organum sub voce* pieces, but the source situation itself may stand in the way of such an interpretation, if a wandering c.f. [can be shown to] occur in the thirteenth-century sources. Moreover, it cannot be understood that organa, so tightly bound by tradition—especially those works stemming from an almost exclusively cloistered musical cultivation—should not have been created out of their own conditioning factors but rather only under a stimulus that had been provided by secular music. In the former art of composition [i.e., organum,] that would not have constituted an insuperable contradiction. In addition, such an opinion [as that advanced by Geering] contradicts the findings of Heinrich Besseler in his article "Ballade," *MGG*, vol. 1 (1949-51), col. 1122, that it was only after 1330 (!) that the polyphonic Ballade gradually took on significance.

[35]Bukofzer, *Geschichte des englischen Diskants*, 115.

formulation as improvisation.[36] Only from this point of view could Bukofzer ever arrive at his hypothesis cited above, since the c.f. in the upper voice and [the concept of] English discant seemed to him to be completely irreconcilable.[37] Above all, it should be understood that in English discant, it is the tenor alone that is always the foundational voice [*Fundamentstimme*] in the sense of [being] a director of sonorities,[38] i.e., it alone is decisive for the building of sonorities. Accordingly, all voices must be consonant with the tenor, although not [necessarily] with each other.[39] The voice leading in fourths between the upper and middle voice in Example 3 is accordingly insignificant, since these voices comprise either an 8-5 or a 6-3 relationship with the tenor. Logically, the theory must always proceed from the tenor in a polyphonic technique such as this. The c.f. *can* be equivalent to the lowest voice, but this is not [to be viewed as] a principle. Also, no debate is required that in the didactic demonstrations of improvisation—which one considers even today as the best method of mastering the theory—the c.f. has to be identical with the tenor.[40] In its simplest form, [then,] English discant became the principle for *res facta*, a fact to which no less prominent an authority than Leonel Power testifies: "This tretis ... for hem that wil by syngers *or makers* or techers."[41]

The decisive thing is that, in English discant, the possibility was given to release the c.f. from its old constructive function as fundamental [voice]. Once the c.f. was freed from these fetters, it could become functional again to the composition in its original role as a melodic entity.

---

[36] Another opinion concerning this has already been given by Georgiades, *Englische Diskanttraktate*, 94.

[37] A further evidence for this is Bukofzer's singular interpretation of the English pieces with c.f. in the middle voice as gymel with added triplum. See below.

[38] It is significant that as early as 1338, Robert Mannyng juxtaposes [the terms] "treble, mene, and bordoun." See Hermann F. Flasdieck, "Französische Fauxbourdon und frühneuenglische Faburden," *Acta Musicologica* 25 (1953): 113, §2.

[39] See Ernst Apfel, "Der klangliche Satz und der freie Diskantsatz im 15. Jahrhundert," *Archiv für Musikwissenschaft* 12 (1955): 302 ff. [Translated above, see essay 5.]

[40] This theoretical one-sidedness is eliminated in the treatise of Pseudo-Chilston (see below, note 46) by the segregated treatment of the added voices, such as countertenor or counter. In this manner the theoretical connection to *res facta* is also effected. The "counter" described in Chapter 3 (which is strictly to be differentiated from "countertenor"), when considered as a true bass part, [shows] the characteristics of a *res facta* in a theoretical sense as well.

[41] London, BM, Landsdowne 763, No. 16, fol. 105v. [The emphasis in the above quotation is Schmidt's].

As Bukofzer has rightly emphasized, the constructive foundations of English discant were the same as those of the older Continental discant treatises.[42] The main difference between the two techniques consisted primarily in the systematically executed alternation between perfect and imperfect sonorities, which brought about a true polarity between harmonic "tension and release."[43] The tendency of the imperfect intervals towards motion acted naturally for the benefit of the melodic qualities of the c.f., particularly when it was no longer situated as the lowest voice.

The above findings are impressively corroborated by the repertory of the Old Hall manuscript (*OH*). Of the fifty mass movements transmitted by this source that are particularly important in this connection (although the others also are composed in a similar fashion), there are only three that incorporate a c.f. in the tenor (lowest voice).[44] Among the surviving three-voice pieces, 22 works place the c.f. in the middle voice. These c.f. are derived either from the [contemporary chants represented in the] *Graduale Romanum* or from the Use of Sarum. In *OH* 53, 55, 92, 93, 100, 103, 104, 106, 120, 122, 123, 126a, 127, and 128, the c.f. is transposed up a fifth with respect to Sarum; in *OH* 121a, the c.f. is transposed up a fifth with respect to [the piece as represented in] *Graduale Romanum*.[45] In this regard, *OH* 105, a Sanctus of Leonel, is also interesting, since in this piece the c.f. appears untransposed with respect to *Graduale Romanum* XVIII, yet it is a third higher (final of C) compared to Sarum 10. The piece as a whole stands in F, so that the c.f. likewise assumes a fifth relationship in connection to the tenor. The above observations are applicable [also] to the fragment London, BM, Add. 40011B (LoF), stemming from about the same time as *OH*. This principle of transposing the c.f. up a fifth represents of course nothing other than the vertical ordering of the c.f. to the tenor (lower voice). In this way the tenor is clearly defined as the director of sonorities, without being a c.f. In the theory of English discant, it is well known that the situation of the middle voice (mene) is thought of as a mental transposition of the c.f. (or tenor, as the case may be) at the fifth.[46] This

---

[42]Bukofzer, "Discantus," *MGG*, vol. 3, col. 573.

[43]Ficker, "Zur Schöpfungsgeschichte des Fauxbourdon," 101. This interpretation is also adopted by Bukofzer, "Discantus," *MGG*, vol. 3, col. 574.

[44]See Bukofzer, *Studies in Medieval and Renaissance Music*, 47-8. The numbering of the pieces as given by Bukofzer will be retained here.

[45]In *OH* 53, 55, 92, 93, 100, 103, 120, 122, and 126a, the c.f. in Sarum is identical with *Graduale Romanum*.

[46]London, BM, Landsdowne 763, no. 16, fol. 113 (Pseudo-Chilston): "The mene beginnyth in a 5te aboue the plainsong in vois and with the plainsong in sighte."

artifice was subsequently applied also in the realm of *res facta* in order to ensure a certain sense of tonal closure among the voices in works created as free and technically polished entities. Later, Ramus de Pareia prescribed this as a generally requisite principle: *Servet quoque modum in arsi et thesi, hoc est, ab inferiori voce ad altiorem sui ipsius sit modus ordinatus ut tropus.*[D] The transposition of a c.f. in a specific interval to the tenor was in discant technique the simplest and most logical realization of this principle.

Bukofzer, who has denied [the possibility of] English discant as *res facta* more than he has affirmed it, was led to surmise, from the conspicuous fact that those pieces with a c.f. in the middle voice fundamentally avoid 6-3 progressions, that these cannot be explained as discant pieces but rather as gymels with an added triplum.[47] Within the sphere of this conception, only the "sixth-chord style" pieces would be considered by him as English discant. In response to this, it should first be remarked that the quality of alternating intervallic qualities [i.e., perfect-imperfect], typical of English discant, can also be produced through the appearance of 5-3 sonorities in the place of 6-3 ones. In this respect, the compositions with c.f. in the middle voice follow exactly the same principles of English discant as do those that carry the c.f. in the upper or lower voice (the latter only occurring occasionally at this point) and are characterized by the "sixth-chord style." Also, those works considered by Bukofzer to be "gymels," consisting of c.f. and tenor, do not display these characteristics. Terminologically, "gymel" refers to "twin song" (Latin: *gemellus*).[48] In principle, this is a two-voice piece, wherein the second part is derived through the doubling of *one* voice in thirds and sixths, chiefly running parallel. Hence, cadences at the unison are typical for this kind of piece, and consequently there is no question here of a real two-voice structure. The crossing of voices, which is often to be observed, seems rather as a stylization but is conditioned precisely by the cadencing at the unison. Gymel is— corresponding to its designation—a special English procedure of voice

---

[D]Johannes Wolf, ed., *Musica Practica Bartolomei Rami de Pareia* [1482], *Beiheft der internationalen Musikgesellschaft* 2 (Leipzig: Breitkopf & Härtel, 1901), 71. [Translation: "Let (the counterpoint) also preserve the mode in raised and lowered (registers), that is, let its mode be ordered as a trope from the lower voice to the higher."]

[47]Bukofzer, *Studies in Medieval and Renaissance Music*, 49 ff. and 101 ff.; "Discantus," *MGG*, vol. 3, col. 575; "Gymel," *MGG*, vol. 5 (1956), col. 1144. In the "Discantus" article, this assertion appears evidently [to have been] qualified.

[48]Bukofzer, "Gymel," *MGG*, col. 1139 ff.

doubling.[49] [Thus,] it is clearly apparent that English compositions with a c.f. in the middle voice, which also manifest the voice pairing of c.f. and tenor, cannot have [anything] in common with a gymel, owing to the dissimilar function of these [two] voices.

The inflection, so to speak, of 6-3 sonorities into 5-3s (established above) and their respective modification into 8-6 or 8-3 sonorities is based quite specifically in the treatment of the c.f. The tendency of the imperfect consonances towards motion has already been discussed. In the 5-3 sonority— and this is strongly preferred in contrast to its variants—the tendency towards motion applies to only one interval (namely, that between the middle and low voices), since the upper voice has a perfect consonance with the low voice. Accordingly, when the c.f. lies in the middle voice, the motion-tendency of the third acts upon this part alone. In the 6-3 sonority, on the other hand, the tendency towards motion is doubled, as it were, namely by the third-relationship between the middle and low voices and the sixth-relationship between the upper and low voices. Thus, the movement tendency overlaps all voices of the complex. It is for this reason that all [such] pieces—regardless of the voice in which their c.f. is placed—are widely characterized by the progression of several 6-3 sonorities at the closing cadences.[50]

From these considerations it is clear why pieces with the c.f. in the middle voice were not amenable to the so-called "sixth-chord style." Otherwise, the c.f. would have been overcast by harmonic considerations. Moreover, the position of the c.f. in the middle voice would still have only been "fictive," since it would have effectively appeared as an octave transposition in the upper voice: fifth-transposition of the c.f. + fourth-relationship [of the middle voice] to the upper = octave.[51] On the other hand, it is clear why an English piece with its c.f. in the upper voice is characterized by its 6-3 sonorities.

---

[49]In the fifteenth century, the sources also designate a voice as gymel when this voice exhibits a two-voice character of its own in certain sections within the composition. This gymel voice follows the same principle as that of the gymel in general.

[50]In this connection it should be noted that the theory always demands the strict resolution of the major sixth to the octave: e.g.,   b' —> c'

                                                                        d —> c

[51]The explanation given in the Pseudo-Chilston treatise (fol. 116 ff.) of the upper-voice position of the c.f. in faburdon as an octave transposition is thus completely normal. See the discussions regarding fauxbourdon in *Acta Musicologica*: [Ficker] 1951, [Besseler] 1952, [Ficker] 1953, [Besseler] 1954 [The first two of these articles are translated elsewhere in this volume]. Additionally, see Bukofzer, *Geschichte des englischen Diskants*, 70 ff., and Georgiades, *Englische Diskanttraktate*, 92 ff.

Within the principles of English discant, the various voice ranges of the c.f. each result in a specific harmonic structure. This diversity, however, presupposes a common conception of the c.f., whose relationship to the counterpoint as a whole is always the same: the preservation of the original melodic integrity of the chant.

The different types of c.f. employment are, in fact, older than the repertory of *OH*.[52] This can be seen, for example, in the two settings of the hymn *Gloria laus* (Edition Vatican) in Worcester 85 (c.f. in the middle voice, transposed up a fifth) and 86 (c.f. in the upper voice).[53] Also noteworthy is the fragment London, BM, Add. 24199, from the fourteenth century, which transmits on fol. 90 two Sanctus (Sarum 8 and 10).[54] In both pieces, the c.f. is set in the middle voice, transposed up a fifth.

Example 4: Benedictus, London, Add. 24199, fol. 90 (■ = ♩)

[52]The opinion previously advanced by [Dom Anselm] Hughes, that the repertory of *OH* in some cases reaches back into the fourteenth century, has received strong documentary support through Brian Trowell, "A fourteenth-century ceremonial motet and its composer," *Acta Musicologica* 29 (1957): 65 ff.

[53]It should of course be kept in mind that, stylistically, Worcester assumes a distinctly unique position within English music. The numbering follows Luther Dittmer, *The Worcester Fragments, Musicological Studies and Documents* 2 (Rome: American Institute of Musicology, 1957).

[54]Bukofzer mentions this manuscript briefly as a new source; see "Changing Aspects of Medieval and Renaissance Music," *Musical Quarterly* 44 (1958): 5.

—ni.   O - san   -   na   in   ex - cel - sis.

In its simplicity, this Sanctus strikes one as a parallel to CbC (Example 3), [but] the difference in its construction of sonorities is clearly recognizable. With the exception of the singular 6-3 in m. 7—which even here is simply passing from the foregoing 5-3—the third is the only imperfect sonority encountered between c.f. and tenor [Schmidt evidently considers the sixths in mm. 3 and 10 as non-structural]. The upper voice, disregarding the non-essential embellishing notes, otherwise exclusively makes perfect consonances with the tenor.[55] Yet it is important that the third always be introduced to a melody tone of the c.f. Already the same in principle, this Sanctus represents a precursor to the technique of the middle-voice c.f. in *OH*. The second Sanctus in this manuscript is somewhat more weighty and correspondingly more stylized, but it does not yet reach the levels of *OH*.

It should also be remarked here that the c.f. is predominantly brought forward in equal breves, without any embellishment, that is, with an awareness of the original rhythmic equality of the chant. This is particularly true when the motion of the other voices is emphasized, as, for example, in the second Sanctus in London, Add 24199. When one connects this characteristic with the coordination between the c.f. and overall harmonic flow, then that [peculiar] character of English music, which Besseler has referred to as "full sonority" [*Vollklang*] and "flowing sonority" [*Klangstrom*], is made explicable.[56]

---

[55]The final cadence (m. 10) is interesting in that here a parallel 6-3 progression is avoided through the wide spacing of the structural 5-3 [i.e., 10-5] sonorities.

[56]Besseler, *Bourdon*, 101 and 103 ff.; see also the following articles of Heinrich Besseler: "Tonalharmonik und Vollklang," *Acta Musicologica* 24 (1952): 136 and 144 [translated above as essay 3, where the following quotation is found]: "Also, the slow tempo of 'flowing rhythm' [*Stromrhythmus*] and the 'cantabile melody' [*kantable Melodik*] that is associated with it (both discussed by me), most probably {!} stem from England"; "Das neue in der Musik des 15. Jahrhunderts," *Acta Musicologica* 26 (1954): 82 ff.; "Dufay in Rom," *Archiv für*

At this point the question arises as to whether there might be any ventures on the Continent outside of the *Ars nova* that are comparable to the English manifestations described above. Among the Continental manuscripts of the fourteenth century, the Codex Apt (Chapter Library, MS 16 bis) assumes a position of special importance;[57] this [quality of uniqueness] is immediately demonstrated in the mere fact that, out of 48 works transmitted in it, only four Latin double motets stand outside the liturgy. Further, it has been ascertained that the generation before Dufay [had] utilized the c.f. in the manner of a chant within a new, homogeneous, songlike form instead of the constructivist and unmelodic technique of dismemberment, which up until that point had been typical.[58] The first evidence for this change in conception of the c.f. on the Continent is found in the Apt manuscript, that is, a chronological point at which the pervasive English influence (judged at least by modern knowledge) had still not become manifest. To be sure, [in this source] the c.f. is principally set in the tenor, i.e., the lowest voice, and remains shackled to the function of potential director of sonorities. A characteristic example of this is [seen in] a Kyrie in Apt ([No. 1,] fols. 1–2),[59] which puts the c.f. (*Graduale Romanum* XI) in the tenor. It is brought forward for the most part in breves, i.e., taking up complete measures [in the modern transcription]. In this respect it comprises a development parallel to the English practice. However, when one considers the sonorities that are built over the c.f., the distinction between this piece and [contemporary] English music becomes evident, namely, that the melodic progress of the c.f. is accompanied predominantly by perfect intervals. The melodic events thus are not coordinated with the harmonic structure. The two elements of counterpoint still stand alone. Insofar as imperfect intervals occur, they are set for the most part as single sonorities between perfect intervals. Solely in the cadential formations does one encounter a series of up to four imperfect sonorities (6-3s) above a descending c.f. Continental discant theory, since about the time of Anonymous 2 and the [treatise] *Compendium magistri Franconis*, had allowed parallel progressions (usually up to three or four) consisting of identical

---

Musikwissenschaft 15 (1958): 18. The English provenance that Besseler always only presumed is now plainly apparent.

[57] See the article of Heinrich Besseler, "Apt," *MGG*, vol. 1 (1949-51), cols. 569-70. According to Besseler, the repertory of this manuscript (although presumably written only in the first quarter of the fifteenth century) reaches far back into the fourteenth century.

[58] Ficker, "Zur Schöpfungsgeschichte des Fauxbourdon," 95 ff.

[59] Amédée Gastoué, *Le Manuscrit de musique du trésor d'Apt* (Paris: Droz, 1936), 1 ff.

imperfect intervals, especially the sixth, over a cantus descending stepwise.[60] This restriction was grounded primarily in the fact that the c.f. was always conceived as a potential director of sonorities. In this respect, the Kyrie [Apt No. 1] is composed in accordance with theory, and the evidence for this is strengthened in the motet-like configuration of the two upper voices. A thoroughly traditional handling of sonorities is particularly elucidated in the hocket section (mm. 90-96), since this passage—with the single exception of a third in m. 93—is comprised exclusively of perfect consonances. The sole aspect of modernity in this piece is that the c.f. is innately melodic and is brought forth in a self-contained and continuous manner. The chant thus regains its full value as a symbol in the composition, and accordingly [the c.f.] begins to divest itself of the simple supporting function under which it had hitherto been governed.

The Kyrie of Chipre in Apt ([no. 5,] fol. 4v)[61] seems noteworthy within the realm of Continental music practice in connection with the question of the alternation of intervallic quality [i.e., perfect vs. imperfect]. Given its conception, the c.f. cannot at present be identified, but it undoubtedly lies in the tenor. At the very least, the tenor is to be considered a *cantus prius factus*. As such, it is in some places even embellished, as a comparison with the second section of the Kyrie shows (m. 31 ff.). Particularly striking in this piece are the frequent progressions of parallel imperfect intervals (up to three) over a tenor descending stepwise, from which, conversely, it can be observed that the piece is conceived from the tenor outwards. The perfect sonorities are concentrated more at the cadence tones of the tenor, and this is much in evidence in the second Kyrie section. It can be seen very clearly that the construction of the tenor is largely built around stepwise descending structural sections,[62] with the help of intervening embellishing notes, in order to make possible, within the scope of theory, a great extension of imperfect intervals upon the total harmonic picture. This proves, incidentally, how close the interrelationships were at that time between theory and practice. The embellishment of a c.f. in the tenor (or indeed of any kind of tenor) as was censured by the curia[63] takes on in this sense a new meaning, since in this

---

[60]*CS* 1, 311b, and *CS* 1, 156b; see also Apfel, *Diskant*, 43, 50, 62, and 88 ff.

[61]Gastoué, *Le Manuscrit de musique du trésor d'Apt*, 15 ff.

[62]Regarding the structure of a cantus in moving forms see Ernst Apfel, "Der Diskant in der Musiktheorie des 12.–15. Jahrhunderts," 53 ff.

[63]See Tundstede, *CS* 4, 295 (Chapter XLIV): "*Modus pronuniandi tenorem secundum artem.*" ["the method of bringing forth a tenor, according to art"]. Georgiades, *Englische Diskanttraktate* (93), interprets this excerpt from Tunstede as a specific case in the English

way a certain equilibrium of intervallic qualities was made possible. Chipre's Kyrie is noticeably characterized by such a tendency, but because of the limitation upon the tenor descending stepwise, an alteration of intervallic quality is only effected on the smallest scale, [occurring] in practically every measure. Consequently, intervallic qualities of "tension" and "release" are in a distinct sense neutralized from the standpoint of the overarching harmonic span. Through the concordance with the Ivrea manuscript (fol. 36r), Chipre's Kyrie is absolutely established as a work of the fourteenth century.[64] Despite the new factors demonstrated above, this piece fits essentially into the milieu of compositional practice on the Continent.

The hymn cycle in Apt (fols. 14v–16v)[65] has heretofore become best known as evidence for the [existence of] "chant-based discant" on the Continent in the fourteenth century.[66] The appearance of the c.f. in the upper voice in nine of the 10 pieces transmitted in this manuscript is indeed noteworthy, but far more decisive is the fact that the upper-voice c.f. stands opposed to tenor in its previous function of director of sonorities. The hymn *Veni creator spiritus* provides clear evidence for this view, considering that the many parallel fourths between c.f. and contra (middle voice)—in mm. 2-4 there are five following contiguously!—are rendered without significance if the responsibility for harmonic coherence is applied solely to the tenor, i.e., if the controlling factor is [considered to be] the [other voices'] consonant relationship to the tenor alone. Seen in this light, only 8-5 or 6-3 sonorities arise—the parallel fourths become transparent, as it were. Superficially, this would imply the same separation of c.f. and [harmonic] foundation that was previously discussed in connection with England; however, there remains a fundamental difference between the two practices. On the Continent, the c.f. as a melodic entity has no functional effect upon harmonic events. The melodic concept and treatment of the c.f. assumes no influence over the treatment of vertical sonorities. This [authority] applies exclusively to the conditioning factors of the tenor. Correspondingly, the imperfect intervals—particularly cases of single imperfect sonorities set between perfect ones—come to have

---

practice. But such a limitation does not square with the tenor's formation in the Chipre piece; this could mean that the special position of Apt has a connection with some English influence that has never before been grasped.

[64]Besseler, "Studien zur Musik des Mittelalters [Part] I," 185 ff.; see also Gilbert Reaney's article "Ivrea," *MGG*, vol. 6 (1957), col. 1581 ff.

[65]Gastoué, *Le Manuscrit de Musique du Trésor d'Apt*, 56-64.

[66]Heinrich Besseler, "Von Dufay bis Josquin," *Zeitschrift für Musikwissenschaft* 11 (1928): 4 ff., and the literature based upon it.

more of a subordinate character. In the hymn *Sanctorum meritis*, several contiguous imperfect sonorities (up to five) do indeed follow each other, but they are of different species, and in some cases they result through voice crossing. The tendency towards motion in imperfect [consonance] varies among the different voices; hence its appearance is not conditioned by factors of the c.f., and this leads one to conclude that Continental music did not recognize specific methods of harmonic treatment based on the various voice ranges of the c.f. The principles of harmonic structure in the hymn *Christe redemptor*, which sets its c.f. in the middle part, are exactly the same as in the other hymns, which have their c.f. in the upper voice.[67]

---

[67]The c.f. in this hymn is also transposed up a fifth in order to place it in the middle voice. Thus, it also has been advanced as evidence for the existence of a Continental practice of discant chant embellishment [*Diskantkolorierung*] in the fourteenth century (see above, note 66). But this view would only apply if one were to identify the discant voice(s) not [just] with one particular voice range, according to discant theory. Moreover, it remains curious that an embellishment of the chant, which does not change its [essential] structure, would occur within the Apt hymn cycle only in the one work which has the c.f. in the middle voice. For this reason the procedure seems, on the contrary, to be founded in the fact that the middle-voice c.f. is intended to be thrown into relief, since if it were brought forth in an unembellished manner, the c.f. absolutely would not be able to act in an "authoritative" capacity within the existing harmonic structure. And this is the main point, in that otherwise the c.f. would have only a purely constructive function. Concerning the upper-voice placement of the c.f.—strictly observed in [the applicable pieces in] Apt—this voice floats naturally above the others and is not amenable to any particular disturbance, not even within the normal treatment of sonorities. The embellishment of the middle-voice c.f. pursues approximately the same goal, whereas in the English practice [this situation] requires a specific harmonic procedure with respect to the c.f. In the variety of the respective practices, the fundamental difference between the c.f. technique of the Continent and that of England could hardly be better demonstrated. The term "discant embellishment" [*Diskantkolorierung*] was first coined by Rudolf von Ficker, "Die Kolorierungstechnik der Trienter Messen," *Studien für Musikwissenschaft* 7 (1920): 5-47, and was indeed introduced as a special constructive technique of English origin. "Discant embellishment" in Ficker's sense signifies a completely new single voice, derived from a c.f. model, which in its essence no longer has a common bond with the model, and which in this form is then used as an upper (discant) voice in a composition. This represents a constructive, intellectual, even a virtually abstract procedure, a unique conception of the c.f. principle. The appearance in Apt has nothing in common with it, because here the chant was not altered structurally. On the contrary, the c.f. [in Chipre's Kyrie] was intended to be emphasized within the flow of sonorities through its (slight) embellishment. Accordingly, in general terminology, particularly for the fifteenth century, discant is largely identified with the upper voice, [so that] one would be well advised to use the term "discant embellishment" only in those instances that have occasioned this characteristic. Conversely, in other cases, such as appear in Apt, one should refer merely to a "chant embellishment" in order that a clear differentiation between these dissimilar processes is ensured.

The repertory of the Apt manuscript and its compositional art occupy a middle position, so to speak, between the typical *Ars nova* and the tradition-bound liturgical music practice. It should be kept in mind that the principles of construction with respect to the building of sonorities do not differ between England and the Continent. This agreement in the purely technical provisions is important for the fifteenth century. In contrast, the c.f. technique is fundamentally differentiated in the two circles of cultivation. While on the Continent no decisive change occurred in this respect, in England it became possible, through effort, to fuse melody (c.f.) and the vertical element into a unified component—a development fundamental to the evolutionary history of the following era.

Outside of the liturgically bound music, however, a newer type of composition, which was structurally different from the previous discant technique, developed on the Continent. Apfel has referred to this as "free discant counterpoint" [*freier Diskantsatz*].[68] In this style, discant and tenor comprise a basic structural framework [*Grundgerüst*] for the composition. Between these structural voices [*Gerüststimmen*], however, no constructive dissonances are allowed. A contratenor fills out the harmony of this foundation counterpoint [*Kernsatz*], but it is entirely dependent upon the tenor and discantus. This dependence of the contratenor is demonstrated, for example, in the chanson *Helas, ma dame par amours* of Dufay.[69] In this piece there is a strange figure, in which the contra, with discantus and tenor, comprises a B minor triad, which seems for us today illogical given its context in the flow of sonorities.[70] According to the rules of theory,[71] when the interval between the structural voices was a major third, the contra could only take the minor third or the octave under the tenor. [But in this case,] in order that the contra not have to make such a wide leap [to reach the octave below the tenor], there remained no other choice than for it to take the B.

The term "free discant counterpoint" denotes the rather free voice-leading possibilities of the discantus, here equivalent with the upper voice. On the other hand, Besseler has, according to evidence from Jacques de Liège, referred

---

[68]Apfel, "Der Diskant in der Musiktheorie des 12.–15. Jahrhunderts," see the section entitled "Der vielstimmige Diskant auf der Grundlage des freien zweistimmigen Diskants (Kontrapunkts)," 156 ff.; these ideas are expanded upon in Apfel's "Der klangliche Satz und der freie Diskantsatz im 15. Jahrhundert," 297 ff.

[69]See Besseler, *Bourdon*, 40 ff., where, however, an analysis according to principles of functional harmony is attempted.

[70]See Heinrich Besseler's transcription, *Bourdon*, 41, m. 27.

[71]See, for example, the rules for the contratenor given by Anonymous XI b, *CS* 3, 466.

to this archetype as "cantilena-style counterpoint" [*Kantilenensatz*], a term that also emphasizes the preeminent role played by secular music.[72] Correspondingly, use of a c.f. is not typical in works conceived in cantilena style. The melody is a self-contained complex in itself, rendered especially prominent simply through its being rhythmically differentiated [from the other voices]. Also, the tenor is in this type of counterpoint not a director of sonorities, for there are no cases in which a simultaneity is entirely conceived around it. The tenor supports the melody in the discant [voice] only in a distinctly linear sense; i.e., to each section of the melody, certain appropriate vertical spacings are laid out, whose goal tones lead to cadence formations. The relationship between melody and verticality is only loose, [and] both components remain to some extent heterogeneous within the composition. The purely vertical-harmonic aspects are more of a secondary consideration.[73] This conception can clearly be seen in the pieces standing closer to the beginning of the fourteenth century, above all in the two-voice pieces.[74] The principle did not in its essence alter when supplementary means of filling out the sonority were realized through the addition of a contratenor. The cantilena style, with which England was *not* familiar, is a typical result of the musical ruminations on the Continent. In the [type of] discant technique that was bound up with c.f. procedures, the purely vertical exigencies stand in the foreground; in the cantilena technique, on the other hand, the melodic element dominates. One of these two main musical determinants [always had to] remain primary, and this also explains why the music of the Continent eschewed that characteristic that Besseler referred to as "full sonority."[75]

---

[72]Besseler, *Bourdon*, 29. The term "cantilena" is also used by Tunstede, *CS* 4, 295, in opposition to motet and rondellus. To effect a more precise demarcation [of genre], the notion of the cantilena style should probably be preferred, because the previous concept of discant circumscribes a unified constructive technique, which is very closely connected with c.f. If the cantilena style also developed out of discant technique, then this would add a new dimension to it, structurally speaking.

[73]This explains above all the Dufay excerpt cited above. The same circumstances must have led Besseler to invoke his so-called "variable quality of the third" [*Terzfreiheit*, i.e., vacillation between major or minor].

[74]See the examples in Annemarie von Königslöw, *Die italienische Madrigalisten des Trecento* (Würzburg: K. Triltsch, 1940); additionally, see Examples nos. 11, 15, 20, 32, 39, 46, and Example I in Erna Dannemann, *Die spätgotische Musiktradition in Frankreich und Burgund vor dem Auftreten Dufays* (Strasbourg: Heitz, 1936).

[75]See above, note 56. The concept of "full sonority," however, is not well suited to the description of English c.f. technique as described here. In Besseler, "Tonalharmonik," 136, note 9, it is also suggested that the technical basis [of "full sonority"] requires further investigation.

Fauxbourdon stands as a remarkable symbol for the mutual encounter between English and Continental music in the first half of the fifteenth century. Independently from the pros and cons of Besseler's and von Ficker's opinions,[76] which have become well known in the literature, it can certainly be said that fauxbourdon still betrays a typical Continental conception. In the c.f. technique as it developed in England, it was always a priority to maintain an equilibrium between the c.f. melody and the harmonic flow of the composition. But it is exactly this equilibrium that is denied in fauxbourdon, where the c.f. melody in the upper voice dominates, dictating the harmonic events on the basis of its own characteristics. From the standpoint of liturgy, this was doubtless seen as a priority, but it led to the acknowledged structural formalism. Thus, fauxbourdon does not document a functional separation of the c.f. from the harmonic foundation. The tenor was only a tenor in an apparent sense, since in all genres it had hitherto been crucial to the formation of [all] harmonic events for which it was responsible or in which it took part, whereas in fauxbourdon it largely had to demur to the c.f. in the upper voice. One must [therefore] agree with Besseler when he avers that the name "fauxbourdon" does not relate to the c.f. and its position, but rather to the fact that the foundation of the harmony is missing.[77] However, the term "harmonic foundation," or more accurately, "sonorous foundation," should be understood only in the sense of the function of the tenor as defined by the theorists. In this context, the entries seen in the manuscripts: *tenor au faux bourdon* ["tenor with fauxbourdon"] and *tenor a faux bourdon* ["tenor in the fauxbourdon style"],[78] mean the same thing, and it is typical that the tenor is expressly mentioned. In fauxbourdon, the structural relationships are precisely reversed with respect to former times, [regardless of] whether one compares it to the conventional discant technique or to the cantilena style. The domination of the c.f. melody [in fauxbourdon] leads one to think more [in terms] of the cantilena style.

When one considers the further evolution [of contrapuntal procedures], the essential issue is clearly not the utilization of the English "sixth-chord style"

---

[76]See above, note 51.

[77]Besseler, *Bourdon*, 99 ff. Here Besseler concedes that if one tries to interpret fauxbourdon according to the tenor, instead of the contratenor (as he suggests), exactly the same set of circumstances will apply. This has already been indicated by Jacques Handschin, "Aus der alten Musiktheorie [Part III:] Zur Ambrosianische Mehrstimmigkeit," *Acta Musicologica* 15 (1943): 14. See also above, note 36. Structurally speaking, however, fauxbourdon encompasses the musical creation as a whole.

[78]Besseler, *Bourdon*, 23. [These terms are also discussed in essay 1 above, 83-4.]

in general but instead the bringing into balance of the melodic and the vertical elements. For this reason, the fauxbourdon technique was accorded only a relatively short life span, as likewise its admittance to the realm of art music was to remain closed. But when melody and the sonorities with which it interacts relate to each other and work to produce a new unified component, then a new chapter in the history of harmony begins. A crucial impetus for this was undoubtedly provided by the c.f. technique developed in England. It is in this sense that we are to understand Tinctoris's remark: *novae artis fons et origo apud Anglicos.*[79]

---

[79]*CS* 4, 154b. [Translation: "the fount and origin of the new art [is to be found] among the English."] The hymns of Dufay are very instructive for [our understanding of] the metamorphosis of c.f. technique on the Continent. *Audivi benigne conditor* and *Christe redemptor* place the c.f. in the contra (middle voice), transposed up a fifth. 6-3 progressions are basically shunned in favor of other imperfect intervals; of course, the 6—>8 cadences and 6-3 sonorities that originate in passing (generally following embellishments) constitute exceptions. The reasons are the same as are set forth above (see note 51 and its accompanying text). This contrasts with the hymns in which the c.f. is placed in the superius, where the 6-3 structure steps into the foreground. The hymn cycle corresponds to the prototypical English practice. See the edition by Rudolf Gerber, *Guillaume Dufay: Sämtliche Hymnen, Das Chorwerk* 49 (Wolfenbüttel: Möseler, 1937).

The future belonged much less to the cantilena-style pieces (predominantly without c.f.) than to English discant, in which the newly developed c.f. technique was manifest. Inherent in the functional distinction between c.f. and harmonic foundation was the possibility of voice groupings, thereby offering new directions in compositional technique. If the voice grouping consisted of a c.f. in the upper voice and a fundament voice, then this type outwardly resembled the cantilena style, but compared to the latter, it had the advantage of [incorporating] a true structural bass function in the fundament voice, and above all, it had the possibility to offer free choices in the contrapuntal treatment of the remaining, subordinate voices. Therein may be said to lie a foundation for the so-called "tonal-free discant counterpoint" [*klanglich-freier Diskantsatz*] as demonstrated by Apfel, the evolutionary development of which has still not been investigated. See Apfel, "Der klangliche Satz und der freie Diskantsatz im 15. Jahrhundert," 306 ff.

7

The Origin of True Four-Voice Counterpoint in England

Ernst Apfel

EDITOR'S PREFACE: *Professor Apfel's concern with compositional techniques gained new impetus from his research into medieval English music, the results of which were published in 1959. The selection translated here comprises a reworked form of some of that material. In essence, it is devoted to comparing procedures of counterpoint in England and on the Continent from the late thirteenth century through the early fifteenth. The contrapuntal paradigms Apfel had previously developed play a large role in his assessments, and again he takes a large number of surviving pieces into consideration. An important point developed here is the differentiation between dispensable and indispensable voice parts, which leads the author to conclude that Continental composers routinely realized multi-voice counterpoint through additive procedures of composition, whereas in England "the subsequent addition of parts to a lesser-voice piece was hardly ever practiced."*

Poets and music theorists of the fifteenth century ascribe a unique contribution to the English in the area of music. Particularly around 1430, English music seems to have exerted influence over that of the Continent. Therefore, with the aid of the music transmitted in Continental sources, music research has attempted to fathom how the special attributes of English music could have manifested themselves. This has brought the author of the present study to the opinion that the Continental chanson style (discussed below) was altered around 1430 according to the model of a certain type of three-voice isorhythmic motet, which at this time was still being cultivated only in England, and which was also employed as so-called "tonal-free discant counterpoint" [*Klanglich-freier Diskantsatz*] in the compositions for the Mass Ordinary.[1] It is this style that became decisive for the genesis of classical

---

[1] The three-voice isorhythmic motet consisting of a tenor cantus firmus (c.f.) and two texted upper voices, particularly as realized in the form of the so-called "tonal-free discant counterpoint" (in which a freely moving, texted discant voice, lying in places lower than the tenor, took over from the tenor at times—along with the uppermost voice, likewise texted—the function of director of sonorities [*Klangträger*] in a manner approximating a structural counterpoint) scarcely existed at this point on the Continent at the beginning of the fifteenth century. In the works of Dufay, at least, this technique does not exist at all within the genre of

vocal polyphony.[2] However, it appears that there was no path leading from chanson composition towards motet and mass composition, and that the type of motet or mass composition that presented itself as a style of "tonal-free discant counterpoint" was still being practiced only in England.[3] The English were in this sense the sole cultivators of a style of composition that was to become decisive for the fifteenth and sixteenth centuries. Against the other hypothesis advanced above (see note 2), that the so-called "tonal discant counterpoint" must have originated in England, [it remains evident] that this type of counterpoint in England appears in the teachings of the theorists only in the fifteenth century, yet on the Continent it is recognizable already in the mass of Machaut. [However, it will be noted that] quite some time ago Handschin had pointed out the fact that English compositions are contained in the Continental motet manuscripts of the thirteenth and fourteenth centuries, probably even as early as the so-called Notre-Dame sources, and that consequently, the English must even at this time have had some musical influence upon the Continent.[4] [In light of subsequent research,] it can now be established that the English even in the thirteenth century were composing four-voice works conceived from the beginning as being four-voiced (see note 3), whereas the musicians on the Continent proceeded from pieces with fewer voices, to which additional voices subsequently were fitted. Whether this latter technique was entirely that of the Continent has not, however, been further pursued. Also, no further research has inquired into the question of why it is that no small number of the early English pieces, conceived from the beginning in four voices and composed according the principles of so-called "tonal counterpoint," [*klanglicher Satz*] consist of two untexted lower voices and two texted upper voices, even though a corroboration of this point would

---

motet-like mass settings, although it was of course practiced by the English. See Heinrich Besseler, *Bourdon und Fauxbourdon* (Leipzig: Breitkopf & Härtel, 1950), 152 ff. and 167 ff. (abbreviation: *Bourdon*), and Ernst Apfel, *Studien zur Satztechnik der mittelalterlichen englischen Musik, Abhandlungen der Heidelberger Akademie der Wissenschaften, Phil.–hist. Klasse, Jahrgang 1959* (Heidelberg: Carl Winter, 1959), vol. I, 89, Gruppe IV 1 b, and vol. I, 92 ff. (abbreviation: *Studien*).

[2]Ernst Apfel, "Der klangliche Satz und der freie Diskantsatz im 15. Jahrhundert," *Archiv für Musikwissenschaft* 12 (1955): 297-313 [translated above, see essay 5]. See also "Der Diskant in der Musiktheorie des 12.–15. Jahrhunderts" (dissertation, University of Heidelberg, 1953; abbreviation: "Der Diskant").

[3]Ernst Apfel, *Studien* I, 90 ff. passim.

[4]Jacques Handschin, "The Summer Canon and Its Background," *Musica Disciplina* 3 (1949): 55, 94, and *Musica Disciplina* 5 (1951): 65.

support the assumption that the technique of tonal counterpoint must have originated in England.

The present study will attempt a comparison of four-voice counterpoint as practiced in England and on the Continent by concentrating on the points of view already alluded to. From the time of the Notre-Dame school until well into the fifteenth century, four-voice works are encountered primarily in the motet [genre], which, beginning in the late fourteenth century in the form of the motet-like mass movement, was to become the most important category of music for the next two hundred years.[5]

If we consider various four-voice motets and motet-like mass settings from the period from approximately 1260 to 1450, we encounter on the one hand a group in which all voices except the tenor are texted and on the other hand, a group in which only two voices are texted. [Editor's note: The following discussion is an extension of ideas developed previously by the author; for an elaboration of these issues, please refer to the citations in notes 1-2 above.]

Taking into account the [respective] positions of the voices added to the tenor (c.f.), three categories can be differentiated:

1) All voices added to the tenor (c.f.) are located above it.
   [= *klanglicher Diskantsatz*, or "tonal discant counterpoint"]
2) One of the voices added to the tenor (c.f.) lies at times under it.
   [= *freier Diskantsatz*, or "free discant counterpoint"]
3) One of the voices added to the tenor (c.f.) moves continually under it.
   [= *klanglich-freier Diskantsatz*, or "tonal-free discant counterpoint"]

When all of the voices added to the tenor (c.f.) are located above it, one may refer to the piece as being in the style of "tonal counterpoint." This technique corresponds at its earliest to that taught by the English theorists: beginning with the uppermost voice, one could successively remove one voice after another as long as the voices are not especially connected texually or musically (see below).

When one of the voices added to the tenor (c.f.) comes to lie underneath it or moves continuously beneath it, then it is in a general sense indispensable to the counterpoint, since it functions as a director of sonorities and must

---

[5]The four-voice works of the Notre-Dame school are founded upon harmonic premises different from those of the succeeding period, and especially of the English (see the set of examples below, Examples 1A-D). The sonority techniques of the Notre-Dame school had a continuing influence only in the early Continental motets.

therefore be the first voice added to the tenor (c.f.), because the consonances taken by the upper voices are subordinate to its consonance with the tenor.

The voice that acts as director of sonorities [in place of the tenor c.f.]— either partially or during the entire composition—can be either with or without text. When it is textless, one can speak of the piece as being "tonal counterpoint"; when it is texted, then we are considering a piece written as "tonal-free counterpoint." The textless sonority-directing voice in tonal counterpoint is rhythmically more akin to a tenor (c.f.), [whereas] the texted low voice in tonal-free counterpoint acts more like the [other] texted voices of the composition. This distinction is, of course, not yet so clearly marked in the early motets, but it became ever more pronounced in the *Ars nova* through increasing use of melisma and the extension of the tenor c.f. (see below).

In tonal counterpoint, the texted [upper] voices are set only loosely to the tenor (c.f.) or to the [composite] sonorous foundation consisting of tenor (c.f.) and the untexted voice [which sometimes acts as] director of sonorities. Therefore, this type of piece was also designated as "multiple two-voice counterpoint" [*mehrfach-zweistimmiger Satz*] (see citation in note 3 above). In tonal-free discant counterpoint—particularly since the *Ars nova*—the uppermost voice forms a structural framework [*Gerüst*] with the lowest discant voice (which is texted and has freedom of motion), wherever this latter voice functions as director of sonorities. This type of piece can accordingly be designated also as "true four-voice (or three-voice) counterpoint" (see note 3).

In the Continental motet—with very few exceptions (discussed below)— every voice added to the tenor (c.f.) is always texted. From among these [added voices], one can be subsequently added or inserted as is the contratenor in the three-voice chanson style of the first half of the fifteenth century (see note 2). This technique, which was first designated [by the author] as "free discant counterpoint" (see note 2) and subsequently as "expanded counterpoint" [*erweiterter Satz*] (see note 3), had not hitherto been established in either motets or in the motet-like mass settings.

The process of adding equivalent upper voices at specific distances from a low-lying tenor (c.f.)—which are independent of each other to the extent that a true four-voice piece does not actually ensue but rather, merely a multiple two-voice piece—is actually described only by the English theorists of the fifteenth century.[6] In contrast to this, the theorists on the Continent either

---

[6]Published by Manfred Bukofzer, *Geschichte des englischen Diskants und des Fauxbourdons nach den theoretischen Quellen* (Strasbourg: Heitz, 1936), and Thrasybulos Georgiades, *Englische Diskanttraktate aus der ersten Hälfte des 15. Jahrhunderts: Untersuchungen zur Entwicklung der Mehrstimmigkeit im Mittelalter* ([Munich]:

deal with a two-voice discant [procedure] based solely on octave consonance, or else their rules for three and (seldom) four voices proceed from those for two voices. This fact confirms that the so-called "tonal counterpoint" [technique] was truly native to England.[7]

Evidence for this is provided by the early *preeminence* of the progression illustrated below in Example 1A (◯ = c.f.), whose two sonorities are to be understood as relating to the lowest tone (i.e., "tonal") because of the dissonance of a fourth between the upper voices. On the Continent, on the other hand, one still frequently encounters in contemporaneous works the progression shown in Example 1B, which must be understood as the result of a rigid resolution of two thirds superimposed upon one another (the major interval resolving to a fifth, the minor to a unison). Compositions of this type are thus conceived as follows:

The tenor c.f. here is only authoritative with respect to the motetus, whereas the triplum is derived as if from a new "tenor c.f."[A] The study just introduced also illustrates progressions such as shown in Example 1C, in which the definitive consonances and progressions are not made between the tenor and the motetus or triplum but rather between the "secondary voices" [themselves]—motetus and triplum. The upper voices of earlier Continental motets certainly correspond to these circumstances, not just because they [all] carry the same text but also because they are notated by themselves in score (without tenor c.f.).[B] The tenor c.f. obtains its full import only as a consequence of the determination of voice ranges. At the same time, the adjustment from the 5-3 sonority (with its resolution to an open fifth) to the 6-3 sonority (with its resolution to an 8-5) was the result of the conception of all sonorities [as proceeding] from the fundamental tone. In the early motets, the more infrequent 6-3 sonority has to be understood [as functioning] similarly to the 5-3 sonority (compare the previous example with

---

Musikwissenschaftliches Seminar der Universität München, 1937; abbreviation: *Diskanttraktate*).

[7] See Apfel "Der klangliche Satz," 302 ff.

[A] See Frieder Zaminer, *Der Vatikanische Organum Traktat, Ottobibliothek lat. 3025: Organum–Praxis der frühen Notre Dame–Schule und ihrer Vorstufen* (Tutzing: Schneider, 1959), 131 ff.: "Zur Entstehung der Dreistimmigkeit."

[B] See Ernst Apfel, "Über einige Zusammenhänge zwischen Text und Musik im Mittelalter, besonders in England," *Festschrift Walther Bulst* (Heidelberg: Carl Winter, 1960), 207 ff.

progressions such as that in Example 1D), since the fourth was at that time still considered a consonance.

Example 1A   **Example 1B**   **Example 1C**   **Example 1D**

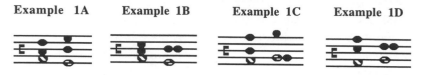

In fact, we encounter no small number of examples of tonal counterpoint among the following four-voice English motets, but we also find ones of the tonal-free type:[8]

Cambridge, Trinity College, MS O.2.1, fol. II: [untexted] / ...*uirtutum spolia* ...*mundo profuit* / [untexted] / *Et confitebor*;

London, Westminster Abbey, Fragments w/Pressmark 33327, Nos. 1-3 and 5-7;[9]

Oxford, Bodleian Library, MS Mus c. 60, fol. 85v.[10]

In the Worcester corpus:[11]

Motets Nos. 10, 18 = 66, 40, 53, 64, 67, 70, 78, and 95.

Of these, the following motets are freely composed: Oxford, Bodleian Library, MS Mus c. 60, and Worcester Nos. 10, 18, 53, and 67. The remaining motets are based on c.f., in some cases not identified (Worcester Nos. 40 and 78). In the motets of Trinity College, MS O.2.1, fol. II, Westminster Abbey Nos. 1 and 2, Bodleian Library, MS Mus c. 60, fol. 85v, and Worcester Nos. 10, 40(?), 64, and 70, none of the voices added to the tenor is labeled. With the exception of the first of these [Trinity], each voice has its own text. Otherwise, one voice besides the tenor is untexted and designated as *Primus tenor, Secundus tenor,* or *Quartus cantus.*[12] In the following motets, the tenor (c.f.) is the lowest voice, all the added voices are

---

[8]See Ernst Apfel, *Studien* I, 23 ff.

[9]Edited by Luther Dittmer, *Veröffentlichungen mittelalterlicher Musikhandschriften*, no. 5 (Worcester Add. 68, Westminster Abbey 33327, Madrid, Bibl. Nac. 192), (Brooklyn: Institute of Mediaeval Music, 1959, abbreviation: *Veröffentlichungen* No. 5).

[10]Edited by Luther Dittmer, "Beiträge zum Studium der Worcester–Fragmente," *Die Musikforschung* 10 (1957): 36.

[11]Luther Dittmer, ed., *The Worcester Fragments, Musicological Studies and Documents* 2 (Rome: American Institute of Musicology, 1957).

[12]The addition of a textless voice designated as *Quartus cantus* is characterized by Dittmer as an exclusively English practice (*Veröffentlichungen*, No. 5, 15), but it still remains to be clarified how the practice originated of adding a textless low voice first to the tenor (c.f.), and of labeling it *Quartus cantus,* or *Primus-* or *Secundus-Tenor.*

located above and none of them takes over from the tenor the function of director of sonorities ([i.e., the technique of] tonal counterpoint): Westminster Abbey Nos. 5 and 7, Bodleian Library, MS Mus c. 60, fol. 85v, and Worcester Nos. 40 and 64. However, in the other works, one of the voices lies either completely, predominantly, or partially under the tenor, thus taking on the function of director of sonorities. Consequently this voice becomes indispensable to the counterpoint, which must be either of the "tonal" or "tonal-free" type, according to whether the voice acting as director of sonorities is with or without text (see following table). The tenor is indispensable in either case.

Motets with a voice set entirely below the tenor:
Worcester No. 10	(unlabeled)

Motets with a voice set predominantly below the tenor:
Westminster Abbey No. 3	(Quartus cantus)
Worcester No. 95	(Primus tenor)

Motets with a voice set partially below the tenor:
Trinity College fol. II	(unlabeled)
Westminster Abbey No. 2	(unlabeled)
Westminster Abbey No. 6	(unlabeled){?}
Worcester No. 18 = 66	(Quartus cantus)
Worcester No. 53	(Quartus cantus)
Worcester No. 67	(Secundus tenor—in versions of Lat. lit d.20 and Gonville & Caius College, MS 543/512)
Worcester No. 70	(unlabeled—notated uppermost)
Worcester No. 78	(Secundus tenor)

In contradistinction to the [type of] tonal counterpoint taught by the English theorists, in which the discant voice is only loosely tied to the tenor (c.f.), none of the upper voices is dispensable in any of the four-voice works listed above. Their direct relationship is reflected in the following ways: [1] they systematically interchange their consonances with the tenor (c.f.) or [with the] director of sonorities; [2] they comprise some kind of voice-exchange; [3] they make exact or analogous phrasing periods; or [4] their texts are identical in content or rhythm or are similar (in their beginnings or through assonance) and so belong together without qualification. In the "tonal" motets with two textless lower voices and two texted upper voices, the balance of the composition would be disturbed with respect to tonal space if one of the upper voices were taken away. (This is, to be sure, an argument that also may apply to the later tonal motets on the Continent.)

Worcester No. 95, of which only two voices survive in the Worcester Fragments, is the only motet that is transmitted also in three voices in another manuscript of Continental origin: *Mo* 4.68.[13] This [latter] version is, however, incomplete: between the tenor c.f. and the upper voices, unsupported fourths occur. If one adds the *primus tenor* transmitted in Worcester to the three-voice version [of *Mo*], then these fourths are mitigated. The *primus tenor* of this motet is thus indispensable to the counterpoint, in contradistinction to the many texted quadrupla and tripla of Continental motets (see below). This voice was most probably left out in the copying of the motet into the Montpellier Codex, on the grounds that untexted low voices were unfamiliar to Continental practice.

With respect to treatment of sonorities, most of the four-voice English motets mentioned above already display characteristics that were to become in large measure typical in the later four-voice English motets, which we will take up presently. These characteristics include the following:

1) Parallel 6-3 sonorities in the place of parallel 5-3s, particularly [to be observed] between the voices added to the tenor, when the latter is resting: [see] Westminster Abbey No. 2, and the four-voice motets of Worcester, except Nos. 70 and 95;

2) Octave added to a 5-3 (or third added to 8-5) instead of doubling a component of the 5-3 (or 8-5) sonority: [see] Westminster Abbey Nos. 2, 6, and 7 (beginning!), Worcester Nos. 64 and 67;

3) Tenth added to an 8-5 sonority: Westminster Abbey Nos. 2 and 6, Worcester Nos. 10, 18 = 66, 53, 64, 67, and probably No. 78;[14]

---

[13]For the siglum of this manuscript, see the edition of *Mo*: Yvonne Rokseth, *Polyphonies du XIIIe siècle, Le Manuscrit H 196 de la Faculté de Médecine du Montpellier*, vol. 2 (Paris: L'Oiseau-Lyre, 1936).

[14]Anonymous 4 describes either one or both of these last two possibilities for the quadruplum, depending on whether the passage in question is interpreted according to Hugo Riemann [see below, Example 2A], *Geschichte der Musiktheorie im IX bis XIX Jahrhundert* (2nd. ed. Leipzig: Max Hesse, 1921 (abbreviation: *Musiktheorie*), 190 ff., or according to Thrasybulos Georgiades [see Example 2B], *Diskanttraktate*, 77, especially note 24. In the same place, Georgiades also mentions another relevant theoretical passage, in which both meanings seem to be admitted: ... *si quadruplum posuerit se in ditono vel semiditono cum tenore vel duplo* [i.e., "... if the quadruplum is placed at a major or minor third's distance from the tenor or duplum"]. The ordering of consonances originating in Georgiades's account one sees early, especially in England, the homeland of the theorist [i.e., Anonymous 4]; the disposition according to Riemann is occasionally encountered also on the Continent. In the instances of sonorities arising in the surviving music corresponding to Riemann's interpretation, however, it is evidently always the sixth that is decisive: it is always connected to the tenor c.f., and it is always major, thus

4) Twelfth added to an 8-5 sonority: Westminster Abbey Nos. 2 and 6, as well as Worcester Nos. 53, 64, and 67.

In these four-voice English motets of which we have been speaking, it should be kept in mind that the role of director of sonorities—an indispensable participant in the counterpoint—can be taken not just by an untexted quartus cantus, primus tenor, or secundus tenor, but also by a texted upper voice (most typically the lowermost). In the former cases, one speaks of tonal discant counterpoint, and in the latter case, of tonal-free discant counterpoint. [But] the indispensability of the upper voices is based on grounds other than that of lower voices (see above).

True four-voice compositions are met with in England in an unbroken series, up to the time in which four-voice writing became the norm. Examples can be seen in the following fragments:[15]

Oxford, New College, MS 362	No. 1 (with quartus cantus) No. 2 (with quartus cantus) No. 8 (all voices texted except tenor c.f.)[16]
Oxford, Bodleian Library, MS Hatton 81	No. 1 (with quadruplex) No. 2 (with quartus cantus) No. 3 (two untexted and unlabeled lower voices)
Cambridge: Gonville & Caius College, MS 543/512	No. 2 No. 3 (see *Studien* I, 52)
London, British Museum, MS Add. 24198[17]	fol. 133v/1 (a—all voices texted except tenor c.f.)

requiring motion to the octave. Its resolution also involves the thirds surrounding the tenor c.f. [see Example 2C]. Thus, the resulting 8-5-3 sonority is only a secondary phenomenon. The third lying below the tenor c.f. is not to be thought of as having a directive function. [Rather,] the sixth-to-octave progression, the two-voice counterpoint, and a definite linear impetus stand in the foreground. In the tone arrangement encountered in England [Example 2B], the sixth arises from secondary considerations and hence does not need to be resolved. The case here involves a 10-8-5 sonority, an aggregation of consonances above a decisive root tone, i.e., a many-voiced intervallic construction. Also noteworthy in this passage of Anonymous 4 is the mention in both cases of the fourth, arising from secondary factors.

Examples: **2 A**   **2 B**   **2 C**

[15]The following motets, unless otherwise indicated, are found in Ernst Apfel, *Studien* II.

[16]Published by Dom Anselm Hughes, ed., *The History of Music in Sound*, vol. 2 (London: Oxford University Press, 1953), 61 ff.

[17]Not reliably transcribable.

Oxford, Bodleian Library,   page VI-VII (a—with quartus cantus)[18]
    MS E Mus. 7   page X-XI (a—with tenor secundus)[19]
Oxford, Bodleian Library,   fol. Ir (actually Iv—with tenor secundus)[20]
    MS Bodley 384

The motets in Hatton 81 and Gonville & Caius 543/512 are freely composed, the others incorporate a c.f.[21] Also, in these motets and the motet-style mass movement in Bodley 384, none of the voices is dispensable, for the reasons given above.

As further [examples of] four-voice English works, mention should also be made here of the rather old Gloria trope, Oxford, Bodleian Library MS Mus. c. 60, fols. IIIv–IVr[22] (actually 84v–85r; not complete), and the somewhat later *Alleluya*, (Verse) *Nativitas gloriose virginis*, Cambridge, Corpus Christi College MS 65, fol. 135.[23] Both of these pieces are notated in score. The former work is of substantial importance in that the actual text of the Gloria was apparently performed monophonically. In the four-voice trope sections, the c.f. proceeds, predominantly in large note values, in the second-lowest (and in places in the lowest) voice. However, the c.f. does not run straight through the movement but rather only at the beginning and end of the sections, which are extended considerably in the middle through free composition. Thus the trope is, as it were, expanded musically yet again, in the course of which voice exchange also takes place. The piece seems interesting above all on account of this, since, rhythmically, it is constructed similarly to the free mass movements in *OH*:[24] The lower voices are rhythmically more ponderous than the upper, and they begin and end the individual sections in large note values. The progression of sonorities at the end of the piece proceeds as follows:

---

[18]Facsimile and transcription in John F.R. Stainer, ed., *Early Bodleian Music* (London: Novello, 1901), vol. I, plates X–XV, and vol. II, 24-43.

[19]Transcribed by Manfred Bukofzer, *Studies in Medieval and Renaissance Music* (New York: Norton, 1950), 30 ff.

[20]This piece, which is untranscribable, probably also belongs on the list. [Editor's note: The piece has since been published, and it does not in fact belong on the list; see *PMFC* 16, No. 28, 47-50.]

[21]These works display more markedly the particular characteristics already appearing in the older four-voice English motets (see above).

[22]Published by Dom Anselm Hughes, ed., *The History of Music in Sound*, vol. 2 (London: Oxford University Press, 1953), 51.

[23]Not published. [This piece is now available in modern edition.]

[24]Alexander Ramsbotham, ed., *The Old Hall Manuscript*, completed by H. B. Collins and Dom Anselm Hughes (Nashdom Abbey: The Plainsong and Medieval Music Society, 1933–38).

In the decidedly later *Alleluya*, (Verse) *Nativitas gloriose virginis* (in which not only semibreves but even minims are plentifully employed), the c.f.— transposed down a fifth and freely rhythmicized—comprises the lowest voice of the piece. The next-lowest voice, which in contrast to the two upper voices moves less quickly than the tenor c.f., occasionally takes over from the latter the function of director of sonorities. As would be expected in a piece where all voices are constrained by the simultaneous declamation of the same text, a condition that does not permit of any independent rests in the parts, the triple-leading-tone cadence is met with quite frequently. All the four-voice works previously introduced—with the possible exception of Oxford, Bodleian Library, MS Hatton 81, No. 2, whose final cadence is [either] incomplete, corrupt, or is meant to be filled in extempore after the repetition of the whole piece—begin and end with a narrow spacing of the voices, whereas the cadence of the *Alleluya* verse incorporates a wide spacing:

The *Alleluya* itself closes with a 5-3 sonority (C-c-g-e', with a penultimate sonority F-c-g-e'). On the Continent, this wide spacing of the voices took hold only gradually during the *Ars nova*.

We shall now turn our attention to the compositions of the Old Hall manuscript and its related fragments (see note 24 above and *Studien* I, 86 ff.).

The first English sources mentioned above correspond to the Continental manuscripts *Mo*, *Ba*,[25] and *Hu*.[26] In *Mo*, the motets in the second fascicle, Nos. 19 through 35, are four-voiced; in *Ba*, No. 92; and in *Hu*, No. 81. *Mo* 2, Nos. 19 and 34 seem, according to Dittmer, to be of English provenance,[27] but this opinion must be open to question, since they are also transmitted with fewer voices (see below). The motets in *Mo* [all] have three texted voices

[25]Pierre Aubry, ed., *Cent motets du XIIIe Siècle, publiès d'après le Manuscrit ed. IV. 6. de Bamberg*, 3 vols. (Paris: Rouert, Lerolle, 1908).

[26]Higini Anglès, ed., *El còdex musical de las Huelgas (Mùsica veus dels segles XIII–XIV), Introducciò, Facsìmil, Transcripciò* (Barcelona: Institut d'Estuis Catalans: Biblioteca de Catalunya, 1931).

[27]See Luther Dittmer, "Binary Rhythm, Musical Theory and the Worcester Fragments," *Musica Disciplina* 7 (1953): 39 ff.

added to a tenor c.f. [On the other hand,] *Ba* No. 92 has two liturgical tenor cantus firmi, which alternatively function as director of sonority, [while] *Hu* No. 81 has a tenor (*Tenura*) and another untexted low voice, which occasionally acts as director of sonorities. The two latter motets are apparently truly four-voiced and precisely because of this, are probably later than those contained in Worcester and *Mo*. The motets in *Mo* exist in four voices for the most part only in that manuscript (and in *Cl* [manuscript *La Clayette*]). In other sources (except perhaps 2:27), they are transmitted in three parts or even only as two-voice works, or else they are based on three- and two-voice clausulae.[28] The "missing" voices would not have been susceptible of being left out if they had been critical to the counterpoint. The four-voice motets in *Mo* (and generally in *Cl*) are thus on the contrary "expanded" two- and three-voice works.[29]

The following discussion is only intended to make a few additional observations regarding the process of transmission [of these works,] and to demonstrate the musical criteria for the subsequent addition of voices: The motet *Mo* 2:19 is apparently based on a three-voice clausula in *F*,[30] which speaks against the English provenance assumed by Dittmer. It is also transmitted in a version for only two voices with another (Latin) motet text, and the phrase periods made by the motetus are the most regular of any of the voices. The (presumably) three-voice clausula in *F* thus probably already represents an expanded two-voice composition. The motet *Mo* 2:20 exists likewise in a three-voice version, and it too is transmitted also in two voices. In *Mo*, the triplum and quadruplum make many parallel octaves and unisons. Therefore, one of the two voices should be left out in performance. *Mo* 2:21 is likewise also transmitted in three (clausula in *F*) and even in two voices. The quadruplum is rhythmically simple and its phrase periods are undifferentiated, being all of identical length. [This voice] also makes many

---

[28]See Friedrich Gennrich, *Bibliographie der ältesten französischen und lateinischen Motetten* (Darmstadt: F. Gennrich, 1957).

[29]In the motets in *Mo*, whenever the voice added last (usually the quadruplum—see above— e.g., *Mo* 2:20, 27, and 35) lying at times below the tenor c.f., seems to support fourths between another voice and the tenor c.f., and thereby to be director of sonorities, one will be able to discover fourths between all voices, and especially between tenor c.f. and motetus, which are the basis of the four-voice version. Such situations are solely the outcome of these pieces having existed previously as older motets.

[30]It does not follow from any of the applicable inventories whether the clausula used as the original basis is three- or only two-voiced. The design of a motet catalogue could in the future be arranged to proceed from the music in such a way that one and the same voice appear under a number, with letters [serving] as indices for its different texts in various motets.

parallel octaves and fifths with the tenor c.f. The Quadruplum of the motet *Mo* 2:22 appears in other versions as a triplum. The triplum in *Mo* is, however, more identifiable with the duplum of the two-voice clausula in *StV* [*St. Victor* manuscript] which is the basis of the motet, and accordingly [the triplum] represents only another version of that voice (in performance one of the two voices should be omitted), whereas the quadruplum, likewise added subsequently, completes the fundamental two-voice structure in a coherent fashion.

In *Mo* 2:23, the quadruplum is a substantially later addition; it moves in simple breves. *Mo* 2:24 exists otherwise only in *Cl*, transmitted in that source without quadruplum, but both the quadruplum and triplum move throughout in breves, in contrast to the motetus and tenor c.f., and thus are later than the two-voice piece [i.e., motetus/tenor] which apparently underlies the composition. Judging from its quick note values (as well as the evidence of manuscript transmission), the motetus of *Mo* 2:25 is the triplum of another version of the motet, whose motetus is evidently lost. The best three-part counterpoint among the four voices in *Mo*, however, is made by the tenor c.f., motetus, and quadruplum. It is unclear at this point how one is to account for this contradiction. In *Mo* 2:26, the quadruplum belongs to the original two-voice version. The duplum and triplum have been subsequently added. In the motet *Mo* 2:27 (see above)—transmitted as a four-voice piece in both sources (*Mo* and *Cl*)—only the motetus displays periodicity throughout in significant measure. Were the triplum and quadruplum, then, really only brought to the piece later? The quadruplum of *Mo* 2:28 is the triplum in other sources. Thus, in *Mo* it is the triplum that is the voice added later. On the other hand, the fact that the quadruplum of *Mo* also moves in semibreves and that its phase periods do not coincide with those of the other voices leads to the interpretation that this voice, too, was only added subsequently. And in fact, this motet survives in a version for two voices. *Mo* 2:29 is founded upon a three-voice clausula in *StV*. The quadruplum of *Mo*—evidently an added voice—manifests a remarkable number of *coniuncturae* and makes many parallel octaves with the tenor c.f. *Mo* 2:30 is transmitted in *Ba* in three voices, without the quadruplum and with Latin texts in the motetus and triplum. *Mo* 2:31 is based upon a two-voice clausula in *F* (intended to have been three-voiced) and is also transmitted in three voices. In *Mo*, the [positions of] motetus and triplum are (mistakenly) reversed. *Mo* 2:32 is also transmitted in two voices (triplum and tenor c.f.). The triplum is of an unusually clear structure, in distinction to the motetus, [which] like the quadruplum [was] apparently added only subsequently. *Mo* 2:33 is transmitted in two- and three-voice versions as well. The quadruplum and triplum in *Mo* make many parallel unisons, so that one of the two voices can be assumed to be omitted during performance. The motet [*Mo*] 2:34 also survives in a version for only three voices. The quadruplum often doubles a consonance of one of the other voices. The clausula underlying the motet *Mo* 2:35 is four-voiced only in W_1; otherwise it is only three-voiced. The motet [itself] is transmitted in *Ma* in two voices (motetus and tenor c.f. of *Mo*). (It should be noted that three-voice clausulae can also be created from two-voiced ones.)

In the four-voice motet from the *Roman de Fauvel* comprising three texted voices added to the tenor c.f.,[C] the quadruplum likewise appears to have been added subsequently, as it often moves in parallel octaves with the tenor c.f. and with the triplum in parallel unisons. Among all the voice possibilities in this archaic, indeed primitively functioning motet, only the motetus and tenor c.f. comprise a relatively good two-voice structure.

Considering their voice designations, the quartus cantus [parts] of English motets correspond to the quadruplum of the motets in Continental manuscripts, and this is also the case in the latter [sources] as far as I can see, whenever the voices are not labeled. However, the so-called quadruplum is always the first voice notated (being in the upper left-hand column, with the other voices ordered successively underneath). A significant distinction thus exists between the two types of voices: The English quartus cantus is untexted but indispensable, [whereas] the French quadruplum is texted but dispensable! According to its name, the English quartus cantus would be the last voice [added to the composition], but along with the tenor c.f. it [actually] comprises the foundation of the counterpoint; [yet] even from a constructive standpoint, the French quadruplum [really] is the last voice added! The contratenor of the later Continental motets, which corresponds to the untexted English quartus cantus, is not encountered until Philippe de Vitry and then only sporadically; not until Machaut does it appear in greater proportion. Constructively, it seems to have been introduced in imitation of the English quartus cantus. Evidence for this can be seen in the fact that [the practice of] tonal counterpoint with two textless lower and two texted upper voices consolidated [at this time] on the Continent, as the frequent occurrence of the

---

[C]Published by Johannes Wolf, *Geschichte der Mensuralnotation von 1250–1460* (Leipzig: Breitkopf & Härtel, 1904), Part II, 8 ff. and Part III, 15 ff. [Also contained in Leo Schrade, ed., *I. The* Roman de Fauvel; *II. The Works of Philippe de Vitry; III. French Cycles of the Ordinarium Missae, PMFC* 1 (critical text in separate volume) (Monaco: L'Oiseau-Lyre, 1956), No. 11, 18-21.]

triple-leading-tone cadence in these works demonstrates.[31] This harmonic progression, stemming from the importance of the lowest tone to the counterpoint, was frequently evaded by the English through rests or special voice leading of one of the participating voices (refined tonal discant counterpoint).[32]

The above observations were pointed out in the present author's *Studien* (chapter III) in connection to the pieces in the Old Hall manuscript and its related fragments. But it is also true of still earlier works,[33] for example: Westminster Abbey Nos. 5 and 6, final cadence, as well as Oxford, Bodleian Library, MS Mus. c. 60, fol. 85v, mm. 19-20, 30-31, and 32-33. The final cadence of Westminster Abbey No. 5 is the basis of the progression of sonorities in Westminster Abbey No. 7 (see below, Example 3A, = c.f.). A further-developed form of this progression, with a sixth instead of a doubled fifth, is displayed in the cadences in Cambridge, Trinity College MS O.2.1, fol. II; Worcester No. 10 (Example 3B-1); and also in *Mo.* 2:19 (Example 3B-2—this piece was discussed above). The progression appears, still further developed, in Oxford, Bodleian Library, MS Mus. c. 60, fol. 85v, mm. 27-8 (Example 3C), and a variant of this is seen in the cadence of Worcester No. 95 (Example 3D). The cadence of Worcester No. 18 = 66, from which the second-highest voice and the tenor are missing in the source, may have been the same progression seen in Oxford, Bodleian Library, MS Mus. c. 60, fol. 85v, mm. 19-20 (Example 3E).

Examples:

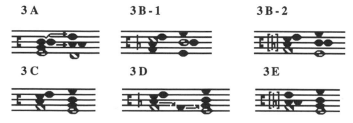

3 A   3 B - 1   3 B - 2

3 C   3 D   3 E

Examples of the evaded triple-leading-tone cadence from the later English motets can be seen in the following places: Oxford, New College MS 362 No. 2, in the cadence at the words *memo*-riam; Oxford, Bodleian Library, MS Hatton 81 No. 1, at hu-*ius ven*-ter; No. 3 at Sal-*ve iu*-bar in the second voice and at *cum iu*-bilo and *famulo* (voice exchange); Oxford, Bodleian Library,

---

[31]See Apfel "Der klangliche Satz," 302 ff.

[32]Ibid., 308 ff.

[33]With regard to the following works, see information relating to notes 15-23 above.

MS E Mus. 7, p. X-XI (a), mm. 6-7 = 20-21 (voice exchange). In these pieces, avoidance [of triple-leading-tone cadences] through use of rests can also be observed.

The evidence presented in *Studien* serves to illustrate that the subsequent addition of parts to a lesser-voice piece was hardly ever practiced in England. Just as the four-voice works were [conceived as] four-voiced from the beginning, so also were the three-voice pieces composed from the beginning as [being] three-voiced. One encounters two-voice pieces only rarely. The French, on the other hand (with the exception of the four-voice motets in tonal discant technique with two untexted lower and two texted upper parts, discussed above), always proceeded from works with a lesser number of voices, to which they added new voice parts.

Accordingly, the majority of three-voice motets in *Mo* are expanded [*erweiterte*] two-voice pieces. Friedrich Ludwig has also ascertained this to be the case for the ballades, rondeaux, and chansons of the fourteenth century, particularly those of Machaut.[34] Aside from the works of these genres in which all voices are texted (Ballades 17 and 29),[35] all of the three-voice works are based on two-voice originals. As the transmission of several works demonstrates, one voice in a three-part piece is subsequently added to a structural framework [*Gerüstsatz*] of texted upper voice and textless tenor. This added voice can be either the contratenor (for example, Ballade No. 4 and Rondeau No. 17) in works—which comprise a statistical majority—with a textless contratenor, or more infrequently it can be a textless triplum (Ballade No. 19 and Rondeau No. 1). The works in question are in some sources either only two-voiced, or else they are transmitted in a three-voice setting with a different triplum or contratenor.[36] One can probably conclude from this that the contratenor (or triplum, as the case may be) was the voice composed last, even in those works existing in all sources as three-voice pieces. Particularly enlightening is the transmission history of the Ballade No. 18 (see also

---

[34]Friedrich Ludwig, "Die mehrstimmige Musik des 14. Jahrhunderts," *Sammelbände der internationalen Musikgesellschaft* 4 (1902–03): 16 ff., especially 35 ff.

[35]Friedrich Ludwig, ed., *Guillaume de Machaut, Musikalische Werke*, vol. 1, *Balladen, Rondeaux und Virelais, Publikationen älterer Musik* I:1 (Leipzig: Breitkopf & Härtel, 1926). See also Leo Schrade, ed. *The Works of Guillaume de Machaut—Second Part: Motets Nos. 17 to 24—Mass—Double Hoquet—Ballades—Rondeaux—Virelais, Polyphonic Music of the Fourteenth Century* 3 (critical text in separate volume) (Monaco: L'Oiseau-Lyre, 1956), 68 ff.

[36]Unfortunately, in Ludwig's edition of Machaut's Ballades, Rondeaux, and Virelais, the transcriptions do not always indicate through system bracing that the works are also transmitted in two- or three- [i.e., fewer-] voice versions. For example, the triplum should be braced by itself in the Ballades Nos. 19 and 21 (and elsewhere), as Ludwig does with No. 31.

Rondeau No. 7): it exists as a two-voice piece in one manuscript, but in most sources it is three-voiced. In some sources, an untexted triplum is added to the two-voice framework of untexted tenor and texted upper voice, in others, it is an untexted contratenor that is added. In one manuscript, the composition appears as a four-voice work, i.e., with both an untexted triplum and untexted contratenor. However, as the dissonances and parallel perfect consonances (arising mostly between the triplum and contratenor) clearly suggest, it is not to be performed as a four-voice piece. The contratenor and triplum merely represent two different options for the completion of the basic two-voice counterpoint.[37] From the standpoint of musical construction, the contratenor and the triplum are essentially equivalent except that they move in different registers.

The transmission of some four-voice works can be traced back only to three-voice versions. In these cases, it is easy to determine which was the last voice added (for example, Ballades No. 23—contratenor last—and No. 31—triplum last). It is more difficult [to determine the order of composition] in works that are extant in all sources in four-voice versions, e.g., Ballade No. 22. But since here there are different contratenors transmitted, I assume that the contratenor was the last voice added. This may also be the case in those works where both upper voices are texted: Ballades Nos. 34 and 41. In Rondeau No. 10, the triplum appears to have been the last voice added. However, composers seem to have recognized the inadequacy of four-voice composition based upon addition of successive voices, since the chansons at the beginning of the fifteenth century are in general only three-voiced, being regularly comprised of tenor, discantus, and contratenor, but without triplum.

Thus it can be seen that, in the earlier motets, the English quartus cantus and the Continental contratenor were equivalent, whereas in the Continental sphere, the triplum and contratenor also had a measure of correspondence. These correlations are also exhibited in the rules—often repeated verbatim—of the motet teachings of the early theorists on the one hand, which speak about the addition of a triplum, and, on the other, of the later theorists of chanson composition, who discuss the addition of a contratenor to a basic two-voice framework.[38] Even in the period of Dufay, the three-voice chansons were still expanded compositions in which the contratenor was added last.

---

[37] It is in this context, which is taught in the *Ars discantus secundum Iohannem de Muris* (*CS* 1, 92b ff.), that both types of expansion of a two-voice counterpoint should most probably be understood (see also Apfel, "Der Diskant," 176 ff.).

[38] See Riemann, *Geschichte der Musiktheorie*, 186 ff., 270 ff., 289 ff., etc., and Apfel, "Der Diskant," 156 ff.

The practice of enlarging a composition [through the addition of subsequent voices], which we first encountered in the motets of the thirteenth century, may have been cultivated even longer on the Continent.

The connections delineated above between motet and chanson (ballade and rondeau) lead one to conclude that the latter genres had their genesis in the (secular) motet.[39] The difference between the two categories [i.e., chanson and motet] becomes awkward only when one considers the chanson from the point of view of an "accompanied melody," in contrast to the motet's being founded on a (liturgical) c.f. in the tenor. But the chanson even in the fifteenth century might also have been composed with the tenor as a point of departure, just like the motet, with the sole difference that the tenor of the chanson would have to be created for the planned song (*cantus prius factus*) and not simply taken over from the ancient stock of (liturgical) melodies. The fact that the upper voice of the chanson was worked out in the sense of a melody has little to do with this. If one grants that the three-voice isorhythmic motet *O livor/Inter amenitatis/Revertenti*, transmitted anonymously in Trent, Codex 87 (No. 177, fol. 231v–232r) is [the same work] transmitted in the *Roman de Fauvel* in a version only with triplum and tenor,[40] then this fact supports the conclusion that the motetus was a subsequent addition, and consequently, the practice of contrapuntal expansion on the Continent would be established also for the isorhythmic motet. In point of fact, the manuscript catalogues showing transmission of some motets in varied numbers of voices also leads to this conclusion,[41] although such a circumstance can sometimes be brought about by the reduction of the two lower voices into a *solus tenor*.

As far as I can see, the Continental four-voice motets and motet-like mass movements [conceived] in tonal discant technique in the fourteenth and early fifteenth centuries always consist of a lower-voice framework of tenor c.f. and contratenor, and two texted upper voices.

Motets and mass settings which have a completely through-composed tenor c.f., without isoperiodicity or isorhythm, are probably to be considered

---

[39] See Gilbert Reaney, "Chanson (II)," *MGG* vol. 2 (1952), cols. 1034-46, especially 1038 ff.

[40] See Rudolf von Ficker, ed., *Sieben Trienter Codices, Geistliche und weltliche Kompositionen des XIV. und XV. Jahrhunderts, Sechste Auswahl, DTÖ* 76 (*Jahrgang* XL) (Vienna: Universal-Edition, 1933), 98. The *Fauvel* version is contained in Schrade, ed., *PMFC* 1, No. 22, 41.

[41] For example, Heinrich Besseler, "Studien zur Musik des Mittelalters [Part] I: Neue Quellen des 14. und beginnenden 15. Jahrhunderts," *Archiv für Musikwissenschaft* 7 (1925): 167 ff., and "Nachtrag zu Studie I," *Archiv für Musikwissenschaft* 8 (1926): 131 ff.

of English provenance.[D] Already in the Worcester corpus—particularly among the so-called "trope-motets"—we find motets based on a free rhythmicization of a completely foreign melody. In connection with the four-voice imitative motet without c.f., which according to Besseler was developed in Italy in response to Italian stimulus (*caccia*) by the Netherlander Johannes Ciconia, we should point here especially to the freely composed four-voice English motets in Oxford, Bodleian Library, MS Hatton 81, whose tenors evince no small measure of "harmonic progressions" (fourths and fifths) and one of which also incorporates short imitations (not simply voice exchange).[E]

On the Continent there existed in the fourteenth and early fifteenth centuries the following types of mass composition, almost exclusively Glorias and Credos. (In the following table, the types seldom represented are counted in each case among the works contained in the codices Ivrea, Apt, and Turin J. II. 9 (=*TuB*), the other types are frequently encountered):

I) Freely Composed

    1) Three-voiced:

        a) One texted upper voice, textless tenor and contratenor: ("ballade-style mass setting").

        b) Two texted upper voices, one textless tenor:

    (Designated as "motet-like mass setting" by Besseler,[F] but a better term would probably be something like "free motet-like piece"). In this type of work it needs to be examined whether the lower-lying of the two texted upper voices occasionally takes over from the tenor the function of director of sonorities, as [happens] in the corresponding pieces in *OH* (Group III 1 c).[G] In this case one really is dealing with a motet-like composition. In the English repertory even as early as the Worcester corpus, one likewise encounters freely composed tenors, running continuously throughout the entire piece.

        c) All voices are texted:

            α) Notated in parts, designated by Besseler likewise as "motet-like mass setting" (see above, 1 b), but which should be called "conductus-style mass setting."

[D] See Besseler, *Bourdon*, 152 ff. Perhaps the pieces in Old Hall, Group III 1 c, whose incorporation of a c.f. is questionable, also belong to this class of pieces; see *Studien* I, 88 and 95 ff.

[E] See Besseler, *Bourdon*, 71 ff.; also Apfel, *Studien* I, 53, and II, 52 ff.

[F] Besseler, "Studien zur Musik des Mittelalters [Part] I," 188 ff.

[G] Apfel, *Studien*, I, 88 and 95 ff.

β) Notated in score (very rare), designated by Besseler likewise as "conductus mass setting": Kyrie, Ivrea no. 49 = Apt No. 5—(this arrangement is seen quite frequently in England).

2) Four-voiced:

a) Two texted upper voices, a repeating, textless tenor (c.f.?) and a contratenor: (Gloria, Ivrea No. 44; Gloria, *TuB*, fol. 29—Similar compositions are encountered even as early as in the Worcester corpus).

b) Two texted upper voices, through-composed textless tenor and contratenor: If the freely composed four-voice mass settings developed out of the three-voice ballade (mass) style, then it is this style that is enlarged through the addition of a second texted voice and would therefore have to be designated as "Four-voice ballade-style mass setting." But if this type came out of the three-voice pieces in motet style, then they would have been expanded through the addition of a textless tenor and would have to be called "four-voice free motet-like [mass] setting." In the latter case, the addition could have followed at first in single pieces, before the four-voice performance became typical, but this [hypothesis] requires further investigation.

c) All four voices are texted: ("four-voice conductus-style mass setting").

II) Works based on a continuous c.f. in the tenor, partially or completely isorhythmic:

1) Three-voiced, two texted voices, one textless tenor c.f.: (Kyrie *rex angelorum*, Ivrea No. 68 = Apt No. 1).

2) Four-voiced, two texted upper voices, textless tenor c.f. and contratenor: (Kyrie, Sanctus, Agnus of Machaut Mass).

III) Works based on a fragment of a foreign melody used as a c.f. in the tenor, which is modally or isorhythmically ordered, whereby the isorhythm can inform the entire composition:

1) Three-voiced, two texted voices, one textless voice (tenor c.f.): (Gloria, Ivrea No. 61 = Apt No. 28; Ivrea No. 34 = *Ite Missa est* of Tournai Mass).

2) Four-voiced, two texted upper voices, two textless tenors (one as carrier of c.f.): (Credo, Ivrea No. 59, with short melismas constantly recurring at the ends of individual sections of the Credo text, which also occurs in England).

From the preceding table it is apparent how rare on the Continent, as opposed to England, were three-voice settings of the Gloria and Credo texts in the form of an isorhythmic motet with a foreign c.f.—particularly when occurring in the form of a tonal-free discant composition. (In the four-voice pieces we see this only once.) Just as striking on the Continent is the propensity towards isorhythm using liturgical Kyrie, Sanctus, and Agnus melodies [as c.f.], carried through in the polyphonic settings of Kyrie, Sanctus, and Agnus.

In contrast, we encounter in the works of Dunstable several so-called tonal-free motets and motet-style mass movements, in which the tenor c.f. comes to lie in places above the lowest of the three texted, freely moving voices added to it, whereby the latter takes over at these places the tenor's function as director of sonorities, comprising a kind of structural counterpoint with the uppermost texted voice. This was most probably a new technique for the Continent in the fifteenth century, although it had its origins in England around 1300.

In a previous study of the present author's, other compositions of this type from Continental sources were noted.[H] [Of this group, however,] the piece by Tapissier[42] and the Marian antiphon [an anonymous *Salve regina*],[43] should be removed from consideration, since: 1) in both pieces, only the two upper voices are texted, and 2) the contratenor *Vale placens* of the work by Tapissier is never the director of sonorities. The fourth of the upper voice with the tenor c.f. in m. 58 is merely a suspension. (No true cadence happens at this place, rather, there is simply a swinging back and forth of the voices above the tenor c.f., whose long note—leapt to from the third below—is held out.) In m. 66, the fourth between the two texted upper voices is also supported by the tenor c.f., not just by the contratenor. This mistake crept in because the notes of both the two lower voices stand in the middle of the measure of the edition instead of at the beginning, where they belong.

In the remaining works introduced in the above citation, the lowest lying, freely moving texted discant voice (the motetus), acts to complement the tenor c.f., from which it takes over the role of director of sonorities. For this reason it was later termed "contratenor," in analogy to the contratenor of tonal counterpoint. In these cases, the motetus thus corresponds to the contratenor, as previously the quartus cantus or the triplum had corresponded [to the contratenor]. Therefore, the English theorists had on the one hand stipulated that, in cases involving a high-lying tenor c.f. and another lower part, one

---

[H]Apfel, *Studien* I, 95.

[42]John F.R. Stainer and C. Stainer, eds., *Dufay and His Contemporaries: 50 Compositions Transcribed from MS Can. misc. 213 in the Bodleian Library* (London: Novello, 1898), 187 ff.

[43]Rudolf von Ficker and Alfred Orel, eds., *Sechs Trienter Codices: Geistliche und weltliche Kompositionen des XV. Jahrhunderts, Vierte Auswahl, DTÖ* 53 (*Jahrgang* XXVII/1) (Vienna: Universal-Edition, 1920), No. 6, 55 ff.

could sing a contratenor instead of a mene (motetus),[44] yet on the other hand, the contratenor of many pieces moves exclusively in a range a fifth above the tenor, i.e., in the range of a motetus. (In such cases, the discantus as a voice type corresponds to the triplum—a point amplified by Anonymous 2.[45]) Two of the pieces introduced in *Studien* (I, 95) are of Binchois, who may have been particularly influenced by the English. The tenor c.f. in the anonymous isorhythmic motet [*O sacrum manna / Ecce panis*],[46] is based on a section of a sequence. Although the tenors on the Continent were, from the time of the *Ars nova*, freely taken from liturgical genres other than the soloistic parts of the Gradual, Responsoria, etc. (which were the customary sources in the organum of the Notre Dame school and in the early motet), it should be pointed out that the use [as c.f.] of sections of sequences, etc. was first practiced by the English. The foregoing observation leads to the further question of whether the French or the English, or both together, had developed the characteristics unique to the *Ars nova* motet, and in this connection, only a few factors need be introduced to demonstrate the independence, if not indeed the leadership, of the English in this development. First of all, it should again be remembered that the English even in the thirteenth century had based their motets on melodic segments derived from sequences and similar sources. Also warranting mention is Handschin's unequivocal observation of isoperiodicity ([i.e.,] predecessor of isorhythm?) as a characteristic pointing to English provenance in motets in Continental manuscripts.[47]

Handschin applies the concept of isoperiodicity in the sense of "analog-periodic," i.e., if only one single voice comprises periods of equal length, then one is not justified in speaking of an isoperiodic motet. [Similarly,] if the periods of the upper voice(s) and the tenor c.f. are [all] of equal length, then one should speak only of simultaneous periodic constructions, but not of an isoperiodic motet. This last category can only come into play when the periods of tenor c.f. and upper voice(s) are of varying lengths, whose relationship to each other must be maintained exactly over several repetitions of the tenor. (In the table below, based on Handschin's, the following symbols are used: -> = (double) measure; ' = rest; / = melodic repetition in the tenor.)

---

[44]See Georgiades, *Diskanttraktate*, 25, line 24 ff., and page 41 ff.

[45]*CS* 1, 309a.

[46]Rudolf von Ficker ed., *Sieben Trienter Codices, Sechste Auswahl*, DTÖ 76, 29 ff.

[47]Jacques Handschin, "The Summer Canon and Its Background" [Part II], *Musica Disciplina* 5 (1951): especially 75.

Mo 7:300

Triplum   -> ->'-> -> ->'->'-> -> ->'->'-> -> ->'->'

Motetus   -> -> ->'->'-> -> ->'->'-> -> ->'->'-> -> ETC.

Tenor c.f.   -> ->'-> ->'-> ->'-> ->'-> ->'/->->'-> ->'

    [1 2 3 4 5 6 7 8 9 10 11 12 13 14]

                (The last repetition is different)

Mo 7:283

Triplum   -> -> ->'-> ->'-> -> ->' -> -> ->'-> ->'-> -> ->' ETC.

Motetus   -> -> ->'-> ->'-> ->'-> ->'-> ->'-> ->'-> ->'->

Tenor c.f. ->'->'->'->'->'->'->'->'/->'->'->'->'->'->'->'->'/

    [1 2 3 4 5 6 7 8 9 10 11 12 13 14 15 16]

Mo 4:56, at the beginning of the repetition of the c.f. in the tenor:

Triplum   (irregular)

Motetus   -> -> ->'-> ->'-> -> ->'   (Triplum in *Mo*)

Tenor (c.f.) -> ->'/-> ->'-> ->'-> ->'

    [1 2   3   4 5 6 7 8]

The same thing also happens in the motet *Tribum quem / Quoniam secta / Tenor* c.f., of Philippe de Vitry, mentioned by Handschin (whose schema, however, is faulty[1]): The periods in the upper voices overlap each other over and over, as well as overlapping the periods of the tenor c.f., due to their varied-length but regular repetitions. They also overlap the repetitions of the tenor c.f. In the isorhythmic motet, however, the periods of the upper voices not only are of the same length, but their content is also similar or even exact to each other, extending even to their rhythms; moreover, [their periods] are for the most part the same length as those of the tenor c.f. (*taleae*). Rarely, [the upper voices] correspond to two or even three tenor c.f. *taleae*. Still less often, they are longer than the fragment employed as tenor c.f. Within a twofold repetition of the c.f., there are usually placed three identical periods in the upper voices and the tenor [i.e., *taleae*]. If the second occurrence of the c.f. is embellished (e.g., diminished), then the periodicity cannot overlap with the successive statements of the tenor c.f. Thus, isoperiodicity in Handschin's sense does not constitute a preliminary step towards isorhythm, since in the isorhythmic motet all voices unfold for the most part in a simultaneous rhythmic phrasing. In addition it must be emphasized, contrary to Handschin and in agreement with Besseler,[J] that there also exists the possibility of the

---

[1]See Jacques Handschin, *Musikgeschichte in Überblick* (Lucerne: Heinrichshofen, [1948]), 202. The piece is also published in Schrade, ed., *PMFC* 1, No. 27, 54-6.

[J]See, respectively, Handschin, *Musikgeschichte*, 203 ff., and Heinrich Besseler, "Studien zur Musik des Mittelalters [Part] II: Die Mottete von Franko von Köln bis Philippe von Vitry,"

tenor alone being isorhythmic. This is the case when the rhythmic construction of the tenor c.f., which had always consisted of periods of equal length, was no longer understood as being subject to the rhythmic modes. In his article "Isorhythmic" in the *Harvard Dictionary of Music*, Willi Apel has pointed to isorhythm in the organa of the Notre Dame school; this will be of some significance to the present discussion.

The type of isoperiodicity characterized by Handschin as primitive, in which the periods and repetitions of the tenor correspond to each other,[K] I have still not been able to trace (*Mo* 8:344?).

Intimations of isorhythm are encountered in England at an early date. In the English polyphonic setting of *Descendit*, (Verse) *Tamquam, Gloria*[48] the tenor c.f. at the beginning of the verse and of the Gloria is laid out in patterns which, due to their length and diversity, cannot be understood as being purely modal. It is this same rhythmicization of the tenor that Apel (see above) has suggested as an example for isorhythm in Perotin. Earlier and more complicated tenor patterns are to be found in the motets Worcester No. 36 (from m. 77), No. 44 (from m. 135), and No. 47 (from mm. 120–32). This same thing is also the case for most of the motets in *Mo* which are probably of English provenance. Here one sees variation in the rhythmicization of the tenor as well, especially the rhythmic shortening of the second (or third, etc.) repetition, a procedure also encountered in the isorhythmic motets. Such variation of the tenor c.f. is, according to Handschin, likewise a distinguishing characteristic of English provenance of motets in Continental sources. In the fragment Oxford, Bodleian Library, MS E Mus. 7, the tenor c.f. of the four-voice motet *Petrum cephas ecclesie* / *Petrus pastor potissimus* / Quartus cantus / [Tenor *Petre amas me*],[L] whose upper voices move throughout in *longa–brevis* rhythms, is in a simple sense isorhythmic; the two texted upper voices always comprise periods of eight beats, offset from each other by a space of two beats. In the motets whose upper voices (or uppermost voice alone) move predominantly in semibreves and which are written in the so-called Petrus de Cruce or *Fauvel* notation, the tenor c.f. is, so to speak, self-evidently isorhythmic. But is it possible that the English could have been so

---

Archiv für Musikwissenschaft 8 (1926): 167, and Heinrich Besseler, *Die Musik des Mittelalters und der Renaissance* (Potsdam: Athenaion, [1931]), 129 ff.

[K] Jacques Handschin, "The Summer Canon and Its Background" [Part II], *Musica Disciplina* 5 (1951): 75.

[48] See Luther Dittmer, "An English Discantuum Volumen," *Musica Disciplina* 8 (1954): 55 ff.

[L] See above, note 18.

conservative in their notation of pieces that they could still have transmitted in Petronian notation works which were clearly of a later date than those of the *Roman de Fauvel* on the Continent? Bukofzer has shown the typically English characteristics of the other four-voice piece contained in this same fragment [MS E Mus. 7].[49] Although the pieces consist of longs, breves, and semibreves, and are written in Franconian mensural, Petronian, and *Fauvel* notation, the upper voices are still syllabic, [and] the two pieces with minims display melismatic sections.[50] The minims, at any rate, do not carry syllables. Melismatic sections are likewise a mark of English provenance.

According to Bukofzer, one type of isorhythm occurs in *OH* that is not met with in Continental sources.[51] As an example see the Gloria No. 21 (III, [32]), in which different *taleae*, each repeated once, are ordered within a melodically through-composed tenor.[52] A similar situation is also seen in the Credo, No. 80 (II, 194). The Gloria, No. 29 (III, [37]), has isorhythm in the last section of [what is otherwise] a "Ballade-style" mass setting. Credo No. 85 (II, 241) systematically alternates textless isorhythmic and texted free sections between the upper voices (voice exchange principle), and this procedure also occurs in *LoF*, Gloria No. 1.[53] The Gloria No. 3 in *LoF* has isorhythm in the two lower voices, which together comprise an ostinato foundation for sonority [*Klangfundament*].

The motets of the *Ars nova* appear to be a phenomenon looking back to organum. Evidence for this assumption can be seen in the fact that their texts are often proses. But for quite some time now, organa according to the models of the Notre Dame school had been composed only in England. In these so-called "new" or "English" organa, the upper voices sometimes only very slightly trope the prose text of the tenor c.f., whereas the tenor c.f. is very melismatic. The English had long since felt no need to underlay a syllable for each note of the upper voices, which moved quicker than the tenor c.f., [but] we see here for the first time, as far as I can ascertain, several notes over a syllable and an independent enunciation of each, or a text only slightly troped

---

[49]Manfred Bukofzer, *Studies in Medieval and Renaissance Music*, 23 ff.

[50]The piece on fol. 529 is incomplete, and that on fol. 530-31 is illegible in places. See Ernst Apfel, *Studien* I, 30 (note 40), and 31; also 54.

[51]Manfred Bukofzer, *Studies in Medieval and Renaissance Music*, 58 ff. passim, and 106 ff.

[52]This type of isorhythm is also encountered in most of the motets in the manuscript Turin, Bibl. Naz. J.II.9, which, moreover, along with certain mass movements from the same source, exhibit connections with west and north Europe, i.e., England. See Richard H. Hoppin, "The Cypriot-French Repertory of the MS Torino, Biblioteca Nazionale, J.II.9," *Musica Disciplina* 11 (1957): 79-125.

[53]See Ernst Apfel, *Studien* I, 86 ff., and *Studien* II, 112 ff.

among the various voices. This is true of Worcester No. 19 (from m. 84) and No. 50 (from m. 16). Thus, in these organa there was no rhythmic-metric unity. The composition did not proceed from syllabification. Similarly to the texts, the music remained that of the prosa. From this point onwards, the composition of the *Ordinarium missae* (prose), and particularly the Gloria and Credo, could proceed in the so-called motet style. Certainly these are new questions, which demand meticulous investigation.

In any case, the English seem to have been the first ones to have developed a true four-voice conception of composition, in which the space under the tenor c.f. was consciously incorporated. [This is true] most particularly in the so-called techniques of "tonal [discant] counterpoint" and "tonal-free discant counterpoint." Moreover, the English seem to have furthered the tradition of organum with its concept of melisma, which may be considered to have been effectively revived in the *Ars nova*.

The present study should not be allowed to conclude without having called to memory the book by Victor Lederer,[M] the conclusions of which, although in some respects modified, have here been demonstrated as [essentially] correct.

[M]See Victor Lederer, *Über Heimat und Ursprung der mehrstimmigen Tonkunst* (Leipzig: Siegel, 1906).

8

Four-Voice Counterpoint
in the Fourteenth and Fifteenth Centuries

Ernst Apfel

EDITOR'S PREFACE: *This selection may be regarded as an extension of the previous one. Together they constitute an essential contribution to the literature on compositional process in the period from about 1300 through 1450. It is precisely in this epoch that four-voice counterpoint had hitherto been rather poorly understood by musicologists, but with these two studies Apfel pointed the way to a clearer understanding of the underlying compositional principles. Both the articles and the concepts developed in them, however, have remained almost entirely outside the scope of research and pedagogy as practiced in the English-speaking world. It might also be mentioned that the figure of Dufay plays a larger role in this article than in any other of Apfel's studies translated in this volume.*

In accordance with the observations in the previous volume of this journal,[1] it may be asserted that the true four-voice type of counterpoint, in which each part conforms to the lowest voice at a specific [intervallic] distance, originated

---

[1] Ernst Apfel, "Zur Entstehung des realen vierstimmigen Satzes in England," *Archiv für Musikwissenschaft* 17 (1960): 81-99 [translated above, see essay 7], where the following corrections should be noted: 85, line 3 should read "in der erstgenannten"; 89, line 2 of the last paragraph should read *"Mo* 2:24"; 90, fifth line from the bottom of the first paragraph should read *"Mo* 2:35"; on page 94 before the words "1) dreistimmig" are missing the words "I) frei komponiert"; on 96, the last line is missing a closing bracket. [These corrections are incorporated into the translation.]

in England around 1300.[2] The few four-voice Continental motets of the *Ars antiqua* are based on three-voice models, which, in turn, originate from two-voice compositions.[3] All four voices in the piece move almost without exception in the space of an octave, and at places of rhythmic emphasis sound together at the unison, fifth, or octave. The sole sonority sometimes occurring that could be designated as four-voiced (notwithstanding the doubling of its lowest tone at the octave) is the 8-5-3. But in this sonority, all imperfect consonances are always resolved to the nearest perfect one:

Example 1   A   or B

In the English compositions, the tenth and the twelfth are also employed as consonances, although the beginnings and endings of the older pieces still stand within the space of an octave.[4] The incorporation of the tenth and twelfth as consonances in motets where the tenor c.f. generally or temporarily lies in a high register was only made possible by employing the third and the fifth below the tenor, due to the restrictions of the available tonal space. The voice that came to lie under the tenor through the use of such consonances

---

[2]The sonorous qualities in the three- and four-voice organa of the Notre Dame school require a special study. Regarding the three- and four-voice types of conductus-motets, see Ernst Apfel, "Zur Entstehung des realen vierstimmigen Satzes in England," 82, note 2 [note 5 in the translation above], and 84, paragraph in small print [in the above translation, this is the paragraph that refers to Examples 1A through 1D]. See also Ernst Apfel, "Über einige Zusammenhänge zwischen Text und Musik im Mittelalter, besonders in England," *Acta Musicologica* 33 (1961): 47-54.

[3]Corresponding to the fact that the motet was the most important category of that time, the following comments are made in connection with this [genre].

[4]The development of "real" voices from doubling practice, outlined by Thrasybulos Georgiades, *Englische Diskanttraktate aus der ersten Hälfte des 15. Jahrhunderts* (Munich: Musikwissenschaftliches Seminar der Universität München, 1937), 67 ff., may be considered to hold true in large measure for England but not for the Continent. On the Continent, with the exception of the three- and four-voice organa of the Notre-Dame school, the two-voice conception of Leonin's *Magnus liber organi* forms the basis of all later composition. The tripla and quadrupla of the four-voice *ars antiqua* motets did not grow out of doubling practice, neither are they "real" voices in the sense of a "real" [four-voice] work. On the contrary, one must ask whether it is not to some degree a question even of alternative voices in order to account for their close placement. [The fact] that a wide placement of the voices was likewise maintained on the Continent at the beginning of the *Ars nova* allows the conclusion that the *Ars nova* was stimulated by English practices, as Handschin has already surmised.

became indispensable to the sonority as its director [*Klangträger*], indeed decisive for the further vertical construction of the piece. This circumstance was a consequence of the concept prevailing in England that sonorities were determined by their lowest part [*grundtönige Auffassung der Klänge*]. The upper voices can have all possible consonances among themselves, including the fourth. Thirds and sixths [occurring] between upper parts do not require resolution to the nearest perfect consonance, but [resolution of these imperfect intervals] is almost inevitably required when [they occur] between an upper part and the lowest part [*Satzfundament*]. Typically the low voice that was added to the tenor c.f. was not texted and was labeled *Quartus cantus*, *Quadruplex*, [or either] *Primus* or *Secundus tenor*. However, it could also be a texted discant voice. The tenor c.f. is tightly bound together with the director of sonorities. For the most part, the other two texted voices of the piece are closely related textually or musically, so that one can speak here of a "true four-voice piece" with the typical "English sound" in open position.

In a work wherein all voices added to the tenor move above it ("multiple two-voice counterpoint" [*mehrfach-zweistimmiger Satz*]), all upper voices would have to be especially closely connected to each other, textually or musically, in order to designate it as a "true four-voice piece."

True four-voice counterpoint is found also on the Continent from the advent of the *Ars nova*, except that here the voice acting as [alternative] director of sonorities—the first one added to the tenor—was designated as "contratenor." However, the two four-voice motets, No. 7 and No. 9 in the Ivrea Codex (Chapter library,[5] fol. 5v–6r: *Apta caro* / *Flos virginum* / tenor: *Alma redemptoris mater* / contratenor, and fol. 6v–7r: *Ida capillorum* / *Porcio nature* / tenor: *Ante tronum* / contratenor) are not really four-voice works. In both, the contratenor was added subsequently to what was essentially a three-voice piece: In the motet No. 7, the contratenor varies considerably between the two manuscripts [in which it is contained, namely] Ivrea and Chantilly, Musée Condé 1047, fol. 60v–61r. In motet No. 9, the respective contratenors are somewhat different at the beginning. In both motets the contratenor is voice led in a very leapwise fashion, and never at any place does it take the third or fifth below the tenor c.f.—[intervals] decisive for the further

---

[5]See Heinrich Besseler, "Studien zur Musik des Mittelalters [Part] I: Neue Quellen des 14. und beginnenden 15. Jahrhunderts," *Archiv für Musikwissenschaft* 7 (1925): 167-252, and especially 188 ff. The following explanatory compositional observations are based on Mildred J. Johnson, "The Motets of the Codex Ivrea," vol. II, "Transcriptions" (dissertation, Indiana University, 1955).

construction of sonorities. In the motets listed below from *Iv*, the contratenor
likewise does not take the third or the fifth under the tenor c.f.

No. 2, fol. 2v–3r: *Altissonis / In principes /* tenor: *Tonans /* contratenor;
No. 70, fol. 55r: *Canenda vulgo / Rex quem metrorum /* tenor / contratenor;
No. 71, fol. 55v a/b: *In virtute / Decens carmen /* tenor: *Clamor meus /* contratenor;
No. 73, fol. 57v: *Trop ay dure / Par sauvage /* tenor / contratenor

To the contrary: in Nos. 2 and 70, it even builds noticeable fourths with the
tenor c.f., so that with the upper voices strange 6-4 sonorities appear.[6] In the
motet No. 18 (fol. 11v–12r: *Almifonis / Rosa sine culpe /* tenor / tenor) the
first tenor is not permitted to play any decisive role in the composition. [On
the other hand,] the contratenor acts as a director of sonorities in the following
motets from *Iv*:

No. 6, fol. 4v–5r: *Impudenter circuivi / Virtutibus laudabilis /* tenor / contratenor / tenor solus;
No. 11, fol. 7v–8r: *Post missarum / Post misse /* tenor / contratenor / tenor solus;
No. 13, fol. 8v–9r: *Vos quid admiramini / Gratissima virginis /* tenor: *Gaude gloriosa /* contratenor / tenor solus.

These are the motets in *Iv* that exhibit a single refined *tenor solus* [built]
from the lowest tones of tenor c.f. and contratenor (which are decisive for the
further construction of the sonorities). The motet No. 1 (fol. 1v–2r: *O
Philippe Franci / O bone dux /* tenor solus) is transmitted only in three voices
with a *tenor solus*. It must thus have been originally four-voiced.[7]

But in all of the Continental motets which have herein been described as
really four-voiced, one detects the "English sound" far more seldom than in
earlier or contemporary English motets. Several of the motets so far discussed
(that is, from among the different types) are attributed to Philippe de Vitry.[8]

---

[6]In No. 2 it is questionable, however, whether the fourths the contratenor makes with the
tenor c.f. are not caused by transcription mistakes in the above-named dissertation.

[7]The bringing together of tenor and contratenor into a *solus tenor*, which reduces a four-
voice motet to one for three voices, is a performance-conditioned measure of necessity, not a
compositional principle as is the subsequent addition of a contratenor to an already complete
three-voice piece that one happens to have at hand. In a three-voice rendition of a four-voice
piece by means of a *tenor solus*, the fifth (for example in an 8-5 or 12-5 sonority) often falls
out, so that in the resulting sonority a void exists, whereas in the motets described above, the
contratenor for the most part simply doubles one component of the already-intact 6-3 or 8-5
sonority, so that the composition, when the contratenor is left out again, remains quite compact.

[8]It must be assumed as eminently plausible that Philippe de Vitry composed in an extremely
varied manner within the category of the motet, both with respect to his own output (youthful
and older works) as well as in connection to the Middle Ages in general (consider Dufay). In
spite of this, and above all since his authorship of the three-voice motets that have been
attributed to him has come into question (see Apfel, "Über einige Zusammenhänge zwischen

Also, the four-voice motets of Machaut[9] (Nos. 5 and 21-23) are "real" four-voice works, just as are the Kyrie, Sanctus, Agnus, and *Ite missa est* of his mass (regarding the Gloria and Credo, see below). But also in Machaut's motets the "English sound" is not so very often to be met with. Instead of this, in No. 5, one of the upper voices often makes a fourth with the tenor c.f., which is not ameliorated by the contratenor. (Also, a remarkable seventh between one of the upper voices and the tenor c.f. occurs.[10]) Even the contratenor itself makes striking fourths with the tenor c.f. The same thing is encountered in motet No. 21. Here, moreover, one of the upper voices forms frequent dissonances with the contratenor. In the motet No. 22, one sees dissonances of significant duration between triplum or motetus and tenor, or (more frequently) contratenor. In the motet No. 23, fourths between the tenor c.f. and contratenor are conspicuous, as well as sevenths between the upper voices and the contratenor, and even with the tenor c.f. Besides [these factors,] in the wide spacing of its sonorities the vertical quality of this piece is reminiscent of the four-voice motets in fascicle 2 of the Codex Montpellier, one of the oldest fascicles of this manuscript. This is also the case in the Sanctus, Agnus, and *Ite missa est* of the Machaut Mass, and to a lesser extent in its Kyrie, whose simultaneities are in this respect more clearly arranged than are those of the pieces mentioned above.

From the time between Machaut and Dufay, there are unfortunately only a few motets accessible in transcription.[11] The edited motets, as well as the manuscript catalogues, lead to the conclusion that the compositional structure of the four-voice isorhythmic motet has not essentially changed during this time. Apparently, however, in these pieces there no longer occur any of those

---

Text und Musik im Mittelalter," 54), the issue of Philippe de Vitry as a composer should be newly examined.

[9]Friedrich Ludwig, ed., *Guillaume de Machaut, Musikalische Werke*, vol. 3, *Motets* (Leipzig: Breitkopf & Härtel, 1929—*Publikationen Älterer Musik* IV 2).

[10]In three-voice motets of the *Ars antiqua* (and correspondingly in four-voice works), the triplum and motetus often have a consonant relationship while one of the two voices, usually the triplum, is dissonant with the tenor c.f. Less often do the triplum and motetus make dissonances while both voices concord with the tenor c.f. (see Götz Dietrich Sasse, *Die Mehrstimmigkeit der Ars antiqua in Theorie und Praxis* (Leipzig: Noske, 1940), 117 ff.). The first-mentioned instance corroborates the suggestion advanced in Ernst Apfel, "Zur Entstehung des realen vierstimmigen Satzes in England," 84, that in the composition of the triplum, attention was often paid only to the motetus. In England, on the other hand, even at an early stage each voice was related individually to the tenor c.f.

[11]See Gilbert Reaney, ed., *Early Fifteenth Century Music, CMM* 11-1 (n.p.: American Institute of Musicology, 1955).

dissonances that disturb the consonant construction of the work, and above all, none of the particularly striking dissonances between the fundamental voices (tenor c.f. and contratenor) such as we have seen in the motets so far discussed.

Special mention is warranted here of the freely composed, imitative four-voice motets, in particular those of Ciconia, which were cultivated especially in Padua and Venice. Moreover, in England as well there are surviving freely composed four-voice motets, which also manifest short imitations.[12] However, a particular [type of] four-voice free counterpoint, proceeding from the discantus or from a discantus-tenor framework [Gerüst] (to be discussed below) may be said to have been more significant for the future than the free, motet-like counterpoint emphasizing the lowest tone (which from the [late] Middle Ages on [was] seen to some extent as a contradiction in itself).

Among the four-voice isorhythmic motets of Dufay, those with a tenor c.f., contratenor, and two texted upper voices set themselves apart from the tradition of the type previously cultivated.[13] In this type the counterpoint is now perfectly realized. In the motets Nos. 1-3 and 7, the contratenor only very seldom takes over from the tenor c.f. the function of director of sonorities with respect to the two texted upper voices. It does so more often in No. 4, and quite often in No. 6. In No. 6 this is a consequence of the fact that the c.f. lies very high. No. 3 and No. 6 manifest a *solus tenor*.

The motets Nos. 8-11 consist of a tenor c.f., a tenor secundus instead of a contratenor, along with a lower- and a higher-lying texted discantus.[14] The

---

[12]See Ernst Apfel, "Zur Entstehung des realen vierstimmigen Satzes in England," 94. The second half of the motet *Salve iubar presulum/Salve cleri speculum* is, to be sure, based on a c.f.; see Frank Ll. Harrison, "English Church Music in the Fourteenth Century," *The New Oxford History of Music*, vol. III, *Ars Nova and the Renaissance: 1300–1540* (London: Oxford University Press, 1960), 89 ff. (abbreviation: *NOHM* III).

[13]Guillaume de Van, ed., *Guglielmi Dufay: Opera Omnia*, Vol. 2, *Motetti qui et cantiones vocantur*, *Corpus Mensurabilis Musicae* 1 (Rome: American Institute of Musicology, 1948), nos. 1-4 and 6-7. The upper-voice incipits of these pieces are as follows:

1) *Vasilissa ergo / Vasilissa ergo*   6) *Rite maiorem / Artubus fumus*

2) *Balsamus et munda / Balsamus et munda*   7) *O gemma lux / O gemma lux*

3) *Introitus Apostolo glorioso / Introitus*

4) *O sancte Sebastiane / O sancte Sebastiane*

[14]Ibid. The upper-voice incipits of these pieces are as follows:

8) *Moribus et genere / Virgo virga virens*   10) *Salve flos / Vos nunc*

9) *Fulgens iubar / Puerpera pura*   11) *Nuper rosarum / Nuper rosarum*

positions of the voices express themselves in their cleffing: No. 11: tenor c.f. (c_4)—tenor secundus and lower texted voice (c_3)—upper texted voice (c_1); No. 10: tenor c.f. and [tenor secundus] (f_3)—lower texted voice (c_4)—upper texted voice (c_2); Nos. 8 and 9: tenor secundus (c_4)—tenor c.f. and lower texted voice (c_3)—upper texted voice (c_1). Whenever the tenor c.f. lies in a high position, the tenor secundus takes over from it the function of director of sonorities. (This happens relatively seldom in No. 11, more often in No. 10, and quite frequently in Nos. 8 and 9). When the tenor c.f. is silent, the lower-lying discant voice sometimes acts as a director of sonorities with respect to the tenor secundus. Occasionally it appears that the lower discant voice, which one could therefore designate as contratenor, has a directive function even with respect to the tenor c.f. However, in these instances the fourth between the uppermost voice and the tenor c.f. is already supported by the tenor secundus:

Example 2   A   or   B

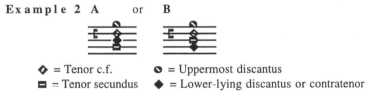

◆ = Tenor c.f.   ◙ = Uppermost discantus
▣ = Tenor secundus   ◆ = Lower-lying discantus or contratenor

The five-voice motet, No. 13 [upper-voice incipits: *Ecclesie militantis / Sanctorum meritis*], stands between the two types of Dufay's motets that we have so far discussed. Like the motets described immediately above, it consists of a tenor [secundus] and a tenor c.f., as well as a lower-lying texted voice expressly designated as contratenor (all c_4), and—corresponding to the motets described first above—two equally high and identically cleffed (c_1) upper voices, both texted.

The use of a harmonically supportive low voice, called tenor secundus, is very reminiscent of the use of such a voice in earlier English motets and in the only two truly four-voice motets in Continental manuscripts, *Ba* No. 92, and *Hu* No. 81, of which the latter is probably of English provenance.[A] The four-voice isorhythmic motet *Salve scema sanctitatis* of Dunstable also has two tenors, whose clefs are as follows: tenor [secundus] (f_3)—tenor [c.f.]

The *Missa Caput* of Ockeghem also belongs to the same type (note the voice designations!) See Ernst Apfel, "Der klangliche Satz und der freie Diskantsatz im 15. Jahrhundert," *Archiv für Musikwissenschaft* 12 (1955): 311 ff. [Translated above, see essay 5.]

[A] See Apfel, "Zur Entstehung des realen vierstimmigen Satzes in England," 88; see also Apfel, "Über einige Zusammenhänge zwischen Text und Musik im Mittelalter," 50, note 13.

(c4)—texted discant voices (c3) and (c2).[15] In *Preco preheminencie* (work No. 29, 78 ff.) the clefs are: tenor c.f. and textless contratenor (c4)—texted discant voices (c2) and (c1); in *Veni creator spiritus* (work No. 32, 88 ff.): tenor c.f. and texted contratenor (low lying *mene* voice with a large ambitus) (c3)— texted discant voices (c2) and (c1); in *Gaude virgo salutata* (work No. 28, 74 ff.): texted contratenor (low-lying *mene* with wide ambitus) (c4)—tenor c.f. (c3)—both texted discant voices (c2).

In the [de Van] edition mentioned above, the isorhythmic motets Nos. 8-11 and 13 by Dufay are dated (in the order of their numbering) as follows: [8] c. 1446, [9] between 1440 and 1450, [10] 1435-36, [11] 1436, [13] 1431. Thus they all fall within the time of possible English influence upon Dufay (No. 13 least so). The harmonic filling notes [*Klangzusatznoten*] in the motets Nos. 8, 10, and 11 just discussed probably are attributable to English influence. In England, we encounter such filling notes in the Old Hall MS and in *LoF* (London, British Museum Add. 40011 B, see also below).[16]

The isorhythmic motet No. 14 [upper-voice incipits: *O gloriose tyre / Divine pastus*] is labeled in this edition as *opus dubium*. The editor, Guillaume de Van, adduces stylistic grounds for his doubt of Dufay's authorship, especially the "dark sonority" of the motet (cleffing: c4, c4, c2, c1). He inclines to the view that it should be regarded as a work of Dunstable's, the more so since its sole transmission is through the main Continental source—*ModB*—containing English motets, although it is not actually present in the English fascicle.[B] And in truth, the following features speak for English origin of the motet: the contratenor leaps almost as that of a chanson, moving practically as fast as the discant voices, and like them, it is texted. [At the same time,] however, it takes over the directive function from the tenor c.f. at very specific places ([so that one can speak of a] tonal-free

---

[15]*John Dunstable: Complete Works*, ed. Manfred F. Bukofzer, *Musica Britannica: A National Collection of Music*, vol. 8 (London: Stainer & Bell, 1953 [revised ed., 1970]), No. 30, 81 ff. Regarding the four-voice isorhythmic motets of Dunstable, see Ernst Apfel, *Studien zur Satztechnik der mitteralterlichen englischen Musik, Abhandlungen der Heidelberger Akademie der Wissenschaften, Phil.-hist. Klasse, Jahrgang 1959, 5. Abhandlung*, Vol. I (Heidelberg: Carl Winter, 1959), 94-5. (Subsequent citations below use the abbreviation *Studien*.)

[16]Handschin has already pointed out that two-voice compositions in the Notre-Dame Codex W1, which are probably English, often cadence in three voices. Strengthening of vertical sonorities is also encountered in the organ pieces in London, British Museum Add. 28550 (Robertsbridge Codex). [Author's note: regarding *Klanszusatznoten*, see the 1987 study by Marianne Danckwardt, cited in the bibliography at the end of this volume.]

[B]Guillaume de Van, ed., *Guglielmi Dufay: Opera Omnia*, Vol. 2, *CMM* 1, XXXII.

[*klanglich-frei*], true four-voice piece).[17] In the fourteenth and early fifteenth centuries, the foregoing characteristics (to which could be added the low range, especially of the motetus) can only be observed in four-voice English motets. According to the English discant treatises of the fifteenth century, the contratenor of a motet is a low *mene* with a wide ambitus. In addition, such motets incorporate notes that are "supplementary" to sonorities (see above). In opposition to de Van, Besseler considers Dufay to be the composer of this motet.[18] In any case, it probably stems from the 1440s, that is, during the time in which influence of English music upon that of the Continent is authenticated.

Binchois, however, appears to have taken over this style of composition from the English even earlier than Dufay.[C] But for the present we will draw upon no. 4 of the above-mentioned edition of Dufay's motets *qui et cantiones vocantur*.[D] This piece [upper-voice incipits: *O proles Yspanie / O sidus Yspanie*] consists of a contratenor secundus, a tenor, and a contratenor primus, all in the same range (c_3), and a higher voice (c_1). All of the voices are texted. Neither of the two contratenors ever takes over from the tenor even once the function of director of sonorities.[19] This corresponds to the subsequent [technique of] four-voice free counterpoint, whose origins we now indeed want to trace. To be sure, the tenor and the upper voice do not [in this piece] constitute a particularly clear framework, and the two contratenors are not spatially separated from each other as in the later four-voice chanson style. This motet is dated by Besseler around 1440.

A special case among the [de Van edition of Dufay's] motets *qui et cantiones vocantur* [Vol. 1] is presented by No. 2, with a mensuration canon in the two upper voices. Between the two canonic voices there occasionally occurs a fourth, which is supported by the [voice labeled] *contra concordans cum fuga et cuilibet per se* [i.e., "contratenor concording with the canonic voices and pleasing in itself"]. The [voice labeled] *secundus contratenor concordans cum omnibus* [i.e., "second contratenor concording with all"] is merely a filling voice.

---

[17]See Apfel, *Studien* I, 90 ff. and 104.

[18]Heinrich Besseler, *Bourdon und Fauxbourdon* (Leipzig: Breitkopf & Härtel, 1950; abbreviation: *Bourdon*), 170 (note 6), 172 (note 3), 174, 176 (with note 3), 191 (note 2), 238 (Thesis 74).

[C]Apfel, "Zur Entstehung des realen vierstimmigen Satzes in England," 96.

[D]Guillaume de Van, ed., *Guglielmi Dufay: Opera Omnia*, Vol. 1, *CMM* 1, 14 ff.

[19]For a contrary argument, see Heinrich Besseler, *Bourdon*, 237, Thesis 68 (summary position).

Additional four-voice pieces include the Introitus (excepting the Repetitio), Alleluya, Offertorium, Sanctus, and Agnus of Dufay's *Missa Sancti Jacobi*.[20] These pieces are based, in traditional fashion (as are the isorhythmic Sanctus and Agnus in Machaut's mass), upon a c.f. in the tenor.[21] In the sections of the Ordinary, all four voices are texted; in the sections of the Proper, the contratenor is untexted. This textless contratenor in the Propers serves only to fill out the sonority. Correspondingly, the decisive voices, tenor c.f. and texted upper voices, begin the Introitus and Alleluya in an 8-5 sonority, that is, in a narrow position, and in the Offertorium, the texted upper voices begin in the manner of structural voices at the octave (the contratenor takes the fifth below, while the tenor rests!). At the beginning of the Sanctus and Agnus, which are texted in all four voices, and at the end of all four-voice sections of the mass, the voices constitute a 12-8-5 sonority, which had been usual for four voices since the *Ars nova* (and which was instigated by the English). The texted voice of the Ordinary sections—which corresponds to the untexted contratenor of the Proper sections—fits particularly well with the underlying three-voice counterpoint.[22] But it is also scarcely possible to ignore the untexted contratenor in the Proper sections, even though it evidently was the last to be added to the contrapuntal fabric. In general, however, it is not the voice pairing of tenor-discant and bassus-altus (later to become typical) that is manifest in these sections from the *Missa Sancti Jacobi*, but rather the older (motet style) consisting of an upper-voice pair over a tenor c.f. with a contratenor.

Four-voice Ordinary sections upon liturgical Ordinary [chant] melodies are also encountered in the Old Hall MS.[23] To begin with, we should quickly consider a group of pieces that exhibit the c.f. in the tenor. In No. 118 (vol. III, 94, by Tyes), all the voices are texted, and none are labeled. The two lowest voices with the same clef are alternate directive voices. The two upper voices likewise share the same clef. In the pieces Nos. 114 and 133 (vol. III,

[20]See Guillaume de Van, ed., *Guglielmi Dufay: Opera Omnia*, Vol. 4, *CMM* 1.

[21]In the Machaut Mass, the Kyrie also can be included; in the *Missa Sancti Jacobi*, certain sections of the Kyrie are founded on a c.f., but others are freely composed.

[22]Still, there are differences between the Sanctus and Agnus. In this connection, see Rudolf Bockholdt, *Die frühen Messenkompositionen von Guillaume Dufay*, *Münchner Veröffentlichungen zur Musikgeschichte*, ed. Thrasybulos Georgiades, vol. 5 (Tutzing: Schneider, 1960), 72 ff. and 166 ff. (abbreviation: *Messenkompositionen*). The study treats the interconnections between rhythm, melody, and sonority in a most illuminating fashion.

[23]See Alexander Ramsbotham, ed., *The Old Hall Manuscript*, completed by H.B. Collins and Dom Anselm Hughes (Nashdom Abbey: The Plainsong and Mediæval Music Society, 1933–38), and, in addition, Apfel, *Studien* I, chap. III, and *Studien* II, 104 ff.

76 and 136, respectively, both by Leonel [Power]), only the contratenor is without text. It never acts as director of sonorities, but in spite of this it is indispensable in the two works, both of which begin and end with a 12-8-5 sonority. The two upper voices at times have identical clefs; in No. 133, this is true also of the tenor c.f. and the contratenor. In No. 114, [however,] the contratenor is lower [than the tenor].

In No. 113 (vol. III, 70, by Leonel), the c.f. is placed in the uppermost voice; the tenor and contratenor are correspondingly without text. Both upper and lower voice pairs have the same clef, and always begin at the unison. Twice during the movement, the contratenor has an unmistakable directive function, and it is also indispensable due to its spatial characteristics [i.e., its being below the tenor].

Of somewhat greater interest are the two works, No. 78 (vol. II, 176, anonymous) and No. 131 (vol. III, 133, anonymous), in which the c.f. is to be found in the cantus secundus. In No. 78, only the two upper voices with identical clefs are texted. The tenor and contratenor likewise have identical clefs, but they are textless. In two places the contratenor is indisputably the director of sonorities. In this c.f. adaptation, notated in parts, with "sectional contrast" (the cadence is five-voiced), the c.f. is handled very freely.

In No. 131, we see a three-voice c.f. adaptation in score notation, with the c.f. in the middle voice, and a texted contratenor, subsequently added, which is independently notated.[24] The three original voices begin and end in a narrow spacing; their cleffing is c5, c3, c1. The clef of the contratenor is c5. The spatial relationship, at least between the two upper voices, thus corresponds to that which later became standard. Because the contratenor was a subsequent addition, it never had the function of director of sonorities; neither did it [have that function] in connection to the middle voice of the basic three-voice structure as later [it did] in four-voice counterpoint in connection to the high contratenor altus, since this [middle voice] is here the carrier of the c.f. The added contratenor moves sometimes under [and] sometimes above the tenor of the basic three-voice structure and would also be dispensable from the standpoint of tonal space. A three-voice composition with c.f. in the middle voice is thus not susceptible of being transformed into a [true] four-voice piece through the addition of a low voice.

As Brian Trowell and the author of the present study have simultaneously but independently ascertained, the middle voice in English faburden was also

---

[24]In the edition, the words *Contratenor de cantu feriali* are inaccurately placed with the c.f. voice instead of with the later contratenor, which was notated separately.

understood as main carrier of the c.f.[25] According to Trowell, the English
gradually began to adopt a c.f. treatment wherein it was placed in the upper
voice even before English music appeared on the Continent.[E] This
transformation was now made possible also at least partially by the
[composers'] inclination to create a four-voice composition through the
addition of a low voice to a three-voice faburden or faburden-like piece, which
from the standpoint of compositional technique was not very possible without
alteration of the middle voice of the basic counterpoint. Guglielmus
Monachus describes in detail how indeed such a four-voice piece would be
composed, in which the subsequently added, low contratenor obtained the
function of director of sonorities in opposition to the middle voice of the
three-voice basic structure (the high contratenor).[F] Tinctoris [can also be cited]
in connection with the use of the fourth in counterpoint, particularly at the
cadences.[26]

Before the early English examples of this type of four-voice
compositional technique are discussed, however, something should be said
about the freely composed mass and chanson works for four voices of the
fourteenth and early fifteenth centuries.

Among the pieces for Mass Ordinary, the Gloria and Credo [genres] are
freely composed in the fourteenth and the beginning of the fifteenth century.
This is also true in the mass of Machaut.[27] With the exception of the "Amen"
[section] of the Gloria, the voices are not specifically labeled in either
movement. But as the facsimile edition of Gennrich shows, the voice
designated in the Gloria as contratenor by de Van in his edition is in reality
the tenor of the movement and that designated as tenor is actually the
contratenor. The voice labeled by de Van as contratenor always takes the tenor

---

[25]Brian Trowell, "Faburden and Fauxbourdon," *Musica Disciplina* 13 (1959): 43-78, and
Apfel, *Studien* I, 82 ff. The English musicians themselves, at any rate, seem to have conceived
things in this manner in connection with the middle-voice c.f. so widely cultivated by them. That
the c.f. in faburden, as in fauxbourdon, actually sounds in both upper voices is not a self-evident
musical phenomenon but is simply a result of contemporary musical practices.

[E]Brian Trowell, "Faburden and Fauxbourdon," 74.

[F]*CS* 3, 293b and 295b ff.

[26]*CS* 4, 84b ff. See also Ernst Apfel, "Der Diskant in der Musiktheorie des 12.–15.
Jahrhunderts" (dissertation, University of Heidelberg, 1953), 183 ff.

[27]See Friedrich Gennrich, ed., *Guillaume de Machaut: Messe de Nostre Dame*, facsimile
edition (Darmstadt: F. Gennrich, 1957); Guillaume de Van, ed., *Guglielmi de Mascaudio:
Opera I: La Messe de Nostre Dame*, CMM 2 (n.p.: American Institute of Musicology, 1949);
Heinrich Besseler, ed., *Guillaume de Machaut, Musikalische Werke, vol. 4, Messe und Lais, aus
der Nachlaß Friedrich Ludwigs* (Leipzig: Breitkopf & Härtel, 1943, retypeset 1954).

cadences, whenever one takes place. The cleffing of the movement runs as follows: "tenor" ($c_{4/5}$), "contratenor" (c_4), upper voices (c_3) and (c_1). Between the real tenor and contratenor there occur rather more unsupported fourths than the relationship of either of the upper voices to the tenor [displays]. Accordingly, the actual contratenor could have been the last voice added to the composition. In the Credo the cleffing runs: tenor (c_5), contratenor ($c_{3/4/5}$), upper voices ($c_{2/1/3}$) and ($c_{2/1}$). At the cadences of individual sections it is primarily the two outer voices (of rather fixed ambitus) that make the decisive sixth-to-octave motion. Accordingly, the "middle voices" (quite flexible in ambitus) have to a certain degree the character of filling or supplementary parts.

The Gloria and Credo of the mass of Machaut are in accord with the Credo No. XXXIII of the Apt Codex (fol. 29v–30r).[28] In this piece, the voices are labeled most interestingly as Tenor, Vᵃ, VIIIᵃ, and XIIᵃ. Here, not only do the two outer voices make a preponderance of the critical sixth-to-octave cadences but also, the two middle voices (especially the one labeled Vᵃ) are rhythmically far more complicated than the [outer voices], thus demonstrating themselves as filling or supplementary voices even in their outward details. Very often the voice marked Vᵃ ends phrases with a short note followed by a rest, while the voice labeled VIIIᵃ conceals the phrase ending with an eliding melodic flourish. One finds unsupported fourths between all voices, but particularly between the two lower parts. Occasionally (and probably fortuitously), the Vᵃ voice supports fourths [occurring] between the tenor and one of the two upper voices.

That conductus-style Glorias and Credos, beginning (and ending) in a wide voice spacing, can also be three-voiced, is demonstrated in the Apt Codex by Nos. XII, XXX, and XXXIV of Gastoué's edition.

In Dufay's freely composed, four-voice Gloria and Credo pairs, Nos. 9/2 and 10/3,[29] the voices are no longer led almost note-against-note; rather, the contratenor, and especially the tenor, move somewhat slower than the two upper voices. (The latter are the only texted voices, excepting occasional places where the contratenor assumes the text.) Accordingly, it appears that, in contrast to the conductus style of the [Apt] Gloria and Credo just discussed, we must speak here more in terms of motet style pieces, as transmitted, for

---

[28] See Amédée Gastoué, ed., *Le Manuscrit de Musique du Trésor d'Apt (XIVᵉ–XVᵉ siècle)*, (Paris: Dróz, 1936), 94 ff. [Editor's note: due to a reversal of the third and fourth fascicles of this manuscript in rebinding, the numbering of this Credo in subsequent editions is Apt 40].

[29] This numbering is based on Bockholdt, *Messenkompositionen*; see 155 ff.; in the edition, 38 ff.

example, in the MS Turin J.II.9 (*TuB*).[G] Tenor and contratenor have in each case the same clef (c3 and c4, respectively) as do the upper voices in the 9/2 pairing, while in the 10/3 pair one of the upper voices lies somewhat lower (c2). The voices are not so dissonant with each other as in the works discussed previously. This moderation of contrapuntal procedure, however, occurred at the expense of the contratenor, which now was led all the more leapwise than before. Regarding the relationship of the contratenor to the counterpoint as a whole, reference can here be made to Rudolf Bockholdt's critical commentary to the Credo 3 (No. 112 of the study cited above), to which only a few amplifying remarks should be added: In measures 68, 77, 98, and 120 of this Credo, the contratenor falsifies the under-third preceding the cadence tone of the upper voice—which in the basic three-voice structure had been consonant—into a dissonance. In m. 101, the contratenor transforms the 6-3 sonority of the basic voices into a 6-4 sonority in wide spacing. In Gloria No. 10, m. 19, the contratenor adds a dissonant quality to the pure 6–3—>8–5 cadence of the other voices. Also, in m. 40 of the same Gloria, the contratenor disturbs the consonance of the other voices. In m. 55, the contratenor continues to rest until just before it enters in a dissonance with the other voices.

In the pairing of Gloria No. 9/Credo No. 2—both movements utilize special compositional devices (imitation, etc.)[30]—there are less of these sorts of things to be found, but here the contratenor leaps and rests at the cadences just as often as in the movements described above. In both pairings, and especially in 9/2, the tenor and the two upper voices make a kind of structural counterpoint (cadencing in close spacing). The positions of the individual voices, however, are not so stratified as those in the four-voice compositions coming into vogue in the fifteenth century. A curious phenomenon that binds Dufay's works with all those previously discussed is that at cadences of phrases, one of the two upper voices sometimes leaps down a fifth.

All the freely composed mass movements for four voices contained in the Old Hall MS, with one exception (No. 31 [old numbering]), display either sectional contrast, imitations, canon between the upper voices, or canon between lower and upper voices.[31] As in Dufay's pieces, the textless, slower,

---

[G] Apfel, "Zur Entstehung des realen vierstimmigen Satzes in England," 94-5.

[30] Regarding the compositional technique of the two pieces, see Bockholdt, *Messenkompositionen*; the corresponding instances mentioned above [occur] in the Gloria, m. 55, and in the Credo, mm. 12 and 45.

[31] See Ernst Apfel, *Studien* I, 88 ff.; for no. 31 (as in *LoF*), *Studien* II (Notenanhang), no. 52, 119 ff. [Regarding the old and new numbering of Old Hall, see *CMM* 46, vol. I, XXVI-XXIX.]

lower voices [on the one hand] and the texted, active, upper voices [on the other] move respectively in the same register, and therefore have the same clefs. The sole exception to this is the contra of the Gloria by Pycard, No. 23 (vol. I, 76 of Ramsbotham's edition), which has a canon in the middle voices.

In No. 31, the voices have the following clefs: tenor (c5)—contratenor (c4)—upper voices (c3/2) and (c2). The contratenor is in some places the director of sonorities and, because of this, is indispensable to the counterpoint. The contratenor acts as director of sonorities also in other pieces, most particularly in Nos. 33 and 73 (with sectional contrast) and less noticeably in Nos. 15 and 71 (with canon in the upper voices). However, [such practices] never amount to a spatial disposition typical for later four-voice counterpoint. Earlier, this is the case in No. 3a, a Gloria notated in score to which a contratenor was subsequently added; this [part], of course, is never a director of sonorities.[32] The beginning of the piece is included by Bukofzer, but unfortunately does not indicate the original clefs, which actually run as follows: (c5), (c5), (c3), (c2), thus corresponding closely to an arrangement typical of the later four-voice works.

We come now to chanson composition. For the rondeaux, ballades, and virelais of Machaut, reference might be made here to a previous study of the author's.[H] In their compositional technique, Dufay's four-voice chansons correspond in their entirety to the works of Machaut. Such is the case in the rondeau *Ma belle dame souverainne*.[33] The piece consists of a low, texted contratenor (c4), and higher-lying tenor, cantus, and triplum parts, all in the same range (c1). Even the voice designations recall the work[s] of Machaut. The sole difference is that the triplum [in the Dufay work] is texted. In analogy to Machaut's works, the tenor and cantus must be [regarded as] the structural or core voices of the composition, as is actually the case. For the placement of the contratenor to this core or structural counterpoint [*Kernsatz*; *Gerüstsatz*], the following places are characteristic: In m. 5, the contratenor turns the F of the cantus into a suspension, further rendering the third of the structural voices into a third-suspension. In m. 6, the cantus and tenor comprise a second-suspension from below. The contratenor makes consonance with the held B-flat of the tenor and the suspension A of the cantus, but it

[32]See Manfred Bukofzer, *Studies in Medieval and Renaissance Music* (New York: Norton, 1950), 36-7 (abbreviation: *Studies*).

[H]Ernst Apfel, "Zur Entstehung des realen vierstimmigen Satzes in England," 92-3.

[33]Edited by Heinrich Besseler, *Bourdon*, 262-3, and discussed in the same volume, 73-4 and 84-5. [Note that all of Dufay's chansons were included in Besseler's later edition, which appeared in 1964; see below, bibliography.]

makes a dissonance with the tenor's note of resolution, C. A particularly instructive example is encountered in m. 20: the cantus makes a suspension a fourth above the tenor; the contratenor takes the fifth under the tenor, as if the fourth were the consonant goal of the structural voices. In reality, their goal is a third, with which the contratenor is of course dissonant. One could point to many other such instances. The contratenor is never director of sonorities. The triplum fits much better with the structural voices. However, in m. 16, it has to adjust itself to a new placement due to the tenor note, although that is only a passing tone. Significantly, the contratenor clings here to the cantus note, so that a further dissonance between contra and triplum is added to the passing-tone dissonance of tenor and cantus. Remarkable sonorities are produced, especially in mm. 13, 16, 21, and 23 ff., through the linking of triplum and contratenor to the structural voices—tenor and cantus.

In *Mon cuer me fait*,[34] all the voices are texted. In essence this piece represents the same type of composition as that which we have discussed, except that here it was evidently the triplum that was added last: In m. 7, the triplum's F could not exist but for the lower F of the contratenor, and equally, in m. 28, its first A (second quarter note) is not conceivable without the contratenor's C. At the beginning of m. 14 the contratenor seems even to support a fourth between the structural voices, tenor and cantus. This, however, is simply a question of a suspension between cantus and tenor. With [respect to] suspensions and passing notes, even the structural voices are rather freely treated, but in spite of this, within the four-voice [complex], the tenor and cantus build by far the best two-voice counterpoint, to which probably first the contratenor, and then the triplum, was added. Tenor and contratenor have the same clefs as do triplum and cantus (c_3 and c_1, respectively).

In *Hé compaignons resvelons nous*,[1] both contratenors appear at times to function as director of sonorities. But since rather free suspensions and passing tones are introduced between the two texted structural voices, both contratenors often have the opportunity to mitigate [the] fourths thereby arising between the structural voices. Some fourths originating in this way, however, [are allowed to] stand without being legitimized by a lower voice (m. 2 cantus: quarter note C; m. 6 tenor: eighth note C; m. 13 cantus: quarter note C and E-flat; m. 17 tenor: half note C; etc.). Moreover, the two contratenors [one is labeled *concordans*] even make irregular fourths between

---

[34]John F.R. Stainer and C. Stainer, *Dufay and His Contemporaries* (London: Novello, 1898), 118 ff. (short title: *Dufay*).

[1]Stainer, *Dufay*, 127 ff. [The note values mentioned below are double those of Besseler's 1964 edition of the Dufay chansons.]

themselves or in relation to one of the other voices (e.g., m. 6: concordans with cantus; m.13: concordans with contratenor; m. 17: concordans and contratenor with the other voices; m. 23: concordans with contratenor; etc.). Even in the very voice designations themselves, [it is apparent that] the contratenor was joined first to the two-voice framework and then the concordans was added to the three-voice piece. The cleffing is: tenor [cantus II] (c4)—contratenor (c4)—concordans (c3)—cantus [I] (c3).

In all three pieces, the spatial relationship of the voices remains unclear throughout. The two structural voices cross each other the least in *Mon cuer me fait*, in which all the voices are texted and where the clefs of the two-voice framework are placed a fifth apart.

Certainly, a four-voice piece created by the addition of a low voice to a real three-voice piece must look different. This type of compositional expansion we encounter only in England or (as the case may be) by English composers.[35]

One of the oldest examples might be the chanson *O rosa bella*, by Dunstable, which has a contratenor secundus and three *concordans* voices attributed to Bedingham.[J] But neither the contratenor secundus nor the three *concordantie* by Bedingham have a contrapuntal effect on the basic three-voice structure. Rather, the contratenor secundus only doubles or takes the third below the lowest voice of the harmony built by the three basic parts. The three *concordantie* fill in gaps in the chords or make parallel thirds with one of the voices (especially by making a gymel with the cantus). As the cleffing shows (c4, c4, c2, + contratenor secundus f4, or *concordantie* f4, c4, c2), from a range standpoint there arises neither a true bass nor a true alto.

---

[35]Characteristically, in the three-voice chansons of Frye and Morton (as well as in other chansons by English composers of the time), the contratenor remains almost always under the tenor (but without being director of sonorities), through which, in turn, the possibility was created to add a contratenor altus between the structural voices. In the chansons [of] Cambridge, Univ. Libr., MS Add. 5943 (from c. 1425—see Bukofzer, *Studies*, 194 ff.) fol. 162v–163r and 165v (with French—or Norman?—text), the contratenor is even the director of sonorities. On fol. 164r it makes dissonances with the upper voice (apparently notated inexactly). It is also noteworthy, as mentioned in Apfel ("Der klangliche Satz und der freie Diskantsatz im 15. Jahrhundert," 308, note 3 [note 25 in the translation above]), that in cases where the contratenor of a three-voice "free discant piece" [*freier Diskantsatz*] legitimizes fourths or diminished fifths of one of the structural voices against the other, these are branded as compositions of English masters.

[J]Manfred Bukofzer, ed., *John Dunstable: Complete Works*, No. 54, 133 ff.

This does happen, however, in the four-voice chanson *L'omme armé* by Robert Morton.[36] The anonymous three-voice chanson with the same text in the Mellon Chansonnier[37] comprises the three upper voices of Morton's four-voice chanson. The only differences are displayed by the alto at cadences (mm. 4-5 and m. 16): The original penultimate third [existing] between the middle part and the tenor of the basic three-voice structure becomes a fourth in the four-voice piece in consideration of the fifth the added bassus makes with the tenor, a procedure that Guglielmus Monachus and Tinctoris expressly describe (see above). The bassus thus becomes responsible for vertical placement with respect to the middle part of the basic three-voice structure—the [part that] later [became known as] altus.

According to Bukofzer, the three-voice version of the piece in the Mellon Chansonnier stems from the early fifteenth century, and the four-voice version from the second half of the century. The three-voice rendition of the chanson in the Mellon Chansonnier is the oldest currently known. Whether it is also the original, and whether Morton is [actually] its composer, Bukofzer leaves undecided.[K] The three-voice composition in the Mellon Chansonnier is a so-called "double chanson."[38] The text of *L'omme armé* and its accompanying melody is divided among the two lower voices of the three-voice version; the upper voice has another text (rondeau *Il sera pour vous*—Morton's four-voice version is untexted). The two lower voices are two equal tenors, as is apparent from the interchangeability of their position in sonorities [see Example 3] and also from their cleffing. Moreover, the "middle voice" of this three-part piece is at one point the director of sonorities.

E x a m p l e 3

---

[36]See Jeanne Marix, ed., *Les Musiciens de la cour de Bourgogne au XVe siècle (1420–1467)* (Paris: L'Oiseau-Lyre, 1937), No. 63, 96.

[37]With respect to the following, see Manfred Bukofzer, "An Unknown Chansonnier of the 15th Century (the Mellon Chansonnier)," *Musical Quarterly* 28 (1942): 14 ff., especially 19 ff.

[K]See Manfred Bukofzer, "Popular and Secular Music in England (to c. 1470)," *New Oxford History of Music*, vol. III (London: Oxford University Press, 1960), 130.

[38]According to Bukofzer (see above, note 37), this term does not apply to the structure of the works in question but rather only to the existence of two (or, in "triple chansons," three) different texts in one chanson. But should one not also consider compositional correlations in analogy to the double structure, particularly of English motets, so clearly formulated by Bukofzer himself? (see Apfel, *Studien* I, 56, note 24).

At least some, if not all, of the above-mentioned facts suggest an English origin or composer of the three-voice version, whether it be Morton or his presumed teacher Dunstable. (The two chansons *O rosa bella* and *L'omme armé* are very similar to each other—[displaying an] exchange of vertical constituents!)[39] The cleffing of the four-voice version runs: contratenor (c4)—tenor (c3)—upper voices (c3) and (c2).

An even better example of the transformation of a three-voice piece into a true four-voice piece is the freely composed (despite the choral intonations) three-movement mass (incomplete Kyrie, Sanctus, and Agnus) in London, British Museum MS Egerton 3307.[40] The basic three-voice structure is extensively wrought in faburden style. However, wherever the bassus (notated in the MS in red) takes the fifth under the tenor of the underlying three-voice framework, the existing third of the middle voice [with the tenor] of the fundamental three-voice framework is typically altered into a fourth, through which the bassus becomes the vertical determinant of this voice—the altus of the four-voice piece—assuming a distance of an octave [below it]. The cadences remain predominantly three-voiced.

It can probably be assumed that the mass represents another stage of this technique as compared to [that of] the chanson described above. But in all three examples wherein a three-voice piece is elevated by English composers into a four-voice piece, we ascertain that tenor and cantus adhere as much as possible to their "natural" octave disposition ([note the] clefs!), since the middle voice of the fundamental structure is placed between them. In Dufay, this relative positioning of the parts only gradually comes into play,[L] but we recognize the tendency of the English to bestow true bass function upon the added low voice at least with reference to the middle voice—the altus—of the underlying three-voice counterpoint. This bass seems indeed rather quickly to have been given

---

[39]Perhaps it is no mere chance that Tinctoris, in one of his examples on proportions, condenses together the upper voice of *O rosa bella* with the beginning of the tenor of *L'omme armé* and the beginning of another chanson tenor (*CS* 4, 173b). The author of the present study may be permitted in this entire connection to see a first confirmation of his hypothesis, that the chanson *L'omme armé* was originally an English song, later set to French text. The original text in England could well have been *O Robert Knollis, per te fit Francia mollis* (which is rhythmically identical and has the same "o" vowel sound at the beginning). With respect to this song and to *L'omme armé*, see Victor Lederer, *Über Heimat und Ursprung der mehrstimmigen Tonkunst*, vol. I (Leipzig: Siegel, 1906; abbreviation: *Heimat*), 82 ff. and 132 ff., respectively, but which unfortunately does not bring the two songs into correlation.

[40]See Manfred Bukofzer, "A Newly Discovered 15th-Century Manuscript of the English Chapel Royal [Egerton 3307]—Part II," *Musical Quarterly* 33 (1947): 38-51.

[L]See Besseler, *Bourdon*.

bass function also in relation to the uppermost voice, whereby a freely composed counterpoint profiling the upper voice was transformed into the configuration of a motet-like c.f. piece emphasizing the lowest voice, so that a fusing of these two structural principles took place, as has been maintained by the present author, and as is the case, for example, in the anonymous *Salve regina*.[41] The German-language incipit in the tenor (*Hilf und gib rat*) cannot prevent us from assuming that the contrapuntal properties of this composition are of English extraction. Similarly, compositional elements in the German lied *Elend du hast umfangen* in the Schedel Liederbuch (Munich, Bayerische Staatsbibliothek, MS 3232) may be of English provenance.[M] The Continental scribes evidently had trouble with the original English texts of such songs and therefore retexted them.[N] A section of the tenor in Tinctoris's example on proportions (see above, note 39), which stands in strong connection to English compositions, is the beginning of the tenor of a song with German text: *Sig, säld und heil*, which is the basis of a tenor c.f. in a mass in *Tr* 91, fols. 216v–225r.[O]

Additional features that speak for the English provenance of the Marian antiphon mentioned above [*Salve regina*] include the variation of the c.f. in the tenor as well as the sectional contrast which manifests itself in highly variable voice combinations. The clefs in this piece run: (c4), tenor (c4), (c3), (g2). From the standpoint of contrapuntal procedure, the same characteristics are also exhibited in Dufay's *Ave regina caelorum* from 1464.

---

[41]Rudolf von Ficker and Alfred Orel, eds., *Sechs Trienter Codices: Geistliche und weltliche Kompositionen des XV Jahrhunderts, Vierte Auswahl, DTÖ 53 (Jahrgang XXVII/1)* (Vienna: Universal-Edition, 1920), 55 ff.; see also Apfel, "Der klangliche Satz," 297-313, especially 299 ff. The Continental composers seem conversely to have proceeded as always in the writing of four-voice free counterpoint (chanson-style) from a two-voice framework of discantus and tenor, to which they added first a lower-lying contratenor bassus, and then, between the structural voices, a contratenor altus. The evidence for this includes octave-leap cadences in the contratenor bassus, contratenor versions which in various manuscripts strongly diverge from one another, or the complete absence in one or more manuscripts of the contratenor altus (see the works listed in Apfel, "Der klangliche Satz," 307, note 4 [note 21 in the translation above], and their critical commentaries).

[M]See Bukofzer, "Popular and Secular Music in England (to c. 1470)," 130.

[N]Ibid., 131.

[O]See the thematic catalogue of Trent 91 in Guido Adler and Oswald Koller, eds., *Sechs Trienter Codices: Geistliche und weltliche Kompositionen des XV. Jahrhunderts, Erste Auswahl, DTÖ 14-15 (Jahrgang VII)* (Vienna: Universal-Edition, 1900), nos. 1338-42 (page 74); see also Victor Lederer, *Über Heimat und Ursprung der mehrstimmigen Tonkunst* (Leipzig: Siegel, 1906), vol. 1, 236 ff.

The contrapuntal procedures described above apply to all of the four-voice *Salve reginas* but particularly to Nos. 4 and 5.[P] The chanson *Le serviteur* is used as a tenor in No. 5.[Q] There exist vertical simultaneities in the three-voice chanson *Le serviteur* of Bedingham,[R] which, however, render it unclear as to whether this [song] represents the original text of the composition.[S]

O rosa bella, *L'omme armé*, and *Le serviteur* are chansons which, even at this early stage, were used as models serving as the basis for masses incorporating parody treatment. According to Bukofzer, the English, after they had developed the [musical] unity of the Mass Ordinary, proceeded to concern themselves with the deployment of parody technique in mass composition.[T]

Besides the four-voice antiphons and one chanson, other works are given in the author's previous study as examples of "true" four-voice counterpoint.[42] These include masses that are partially based on the above-named chansons. Of the three masses in *DTÖ* 22 utilizing either single voices from *O rosa bella*, or else making a parody construction from it, [two of them, namely] No. II (three-voiced) and No. III (four-voiced), are very probably of English provenance, since they are [conceived as] "real" counterpoint.[U] These questions warrant further exploration, but that cannot be a task of the present study.

In summary, however, a few things should be remarked: The main characteristic of English music [of this time] is a rather clear construction of simultaneities, as much as possible under the influence of the lowest tones as a foundation—regardless of which voice [they appear in]; [this attribute is understood within an overall concept of] polyphony, associated with a certain

---

[P]These compositions are published in Rudolf von Ficker and Alfred Orel, eds., *Sechs Trienter Codices, Vierte Auswahl, DTÖ* 53, 39 ff. (no. 4, 50 ff., no. 5, 52 ff.). See also Ernst Apfel, "Der klangliche Satz," 308, note 1 [Note 23 in the translation above].

[Q]See the edition attributed to "Isaac" in Guido Adler and Oswald Koller, eds., *Sechs Trienter Codices, DTÖ* 14-15, 238 ff.

[R]Ibid., 239 ff.

[S]See Bukofzer, "Popular and Secular Music in England (to c. 1470)," 129, note 4.

[T]Bukofzer, "English Church Music of the Fifteenth Century," *New Oxford History of Music*, Vol. III (London: Oxford University Press, 1960), 208 ff.

[42]See Ernst Apfel, "Der klangliche Satz," 308, note 1 [Note 23 in the translation above]. The German-texted chanson entitled *Heya Heya, nu wie sie grollen*, evidently quite late, has imitation through all the parts aside from the *cantus prius factus* tenor, which sounds in sonorous semibreves until almost the final cadence; the piece is edited in Guido Adler and Oswald Koller, eds., *Sechs Trienter Codices: Geistliche und weltliche Kompositionen des XV. Jahrhunderts, Zweite Auswahl, DTÖ* 22 (*Jahrgang* XI/1) (Vienna: Universal-Edition, 1904), 118 ff.

[U]See also Lederer, *Über Heimat und Ursprung*, 239 ff.

wide-ranging quality of the voices, generally linked with a clear separation of the various voice registers, and no great differentiation in rhythmic activity among the parts. The motions of the individual voices are motions in consonances—vertical sonorities resting upon their lowest tones—and are not determined by any particular progression tendency of thirds or sixths. In this manner "pentatonic figures" are often produced:[43]

E x a m p l e 4

5 6 8

[Such figures appear as above] and inverted, in other words: motion in consonances!

In accordance with the present author's *Studien* and his article "Der klangliche Satz," it could seem as if the achievements of the English in the fifteenth century affected solely, or almost solely, the motet-style compositions, i.e., [those] based on a pre-ordained melody as a c.f. As we have attempted to point out above, these [achievements] also affected the freely composed masses, and even the chanson composition[s], although the English did not occupy themselves much with the latter until after their encounter with Continental music around 1420–30. Collectively speaking, the accomplishments of the English consist rather in the creation of the true four-voice style of counterpoint, wherein the foundation was laid for further development of the technique all the way through the style of Palestrina, in whose prevailingly freely composed works not based on a c.f., the genesis of true four-voice counterpoint out of the true three-voice technique can still be discerned.[44]

---

[43]See Bockholdt, *Messenkompositionen*, 89-90 and 137-8, where, regarding the three-voice mass sections published at the end of his Dufay edition (58 ff.), similar phenomena were mentioned in connection with rhythmic elements, and these must presuppose English influences. The author's point of view in the present study is that the Dufay works just mentioned (as distinct from the previous Kyrie, Sanctus, and Agnus, which are composed more in a chanson style with a two-voice framework as foundation—the Gloria and Credo display special characteristics in any case), retain the so-called "free treble-style": they exist less as a two-voice framework than as a freely composed upper voice provided with two supporting voices. The reduced prominence—indeed, complete lack—of the octave-leap cadence in the contratenor (especially in the *Missa Sancti Antonii Viennensis*) is indeed noticeable.

[44]Through the transformation of a three-voice piece into one for four voices was created the voice pairings: tenor–discantus vs. bassus–altus, which displaced the old motet order [consisting of a] foundation [proceeding] from tenor c.f. and contratenor [and incorporating

The question of the bass is, in fact, decisive for our research into the history of early music: composition from the bass outward (a predominantly leaping low voice) was definitively carried through in a true sense only around 1600 (that is, with decisive [moment] for the new music at this time). It became possible to proceed with composition [conceived] from the bass only when it had become the lowest voice throughout the piece—a true "bass part." This is the case at any rate in all of the published sacred concertos of Viadana, for example. Viadana's bass, then, is an actual "basso continuo," whereas in the compositions of classical vocal polyphony, the tenor (or even some other higher voice) can also in places assume the function of the bass. Correspondingly, the bass lines set down by organists for the accompaniment of motets, etc., were extracted—some from the bass, some from the tenor (or even from some higher voice)—and placed together from whatever tones happened to be lowest at any given point in the piece (analogous to the *solus tenor* of the older motet). The new bass effected a new conception of vertical sonorities and became the cornerstone of our modern system of harmony. Accordingly, the solo voices of Viadana are true tenor, alto, bass, or (and) soprano parts in the sense of classical vocal polyphony. On the other hand, the solo voices in the works of various composers, where the thoroughbass contains figures above "9," juxtapose a composite of different upper voices ([i.e., a given voice] assuming different chordal components at different times) of what is in the background a three- or four-voice piece. Thus, sometimes [a given voice] is the highest part of the composition ([such that] the other "voices" have smaller figures), and other times [it] is a middle voice ([so that] other "voices" have higher figures).[45]

---

an] upper-voice duet. This process is still discernible in the Palestrina style, as was mentioned above (see Ernst Apfel, "Zur Entstehungsgeschichte des Palestrinasatzes," *Archiv für Musikwissenschaft* 14 (1957): 30-45, where, however, the two-voice chanson style, not the three-voice faburden-like style, was considered to be the foundation of the [necessary] component of free composition in contrast to the motet technique). This, however, does not mean that the Palestrina style did not constitute a unity of interaction between simultaneity, melody, and rhythm (language, declamation) (see Reinhold Schlötterer, "Struktur und Kompositionsverfahren in der Musik Palestrinas," *Archiv für Musikwissenschaft* 17 (1960): 40-50.

[45] See also Hans Heinrich Eggebrecht, "Arten des Generalbasses im frühen und mittleren 17. Jahrhunderts," *Archiv für Musikwissenschaft* 14 (1957): 62-82.

The Harmonic Structure of Late Medieval Music as a Foundation of Major-Minor Tonality

Ernst Apfel

EDITOR'S PREFACE: *The study translated here is possibly the most interesting one in this book. In many respects, however, it is also the most speculative, since it attempts a comprehensive interpretation of harmonic developments over a period stretching from the thirteenth through the seventeenth century. Obviously, the success of these ideas depends to a great degree on the validity of generalized concepts advanced by the author but not necessarily substantiated. Until these hypotheses are thoroughly reevaluated, we are probably not in a position to assess the author's conclusions fully. Even so, the interpretation advanced here will likely prove more tenable than Besseler's hypothesis of the genesis of "dominant tonality." In the translation, the musical examples have been numbered consecutively throughout the text. It should also be noted that in the original article, Example 6B was printed upside down.*

In the following [essay], the author's researches into compositional process of the music of the thirteenth through the seventeenth centuries, particularly regarding the question of the genesis of the major-minor tonal system [*Dur-Moll Tonalität*] of later music, will be summarized and complemented.[1] We

---

[1]Of the studies comprising the basis of the present author's work, the following should be named here: Ernst Apfel, "Der Diskant in der Musiktheorie des 12. – 15. Jahrhunderts" (dissertation, University of Heidelberg, 1953); Ernst Apfel, "Der klangliche Satz und der freie Diskantsatz im 15. Jahrhundert," *Archiv für Musikwissenschaft* 12 (1955): 297-313 [Translated elsewhere in this volume]; Ernst Apfel, *Studien zur Satztechnik der mittelalterlichen englischen Musik, Abhandlungen der Heidelberger Akademie der Wissenschaften, Phil.–hist. Klasse, Jahrgang 1959, 5. Abhandlung*, 2 vols. (Heidelberg: Carl Winter, 1959); Ernst Apfel, "Zur Entstehungsgeschichte des Palastrinasatzes," *Archiv für Musikwissenschaft* 14 (1957): 30-45; Ernst Apfel, "Zur Entstehung des realen vierstimmigen Satzes in England," *Archiv für Musikwissenschaft* 17 (1960): 81-99; Ernst Apfel, "Über den vierstimmigen Satz im 14. und 15. Jahrhundert," *Archiv für Musikwissenschaft* 18 (1961): 34-51. [The last two articles named are translated elsewhere in this volume.] See also especially Heinrich Besseler, *Bourdon und Fauxbourdon: Studien zum Ursprung der niederländischen Musik* (Leipzig: Breitkopf & Härtel, 1950); and Thrasybulos Georgiades, *Englische Diskanttraktate aus der ersten Hälfte des 15.*

will begin with the transition from organum to the motet in the thirteenth century, when composition is [cultivated consistently] in three voices.

The most frequent sonority progressions in the three-voice motets of the thirteenth through the fifteenth century, and also in pieces belonging to the secular genres, are the following:

Examples

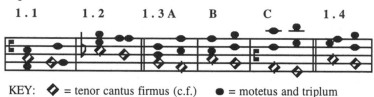

1.1   1.2   1.3 A   B   C   1.4

KEY: ◆ = tenor cantus firmus (c.f.)   ● = motetus and triplum

Even a first glimpse shows that with the exception of Example 1.3A, the minor third always proceeds to the unison, the major [third] to the fifth, and the major sixth to the octave.[2] As a result [one deduces that] all imperfect consonances must be resolved to the nearest perfect [consonance]. (This is true until into the seventeenth century.) Conversely, this [also] means that thirds before unisons must be minor, and thirds before fifths, as well as sixths before octaves, must be major. Accordingly, the sonority progressions with stepwise motion in all voices (neighbor-relationship of sonorities [*Nachbarschafts-verhältnis der Klänge*]), which stood in the foreground until well in the fifteenth century, give rise to a plethora of leading-tone motion. The most natural [example of this] is the simultaneous use of E and B in the penultimate sonority. These progressions just introduced should now be discussed individually.

Example 1.1: is also found with the tenor c.f. moving D—C, seldom with E—D; the motetus is usually the lowest voice.[3] When the tenor c.f. moves G—F and D—C, the third the motetus takes below the tenor c.f. is

---

Jahrhunderts: Untersuchungen zur Entwicklung der Mehrstimmigkeit im Mittelalter (Munich: Musikwissenschaftliches Seminar der Universität München, 1937).

[2]As is known, previous practice had voice-led the major third, or even the fourth, to the unison (and this is still true of the tenor cantus firmus and motetus in the early motets). Particularly the cadence of the major third to the unison may be said to have belonged to a musical culture that not only was older than the one that cadenced using the minor third but which also was different in type.

[3]It is located at a minor third below the tenor (c.f.). Several motets of the *Ars antiqua* require the motetus [to be placed] up to a fourth below the tenor (c.f.), which in these cases apparently must be considered a consonance. Voice crossings [wherein the motetus proceeds lower] than a fifth appear to point to English provenance of the [applicable] motet (see note 4).

natually minor, and the third of the triplum above the tenor c.f. is major (e.g., F# over a D—C progression). Thus, when the tenor c.f. moves E—D, the E must probably be inflected to an Eb, although the lesser possibility remains of inflecting the motetus C to C# and the triplum G to G#.

Example 1.2: is usually embellished; the third between motetus and tenor is major and that between motetus and triplum is minor.

Example 1.3A: Here the fifth of the triad F–A–C (a minor third above A) is voice-led not as previously to the unison with the motetus's B on the fifth of the final sonority but moves vigorously [by leap of a third] to its octave F; this is brought about by a separation, as it were, of [motetus and triplum] voice registers. This [progression] indicates something completely new, developed most likely by the English, which probably led to the embellishing usage of the sixth between the fifth of the penultimate sonority and the octave of the final one.

Examples 1.3B and 3C: Either the motetus or triplum may have the major third or sixth; both voices have leading-tone motion.

Example 1.4: motetus and triplum are at a major second's distance [and] are at a perfect fifth and a sixth above the tenor c.f., respectively.

These sonority progressions presuppose a descending stepwise motion of the tenor. The two-and three-note groups, in which the melodies composed as tenors of motets (cantus firmus or *cantus prius factus*) using borrowed or newly composed material were brought forward according to the rhythmic modes, rarely cadence with a descending stepwise motion, so that the sonority progressions [shown] above could not always be put into effect.

In not a few cases the tenor (c.f.) even moves by ascending stepwise motion. In this case, the sonority progressions typically look as follows:

Examples

N.B.: diagonal lines indicate voice crossings

Example 2.1A and B: The tenor has mostly C—D and F—G, sometimes G—A (with Bb in the motetus), and E—F. In the two last cases either the motetus or the tenor c.f. must have a leading-tone motion, with the result that when the tenor c.f. motion is C—D, either the motetus must have an Eb or else the tenor (c.f.) must have a C#, in which case the G of the triplum must be inflected to G# (in Example 2.1B, the triplum would have to be inflected from C to C#). When the tenor's motion is F—G, the motetus must probably have Ab or the tenor (c.f.) an F#, whereby the C of the triplum would have to be inflected to C# (which is more reasonable than the Ab in the motetus).

Example 2.2: Two voices, particularly tenor (c.f.) and motetus, make the progression octave—fifth, which is also demanded by the medieval theorists for ascending c.f. motion, [as it] is the only possible progression except for the minor third—unison. (The triplum acts incorrectly in these cases, since it is the last voice added to the composition.) Example 2.2B is found also without voice crossing, thus incorporating parallel fifths and octaves.

However, when even the tenor leaps, and especially when it ascends leapwise, no imperfect consonances requiring stepwise resolution can be used at all. Rather, when the tenor (c.f.) leaps upward, the two most important voices (almost always tenor c.f. and motetus) make the progression fifth—unison, or octave—fifth. When the tenor leaps downward, these voices make the progression fifth—octave. The third voice, typically a triplum, moves freely even if incorrectly. The English were evidently the first to hit upon the idea of leading one of the two added voices (motetus or triplum) under the tenor (c.f.) when the latter ascends by a minor or major second and to give the descending stepwise motion—the so-called "tenor cadence"—to one of these parts in place of the tenor. [In this case,] whichever voice acts as the third part is allowed to ascend stepwise in parallel fourths with the tenor (c.f.).[4]

Example 3

In this way, the stepwise ascent of the tenor (c.f.) also has its own sonority progression with imperfect consonances. The "tenor principle" mentioned above (as one might call it) was in evidence in England in other genres besides the motet, as, for example, in the simple cantus firmus

---

[4]Manfred Bukofzer, in "Popular Polyphony in the Middle Ages," *Musical Quarterly* 26 (1940): 31-49, and elsewhere, has already pointed to the frequent voice crossings between tenor (c.f.) and discantus (or in three-voice pieces, one of the [two] discant voices) in the English cantus firmus settings, songs, and motets. Theodor Göllner also makes reference to the "interplay" between cantus firmus and added voices in the Gymel; see *Formen früher Mehrstimmigkeit in deutschen Handschriften des späten Mittelalters, Münchner Veröffentlichungen zur Musikgeschichte* 6, ed. Thrasybulos Georgiades (Tutzing: Schneider, 1961), 125 ff.

settings. The [parallel] fourths of the upper discant voice are an expression of the tenor (c.f.) role being played by the other [lower discant voice]. Rather quickly, however, the triplum was placed somewhat higher as an entity and so was freed from the registral equality of all voices that hitherto had prevailed. The role of one of the discant voices as the director of sonorities [*Klangträger*] (described above) was from now on taken over at the applicable places only by the motetus. And so it remained in the three-voice motet into the fifteenth century, especially in England ([as a] tonal-free [*klanglich-frei*], truly three-voice composition).

However, while still in the thirteenth century the English apparently switched over to [a process] of adding a low voice (at first textless) to the tenor (c.f.); this [added voice then] made the descending stepwise motion (i.e., the tenor cadence), under the tenor (c.f.), when the latter ascended stepwise. Since this added low voice moved in the range of the tenor (c.f.), the space above became freer, so that now a fourth voice could join in. (Four-voice composition thus originated hand in hand with the technique mentioned above.) Although the English designated this low voice as *secundus tenor*, *quartus cantus*, or *quadruplex*, it had to be added first to the tenor (c.f.) on account of its contrapuntal significance (i.e., as occasional substitute for the tenor c.f. as director of sonorities). This [function is] in contradistinction to the quadruplum of those few four-voice motets on the Continent, which was usually added last, indeed subsequently, in the register of the motetus and triplum to an existing three-voice composition.

The most frequent sonority progression of what is now a four-voice composition (in analogy to the three-voice techniques discussed above) is this:

Ex a m p l e 4

KEY: ◇ = tenor (c.f.)   ◆ = quadruplex

Early four-voice compositions of this type, however, still begin with an 8-5 sonority with one component doubled as a fourth voice and close according to the position of the cantus firmus, as here:

Ex a m p l es   5 A   B

or:

Example 5B shows a sonority progression that is occasionally encountered even in four-voice (presumably) Continental motets of the *Ars antiqua*.

At the beginning of the fourteenth century, the Continental composers appropriated the technique described above from the English (at the beginning of the *Ars nova*), except that they designated as "contratenor" the voice alternating with the tenor (c.f.) in the role of director of sonorities. However, the total sonorous effect of the relevant Continental motets is seldom as pure as is that of the English, insofar as (among other things) the foundation voices [*Fundamentstimmen*], tenor (c.f.) and contratenor, often make dissonances (e.g., fourths) with each other. In not a few Continental motets, the contratenor is even a later addition to the piece. This condition is evinced by [the following factors: 1)] that in another manuscript it is missing entirely or exists in an altered form; [2] that it is predominantly of leapwise character; [3] that it is not director of sonorities (i.e., does not take the third or fifth below the tenor c.f. when the latter makes fourths with the upper voices); or [4] that it even disturbs the consonance of the underlying three-voice composition.

This is even the case with the four-voice pieces of Johannes Ciconia, the early Netherlander who lived primarily in Italy.[5] In his works there are no cases of the philological argument (mentioned above) for the subsequent addition of a contratenor (which in his three-voice works is also only a filling voice). Indeed, this [contratenor in the four-voice works of Ciconia] is never a director of sonorities; rather, it is more likely to make the other voices (which together comprise a thoroughly pure three-part counterpoint) problematic in

---

[5]See Suzanne Clercx, *Johannes Ciconia, Un musicien liègeois et son temps (vers 1335-1411)*, vol. I: *La vie et l'œuvre*, vol. II: *Transcriptions et notes critiques* (Brussels: Académie, 1960); see also Kurt von Fischer, "Zur Ciconia-Forschung," *Die Musikforschung* 14 (1961): 316-22. To call the cantus II in Ciconia's four-voice pieces a "filling voice," as is done in the study just named, is problematic. In the works of the present author, the triplum (cantus I) in motet-style pieces is the only part compared to the discantus of chanson pieces in its relationship to the tenor (c.f.), although the motetus (cantus II) of the four-voice motet-style pieces since the *Ars nova* is certainly equal to the triplum (cantus I) both in terms of its compositional status and its register. This [use of terminology] is intended only for the sake of simplicity. However, whatever is true of the triplum (cantus I) is also true of the motetus (cantus II), whereas the contratenor altus of the four-voice chanson as a filling voice (which it normally is) corresponds to the motetus (cantus II) in only a very limited fashion, since the former is conditioned by very different compositional factors. However, even as early as Dunstable and Dufay, the motetus (cantus II) in motet-style pieces obtains a somewhat lower ambitus than the triplum (cantus I) and thus begins to approach the altus of the four-voice chanson-style pieces with respect to register.

the four-voice version: [In Ciconia's *Et in terra*,] m. 73, the [contratenor's position a] fifth lower [than the tenor] makes a dissonance with the 6-3 sonority of the other voices—or, as one could perhaps better put it: the cantus II is not yet oriented to the [low position of the] contratenor.[A] In m. 83, the contratenor even takes the fourth lower than the tenor, and thus disturbs the 6-3 chord of the other voices in a fashion that cannot be ameliorated. In m. 94, the contra supports the fourth existing between the cantus II and tenor by taking the fifth below [the tenor]—but in so doing it creates here (among other places) parallel octaves with the cantus I in mm. 94-5.[6] In m. 145, and elsewhere, the contratenor is placed a fifth below the tenor but without being decisive for the consonance of the other voices. The fifth of the contratenor under the tenor in [a three-voice *Patrem* of Ciconia], m. 65 also does not support a dissonance between cantus I and tenor.[B] The reinsertion of the cantus I in m. 125 seems more likely to have been justified by the lower D of the contratenor, [and,] if one wants to take into consideration the fourth between the tenor and cantus I in the last quarter note, the contratenor sometimes even makes fourths with the tenor. In m. 132, the contratenor disturbs the consonance between cantus I and tenor, etc.

The contratenor must also be left out of the question of placement of accidentals. The vertical sonority seems to be more decisive to the assignment of accidentals than the motion of voices, upon which the rule *una nota super la, semper est canendum fa* (used by Clercx to justify many editorial accidentals) is grounded. Thus, in [Ciconia's four-voice motet *O virum*

[A]Suzanne Clercx, *Johannes Ciconia*, vol. II, No. 20, 92-7; the passage occurs on 94.

[6]Thus, a triple-leading-tone cadence results. [This cadence] actually seems to have been invented by the English, and its fundamental element was that which was designated as "real four-voice counterpoint": The voices are separated from each other registrally, so that fewer doublings of the unison occur than of the octave. (The fourth voice, quadruplex, quartus cantus, or secundus tenor, as a compositionally secondary voice, has its own ambitus, mostly under the tenor c.f.). The same thing is very much true in the following sonority progression (influenced by the English), encountered frequently on the Continent in the few four-voice motets of the *Ars antiqua* and in the somewhat more numerous *Ars nova* motets, which is an extension of the progression shown above in Example 1.1:

Example N-1

As is mentioned above, the English seem very quickly to have developed other four-voice sonority progressions besides the triple-leading-tone cadence, so that they avoided these types.

[B]Clercx, *Johannes Ciconia*, vol. II, No. 28, 133-42; this passage occurs on page 135.

omnimoda veneracione], m. 42, the contratenor should probably be altered according to the B natural in the cantus I, not vice versa.[C] In [*Albane misse celitus*, another Ciconia motet in four voices], m. 16, the cantus I must probably read B natural (perfect fifth above the tenor) in spite of the contratenor's C.[D] Likewise, the two upper voices in mm. 73-4 must have B natural, not Bb, and so forth. Outside of octaves and unisons, the contratenor mostly makes thirds with the tenor, but these have no influence upon the sonority construction of the piece, since they are not exploited for the placing of fourths between the upper voices and the tenor, as is the case with the English. Ciconia's achievement may be said to lie less in the realm of sonority treatment than in the areas of imitation and rhythm, etc.

Rather quickly, however, the English transformed the earlier triple-leading-tone cadence into the following two cadential types.

Examples   6 A   B

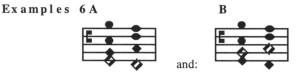

and:

Indeed, the English actually evaded [triple-leading-tone cadences] insofar as they allowed the contratenor to pause at the end, or else no longer even had any tenor cadence [i.e., descending stepwise motion] under the tenor [voice]. This meant that now the director of sonorities, now designated contratenor even by the English, had to proceed more leapwise than its predecessor, the quadruplex (also known by other names as indicated above). This voice, however, still remained the director of sonorities as always, and this fact remained characteristic of English compositional technique. The new English contratenor is, so to speak, a hybrid of the English quadruplex and the Continental contratenor, which was subsequently added [to a composition]. In differentiation from both of these, it is usually texted and moves more like the discant voices, less like the tenor, which is reminiscent of the motetus [voice] that earlier had been used as a director of sonorities (see above). According to the English theorists of the fifteenth century, it is really to be considered a lower-lying mene (i.e., motetus).[7] As cadences, the following [types] result,

---

[C]Clercx, *Johannes Ciconia*, vol. II, No. 38, 173-6; this passage occurs on page 174.

[D]Clercx, *Johannes Ciconia*, vol. II, No. 39, 177-82; this passage occurs on page 177.

[7]Since [the time of] Dunstable, the contratenor is designated also as contra bassus, secundus tenor, tenor bassus, or simply as bassus, whereas the lower-lying discant voice of the time (motetus) was also designated as contratenor or contra. These usages correspond thoroughly to the teachings of the English theorists.

corresponding to the various motions of the cantus firmus in the tenor:

Examples   7.1   7.2   7.3   7.4

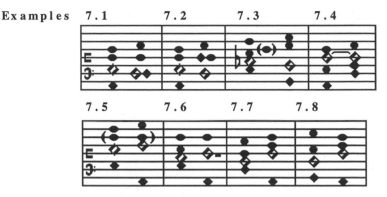

7.5   7.6   7.7   7.8

(One can see how closely the sonority progressions depend on the motions of the cantus firmus—see above, Examples 1 and 2, regarding the motets of the *Ars antiqua*.) One sees progressions 7.1–7.3 and 7.7–7.8 in the motets of Dunstable, whereas progressions 7.4–7.6 are found in Dufay (*Missa se la face ay pale*, which uses the chanson of the same name as its tenor). Progressions 7.1–7.3 are also found later in chanson composition[8] (regarding Example 7.3, see below, Example 14).

The main cadences of song composition in the fourteenth century (see Examples 1.1 and 1.2 above), which seem to stem from the secular motet (with French text) on the Continent, are apparently composed voice by voice like the latter and accordingly do not display a clear relationship of sonorities. In the three-voice Continental chanson of the fifteenth century, on the other hand, the voice relationships are clarified, so that tenor and discantus comprise a pure two-voice counterpoint, to which the contratenor is added as a mere filling voice, moving in alternation between the two structural voices [*Gerüststimmen*] (tenor and discantus) and below the tenor. When it lies between the structural voices, [the contratenor] must be consonant with the tenor, but it may take the dissonant fourth with the discantus (not, however, the dissonant second):

---

[8] The technique of composition in the chanson became transformed in the fifteenth century according to the model of the motet, so that one can speak of a fusing of the two techniques, as is maintained in my almost entirely unnoticed article "Der klangliche Satz und der freie Diskantsatz im 15. Jahrhundert," 297–313, but which meanwhile was again subjected to doubt since the genre of the chanson in itself has nothing to do with the motet (Ernst Apfel, *Studien* I, 90 ff.). The compositional mingling of the two genres does, however, find a palpable expression in the parody mass, which was created by the English.

Example 8

When it is under the structural voices, [the contratenor] must be concordant with both. However, as a filling voice, [the contratenor] does not function as director of sonorities even when it is placed under the tenor. The two structural voices can exist without it. In song composition on the Continent, the contratenor attains the status of director of sonorities only in the late fifteenth century, under English influence.

In the first half of the fifteenth century, the type of counterpoint just described was subjected to transformations, to the effect that the leaping contratenor remained more and more under the tenor (but still never being the director of sonorities);[9] this can be read from the development of its most typical cadence [forms]:

Examples   9 A   B   C

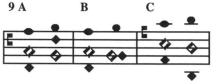

Since now the two structural voices did not have very many possibilities to set up their decisive sixth-octave cadence progression, several sonorities soon presented themselves as uniquely suited for the antepenultimate; indeed, this development extended back to the fourth sonority from the final, for there were not all that many possibilities for [any of] these:[10]

---

[9]The voice structure of the contratenor in Dufay's works that was especially emphasized by Besseler (see *Bourdon und Fauxbourdon*)—ambitus of an octave or twelfth, emphasis of the fifth, triadic melody, etc.—is not meant to be denied by this observation. It did not disappear even after 1440 but rather was merely veiled by the tendency towards stepwise motion (vocalization) due to the increased possibilities for the contratenor (bassus) in vertical sonorities and by the [melodic] filling in of the leaps. That the contratenor (bassus) takes over the tenor cadence and also can make leading-tone motion are thus (apart from its function as director of sonorities) further signs of its gathering strength to [become] the decisive voice of the counterpoint. Previously it was mentioned that, as a bass, it can fashion syncopations in the upper voices into dissonances and that, since it is a bass, the structural voices no longer have to begin or close at the octave or unison but rather can end at, say, the third or sixth, which the bass turns into full triads by taking the third below.

[10]The sonority progressions 10.1 and 10.4 are only possible in a C tonality. In Dorian, Example 10.1 would result in the first sonority having double leading tones, and Example 10.4

Examples

10.1   10.2   10.3   10.4

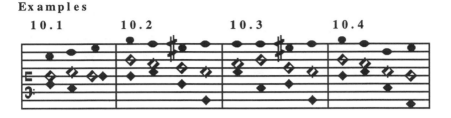

In the second half of the fifteenth century, the Continental composers, under the influence of the English, introduced the two half-consonances, fourth and diminished fifth, into the structural voices—the fourth, supported by the third or fifth below [the tenor], and the diminished fifth, supported by the major sixth [below the tenor] in the lower-lying contratenor (bassus).[11] The inclusion of the fourth and the diminished fifth, with their tendency of resolution toward the third, greatly extended the given possibilities (which already included the unison, third, and perfect fifth) for voice-leading the structural voices (tenor and discantus) within a narrow [as well as a wider] compass; this even includes an exchange of their relative [registral] positions. At the same time, the contra was directly forced by this to remain under the tenor. The contratenor's taking the major sixth under the tenor is itself a novelty, since this [interval] always requires resolution to the octave: the contra has to descend stepwise under the tenor and thus makes a tenor close [*Tenorklausel*], whereas the latter assumes the discant close [*Diskantklausel*, or stepwise ascent], resulting in these sonority progressions:

---

would result in the second sonority having them (in the contratenor and discantus, B or E). If one were to lower the two Bs to B flats in [a Dorian version of] Example 10.1, it would yield double leading tones towards the low note; the structural voices would have a minor sixth (still not permitted), and the discantus would have to progess from B-flat to C-sharp! But in fact many chansons exist in a C tonality, which is why other examples above are in C.

[11]The evolution within the chanson of a counterpoint without fourths, demonstrated by Charles Warren Fox, ("Non-Quartal Harmony in the Renaissance," *Musical Quarterly* 31 (1945): 33-53), through which it became possible to perform any two voices out of a three- or four-voice piece, resulted quite naturally from French chanson composition: tenor and discantus, as structural voices, already were always consonant with each other, and the contratenor (bassus) is obligated to [be consonant with] both tenor and discantus when it is beneath the former. This results primarily in the following sonorities:

Example N-2

Examples

better on C!

To place a sixth in the contratenor (bassus) beneath the perfect fifth of the structural voices would, in itself, already have been conceivable, since otherwise [the tenor and discantus] could only have been filled into a "triad" (again used in the sense of modern terminology) by the placing [the contra] at the third [above the low note].[12] Thus, it would seem that one could have voice-led the contratenor below the fifth of the structural voices into an octave, but this was not customary. [Such a progression] would have yielded only a minor sixth under almost all conceivable fifths between the structural voices, but this interval was not yet recognized as a consonance, and wherever a major [sixth] would have been involved, [this] would also have entailed a [melodic step of a] minor second [in the low voice]—a progression that at first was even less allowable to the contratenor (bassus) than was the tenor close or [the presence of] a minor sixth in a vertical sonority.

All of the resulting sonorities should now be introduced and discussed:

---

[12]The octave and unison also yield a usable sonority through the placement of a third below (see below, Example 16). However, the placing of a sixth under the tenor below a perfect fifth in the structural voices (or the combination of fifth and unison or octave if [the composition] proceeds from the higher-lying voices of a three-part piece, to which the contratenor is added) is problematic also in that a contradiction ensues: the tenor tone, which has a perfect fifth above it, wants to be felt as a ground-tone [*Grundton*], but a sixth is placed below it, and this tends towards forward motion. Accordingly, the fifth (and its combinations with unison or octave) lost in importance for the structural voices, and the third—and particularly the sixth—gained to the same extent. The placement of the forward-tending imperfect consonances in the upper parts above the more stable perfect [consonances] was adopted first by the English, namely in motet-style compositions. The above-mentioned quality of the lower tone of the fifth to appear as a ground-tone is shown by the importance of the addition of structural-voice sonorities with fifth below. That tendency also comes to expression in the addition of a lower third to a 6-3 sonority, whereby a full triad originates. The fifth acts as a ground-tone under the sixth (and fourth), as does the major third under the minor third and sixth; the fourth is supported by a third (or fifth) below; the diminished fifth [is supported] by a major sixth below. The major sixth acts as a supplementary [pitch when placed below] the perfect fifth, and the minor third [acts similarly when placed] beneath the major third or sixth. How one should describe these various functions of the bass is difficult. In connection to the fourth and diminished fifth, I refer to the bass as director of sonorities.

Examples

	12.1	12.2	12.3	12.4
Dc:	A　—B (G#)	B　—C	Bb　—A	C　D　—E (C#)
Tn:	D　—E	E　—F	E　—F	F　G　—A
Ct:	F+　—E	G+　—F	G+　—F	A-　Bb+　—A

	12.5	12.6	12.7	12.8	12.9
	D　—C (E)	E　—F	E　—D (F)	F　F　—E	G　G　—F#
	G　—G	A　—Bb	A　—A	Bb　H　—C	C　C#　—D
	B-　—C	C+　—Bb	C#-　—D	D-　D+　—C	E-　E+　—D

KEY: − = minor sixth above
　　　+ = major sixth above
　　　— = progression tendencies

　　The sonority E–B with a major sixth below creates a double-leading-tone progression [Example 12.2], so that B natural is better replaced by B flat, which produces a strong tendency towards the F sonority [Example 12.3]. The C# in the sonority C#–G with the lower sixth E and the resolution tendency to the D sonority (with major third!) occurs only *per accidens* [Example 12.9]. The fifth A–E with the lower sixth C has a tendency towards the Bb sonority [Example 12.6], but the E cannot be inflected to Eb, since this would lead out of the tonality. D under B–F [Example 12.8, second sonority] corresponds to G under E–Bb [Example 12.3], and [the former] resolves to a C sonority. The major sixth thus is most reasonably placed under the diminished fifth. In fact, the introduction of the diminished fifth into the structural counterpoint goes hand in hand with [the inclusion of] the major sixth into the stock of consonances for the contratenor. But at the same time, the C and F sonorities rose to prominence within the Dorian [tonality]—or to put it precipitously, F major and C major.[13] As was already mentioned, the Dorian sonority on D is only produced very artificially, that is, *per accidens*.

　　A similar tendency towards major results also from the placing of all conceivable [types of] thirds below [thirds of the structural voices] in the Dorian tonality:[E]

---

[13]The "major" thus actually lies latent since the Greek Greater Perfect System—the [initial] ordering of complete tonal resources. It is only that the latter was interpreted differently insofar as it was divided up primarily into various segments. E and B are already in themselves leading tones toward F and C [respectively] (but the latter do not necessarily presuppose E and B as leading tones). Their progression tendency became greatly stronger, however, through the addition of the minor (major) third and the major sixth [as consonances], and as a result of this tendency, F and C step into the foreground among all the so-called "church modes."

[E]A third between the structural voices could otherwise be fashioned into a three-voice sonority only by placing the contratenor an octave below—and this was not very reasonable. It

Example 13

	A	B	C	D	E	F	G	H	I	J	K	L
Dc:	F	F	G	G	A	B	Bb	C	D	D	E	E
Tn:	D	D	E	E	F	G	G	A	B	Bb	C	C#
Ct:	B	Bb	C	C#	D	E	E	F	G	G	A	A

The D–F and G–Bb intervals [between tenor and discantus; see Examples 13A and G], when joined by a [diatonic] lower third [in the contratenor] result in diminished triads, which were only incorporated into composition after 1500; this also applies to E–G with C# *per accidens* [Example 13D]. (B–D–F leads to a C sonority, E–G–Bb *per accidens* to an F sonority, and C#–E–G *per accidens* to a D sonority—usually with a major third *per accidens*.) In [the structural-voice intervals] F–A, G–B, Bb–D *per accidens*, and C–E [Examples 13E, F, J, and K, respectively], the [diatonic] lower third is minor. (Thus, with the addition of a minor third [in the contratenor] below [a major third formed by the tenor and discantus], minor triads originate.[14]) The minor third below has a forward-driving tendency; indeed, in the sonority E–G–B, the lower third of the contratenor (bassus) is even a *subsemitonium*, and this at first gave the contratenor (bassus) an overwhelming power. In order to mitigate the forward-driving tendency of the minor third in the low position (particularly at cadences of Dorian, Aeolian, and Phrygian pieces) and still to [provide for] the leading tone in the contratenor (bassus), the [thirds in the

would seem, then, that one might have voice-led the contratenor *above* the third in the structural voices into a fifth or even an octave, but this was unusual. [Emphasis added.]

[14]Besides G–Bb–D, there are also the minor triads of C major as well as the tonic, subdominant, and dominant of the relative minor tonality, A minor. That these minor triads in C major are really conditioned by adding a third below a major third [in the structural voices] is shown by the fact that their third can be doubled without any further consideration. However, D–F–A constitutes a special case: D has no major third below it that one could conceive of as a ground-tone of the lower minor third, in the role F plays to the A minor triad or C does to the E minor triad. The ground-tone of D is G, and that of A is the F that needs to be doubled, and for this reason the fifth [compass] D–A of the triad is too small. Thus, one can conceive of it as a doubled and truncated dominant seventh chord or raise the F to F#, so that the sonority becomes a double [i.e., secondary] dominant, and a progressive striving towards the dominant arises. For these reasons it is both "theoretically" as well as historically justified to conceive of [the sonority] F (doubled)–A–D not as an inversion of D–F–A, but as a root-position chord (subdominant sixth) with a sixth in the place of the fifth (as is [the case with] the 6-3 sonority in the Middle Ages in general). Also, in order to impart to the D minor sonority within [the key of] A minor the forward-moving tendency of the lower minor third and also [to impart] a leading-tone quality to the E-minor triad, both sonorities were probably transformed into major triads. Here it should also be noted that in melodic minor, all sixths are minor with one exception, whereas the thirds exist in approximately equal numbers, etc.

cadential] sonorities on D, A, and E were almost always inflected from F to F#, C to C#, and G to G#, respectively, [all thus being transformed] into a major triad.[15] In other cases, the addition of a lower third results in major triads on Bb, C, F, and G, which belong to F major and C major. It must again be emphasized that the major third is neutral—so neutral that the contratenor (bassus) can leap away from it.[16] This [circumstance exists] already in the typical chanson cadence if one looks at the contratenor (bassus) in relation to the discantus, as was done later. This is an essential precondition for the genesis of the dominant-tonic cadence.

The composing-out of the sixth between the structural voices into a "triad" constitutes a unique problem. At first, only the major sixth [as opposed to the minor] was permitted between the structural voices, which occurs naturally only over the tones D, F, G and C of the Dorian scale, and over E only *per accidens* (C#).[17] The least problematic thing was the insertion

---

[15]With G#, the Phrygian final cadence acts as a dominant and can well be brought in as such in Aeolian in the form of the so-called "Phrygian cadence." In the final analysis, however, this fact leads in the direction of a Phrygian function and to [a recognition] that in the realm of the natural tone system the "white notes" of C major on E (or on the corresponding tones of the transposed scales), no triad was erected on principle (on B this was not possible anyway) but rather always only a sixth chord, so that later the E triad became the weakest of all sonorities in the C tonality. Possibly the problematic aspect of the sonority on E also contributed to the entrenchment of Bb in Dorian and Lydian (regarding the sixth chords G–B–E and G–E–B, see the discussion of Examples 1.3B and C, above).

[16]The progression major third—fifth was largely replaced by the progression major third—octave, with a falling fifth in the lower voice, here contratenor (bassus). Since about 1500, the major third was voice-led to the fifth only when its leading tone was in the lower voice, as in the cadence from F–A to E–B and from Bb–D to A–E (the so-called "Phrygian cadence" with a major sixth to major third). In the place of the neighbor relationship of tones, which previously was customary, the fifth–relationship had in the meantime appeared. Furthermore, the fifth, to which the major third had hitherto been voice-led, is not as perfect a consonance as the octave (or unison), to which the major third and almost always the major sixth (or minor third) was led. The fifth contains one half-tone, as do the imperfect consonances, [whereas] the octave [contains] two half-tones, which either counterbalance each other or complement each other into a whole-tone.

[17]Likewise over A and B, where F must be raised to F# and G to G#. C#, F#, and G# are also major thirds over A, D, and E in place of those [occurring naturally as] minor. This is important for the creation of the double- (and triple-) leading tone cadence, particularly characteristic of motet-style composition in the fourteenth and early fifteenth centuries. Together with Bb and its perfect lower fifth, Eb, these pitches circumscribe the normative accidentals used in the later Middle Ages: D# over B was, however, brought in as well. With this [inclusion], the now long-standard "chromatic scale" was produced. Minor thirds have the leading tone most naturally below. They exist only under D and G naturally (and by acceptance of Bb, also under C), and

of thirds, or in the case of D–B, G–E, and C–A [intervals], the addition of a lower fifth. (Below F, the fifth—B—is not perfect, it should thus be lowered to Bb, but this makes the resolution of the major sixth, F–D impossible, since [one cannot decide] which tone the third voice should take under e–e'. Therefore, the following progression was made for the succession f–d'—e–e' in the structural voices:[F]

Example 14

The major sixth C–A with the lower fifth F has a tendency [to progress] to Bb/Bb–Bb, i.e., to the octave over a tone that in Dorian is only available *per accidens*.

To furnish the major sixth just mentioned, with the necessary minor third below is indeed impossible: it would entail a doubled leading tone with a doubled tendency toward resolution out of the sonority (major sixth—octave, minor third—unison), and in this succession, parallel octaves would arise.

The insertion of a minor sixth into the structural voices, which tends back to the fifth, is different: minor sixths are found in the Dorian scale on D (with Bb), E, A, and B. In [the intervals] D–Bb and A–F, the leading tone is above; in [the interval] A–F, [the leading tone] also exists below (if one assumes a Bb above A); in [the interval] E–C [the leading tone] exists both above and below, and in [the interval] B–G [it exists] only below. If the leading-tone step lies above (or if one interprets it as lying above), then the addition to the minor sixth of the structural voices with the necessary major third below is pointless; it would result in an incoherent progression. But if the leading-tone step lies below (or if one interprets it as lying below), so that the tenor has it, and the discantus remains unaltered (exchange of voice functions), then the possibility of a downward fifth leap in the contratenor (bassus) is connected with the tendency of the minor sixth to return [to the

---

are produced beneath E, A, and B through the use of the "artificial" tones C#, F#, and G# (mentioned above). The minor thirds below F and C are problematic, and the corresponding major sixths above [these notes] are likewise, as is the major third below A (by adoption of B) and D (with Bb). Among the major thirds, it is precisely those just mentioned, having the leading tone below, which act as a Phrygian cadence, since they have the leading tone in an "incorrect" place (see above, notes 11, 13, and 15–17).

[F]See above, Example 7.3.

fifth], so that the succession major third—octave arises between the contra and the tenor. Here again, the C and F sonorities (as well as Bb) are thrust into the foreground.

The mirror-image, so to speak, of these relationships results from the inclusion of the fourth into the structural voices and its sole coherent [three-voice] realization incorporating a lower third:

Example 15

	A	B	C	D	E	F	G	H	I	J	K	L	M
Dc:	G	G	A	A	B	Bb	C	C#	D	E	E	F	F
Tn:	D	D	E	E	F	F	G	G	A	B	Bb	C	C#
Ct:	B	Bb	C	C#	D	D	E	E	F	G	G	A	A

If, in the succession 6-3—8-5, both upper voices should have had as much as possible the leading-tone step above (see above, G–B–E, or with Bb as a target pitch: C–E–A), then the [succession] was soon recognized by which the lowest voice, the contratenor (bassus), has a leading-tone motion directed downwards (Bb–D–G and F–A–D). Then followed that type in which only the uppermost voice had leading-tone motion (D–F–B, E–G–C#, and G–Bb–E *per accidens*). In the sixteenth century, however, the contratenor (bassus) could also take the leading-tone motion upwards, and thus make a minor third with the tenor and a minor sixth with the discantus (in a wide voicing, these dispositions could be reversed): B–D–G toward a C sonority, C#–E–A *per accidens* toward a D sonority, E–G–C toward an F sonority, and A–C–F toward a Bb sonority, which in Dorian is only available *per accidens*.

In the fifteenth century, our so-called deceptive cadence appeared in chanson composition: the structural voices, tenor and discantus, cadence in a wide voicing from the major sixth to the octave, and in a restricted voicing from the minor third to the unison. In the wide voicing, the contratenor (bassus) does not leap up to the fifth above the tenor (octave-leap cadence), nor [does it move] to a unison with the tenor (also in a narrow voicing of the structural parts), nor does it fall to the fifth below the tenor. Rather, it progresses to the third beneath the tenor, thus providing the lower third to the octave or the unison of the structural voices:

Examples 16A   B

In a narrow voicing of the structural parts, the tenor has the leading tone in the penultimate minor third and, thereby, the discant cadence, and the discantus [has] the whole-tone and, thereby, the tenor cadence. Both progressions are produced in Dorian particularly on C and F (see above); the lower third yields the A minor and D minor sonorities (see above, note 14).

Since the contratenor (as contratenor bassus) in three-voice composition remained more and more beneath the tenor even in wide voicings, the possibility was opened of introducing yet another contratenor between the structural voices—[one] whose consonance was determined less by the structural voices than by the tone of the contratenor bassus. The cadences of four-voice chanson-style counterpoint follow:[18]

Examples

17.1   17.2   17.3   17.4   17.5

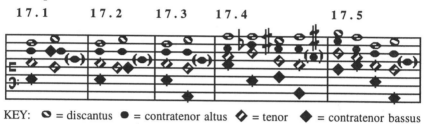

KEY: ◐ = discantus ● = contratenor altus ◆ = tenor ◆ = contratenor bassus

On the other hand, in the composition of four-voice pieces (usually conceived from the beginning in four voices, particularly in motet-style composition) the English sometimes proceeded from a compact, faburden-like three-voice piece of tenor, contratenor (altus), and discantus, to which (in conjunction with requisite alterations of the contratenor altus), they added a contratenor bassus. Soon, however, they gave the contratenor bassus the function of director of sonorities also with respect to the tenor and discantus, whereby they placed even fourths and diminished fifths between these two voices. In this way, the possibility to voice-lead the structural parts in narrow intervals was enhanced even in four-voice counterpoint, as was the case especially in the frottola and its descendant, the madrigal. (Sometimes these voices were composed such that the contratenor altus came to lie above even the discantus.) The following sonority progressions thus resulted:[19]

---

[18]The progression in Example 17.4 became possible on C after the minor sixth was incorporated [as a consonance] in the structural counterpoint (here the structural voices make a minor sixth in the first sonority). Finally, the contratenor could even have the leading-tone step in place of the tenor and thus make a minor sixth with the discantus.

[19]Example 18A corresponds entirely to Example 6B, from four-voice motet-style composition. But note the voicing here! The tenor and the upper voice (structural voices in chanson composition) cadence in Example 6B at the major sixth, which was unthinkable in chanson composition until around 1500. In the present example (18A), the structural voices

Examples 18 A   B

The use of lower thirds below 6-3 sonorities based on a tenor cantus firmus now also occurs in the Spanish *falsobordones* so that, for example, in a 6-3 sonority over a *repercussio* C, A-minor sonorities arise, etc. It is precisely at this time that the triad as an entity is first truly discovered, and equally, only from this time forward were the sonorities conceived on principle in root position. As soon as this was the case, however, it was logical to conceive of the cantus firmus as lowest voice and above it to erect full (actually four-voice) sonorities, which now also in the church modes are predominantly major triads. The entire sonorous component now commences with [the interval of] a third. The church modes are thus transformed under the influence of the development of polyphony as follows:

Dorian becomes the same as Aeolian through the progressively more frequent use of a Bb in the lower fifth register (Aeolian plagal = Phrygian, and Dorian plagal with Bb = Phrygian on the lower fifth; Phrygian is also contained in C major). Lydian becomes Ionian through habitual use of Bb in the lower fifth register. Mixolydian becomes Ionian through habitual use of the *subsemitonium modi* F# in the upper fifth register.

On the basis of the aggregate scale (solidified since ancient Greek times), in which the half-tones lay between E–F and B–C, all of the so-called church modes have had since the beginning of Western polyphony a tendency toward the C and F sonorities (F under C aspect), and the Dorian through the use of Bb has had a tendency towards the F sonority under F aspect.[20]

We have seen above that the typical bass progressions of the various realizations of our harmonic cadence are the result of the addition of consonances to dyads or triads (in the larger sense) and their consequences in the higher voices. This is also true for the following, more complex, variant:

---

close at the major third!

[20]Polyphony and its development had to lead to a fusing of the church modes into progressively fewer genera until [the system of] major-minor tonality [was attained]: Generally speaking, the more voices the composition encompassed (i.e., the more multifarious its sonorities had become), the less areas among the total tonal resources they could belong to. (The melody tone E can possess very many melodic properties, [but] the sonority E–G–B–E, for example, is conceivable only in the A, C, and E tonal areas.

Example 19

The subdominant 6–5 chord actually originated through a suspension of the earlier structural voices, tenor and discantus, in close position:

Example 20

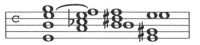

In both cases, the note held over between the subdominant and dominant is the only element binding both sonorities. Considered purely as such, the cadence Tonic–Subdominant–Dominant–Tonic is a case of the contiguous placement of two dominant–tonic progressions, [i.e., of] two [disjunct] descending fifth-leaps. Even more so is the cadence with the supertonic chord in Example 17.5, which represents two unmediated successive fifth-leaps, [a progression that arises] as soon as the chord built on the supertonic becomes a major triad *per accidens*, and thus becomes a secondary dominant, which was only conceivable with the genesis of modern major-minor tonality in the sixteenth century.[21] The voices not taking part in the syncopation dissonances of the previous examples must always progress at the point of dissonance resolution lest a chain of syncopation dissonances be created.

Therefore, the following progression cannot exist:

---

[21]In the progression Tonic–Supertonic–Dominant–Tonic, or even Tonic–Secondary dominant–Dominant–Tonic, the problem of the double fifth-leap from the subdominant [to the dominant] in the progression Tonic–Subdominant–Dominant–Tonic is displaced to the beginning of the cadence; that is to say, the inner lack of connection of the two falling fifths [characteristic of the progression] Tonic–Subdominant–Dominant–Tonic is overcome, particularly since the supertonic and the secondary dominant [both] have a tone in common with the dominant, and [the supertonic] has as many as two tones in common with the truncated dominant-seventh chord, which is usually used as a sixth chord with "root" doubling. Also, the subdominant 6-5 arising from an anticipation and the dominant have a common tone, as do the subdominant and the dominant seventh arising from a suspension.

Example 21

Rather, the entire dominant-seventh chord is immediately resolved to the tonic. With the tendency toward resolution of the imperfect sonorities with respect to the bass, the 2–1 suspension is bound to the tritone resulting from it. The perfect consonances with the bass are free in their [possibilities of] progression, but they are carried along with it. In the unmediated progression Tonic–Dominant–Tonic, the dominant-seventh chord is not created out of the subdominant through a suspension but rather through the frequent employment of a passing tone, which finally could appear simultaneously with the rest of the chord as well:

Example 22

In the early music for polyphonic instruments, the following cadence now appears frequently:

Example 23

The voices appear to be intended to progress according to the arrows as shown. Leading this back to composition in parts, however, the sonority progression is conceived as follows (see also above, Example 17.1):

Example 24

On the polyphonic instruments (apart from those with several keyboards), the voice-like conception does not come to expression. This finally resulted in the "triad" being perceived as a sonorous entity and no longer as the result of the joining of individual consonances to a basic tone or as the result of the placing together of consonances.[22] The seed of the new conception, however, lay in [the triad] itself: the half-dissonance of the fourth, only appearing in its four-voice realization in octave and third position, is well concealed between full-voiced consonances; in close position and in three-voice execution, the fourth does not appear even once.[23] (In sixth chords, the fourth is missing only in a wide voicing; in a narrow voicing it is already present even in three-voice performance, although well veiled.)

As was previously suggested, the *Basse fondamentale* of Rameau is derived, so to speak, from a tenor or discantus (a pitch set that one can conceive of as an upper voice), just as the contratenor (bassus) in chanson composition [is derived] from a two-voice contrapuntal framework of tenor and discantus. Rameau's *Basse fondamental*, however, employs only the lower third and lower fifth (just as the contratenor had previously done), but never the lower sixth, which always remained problematic.[24]

Now, the interval A–B in the C-major scale, when considered in relation to the *Basse fondamentale,* presents difficulties that do not appear when one conceives of the scale as proceeding from B–A (in F major from E–D, in G major from F#–E, etc.)—Rameau's "natural scale." The C-major scale consists of the two identical disjunct tetrachords, C–F and G–C, both with the half-step above. Regarding the A–B interval, the difficulty of the *Basse fondamentale* thus corresponds to the disjunction of the two tetrachords just named. It is otherwise in Rameau's "natural scale": It consists, so to speak, of

---

[22]A dissonant suspension no longer needs to be resolved in the same voice in which it had been introduced. Rather, it is sufficient that the tone of resolution be present somewhere in the following chord. Regarding the harmony of the early thoroughbass era in Germany, see also Lars Ulrich Abraham, *Die Generalbaß im Schaffen des Michael Praetorius und seine harmonischen Voraussetzungen*, Berliner Studien zur Musikwissenschaft 3, ed. Adam Adrio (Berlin: Merseberger, 1961), where historical and systematic research are joined in a fruitful manner.

[23]The close root position of the triad is, so to speak, its weakest position: the alto thus has the third of the sonority, the bass merely doubles the tone of the tenor at the unison or at the octave below, the discantus as upper voice has the fifth, which is inherently stable.

[24]On the other hand, the *Regula dell'ottave* (*Règle de l'octave*, Rule of the octave), which probably came into vogue in the seventeenth century in Italy, is understood in relation to the major or minor scale as a bass, and accordingly incorporates the sixth chord in the "harmonization."

the *hexachordum naturale* (C–A) with [the addition of the] *subsemitonium modi*. As a whole, the "natural scale" consists of the two identical conjunct tetrachords, B–E and E–A, both with the half-tone below. Because of the difficulty of the interval A–B in the scale from C–C, it corresponds to the disjunction (F/G) in the tetrachords C–F and G–C.[25] The tenor in chanson composition of the fifteenth century actually moves predominantly over its ground–tone and closes much more rarely than the discantus by rising over the sixth to the seventh to the ground–tone. Indeed, in classical vocal polyphony the discantus is not permitted to leap to the seventh from the fifth. Tenor and discantus thus lie truly at any given time above C, and B is merely the *subsemitonium modi*. This is demonstrated by our cadence examples above.

We now conclude: Regarding the development represented in the foregoing, one may consider as decisive the incorporation of the so-called imperfect consonances into musical composition. They are of a dual nature—they are consonances, but they contain a half-tone, a "leading tone," which wants to be voice-led into stability. The imperfect consonances thus are particularly amenable to being placed easily into all of the so-called church

---

[25]Thus, Bb should be placed [in this scale]. Thereby result the two conjunct tetrachords C–F and F–Bb, with the half-tone above (in Mixolydian this is true in any case—F must be raised here to F# as a leading tone). Accordingly, our basic scale actually runs C ... A–Bb–B–C; that is, C major is already a decisive move upwards, F major acts similarly going downwards. With the inclusion of B (possibly due to the use of the note F# in secondary dominants, which is eminently a possibility, see note 21), the basis of the upper tetrachord of the basic scale C–Bb (in minor, C#–Bb; our F-major scale probably originated through placing the tetrachord F–Bb below the C–F tetrachord) is pushed up a whole-tone from F to G, and it is just this whole-tone that renders the distance between F and B as "excessive." This is the reason why both F and G were ground–tones of hexachords. If one takes Rameau's natural scale on B and fits it at the same time on C (with Bb above), one obtains the scale B/C—A/Bb. The germ of this scale is the hexachord naturale with sub- and supersemitonium. If, simultaneously, one proceeds constantly downwards stepwise from Bb and constantly upwards stepwise from B, then the half-tones appear at the same time. One could pursue these inquiries *ad infinitum*. The dual character of Bb/B, however, as is generally known, was known even to the ancient Greeks. This fact is also decisive for the theme answer in the fugue. The tetrachords correspond to each other as follows (C-major scale):

C D E F =x   y= G A B C   B C D E =x   y= E F G A
G A B C =y   x= C D E F   Rameau's "natural" scale: E F G A =y   x= B C D E

The result of combining the two scales is that A, C, D, E, and G can be answered tonally at the fourth or fifth below, and vice versa, according to the melodic context:

A B C D E F G
E   G A B C D
D E F G A   C

At the beginning of a C-major fugue, one of course answers C with G and not F, etc.

modes having half-tones (consolidated at least since the ancient Greek music), so that they became more and more crucial. The tendency of the imperfect consonances towards progression led, with their stricter observation in multi-voice counterpoint, to parallel fifths and octaves. The English circumvented these [parallels] by placing the parts in wide voicings or by no longer resolving rigorously all imperfect consonances within the composition. In the four-voice motet style of composition, they then at first (around 1400) voice-led one part predominantly leapwise into perfect consonances with the other voices. The Continental [musicians]—probably on account of the reason named above—composed since about the middle of the thirteenth century at first only two-voice [pieces], and only then did they [recompose] them into three- and four-voice works. [This two-voice conception on the Continent] is also valid since the beginning of the fifteenth century, since [composers] voice-led the third voice predominantly leapwise into perfect consonances based on the dyads of the structural voices. Only gradually were the third voice (the bass) and the fourth (the alto) endowed with all [the contrapuntal] privileges which hitherto only the structural voices had possessed.

This process led to a linearization and hence a vocalization of the [bassus and altus] with respect to the structural voices [tenor and discantus], and the "tonality," which previously had been determined by the vertical sonorities and their progression tendencies, [now] was becoming a linear tonal order as [techniques moved] towards classical vocal polyphony. The music for harmonic instruments, which was coming more and more into fashion in the fifteenth and sixteenth centuries, was, however, in general composed according to the principle of the chanson, so that here the [older conception of] tonality conditioned by vertical sonority and its progression tendency still survived. The sonorous uniqueness of the harmonic instruments led as far as to make the sonority be perceived as a self-propelled quantity even more than before. Without the harmonic instruments, however, the new music coming into style in the sixteenth century and the entire succeeding era of thoroughbass would not have been conceivable. In [the thoroughbass era], the tendency towards repetition of specific sonority progressions—already present [in the earlier music]—finally won the upper hand (although not without "reversions" [such as] Bach). But now the motive force was no longer the tenor (cantus firmus); rather, [the sonority progressions developed] out of themselves. Conversely, the facts just mentioned offer the most fitting confirmation for the fact (still not demonstrated in all its particulars) that the developing music for harmonic instruments—of decisive importance since the fifteenth century—was founded on the compositional principle of the chanson.

Late Medieval Harmonic Structure
and Major-Minor Tonality

Ernst Apfel

EDITOR'S PREFACE: *This and the previous selection comprise not two separate studies but rather one article with an addendum. For general information regarding the issues discussed below, please refer to the preface of the preceding translation.*

In the following [essay], a few additional concluding observations should be made to an article of mine which previously appeared in this journal.[A]

Construction and movement of sonorities comprise the [property of] so-called tonality. Decisive for both is the lowest voice of the composition. The progression of sonorities based on motion in intervals of a second,[B] which predominated in the period from the thirteenth century through the beginning of the fifteenth, also comprises a kind of "tonality," although a very short-winded one. It is based on stepwise motion of the lowest voice of the composition, which is always preexistent as a cantus firmus or *cantus prius factus*. [This stepwise motion] can in the best case be extended only somewhat, [being restricted] to segments where the preexistent voice rises or falls by several consecutive seconds, as here:

Example 1

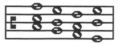

Wherever the preexistent voice leaps and therefore only permits a succession of perfect consonances, the [property of] "tonality" is dormant, so to speak.

[A]Ernst Apfel, "Die Klangstruktur der spätmittelalterlichen Musik als Grundlage der Dur-Moll Tonalität," *Die Musikforschung* 15 (1962): 212-27 [translated above; see the previous selection.]

[B]This type of progression is also characterizable by the term "neighbor-relationship of sonorities" [*Nachbarschaftsverhältnis der Klänge*], i.e., the double- and triple-leading-tone cadences.

The lowest voice of the composition always takes part very much in the motion of sonorities, although it proceeds mostly by major second, whereas the other voices make leading tone progressions. [The lowest voice] is in fact a melodic part. If it were static, the composition would become rigid. The most frequent sonority in this type of counterpoint is the dynamic 6-3, which tends toward motion.

The layered thirds and sixths in the sonorous principle just suggested must at any given time be resolved strictly into the closest available perfect consonances through half-tone motion in one voice and whole-tone motion in the other. Thus, sonorities tending toward pure motion and pure stasis follow each other, or in other words, stasis and motion were separated from each other *vertically*. In the fourteenth and fifteenth centuries, a new low voice—the so-called contratenor and afterwards bass—came into being especially in chanson composition. At first it was always only subsequently added *ad libitum* to already-existing pieces. (In Dunstable this leaping contratenor appears in the motet as well, but as a complement to the tenor cantus firmus [in its role] as director of sonorities [*Klangträger*].) This contratenor, added subsequently to a given piece, cannot, however, be considered to have had from the beginning the same compositional status as the preexisting voices. At first it was not even a true voice, since its individual tones only served to fill out the individual sonorities of the piece at hand. Hence, dynamic melodic motion was not its entitlement, so that it was allowed to have neither the stepwise descent allotted to the tenor nor the rising leading-tone progression identified with the discantus. The propulsive element was retained by the voices of the so-called basic contrapuntal framework [*Gerüstsatz*], which at first lay mostly—and later always—above [the added contratenor]. This meant, in fact, that the contratenor was allowed to make absolutely no imperfect consonances below the tenor that would have to be resolved, through motion in the contratenor such as is described above and a corresponding motion in the tenor, into the closest available perfect consonances. The only usable consonances for the contratenor [as low voice] were the perfect ones—octave and fifth below the tenor and the unison with it. The major third only became a possibility when it was discovered that one could satisfactorily voice-lead the upper voice with semitone motion and the lower voice to the octave [below] by leaping down a fifth (Example 2A) instead of voice-leading one of the voices by half-step motion the other by whole-tone motion into a [perfect] fifth (Example 2B).

Examples 2 A B

The minor third in root position [i.e., when it is the lowest interval of a multi-voice sonority] really only possesses sufficient independence when it is circumscribed by whole tones [on either side], as [it is] within the natural tonal system in the D-minor and A-minor sonorities. The E-minor sonority is problematic as its "ground–tone" is a leading tone.

The two [types of] sixths were almost entirely unavailable to the contratenor [when lying below the tenor], especially when it thereby would occupy the leading tone, which would usually have been the case with the minor sixth, since it predominantly has the leading tone below. [The contratenor] cannot leap out of a sixth [with the tenor], especially when it has the leading tone. The sixths comprise yet another exception compared to the other consonances: they always [must] concord with all upper components of all sonorities as imperfect [consonances], whereas the octave, fifth, third, and unison make a perfect consonance with at least one of the upper voices (Example 3A) or combined (so that Example 3B becomes Example 3C).

Examples 3 A B C

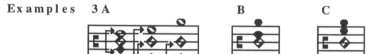

In this way, the contratenor became [in places] the foundation of the sonorities, and later also [throughout] the entire piece, so that it became indispensable to the composition as a whole. Through this, a moment of stasis entered into the sonorities, which hitherto had always acted in a manner serving to propel the piece forward. It is also important here that the major third was recognized with the octave and fifth equally as a foundational consonance. After the strengthening of the new bass, [the major third] was even permitted even in the last sonority of a piece, so that a propelling element (to the extent that such was still operative in the major third) was even introduced in the final sonority. With the genesis of the bass, composers now went over to using only one leading tone in each sonority (devolving upon one of the upper voices—particularly the highest), so that the double- and triple-leading-tone cadences were replaced by the one shown in Example 4:

Example 4

Motion and stasis are now present in all sonorities but separated from each other *horizontally*: the upper voices comprise the propulsive element, the bass the static. The sonorities thereby are amalgamated more than previously. They gradually become conceived of as chords. This conception then is conclusively carried out with the incorporation of the chordal instruments.

The reversion to a two-voice conception that was a consequence of the Continental approach to chanson composition was very significant. It led to the restriction to *one* leading tone per sonority. The strict resolution of thirds and sixths through stepwise motion of the participating "voices" into the unison, fifth, and octave was permitted only in two-voice counterpoint, or at most in multiple two-voice counterpoint, as for example:

Example 5

Only when composers voice-led the fifth through the sixth into the octave did a true three-voice conception arise. A true four-voice conception, however, was not possible without a mixture of perfect and imperfect consonances in all sonorities. When this [principle] was undertaken, the neighbor-relationship of sonorities had to be eschewed, i.e., the imperfect consonances were no longer amenable of resolution into the nearest available perfect consonance through stepwise motion in all participating voices. In the place of the progressions shown in Example 6A, the ones in Example 6B were required.

Examples   6 A   B

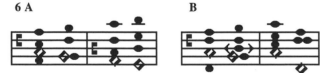

In the G sonority, B no longer acts as a leading tone with respect to both G and D but now only with respect to D, [that is, in the interval] B–D or its inversion; G is added in the contratenor (bassus) as the major third, fifth, or [major] tenth below. The 6-3 sonority (sixth chord) lost ever more in significance due to the creation of the harmonic bass, precisely because [this bass] was no longer composed as a sonorous foundation moving in stepwise melodies as the lowest voice of the composition. In the sixth chord, the lowest voice of the counterpoint is the factor influencing motion, whereas the harmonic bass supports the motion of the upper voices with the octave, fifth, and major third (and with the minor third only when it is circumscribed by whole tones [see above]). The [harmonic bass] is [thus] the foundation of the composition.

Also important for the fusing of the triad into a corporeal entity, so that it became the definitive sonority of music, was the following: The fourth-suspension before the third within a close-position triad is simultaneously a second-suspension (Example 7A), so that one is not certain which structure is the primary one, and [thus] a contrapuntal framework [*Satzgerüst*] is no longer ascertainable. This is doubly true of the progression in Example 7B:

Examples

7 A   B

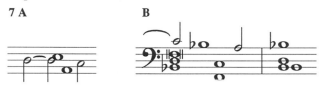

From the standpoint of the structural framework, intervallic composition proceeding out from the individual voices placed the syncopated seventh dissonance between tenor and discantus in the foreground of events in both sonorities. However, the bass, and with it the triad, pervade the sonorous element in such a manner as to render the structural framework meaningless, and one can conceive of the first suspension in Example 7B as a ninth–suspension and the second as a fourth– [actually eleventh–] suspension between the discantus and bass. On the other hand, in both of the following examples no doubt arises as to the voice crucial to the suspension:

Examples

8 A   B

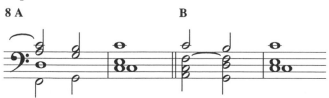

In Example 8A, the seventh–suspension of the discantus is referenced to the tenor's D, which concords with both other voices. The two structural voices stand unequivocally in the foreground of events. In Example 8B, the alto's seventh–suspension is referenced to the bass's G. The two structural voices—

tenor and discantus—concord with each other, but they also could be referenced to the G in the bass. In both cases, all voices must progress with the resolution of the syncopated seventh dissonance; otherwise its tone of resolution would be dissonant with one of the other voices. (This is also true of the following sonority progressions):

Example 9

On the basis of the facts just mentioned, the subdominant sixth chord and the dominant seventh chord could be adopted as four-note entities—dissonant, yes, but thoroughly usable—into the sonorous palette of Western European music.

Several additional observations regarding individual points remain to be addressed: Godfroy Keller, in [a treatise entitled] *Rules for Playing a Thorough Bass*, designates the notes B, E, and A as "sharp notes."[C] He thus assumes Bb [as the default note to be placed] over A, and the succession in which he names these pitches, as well as the fact just mentioned, permit the conclusion that he has Rameau's natural scale in mind. This scale, along with the difficulty of the progression from A to B and vice versa, was overcome in the conception of the so-called C-major scale as follows: C D E F# G A B C Bb A G F E D C (ascending with the Lydian fourth and descending with the Dorian—?—Bb). In the [technique of fugal] imitation, the tonal answer demonstrates the omnipotence of the octave divided unequally: if the theme remains in the realm of a fourth, then it can be answered in a "real" fashion, since the octave contains two identical tetrachords, otherwise it cannot. The real answer corresponds to the intervallic construction, whereby the position within the total tonal space is equally decisive; the tonal answer [corresponds] to the chordal [construction] with the octave as the crucial quantity.

It remains to enter briefly into the study of Edward Lowinsky, *Tonality and Atonality in Sixteenth-Century Music.*[D] Lowinsky considers the pieces he cites as completed compositions. Tonality (and also "atonality") originates, however, in the methods employed in composition. In my opinion, tonality—conditioned by [the concepts of] triad and cadence, and thus by a tonal center (first [expressed] modally and later through the two tonal realms major and

[C]Hugo Riemann, *Geschichte der Musiktheorie* (Berlin: Max Hesse, 1921), 448 ff., point 4.

[D]Edward Lowinsky, *Tonality and Atonality in Sixteenth-Century Music* (Berkeley and Los Angeles: University of California Press, 1961).

minor)—originated through the method of composition expressed in chanson composition (which also came into use in certain motets and in the early instrumental music), namely [a type of composing] according to [separate] voices. Thus, most of the examples adduced by Lowinsky (apart from those taken from madrigals) still permit the recognition throughout of a two-voice structural framework. In [Lowinsky's] Examples 4 and 14,[E] the dissonances mentioned specifically by Lowinsky are the very ones that betray composition by voices, although in Example 4, the altus also makes a cadence with the discantus, and the fourth in the structural voices is incorporated [into the counterpoint]. In m. 2 of Example 4, the structural voices (tenor and discantus) make the wholly consonant sixth, while the two filling and completing voices (bassus and altus) have the likewise-consonant octave. The dissonance originates only through the juxtaposition of these two consonances. In m. 8, the two structural voices concord at the fifth, in the second place the cadencing voices (altus and discantus) concord at the third, and the bassus and tenor in turn concord at the fifth. In m. 6 of Example 14, the discantus, moving along together with the altus, is referenced to the held C of the tenor, but the bassus makes the passing dissonance with a half-note D. In Example 40,[F] many dissonances occur only because the pitch of the counter-voice is constantly repeated instead of being held over.

In the article mentioned above (see above, note A), I have explicated how the later major-minor tonality originated within chanson-style composition. The madrigal, on the other hand, was (as Lowinsky also remarks) more indebted in a compositional sense to the motet [than to the chanson].

All of the problems [discussed here are intended] only as a small point of departure [for a dialogue on compositional technique, a topic] regarding which musicology finds itself decidedly in a phase of delivering opinions rather than [one of] true discussion.

[E]Ibid., see 5 and 12, respectively.
[F]Ibid., 52-3.

Tonality and Harmony in the French Chanson
between Machaut and Dufay

Wolfgang Marggraf

EDITOR'S PREFACE: *The author of this study was a student of Besseler, and many of the latter's ideas find a strong echo here. One of Marggraf's primary goals is to confirm Besseler's view that the so-called "dominant-tonal sonority system" is discernible within the Franco-Flemish musical sphere beginning in the late fourteenth century. Through a series of chronological tables, Marggraf examines tonal coherence in various sets of chansons and concludes that a trend is evident towards increasing emphasis on the fifth scale degree. This the author interprets as a clear "result of a new harmonic and tonal sensitivity." He further asserts that "the dominant-tonal ordering of sonorities was developed in courtly song and not in sacred music." The lack of text underlay in the musical examples makes it difficult to evaluate certain arguments, however, since a crucial element of cadences is precisely the manner by which the grammatical sense of the text is articulated. In Marggraf's article as originally published, footnote number 48 appears twice, so that here the final three footnotes have been renumbered 49-51.*

In his *Bourdon und Fauxbourdon*, a work so thoroughly significant for the early history of Netherlandish music, Heinrich Besseler directed the gaze of research for the first time upon the secular works of Guillaume Dufay—a composer whose harmony is based in large measure on exploiting dominant relations [*Dominantbeziehungen*].[1] As is the case with Dufay's other output, these chansons stand likewise isolated in their time. The breakthrough of the dominant-tonal ordering of sonorities [*dominantisch-tonale Klangordnung*] occurred, however, in [the chanson] with such convincing power that it is inescapable to think [that it is the result of] a working-out of specific initial ideas. The search for possible prototypes was previously pointed to by Besseler himself above all in Italy, where—as has long been known—rudiments of the dominant ordering of sonorities are found as early as in the

---

[1]Heinrich Besseler, *Bourdon und Fauxbourdon* (Leipzig: Breitkopf & Härtel, 1950), 38 ff.

music of the Trecento.[2] As an intermediary between the Italian and the Burgundian-French music traditions, great significance is apparently due to the Netherlander Johannes Ciconia. Besseler has vigorously pointed to his output as an archetype for the works of Dufay.

On the other hand, in Besseler's inquiry the question remains open as to the relationship Dufay's works manifesting the dominant system of harmony [*dominantische Harmonik*] stand with respect to the tradition out of which Dufay immediately came. Historical experience teaches that wherever a new phenomenon seems to spring suddenly and decisively into the light of history, partial manifestations of this phenomenon are already at hand, at least as latent tendencies of development. Even the genius does not find something that does not already exist at least as a desideratum. Thus, one had to presume that, with appropriate methods, a developmental process in the French music between Machaut and Dufay can be traced—a process that aimed at a progressively stronger dominant-tonal organization in composition [*dominantisch-tonale Durchorganisierung*].

The evidence for such a development can only be derived by a method that is realized out of the phenomenon itself, [a procedure which] thus invalidates from the beginning any criticism that foreign or inadequate standards of measure might have been applied to a historical manifestation. But this requisite is in no way identical to the one that serves solely the [intellectual] concepts provided by the contemporary music theory. The relationship between the musical creations and the theory of an epoch is not as literal as Ernst Apfel represents it.[3] Without doubt he overestimates the level of recognition the theory [had] for the contemporary [musical] practice when he makes the severe formulation that: "the absolute in what is not said in {the rules of the theorists} is also not important to the applicable compositions, although it may be contained in them."[4] The complicated and many-layered dialectic of the relationship between theory and practice cannot be represented here,[5] but it is certain that the view that comprehends theory and practice as always parallel must result in relinquishing [the possibility] to describe phenomena that have developed only vaguely and gradually. Rather, these can

---

[2]See also Annemarie V. Königslöw, "Die italienischen Madrigalisten des Trecento" [Würzburg: K. Triltsch, 1940]; (Dissertation, University of Munich, 1941).

[3]Ernst Apfel, "Über das Verhältnis von Musiktheorie und Kompositionspraxis im späten Mittelalter (etwa 1200–1500)," *Kongreßbericht Kassel 1962* (Kassel: Bärenreiter, 1963), 354.

[4]Ibid., 356.

[5]Reference might be made here to the seminal account by Hans Heinrich Eggebrecht, "Musik als Tonsprache," *Archiv für Musikwissenschaft* 18 (1961): 73.

only be understood when the works are approached and examined empirically, [so that] out of a familiarity with their essential characteristics, points of departure for methodology and description can be found.

Such starting points for such an understanding of tonal relationships, empirical in the sense that they are not influenced by preexisting system of theory, are doubtless represented in the fourteenth and fifteenth centuries by the cadences of the [actual] works. In them the melodic process is solidified in constantly returning, stereotypical formulae, whereby the attention of the listener is directed away from the melodic [element and] more strongly towards the vertical sonority. In the compelling confluence of all voices towards the goal-tone of the cadence, the [element of] tonality is most strikingly experienced. Thus, the cadences of the composition comprise a complex of fixed tonal points. From [these fixed points] and their respective context, one can proceed with an empirically oriented representation of tonal relationships.

The chanson forms of the fourteenth and fifteenth centuries thus offer ideal material for such an inquiry into cadential scale degrees, primarily because in their very nature a clear hierarchical gradation in the significance of cadential points is manifest; [this hierarchy is] identifiable through the clear differentiation between half- and full-cadences, which is conditioned by the form of the text. The relationship between *ouvert* and *clos* [cadences] in the ballade, between full- and middle-closes in rondeaux,[6] gives clear testimony of the hierarchy that exists between the individual scale degrees of the tonal system. Because this evidence about the relationship of the scale degrees to each other carries a weight in proportion to the quantity of materials researched, the opportunity to employ statistical methods is clearly offered here. In this way a secure foundation will be laid, upon which individual observations can be superposed.

The basis of the present study therefore is comprised of three-voice cantilena [i.e., treble-dominated song] composition in its normal form, with cantus, tenor, and contratenor—[a voice disposition] that was *de rigueur* for the chanson art of the fourteenth and fifteenth centuries.[7] In order to achieve out of the extensive material a selection of pieces uninfluenced as much as possible by the axioms of the inquiry, [the works chosen] are restricted to those available in modern editions.

---

[6]That *ouvert* and middle-closes in the fourteenth century were perceived as an analog to their relationship to the tonic scale degree is witnessed by Egidius de Murino, who refers to both as *apertum* (*CS* 3, 128).

[7]For definitions [of these voice types], see Besseler, *Bourdon*, 30.

The concept of "tonality" requires a refinement even in its modern context. It in no way implies necessarily a conception in the sense of the later system of major-minor harmony [*Dur-Moll-Harmonik*] but rather should at first be defined as generally as possible as the aggregate of the connections that exist between the individual elements of a tonal system. In this comprehensive meaning, and only here, is it usable with respect to the most varying musical phenomena.[8] Moreover, a differentiation of the concept of tonality is only ever possible for a specific historical form of tonality; it can be won anew [for any given repertory] only empirically out of analysis of the materials. Even Fétis, the originator of the conception of "tonality," knew that various possibilities of tonal order were immanent in history.[9] Unfortunately, systematic research into this [phenomenon] still has not so far been achieved.[10] We will not make use of any concept that might be suitable to characterize accurately the form of tonality occurring in the chansons of the masters examined here. Thus, in this study, when "tonality" is spoken of without further proviso, the concept is intended in its most general sense, according to the above definition. On the other hand, dominant tonality [*dominantische Tonalität*] represents a special form and must be designated as such. It is [here] defined as a form of "central" tonality, in which, along with the tonic scale degree, the fifth scale degree plays a dominant role in the construction of the piece. The gravitational effect towards the tonic scale degree, which results from psychological factors that are peculiar to the chord on the fifth scale degree, is realized and used [by composers] in an artistically aware fashion. That this gravitational effect was already experienced relatively early (at the latest around the turn of the fourteenth to the fifteenth century) is attested to not only by the [presence of] the decisive chord progression [i.e., V–I, which is] often laid out very distinctly, but also by the occurrence of the so-called "octave-leap cadence," in which the cadential power of the dominant relationship is realized for the first time.

---

[8]Even a definition proceeding from the concept of a tonal center would not be comprehensive, since the [concept of a] central gravitation of tones already represents a special case, along with which there exists other forms of tonality not incorporating a tonic (e.g., pentatonicism).

[9]Hermann Lang, "Begriffsgeschichte des Terminus 'Tonalität'" (dissertation, University of Freiburg im Breisgau, 1956).

[10]How imprecise our terminology is with respect to the tonal context is demonstrated, for example, by the laxity by which the concepts "tonal harmony" [*Tonalharmonik*] and "dominant tonality" [*dominantische Tonalität*] are frequently used as synonyms.

I. Guillaume de Machaut

It is appropriate to begin the inquiry with Guillaume de Machaut, particularly with his late works, which apparently represent the end stage of a development aimed at increasing tonal consolidation. This [process] shows itself most clearly over the total span of the piece. In this respect, four possibilities can be fundamentally differentiated:

A) The piece is tonally closed—the beginning and ending chords are identical.
B) The tonality of the piece is manifest through the first interior cadence, whose goal tone corresponds to the final chord.
C) The cantus of the piece is tonally closed, while the tonality of the lower voices diverges at the beginning or at the end.
D) The piece is tonally unclosed.

An overview of the division of these fundamental categories of tonal process with respect to the four chronological groups of works, according to which Machaut's output can be classified, results in the following picture:

Table I[11]

Group	A Closed	B 1st Cadence	C Diverging	D Unclosed
I: B 3, 4	—	—	B 4	B 3
2 TOTALS:	0	0	1	1
II: B 18-23	B 18, 19, 21	—	B 22, 23	B 20
R 1, 7,	R 10	—	R 7, 9	R 1
9, 10				
10 TOTALS:	4	0	4	2
III: B 25-28, 30-36	B 33, 34, 35	B 26, 28, 32	B 27, 31, 36	B 25, 30
R 8, 11, 13-15, 17	R 11, 13, 14 15, 17	—	R 8	—
V 26	V 26	—	—	—
18 TOTALS:	9	3	4	2
IV: B 38-40	—	B 38, 39	—	B 40
R 18, 19, 21	R 18, 21	R 19	—	—
6 TOTALS:	2	3	0	1

---

[11]The division into four [chronological] groups of works was established on the basis of the source situation by Ursula Günther, "Der musikalische Stilwandel der französischen Liedkunst in der zweiten Hälfte des 14. Jahrhunderts" (dissertation, University of Hamburg, 1957), 45 ff. [In the table, B=ballade, R=rondeau, V=virelai, followed by the number of Ludwig's edition (see below, note 14).]

The diminishing quantity of the tonally unclosed pieces as well as the ones with diverging [tonality] is unquestionably manifest from the table. Next to closed works, one sees frequently in the two latest work groups [III and IV] one in which the tonality is solidified through the first cadence. [The fact] that this circumstance does not occur in the first group of works strengthens the presumption that the development of Machaut's chanson output was aimed at tonal consolidation, since the tonality is vigorously strengthened by cadencing to the tonic scale degree at the cadence appearing at the beginning of the piece.

No clear developmental tendency can be ascertained with respect to sectionalization according to the individual tonalities. In all groups of works, the C tonality dominates, followed by the D, Bb, and G tonalities. Compositions in F are completely absent from group II.

At the *ouvert* [closes] of the ballades and virelais, as well as the middle close of the rondeaux, the second scale degree appears [to be] fundamental in the complete chanson output, [although] it can be replaced by the third [scale degree] in works of the C, F, and Bb tonalities. In group IV, however, the second scale degree has almost absolute priority; the sole exception is Rondeau 18, whose middle close leads back to the beginning with cadential effect, in the manner of a double-leading-tone cadence.

The great significance of the second scale degree as a cadential goal and thus for the construction of the composition is displayed not only at *ouvert* and middle closes but is emphasized especially throughout [Machaut's] late works. Virtually all the collected works of group IV, but also many [works] of the preceding third [group] (for example, Ballades 28 and 33), evince two cadential goal tones: the second scale degree and the tonic. This restriction is certainly a result of artistic economy as likewise is the strong tonal orientation that Machaut achieved in his late works.

All chansons in the latest group of works are very clearly structured through their cadences; typically, a cadence is placed at any given time after approximately three breves. In particular, the end of the first verse line is always marked by a cadence acting as a caesura. The musical structuring of the composition thus coincides with the formal construction of the text.

Many examples of dominant sonority progressions [*dominantische Klangfortschreitungen*] are found, often at conspicuous places. Ballade 38 has, at the beginning of the second line (mm. 26-27) the progression g+ — c over the contratenor's foundation, [while] Ballade 39 (mm. 41-42) has the progression a+ — d over the tenor. In both cases, the effect seems to have been consciously laid out: it is intended either to confirm the basic tonality [*Grundtonalität*] or to lead back inexorably to it. In Machaut's compositions, each of the two instrumental lower voices has the capability of serving as a foundation of dominant progressions; [of the two,] the tenor is clearly more frequent in this function. The dominant connection of sonorities [*dominantische Klangverbindung*], however, can also be effected through a leap upwards of the contratenor, as in the later octave-leap cadence,[12] as, for example, in Ballade 34, mm. 5-6 and 6-7.

II. French Late Period

In the musical transmission from the epoch after Machaut's death, the "French Late Period" [*französische Spätzeit*], two large stylistic groups are clearly discernible. The first group is comprised of those compositions that carry on Machaut's style with little modification, while the representatives of the second group project that extraordinary differentiation and complication of rhythm that justifies the designation "*Ars subtilior*," which has recently been suggested.[13] The manuscript Chantilly, Musée Condé 1047 (*Ch*)—a central [source] for French music in the last quarter of the fourteenth century— transmits works in both the Machaut and the *Ars subtilior* styles. The following inventory attempts [to make] an assignment of the composers named in *Ch* to one of the groups. A separate inquiry into the two groups can be dispensed with, however, since (as will soon be shown) characteristic departures from Machaut's tonal and harmonic technique are already found in works that still stand close to his style in their overall lines.

The material will be enlarged through several anonymous works from the [following] peripheral manuscripts: Paris, Bibl. Nat., n.a.frç. 6771 (*PR*) and Bibl. Nat., f. it. 568 (*Pit*); Prague, University Library, Codex XI. E. 9 (*Prag*); London, Brit. Mus., Cotton Titus A XXVI (*Tit*); and Cambrai, MS 1328 (*CaB*).

---

[12]See my study "Zur Vorgeschichte der Oktavsprungkadenz," *Die Musikforschung* 18 (1965): 399.

[13]Ursula Günther, "Das Ende der Ars nova," *Die Musikforschung* 16 (1963): 105-20. The concept of *Ars subtilior* is differentiated from the term "mannered style" used by Willi Apel, *French Secular Music of the Late Fourteenth Century* (Cambridge, Mass.: American Institute of Musicology, 1950), which will not be employed here due to its somewhat pejorative overtones.

[I] Codex Chantilly[14]

A) Machaut style

Solage (10: Apel Nos. 31-40); Trebor (6: Apel Nos. 41-46); Vaillant (3: Apel Nos. 69, 76; Günther No. 7); Grimace (1: Apel No. 72); Magister Franciscus (2: Apel No. 55; *MD* 8, p. 98); Andrieu (1: Ludwig I, p. 49); Anonymous (1: *MD* 8, p. 100).

B) Ars subtilior

Jacob de Senleches (5: Apel Nos. 47-51); Philipoctus de Caserta (4: Apel Nos. 59, 60; WolfM p. 27; Günther No. 10); Magister Egidius (2: Apel No. 57; Günther No. 8); Borlet (2: Apel No. 67, 68); Galiot (1: Apel No. 56); Cuvelier (1: WolfM p. 65); Hasprois (1: Reaney II, p. 28); Haucourt (1: Reaney II, p. 34); Guido (2: WolfM p. 64; *Mf* 16, p. 117); Garinus (1: Apel No. 78); Anonymous (5: Apel No. 61; WolfN I, p. 365; ApelN, p. 465; *MD* 8, p. 104; Günther No. 4).

[II] Peripheral Sources (all anonymous)

Apel Nos. 52, 63-65, 70, 71, 73-75, 77	(= 10 works)
Günther Nos. 1-3, 5, 6	(= 5 works)
Kammerer Nos. 12, 18, 27, 40	(= 4 works)

Thus, 68 works are available from the French Late Period: 39 ballades, 18 virelais, and 11 rondeaux. Table II shows their relationships with respect to overall structure, ordered according to tonalities.[15]

---

[14]All published works of a [given] composer are taken into consideration, including those that are transmitted in other sources (primarily Modena, Bibl. Estense M.5.24). The first count [in parenthesis] following a composer's name is the number of works analyzed. Since a precise accounting of the chansons with concordances cannot be given here, only the publication in which they are found is cited. The abbreviations designate the following editions: Willi Apel, *French Secular Music of the Late Fourteenth Century* (cited above = Apel); Willi Apel, *Die Notation der Polyphonen Musik* (Leipzig: Breitkopf & Härtel, 1962) (= ApelN); Ursula Günther, *Zehn datierbare Kompositionen der ars nova* (Hamburg: Musikwissenschaftliches Institut der Universität, 1959); Friedrich Kammerer, *Die Musikstücke des Prager Kodex XI. E. 9* (Augsburg: B. Filser, 1931); Friedrich Ludwig, *Guillaume de Machaut, Musikalische Werke* (Leipzig: Breitkopf & Härtel, 1926); Gilbert Reaney, *Early Fifteenth-Century Music*, Vols. I and II (Rome: American Institute of Musicology, 1955/59); Johannes Wolf, *Geschichte der Mensuralnotation von 1250–1460* (Leipzig: Breitkopf & Härtel, 1904) (WolfM); Johannes Wolf, *Handbuch der Notationskunde*, Vol. I (Leipzig: Breitkopf & Härtel, 1913) (WolfN).

[15]Since it is not possible here to give particulars for each individual work, reference should be made to my dissertation: Wolfgang Marggraf, "Tonalität und Harmonik in der französischen Chanson vom Tode Machauts bis zum frühen Dufay" (University of Leipzig, 1964).

Table II

Tonality	Works	A) Closed	B) 1st cadence	C) Diverging	(D) Unclosed
C	30	10	7	3	10
G	20	5	5	2	8
D	9	7	1	1	–
F	6	3	1	–	2
Bb	3	2	–	1	–
TOTALS	68	27	14	7	20

The relative numbers correspond roughly to those of Machaut's late works. Approximately 60% of all pieces are tonally closed or establish the tonality with the first cadence. Conversely, around 30% of the works stand in unclosed tonality. The high proportion of unclosed pieces in the G tonality (40%) is striking. The chansons with diverging tonality are noticeably reduced (10%).

Table III contains information concerning the *ouvert* [cadences] of the ballades and virelais.

Table III

Tonality	Works	I	II	III	IV	V	[VI]	VII
C	23	1	18	3	–	–	[–]	1
G	17	1	13	–	1	1	[–]	1
D	9	2	4	1	1	1	[–]	–
F	5	1	–	3	–	1	[–]	–
Bb	3	–	–	3	–	–	[–]	–
TOTALS	57	5	35	10	2	3	[0]	2

Here, as before, the second and third scale degrees determine the picture, with a total of 79%. The fifth scale degree is very rare; it does appear somewhat more frequently, however, at the close of the *Abgesang*, namely in five of the 32 ballades that have a clearly demarcated refrain.[16]

Also, the second and third scale degrees predominate in the rondeaux, with 64% of the middle closes.

Thus, in the total disposition of the Late-Period chansons, no change can be registered with respect to the works of Machaut. The situation within the compositions, however, is revealed even more clearly, [where] above all it should be emphasized that the cadences are losing their function as clarifiers of form. [Rather,] they comprise an essentially autonomous framework [*Gerüst*], which is set up independently from [the works'] formal construction.[17]

---

[16]For example, Trebor, *En seumeillant, Quant joyne cuer*; Philipoctus de Caserta, *Par les bons Gedeon.*

[17]See particularly the works of Solage, Jacob de Senleches, and Philipoctus de Caserta.

Simultaneously, the frequency of the cadences and their density within the composition diminishes. The flow of voices, largely independent of each other and [moving] ceaselessly as much as possible, appears evidently in the Late Period to have been an ideal, which is fulfilled in not a few pieces evincing a complete lack of articulating cadences.[18] The toying with and camouflaging of cadences, which one finds particularly in [the works of] Philipoctus de Caserta, serves the same intent, [namely,] if not to avoid clear articulative breaks, at least to attenuate them.

E x a m p l e   1 A : Philipoctus, *Par les bons gedeon*, mm. 24-5

E x a m p l e   1 B : *De ma dolour*, mm. 36-8

[Examples 1A and 1B (lower staff): contratenor = stems up; tenor = stems down.]

Frequently one now encounters chansons with numerous cadences as well. All of these [procedures] point to an intention of obfuscating tonality and form as much as possible.

A tonal layout very typical of the Late Period is displayed by Solage's ballade *Calextone qui fut*, whose cadence plan can be represented as follows:[19]

SECTION A						I1.	I2.		SECTION B				
‖ G	D	G	C	(A°)	D	Bb+ :‖	C	‖ G	D	Bb+ ‖	D°	C	‖
m. 4	10	14	19	23	31		39		63	71			90

---

[18]For example, Solage, *Le basile*; Vaillant, *Tres doulz amis*; Magister Egidius, *Roses et lis*.
[19]Irregular cadences stand in parenthesis.

This work serves well to illustrate our hypothesis: the high number of cadential target pitches as well as the loose density of cadences, especially in section B, is unmistakable from the diagram. But particularly striking is that the basic tonality of the piece, C, is not emphasized anywhere; as a cadence it is manifest neither at the beginning, nor is it expressly given prominence elsewhere, since the sole interior cadence on C [m. 39] has an entirely transitory character. In view of such a disposition [of sonorities] throughout the piece, one might suggest speaking of this composition in terms of an *appended tonality [angehängte Tonalität]*. This is so frequent in the Late Period that one can refer to [it as] a typical phenomenon.[20] Dominant progressions within a piece are to be found more often in works of the Machaut style than in those of the *ars subtilior*. They are supported primarily by the tenor, but the contratenor can certainly also be the foundation [of sonorities]. When both [lower] voices split the bass role, the contratenor usually leaps up an octave. Progressions based exclusively upon fifth–relations over an extended stretch, such as those occurring at the beginning of Solage's four-voice ballade *Le basile* (supported by the contratenor), are still very rare:

E x a m p l e 2 :   Solage, *Le basile*

[KEY: (upper staff): triplum = stems up; cantus = stems down
        (lower staff): contratenor = stems up, tenor = stems down]

If one [can still] be in doubt as to whether such dominant influences [*Dominantwirkungen*] within a piece were intended by composers or are more the result of caprice, the character of the dominant progression [*dominantischer Schritt*] is unquestionably clearly recognized here: where[ever] it stands at the end, its power to make closure is utilized. For example, one sees dominant final cadences (still completely absent in Machaut) in Solage's *Le basile*,

---

[20]As examples the following pieces can be named: Solage, *Corps femenin* and *En l'amoureux*; Philipoctus de Caserta, *De ma dolour*; Anonymous, *Le mont Aon, Un orible plein*.

Philipoctus's *Par les bons Gedeon* and *De ma dolour,* Vaillant's *Tres doulz amis*; sometimes [the effect of these cadences is] slightly muddied. In the closing cadence to the anonymous *Le mont Aon,* likewise a dominant [progression], the contratenor remains under the tenor: this already heralds the later double-octave cadence.

Although this example is singular, it may be taken as symptomatic of the fact that the contratenor, even as early as this Late Period [*ars subtilior* style], takes on more and more significance for the counterpoint. In the chansons of Machaut, it still always had the character and the function of a voice added to a two-voice contrapuntal framework [*Gerüstsatz*] of cantus and tenor, a fact confirmed by the fact that some chansons in individual sources are transmitted as two-voice compositions, without the contratenor. Already in the Late Period, however, it became more and more indispensable. It is very revealing that in the compositions examined here, examples of two-voice transmission are no longer found. In the latticework of voices, generally quite complex, of these late works, the omission of the contratenor would be most palpably apparent. If one were to leave it out, a [bare contrapuntal] framework would result—one which would suffice as far as the rules of the theorists were concerned, but which musically would be insufficient. That the contratenor now occasionally is assigned the ascending leading-tone progression in the cadence (which hitherto had exclusively been the province of the cantus), underlines its new importance (see Example 3).[21]

E x a m p l e 3 : Jacob de Senleches, *Je ne merveil,* mm. 5-6

A very characteristic phenomenon of the musical sensitivity of this Late Period is the frequent exploitation of a harmonic fascination that results from the succession of sonorities that are little related to each other. For similar

---

[21]Ernst Apfel, in *Beiträge zu einer Geschichte der Satztechnik von der frühen Motette bis Bach* (Munich: Eidos, 1964), maintains that Dufay's chansons are still "expanded" [*erweiterte*] two-voice compositions. The introduction of the leading-tone progression in the contratenor he recognizes as symptomatic of the "growing strength" of this voice (59), but he mistakenly places this [procedure] only in the middle of the fifteenth century.

phenomena in the harmony of the nineteenth century, Ernst Kurth has coined the term "absolute progression effect"[22] [*absolute Fortschreitungswirkung*], which will be used here, since without doubt it characterizes the phenomenon quite appropriately. In the late-period, sonority progressions such as Eb+— C+, Bb+—C+ were made possible predominantly through the partial signature of two flats in the lower voices as opposed to one in the cantus; [this signature] occurs exclusively in pieces in Bb or C tonality, that is, always in pieces in Bb and in about 30% of those in C. In almost all of these works, the illuminating power of absolute progression effects is used.[23] Machaut made use neither of these kinds of partial signatures nor of prominent coloristic sonority progressions.[24] Their surprise effects may be said to be a concession to the music ideal of the Late Period, which proceeded from [a striving for] abundance and boundlessness.

The very frequent partial signature of a flat in each of the lower voices serves almost exclusively to enable the variability of the third in sonorities [i.e., Besseler's *Terzfreiheit*]. In the majority of the chansons examined, several chords have a variable third. It seems as though the distinction between sonorities with minor or major third was understood not in the sense of polar opposites but rather as shades of color. The frequent suppression of accidentals in individual sources, as for example in *De Narcissus* of Franciscus, leads to the conclusion that in the second half of the fourteenth century, no essential significance was attached to whether the third should be taken as major or minor, [and that] the question was truly "accidental."

In the masters by whom we possess several works, personal characteristics of harmony and tonality can be clearly ascertained. The most interesting composer is probably Solage. Although his rhythm is still very much fettered to the Machaut style, he was an active participant in the style transformation. In his compositions, the count of tonally unclosed works is strikingly high, and these are mostly characterized by "appended tonality" and by a large number of cadential target pitches. Solage loves coloristic play and surprise effects in the connection of sonorities just as [he loves] the illuminating power of complete major and minor chords, which he also likes

---

[22]Ernst Kurth, *Romantische Harmonik und ihre Krise in Wagners "Tristan"* (Berlin: Max Hesse, 1923), 262.

[23][This occurs] particularly frequently in Jacob de Senleches, see *Tel me voit, En ce gracieux tamps, Fuions de ci*.

[24]The chord progressions of Machaut cited by Besseler (*Bourdon*, 58) are more characteristic of his motets than of the chansons.

to employ as cadential goals. Also, he makes relatively rich use of dominant chord relationships [*dominantische Akkordverbindungen*].

On the other hand, in the chansons of Trebor, the tonality is for the most part clearly marked; he restricts himself almost always to two cadential goal tones and makes only sparse use both of absolute progression effects and [of the system of] dominant harmony [*Dominantik*]. Of all the masters of the Late Period, he is the one whose harmony stands closest to Machaut's.

In the chansons of Jacob de Senleches and Philipoctus de Caserta, who stand very close together stylistically, one encounters the mature style of the *ars subtilior*, proceeding from luxuriance and richness of harmony. Coloristic chordal successions and harmonic surprise effects play an unusually large role as opposed to the [use of] dominant harmony, which recedes noticeably. A typical phenomenon of the Late Period is the frequent overlapping of caesuras.

III. Pre-Netherlandish Transition Period

In accordance with a suggestion of Heinrich Besseler, the era from the beginning of the fifteenth century up to about 1430 will be designated as the "Pre-Netherlandish Transition Period" [*vorniederländische Übergangszeit*].[25] Central sources for the chanson oeuvre of this time are the manuscripts Modena, Bibl. Estense, M. 5. 24. (*Mod*)[26] and Oxford, Bodl. Library, Can. Misc. 213 (*O*). Numerous chansons from both codices have been published.[27]

---

[25]Heinrich Besseler, "Niederländische Musik," *Riemann Musik Lexikon*, Section ed. Hans Heinrich Eggebrecht (12th ed., Mainz: B. Schott's Söhne, 1960), vol. 3, 633-4.

[26]Regarding the dating of *Mod*, whose repertoire belongs right at the beginning of the fifteenth century, see Kurt von Fischer, Review of G. Cesari and F. Fano, *La cappella del duomo di milano* I: *Le Origini il primo maestro di cappella: Matteo da Perugia*, *Die Musikforschung* 12 (1959): 226. Willi Apel's excessively early dating of the manuscript was rejected by Heinrich Besseler, "Hat Matheus de Perusio Epoche gemacht?," *Die Musikforschung* 8 (1955): 19.

[27]To the publications mentioned above in note 14 must be added: Wolfgang Rehm, *Die Chansons von Gilles Binchois, Musikalische Denkmähler* 2 (Mainz: B. Schott's Söhne, 1957); Charles van den Borren, *Pièces polyphoniques profanes de provenance liègoise* (Brussels: Editions de la Librarie Encyclopedique, 1950); Erna Dannemann, *Die spätgotische Musiktradition in Frankreich und Burgund vor dem Auftreten Dufays* (Strasbourg: Heitz, 1936); Jeanne Marix, *Les musiciens de la cour de Bourgogne au XVe siècle* (Paris: L'Oiseau-Lyre, 1937); John F.R. Stainer, *Dufay and His Contemporaries* (London: Novello, 1898). Chansons from *Mod* with concordances in *Ch* or *PR* were treated in the above section. Those works of Dufay that are transmitted in *O* are not included here; they will be discussed below.

Modena, Bibl. Estense, M. 5. 24

Matheus de Perusio (17; Apel 1-9, 11-18); Anthonellus de Caserta (8; Apel 23-30); Johannes Ciconia (1; Apel 66); Johannes de Janua (1; Apel 58); Anonymous (2; Apel 53; ApelN, facs. 82).

Oxford, Bodl. Library, Can. Misc. 213

Binchois (28; Rehm 1, 3, 6-9, 12, 13, 17, 18, 20, 21, 24-26, 28, 31, 32, 33, 37, 38, 43-45, 49, 51, 52, 54); Arnold de Lantins (14; Borren 1-14); Hugo de Lantins (14; Borren 15-28); Cordier (9; Reney II, p. 1-12); Fontaine (7; Marix 5-9; *ActM* 22, p. 35; WolfM 33); Cesaris (6; Reaney I, p. 19-30); Vide (5; Marix 11, 13, 14, 16, 17); Johannes Le Grant (5; Reaney II, p. 68-73); Malbecque (5; Reaney II, p. 94-100); Grenon (5; Stainer, p. 162; Marix 1-4); Lebertoul (4; Reaney II, p. 41-45); Velut (4; Reaney II, p. 118-25); Francus de Insula (3; Reaney II, p. 22-5); Guillaume Le Grant (3; Reaney II, p. 49-50); Franchois (3; Borren 33-5); Adam (3; Reaney II, p. 1-3); Hasprois (2; Reaney II, p. 30-2); Haucourt (2; Reaney II, p. 36-8); Loqueville (1; Dannemann III); Cardot (1; Stainer, p. 85); Charité (1; Reaney II, p. 20); La Beausse (1; Reaney II, p. 39); Paullet (1; Reaney II, p. 102); Libert (1; Stainer, p. 176); Rezon (1; Reaney II, p. 105); Grossim (1; Stainer, p. 172); Passet (1; Reaney II, p. 101); Coutreman (1; Reaney II, p. 21).

A total of 161 works is available: 116 rondeaux, 31 ballades, and 14 virelais.

Again, the occurrence of the four possibilities of tonal process will be illustrated in a table, wherein [the works in] *Mod* and *O* are differentiated. Compared to the French Late Period, the rapid recession of [instances of] the divergent and unclosed tonalities (2% and 13%, respectively) can hardly be overlooked.

Table IV

Source	Tonality	Works	A Closed	B 1st cadence[28]	C Diverging	D Unclosed
Mod	G	11	3	4	–	4
	C	7	3	4	–	–
	D	6	5	1	–	–
	F	4	3	1	–	–
	Bb	1	1	–	–	–
TOTALS		29	15	10	–	4

[28]Since cadences within the [text] lines are very rare in this transitional period, the first cadence serving to solidify the tonality is almost always closing cadence of the instrumental prelude or the [end of the] first line.

O	G	42	16	16	1	9
	D	37	29	5	1	2
	F	29	22	5	1	1
	C	20	9	6	–	5
	Bb	3	2	1	–	–
	A	1	1	–	–	–
TOTALS		132	79	33	3	17

It is also striking that the representation of tonalities should be so strongly at variance with the Late Period; particularly so is the strong decrease in pieces in C.

Table V gives an overview of scale degrees in the middle closes of the rondeaux.

Table V

Tonality	Works	I	II	III	IV	V	[VI]	VII
G	35	7	18	–	2	5	–	3
D	32	6	9	4	3	9	–	1
F	27	3	3	13	–	4	3	1
C	17	3	6	–	2	4	1	1
Bb	4	–	–	3	1	–	–	–
A	1	–	–	–	1	–	–	–
TOTALS	116	19	36	20	9	22	4	6

Here, the fifth scale degree has attained a noticeable significance (19%); it stands already in second place, behind the second scale degree, which leads as always. An overview of the *ouvert* [cadences] in the ballades and virelais offers a similar scenario:

Table VI

Tonality	Works	I	II	III	IV	V	VI	VII
G	18	2	11	1	–	3	–	1
D	11	1	5	1	2	2	–	–
C	10	–	3	3	2	1	–	1
F	6	–	1	4	–	–	1	–
TOTALS	45	3	20	9	4	6	1	2

The style transformation that was brought to fruition in the first decades of the fifteenth century has been exhaustively described.[29] Thus, only certain revisions having consequences for harmony need to be named here. In the first place, the clear structuring of the composition needs to be mentioned; this was

---

[29]See particularly Erna Dannemann, *Die spätgotische Musiktradition* (cited above).

a reaction to the caesuraless flow of the chanson art of the Late Period. In essence, the musical structure of the works examined here follows rigorously the construction of the text: the end of every line is typically marked by a cadence. Apparently, this agreement between textual and musical structure is the stylistic attribute that developed first, since it is displayed very markedly even in such earlier works [as those] by Matheus de Perusio and Anthonellus de Caserta, whose rhythm still carries characteristics of the Late Period. Next to the cadences at the closes of lines, cadences within the line are still thoroughly frequent in Matheus and Anthonellus, whereas they recede completely even in the oldest fascicles of *O*. One might conclude from this that the caesura effect of the cadence was now felt very strongly; through the elimination of the interior cadences, the cadences at the line endings obtain a heightened significance.

The closing cadence of the first [text] line (or of the instrumental prelude) is particularly important for the consolidation of tonal perception. Table VII indicates the scale degrees to which these [cadences] are voice-led.

Table VII

Tonality	Works	I	II	III	IV	V	VI	VII
G	48	29	5	–	6	7	–	1
D	42	31	1	1	5	4	–	–
F	32	16	3	5	2	5	–	1
C	24	16	1	1	1	4	1	–
Bb	4	3	–	–	1	–	–	–
A	1	–	–	–	1	–	–	–
TOTALS	151[30]	95	10	7	16	20	1	2

Here, the first scale degree [*Grundstufe*] dominates. Next to it, the fifth [scale degree] steps clearly to the fore, while the second scale degree, which previously had predominated next to the tonic as a cadential goal, has completely lost its importance.

The new valuation of the fifth scale degree, which is visible at the decisive points of the chanson form, is doubtless a result of a new harmonic and tonal sensitivity, which announces itself more or less cautiously. Naturally, individual differences between the various masters play a large role here. But even so, a glance at the chansons of the transition period will reveal the growing importance of the fifth scale degree as a cadential goal. Several

---

[30]Here the total count is not complete, since those few works that do not have a clearly articulated first line or prelude have been left out.

pieces cadence only on the tonic and its fifth,[31] whereby the latter is usually strongly emphasized. Other [pieces] not restricting themselves to these two scale degrees still accord a decisive role to the fifth degree.[32] It is completely lacking as a cadential goal in only around 40% of the works of the transitional period examined [here], whereas in the Late Period, about 70% of all chansons do not incorporate it.

A further important characteristic of the chanson art of the fifteenth century is the shortening of form. The individual sections, as conditioned by the verse lines, become definitely shorter, whereby the cadences draw closer together. Thus, their relationship and the tonal construction of the piece become much stronger than was previously known. The construction with "appended tonality," characteristic of many works from the late-period, is found after 1400 only very seldom.[33] Instead, the rondeaux evince a kind of formal construction that can be elucidated with the aid of Loqueville's *Je vous pri*. This rondeau has the following cadence plan:

| ‖ | D — D | D — D | D — G | ‖ | G — A | A — D | ‖ |
| | [A] Prelude | Line I | Line II | [B] | Line III | Line IV | |

The outer lines cadencing to the tonic enclose two inner lines of variable tonality. This thoroughly typical construction could be designated as *frame-structure* [*Rahmenstruktur*]. It corresponds to the rhyme scheme ABBA, which very often is employed in the rondeau. A connection is not unlikely if one calls to mind the close relationship between textual and musical structure in the transitional period.

Rondeaux with "frame-structure" are still not found in the Late Period; even in *Mod* they are very rare.[34] But as early as the oldest fascicles of *O*, this [type of] construction is so absolutely predominant that any evidence given here would be superfluous. This formal principle was doubtless one of the most important innovations of the transitional period; it provided for tonal closure without requiring the variety of cadence goal tones to be given up.[35]

---

[31]For example, Cordier, *Ce jour de l'an*; Velut, *Un petit oyselet*; Coutreman, *Vaylle que vaylle*.

[32]For example, Ciconia, *Sus une fonteyne*; Arnold de Lantins, *Amour servir, Ne me vueilliès*; Passet, *Si me fault*.

[33]Three of the few examples could be named here: Matheus de Perusio, *Se je me plaing*; Lebertoul, *Ma doulce amour*; Vide, *Espoir m'est*.

[34]One of the very few examples is *Trouver ne puis* of Matheus de Perusio.

[35]A dissimilar and more primitive solution of the problem of a more convincing tonal symmetry is offered by those chansons—not a few—that, apart from the middle close or *ouvert*, restrict themselves to one cadential goal tone (for example, Matheus de Perusio, *Le greygnour*

With this, a blueprint was achieved, which immediately illuminated the tonal perception of the time, and was capable of progressing in the direction of a dominant-tonal conception. It is certainly no accident that Dufay also avails himself of this formal principle in his chansons displaying dominant tonality.

If in the Late Period the contratenor stood as it were between cantus and tenor with respect to its melodic flow, so now it approaches the tenor in ambitus and rhythmic profile. [The contratenor] comprises a framework [*Gerüst*] with the tenor, supporting the songlike cantus, which is always the first [voice] conceived.[36] It is extremely noteworthy that the contratenor in the transitional period takes the foundation of dominant progressions far more often than the tenor. In the later fascicles of *O*, such sonority progressions over the tenor are met with now only very seldom, even though dominant progressions effected by the lower voices through voice crossing (usually with an octave leap in the contratenor) are very frequent. Sometimes the contratenor also serves as a "harmonic bass," which over long stretches is based exclusively upon fifth–relations.[37]

E x a m p l e 4 : Fontaine, *Mon cuer pleure*, m. 5 ff.

---

bien; Cordier, *Belle bonne*; *Se cuiur d'amant*). Fontaine's *J'ayme bien* seems to indicate that such compositions were soon felt as monotonous, [since] in the source Escorial ms. V.III.24 a new contratenor is added by an apparently foreign hand—one that revises the cadences in places to other goal tones.

[36]The compositional priority of the cantus with respect to the lower voices is vouched for by an unknown theorist of the early fifteenth century as an essential difference between chanson and motet composition; see Manfred Bukofzer, "Fauxbourdon Revisited," *Musical Quarterly* 38 (1952): 38; *Qui vult condere modulum fiat primo tenor.... Et qui vult condere baladam, rotundellum, viriledum, psalmodium fiat primo discantus.* ["He who wants to compose a motet fashions the tenor first.... But he who wants to compose ballades, rondelli, virelais, and psalms, fashions the discantus first."]

[37]See also the opening measures of Arnold de Lantins's *Amour servir* and Johannes le Grant's *Seliesse est.*

In view of such places, one gets the impression that the foundational role
of the contratenor in dominant harmony has already been tested in individual
progressions and shorter passages, before Dufay raised it to a principle in his
works with a bourdon-contratenor. The reason for this preference for the
contratenor may well be sought in the fact that the melodic flow of the tenor
was too much established for the late medieval musician. It was understood as
a primary voice, melodically fashioned; frequent leaps of fifths and fourths,
which are necessary in dominant harmony, would have contradicted its
essence. On the other hand, the contratenor as the sole filling voice was by
tradition less rigorously [pre-]determined. It could be voice-led in leaps
without a second thought, as its very frequent ascending leap of an octave
demonstrates.

In the pre-Netherlandish transitional period, stereotypical chord
progressions are fashioned directly before the cadence. The harmonic force of
the cadence radiates back to the sonorities preceding it. Such constantly
recurring progressions of sonorities might well be named "cadence sequences"
[*Kadenzfolgen*]. Its simplest forms are the chains of sixth chords, which are
very frequent even in the oldest fascicles of *O*,[38] yet which are only seldom
encountered even as late as *Mod*,[39] and are almost completely lacking in the
French Late Period.[40] Typically, the successions of sixth chords are slightly
masked so that one voice "counters" the prevailing pulse. Fully "compact"
sixth-chord successions are rare. As a rule, no more than three sixth chords
follow each other directly.

The parallel [i.e., double-leading-tone] cadence, which in *Mod* is still the
sole type prevailing, gives way first in the early fascicles of *O* to the
dominant octave-leap cadence and—although at first much more infrequently—
the double-octave cadence.[41] The appraisal of all these cadence forms varies
according the individual composers. Thus, the octave-leap cadence is placed
only at interior locations in the works of Vide, Velut, Johannes Le Grant, and
Arnold de Lantins and never leads to the ground-tone (which is always
approached with the parallel cadence). The closing effect of the dominant
progression [*dominantische Fortschreitung*] is apparently yet unknown to
these composers. Also, the double-octave cadence is introduced in a

---

[38]For example, Velut, *Un petit oyselet* (mm. 5-6, 46-47); Guillaume le Grant, *Ma chiere
mestresse* (before almost every cadence).

[39]Matheus de Perusio offers not a few examples: *Trover ne puis*, *Pour dieu*, both times at the
middle close, and the final cadence of *Helas avril*.

[40]The final cadences of Solage's *Corps femenin* and *Calextone qui fut* are totally singular.

[41]Regarding the cadence forms, see Besseler, *Bourdon*, 27 ff.

contradictory fashion: in [works of] Lebertoul and Coutreman it appears at the final close, whereas Arnold de Lantins uses it only to approach the ground-tone. In the rondeaux of Adam, the octave-leap cadence is applied solely to the ground-tone; in all other scale degrees, parallel cadences are placed. This insecurity in the use of cadence forms probably should be viewed as a typical phenomenon of the transition period.

Absolute progression effects that are emphasized are rare in the transitional period. The partial signatures occurring in the majority of chansons examined [here] typically produces only a variable third in individual sonorities.

IV. Guillaume Dufay

An inquiry into the complete chanson production of Guillaume Dufay does not lie within the plan of this study, since its intent is to show the historical development that led to his oeuvre. In order to facilitate a comparison of Dufay's harmony with his direct predecessors and contemporaries, a restriction upon this study's empirical basis is necessary, which means that discussion will be limited to the works transmitted in O.[42] There are 31 rondeaux and seven ballades. Following is an overview of tonal progress over the span of entire pieces:

Table VIII

Tonality	Works	A) Closed	B) 1st cadence	C) Unclosed
G	11	6	2	3
F	11	9	2	–
D	9	7	1	1
C	5	5	–	–
A	2	–	1	1
TOTALS	38	27	6	5

The frequency of [occurrence of] the individual tonalities, as well as the division of possibilities for tonal progress, correspond almost totally to the transitional period.

Table IX has relevant information regarding the middle closes of the rondeaux.

---

[42]See the source commentary in Heinrich Besseler, *Guilielmus Dufay: Opera Omnia*, vol. 6, *Cantiones, Corpus Mensurabili Musicae* 1 (Rome: American Institute of Musicology, 1964). Whenever individual works are mentioned [in the present study], the number of the applicable piece within the complete edition [of Dufay's secular works] is given in parenthesis.

Table IX

Tonality	Works	I	II	III	IV	V
G	9	1	3	–	2	3
F	9	3	–	3	–	3
D	7	3	2	–	–	2
C	5	2	–	–	1	2
A	1	1	–	–	–	–
TOTALS	31	10	5	3	3	10

The striking thing here is the high count of middle closes on the ground-tone and its fifth.

In four of the seven ballades, *ouvert* and *clos* are not differentiated. The other three have [cadences on] the second or third scale degree at this place.

At the close of the first line (or prelude), the first scale degree predominates, just as [it does] generally in the transitional period. Next to that, however, the fifth scale degree has great significance, as Table X shows:

Table X

Tonality	I	II	[III]	IV	V
G	6	1	[–]	3	3
F	9	–	[–]	–	2
D	9	–	[–]	–	1
C	3	–	[–]	1	2
A	2	–	[–]	–	–
TOTALS	29	1	[0]	4	8

A decisive majority of the rondeaux under consideration have a frame-structure, in which the fifth scale degree appears again to be preferred as a cadence goal of the inner lines: in five pieces it is the sole cadence goal outside of the first scale degree.[43] Only about 30% of all [Dufay's] chansons eschew a cadence on the fifth. Conversely, works in which the second scale degree is prominent are few. Only at the middle close of the rondeaux and at the *ouvert* of the ballades does it preserve a modest role—otherwise the fifth scale degree has replaced it almost everywhere.

Dominant progressions are found more or less frequently in almost all Dufay's works.[44] In *Ma belle dame souverainne* (44) and *Estrines moy* (58), dominant progressions are supported exclusively by the contratenor, whereas

---

[43]In the following observations, the works with a *Bourdon* contratenor were not taken into consideration. Regarding their special position, see below.

[44]Exceptions [include]: *Belle veullies moy retenir* (30), *Ce moys de may* (39), *Resvelons nous* (28), *C'est bien raison* (16), *Entre vous, gentils* (26), *Je ne puis plus* (29), *La belle se siet* (12).

[such progressions] as for example, in *Navré je suy* (77) and *Pouray je avoir* (33), are almost always accomplished with an octave leap of the contratenor. Chord progressions [*Akkordfolgen*] based exclusively on fifth-relations over rather long stretches are found in *Ce jour de l'an* (38, prelude), *Je donne a tous* (52, beginning), and *Pouray je avoir* (33, m. 5 ff.). Dufay uses the tension of the dominant to bridge over caesuras more often than his contemporaries.[45]

Dufay was more confident in his assessment of cadence forms than his direct predecessors and contemporaries. The cadential effect of the octave-leap cadence—decisive in comparison to the parallel cadence—is almost always used sensibly, insofar as the cadence to the ground-tone is approached by octave-leap motion, whereas the other scale degrees [are approached] by parallel cadences.[46] Double-octave cadences are more frequent within the composition than at its end. Works restricting themselves to parallel cadences are still relatively numerous. *Resvellies vous* (11), which is doubtless an early work on the strength of its transmission in the oldest fascicles of *O*, employs parallel cadences exclusively but incorporates a number of dominant progressions within [the counterpoint], with an octave leap in the contratenor.

The successions of sixth chords before the cadences, usually slightly veiled, which are often to be observed in the transitional period are also not rare in Dufay, although for the most part he avoids their overuse. As a rule he does not place more than two sixth chords contiguously. Only *Ce jour de l'an* (38) and *Pouray je avoir* (33) employ a relatively large number of sixth chords.

The characteristic cadential progressions that Besseler has pointed to in Dufay's works as [manifesting] the "technique of bourdon harmony" [*Bourdon-Harmonik*][47] are very rare in other pieces [of the composer]. Apart from the cases cited by Besseler, the progression Subdominant–Tonic–Dominant–Tonic is found only in *J'ay mis mon cuer* (13) and *Pour ce que veoir* (41), each time at the final cadence. An orthodox full cadence, in which subdominant and dominant stand next to each other, is seen twice in *Estrines moy* (58), that is, with both major (mm. 3-4) and minor subdominant (final cadence).

If one looks in Dufay's works for vestiges of the coloristic harmony based on absolute progression effects, which are especially typical of the Late Period, then one will first turn to the chansons whose partial signatures are

---

[45]For example, in *Belle plaissant* (40), *Ce jour de l'an* (38), *Estrines moy* (58), *Je me complains* (14), *Las, que feray* (69).

[46]Exceptions [include]: *Belle, vueillies vostre mercy* (47), *Adieu ces bons* (27), *C'est bien raison* (16), *Entre vous, gentils* (26), *Mon chier amy* (15).

[47]Besseler, *Bourdon*, 61 ff.

unusual. But these are quite rare. Only *Belle veullies moy retenir* (30) has two flats in both lower voices with no signature in the cantus; *Or pleust a dieu* (60) likewise prescribes two flats in the lower voices but also has one flat in the cantus. Examining the sonorous content of this work, one ascertains that the variable tones are almost without exception used as thirds in chords and scarcely ever as their ground-tone. Chords on B-flat and E-flat are very rare and even then always completely unemphasized. The partial signature thus serves in these works exclusively [to facilitate] the variability of the third. The same thing is true for the ballade *C'est bien raison* (16), which is provided with a relatively large number of supplementary accidentals.

Taken together, Dufay's chansons present a picture not fundamentally different from the one developed by his predecessors and contemporaries. However, [these chansons] possess certain features pointing to [Dufay's] more secure recognition of the driving forces of historical development. The large role played by the fifth scale degree and the system of dominant harmony [*Dominantik*], the fluency in utilization of cadence forms, the renunciation of absolute progression effects[48]—all these things in no way represent a break with tradition but rather result as their natural consequence. Those works incorporating six-line and deep-clef contratenors go even further in this direction [to the extent that] the multifarious potentialities found in Dufay's other works, as generally in his time, are reformulated to a principle. Even if the foundational role of the contratenor in certain respects had already been explored, it is nevertheless certain that the thoroughgoing employment of a low voice acting as a director of sonorities [*klangtragende Tiefstimme*] was an innovation of surpassing import. Besseler has extensively described [Dufay's] evident development from early stages such as the Italian ballades *Passato e il tempo* (3) and *Vergine bella* (5), up through the mature Bourdon compositions such as *He compaignons* (49), *Helas ma dame* (45), and *Je languis en piteux* (17), with their surprisingly modern harmony, and for this reason reference can be made [here] to those arguments. It should, however, be emphasized that almost all of these works adhere to a layout that we have designated as "frame-structure." In this respect also, Dufay only developed further forms that had already become a common currency of his time.

If it has been attempted here to show that Dufay's innovations lay at hand in the musical tradition from which he stemmed, then the presumption of

---

[48]In this renunciation, Dufay differentiates himself clearly from his greatest contemporary, Gilles Binchois, in whose works a substantially greater role is played by absolute progression effects (in this regard, see the particularly interesting rondeau *Ay douloureux disant helas*).

Italian stimulus does not present insuperable difficulties. It is, however, questionable whether this [stimulus] could have been so fruitful had there not been a predisposition toward a dominant-tonal ordering [*dominantisch-tonale Klangordnung*] within the Franco-Burgundian musical development, [i.e.,] if the ground for this had not already been prepared. On the other hand, an English influence upon the development described here may be taken as having been entirely out of the question. It is no coincidence that the dominant-tonal system of harmony [*dominantisch-tonale Harmonik*] was developed in courtly song and not in sacred music, whose forms were not conducive to a hierarchical differentiation of cadences. However, it was precisely in the area of secular song that there existed in England no models worth mentioning that could compare to the highly developed French chanson art. An influence upon chanson composition of the motet, which almost always was bound to a cantus firmus, is neither demonstrable nor even likely, since late medieval music theory sharply differentiates between the two compositional techniques with respect to the order of conceiving voice functions, as the [comments of the] theorist cited above attest.[49] In the fifteenth century, the cantus was the fundamental voice [*kostitutive Stimme*] in chanson composition; [chansons] were never composed "from the tenor outward." In England, on the other hand, the [technique of] working from a cantus firmus, which did proceed from the tenor, always retained priority. For all these reasons the thesis suggested by Ernst Apfel, whereby the contratenor is supposed to have become the director of sonorities [*Klangträger*] only under English influence,[50] is lacking in cogency. Brian Trowell also goes awry when he proposes "Besseler's *Bourdonkontratenor*" [as] already [implied] in a description of Pseudo-Tunstede, even though his explanations reveal clearly that this is simply a case of a cantus-firmus setting "discanting beneath the Plainsong."[51] But the new [element] of Bourdon is precisely that it supports an autonomous harmony, which does not result secondarily from laying out a cantus firmus but rather thrusts the primary harmonic forces into being.

---

[49]See above, note 36.

[50]Ernst Apfel, *Beiträge*, 59. He grounds his assumptions of an English influence upon the Continent, discernible almost everywhere since about 1300, exclusively upon examinations of compositional processes that proceed from contemplations of the contemporary music theory and particularly from the context of the contratenor, which allegedly was always the last voice added to a two-voice contrapuntal framework of cantus and tenor. This basis, which is doubtless very narrow, leads to historical conclusions that have no support in other observations.

[51]Brian Trowell, "Faburden and Fauxbourdon," *Musica Disciplina* 13 (1959): 52.

12

The Effect of Medieval English Polyphony upon the Development of Continental Cantus-Firmus Techniques and Tonal Structure

Ernest H. Sanders

EDITOR'S PREFACE: *This study is drawn extensively from the last chapter (V B) of Professor Sanders's Columbia University dissertation, although certain cuts and revisions were made by the author. I have adhered to the original English text from the dissertation wherever possible. In those passages where the German version deviates from the dissertation, I have simply translated what stands in the article as published in* Archiv für Musikwissenschaft. *All quotations from German sources are given in Professor Sanders's own translations, excepting only those few instances where passages not present in the dissertation were inserted into the article. The footnote numbering in the journal is faulty due to the insertion of a note 35a after note 35; this anomaly has been corrected below, which, of course, means that all subsequent footnote numbers are greater by one. Professor Sanders has altered the title slightly from the original and has offered a number of additional corrections, emendations, and other suggestions in preparing the article for publication in its present form.*

The role of the cantus-firmus principle in Western music has long been recognized as singularly significant and instructive. Numerous writers have marveled at its durability and fecundity in the realm of polyphony. And indeed, the variety of styles and procedures with which it has been involved—from the twelfth century to the eighteenth—attests to its longevity and productive power.

However, an equally important compensatory phenomenon has been stressed rarely; manipulation of a plain song, so as to make it suitable for polyphonic elaboration, invariably does violence to it, often reducing it to the point of unrecognizability. In fact, the history of discant against a cantus firmus as well as of post-medieval techniques of cantus-firmus elaboration can be described as so many chapters in the fascinating story how composers, in effect, bent the chant to their purposes, a process that ultimately resulted in the elimination of the cantus firmus in the eighteenth century. For Gregorian chant, polyphony proved to be a most powerful agent of decomposition.

Thrasybulos Georgiades has pointed out that the art of music does not fulfill its potential properly without polyphony, i.e., organized simultaneity of tones:

> The sound of speech ... can exist only by itself; it does not tolerate the simultaneity of another speech sound. The {musical} tone, however ... can indeed be combined with another, can sound simultaneously with it.... Only in polyphony {in the inclusive sense of *Mehrstimmigkeit*} do the consequences of the inherent properties of the tone in its function of purveying musical meaning reveal themselves.[1]

In general, the known Western music of the Christian era was not independent of speech prior to Carolingian times; the limitations of cheironomic and ecphonetic notation are symptomatic, since such notation is "meaningful only in conjunction with the text" and has "no intrinsically musical origin."[2] Only staff or letter notation corresponds to a fully developed awareness of discrete pitches and, presumably, to the desire for their distinct rendition in performance.[3]

It is obvious, therefore, that some of the often-cited parallels between certain Near-Eastern chants and Gregorian melodies must not be taken too literally. Idelsohn himself pointed out with respect to one such case that the "movable [interval of a] second" gave the oriental version a suppleness "totally lacking in the Gregorian tune in the presently fixed form of its scale."[4] In his discussion of the chants of the Yemenite Jews, several of which have often been referred to as similar or identical to Gregorian melodies, he has repeatedly emphasized the habit of Yemenite singers to raise pitches progressively as they waxed more and more ecstatic. While absence of precise pitch notation by no means needs to betoken lack of precision in the

---

[1]Thrasybulos Georgiades, "Sprache, Musik, schriftliche Musikdarstellung," *Archiv für Musikwissenschaft* 14 (1957): 224-5. However, to justify with this the converse axiom that only polyphony has musical validity would be an obvious fallacy.

[2]Ibid.

[3]"None of the ecphonetic systems can be transcribed in modern notation without the help of oral tradition"; Eric Werner, *The Sacred Bridge* (London and New York: Dobson, 1959), 105; see also 357-9 and 410-1.

[4]Abraham Z. Idelsohn, "Parallele zwischen gregorianischen und hebräisch-orientalischen Gesangsweisen," *Zeitschrift für Musikwissenschaft* 4 (1922): 515. The melody in question is partly reprinted in Gustave Reese, *Music of the Middle Ages* (New York: Norton, 1940), 114.

cognition and performance of pitches,[5] imprecisions and deviations are frequent concomitants of monophony.[6]

On the other hand, the necessary precondition for polyphonic elaboration of a chant is that it is regarded as consisting of fixed, mutually related pitches, which ordinarily can be fitted into a scalar system. It is only through some scientific system of pitches and their relations that an ordered simultaneity of tones becomes possible. Thus, the evolution of diastematic notation, together with the adoption of the concept of scale, constitutes *the* fundamental revolution in the Western music of the Christian era. Significantly, Peter Wagner has called attention to evidence of "chromatic" ambiguities in a number of chants that were, in one way or another, eliminated by staff notation.[7] The appearance of heighted neumes, Daseian notation, and staff notation undoubtedly reflects necessities created by preexisting improvisational practices[8] (perhaps instrumental[9]), which, in turn, were probably related to indigenous secular customs divergent from Gregorian traditions.[10] It is important to bear in mind that, "when the Western church attempted to systematize its songs according to the misunderstood teachings of the Greek theorists, it was the melismatic type which suffered most. Forced into the procrustean bed of the eight Church Tones, it was modified and mutilated."[11] "Very few, if any, of the Western Alleluia melodies can be traced back to synagogal or even Syro-Byzantine sources. Here again the West systematized and brought order to the endless, often improvised, flourishes...."

---

[5] Jacques Handschin, *Der Toncharakter* (Zurich: Atlantis, 1948), 312 ff.

[6] Abraham Z. Idelsohn, *Gesänge der jemenischen Juden, Hebräisch-Orientalischer Melodienschatz*, vol. 1 (Leipzig: Breitkopf & Härtel, 1914): 19, 28, 30-1, 34, etc.

[7] The article in question (Peter Wagner, "Die Diatonisierung des gregorianischen Gesanges durch das Liniensystem") appeared in three journals; see Willi Apel, *Gregorian Chant* (Bloomington: Indiana University Press, 1958), 108, note 13.

[8] According to Ernest Ferand, the genesis of polyphony goes back to this kind of tradition; see *Die Improvisation in Beispielen* (Cologne: Arno Volk, 1956), 5.

[9] Jacques Handschin, "Zur Geschichte der Lehre vom Organum," *Zeitschrift für Musikwissenschaft* 8 (1926): 324 ff. and 328.

[10] "It is of the greatest importance that in the first centuries {of polyphony} sequences, tropes, and conducti, i.e., the new tributary species, were preferred for polyphonic elaboration;" see Walter Wiora, *Europäische Volksmusik und abendländische Tonkunst, Die Musik im alten und neuen Europa* 1 (Kassel: Hinnenthal, 1957), 81. Concerning the tropes, it should be mentioned here that Richard L. Crocker recently has emphasized their effect upon the chant, related to [the effect produced by] polyphony, in that "the tropes tend to overrun the Gregorian original, swallowing it up into their own substance;" see "The Troping Hypothesis," *Musical Quarterly* 52 (1966): 190.

[11] Werner, *The Sacred Bridge*, 352.

The same organizing hand of the Occident is discernible in simpler chants of more archaic character...."[12]

Once the firmness of its constituent pitches and their relationships was guaranteed, the chant could be turned into a cantus firmus to subserve the composer's creativity. But this involved a sacrifice of its original character; only through isolation and individualization of its ingredients could it become the instrument of the polyphonists. "Organum came into being, a species of historic music, which for the first time must be understood *qua* music, which contains autonomous meaning."[13]

With its original melodic character transformed, the cantus firmus increasingly had to surrender the chant's essential quality in order to be subservient to the product of simultaneity. The term *discantus*, which appears in the twelfth century, describes the new situation very well: not only does it designate the divergent added voice (*dis-* = in two, in different directions) but it can also be understood to refer to the polyphonic technique as such, which dissolves the cantus [i.e., cantus firmus] as a melodic entity (*dis-* = apart, asunder). Perhaps Franco's striking choice of words is relevant in this connection: *Sed discantus dicitur dupliciter; primo dicitur discantus quasi diversorum cantus, secundo dicitur discantus quasi de cantu sumptus.*[14] Simultaneity is the preeminent compositional problem, and each pitch of the cantus firmus becomes the constituent element of a consonant interval.[15] The chant tune now becomes a "tenor," which sustains consonances.[16]

---

[12]Ibid., 579. See also Rudolf von Ficker's definition of what he called the "primäre Melodietypus," in "Primäre Klangformen," *Jahrbuch Peters* 36 (1929): 24.

[13]Georgiades, "Sprache, Musik, schriftliche Musikdarstellung," 225; naturally the wording is to be understood as hyperbolic (see above, note 1).

[14]*CS* 1, 130b; Simon M. Cserba, *Hieronymus de Moravia O.P.: Tractatus de Musica* (Regensburg: Pustet, 1935), 252. [Author's 1996 addition: The pertinence of Franco's statement was based on a faulty reading. Translation: "Discant has a twofold meaning; in the first place it is called discant to designate a vocal piece of diverse parts {i.e. a discant composition}, and secondly it is called discant when understood in functional relation to a cantus {i.e. as a discant voice above a bottom voice of a discant composition}."]

[15]Aspects of technique and style of polyphony prior to Notre Dame have been treated searchingly by Günther Schmidt, "Strukturprobleme der Mehrstimmigkeit im Repertoire von St. Martial," *Die Musikforschung* 15 (1962): 11-39.

[16]See the relevant observations in Günther Schmidt, "Zur Frage des Cantus firmus im 14. und beginnenden 15. Jahrhunderts," *Archiv für Musikwissenschaft* 15 (1958): 231-2 [translated elsewhere in this volume]. It is astonishing how many modern transcriptions of pre-Franconian polyphony, particularly that of the twelfth century (St. Martial, Codex Calixtinus, *Magnus Liber*), do not attach the necessary significance to this important, and actually self-evident, condition. The coincidence of a tenor note with that of the duplum is basically—with few

Discant is not only the technique of *punctus contra punctum* but of setting one contrapuntal cell (i.e., interval) after the other—the connection of sonorities. The composer's task is circumscribed and his ingenuity challenged by the exigencies set out by the band of notes of the *cantus prius factus* and by the two-voice framework, which generally does not exceed an octave before the end of the thirteenth century. Necessarily, contrapuntal propriety demands contrary motion wherever possible. In principle at least, each progression from perfect consonance to perfect consonance has no cohesion other than that provided extraneously and, as it were, accidentally, by the authoritative cantus firmus. "For since the consonances {*Klänge*} are complete in themselves like mathematical relationships, no causality, necessity, or logical inevitability relates one to the other."[17]

However, Eggebrecht's characterization of medieval *contrapunctus* on the Continent as "setting tone *against* tone…, each such action complete in itself: the static fixation of two quantities, which requires no further action (and is incapable of sparking any 'development')"[18] clearly excludes the connecting tissues too rigorously. It is true that, notwithstanding the disappearance from the French sources of homorhythmic counterpoint over a cantus firmus and the corresponding appearance of systems of rhythmic organization (modal patterns in the thirteenth century, isorhythm in the fourteenth century), medieval motets are still discants, but they are fleshed-out discants, with cantus firmi whose melodic qualities have been destroyed completely.[19] Eggebrecht thinks that the connections between the consonances of discant, as for example in a motet, "though seemingly foreground for the sensuous perception, are nonetheless of subordinate validity, not only in theory but also in practice and in their effect."[20] He apparently concludes that the notes of a duplum or triplum can only be referred to whatever note of the cantus firmus sustains them and that voice-leading considerations are inappropriate. But relative insignificance of function and causality does not mean total isolation of each consonance. This becomes more evident in view of the undeniable

---

exceptions—a matter of consonance, which often occurs at the end of ligatures or phrases of the duplum.

[17]Hans Heinrich Eggebrecht, "Musik als Tonsprache," *Archiv für Musikwissenschaft* 18 (1961): 83. He had previously pointed out that his remarks concerned only "the chiefly important French tradition of polyphonic music of the thirteenth and fourteenth centuries" (82).

[18]Ibid., 82. [The emphasis in this quotation is present in Eggebrecht's article.]

[19]See Rudolf von Ficker, "Formprobleme der mittelalterlichen Musik," *Zeitschrift für Musikwissenschaft* 7 (1925): 205.

[20]Eggebrecht, "Musik als Tonsprache," 83.

qualitative differences between what the author of the *Discantus positio vulgaris* calls *pure discantus*, or *discantus ipse* (i.e., note-against-note counterpoint),[21] and a Notre-Dame motet. In the latter, "because it was only the first interval of the rhythmic foot that was required to be consonant, the intervals in between enjoyed unlimited freedom.... The movement between perfect consonances was thus relieved by {passing} imperfect consonances and even by dissonances."[22] Undoubtedly, the conductus, which, though *"super unum metrum... etiam secundarias recipit consonantias,"*[23] had a good deal to do with this loosening of the rules of discant. However, the usual restriction of structural intervals to perfect consonances prevents truly functional intervallic relationships; the consonances are strung together successively, each representing a new "tonic," as it were. Functional aspects of structure proceed only from the manipulation of rhythm and phraseology (*modus* and *ordo*). *Mutatis mutandis*, these considerations apply equally to the motets of the *Ars antiqua* and the fourteenth century (with the significant exception that secular tenors retain their original rhythm).[24] Modal rhythm having been exploded by the semibreve, the long-sustained notes of the cantus firmus, when first sounded, almost always produce perfect consonances.

"Pure discant" (*discantus ipse*) was of course affected by the intervention of imperfect consonances and dissonances in modal and isorhythmic music; gradually, the thirds and sixths were admitted.[25] But a system of "harmonic" functions could hardly be expected in polyphony based on monophonic modal

---

[21] *CS* 1, 96a; Cserba, *Hieronymus de Moravia O.P.: Tractatus de Musica*, 192.

[22] Sylvia W. Kenney, "English Discant and Discant in England," *Musical Quarterly* 45 (1959): 43. Pertinent passages exist in the *Discantus positio vulgaris*, in [Johannes de] Garlandia's *De musica mensurabili positio*, and in the treatise of Anonymous 4 (see *CS* 1, 95a, 107a, 359b; Cserba, *Hieronymus de Moravia O.P.: Tractatus de Musica*, 191, 211-2). Coussemaker's reading of the passage in Garlandia's tract (*omne quod fit impari*) makes more sense and accords better with the passages from the other treatises than does Cserba's.

[23] *CS* 1, 96b; Cserba, *Hieronymus de Moravia O.P.: Tractatus de Musica*, 193. [Translation: "upon one single unit of measurement... also admits secondary consonances."]

[24] See Eggebrecht, "Musik als Tonsprache," 83-5. Significantly, the tenor rhythm of the two examples he quotes is isochronous or nearly so, resulting in the greatest possible structural neutrality. The reasons for the composers' selection of particular cantus firmi and the considerations accounting for their various rhythmic arrangements still await systematic investigation.

[25] Kenney, "English Discant," 43-4; Richard L. Crocker, "Discant, Counterpoint, and Harmony," *Journal of the American Musicological Society* 15 (1962): 3-7; Frieder Zaminer, *Der Vatikanische Organumtraktat...*, *Münchner Veröffentlichungen zur Musikgeschichte* 2 (Tutzing: Schneider, 1959), 153.

melodies, which had been composed without any vision of specific vertical functionality.[26]

The problem of melodic functionality is more complex. Eggebrecht's denial of its existence is not new; Besseler had pointed out long ago regarding the motet duplum of the thirteenth century that "goal tones, melodic sequences, axes around which it moves {*Bewegungsachsen*}, climaxes, contrasts, etc., are either completely absent, or else play only now and again a random role that is in no way constructive.... Every tone can serve as a conclusion as long as it is properly consonant."[27]

The basic procedures of discant would indeed seem to prevent the voice added to a cantus firmus from being primarily a melody (the cantus firmus no longer is, the upper voice not quite); thus Besseler came to describe the melodic style of the upper voices of thirteenth-century motets as a series of points [*punkthaft*]. Eggebrecht, using a different route, arrives at the same conclusion,[28] but his categorical denial of all progression again seems too rigid. Not only does he thus disregard the cadence (vertical and horizontal), but he denies the possibility of melodic tendencies from one consonance to the next. What Eggebrecht takes to be an illusory foreground, is often, especially in compositions in Perotin's style, too persuasive to allow us to look the other way, quite apart from those motets which manage to accommodate a preexisting secular tune in an upper voice.[29] Perhaps the discant technique of motets is best described as reticular, with the vertical strands as a rule connecting the knots firmly and the horizontal threads more fanciful and

---

[26]Crocker offers the opposite opinion, but does not bring in any sort of evidence: "Without being able to demonstrate it, I venture to assert that the tonal plans of Philippe de Vitry... are substantially more convincing than Dunstable's." This quotation is from Richard L. Crocker, Review of Edward Lowinsky, *Tonality and Atonality in Sixteenth-Century Music, Journal of Music Theory* 6 (1962): 147. Tonal unity is, in any case, atypical of Vitry's motets and is also not discernible in many chansons of Machaut.

[27]Heinrich Besseler, "Studien zur Musik des Mittelalters, [Part] II: Die Motette von Franko von Köln bis Philippe von Vitry," *Archiv für Musikwissenschaft* 8 (1926): 172-3; see also 177.

[28]Eggebrecht, "Musik als Tonsprache," 81-2.

[29]Thus, Crocker's argument that discant does not represent the combination of two melodies ("Discant, Counterpoint, and Harmony," 8 ff.) must be treated with reserve in a good many cases of "fleshed-out" discant. On the contrary, in several manuscripts there exist motets, which, because of the subordinate accompanimental role of the cantus firmus, are transmitted simply without tenors or else with corrupt tenors completely misunderstood by the scribe; occasionally one also finds a motet whose cantus firmus was replaced in one manuscript by a newly composed tenor (e.g., MS *Las Huelgas*, no. 83).

generally less solid. In this connection a perspicacious observation in
Zaminer's book on the Vatican Organum treatise should be cited:

> That the *organizator* [compiler] did not cling pedantically to fixed
> principles of progression is ready-made proof that for him something else
> was involved, namely a well-formed melody. Just as the cantor sings a
> coherent melody, so the *organizator* for his part endeavors to fashion a
> melodic unit. Of course, the organum melody (... discantus melody) does not
> unfold freely in great arches but, as it were, haltingly, with constant regard
> to the cantus [firmus]; even so, an unmistakable impulse lies in it to
> fashion coherences beyond the individual progressions and to assert itself
> as a melody alongside the chant tune.[30]

*   *   *

Medieval discant techniques undermined the essence of plainsong by
disassembling it, but the sacrosanct authority of the resulting ingredients was,
in general, strictly observed. In the first decades of the fifteenth century,
however, a decisive reorientation began to evolve.

Professor Lowinsky has observed that "to employ *cantus firmus* technique
meant first to lay out the cantus firmus and then add the other voices to it.
Thus it was impossible to conceive of a harmonic whole as long as *cantus
firmus* technique was used."[31] Beginning in the early 1400's, however, the
"melodic" tonality of the church modes, which had produced medieval discant,
gradually gave way to the "harmonic" tonality of the major-minor system.[32]
What motivated the gradual establishment of "harmonic tonality" and the
concomitant gradual elimination of cantus-firmus technique? Besseler has
argued paradoxically that "tonal harmony seems somehow related to the
characteristic features of song {*dem Liedmässigen*}"[33] and that "tonal harmony
in the fifteenth century was closely connected with instrumental music."[34]
Lowinsky thinks "tonality should be most conspicuous in ... the social
dance."[35] An attempt to resolve these apparent contradictions might well
begin by referring once again to Georgiades's meaningful comment that, in

---

[30]Zaminer, *Der Vatikanische Organumtraktat...*, 95.

[31]Edward Lowinsky, "The Concept of Physical and Musical Space in the Renaissance (A
Preliminary Study)," *Papers of the American Musicological Society* (1940–41): 69.

[32]Eggebrecht, "Musik als Tonsprache," 87.

[33]Heinrich Besseler, *Bourdon und Fauxbourdon* (Leipzig: Breitkopf & Härtel, 1950), 210.

[34]Heinrich Besseler, "Dufay in Rom," *Archiv für Musikwissenschaft* 15 (1958): 17.

[35]Edward Lowinsky, *Tonality and Atonality in Sixteenth-Century Music* (Berkeley and Los
Angeles: University of California Press, 1961), 61.

contrast to speech, polyphony is an eminently and exclusively musical phenomenon. The rational ordering of tonal material—the precondition of polyphony—detaches pitch from language by considering pitch as a separate entity. According to legend, Pythagoras discovered the affinity between music and number in a blacksmith shop, when he noticed that a heavier hammer sounded a deeper tone than did a lighter one. This fable, which goes back to Asiatic sources, indicates that organization and systemization of discrete pitches is inconceivable on the basis of the human voice primarily as speech medium, since without the intercession of essentially instrumental factors it projects only indeterminate pitches in conjunction with words. The voice can be "fretted" only after the model of a string (e.g., monochord).[36] Due to their twofold nature the human vocal chords are available as phonetic agent (vowels) and as the most personal of musical instruments, just as our lips, lungs, and teeth can be used phonetically (voiceless consonants) or musically (whistling). Hence, performance and perception of distinctly different pitches admittedly need not depend on man-made instruments. But systemization of pitches necessarily is an instrumental function in the more restricted sense of that term.[37] "Therefore, the notion of the instrumental is essential for the proper conception of music, of polyphony. *Organum* (*organon* Latinized), the first term to appear in the manuscripts as a designation for Western polyphony, can be understood as pointing to the essence of music: polyphonic, instrumental."[38] Here, then, lies the recognizable origin of music as an autonomous language and art (rather than ingredient), whose tendencies are increasingly instrumental.[39]

Besseler's observation that tonal harmony in the fifteenth century was closely connected with instrumental music therefore proves the stylistic revolution of the early fifteenth century to be an important waystation in the gradual instrumentalization of Western music. Nonetheless, his apparently contradictory association of tonal harmony with the *Liedprinzip* is also

---

[36]Note, in the treatise of Odo of Cluny, the teacher's reply to the pupil's astonished question, why a string can teach better than a man ("*Qua ratione fieri potest ut melius quam homo doceat chorda?*"); *GS* 1, 253a.

[37]See Walter Wiora, *Die vier Weltalter der Musik* (Stuttgart: W. Kohlhammer, 1961): 22. Conjunct melodic style and irregular "prose" phrasing (see below) are qualities that are, as it were, reminiscent of speech; hence, the Catholic church considers Gregorian chant and the *stile alla Palestrina* as especially appropriate for the liturgy; both serve "the word."

[38]Georgiades, "Sprache, Musik, schriftliche Musikdarstellung," 225.

[39]Curt Sachs characterizes Europe as a typical "nonsingers' land," *The Rise of Music in the Ancient World, East and West* (New York: Norton, 1943), 307.

appropriate and will be seen to be intrinsically related. "The Lied as a fundamental type," says Besseler, "is found in lay song as well as in the most complex art forms. A glimpse at the epochs of Western history reveals its variegated manifestations. Yet, in all cases a relatively small, closed form is involved...."[40] Elsewhere, Besseler has pointed out that "the Christian ritual chant {apart from hymns} has no poetic texts. It is based on scriptural prose."[41] By analogy, he saw fit to apply the term "prose" to the melodic style of the melismatic and neumatic items of the *Proprium Missae*.[42] Any attempt at defining the counterpole of prose "will concern itself with the concepts of rule and order, of matter bound and delimited in the widest sense.... Here there are 'members,' which are subject to cognition and recognition.... It is essential that such a member is related to other members."[43] Besseler has coined the term *Korrespondenzmelodik* for styles in which the smallest members are balanced against one another, a musical procedure that is antithetical to melismatic chant. Not only pitches and phrases are arranged in orderly patterns in such music, but at least an underlying awareness of a system of time values must likewise exist. Order and proportion prevail in musical space and time according to fundamental numerical relationships. Such "poetic" melodic style is the peculiar characteristic of Western dance music,[44] which Besseler, in effect, considers its *fons et origo*.

---

[40]Besseler, *Bourdon und Fauxbourdon*, 29.

[41]Heinrich Besseler, "Singstil und Instrumentalstil in der europäischen Musik," *Bericht über den internationalen musikwissenschaftlichen Kongreß, Bamberg 1953* (Kassel and Basel: Bärenreiter, 1954), 225. For the background of this circumstance see Wiora, *Die vier Weltalter der Musik*, 74-7.

[42]Besseler, "Singstil und Instrumentalstil," 226. These [texts] have thus suffered particularly under their adoption in the West (see above, notes 11-13 and their accompanying discussion). Willi Apel has noted that Alleluias with clear structure and Offertories that include melismas formed by repetitions, "are of a fairly late date, probably not earlier than the eighth or ninth centuries..." (*Gregorian Chant*, 369 ff. and 388 ff., especially 390). The same may also be assumed to apply to the neumes of the Responsories; most of them have likewise a repetitive form and apparently originated as supplementary tropes; see Hans-Jörgen Holman, "Melismatic Tropes in the Responsories for Matins," *Journal of the American Musicological Society* 16 (1963): 36-46, especially 41; Example 2 [in the article just cited] is faulty: in line 4 read "confessor" and in line 8, the "R" is missing after "Christi;" afterwards, read "Presta."

[43]Besseler, "Singstil und Instrumentalstil," 230 ff.

[44]Ποιεῖν (to create, to fashion) and ποίησις (a making, creation, fabrication) carry the connotation of tools and instruments; composition is a "putting together" of measured, related, and balanced ingredients and members (see Eggebrecht, "Musik als Tonsprache," 80).

Having pointed to the dance as the basis of the [classic] Viennese instrumental style, Besseler remarks that "the Lied art of the Middle Ages, which to a large extent was based on *Korrespondenzmelodik*,[45] contains surprising parallels to modern times."[46] The inevitable conclusion is that what Besseler calls *liedmässig* ["songlike"] is in effect synonomous with *tanzliedhaft* ["dancelike"]. Particularly compelling in this connection is Curt Sachs's observation that the contrast between semicadence and cadence (e.g., *ouvert* and *clos* endings) "finds no better illustration, except in the dance. In many dances all over the world, the performers take a few steps forward, then return to the starting point;.... By uniting two phrases with cadential distinction to form what musical theory calls a *period*, primitive peoples at a very low level of civilization had created the most fertile of musical structure schemes, the lied form."[47] Western dance song and the *Liedprinzip* (closed form)—all tending toward the major-minor system—are fundamentally the same thing, and thus the Lied, in its antithesis to the modal prose music of chant, is actually beholden to the dance and instrumental principles. Conversely, instruments and dance are foreign to chant and the divine service and were so regarded by the church fathers, for whom synagogal practices were still living traditions.[48] Significantly, Werner points out that in Jewish sources of the Hellenistic (-Talmudic) era, "Greek musical terms are used almost exclusively for instruments, their parts, their tuning, etc. The Hebrew vocabulary was perfectly sufficient to express all of the nuances of *vocal* music."[49]

The decisive importance of the instrumental element in Western music and the consequent process of its increasing instrumentalization provide a

---

[45]Jacques Handschin repeatedly proposed the main subdivisions of medieval polyphony as: 1) chant settings; 2) "compositions with rhythmic text." See, for example, "Was brachte die Notre-Dame-Schule Neues?" *Zeitschrift für Musikwissenschaft* 6 (1924): 545 ff.; "Eine wenig beachtete Stilrichtung innerhalb der mittelalterlichen Mehrstimmigkeit," *Schweizerisches Jahrbuch für Musikwissenschaft* 1 (1924): 70; "Über Voraussetzungen, sowie Früh und Hochblüte...," *Schweizerisches Jahrbuch für Musikwissenschaft* 3 (1927): 13.

[46]Besseler, "Singstil und Instrumentalstil," 238.

[47]Sachs, *The Rise of Music*, 35.

[48]See Wiora, *Die vier Weltalter der Musik*, 74-7, 80-3. Both Wiora (ibid., 118 ff.) and Georgiades have emphasized the perpetual dynamic tension between the sacred and the secular, to which Western music—and Western culture as a whole—owe their singular evolution and their specific phenomena. See Thrasybulos Georgiades, *Sakral und Profan in der Musik, Münchner Universitätsreden, Neue Folge, Heft 28* (Munich: Ludwig–Maximillians–Universität, 1960), 6.

[49]Werner, *The Sacred Bridge*, 334.

frame of reference for the explanation of many a phenomenon. With respect to the gradual evolution of harmonic tonality and the major-minor system, Besseler has called attention to the role played ca. 1400 by the newly developed slide trumpet—predecessor of the trombone—in the creation of a new style for one or both of the accompanying voices of chansons; the accompaniment often exhibits striking qualities of a harmonic support voice with considerable ambitus, large skips, and V–I cadences.[50] (It may well be, therefore, that the expansion of the two-voice framework to two octaves was brought about under the influence of specific instrumental practices.)

The conflict between this novel style and centuries-old conventions is clearly demonstrated by a new cadence progression; "in order to achieve a dominant-tonic formula with the parallel {i.e., II–I tenor} cadence, that ingenious octave skip [octave-leap cadence] was invented...."[51] This interpretation was promptly attacked by Ficker, who argued that superius and tenor, which generally exhibit flawless counterpoint, are therefore, as regards compositional technique, the two essential voices, while the contratenor has no role as harmonic support and "in that respect would be entirely dispensable. Its function is mainly restricted to filling and clarifying the framework provided by the essential voices, which consists of already complete composite sounds. Only relatively rarely does it happen that here and there the original harmonic relationships are altered by the filler contratenor...."[52] Having studied the discant treatises of the time, Ernst Apfel on several occasions has presented similar arguments. "In the fifteenth century ... the tenor determines all musical events." Hence, the first chord of Example 1 is "by no means a dominant, as we understand it."[53]

---

[50]Heinrich Besseler, "Die Entstehung der Posaune," *Acta Musicologica* 22 (1950): 8-35; see also Besseler, "Dufay in Rom," 17.

[51]Besseler, *Bourdon und Fauxbourdon*, 33. This cadence first appears in works of the generation before Dufay. Several examples can be found in Gilbert Reaney's edition of *Early Fifteenth-Century Music*, 7 vols., *Corpus Mensurabili Musicae* 11 (n.p.: American Institute of Musicology, 1955-79).

[52]Rudolf von Ficker, "Zur Schöpfungsgeschichte des Fauxbourdon," *Acta Musicologica* 23 (1951): 116. [Translated elsewhere in this volume; the translations above are Sanders's.]

[53]Ernst Apfel, "Der Diskant in der Musiktheorie des 12.–15. Jahrhunderts" (dissertation, University of Heidelberg, 1953), 2; see also Ernst Apfel, "Über das Verhältnis von Musiktheorie und Kompositionspraxis...," *Kongreßbericht Kassel 1962* (Kassel: Bärenreiter, 1963), 356.

Example 1

KEY: ○ = superius   ◇ = tenor   ◆ = contratenor

"But in its quality as a filler voice {the contratenor}, regardless of whether it lies above or below the tenor, has no bass function {*Klangträgerfunktion*}. The two structural voices {*Gerüststimmen*} can exist without it."[54] The impression created by Apfel is that the contratenor is never essential and hence dispensable. "For us today {it is} more important to know how people composed in the fourteenth and fifteenth centuries, i.e., what was the compositional genesis of chords, and what method determined the manner of adding the contratenor to the structural voices, than to know what chords resulted...."[55] And so he concludes that the music of 1400 to 1440 cannot be called "harmonic."[56] But discant treatises were manuals for the techniques of counterpoint as are harmony books for techniques of chord progression. In both cases the rules they contain are notoriously poor tools for analysis. Quite obviously, the composers of the first half of the fifteenth century adapted new concepts to traditional techniques, which were becoming atavistic; to lead the tenor 2–1 in a V–I cadence of a chanson is no more (or less) meaningful than Schönberg's failure to replace the convention of sharps and flats with a new system of "panchromatic" notation. Some of the old functions and tendencies occasionally seem to lead a sort of ghost existence, but they are no longer essential. Besseler's rebuttal of Ficker clearly has the better of the argument; it faces the facts: in such a piece "no voice is dispensable any longer, since

---

[54] Ernst Apfel, "Die klangliche Struktur der spätmittelalterlichen Musik...," *Die Musikforschung* 15 (1962): 217 [translated elsewhere in this volume]; also Ernst Apfel, "Der klangliche Satz und der freie Diskantsatz im 15. Jahrhundert," *Archiv für Musikwissenschaft* 12 (1955): 305 ff. [translated elsewhere in this volume]; and Sylvia Kenney, "Ely Cathedral and the 'Contenance Angloise,'" *Musik und Geschichte* (Cologne: Arno Volk, 1963): 45-8. One can scarcely accept, as Ms. Kenney does, Tinctoris's report about Gerard von Brabant, who allegedly sang simultaneously the discant and the tenor of a three-voice rondeau, as evidence for the inessentiality of the contratenor; one must also consider that he would not have been able to surpass this miraculous deed by singing all three voices at the same time!

[55] Apfel, "Der Diskant in der Musiktheorie des 12.–15. Jahrhunderts," 179.

[56] Ernst Apfel, *Studien zur Satztechnik der mittelalterlichen englischen Musik*, 2 vols. *Abhandlungen der Heidelberger Akademie der Wissenschaft, Phil.-hist. Klasse, Jahrgang 1959, 5. Abhandlung* (Heidelberg: Carl Winter, 1959), vol. 1, 84, note 24.

otherwise the character of the composition would be destroyed."[57] Ficker's and Apfel's denial of the musical realities is the more surprising when it is realized that V–I cadences already appear in a number of Machaut's chansons.[58] Moreover, both authors fail to explain why the double-leading-tone cadence did not retain its prominence. It is particularly strange to see their position adopted by Crocker,[59] since he repeatedly emphasized the importance of the ear[60] and pointed out that "the discant treatise does not describe what the listener hears, any more than does the treatise on traditional harmony. In both cases the teacher tells the student how to proceed; he does not analyze the result as it strikes the ear." "... Successiveness ... is a feature of teaching rather than of listening."[61]

That [theorists] in the Middle Ages were not rigidly dogmatic is also evident from the observation of Anonymous XIb that *contratenor in quantum est gravior tenore dicitur tenor*.[62] "However," says Apfel, "this remark together with its content {sic} is not decisive,"[63] and comments similarly on a comparable passage from another treatise.[64] He acknowledges that in the notation of early keyboard and lute music the V–I cadence can no longer be considered the result of a contrapuntal accident.[65] But it seems quite unlikely that these instruments brought about a change in the perception of such cadences, while in prior and contemporaneous ensemble music they were presumably still heard as special configurations of the old tenor cadence. Likewise, whenever compositions from this period contain non-cadential passages with strong chord progressions based on a fundament moving in skips, it would seem impossible to assume that the listener of the time was

---

[57]Heinrich Besseler, "Tonalharmonik und Vollklang," *Acta Musicologica* 24 (1952): 141 [translated elsewhere in this volume]. See also Wolfgang Marggraf, "Tonalität und Harmonik in der französischen Chanson zwischen Machaut und Dufay," *Archiv für Musikwissenschaft* 23 (1966): 12, 19 [translated elsewhere in this volume].

[58]Armand Machabey, "Machaut," *MGG*, vol. 8, col. 1397; Marggraf, "Tonalität und Harmonik in der französischen Chanson," 15.

[59]Crocker, "Discant, Counterpoint, and Harmony," 13 ff.

[60]Ibid., 4.

[61]Ibid., 9; see also 13.

[62]*CS* 3, 466a. [Translation: "insofar as the contratenor is lower than the tenor it is called tenor."]

[63]Apfel, "Der Diskant in der Musiktheorie des 12.–15. Jahrhunderts," 173. [The original quotation reads as follows: "Jedoch ist diese Bemerkung samt ihrem Inhalt nicht entscheidend."]

[64]Ibid., 178.

[65]Apfel, "Die klangliche Struktur," 225.

always capable of, or even intent upon, sorting out the voices so as to recognize the *Gerüststimmen*; the frequent crossings of tenor and contratenor alone reduce such an assumption to absurdity, regardless of the frequency of the mixture of timbres in musical performance.[66]

According to Crocker, the cadence progression of the contratenor, whether it jumps an octave or moves from dominant to tonic "merely enriches the sonority. It cannot be said to have any function—save from an 18th-century point of view."[67] But there can hardly be any question that the appearance of the V–I cadence, no matter in what guise, indicates a change. On the other hand, Lowinsky's thesis that the V–I cadence "is the cradle of tonality,"[68] and that without it tonality is impossible, should be seen as a restrictive and partisan formulation requiring critical examination.

Professor Lowinsky's book has been criticized for a "not very informative" definition of tonality,[69] loose enough to permit "the author to hide the fixity of his concepts."[70] Lowinsky has defended himself by pointing out that "tonality" connotes the long and complex story of an evolution. That the road to Vienna traverses many kinds of tonality is obvious. Nevertheless, Lowinsky's admittedly incomplete definition of tonality as "tonally centered organization"[71] is so unfocused as to add nothing to his own thesis; on the contrary, the same thing is also true of the majority of chant melodies.

For a comprehensive definition of the concept of "tonality," a second point is of central importance, namely that tonality, in the customary sense of that term, concerns the method and manner in which the members of a composition define the tonal center, i.e., the tonic. In their ordered relationship to the tonic, they are at the same time mutually related; balance and proportion of the component members, articulated by cadences, are necessary concomitants of a musical tradition that, having fixed pitches and their relationships, increasingly views them as a graded hierarchy (in contrast

---

[66]The effect of this practice has doubtless been overvalued; see Arnold Salop, "Jacob Obrecht and the Early Development of Harmonic Polyphony," *Journal of the American Musicological Society* 17 (1964): 289-90 and note 3.

[67]Crocker, "Discant, Counterpoint, and Harmony," 14.

[68]Lowinsky, *Tonality and Atonality*, 4.

[69]H[erbert] K. Andrews, Review of Edward Lowinsky, *Tonality and Atonality in Sixteenth-Century Music*, *Music and Letters* 43 (1962): 64.

[70]Richard L. Crocker, Review of Edward Lowinsky, *Tonality and Atonality in Sixteenth-Century Music*, 144.

[71]Lowinsky, *Tonality and Atonality*, XII.

to the attitude that produced discant and the medieval motet in France).[72] Tonal music is necessarily "poetic" in Besseler's sense[73] and, therefore, also fundamentally *liedmässig*.

Significant as the emergence of the V–I cadence is, tonal articulation need not depend on it or, for that matter, on the major mode. Lowinsky clearly regards any works with tonal organization prior to "the turn to dominantic tonality"[74] as relatively primitive evolutionary predecessors. He quite rightly takes Besseler to task for overlooking "Dunstable's new contribution in organizing a work by the distribution of well-placed cadences in clear tonal relation to each other,"[75] but then calls Dunstable's tonal organization "astonishing"[76] and points out that most of his cadences "do not have the force and direction of a V–I cadence."[77]

Two misconceptions are involved, one historic, the other systematic. It is, of course, incorrect to say that Dunstable's contribution was new, except for "some modest precedents—for example in the early fifteenth-century chanson."[78] In addition, it is precarious to consider "a net of cadences on varying degrees related to the tonic" as coming "closer to defining tonality,"[79] since multiplicity of degrees is not an inevitable condition; furthermore it seems unnecessarily parochial to consider modality as essentially incompatible with tonal organization.[80] The Summer canon is tonal throughout, and the fact that only one scale degree (the supertonic) occurs apart from the tonic does not alter that fact.[81] On the other hand, hymns such as *Pange lingua gloriosi lauream certaminis* or, for that matter, any number of folk songs and medieval Latin songs are no less tonal than the trouvère chanson *Ce fut en mai*,

---

[72]"Tonality is the construction from tonally related scale degrees with a center of reference; functions are values of placement and obligations of scale degrees within an ordering and as nodes of a whole"; Wiora, *Die vier Weltalter der Musik*, 24.

[73]See above, note 43, and its accompanying explanation.

[74]Lowinsky, *Tonality and Atonality*, 83 (note 3 for page 15).

[75]Ibid., 83.

[76]Ibid., 15.

[77]Ibid., 16.

[78]Ibid., 16.

[79]Ibid., 15.

[80]"It is of undeniable significance that cadences on the tonic and dominant occur thrice, whereas cadences on the fourth and second scale degrees only occur twice..." (ibid., 16).

[81]While Lowinsky convincingly describes ostinato patterns as "the playground in which {tonality} grew strong and self-confident" (ibid., 5), it is, in view of the Worcester repertoire, not correct to consider Renaissance Italy as "the home of all ostinato patterns."

although only the latter proceeds in major.[82] The tonal aspects differ, but the principle of tonality is apparent in all such pieces.

Lowinsky begins the concluding paragraph of his fifth chapter ("Consolidation of Tonality in Balletto and Lute Ayre") as follows:

> Unquestionably, a new sense of direction is the strongest underlying principle that sets off tonality from modality. The use of the tonic reserved for points of departure and arrival, the dynamic character of the sequence, the marked and regular distinction between weak and strong beats rendered more conspicuous by light and springy upbeats—they contribute as much

---

[82]Significantly, Ernst Krenek's restricted view of tonality is similar to Lowinsky's: "A tone becomes a tonic only when the central triad is built over it"; see *Music Here and Now* (New York: Norton, 1939), 110. This formulation is evidently imprecise; see William Thomson, "The Problem of Tonality in Pre-Baroque and Primitive Music," *Journal of Music Theory* 2 (1958): 40. That modality does not need to stand in the way of tonal organization and that, in fact, tonality was viewed as early as c. 1000 as a main factor of musical shaping is shown by the following quotation from the treatise of Odo of Cluny (*GS* 1, 257b-258a):

> Distinctiones quoque, id est loca, in quibus repausamus in cantu et in quibus cantum dividimus, in eisdem vocibus debere finiri in unoquoque modo in quibus possunt incipi cantus eius modi manifestum est. Et ubi melius et sepius incipit unusquisque modus ibi melius et decentius suas distinctiones incipere vel finire consuevit. Plures autem distinctiones in eam vocem que modum terminat debere finire magistri tradunt, ne si in alia aliqua voce plures distinctiones quam in ipsa fiant, in eandem {eadem?} quoque et cantum finiri expetant et a modo in quo fuerant mutari compellant. Ad eum denique modum magis cantus pertinet ad quem sue distinctiones amplius currunt. Nam et principia sepius et decentius in eadem voce que cantum terminat inveniuntur. Dicte rei exemplum in hac antiphona comprobabis: Tribus miraculis....

> ["Phrase endings, too, that is, the places at which we repeatedly pause in a melody and at which we divide it, ought obviously to end in each mode with the same pitches with which a melody in that mode may begin. And where each mode best and most often begins, there as a rule it best and most suitably begins and ends its phrases. The majority of phrases ought to end with the pitch which concludes the mode, the masters teach, lest, if more phrase endings are made on any pitch rather than on this one, they also desire the melody to be ended on that other pitch and compel it to be changed from the mode in which it was. A melody, in other words, belongs most to the mode in which the majority of its phrases lie. For the beginnings, too, are most often and most suitably on the pitch which concludes the melody. You may confirm what has been said by example in the antiphon *Tribis miraculis*...." Translation adapted by the author from Oliver Strunk, *Source Readings in Music History*, Vol. 1, *Antiquity and the Middle Ages* (New York: Norton, 1950), 113-4.]

Subsequently [Odo] enumerates the *distinctiones* of this particularly appropriate chant.

to the effect of tonality as does the change of mode and of harmonic vocabulary.[83]

And he goes on to point out that in the lute and keyboard dances of the earlier sixteenth century, "the process of tonal clarification and the emergence of major and minor go hand in hand with modern phrase structure and formal symmetry. The dances are built up in units of four measures. Repetition and symmetry ... are part and parcel of tonality. Together with regular accentuation they are, of course, an integral part of the art of dance."[84]

Here, in effect, Lowinsky describes the second of the two fundamental principles of tonality. Elsewhere, he describes compositions of the first quarter of the sixteenth century as possessing "tonal logic through a carefully constructed order of cadential relations."[85] However, it is simply not true (to cite Lowinsky once again) that "the earliest and most surprisingly mature examples of tonality can be found in the dances tabulated for lute or for keyboard instruments ... of circa 1500."[86] A large number of freely composed English pieces of the thirteenth and fourteenth centuries have survived whose tonal characteristics clearly accord with Lowinsky's specifications, if his insistence on V–I cadences is discounted. The following examples should serve to make Dunstable's tonal organization appear less "astonishing" (see Examples 2-7).[87]

---

[83]Lowinsky, *Tonality and Atonality*, 61.

[84]Ibid., 65 ff.

[85]Ibid., 34. Ingmar Bengtsson has remarked that regular measures and major-minor tonality belong together; see "On Relationships between Tonal and Rhythmic Structures in Western Multipart Music," *Studier: Tillägnade Carl-Allan Moberg, Svensk Tidskrift för Musikforskning* 43 (1961): 56. [Moreover, he says that] "it seems effectively impossible to describe tonality solely as a 'harmonic' or 'melodic and harmonic' phenomenon" (ibid., 75). His concept of "pulse groups" and "super groups" refer to the same facts to which Besseler applies terms such as "Glieder" and "Correspondence melody" (ibid., 57).

[86]Lowinsky, *Tonality and Atonality*, 62.

[87]The six examples come from six different manuscripts of the first half of the fourteenth century. Further examples could easily be adduced from the Worcester repertoire. Also, the variation motet published in Ernest Sanders, "Tonal Aspects of 13th-Century English Polyphony," *Acta Musicologica* 37 (1965): 28-30, should be mentioned here.

Example 2: Cambridge, St. John's College 84, front flyleaf r–v
(London, British Library, Sloane 1210, fol. 143v)

[A]b-o - ra sum me nun - ci - us a sum- mo pa - tre mit - ti - tur ad
A - ve tu ple - na gra - ci a ma - ri - a te - cum do - mi - nus e—

ma ri - am se - cre - ci - us et i - psam sic al - lo - qui- tur:
ris ma - ter e - gre - gi - a sed vir - go ni - hi - lo - mi - nus.

Example 3: London, British Library 62132 A, fol. 229v (* = f in MS)
(*olim* Studley Royal Fragment, fol. 2v)

A- ve ma-ter sum- mi re- gis de- i - ta-tis cel- lu- la lux et vi- ta for-ma le - gis
Lux ce- co-rum mo - ri- en-tis vi- ta qua-re vi - vi- tur spes sa-cra-ta men-tis gen- tis

Example 4:

Cambridge University, Pembroke College 228, fol. ar, av, br, 3rd strophe
(The end of the first strophe and the beginning of the second are missing)

Noser-go la-bi-les cau-sa pecca vi-mus a-de vel cri-mi-nis e-ve pri-ma-ri-e

fac fo-re sta-bi-les do-no spi-ra-mi-nis tu ma-ter lu-mi-nis et re-gis glo-ri-e.

Example 5:

Brussels, Bibl. Royale, II 266, No. 10 ("Fragment Coussemaker"), fol. 2r

Sal-ve vir-go sin-gu-la-ris sal-ve pa-rens ex-pers pa-ris cu-ius

men-tem sa-lu-ta-ris per-tran-si-vit gla-di-us. Tur-pi mor-te

con-demp-na - ti te co - e - git a-mor na - ti pro sa-lu- te no-stra pa - ti

cum pa-scha- li vic - ti - ma. Hinc ru - 'i - na re-pro-bo - rum re-sur-rec-ti—

o iu-sto - rum cum mer-ce-de sin-gu-lo - rum me - ri-tis com pen - de - ret.

Example 6: Oxford University, Selden B.14, fol. I, col. 2
(End of an incompletely preserved Kyrie-trope)

Ky - ri - e cre - den - ci - um sal-va - tor vir-gi-num con-ser-va - tor

a - ni- me   sum - me   rex e- ter - ne glo- ri - e   e - ley - son.

Example 7:

Cambridge University, Gonville and Caius College 727/334, fol. 199
(Only the last strophe survives)

Ma   ter Chri- sti no - bi- lis   o vir- go ma- ri - a   tu - is e- sto
Ut   sic pos- sint vi - ve- re   vi - te vi- va me - ta   qua - ti - nus per–

+This note is d in the fragmentary concordance Oxford, Bod. Lib., Bodley 548

fa   -   mu - lis   mi - se - ra - trix pi -   a.
ci   -   pe - re   que- ant ce - li le -   ta.

The English sense of tonality necessarily produced approaches to the
cantus firmus that were fundamentally different from the practices prevailing
in France. In the first place, it is of primary importance that this tonal sense
is itself an aspect of the English medieval penchant for tangible cohesion,
which accounts for the relative rarity of motets in the French sense of the
word, i.e., polyphonic compositions based on melismatic segments of chant.
Most English cantus-firmus compositions are elaborated discants in a more

real sense than are French motets, as the English composers usually set an entire chant or a monophonically meaningful portion. The earliest preserved Worcester compositions demonstrate the respect for the essential integrity of the cantus firmus by the phrasing and text treatment in the tenor and through the frequent confluence of the tropic text of the upper voices with that of the cantus firmus.

Most palpably cohesive in the English medieval repertoire are the freely composed fourteenth-century pieces that: 1) have a tonal center, and 2) consist of a series of balanced phrases, which are mutually related and with their various cadences define the tonic. But much of the cantus-firmus polyphony in the Worcester repertoire also evinces the importance of both factors. The conductus, which is so centrally influential in thirteenth-century English music, is responsible for the various manifestations of balanced phrasing in cantus-firmus settings.[88] Compositions in which the phrase structure of the duplum not only determines the phrase design of the tenor but apparently even accounts for pitch changes in the cantus firmus include the internationally circulated *Ave gloriosa mater* and an *Alleluia: Ave Maria* in MS Cambridge University, Jesus College, Q.B. 1.[89] Of further interest in this connection is the treatment of the cantus firmus in the English motet *In odorem*, transmitted in the MS Oxford, Bodleian Library, Corpus Christi College 497, and in Montpellier, Bibl. de l'École de Médecine H 196 (*Mo*), No. 70. Example 8 compares the layout of this cantus firmus (*Mo*, No. 70) with that in *Mo*, No. 95, a Continental composition, probably by Perotin.

Example 8 : Cantus-firmus disposition in *Mo*, No. 70 and *Mo*, No. 95

<hr>

[88]The topic of tonal unity in English cantus-firmus settings was discussed in my article "Tonal Aspects of 13th-Century English Polyphony," *Acta Musicologica* 37 (1965): 27 ff.

[89]See Ernest H. Sanders, "Peripheral Polyphony of the Thirteenth Century," *Journal of the American Musicological Society* 17 (1964): 279-82.

The final section of the other Alleluia setting partially preserved in the Jesus College manuscript (*Alleluia: Hodie Maria*), disposes the tenor in a more bouncy pattern that mixes the fifth and first modes, i.e., Franco's first mode:

This figure is widespread in Notre-Dame clausulae and in motets. What these and similar figures have in common is their balanced regularity, reminiscent of ostinato dance patterns. The tenors of the Ordinary tropes in MS Cambridge University, University Library, Ff. 2. 29 D (presumably of English provenance), are even more strikingly disposed:

Example 9: Cambridge University, University Library, Ff. 2. 29 D, fol. 2r

Such active and variegated dance figures occur in the tenors of the melismatic closing sections of many tropes. However, the English repertoire from the later thirteenth century contains a few instances in which dancelike patterns are applied to the chant tenor itself, for example, *WF*, Nos. 2 and 37[90] and the English-texted motet *Worldes blisce / Domino*.[91]

Example 10: *WF*, No. 2 (Kyrie setting)

These tenors are obviously shaped like certain *pedes* of freely composed motets, a few of which are demonstrably related to secular songs or dances.

Example 11a: *Pes* from *WF*, No. 10 (freely composed motet)

Example 11b:
One of the *puncta* of the dance in Oxford, Bodleian Library, Douce 139

Example 11c: Tenor of the first strophe of the conductus *WF*, No. 92

---

[90]Luther A. Dittmer, *The Worcester Fragments, Musicological Studies and Documents* 2 (Dallas: American Institute of Musicology, 1957); siglum: *WF*.

[91]See Manfred F. Bukofzer, "The First Motet with English Words," *Music and Letters* 17 (1936): 225-33. The part of the folio preserving this motet is a recto. Evidently this was originally a three-voice piece.

Example 12: *Pes* of *WF*, No. 65 (freely composed motet)[92]

Example 13a: *WF*, No. 36, third phrase of the *pes* and its later diminution

Example 13b:
Tenor of a fragmentary motet (Princeton, University Library, Garrett 119, Frag. B; London, British Museum, Gotton Frag. XXIX, fol. 36)

Dou way ro - bin the   child   wi - le   we - pe dou - way Ro - bin

A further noteworthy example of a cantus firmus with dancelike rhythm and phrasing is the fragmentary Sanctus setting *WF*, No. 60.

Example 14:
Beginning of the tenor of *WF*, No. 60 (setting of the Sanctus Sarum No. 5)

Sanc   -   -   -   - tus Sanc   - tus Sanc   - tus

The extraordinary aspect of this composition is not only the shaping of the Gregorian cantus firmus, but also the fact that the first phrase of the tenor is not Gregorian at all but freely invented, thus producing for the beginning of the tenor and the triplum—the duplum is missing—an a b a' b form. Handschin was surely right in attributing this tampering with the cantus firmus to considerations of tonal unification;[93] but beyond this, it also exhibits the evident desire for balanced phrasing. As a rule, most English compositions of the thirteenth century are differentiated from the contemporary French polyphony in the following points: 1) reciprocal musical and textual relatedness and assimilation of all voices; 2) preference for the [interval of a]

---

[92]Jacques Handschin has drawn attention to the fact that the *pes* of *WF*, No. 65, recalls the form of the estampie; see "The Summer Canon and Its Background," Part II, *Musica Disciplina* 5 (1951): 72.

[93]See Sanders, "Tonal Aspects of 13th-Century English Polyphony," 32.

third; 3) compact sonorities with relatively frequent triads; 4) tonal unity in free composition and in cantus-firmus settings; 5) prominence of trochaic rhythms; 6) predominance of regular periodicity, often with dancelike rhythms and phrases.

*   *   *

By the middle of the fourteenth century, the English art of troped cantus-firmus treatment seems to have subsided almost completely.[94] An exclusively English type of cantus-firmus composition arose, that is, the three-voice discant setting that generally maintained a strict note-against-note style.[95] The chant, placed in the middle voice, is surrounded by a discantus and a countervoice (called "counter"). Two marginal circumstances may have contributed to the growth of the novel practice of placing the cantus firmus in the middle. First, one must adduce the popularity of a cantus firmus with a high tessitura, which inevitably removed it from the bottom; the Gloria trope

---

[94]A convincing explanation for this apparent reversal is still lacking. It would be tempting to attribute it to the famous Bull of [pope] John XXII, but none of the English synods of the time concerned themselves with musical questions. Frank Ll. Harrison has noted that the monasteries were gradually being overshadowed in musical matters by the secular churches; see "English Church Music in the Fourteenth Century," *New Oxford History of Music*, vol. III: *Ars Nova and the Renaissance, 1300–1540* (London: Oxford University Press, 1960), 82. One wonders, however, whether such a change might not have begun to appear even earlier.

[95]Ibid., 97. Günther Schmidt mentions three-voice cantus-firmus settings in Continental manuscripts of the fourteenth century ("Zur Frage des Cantus firmus," 236 ff., 238). However, the English material, particularly in view of the mutilated sources, is incomparably richer and more variegated than the production on the Continent, where, moreover, two-voice pieces predominated. Chant settings in simple discant style have a long international tradition (Sanders, "Peripheral Polyphony," 261 ff.), but, to judge from the Continental source material, they were cultivated especially in England; see Ernst Apfel, "Über einige Zusammenhänge zwischen Text und Musik im Mittelalter, besonders in England," *Acta Musicologica* 33 (1961): 52 ff. According to Harrison, the Old Hall manuscript rests on French traditions, mainly because in the years preceding his coronation Henry IV had had extensive opportunity to become acquainted with the musical practices of the Continental court chapels; see Frank Ll. Harrison, *Music in Medieval Britain* (London: Routledge & Paul, 1958), 222 ff., and Frank Ll. Harrison, "Old-Hall-Manuskript," *MGG*, vol. 9 (1961), col. 1922. He particularly notes that these chapels "were well provided with competent composers and singers and with organs" (*Music in Medieval Britain*, 223). However, one must ask whether the composers wrote polyphony for the rite, whether the singers sang such compositions, and, in that case, whether the organ took part. Furthermore, Henry's journeys took place only in the 1390s—after the creation of the earliest works in the Old Hall codex. And finally, the Old-Hall repertoire can scarcely [be taken to] assume a singular position in England, since it is the only manuscript that survives almost in its entirety.

Spiritus et alme is such a case, which one encounters again and again. Secondly, the emergence of the sixth as a favored interval and the cultivation of parallel sixths[96] made it inevitable that a composer wishing to combine two voices largely in parallel sixths with a slower cantus firmus would find it more convenient to drape such a duet around the cantus firmus rather than to retain the traditional arrangement; many examples of such pieces could be cited.[97] A related and, at the same time, perhaps more compelling reason is that, in contrast to the Continental motet, the gradual expansion of the overall range allowed composers to turn more or less tentatively to designing bottom voices with more of a support quality than the generally conjunct style of Gregorian melodies could yield.[98] The rather extensive repertoire seems to confirm this assumption; usually the lowest voice is the most disjunct of the three,[99] a feature often due not to contrapuntal necessity but to the composer's preference.[100]

Whatever the reasons may have been that led to a lower voice being placed under the cantus firmus, it was thus enveloped and concealed. In the attempt to assimilate the cantus firmus, a number of compositions with migrant cantus firmus make the greatest strides forward. If one examines the

---

[96]Ernest H. Sanders, "Cantilena and Discant in 14th-Century England," *Musica Disciplina* 19 (1965): 10 ff.

[97]See Sanders, "Medieval English Polyphony and Its Significance for the Continent," 231 ff., 250-1.

[98]Manfred Bukofzer's hypothesis that such settings are "gymels" with an added treble is untenable; see *Studies in Medieval Music* (New York: Norton, 1950), 49. Apart from the incorrect application of the term (see Sanders, "Cantilena and Discant in 14th-Century England," note 17), no tradition exists in which a cantus firmus was placed—transposed if necessary—in the upper of two voices. Moreover, contrary to Bukofzer's implication, parallel fifths occur between all voices, not only between the "subsidiary" treble and the cantus firmus (see Apfel, *Studien*, vol. 1, 64 and 101). Finally, his statement that "the two lower voices come often to the essential sixth-octave cadence which proves their structural function" is incomprehensible, since this hardly ever happens.

[99]Evidently, Besseler was not aware of the prevailing English custom of placing a counter below the cantus firmus, since he considers countertenors with low clefs to be an innovation of Burgundian composers that had been unknown in England. (See *Bourdon and Fauxbourdon*, 52-4 and 70-2; see also Marggraf, "Tonality and Harmony in the French Chanson," 26, where in his discussion of pre-Burgundian contratenors with fifth- and fourth-leaps, the English "counters" remain likewise unmentioned.) Moreover, as early as the late thirteenth century some of the freely composed Worcester pieces (for example, *WF*, Nos. 88 and 91) already have clef arrangements that are comparable to ones listed in Besseler's book (*Bourdon and Fauxbourdon*, 53).

[100]See Sanders, "Medieval English Polyphony and Its Significance for the Continent," 405, note 149.

English compositions written up to the end of the fourteenth century, No. 47 of the Old Hall manuscript, written around 1400 by that remarkable composer, Byttering, displays progressive tendencies that are especially instructive. This setting of the antiphon *Nesciens mater* illustrates the propensity, which can be observed in many English compositions of the fourteenth century, to give the highest voice the most marked profile, ultimately coming together with traditions of style by which the cantus in contemporary French chansons were modeled. What is striking, however, is the singular treatment of the cantus firmus. The numerous transpositions and migrations from one voice to another can be explained, at least in part, as the consequence of requirements that derived both from the relatively high position of the cantus firmus and from the basic tonal plan of the composer; in other words, where the cantus firmus does not fit, the composer transposes it or places it in another voice or does both simultaneously.[101] Yet, similar results could unquestionably have been achieved had the cantus firmus been treated less capriciously. It is hard to avoid the conclusion that another prominent compositional principle must have been the composer's desire to employ every known artifice in his treatment of the cantus firmus, with the result that not only its melodic essence but even its pitch progressions are totally destroyed, particularly as it is also subjected to paraphrasing. The resultant composition sounds like a singularly appealing amalgam of English cantilena and early Burgundian chanson.[102] The new fluency, suavity, and grace attributed by Harrison to the works of the second layer of the Old Hall codex[103] is surely already in captivating evidence in this composition by Byttering.

$$* \qquad * \qquad *$$

It is one of the cardinal facts in the history of Western music that the beginning of the fifteenth century is a period of nodal significance. It witnessed not only absorption of French practices in England but also a reverse flow of influences. The early years of the century constitute an extraordinary stylistic watershed. A large part of Heinrich Besseler's research, culminating in his book *Bourdon and Fauxbourdon*, has been devoted to the investigation of the formation of the Burgundian musical styles (sacred and secular). It is his conclusion that after the assimilation of Italian traditions in

---

[101] See ibid., 406-8, where this composition as well as two other relevant works are discussed in depth.

[102] See Sanders, "Cantilena and Discant in 14th-Century England," 13.

[103] Harrison, *Music in Medieval Britain*, 246, 247, 250.

Burgundy, English influences began to exert an effect on Continental composers in the 1420s.[104] To Besseler, whose point of departure was fauxbourdon, the English composers' contribution to Burgundian music was their predilection for the sensuous quality of rich chordal sonorities replete with thirds and sixths {*Vollklang, Klangsinnlichkeit*}.[105] Contact with Italy, according to Besseler, caused the Franco-Flemish composers to adopt the typically Italian feeling for tonal space and its ordering {*Tonraumgefühl, Tonraumordnung*}; he adds that this tonal sensitivity, in which the dominant functions as the primary subdivision of available tonal space (after the octave), determines the style of the melodies as well as of the harmonically supporting instrumental tenors having "bass function" {*Harmonieträger, Baßfunktion*}. "Dominant tonality" is for Besseler quite simply the essential substance of tonality.[106]

Undeniably, predilection for chordal sonorities had been a characteristic feature of English music ever since rondellus and rota appeared in medieval sources. In addition, it is difficult to contest Besseler's contention that Dufay's "bourdon" contratenor {*Bourdon-Tiefstimme*} reflects assimilation of Italian influences.[107] But Besseler's disavowal of any significant role of "Bourdon and dominantic tonality" in medieval English music is surely one-sided and

---

[104]Besseler, *Bourdon und Fauxbourdon*, 73 ff., 15, 70. See also Gilbert Reaney, "Musica ficta in the Works of Guillaume de Machaut," *L'Ars nova, Les Colloques de Wégimont 2* (1955), (Paris: Société d'Editon "Les Belles Lettres," 1959), 209-11.

[105]Ibid., 71-2.

[106]Ibid., 72-85, 99. Leo Treitler has shown that the dominant functions as the main subdivision of the octave even in the monophonic songs of the "St. Martial" repertoire, which is of southern French provenance; see "Tone System in the Secular Works of Dufay," *Journal of the American Musicological Society* 18 (1965): 134 ff. However, prototypes of melody organized in this manner probably existed even in the ancient world (see Wiora, *Die vier Weltalter der Musik*, 69).

[107]Understandably, Besseler's deductions regarding the presumptive existence of the term *bordone* to designate such contratenors has been met with distrust; see Rudolf von Ficker, "Zur Schöpfungsgeschichte des Fauxbourdon," 114; also Manfred Bukofzer, "Fauxbourdon Revisited," *Musical Quarterly* 38 (1952): 26. [Besseler's] semantic discussion, which is limited to Latin and French forms of the word, confirms only that it denoted "drone" or perhaps "drone register (= bass register)." But what may lend Besseler's argument slight support is the fact that at least since Dante's time the Italian locution *fare bourdon* meant "to accompany a melody with low notes, to sound the bass"; see Salvatore Battaglia, *Grande Dizionario della Lingua Italiana*, vol. 2 (Turin: Unione tipografico-editrice torinese, {1962}), 312. Nonetheless, Besseler's imaginative hypothesis remains shaky as long as the term cannot be proved to have been used specifically as he assumes (e.g., *Bourdon und Fauxbourdon*, 46).

requires revision,[108] just as much as his assertion that "the fundament of dominant tonality stems from Italy" is untenable.[109] The state of English sources of the late fourteenth century is too fragmentary to reveal to what extent England contributed to the development of "harmonic tonality" on the Continent, but that it was known and cultivated in England at least as early as in Italy is proved not only by many of the examples adduced above but further by such compositions as *WF*, No. 67, the cantilena *Gemma nitens*,[110] and the dance in MS Oxford, Bodleian Library, Douce 139.[111] Thus, insofar as the Italian style opposes a sustaining instrumental part (or, in the case of a "dual harmonic fundament" {*Harmonieträgerduo*}, two voices)[112] to a stylistically distinct vocal melody, it features polarity between the outer voices more markedly than does the English repertoire. But what distinguishes English from Italian usage is not only its typical chordal richness,[113] but its considerable attention to balanced phrasing and clear structural divisions. To conceive a composition as a tonal unit is far more characteristic of English than of Italian medieval polyphony; likewise, the layout of phrases and the disposition of intermediate cadences often makes more of an impression of tonal purposiveness than in much of Trecento music.[114] There can be no question that the slow tenors in Italian *cacce* and other works function as bass supports. But they cannot, as a rule, be demonstrated to produce tonal organization. A disjunctly written bottom voice provides solid support but

---

[108]Besseler, *Bourdon und Fauxbourdon*, 112-8.

[109]Ibid., 99.

[110]Published in part in Handschin, *Der Toncharakter*, 257-8, and, in an even more abbreviated fashion, in *Musikgeschichte im Überblick* (Lucerne: Heinrichshofen, 1948): 214.

[111]See Ernest H. Sanders, "Duple Rhythm and Alternate Third Mode in the Thirteenth Century," *Journal of the American Musicological Society* 15 (1962): 288 ff.

[112]Besseler, *Bourdon und Fauxbourdon*, 82.

[113]A three-voice style with rich sonorities developed in Italian music only in the later fourteenth century. Strangely, Kurt von Fischer seems to trace this style back to "rather old traditions," even though the Italian polyphony of the early fourteenth century is generally two-voiced; see "On the Technique, Origin, and Evolution of Italian Trecento Music," *Musical Quarterly* 47 (1961): 53. The earliest known examples (c. 1300) are either for two dissimilar voices, which are set note against note with a maximum [vertical] interval of an octave (rarely, a twelfth) or for two equal voices, which, therefore, cross frequently. See Giussepe Vecchi, *Uffici Drammatici Padovani, Biblioteca dell' "Archivum Romanum,"* series 1, vol. 41 (Florence: Olschki, 1954), 26, 30, 106, 108, 110.

[114]Besseler's opinion that England possessed no song art in the Middle Ages (*Bourdon und Fauxbourdon*, 118) can hardly be said to correspond with the facts; see Sanders, "Cantilena and Discant in 14th-Century England," 21. In this connection, it is immaterial whether [or not] "soloistic, instrumentally accompanied" characteristics can be identified.

does not guarantee tonality and, therefore, is not its inevitable precondition.[115] This is proved when one realizes that some of the outstandingly tonal English pieces of the fourteenth century can easily be equipped with a disjunct "functional" bass, which is, however, no essential tonal ingredient.

What makes many of the English medieval compositions so remarkable is that they demonstrate the existence of tonal concepts, melodically as well as harmonically. Within the musical space available in the first half of the fourteenth century, one cannot expect a disjunct fundamental bass in a three-voice piece. But there can be no doubt that the English, in contrast to the Italians, did manage to give tonal organization to a good many of their richly chordal compositions, that they knew how to harmonize a tonal melodic organism. The more modern—and perhaps ideal—type of tonality, i.e., with a functional bass, could only begin to evolve when in the second half of the fifteenth century, the needed tonal space had become available, probably as a result of instrumental practice (as for example the slide trumpet). Here, as Lowinsky has pointed out, "both frottola and villancico take a place of honor,"[116] although these pieces, on account of the predominance of triads in root position, are harmonically less interesting than the examples of English fourteenth-century music cited above.

As stated earlier, Lowinsky's conception of tonality cannot be adopted uncritically and, in fact, has been criticized many times, but its teleological slant is nevertheless defensible. He has been dismissed on the grounds that he is supposed to have been intent upon basing his discussion of villancico and frottola on the tonality of the eighteenth century.[117] This may well be true, but solid reasons can be adduced for his view. The advantage of historical hindsight is that it can and must at least suggest, if not plausibly demonstrate, lines of evolution.[118] Since an evolutionary peak of tonal organization is

---

[115]In contrast to the applicable English compositions, the three voices of the *cacce* were apparently not conceived together as a unit but rather as a canonic duet with a supporting voice added subsequently, which moves relatively sluggishly. The disjunct style of the "counter" in Old Hall and comparable English sources likewise has no effect upon tonal construction.

[116]Lowinsky, *Tonality and Atonality*, 14.

[117]Richard L. Crocker, Review of Edward Lowinsky, *Tonality and Atonality in Sixteenth-Century Music*, 146.

[118]It seems especially capricious to attack the position that the frottola can be viewed as a predecessor of another style, if nonetheless the frottole are brought into relation with their own stylistic forebears. ("The real problem is to show how these little frottole were produced out of their own stylistic past, not how they anticipated something that had not yet happened"; ibid., 146.)

represented by the Viennese classic composers,[119] a definition of tonality that makes major essential is comprehensible and not quite so "trivial" as Crocker describes it.[120] Any tonal order rooted in the naturally available simple relationships that it exploits and elaborates has its primary melodic corollary in the major mode.[121] It is highly significant that most of the freely composed pieces in the medieval English repertoire are not only tonal, but in major, and feature prominently the latter's companion, the major third, as consonance.[122]

$$*\quad\quad*\quad\quad*$$

The chief factor of Western music, its rational and distinguishing mark, is the role of the harmonic frequency relationships,... which has its source both in hearing and in the physical world. In hearing we find it in the qualitative identity experienced in the octave, in the degrees of consonance of intervals and chords, and in the unified sound of a complex tone. And in the physical world, we find it in the frequency relationships of the sounds produced by sources of regular and simple shape.[123]

The principle of the "harmonic," that is, measured relationships of consonance, naturally includes both horizontal and vertical intervallic structures.[124] Cognate considerations have caused the turn from the "melodic tonality" of the church modes to the "harmonic tonality" of the major-minor system to be described as symptomatic of the recognition of the inherent

---

[119]Walter Wiora, "Der tonale Logos," *Die Musikforschung* 4 (1951): 157; Bengtsson, "On Relationships Between Tonal and Rhythmic Structures...," 63.

[120]Crocker, Review of Edward Lowinsky, *Tonality and Atonality in Sixteenth-Century Music*, 148.

[121]Marchettus de Padua maintained that the C Hexachord was called *naturale*, since melodies with the half step between the third and fourth scale degrees are natural; see Jacques Handschin, "Dur-Moll," *MGG*, vol. 3, col. 977; see also Wiora, "Der tonale Logos," 33.

[122]See Carl Dahlhaus, "Die Natur der Musik und die Konsonanz," *Die Natur der Musik als Problem der Wissenschaft, Musikalische Zeitfragen* 10 (Kassel and Basel: Bärenreiter, 1962): 22.

[123]Edward A. Lippman, "Music and Space" (Ph.D. dissertation, Columbia University, 1952), 237-8.

[124]"Consonances should not be conceived initially as vertical sonorities and only later as successive, but rather as relationships of quality conditioned by number which appear equally in melody and in polyphony"; see Walter Wiora, "Älter als die Pentatonik," *Studia Memoriae Belae Bartok Sacra* (Budapest: Academia Scientarum Hungaricae, 1957), 195; see also 197-8, and Wiora, *Die vier Weltalter der Musik,* 58-9, 69. Sachs names the octave, fifth, and fourth "the three innate intervals," *The Rise of Music*, 64; see also 42.

instrumental qualities of the tone, i.e., of its nature as a composite entity.[125] "The simultaneous sounding of tones is no longer the result of setting *punctus contra punctum*, i.e., an intervallic structure, with each establishment of *rationes* a self-sufficient entity, but chord {*Akkord*}: congruence of tones in the sense that it makes patent what is latent 'in nature.'"[126] Besseler describes the "'natural' system of our tonal harmony" as follows:

> Its essence is the polar opposition of tension and relaxation. The fundamental relationship, recurring in manifold shadings and colorings, is formed by dominant and tonic, the one sharpened by the leading tone and carried along by the fifth in the bass, the other more stable, abating the motion of the heavy beat. In view of the musical polarity of dominant-tonic or arsis-thesis Goethe had already pointed to the living organism that everywhere lives in alternating tension and relaxation, in accordance with the primordial example of the heart (systole and diastole).... This activity of the heart and its pulse, but also inhaling and exhaling, even the right-left of the ordinary stride—all these belong to the polar physical acts that directly affect music.[127]

When seen in this light, it is evident that tonal music[128] (*musica instrumentalis*) is fundamentally in harmony with what Boethius called *musica humana*. And Besseler indeed concludes that it [i.e., tonal music][129] is "the musical system {*Klangsystem*} of *humanitas*."[130]

---

[125]The phenomenon of partials is "parallel" to the principle of the geometric division of a string; see Sachs, *The Rise of Music*, 78; see also 75.

[126]Eggebrecht, "Musik als Tonsprache," 86-7.

[127]Besseler, *Bourdon und Fauxbourdon*, 216.

[128]The practice of extending the term "tonality" to the discretionary establishment of tonal relations (as in serial music), is not justifiable from the standpoint of the history of that terminology and thus only serves to becloud the issue. Music emancipated from a tonic is music without tonality. In view of its atomistic nature and tendencies, it is a clear forerunner of electronic music; see Wiora, "Der tonale Logos," 15-6, and the reference of the same author to the composers' "conscious suppression of natural entities"; see Wiora, "Natur der Musik? Unnatur heutiger Musik?" *Die Natur der Musik als Problem der Wissenschaft, Musikalische Zeitfragen* 10 [1962]: 17. Thus, the customary separation by many contemporary composers of musical materials from the significant relationships to be established with them is symptomatic; see Leon Kirchner, "The Lag of Theory Behind Practice," *College Music Symposium* 1 (1961): 25; also George Rochberg's relevant observations in his letter to the editor, *College Music Symposium* 2 (1962): 122.

[129]In his article "Dufay in Rom" (18), Besseler characterizes tonal music as the "customary instrumental style ingrained in us."

[130]Besseler, *Bourdon und Fauxbourdon*, 217.

A short excerpt from an article of Walter Wiora's should be cited here, in which he has fittingly expressed the universal potential of Western music:

> One side of this universality is rational forming, which Max Weber especially has emphasized as a fundamental trait of Western music and culture. It is primarily a matter of... revealing and setting off "natural" structures based on simple number relationships, that is to say, the logical side of nature. Since the early age [of Western music] such structures have prevailed in dance and folk song, e.g., square rhythm and scales approximating major.... But particularly characteristic of the West is the habit of creating pregnant shapes.... Pregnancy, however (as in geometric figures), is no less an aspect of universality than rationality (as in simple number relationships).[131]

The earliest compositions known to us that must be called tonal organisms, melodically and harmonically, stem from the "Westcuntre," as Anonymous 4 calls it, [and] the "Summer Canon" is without doubt the most telling example. It richly and obviously warrants the extraordinary impression it has made on scholars and listeners since Hawkins's and Burney's day. Due to freakish luck, this rota was preserved through the centuries to attest to a flourishing musical culture that evidently was an important tributary to the second generation of Notre-Dame composers.[132] "Naturally{!}," says Lowinsky, "English ears had an affinity with the major mode ever since the days of the Summer Canon,"[133] implying that there must be a connection between the Summer Canon and the avowedly tonal English lute ayre of the sixteenth century. But since to him an essential ingredient of tonality is the V–I cadence, he has failed to consider the earlier English tonal tradition. Such compositions as the Summer Canon, however, "played an early and decisive role... in the interpenetration of song melody {*Liedmelodik*} and harmonic thinking...."[134]

---

[131]Walter Wiora, "Zur Grundlegung der allgemeinen Musikgeschichte," *Deutsches Jahrbuch der Musikwissenschaft* 1 (1956): 99-100. See also Wiora, "Der tonale Logos," 13-5, 22; *Die vier Weltalter der Musik*, 11, 24, 107-9, 111 ff.; "Natur der Musik?" 13; "Europäische Volksmusik und abendländische Tonkunst," 14-5. In this last study, he declares that "the human voice and ear are structural by nature, like crystals and plants." (92).

[132]See Sanders, "Peripheral Polyphony," 264 ff.

[133]Edward Lowinsky, "Awareness of Tonality in the 16th Century," *Kongreßbericht New York 1961*, vol. 1 (Basel, London, New York: Bärenreiter, 1961): 52.

[134]Walter Wiora, "Der mittelalterliche Liedkanon," *Kongreßbericht Lüneburg 1950* (Kassel and Basel: Bärenreiter, n.d.): 75. It seems to me particularly important in this connection to emphasize once again that the designation of the Summer Canon as a Latin cantus-firmus motet

While the contributions of Italy to Burgundian and Franco-Flemish music are undeniable, it is noteworthy that the famous passage in Martin Le Franc's *Le Champion des Dames* makes no mention of Italians, but indicates that the English were notable not only for *frisque concordance* but for *fainte, pause, et muance*—all these terms concern melody and phrasing. Clearly, the tonal and chordal features of a good deal of English music—manifestations of the English medieval bent for tangible cohesion—fructified Continental music not once but twice: first in Perotin's time and again in the fifteenth century, when the English decisively contributed to the reorientation of Continental musical practices that seemed incapable of further refinement.[135]

Nearly sixty years ago Victor Lederer called Wales the homeland of tonal polyphony and insisted on the crucial importance of Dunstable and his English contemporaries for the further development of Western music.[136] The book in which he sought to demonstrate his views unquestionably suffers from its author's mercurial imagination, but his main thesis reveals respectable intuition and insight, and may well be acknowledged in many respects as correct.[137]

---

reflects neither the facts nor the historical circumstances represented here. All evidence indicates that it should be looked upon as a freely invented composition—the quintessence, so to speak, of English music of the thirteenth century; see Sanders, "Tonal Aspects," 20-1.

[135]In contrast to the English tradition, where the parallelism of 6-3 sonorities for the most part appears in *cantilenae* (i.e., compositions without a cantus firmus), the Burgundian composers experimented with such sonorities first in chant settings, that is, in fauxbourdon compositions; see Sanders, "Cantilena and Discant in 14th-Century England," 50. That the hymn played such a prominent role in this class of works (i.e., fauxbourdon) is a fact of considerable interest with respect to the English tradition.

[136]Victor Lederer, *Über Heimat und Ursprung der mehrstimmigen Tonkunst* (Leipzig: Siegel, 1906), vol. I, 4.

[137]See Ernst Apfel, "England und der Kontinent in der Musik des späten Mittelalters," *Die Musikforschung* 14 (1961): 289.

APPENDIX

Glossary and Concordance of Specialized Terms

The purpose of this glossary is to compare terminological usage in the essays translated above. It is chiefly restricted to terms used by the various authors in connection with counterpoint and tonality in late medieval polyphony, especially those identifiable with basic axioms and principles underlying the respective arguments. Each German term (typically presented in the nominative singular regardless of its original grammatical guise) is shown along with the translation normally assigned to it. Wherever applicable, I have provided certain equivalent expressions (noted by asterisks), many of which I myself have developed to facilitate comparison of concepts. These abstract equivalents are not used in the translations but are explained at length in the editor's introduction. Each term in the glossary is also provided with a citation of its *first appearance* in every article in which it occurs (i.e., the original journal citation, not the translation). In a few cases a given term is used in more than one sense in a given article.

TERM	STANDARD TRANSLATION

Absolute Fortschreitungswirkung = "Absolute progression effect"
    Marggraf 1966   20

Angehängte Tonalität = "Appended tonality"
    Marggraf 1966   18-9

Bassfunktion = "Bass function"
    *Function of voice occupying referential pitch
    Besseler 1952   141
    Schmidt 1958   250, note 1 (note 79 of translation)
    Sanders 1967   47, quotation of Besseler

Bourdon-Harmonik = "Technique of bourdon harmony"
    *Referential-pitch line placed below tenor
    Marggraf 1966   29, reference to Besseler

Bourdon-Kontratenor = "Bourdon (low-voice) contratenor"
    *Contra consistently taking referential pitches
    Marggraf 1966   26

TERM	STANDARD TRANSLATION

Bourdon-Tiefstimme   = "Bourdon low-voice"
                  *Voice taking referential pitches below tenor
   Besseler 1948   44
   Sanders 1967   47, quotation of Besseler

Diskantklausel   = "Discantus close"
                  *Stepwise melodic ascent at point of cadence
   Apfel 1962   218

Diskantkolorierung   = "Discant (cantus-firmus) embellishment"
   Besseler 1948   37
   Ficker 1951   95
   Besseler 1952   143, reference to Ficker
   Schmidt 1958   246, note 3 (note 67 of translation)

Dominantbeziehung   = "Dominant relation"
   Marggraf 1966   11

Dominantik   = "(System of) Dominant harmony"
   Marggraf 1966   21

Dominantisch-tonale Durchorganasierung = "Dominant-tonal organization"
   Marggraf 1966   11

Dominantisch-tonale Harmonik   = "Dominant-tonal system of harmony"
   Marggraf 1966   30

Dominantisch-tonale Klangordnung = "Dominant-tonal sonority ordering"
   Marggraf 1966   11

Dominantische Akkordverbindung = "Dominant chord relationship"
   Marggraf 1966   21

Dominantische Fortschreitung   = "Dominant progression"
   Marggraf 1966   26

Dominantische Harmonik   = "System of dominant harmony"
   Meier 1952   30
   Marggraf 1966   11

Dominantische Klangfortschreitung = "Dominant sonority progression"
   Marggraf 1966   15

Dominantische Klangverbindung   = "Dominant connection of sonorities"
   Marggraf 1966   15

Dominantische Klangordnung   = "Dominant ordering of sonorities"
   Marggraf 1966   11

Dominantische Tonalität   = "System of dominant tonality"
   Besseler 1948   45
   Ficker 1951   98, note 20, quotation of Besseler
   Besseler 1952   135
   Marggraf 1966   13
   Sanders 1967   47, quotation of Besseler

TERM	STANDARD TRANSLATION

Dominantischer Schritt = "Dominant progression"
Marggraf 1966   19

Dominantwirkung = "Dominant influence"
Marggraf 1966   19

Dur-Moll-Harmonik = "Major-minor system of harmony"
Marggraf 1966   13

Ergänzungsstimme = "Supplementary voice"
Apfel 1963   156

Erweiterter Satz = "Expanded two-voice counterpoint"
Apfel 1960   83   *Same as *Freier (Discant)Satz*

Freier (Diskant)Satz = "Free (discant) counterpoint"
          *Same as "Expanded two-voice counterpoint" (*Erweiterter Satz*)
Apfel 1955   302, note 3 (note 9 of translation)
Schmidt 1958   247
Apfel 1960   83
Apfel 1961   46, note 2 (note 35 of translation)

Fundament(stimme) = "Fundament(-voice)"
Schmidt 1958   239   *Voice(s) consistently taking referential pitches
Apfel 1961   35, *Satzfundament*
Apfel 1962   215
Apfel 1963   154
Marggraf 1966   15
Sanders 1967   35

Gerüst(stimmen) = "Contrapuntal (or structural) framework"
Ficker 1951   116
Besseler 1952   135, *Gerüst* in the sense of melodic nodes
Besseler 1952   140, *Cantus-Tenorgerüst* (contrapuntal framework)
Meier 1952   32
Apfel 1955   299
Schmidt 1958   247
Apfel 1961   38
Apfel 1962   217
Apfel 1963   155
Marggraf 1966   18, *Gerüst* as an overall plan of cadential pitches
Marggraf 1966   19, *Gerüst* as a discantus-tenor contrapuntal framework
Marggraf 1966   25, *Gerüst* as composite lower voice (tenor-contra)
Sanders 1967   34, reference to Ficker

Gerüstsatz = "(Two-voice) Contrapuntal framework"
Apfel 1955   302, note 4 (note 10 of translation)
Apfel 1960   92
Apfel 1961   44
Apfel 1962   221
Apfel 1963   153
Marggraf 1966   19

TERM		STANDARD TRANSLATION

Grundfunktionen = "Basic (Harmonic) Functions"
Besseler 1952   135   *Tonic and Dominant

Grundkonsonanz = "Basic consonance" (of two-voice framework)
Apfel 1955   305   *Octave; less often, unison

Grundstimme = "Ground-voice"
*Voice consistently taking referential pitches
Besseler 1952   141, also *Grundstimmentypus* ("G.-v. archetype")
Schmidt 1958   232, also with sense of "preexistent voice"
Sanders 1967   33, *Harmonische Grundstimme*

Grundton = "Ground-tone"; or "First scale degree" [= final]
*Referential pitch; alternatively: Final
Besseler 1952   135, in sense of final
Apfel 1955   307, note 1 (note 18 of translation)
Apfel 1960   91, *Grundtönigkeit*
Apfel 1961   35, *Grundtönige Auffassung der Klänge*
Apfel 1962   219, note 12
Marggraf 1966   24, in sense of final

Grundtonalität = "Basic tonality [i.e., of the final]"
Marggraf 1966   15

Harmoniefundament = "Harmonic foundation"
Besseler 1948   44   *Referential pitch or sequence of referential pitches
Besseler 1952   141
Schmidt 1958   249, reference to Besseler

Harmonieträger = "Director of harmony"
*Voice(s) comprising sequence of referential pitches (= referential voice)
Ficker 1951   114, reference to Besseler
Besseler 1952   136
Sanders 1967   47, quotation of Besseler

Harmonischer Bass = "Harmonic bass"
Apfel 1963   154   *Fundamental bass in Rameau's sense

Kantilenensatz = "Cantilena-style counterpoint"
Schmidt 1958   248, quotation of Besseler

Kernsatz = "(Two-voice) Contrapuntal framework"
Ficker 1951   113
Besseler 1952   133, reference to Ficker
Schmidt 1958   247
Apfel 1961   45
Sanders 1967   34, quotation of Ficker

Kernstimme = "Core-voice"
Besseler 1952   140, *Tenor-Kernstimme*
Schmidt 1958   232, with sense of referential and preexistent voice
Apfel 1961   45, *Kernstimmen*, equivalent to *Gerüststimmen*
Sanders 1967   34, reference to Ficker

TERM	STANDARD TRANSLATION

Klangfundament = "Sonorous foundation"
  *Referential pitch or sequence of referential pitches
Besseler 1952   140
Schmidt 1958   236
Apfel 1960   83

Klanghalter = "Proprietor of sonorities"
  *Referential voice
Apfel 1955   304, note 2 (note 13 of translation)

Klanglicher (Diskant)Satz = "Tonal (Discant) Counterpoint"
  *Same as "Multiple two-voice counterpoint" (*Mehrfach-zweistimmiger Satz*)
Apfel 1955   302, note 3 (note 9 of translation)
Apfel 1960   82

Klanglich-freier Satz = "Tonal-free [discant] counterpoint"
Apfel 1955   307   *Consolidated (discant) counterpoint
Schmidt 1958   250, note 1 (note 79 of translation), Apfel quotation
Apfel 1960   81
Apfel 1961   40
Apfel 1962   214

Klangstrom = "Flowing sonority"
Schmidt 1958   244, quotation of Besseler

Klangträger = "Director of sonorities"
  *Referential pitch; alternatively: Referential voice
Apfel 1955   300, note 1 (note 6 of translation)
Schmidt 1958   235, identified with tenor
Apfel 1960   81, note 1 (note 1 of translation)
Apfel 1961   35
Apfel 1962   214, *Klangträgerrolle*
Apfel 1963   153
Marggraf 1966   30, *klangtragende Tiefstimme*
Sanders 1967   34, *Klangträgerfunktion*, quotation of Apfel

Klassische Harmonieführung = "Classical harmonic voice leading"
Ficker 1951   103
Besseler 1952   136, reference to Ficker

Kombinationsbass = "Composite bass line"
  *Sequence of referential pitches as composite of more than one voice part
Besseler 1948   44
Besseler 1952   141

Kombinierte Tiefstimme = "Composite low-voice"
  *Sequence of referential pitches as composite of more than one voice part
Apfel 1955   303

Linienwert = "Linear value"
Besseler 1952   133

TERM	STANDARD TRANSLATION

Mehrfach-zweistimmiger Satz = "Multiple two-voice counterpoint"
Apfel 1960   83   *Same as *Klanglicher (Diskant)Satz*
Apfel 1961   35

Nachbarschaftsverhältnis der Klänge = "Neighbor-relationship of sonorities"
Apfel 1955   303   *Stepwise relationship of sonorities
Apfel 1962   220
Apfel 1963   153

Ruheklang   = "Sonority of repose"
Besseler 1952   137

Tenorklausel   = "Tenor close"
                                 *Stepwise melodic descent at point of cadence
Apfel 1962   218

Terzfreiheit   = "Variable quality of the third"
Besseler 1952   137
Schmidt 1958   248, quotation of Bessler
Marggraf 1966   20, using the term *Variabilität der Terz*

Tonale Grundordnung   = "Fundamental tonal ordering"
                                 *Tonal orientation of referential-pitch sequence
Besseler 1948   44

Tonale Harmonieführung   = "Tonal-harmonic voice leading"
Besseler 1952   137

Tonalharmonik   = "Tonal system of harmony"
Besseler 1948   44
Besseler 1952   135
Marggraf 1966   13, in connection with *Dominantische Tonalität*
Sanders 1967   30, quotation of Besseler

Tonalität   = "Tonality"
Besseler 1952   137
Meier 1952   34
Apfel 1962   212, *Dur-Moll-Tonalität*
Apfel 1963   153
Marggraf 1966   12
Sanders 1967   30, *Harmonische Tonalität*

Tonika-dominant-Harmonik   = "Tonic-dominant harmonic system"
Besseler 1952   137

Vollklang   = "Full sonority"
            *Sonority rich in thirds and sixths (characteristic of fauxbourdon)
Besseler 1948   37
Ficker 1951   98, quotation of Besseler
Besseler 1952   135
Schmidt 1958   244, quotation of Besseler
Sanders 1967   48, reference to Besseler

BIBLIOGRAPHY

List of Works Cited and
Supplementary Modern Editions

The following list includes every secondary source cited in the essays contained above (including the editor's introduction). In addition are cited a number of modern editions of music and theory, whose purpose is to augment the citations in the selections translated.

Abraham, Lars Ulrich. *Die Generalbaß im Schaffen des Michael Praetorius und seine harmonischen Voraussetzungen. Berliner Studien zur Musikwissenschaft* 3. Ed. Adam Adrio. Berlin: Merseberger, 1961.

Adler, Guido. *Der Stil in der Musik.* Leipzig: Breitkopf & Härtel, 1911.

——. *Studien zur Geschichte der Harmonie. Sitzungsberichte der kaiserlichen Akademie, Philosophisch-historische Classe* 98. Vienna: Carl Gerold's Sohn, 1881, 781-830 (with appended musical examples, pages I-XXXI).

——, and Oswald Koller, eds. *Sechs Trienter Codices: Geistliche und weltliche Kompositionen des XV. Jahrhunderts. Erste Auswahl. DTÖ* 14-15 (Jahrgang VII). Vienna: Universal-Edition, 1900.

——, and Oswald Koller, eds. *Sechs Trienter Codices: Geistliche und weltliche Kompositionen des XV. Jahrhunderts. Zweite Auswahl. DTÖ* 22 (Jahrgang XI/1). Vienna: Universal-Edition, 1904.

Agricola, Alexander. *Opera omnia.* 5 vols. *Corpus Mensurabilis Musicae* 22. Ed. Edward J. Lerner. N.p.: American Institute of Musicology, 1961-70.

Ambros, August. *Geschichte der Musik.* 5 vols. Leipzig: Breitkopf & Härtel, 1864–89.

Anderson, Gordon A., ed. *The Las Huelgas Manuscript (Burgos, Monasterio de Las Huelgas).* 2 vols. *Corpus Mensurabilis Musicae* 79. N.p.: American Institute of Musicology, 1982.

——, ed. *Motets of the Manuscript La Clayette.* Texts ed. and trans. Elizabeth A. Close. *Corpus Mensurabilis Musicae* 68. N.p.: American Institute of Musicology, 1975.

Andrews, H[erbert] K. Review of Edward Lowinsky, *Tonality and Atonality in Sixteenth-Century Music. Music and Letters* 43 (1962): 64-6.

Anglès, Higini, ed. *El còdex musical de las Huelgas (Mùsica veus dels segles XIII–XIV), Introducciò, Facsìmil, Transcripciò.* Barcelona: Institut d'Estuis Catalans: Biblioteca de Catalunya, 1931.

Apel, Willi.*Gregorian Chant.* Bloomington: Indiana University Press, 1958.

————. *Die Notation der Polyphonen Musik.* Leipzig: Breitkopf & Härtel, 1962. (English version, *The Notation of Polyphonic Music: 800–1600.* Cambridge, Mass.: The Mediaeval Academy of America, 1942.)

————, ed. *French Secular Compositions of the Fourteenth Century.* 3 vols. *Corpus Mensurabilis Musicae* 53. N.p.: American Institute of Musicology, 1970–72.

————, ed. *French Secular Music of the Late Fourteenth Century.* Cambridge, Mass.: American Institute of Musicology, 1950.

Apfel, Ernst. *Anlage und Struktur der Motetten im Codex Montpellier. Annales Universitatis Saraviensis, Reihe: Philosophische Fakultät* 10. Ed. August Langen. Heidelberg: Carl Winter, 1970.

————. *Beiträge zu einer Geschichte der Satztechnik von der frühen Motette bis Bach.* 2 vols. Munich: Eidos, 1964/65.

————. "Bemerkungen zum geschichtlichen Zusammenhang zwischen dem barocken und mittelalterlichen modalen Rhythmus." *Zum 70. Geburtstag von J. Müller-Blattau.* Ed. Christoph-Hellmut Mahling. *Saarbrücker Studien zur Musikwissenschaft* 1. Ed. Walter Wiora. Kassel: Bärenreiter, 1966, 34-45.

————. "Der Diskant in der Musiktheorie des 12.–15. Jahrhunderts." Dissertation, University of Heidelberg, 1953. Published as *Diskant und Kontrapunkt in der Musiktheorie des 12. bis 15. Jahrhunderts. Taschenbücher zur Musikwissenschaft* 82. Ed. Richard Schaal. Wilhelmshaven: Heinrichshofen, 1982. Second, revised and expanded ed., Saarbrücken: Universitätsbibliothek der Universität des Saarlandes, 1994.

————. "England und der Kontinent in der Musik des späten Mittelalters." *Die Musikforschung* 14 (1961): 276-89.

————. *Geschichte der Kompositionslehre: Von den Anfängen bis gegen 1700.* 3 vols. *Taschenbücher zur Musikwissenschaft* 75-77. Ed. Richard Schaal. Wilhelmshaven, Heinrichshofen, 1981. Revised ed. 5 vols. Saarbrücken: Universitätsbibliothek der Universität des Saarlandes, 1985. Subsequent revised eds., 1987, 1989. Supplementary vol., *Nachträge zu Geschichte der Kompositionslehre von den Anfängen bis gegen 1700.* Saarbrücken: Universitätsbibliothek der Universität des Saarlandes, 1995.

————. *Grundlagen einer Geschichte der Satztechnik* [Part I:] *vom 13. bis zum 16. Jahrhundert.* Saarbrücken: Universitätsbibliothek der Universität des Saarlandes, 1974. Second ed. with revisions, 1988. Part II: *Polyphonie und Monodie, Voraussetzungen und Folgen des Wandels um 1600.* Publication data as above, 1974. Part III: *Untersuchungen zur Entstehung und Frühgeschichte des Ostinato in der komponierten Mehrstimmigkeit.* Publication data as above, 1976. Appendix to Part III: *Entwurf eines*

Verzeichnisses aller Ostinato-Stücke zu Grundlagen einer Geschichte der Satztechnik, Teil III. Publication data as above, 1977.

―――――. "H. Besseler, Bourdon und Fauxbourdon und die Tonalität." *Aufsätze und Vorträge zur Musikgeschichte und historischen Musiktheorie.* Saarbrücken: Selbstverlag Ernst Apfel, 1977, 111-22.

―――――. "Der klangliche Satz und der freie Diskantsatz im 15. Jahrhundert." *Archiv für Musikwissenshcaft* 12 (1955): 297-313. (Essay 5.)

―――――. "Die klangliche Struktur der spätmittelalterlichen Musik als Grundlage der Dur-Moll Tonalität." *Die Musikforschung* 15 (1962): 212-27. (Essay 9.)

―――――. *Die Lehre vom Organum, Diskant, Kontrapunkt und von der Komposition bis um 1480.* Saarbrücken: Universitätsbibliothek der Universität des Saarlandes, 1987. Revised and expanded 4th ed., 1993. Separate vol. of musical examples, *Notenbeispiele zu Die Lehre vom Organum, Diskant, Kontrapunkt und von der Komposition bis um 1480.* Publication data as above, 1993.

―――――. "Nochmals zum Fauxbourdon (Faburden) bei Guillelmus Monachus." *Die Musikforschung* 19 (1966): 284-8.

―――――. "Ostinato und Kompositionstechnik bei den englischen Virginalisten der elisabethanischen Zeit." *Archiv für Musikwissenschaft* 19-20 (1962–63): 29-39.

―――――. "Probleme der theoretischen Harmonik aus geschichtlich-satztechnischer Sicht." *Festschrift für Walter Wiora zum 30. Dezember 1966.* Eds. Ludwig Finscher and Christoph-Hellmut Mahling. Kassel: Bärenreiter, 1967, 140-8.

―――――. *Sämtliche herausgegebenen musikalischen Satzlehren vom 12. bis gegen Ende des 15. Jahrhunderts in deutschen Übersetzungen.* Saarbrücken: Universitätsbibliothek der Universität des Saarlandes, 1986. Revised 4th ed. 1992. Separate vol. of musical examples, *Notenbeispiele zu Sämtliche herausgegebenen musikalischen Satzlehren vom 12. bis gegen Ende des 15. Jahrhunderts in deutschen Übersetzungen.* Publication data as above, 1992.

―――――. "Satztechnische Grundlagen der neuen Musik des 17. Jahrhunderts." *Acta Musicologica* 34 (1962): 67-78.

―――――. "Spätmittelalterliche Klangstruktur und Dur-Moll Tonalität." *Die Musikforschung* 16 (1963): 153-6. (Essay 10.)

―――――. *Studien zur Satztechnik der mittelalterlichen englischen Musik.* 2 vols. *Abhandlungen der Heidelberger Akademie der Wissenschaft, Philosophisch-historische Klasse 5, Jahrgang 1959.* Heidelberg: Carl Winter, 1959.

―――――. "Über das Verhältnis von Musiktheorie und Kompositionspraxis im späteren Mittelalter (etwa 1200–1500)." *Bericht über den Internationalen musikwissenschaftlichen Kongreß Basel, 1962.* Eds. Georg Reichert and Martin Just. Kassel: Bärenreiter, 1964, 354-6.

————. "Über den vierstimmigen Satz im 14. und 15. Jahrhundert." *Archiv für Musikwissenschaft* 18 (1961): 34-51. (Essay 8.)

————. "Über einige Zusammenhänge zwischen Text und Musik im Mittelalter, besonders in England." *Acta Musicologica* 33 (1961): 47-54. (Also in *Medium Aevum Vivum: Festschrift für Walther Bulst.* Eds. Hans Robert Jauss and Dieter Schaller. Heidelberg: Carl Winter, 1960, 207-11).

————. "Wandlungen der Polyphonie von Palestrina zu Bach." *Archiv für Musikwissenschaft* 21 (1964): 60-76.

————. "Wandlungen des Gerüstsatzes vom 16. zum 17. Jahrhundert." *Archiv für Musikwissenschaft* 26 (1969): Part I, 81-104; Part II, 209-35.

————. "Zur Entstehung des realen vierstimmigen Satzes in England." *Archiv für Musikwissenschaft* 17 (1960): 81-99. (Essay 7.)

————. "Zur Entstehungsgeschichte des Palestrinasatzes." *Archiv für Musikwissenschaft* 14 (1957): 30-45.

————. "Zur Vorgeschichte der Triosonate, Ein Versuch." *Die Musikforschung* 18 (1965): 33-6.

Aubry, Pierre. *Cent motets du XIIIe Siècle, publiès d'après le Manuscrit ed. IV. 6. de Bamberg.* 3 vols. Paris: Rouert, Lerolle, 1908.

————. "Iter Hispanicum: Notices et extraits de manuscrits de musique ancienne conservés dans les bibliothèques d'Espagne [Part] II: Deux chansonniers français à la Bibliotheque de l'Escorial." *Sammelbände der internationalen Musikgesellschaft* 8 (1906–07): 517-34.

Barbireau, Jacobus, *Opera omnia.* 2 vols. Ed. Bernhard Meier. *Corpus Mensurabilis Musicae* 7. Rome: American Institute of Musicology, 1954/57.

Battaglia, Salvatore, ed. *Grande Dizionario della Ligua Italiana.* 17 vols. Turin: Unione tipografico-editrice torinese, [1962].

Beenken, Hermann. *Hubert und Jan van Eyck.* Munich: F. Bruckmann, 1941.

Bengtsson, Ingmar. "On Relationships Between Tonal and Rhythmic Structures in Western Multipart Music." *Studier: Tillägnade Carl-Allan Moberg, 5 Juni 1961. Svensk Tidskrift för Musikforskning* 43 (1961): 49-76.

Bent, Margaret, ed. *Fifteenth-Century Liturgical Music II: Four Anonymous Masses. Early English Church Music* 22. London: Stainer and Bell, 1979.

Berger, Christian. *Hexachord, Mensur und Textstruktur. Beihefte zum Archiv für Musikwissenschaft* 35. Stuttgart: Franz Steiner, 1992.

Berger, Karol. *Musica ficta.* Cambridge: Cambridge University Press, 1987.

Besseler, Heinrich. "Apt." *MGG*, vol. 1 (1949–51), cols. 569-70.

————. "Ars Antiqua." *MGG*, vol. 1 (1949–51), cols. 679-98.

————. "Ars nova." *MGG*, vol. 1 (1949–51), cols. 702-29.

————. "Ballade." *MGG*, vol. 1, (1949–51), cols. 1115-27.

————. "Bedingham." *MGG*, vol. 1 (1949–51), cols. 1493-94.

————. *Bourdon und Fauxbourdon: Studien zum Ursprung der niederländischen Musik*. Leipzig: Breitkopf & Härtel, 1950. Second ed. based on author's revisions, ed. Peter Gülke. Leipzig: VEB Breitkopf & Härtel, 1974.

————. "Cesaris." *MGG*, vol. 2 (1952), cols. 983-9.

————. "Ciconia." *MGG*, vol. 2 (1952), cols. 1423-34.

————. "Dufay in Rom." *Archiv für Musikwissenschaft* 15 (1958): 1-19.

————. "Dufay Schöpfer des Fauxbourdons." *Acta Musicologica* 20 (1948): 26-45. (Essay 1.)

————. "Die Entstehung der Posaune." *Acta Musicologica* 22 (1950): 8-35.

————. "Hat Matheus de Perusio Epoche gemacht?" *Die Musikforschung* 8 (1955): 19-23.

————. *Die Musik des Mitelalters und der Renaissance*. Potsdam: Athenaion, [1931].

————. "Neue Dokumente zum Leben und Schaffen Dufays." *Archiv für Musikwissenschaft* 9 (1952): 160-76.

————. "Das Neue in der Musik des 15. Jahrhunderts." *Acta Musicologica* 26 (1954): 75-85.

————. "Niederländische Musik." *Riemann Musik Lexikon*. 12th ed. 5 vols. Section ed. Hans Heinrich Eggebrecht. Mainz: B. Schotts Söhne, 1960, vol. 3, 633-4.

————. "Singstil und Instrumentalstil in der europäischen Musik." *Bericht über den internationalen musikwissenschaftlichen Kongreß, Bamberg 1953*. Kassel and Basel: Bärenreiter, 1954, 223-40.

————. "Studien zur Musik des Mittelalters [Part] I: Neue Quellen des 14. und beginnenden 15. Jahrhunderts." *Archiv für Musikwissenschaft* 7 (1925): 167-252; "Nachtrag zu Studie zur Musik des Mittelalters [Part I]: Neue Quellen des 14. und beginnenden 15. Jahrhunderts." *Archiv für Musikwissenschaft* 8 (1926): 233-58.

————. "Studien zur Musik des Mittelalters [Part] II: Die Motette von Franko von Köln bis Philippe von Vitry." *Archiv für Musikwissenschaft* 8 (1926): 137-232.

————. "Tonalharmonik und Vollklang." *Acta Musicologica* 24 (1952): 131-46. (Essay 3.)

————. "Der Ursprung des Fauxbourdons." *Die Musikforschung* 2 (1948): 106-12.

————. "Von Dufay bis Josquin." *Zeitschrift für Musikwissenschaft* 11 (1928/29): 1-22.

Binchois, Gilles. *Die Chansons.* Ed. Wolfgang Rehm. *Musikalische Denkmähler* 2. Mainz: Schott, 1957.

Blackburn, Bonnie J. "On Compositional Process in the Fifteenth Century." *Journal of the American Musicological Society* 40 (1987): 210-84.

Blume, Friedrich, ed. *Die Musik in Geschichte und Gegenwart.* 17 vols. Kassel: Bärenreiter, 1949–68. (Individual citations are given separately by author; abbreviation *MGG.*)

Bockholdt, Rudolf. "Französische und niederländische Musik des 14. und 15. Jahrhunderts." *Musikalische Edition im Wandel des historischen Bewusstseins.* Ed. Thrasybulos Georgiades. Kassel: Bärenreiter, 1971, 148-54.

————. *Die frühen Messenkompositionen von Guillaume Dufay.* 2 vols. *Münchner Veröffentlichungen zur Musikgeschichte* 5. Ed. Thrasybulos Georgiades. Tutzing: Schneider, 1960.

Boen, Johannes. *Ars [musicae].* Ed. F. Alberto Gallo. *Corpus Scriptorum de Musica* 19. N.p.: American Institute of Musicology, 1972.

Borren, Charles van den. "Dufay and his School." *Ars Nova and the Renaissance, 1300–1540.* New Oxford History of Music, Vol. III. General eds. Dom Anselm Hughes and Gerald Abraham. London: Oxford University Press, 1960, 214-38.

————, ed. *Missa Tornacensis [Mass of Tournai].* Corpus Mensurabilis Musicae 13. N.p.: American Institute of Musicology, 1957.

————, ed. *Pièces polyphoniques profanes de provenance liègoise.* Brussels: Editions de la Librarie Encyclopedique, 1950.

————, ed. *Polyphonia Sacra* [Latin-texted works of MS Oxford 213]. 1932. Revised ed. London: The Plainsong and Mediaeval Music Society, 1962.

Brown, Howard M. "A Ballade for Mathieu de Foix: Style and Structure in a Composition by Trebor." *Musica Disciplina* 41 (1987): 75-107.

Bukofzer, Manfred F. "Changing Aspects of Medieval and Renaissance Music." *Musical Quarterly* 44 (1958): 1-18.

————. "Discantus." *MGG,* vol. 3 (1954), cols. 559-78.

————. "English Church Music of the Fifteenth Century." *Ars Nova and the Renaissance, 1300–1540.* New Oxford History of Music, Vol. III. General eds. Dom Anselm Hughes and Gerald Abraham. London: Oxford University Press, 1960, 165-213.

————. "Fauxbourdon Revisited." *Musical Quarterly* 38 (1952): 22-47.

————. "The First Motet with English Words." *Music and Letters* 17 (1936): 225-33.

————. *Geschichte des englischen Diskants und des Fauxbourdons nach den theoretischen Quellen. Sammlung musikwissenschaftlicher Abhandlungen* 21. Strasbourg: Heitz, 1936; reprint Baden-Baden: Valentin Koerner, 1973. (Dissertation, University of Basle, 1935.)

————. "Gymel." *MGG*, vol. 5 (1956), cols. 1139-46.

————. "A Newly Discovered 15th-Century Manuscript of the English Chapel Royal [Egerton 3307]—Part II." *Musical Quarterly* 33 (1947): 38-51. [Part I, see under Schofield.]

————. "Popular and Secular Music in England (to c. 1470)." *Ars Nova and the Renaissance, 1300–1540. New Oxford History of Music*, Vol. III. General eds. Dom Anselm Hughes and Gerald Abraham. London: Oxford University Press, 1960, 107-33.

————. "Popular Polyphony in the Middle Ages." *Musical Quarterly* 26 (1940): 31-49.

————. *Studies in Medieval and Renaissance Music.* New York: Norton, 1950.

————. "An Unknown Chansonnier of the 15th Century (the Mellon Chansonnier)." *Musical Quarterly* 28 (1942): 14-49.

————. "Über Leben und Werke von Dunstable," *Acta Musicologica* 8 (1936): 102-19.

Cattin, Giulio, Francesco Facchin, et al., eds. *French Sacred Music [Settings of the Ordinary of the Mass, Hymns, Miscellaneous, Llibre Vermell].* 2 vols. *Polyphonic Music of the Fourteenth Century* 23 A/B. Monaco: L'Oiseau-Lyre, 1989/91.

Ciconia, Johannes. *Nova musica* [c. 1400] and *De proportionibus* [revision of Book III of *Nova musica*]. Ed. and trans. Oliver B. Ellsworth. *Greek and Latin Music Theory* 9. General ed. Thomas J. Mathiesen. Lincoln: University of Nebraska Press, 1993; 42-411.

————. *The Works of Johannes Ciconia.* Eds. Margaret Bent and Anne Hallmark. *Polyphonic Music of the Fourteenth Century* 24. Monaco: L'Oiseau-Lyre, 1985.

Clercx, Suzanne. *Johannes Ciconia, Un musicien liègeois et son temps (vers 1335–1411)*, Vol. I: *La vie et l'œuvre*; Vol. II: *Transcriptions et notes critiques.* Brussels: Académie, 1960.

Closson, Ernest. "L'origine de Gilles Binchois." *Revue de Musicologie* 5 (1924): 149-51.

Cochlaeus, Johannes. *Musica active, pars tertia: De arte componendi et contrapunctus.* Cologne: Johannes Landen, 1507.

————. *Tetrachordum musices.* [Nuremburg: Johannes Weyßenbürger, 1511.] Ed. and trans. Clement A. Miller. *Musicological Studies and Documents* 23. N.p.: American Institute of Musicology, 1970.

Codex Tridentinus 87-92. 7 vols. Rome: Vivarelli e Gullà, 1970. (Facsimile edition of Trent MSS, no editor cited.)

Coussemaker, Edmond de. *Histoire de l'harmonie au moyen âge.* Paris: Didron, 1852.

————. *Scriptorum de musica medii aevi.* 4 vols. Paris: Durand & Pedone-Lauriel, 1864–76. (Citations identified through the following system of abbreviation: *CS*, volume no., column.)

————, ed. *Messe du XIII siècle* [Tournai Mass]. Tournai: Malo et Levasseur, 1861.

Crocker, Richard L. "Discant, Counterpoint, and Harmony." *Journal of the American Musicological Society* 15 (1962): 1-21.

————. "French Polyphony of the Thirteenth Century." *The New Oxford History of Music,* Vol. II. *The Early Middle Ages to 1300* [Revised ed.]. Eds. Richard L. Crocker and David Hiley. Oxford: Oxford University Press, 1990, 636-78.

————. *A History of Musical Style.* 1966. Reprint New York: Dover, 1986.

————. "The Troping Hypothesis." *Musical Quarterly* 52 (1966): 183-203.

————. Review of Edward Lowinsky, *Tonality and Atonality in Sixteenth-Century Music. Journal of Music Theory* 6 (1962): 142-53.

Cserba, Simon M. *Hieronymus de Moravia O.P.: Tractatus de Musica.* Regensburg: Pustet, 1935.

Dahlhaus, Carl. "Die Natur der Musik und die Konsonanz." *Musikalische Zeitfragen* 10. *Die Natur der Musik als Problem der Wissenschaft.* Ed. Walter Wiora. Kassel and Basel: Bärenreiter, 1962, 19-26.

————. *Über die Entstehung der harmonischen Tonalität.* Kassel: Bärenreiter, 1968. English translation as *Studies on the Origin of Harmonic Tonality.* Trans. Robert O. Gjerdingen. Princeton: Princeton University Press, 1990.

Danckwardt, Marianne. "Zur Cantus-firmus-Behandlung in der Musik des Old-Hall Manuscripts." *Bericht über den internationalen musikwissenschaftlichen Kongreß Stuttgart.* 2 vols. Eds. Dietrich Berke and Dorothee Hanemann. Kassel: Bärenreiter, 1987, vol. 2, 217-29.

Dannemann, Erna. *Die spätgotische Musiktradition in Frankreich und Burgund.* Strasbourg: Heitz, 1936.

Davey, Henry. *History of English Music.* 2nd ed. London: Curwen, 1921.

Dèzes, Karl. "Das Dufay zugeschriebene Salve regina eine deutsche Komposition." *Zeitschrift für Musikwissenschaft* 10 (1927–28): 327-62.

————. "Der Mensuralkodex des Benediktinerklosters Sancti Emmerani zu Regensburg." *Zeitschrift für Musikwissenschaft* 10 (1927–28): 65-105.

————. "Van den Borrens 'Dufay.'" *Zeitschrift für Musikwissenschaft* 9 (1926–27): 294-307.

Dittmer, Luther A. "Beiträge zum Studium der Worcester–Fragmente." *Die Musikforschung* 10 (1957): 29-39.

————. "Binary Rhythm, Musical Theory and the Worcester Fragments." *Musica Disciplina* 7 (1953): 39-57.

————. "An English Discantuum Volumen." *Musica Disciplina* 8 (1954): 19-58.

————, ed. *Worcester Add. 68, Westminster Abbey 33327, Madrid Bibl. Nac. 192* [facsimile]. *Veröffentlichungen mittelalterlicher Musikhandschriften* 5. Brooklyn: Institute of Mediaeval Music, 1959.

————, ed. *The Worcester Fragments. Musicological Studies and Documents* 2. [Rome]: American Institute of Musicology, 1957.

————, ed and trans. *Anonymous IV. Music Theorists in Translation* 1. Brooklyn: Institute of Mediaeval Music, 1959.

Dufay, Guillaume. *Guglielmi Dufay: Opera Omnia*. 4 vols. Ed. Guillaume de Van. *Corpus Mensurabili Musicae* 1. Rome: American Institute of Musicology, 1947–49.

> Vol. 1 (1947): *Motetti qui et cantiones vocantur.*
> Vol. 2 (1948): *Motetti qui et cantiones vocantur.*
> Vol. 3 (1949): *Missa Sine nomine.*
> Vol. 4 (1949): *Missa Sancti Jacobi.*

————. *Guilielmus Dufay: Opera Omnia*. 6 vols. Ed. Heinrich Besseler. *Corpus Mensurabilis Musicae* 1. Rome: American Institute of Musicology, 1951–66.

> Vol. 1 (1966): *Motetti.*
> Vol. 2 (1960): *Missarum Pars Prior.*
> Vol. 3 (1951): *Missarum Pars Altera.*
> Vol. 4 (1962): *Fragmenta Missarum.*
> Vol. 5 (1966): *Compositiones Liturgicae Minores.*
> Vol. 6 (1964): *Cantiones.*

————. *Zwölf geistliche und weltliche Werke*. Ed. Heinrich Besseler. *Das Chorwork* 19. Wolfenbüttel: Möseler, 1932.

Dufourcq, Norbert. *Documents inédits relatifs à l'orgue français*, vol. 1. Paris: Droz, 1932.

Dunstable, John. *Complete Works*. Ed. Manfred Bukofzer. *Musica Britannica* 8. London: Stainer & Bell, 1953. (Revised ed. 1970, eds. Margaret Bent, Ian Bent, and Brian Trowell.)

Eggebrecht, Hans Heinrich. "Musik als Tonsprache." *Archiv für Musikwissenschaft* 18 (1961): 73-100.

————, and Frieder Zaminer, eds. *Ad organum faciendum: Lehrschriften der Mehrstimmigkeit in nachguidonischer Zeit. Neue Studien zur Musikwissenschaft* 3. Mainz: B. Schott's Söhne, 1970.

Egidius de Murino. [*De motetti*] (excerpts). Ed. and trans. Daniel Leech-Wilkinson. *Compositional Techniques in the Four-Part Isorhythmic Motets of Philippe de Vitry and His Contemporaries*. New York: Garland, 1989, 18-23, critical notes in Appendix I. (A complete but less dependable text of this treatise is given as *Tractatus cantus mensurabilis, CS* 3, 124-8.)

Eisner, Andreas. "Zur Geschichte des musikwissenschaftlichen Lehrstuhls an der Universität München." Dissertation, University of Munich, 1982.

Elling, Alwin. "Die Messen, Hymnen und Motetten der Handschrift von Apt." Dissertation, University of Göttingen, 1924.

Fallows, David. *Dufay. The Master Musicians.* New York: Vintage, 1982.

Feininger, Laurence K. *Die Frühgeschichte des Kanons bis Josquin des Prez.* Emsdetten: Lechte, 1937. (Dissertation, University of Heidelberg, 1935.)

Ferand, Ernest. *Die Improvisation in Beispielen.* Cologne: Arno Volk, 1956.

Ficker, Rudolf von. "Formprobleme der mitteralterlichen Musik." *Zeitschrift für Musikwissenschaft* 7 (1924–25): 195-213.

————. "Die frühen Messenkompositionen der Trienter Codices." *Studien zur Musikwissenschaft* 11 (1924): 3-58.

————. "Guido Adler und die Wiener Schule der Musikwissenschaft." *Österreichische Musikzeitung* 1 (1946): 185-7.

————. "Die Kolorierungstechnik der Trienter Messen." *Studien zur Musikwissenschaft* 7 (1920): 5-47.

————. "Die Musik des Mitelalters und ihre Beziehungen zum Geistesleben." *Deutsche Vierteljahrschrift für Literaturwissenschaft und Geistesgeschichte* 3 (1925): 501-35.

————. "Der Organumtraktat der Vatikanischen Bibliothek (Ottob. 3025)." *Kirchenmusikalisches Jahrbuch* 27 (1932): 64-74.

————. "Primäre Klangformen." *Jahrbuch der Musikbibliothek Peters* 36 (1929): 21-34.

————. "The Transition on the Continent." *Ars Nova and the Renaissance, 1300–1540.* New Oxford History of Music, Vol. III. General eds. Dom Anselm Hughes and Gerald Abraham. London: Oxford University Press, 1960, 134-64.

————. "Zur Schöpfungsgeschichte des Fauxbourdon." *Acta Musicologica* 23 (1951): 93-123. (Essay 2.)

————, ed. *Sieben Trienter Codices: Geistliche und weltliche Kompositionen des XIV. und XV. Jahrhunderts. Fünfte Auswahl. DTÖ* 61 *(Jahrgang* XXXI). Vienna: Universal-Edition, 1924.

————, ed. *Sieben Trienter Codices: Geistliche und weltliche Kompositionen des XIV. und XV. Jahrhunderts. Sechste Auswahl. DTÖ* 76 *(Jahrgang* XL). Vienna: Universal-Edition, 1933.

————, and Alfred Orel, eds. *Sechs Trienter Codices: Geistliche und weltliche Kompositionen des XV. Jahrhunderts. Vierte Auswahl. DTÖ* 53 *(Jahrgang* XXVII/1). Vienna: Universal-Edition, 1920.

Finscher, Ludwig, ed., "Die Musik des 15. und 16. Jahrhunderts." *Neues Handbuch der Musikwissenschaft* 3/1 and 3/2. General ed. Carl Dahlhaus, continued by Hermann Danuser. Laaber: Laaber Verlag, n.d.

Fischer, Kurt von. "Zur Ciconia-Forschung." *Die Musikforschung* 14 (1961): 316-22.

—————. "On the Technique, Origin, and Evolution of Italitan Trecento Music." *Musical Quarterly* 47 (1961): 41-57.

—————. Review of G. Cesari and F. Fano, *La Cappella musicale del duomo di milano*, Part 1. Fabio Fano: *Le Origini il primo maestro di cappella: Matteo da Perugia*. *Die Musikforschung* 12 (1959): 223-30.

—————, and F. Alberto Gallo, eds. *Italian Sacred Music [Settings of the Ordinary of the Mass, Benedicamus Settings, Settings for the Proper of the Mass and for Processions, Motets and other Sacred Pieces, Liturgical Pieces from the Faenza Codex]*. Polyphonic Music of the Fourteenth Century 12. Monaco: L'Oiseau-Lyre, 1976.

—————, and F. Alberto Gallo, eds. *Italian Sacred and Ceremonial Music [Settings of the Ordinary of the Mass, Other Liturgical Settings, Motets and Ceremonial Pieces, Instrumental Pieces and Fragments]*. Polyphonic Music of the Fourteenth Century 13. Monaco: L'Oiseau-Lyre, 1987.

Flasdieck, Hermann M. "Elisab. *Faburden* 'Fauxbourdon' and NE. *Burden* 'Refrain.'" *Anglia* 74 (1956): 188-238.

—————. "Franzosische Fauxbourdon und frühneuengl. Faburden: Ein sprachwissenschaftlicher Beitrag zur europäischer Musikgeschichte." *Acta Musicologica* 25 (1953): 111-27.

Flotzinger, Rudolf. *Der Discantus-Satz im Magnus liber und seiner Nachfolge*. Wiener Musikwissenshaftliche Beiträge 8. Ed. Erich Schenk. Vienna: Hermann Böhlaus Nachfolger, 1969.

Fox, Charles Warren. "Non-Quartal Harmony in the Renaissance." *Musical Quarterly* 31 (1945): 33-53.

Franco of Cologne. *Ars cantus mensurabilis*. Ed. Gilbert Reaney and André Gilles. Corpus Scriptorum de Musica 18. N.p.: American Institute of Musicology, 1974.

Frobenius, Wolf. *Johannes Boens Musica und seine Konsonanzenlehre*. Freiburger Schriften zur Musikwissenschaft 2. Ed. Hans Heinrich Eggebrecht. Stuttgart: Musikwissenschaftliche Verlags-Gesellschaft, 1971.

—————. Review of Christian Berger, *Hexachord, Mensur und Textstruktur*, Beihefte zum Archiv für Musikwissenschaft 35 (Stuttgart: Franz Steiner, 1992). *Die Musikforschung* 48 (1995): 415-7.

Fuller, Sarah. "On Sonority in Fourteenth-Century Polyphony: Some Preliminary Reflections." *Journal of Music Theory* 30 (1986): 35-70.

—————. "Tendencies and Resolutions: The Directed Progression in *Ars Nova* Music." *Journal of Music Theory* 36 (1992): 229-58.

Gallo, F. Alberto, ed. *Il Codice Musicale 2216 della Biblioteca Universitaria di Bologna*. 2 vols. (facsimile and commentary). Bologna: Forni, 1968.

Gastoué, Amédée. *L'Orgue en France de l'antiquité au début de la périod classique.* Paris: Au Bureau d'edition de la 'Schola,' 1921.

──────, ed. *Le Manuscrit de Musique du Trésor d'Apt (XIVe–XVe Siecle).* La *Société française de Musicologie,* Series 1, vol. 10. Paris: Droz, 1936.

Geering, Arnold. *Die Organa und mehrstimmigen Conductus in den Handschriften des deutschen Sprachgebietes vom 13. bis 16. Jahrhunderts.* Bern: Haupt, 1952.

Gennrich, Friedrich. *Bibliographie der ältesten französischen und lateinischen Motetten. Summa Musicae Medii Aevi* 2. Darmstadt: F. Gennrich, 1957.

──────, ed. *Guillaume de Machaut: Messe de Nostre Dame* [facsimile ed.]. *Summa Musicae Medii Aevi* 1. Darmstadt: F. Gennrich, 1957.

Georgiades, Thrasybulos. *Englische Diskanttraktate aus der ersten Hälfte des 15. Jahrhunderts. Schriftenreihe des musikwissenschaftlichen Seminars der Universität München.* Ed. Rudolf von Ficker. Munich: Musikwissenschaftliches Seminar der Universität München, 1937. (Dissertation, University of Munich, 1935.)

──────. *Sakral und profan in der Musik. Münchner Universitätsreden, Neue Folge, Heft 28.* Munich: Ludwig-Maximillians-Universität, 1960.

──────. "Sprache, Musik, schriftliche Musikdarstellung." *Archiv für Musikwissenschaft* 14 (1957): 223-9.

Gerber, Rudolf, ed. *Guillaume Dufay: Sämtliche Hymnen. Das Chorwerk* 49. Wolfenbüttel: Möseler, 1937.

Gerbert, Martin. *Scriptores ecclesiastici de musica sacra potissimum.* 3 vols. 1784. Reprinted Milan: Bolletino bibliografica musicale, 1931. (Citations identified as follows: *GS*, volume no., column.)

Göllner, Theodor. *Formen früher Mehrstimmigkeit in deutschen Handschriften des späten Mittelalters, Münchner Veröffentlichungen zur Musikgeschichte* 6. Ed. Thrasybulos Georgiades. Tutzing: Schneider, 1961.

Goscalcus [attrib.]. *The Berkeley Manuscript [Tractatus secundus].* 1375. Ed. and trans. Oliver B. Ellsworth. *Greek and Latin Music Theory* [2]. General ed. Thomas J. Mathiesen. Lincoln: University of Nebraska Press, 1984.

Green, Gordon K., ed. *French Secular Music: Ballades and Canons. Polyphonic Music of the Fourteenth Century* 20. Monaco: L'Oiseau-Lyre, 1982.

──────, ed. *French Secular Music: MS Chantilly Musée Condée 564. First Part: Nos. 1–50. Polyphonic Music of the Fourteenth Century* 18. Monaco: L'Oiseau-Lyre, 1981.

──────, ed. *French Secular Music: MS Chantilly Musée Condée 564. Second Part: Nos. 51–100. Polyphonic Music of the Fourteenth Century* 19. Monaco: L'Oiseau-Lyre, 1982.

──────, ed. *French Secular Music: Rondeaux and Misc. Pieces. Polyphonic Music of the Fourteenth Century* 22. Monaco: L'Oiseau-Lyre, 1989.

_____, ed. *French Secular Music: Virelais. Polyphonic Music of the Fourteenth Century* 21. Monaco: L'Oiseau Lyre, 1987.

Günther, Ursula. "Das Ende der Ars nova." *Die Musikforschung* 16 (1963): 105-20.

_____. "Der musikalische Stilwandel der französischen Liedkunst in der zweiten Hälfte des 14. Jahrhunderts." Dissertation, University of Hamburg, 1957.

_____, ed. *The Motets of the Manuscripts Chantilly, Musée Condé, 564 (olim 1047) and Modena, Biblioteca Estense, a.M.5.24 (olim Lat. 568). Corpus Mensurabilis Musicae* 39. N.p.: American Institute of Musicology, 1965.

_____, ed. *Zehn datierbare Kompositionen der Ars Nova*. Hamburg: Musikwissenschaftliches Institut der Universität, 1959.

Guglielmi de Mascaudio [= Guillaume de Machaut]. *Opera I: La Messe de Nostre Dame. Corpus Mensurabilis Musicae* 2. Ed. Guglielmus [Guillaume] de Van. Rome: American Institute of Musicology, 1949.

Guillaume de Machaut. *Guillaume de Machaut: Musikalische Werke.* 4 vols. Ed. Friedrich Ludwig. *Publikationen älterer Musik* I/1-4. 1926–43. Reprint Leipzig: Breitkopf & Härtel, 1954.

Vol. 1 (1926): *Balladen, Rondeaux und Virelais*
Vol. 2 (1928): Introduction and Critical Apparatus
Vol. 3 (1929): *Motetten*
Vol. 4 (1943): *Messe und Lais* (plates destroyed 1943, retypeset 1954, ed. H. Besseler.)

_____. *The Works of Guillaume de Machaut—First Part: Lais – Complainte – Chanson Royale – Motets Nos. 1 to 16.* Ed. Leo Schrade. *Polyphonic Music of the Fourteenth Century* 2 (with separate commentary volume). Monaco: L'Oiseau-Lyre, 1956.

_____. *The Works of Guillaume de Machaut—Second Part: Motets Nos. 17 to 24 – Mass – Double Hoquet – Ballades – Rondeaux – Virelais.* Ed. Leo Schrade. *Polyphonic Music of the Fourteenth Century* 3 (with separate commentary volume). Monaco: L'Oiseau-Lyre, 1956.

Guillielmus Monachus. *De preceptis artis musicae.* Ed. Albert Seay. *Corpus Scriptorum de Musica* 11. N.p.: American Institute of Musicology, 1965.

Haberl, Franz X. "Die römische 'schola cantorum' und die päpstlichen Kapellsänger bis zur Mitte des 16. Jahrhunderts." *Vierteljahrsschrift für Musikwissenschaft* 3 (1887): 189-296.

_____. "Wilhelm du Fay: Monographische Studie über dessen Leben und Werke." *Vierteljahrsschrift für Musikwissenschaft* 1 (1885): 397-530.

Hanboys, Johannes. *Summa.* Ed. and trans. Peter M. Lefferts. *Greek and Latin Music Theory* [7]. General ed. Thomas J. Mathiesen. Lincoln: University of Nebraska Press, 1991, 180-345.

Handschin, Jacques. "Aus der alten Musiktheorie." 5 parts. *Acta Musicologica* 14-17 (1942–45).

_____. "Dur-Moll." *MGG*, vol. 3 (1954), cols. 975-83.

_____. *Musikgeschichte im Überblick.* Lucerne: Heinrichshofen, 1948.

————. "Die Rolle der Nationen in der mittelalterlichen Musikgeschichte." *Schweizerisches Jahrbuch für Musikwissenschaft* 5 (1931): 1-42.

————. "The Summer Canon and Its Background." [Part I], *Musica Disciplina* 3 (1949): 55-94; [Part II] *Musica Disciplina* 5 (1951): 65-113.

————. *Der Toncharakter.* Zurich: Atlantis, 1948.

————. "Über Voraussetzungen, sowie Früh und Hochblüte der mittelalterlichen Mehrstimmigkeit." *Schweizerisches Jahrbuch für Musikwissenschaft* 2 (1927): 5-42.

————. "Was brachte die Notre-Dame-Schule Neues?" *Zeitschrift für Musikwissenschaft* 6 (1924): 545-58.

————. "Eine wenig beachtete Stilrichtung innerhalb der mittelalterlichen Mehrstimmigkeit." *Schweizerisches Jahrbuch für Musikwissenschaft* 1 (1924): 56-75.

————. "Zur Frage der melodischen Paraphrasierung im Mittelalter," *Zeitschrift für Musikwissenschaft* 10 (1928): 513-59.

————. "Zur Geschichte der Lehre vom Organum." *Zeitschrift für Musikwissenschaft* 8 (1926): 321-41.

————. "Zur Geschichte von Notre-Dame." *Acta Musicologica* 4 (1932): 5-17; 49-55; 104-5.

Harrison, Frank Ll. "English Church Music in the Fourteenth Century." *Ars Nova and the Renaissance, 1300-1540. New Oxford History of Music,* Vol. III. General eds. Dom Anselm Hughes and Gerald Abraham. London: Oxford University Press, 1960, 82-106.

————. *Music in Medieval Britain.* London: Routledge & Paul, 1958.

————. "Old-Hall-Manuskript." *MGG,* vol. 9 (1961), cols. 1919-25.

————, ed. *Motets of English Provenance. Polyphonic Music of the Fourteenth Century* 15. Monaco: L'Oiseau-Lyre, 1980.

————, ed. *Motets of French Provenance. Polyphonic Music of the Fourteenth Century* 5. Monaco: L'Oiseau-Lyre, 1968.

————, Ernest H. Sanders, and Peter M. Lefferts, eds. *English Music for Mass and Offices* (I). *Polyphonic Music of the Fourteenth Century* 16. Monaco: L'Oiseau-Lyre, 1983.

————, Ernest H. Sanders, and Peter M. Lefferts, eds. *English Music for Mass and Offices* (II) *and Music for Other Ceremonials. Polyphonic Music of the Fourteenth Century* 17. Monaco: L'Oiseau-Lyre, 1986.

————, and Roger Wibberly, eds. *Manuscripts of Fourteenth-Century English Polyphony: A Selection of Facsimiles. Early English Church Music* 26. London: British Academy, 1981.

Hirshberg, Jeohash. "Hexachordal and Modal Structure in Machaut's Polyphonic Chansons." *Studies in Musicology in Honor of Otto E. Albrecht.* Ed. John Walter Hill. Kassel: Bärenreiter, 1980, 19-42.

Hoffmann, Rolf. "Form und Gestalt in der frühen Kunstmusik, Beiträge zur äesthetischen Wertung der gotischen Musik in Form von Analysen ausgewählter Beispiele der Epoche Leonin bis Machaut." Dissertation, University of Marburg, 1943.

Hoffmann-Axthelm, Dagmar. "Tenor/Contratenor und Bourdon/Fauxbourdon." Dissertation, University of Freiburg im Breisgau, 1970.

Holman, Hans-Jörgen. "Melismatic Tropes in the Responsories for Matins." *Journal of the American Musicological Society* 16 (1963): 36-46.

Hoppin, Richard H. "The Cypriot-French Repertory of the MS Torino, Biblioteca Nazionale, J.II.9." *Musica Disciplina* 11 (1957): 79-125.

————, ed. *The Cypriot-French Repertory of the Manuscript Torino, Biblioteca Nazionale J. II-9.* 4 vols. *Corpus Mensurabilis Musicae* 21. Rome: American Institute of Musicology, 1960.

Hughes, Andrew. "Some Notes on the Early Fifteenth Century Contratenor." *Music and Letters* 50 (1969): 376-82.

————, and Margaret Bent, eds. *The Old Hall Manuscript.* 3 vols. *Corpus Mensurabilis Musicae* 46. N.p.: American Institute of Musicology, 1969.

Hughes, Dom Anselm, ed. *The History of Music in Sound,* vol. 2 [program booklet accompanying set of records]. London: Oxford University Press, 1953.

Hughes, David. "A View of the Passing of Gothic Music: Line and Counterpoint 1380-1430." Ph.D. dissertation, Harvard University, 1956.

Husmann, Heinrich. "Cantus Firmus." *MGG,* vol. 3 (1954), cols. 784-99.

————. "Zur Rhythmik des Trouvèregesanges." *Die Musikforschung* 5 (1952): 110-31.

Idelsohn, Abraham Z. *Gesänge der jemenischen Juden. Hebräisch-Orientalischer Melodienschatz,* vol. 1. Leipzig: Breitkopf & Härtel, 1914.

————. "Parallele zwischen gregorianischen und hebräisch-orientalischen Gesangweisen." *Zeitschrift für Musikwissenschaft* 4 (1922): 515-24.

Jacques de Liège. *Speculum musicae* [c. 1320.] 7 vols. Ed. Roger Bragard. *Corpus Scriptorum de Musica* 3. N.p.: American Institute of Musicology, 1961–73.

Jeppesen, Knud. *Der Palastrinastil und die Dissonanz.* Leipzig: Breitkopf & Härtel, 1925.

————, ed. *Der Kopenhagener Chansonnier.* Copenhagen: Levin & Munksgaard, 1927.

Johannes de Grocheo. *Concerning Music [De musica].* Trans. Albert Seay. Colorado Springs: Colorado College of Music Press, 1973.

————. *Die Quellenhandschiften zum Musiktraktat [De musica] des Johannes de Grocheio*. Ed. and trans. Ernst Rohloff. Leipzig: VEB Deutscher Verlag für Musik, 1967.

Johannes de Muris. [1] *Notitia artis musicae* [2] *Compendium musicae practicae* [with Appendix: *Tractatus de musica*, attrib. Petrus de Sancto Dionysio.] Ed. Ulrich Michels. *Corpus Scriptorum de Musica* 17. N.p.: American Institute of Musicology, 1972.

Johnson, Mildred J. "The Motets of the Codex Ivrea." 2 vols. Ph.D. Dissertation, Indiana University, 1955.

Kammerer, Friedrich. *Die Musikstücke des Prager Kodex XI. E. 9*. Augsburg: B. Filser, 1931.

Kenney, Sylvia. "Ely Cathedral and the Contenance Angloise." *Musik und Geschichte*. Cologne: Arno Volk, 1963, 35-49.

————. "English Discant and Discant in England." *Musical Quarterly* 45 (1959): 26-48.

————. *Walter Frye and the* Contenance Angloise. *Yale Studies in the History of Music* 3. Ed. William G. Waite. New Haven and London: Yale University Press, 1964.

Kiesewetter, Raphael. *Schicksal und Beschaffenheit des weltlichen Gesanges*. Leipzig: Breitkopf und Härtel, 1841.

Kirchner, Leon. "The Lag of Theory Behind Practice." *College Music Symposium* 1 (1961): 23-5.

Koller, Oswald, et al., eds. *Sechs Trienter Codices: Geistliche und weltliche Kompositionen des XV. Jahrhunderts. Dritte Auswahl. DTÖ* 38 (*Jahrgang* XIX/1). Vienna: Universal-Edition, 1912.

Königslöw, Annemarie von. *Die italienische Madrigalisten des Trecento*. Würzburg: Triltsch, 1940. (Dissertation, University of Munich, 1941.)

Korte, Werner. *Die Harmonik des frühen 15. Jahrhunderts in ihrem Zusammenhang mit der Formtechnik*. Münster: Suhrbier & Bröcker, 1929.

————. *Studie zur Geschichte der Musik in Italien*. Kassel: Bärenreiter, 1933.

Korth, Hans-Otto. *Studien zum Kantilenensatz im frühen 15. Jahrhundert. Berliner Musikwissenschaftliche Arbeiten* 29. Eds. Carl Dahlhaus and Rudolf Stephan. Munich–Salzburg: Emil Katzbichler, 1986.

Krenek, Ernst. *Music Here and Now*. New York: Norton, 1939.

Kresteff, Assen. "Die mehrstimmigen Messkompositionen des Codex Ivrea." Dissertation, University of Munich, 1942. (Destroyed in 1944–45; exists only as a six-page summary, 1947.)

Kroyer, Theodor. "Die threnodische Bedeutung der Quart in der Mensuralmusik." *Bericht über den musikwissenschaftlichen Kongreß in Basel* [1924]. Leipzig: Breitkopf & Härtel, 1925, 231-42.

Kühn, Hellmut. *Die Harmonik der Ars nova: Zur Theorie der isorhythmischen Motette. Berliner musikwissenschaftliche Arbeiten* 5. Eds. Carl Dahlhaus and Rudolf Stephan. Munich: Emil Katzbichler, 1973.

Kurth, Ernst. *Grundlagen des linearen Kontrapunktes.* Bern: Krompholz, [1917].

———. *Romantische Harmonik und ihre Krise in Wagners "Tristan."* Berlin: Max Hesse, 1923.

Lang, Hermann. "Begriffsgeschichte des Terminus 'Tonalität.'" Dissertation, University of Freiburg in Breisgau, 1956.

Le Cerf, Georges, and Edmond-Renée Labande. *Instrumente de musique du XVe siècle.* Paris: A. Picard, 1932.

Lederer, Victor. *Über Heimat und Ursprung der mehrstimmigen Tonkunst.* 2 vols. Leipzig: Siegel, 1906.

Leech-Wilkinson, Daniel. *Machaut's Mass: An Introduction* [and Edition]. Oxford: Clarendon Press, 1990.

———. "Machaut's *Rose, lis* and Early Music Analysis." *Music Analysis* 3 (1984): 9-28.

Lefferts, Peter M. "Signature-systems and Tonal Types in the Fourteenth-century French Chanson." *Plainsong and Medieval Music* 4 (1995): 117-47.

Lippman, Edward A. "Music and Space." Ph.D. dissertation, Columbia University, 1952.

Lowinsky, Edward. "Awareness of Tonality in the 16th Century." *Report of the Eighth* [International Musicological Society] *Congress: New York 1961.* 2 vols. Kassel: Bärenreiter, 1961, vol. 1, 44-52.

———. "Canon Technique and Simultaneous Conception in Fifteenth-Century Music: A Comparison of North and South." *Essays on the Music of J.S. Bach and Other Divers Subjects: A Tribute to Gerard Herz.* Ed. Robert L. Weaver. Louisville: University of Louisville Press, 1981, 181-222.

———. "The Concept of Physical and Musical Space in the Renaissance (A Preliminary Study)." *Papers of the American Musicological Society* (1940–41). Ed. Gustave Reese. N.p., 1946, 57-84.

———. *Tonality and Atonality in Sixteenth-Century Music.* Berkeley and Los Angeles: University of California Press, 1961.

Ludwig, Friedrich. "Die mehrstimmige Musik des 14. Jahrhunderts," *Sammelbände der internationalen Musikgesellschaft* 4 (1902–03): 16-69.

———. *Repertorium Organorum Recentioris et Motetorum Vetusissimi Stili.* 3 vols. Halle: Niemeyer, 1910.

———. Review of Victor Lederer, *Über Heimat und Ursprung der mehrstimmigen Tonkunst* (Leipzig: Siegel, 1906). *Zeitschrift der internationalen Musikgesellschaft* 7 (1905–06): 404-14.

Lütolf, Max. *Die mehrstimmigen Ordinarium Missae--Sätze vom ausgehenden 11. bis zur Wende des 13. zum 14. Jahrhundert.* 2 vols. Vol. I: *Studien zu den Quellen und Darstellung der Sätze,* Vol. II, *Übertragungen.* Bern: Paul Haupt, 1970.

Machabey, Armand. *Genèse de la tonalité musicale classique des origines au XVe siècle.* Paris: Masse, 1955.

——————. "Machault." *MGG,* vol. 8 (1960), cols. 1392-9.

Mahrt, William P. "Guillaume Dufay's Chansons in the Phrygian Mode." *Studies in Music from the University of Western Ontario* 5 (1980): 81-98.

Marchetto da Padova. *Lucidarium in arte musicae planae.* Ed. and trans. Jan W. Herlinger. Lincoln: University of Nebraska Press, 1987. (Text also in *GS* III, 64-121.)

——————. *Pomerium in arte musicae mensurate. Corpus Scriptorum de Musica* 6. Ed. Guiseppe Vecchi. N.p.: American Institute of Musicology, 1961. (Text also in *GS* III, 121-88.)

Marggraf, Wolfgang. "Tonalität und Harmonik in der französischen Chanson vom Tode Machauts bis zum frühen Dufay." Dissertation, University of Leipzig, 1964.

——————. "Tonalität und Harmonik in der französischen Chanson zwischen Machaut und Dufay." *Archiv für Musikwissenschaft* 23 (1966): 11-31. (Essay 11.)

——————. "Zur Vorgeschichte der Oktavsprungkadenz." *Die Musikforschung* 18 (1965): 399-400.

Marix, Jeanne. *Histoire de la musique et des musiciens de la Cour de Bourgogne sous le règne de Philipe le Bon (1420–67). Collection d'études musicologiques* 28. Strasbourg: Heitz, 1939.

——————, ed. *Les musiciens de la Cour de Bourgogne au XVe siècle (1420–1467).* Paris: L'Oiseau-Lyre, 1937.

Marrocco, W. Thomas, ed. *Fourteenth-Century Italian Cacce.* Cambridge, Mass.: Mediaeval Academy of America, 1961.

——————, ed. *Italian Secular Music: By Magister Piero, Giovanni da Firenze, Jacopo da Bologna. Polyphonic Music of the Fourteenth Century* 6. Monaco: L'Oiseau-Lyre, 1967.

——————, ed. *Italian Secular Music: By Vincenzo da Rimini, rosso de Chollegrana, Donato da Firenze, Gherardello da Firenze, Lorenzo da Firenze. Polyphonic Music of the Fourteenth Century* 7. Monaco: L'Oiseau-Lyre, 1971.

——————, ed. *Italian Secular Music [Anonymous Madrigales and Cacce; The Works of Niccolò da Perugia]. Polyphonic Music of the Fourteenth Century* 8. Monaco: L'Oiseau-Lyre, 1972.

————, ed. *Italian Secular Music: Bartolino da Padova, Egidius de Francia, Guilelmus de Francia, Don Paolo da Firenze*. *Polyphonic Music of the Fourteenth Century* 9. Monaco: L'Oiseau-Lyre, 1975.

————, ed. *Italian Secular Music* [Andrea da Firenze, Andrea Stefani, Antonellas da Caserta, Anthonius Clericus Apostolicus, Arrigo (Henricus), Jacobelas Bianchi, Bonaiuto Carsini, Ser Feo, Jovannes de Florentia, Gian Toncano, Johannes Fulginatus, Jacopo Pianelaio da Firenze, Johannes Baçus Correçcarius de Bononia, Mattheo da Perugia, Nucella, Franciscus Reynaldus, Antonius Zacharia da Teramo, Magister Zacharias (Chantor), Nicholaus Zacharie, Zaninus de Peraga de Padua, and Attributed Fragments]. *Polyphonic Music of the Fourteenth Century* 10. Monaco: L'Oiseau-Lyre, 1977.

————, ed. *Italian Secular Music* [*Anonymous Ballate, Anonymous Fragments*]. *Polyphonic Music of the Fourteenth Century* 11. Monaco: L'Oiseau-Lyre, 1978.

Martinez [Göllner], Marie Louise. *Die Musik des frühen Trecento*. *Münchner Veröffentlichungen zur Musikgeschichte* 9. Ed. Thrasybulos Georgiades. Tutzing: Schneider, 1963.

McPeek, Gywnn S., ed. *The British Museum Manuscript Egerton 3307*. London: Oxford University Press, 1963.

Meier, Bernhard. "Die Harmonik im cantus-firmus-haltigen Satz des 15. Jahrhunderts." *Archiv für Musikwissenschaft* 9 (1952): 27-44. (Essay 4.)

————. *Die Tonarten der klassischen Vokalpolyphonie*. Utrecht: Oosthoek, Scheltema & Holkema, 1974. English translation as *The Modes of Classical Vocal Polyphony*. Trans. Ellen S. Beebe. New York: Broude Brothers, 1988.

Michels, Ulrich. *Die Musiktraktate des Johannes de Muris*. *Beihefte zum Archiv für Musikwissenschaft* 8. Wiesbaden: Franz Steiner, 1970.

Moll, Kevin N. "Analyzing Four-Voice Vertical Sonorities in Fifteenth-Century Sacred Polyphony: A Comparison of Selected Ockeghem Kyries According to Contrapuntal Theory of Pietro Aron." M.M. thesis, New England Conservatory, 1988. UMI version with minor revisions, 1995.

————. "Structural Determinants in Polyphony for the Mass Ordinary from French and Related Sources (ca. 1320–1410)." Ph.D. dissertation, Stanford University, 1994.

————. "Voice Leading, Sonority, and Contrapuntal Referentiality in Late-Medieval Polyphony." Forthcoming.

Murray, Sir James A.H., and Henry Bradley, et al., eds. "Burden and Faburdon." *A New English Dictionary on Historical Principles*. Oxford: Clarendon Press, 1895.

Obrecht, Jacob. *New Obrecht Edition*. 18 vols. Eds. Christopher Maas, Barton Hudson, and Thomas Noblitt. Utrecht: Koninklijke VNM, 1983–in progress.

————. *Werken van Jacob Obrecht.* 26 vols. (1908–21). Ed. Johannes Wolf. Reprinted in 7 vols., Westmead, GB: Gregg International, 1968.

Ockeghem, Johannes. *Collected Works.* 3 vols. Vol. I, *Masses I–VIII* (1927); Vol. II, *Masses and Mass Sections IX–XVI* (1947). Ed. Dragan Plamenac. Second, corrected editions. N.p.: American Musicological Society, 1959/66. Vol. III, *Motets and Chansons.* Eds. Richard Wexler and Dragan Plamenac. N.p.: American Musicological Society, 1992.

————. *Masses and Mass Sections.* 3 vols. Ed. Jaap van Benthem. Utrecht: Koninklijke VNM, 1994–in progress.

Orel, Alfred. "Einige Grundformen der Motettkomposition im XV. Jahrhundert." *Studien zur Musikwissenschaft* 7 (1920): 48-101.

————. "Die mehrstimmige geistliche (katholische) Musik von 1430–1600." *Handbuch der Musikgeschichte.* 2 vols. Ed. Guido Adler. Berlin: Keller, 1930, vol. 1, 295-357.

Otterbach, Friedemann. *Kadenzierung und Tonalität im Kantilenensatz Dufays. Freiburger Schriften zur Musikwissenschaft* 7. Ed. Hans Heinrich Eggebrecht. Munich: Emil Katzbichler, 1975.

Pelinski, Ramón. "Zusammenklang und Aufbau in den Motetten Machauts." *Die Musikforschung* 28 (1975): 62-71.

Perkins, Leeman L., and Howard Garey, eds. *The Mellon Chansonnier.* 2 vols. New Haven and London: Yale University Press, 1979.

Pesce, Dolores. "A Case for Coherent Pitch Organization in the Thirteenth-Century Double Motet." *Music Analysis* 9 (1990): 287-318.

Petrus dictus Palma ociosa. *Compendium de discantu mensurabili.* 1336. Ed. Johannes Wolf. "Ein Beitrag zur Diskantlehre des 14. Jahrhunderts." *Sammelbände der internationalen Musikgesellschaft* 15 (1913–14): 504-34.

Philippe de Vitry [attrib.]. *Ars nova.* Eds. Gilbert Reaney, André Gilles, and Jean Maillard. *Corpus Scriptorum de Musica* 8. N.p.: American Institute of Musicology, 1964.

Pirro, André. *Histoire de la musique de la fin du XIVe siècle à la fin du XVIe.* Paris: Renouard, 1940.

————. *La musique à Paris sous le règne de Charles VI.* Strasbourg: Heitz, 1930.

Planchart, Alejandro E., ed. *Missae Caput.* New Haven and London: Yale University Press, 1974.

Power, Leonel. *Complete Works.* 2 vols. (projected). Ed. Charles Hamm. Vol. 1: *The Motets. Corpus Mensurabilis Musicae* 50. Rome: American Institute of Musicology, 1969.

Prosdocimus de Beldemandis. *Contrapunctus.* 1412. Ed. and trans. Jan Herlinger. *Greek and Latin Music Theory* [2]. General ed. Thomas J. Mathiesen. Lincoln: University of Nebraska Press, 1984.

Ramsbotham, Alexander. *The Old Hall Manuscript.* Completed by H. B. Collins and Dom Anselm Hughes. 3 vols. Nashdom Abbey: The Plainsong and Mediæval Music Society, 1933–38.

Randel, Don. "Emerging Triadic Tonality in the Fifteenth Century." *Musical Quarterly* 57 (1971): 73-86.

Reaney, Gilbert. "The Ballades, Rondeaux and Virelais of Guillaume de Machaut: Melody, Rhythm and Form." *Acta Musicologica* 27 (1955): 40-58.

————. "Chanson (II)," *MGG*, vol. 2 (1952), cols. 1034-46.

————. "Fourteenth Century Harmony and the Ballades, Rondeaux and Virelais of Guillaume de Machaut." *Musica Disciplina* 7 (1953): 129-46.

————. "Ivrea," *MGG*, vol. 6 (1957), cols. 1581-4.

————. "Modes in the Fourteenth Century, in particular in the Music of Guillaume de Machaut." *Organices Voces: Festschrift Joseph Smits van Waesberghe.* Ed. Pieter Fischer. Amsterdam: I.M.M. Institut voor Middeleeuwse Musziekwetenschap, 1963, 137-43.

————. "Musica Ficta in the Works of Guillaume de Machaut," *L'Ars Nova. Les Colloques de Wégimont* 2 (1955). Paris: Société d'Edition "Les Belles Lettres," 1959, 196-203.

————. "Notes on the Harmonic Technique of Guillaume de Machaut." *Essays in Musicology: A Birthday Offering for Willi Apel.* Ed. Hans Tischler. Bloomington: Indiana University Press, 1968, 63-8.

————. "Transposition and 'Key' Signatures in Late Medieval Music." *Musica Disciplina* 33 (1979): 27-41.

————, ed. [1] *Anonymous: De valore notularum tam veteris quam novae artis (Ms. Paris, Bibl. Nat., lat. 15128;* [2] *Anonymous: Compendium musicae mensurabilis tam veteris quam novae artis (Ms. Paris, Bibl. Nat., lat. 15128);* [3] *Anonymous: De diversis maneriebus in musica mensurabili (Ms. Saint-Dié, Bibl. Municipale 42).* [Three theoretical treatises: *CS* 3, Anon. II, III, IV.] *Corpus Scriptorum de Musica* 30. Neuhausen-Stuttgart: American Institute of Musicology/Hänssler Verlag, 1982.

————, ed. *Early Fifteenth-Century Music.* 7 vols. *Corpus Mensurabilis Musicae* 11. N.p.: American Institute of Musicology, 1955–79.

Reckow, Fritz. *Der Musiktraktat des Anonymus 4.* 2 vols.: Vol. I: *Edition,* Vol. II: *Interpretation der Organum-Purum-Lehre. Beihefte zum Archiv für Musikwissenschaft* 4-5. Wiesbaden: Franz Steiner, 1967.

Reese, Gustave. *Music in the Middle Ages.* New York: Norton, 1940.

Rehm, Wolfgang. *Die Chansons von Gilles Binchois. Musikalische Denkmähler* 2. Mainz: B. Schott's Söhne, 1957.

Reimer, Erich. *Johannes de Garlandia: De mensurabili musica.* 2 vols. Vol. I: *Quellenuntersuchungen und Edition;* Vol. II: *Kommentar und Interpretation der Notationslehre. Beihefte zum Archiv für Musikwissenschaft* 10-11. Wiesbaden: Franz Steiner, 1972.

Riemann, Hugo. *Geschichte der Musiktheorie*. 2 vols. Berlin: Max Hesse, 1898 (2nd ed. 1920). *History of Music Theory*. Trans. Raymond Haggh. Lincoln: University of Nebraska Press, 1962.

—————. *Handbuch der Musikgeschichte*. 2 vols. Leipzig: Breitkopf & Härtel, 1919.

—————, ed. "Anonymi Introductorium musicae," *Monatshefte für Musik-geschichte* 30 (1898): 1-21.

Robert[us] de Handlo. *Regule* [*The Rules*]. Ed. and trans. Peter M. Lefferts. *Greek and Latin Music Theory* [7]. General ed. Thomas J. Mathiesen. Lincoln: University of Nebraska Press, 1991, 80-179.

—————. [*Theoretical Works*.] Ed. Luther Dittmer. *Music Theorists in Translation* 2. Brooklyn: Institute of Medieval Music, 1959.

Rochberg, George. Letter to Editor. *College Music Symposium* 2 (1962): 121-2.

Rohloff, Ernst. *Studien zum Musiktraktat des Johannes de Grocheo*. Leipzig: Reinecke, 1930.

—————. *Der Musiktraktat des Johannes de Grocheo*. Leipzig: Reinecke, 1943.

Rokseth, Yvonne. *Polyphonies du XIIIe siècle, Le Manuscrit H 196 de la Faculté de Médecine du Montpellier*. 4 vols. Paris: L'Oiseau Lyre, 1935–39.

Rosen, W. H. "Die liturgischen Werke des Johannes von Lymburgia." Dissertation, University of Innsbruck, 1929.

Saar, Johannes du. *Het leven en de composities van Jacobus Barbireau*. Utrecht: W. de Haan, 1946.

Sachs, Curt. *Reallexikon der Musikinstrumente*. Berlin: Bard, 1913.

—————. *The Rise of Music in the Ancient World, East and West*. New York: Norton, 1943.

Sachs, Klaus-Jürgen. *Der Contrapunctus im 14. und 15. Jahrhundert: Untersuchungen zum Terminus, zur Lehre und zu den Quellen. Beihefte zum Archiv für Musikwissenschaft* 13. Wiesbaden: Franz Steiner, 1974.

Salop, Arnold. "Jacob Obrecht and the Early Development of Harmonic Polyphony." *Journal of the American Musicological Society* 17 (1964): 288-309.

Sanders, Ernest H. "Cantilena and Discant in 14th-Century England." *Musica Disciplina* 19 (1965): 7-51.

—————. "Duple Rhythm and Alternate Third Mode in the Thirteenth Century." *Journal of the American Musicological Society* 15 (1962): 249-91.

—————. "Medieval English Polyphony and Its Significance for the Continent." Ph.D. dissertation, Columbia University, 1963.

—————. "Peripheral Polyphony of the Thirteenth Century." *Journal of the American Musicological Society* 17 (1964): 261-87.

————. "Die Rolle der englischen Mehrstimmigkeit des Mittelalters in der Entwicklung von cantus-firmus-Satz und Tonalitätsstruktur." *Archiv für Musikwissenschaft* 24 (1967): 24-53. (Essay 12.)

————. "Tonal Aspects of 13th-Century English Polyphony." *Acta Musicologica* 37 (1965): 19-34.

————, ed. *English Music of the Thirteenth and Early Fourteenth Centuries. Polyphonic Music of the Fourteenth Century* 14. Monaco: L'Oiseau-Lyre, 1979.

Sasse, Götz Dietrich. *Die Mehrstimmigkeit der Ars antiqua in Theorie und Praxis.* Leipzig: Noske, 1940.

Schering, Arnold. *Aufführungspraxis alter Musik.* 1931. Reprint Wilhelmshaven: Heinrichshofen, 1975.

————. *Geschichte der Musik in Beispielen.* Leipzig: Breitkopf & Härtel, 1931.

————. "Das kolorierte Orgelmadrigal des Trecento." *Sammelbände der internationalen Musikgesellschaft* 13 (1911–12): 172-90.

————. *Studien zur Musikgeschichte der Frührenaissance.* Leipzig: Kahnt, 1914.

Schlötterer, Reinhold. "Struktur und Kompositionsverfahren in der Musik Palestrinas." *Archiv für Musikwissenschaft* 17 (1960): 40-50.

Schmidt, Günther. "Strukturprobleme der Mehrstimmigkeit im Repertoire von St. Martial." *Die Musikforschung* 15 (1962): 11-39.

————. "Zur Frage des Cantus firmus im 14. und beginnenden 15. Jahrhunderts." *Archiv für Musikwissenschaft* 15 (1958): 230-50. (Essay 6.)

Schofield, Bertram. "A Newly Discovered 15th-Century Manuscript of the English Chapel Royal [Egerton 3307]—Part I." *Musical Quarterly* 32 (1946): 509-36. [For citation of Part II, see under Bukofzer.]

Schrade, Leo, ed. *I.* The *Roman de Fauvel; II.* The *Works of Philippe de Vitry; III. French Cycles of the* Ordinarium Missae. *Polyphonic Music of the Fourteenth Century* 1 (with separate commentary volume). Monaco: L'Oiseau-Lyre, 1956.

————, ed. *The Works of Francesco Landini. Polyphonic Music of the Fourteenth Century* 4. Monaco: L'Oiseau-Lyre, 1958.

Scott, Anne Besser. "The Beginnings of Fauxbourdon: A New Interpretation." *Journal of the American Musicological Society* 24 (1971): 345-63.

Smijers, Albert. *Van Ockeghem tot Sweelinck.* 1939 Amsterdam: Alsbach, 1951.

Solesmes, [Benedictines of the] Abbaye Saint-Pierre de, eds. *Antiphonale Monasticum pro Diurnis Horis* [=AM]. Paris: Desclée, 1934.

————, eds. *Graduale Sacrosanctæ Romanæ Ecclesiæ de Tempore & de Sanctis* [=GR]. Tournai: Desclée, 1974.

————, eds. *Liber Usualis* [=LU]. Tournai: Desclée, 1952.

Sowa, Heinrich. *Ein anonymer glossierter Mensuraltraktat 1279*. Kassel: Bärenreiter, 1930.

Sparks, Edgar. *Cantus Firmus in Mass and Motet: 1420–1520*. Berkeley and Los Angeles: University of California Press, 1963.

Stäblein-Harder, Hanna, ed. *Fourteenth-Century Mass Music in France. Corpus Mensurabilis Musicae* 29 (Commentary and Critical Text under identical title in *Musicological Studies and Documents* 7). N.p.: American Institute of Musicology, 1962.

Stainer, John F.R., and Cecilia Stainer, eds. *Early Bodleian Music*. 2 vols. London: Novello, 1901. (Vol. 3: Critical commentary and facsimiles. Ed. Edward W.B. Nicholson, 1913.)

————, and C[ecilia] Stainer, eds. *Dufay and His Contemporaries: 50 Compositions Transcribed from MS Can. Misc. 213 in the Bodleian Library*. London: Novello, 1898.

Stenzl, Jürg. *Die vierzig Clausulae der Handschrift Paris, Bibliothèque Nationale latin 15139 (Saint Victor–Clausulae). Publikationen der schweizerischen musikforschenden Gesellschaft/Publications de la Société de Musicologie*, II/22. Bern and Stuttgart: Paul Haupt, 1970.

Stephan, Wolfgang. *Die burgundisch–niederländische Mottete zur Zeit Ockeghems*. Kassel: Bärenreiter, 1937.

Strohm, Reinhard. *The Rise of European Music, 1380–1500*. Cambridge: Cambridge University Press, 1993.

Strunk, Oliver, ed. *Source Readings in Music History*. 1950. Reprinted in 5 vols, New York: Norton, 1965.

Sweeney, Cecily, and André Gilles, eds. [1] *Anonymous: De musica mensurabili*; [2] *Anonymous: De semibrevibus caudatis. Corpus Scriptorum de Musica* 13. N.p.: American Institute of Musicology, 1971.

Thomson, William. "The Problem of Tonality in Pre-Baroque and Primitive Music." *Journal of Music Theory* 2 (1958): 36-46.

Tinctoris, Johannes. *The Art of Counterpoint [Liber de arte contrapuncti]*. 1477. Ed. and trans. Albert Seay. [Rome:] American Institute of Musicology, 1961.

————. *Opera omnia*. Ed. W. Melin. *Corpus Mensurabilis Musicae* 18. Rome: American Institute of Musicology, 1976.

————. *Opera theoretica*. 3 vols. Ed. Albert Seay. *Corpus Scriptorum de Musica* 22. N.p.: American Institute of Musicology, 1975.

Tischler, Hans, ed. *The Montpellier Codex*. 4 Parts. Part 4 ed. and trans. Susan Stakel and Joel C. Relihan. *Recent Researches in the Music of the Middle Ages and Early Renaissance* 2-8. Madison: A-R Editions, 1978-85.

Tolnay, Charles de. *Le maître de Flémalle et les frères van Eyck*. Brussels: Editions de la connaissance, 1939.

Treitler, Leo. "Tone System in the Secular Works of Guillaume Dufay." *Journal of the American Musicological Society* 18 (1965): 131-69.

Tröller, Josef. "Untersuchungen zur Satztechnik von den Niederländern bis zu Monteverdi." Dissertation, University of Heidelberg, 1953.

Trowell, Brian. "Faburdon and Fauxbourdon." *Musica Disciplina* 13 (1959): 43-78.

——. "A Fourteenth-century Ceremonial Motet and Its Composer." *Acta Musicologica* 29 (1957): 65-75.

Trumble, Ernest. "Authentic and Spurious Faburden." *Revue Belge de Musicologie* 14 (1960): 3-29.

Tunstede, Simon [formerly attrib.]. *Quatuor principalia. CS* IV, 200-98; another version of Part IV of this treatise exists as *De musica antiqua et nova*, Anonymous 1, *CS* III, 334-64.

Ursprung, Otto. *Die katholischen Kirchenmusik*. Potsdam: Athenaion, 1931.

Van, Guillaume de. "Inventory of Manuscript Bologna, Liceo Musicale, Q15 (*olim* 37)." *Musica Disciplina* 2 (1948): 231-57.

——. "A Recently Discovered Source of Early Fifteenth Century Polyphonic Music [The Aosta Codex]," *Musica Disciplina* 2 (1948): 5-74.

Vecchi, Guissepe. *Uffici Drammatici Padovani, Biblioteca dell' "Archivum Romanum,"* series 1, vol. 41. Florence: Olschki, 1954.

Wagner, Peter. "Die Diatonisierung des gregorianischen Gesanges durch das Liniensystem." *Rassegna gregoriana* 3 [1903]: 245 ff. This study also appeared in two other journals from 1904; see Willi Apel, *Gregorian Chant* (Bloomington: Indiana University Press, 1958), 108, note 13.

——. *Geschichte der Messe*. Leipzig: Breitkopf & Härtel, 1913.

Werner, Eric. *The Sacred Bridge*. London and New York: Dobson, 1959.

Wilkins, Nigel E., ed. *A 15th-Century Repertory from the Codex Reina (Paris, Bibl. Nat., Nov. Acq. Fr., 6771). Corpus Mensurabilis Musicae* 37. N.p.: American Institute of Musicology, 1966.

——, ed. *A 14th-Century Repertory (52 Ballades, Virelais, Rondeaux) from the Codex Reina (Paris, Bibl. Nat., Nov. Acq. Fr., 6771). Corpus Mensurabilis Musicae* 36. N.p.: American Institute of Musicology, 1966.

Wilson, David F. *Music of the Middle Ages: Style and Structure*. New York: Schirmer, 1990.

Wingell, Richard J. "Anonymous XI (CS III): An Edition, Translation, and Commentary." 3 vols. Ph.D. dissertation (Music), University of Southern California, 1973.

Wiora, Walter. "Älter als die Pentatonik." *Studia Memoriae Belae Bartok Sacra*. Budapest: Academia Scientarum Hungaricae, 1957, 185-208.

——. *Europäische Volksmusik und abendländische Tonkunst. Die Musik im alten und neuen Europa* 1. Kassel: Hinnenthal, 1957.

————. "Der mittelalterliche Liedkanon." *Kongress-Bericht Lüneburg 1950*. Ed. Hans Albrecht, et al. Kassel and Basel: Bärenreiter, n.d., 71-5.

————. "Natur der Musik? Unnatur heutiger Musik?" *Musikalische Zeitfragen* 10. *Die Natur der Musik als Problem der Wissenschaft*. Ed. Walter Wiora. Kassel and Basel: Bärenreiter, 1962, 7-18.

————. "Der tonale Logos." *Die Musikforschung* 4 (1951): 1-35; 153-75.

————. *Die vier Weltalter der Musik*. Stuttgart: W. Kohlhammer, 1961.

————. "Zur Grundlegung der allgemeinen Musikgeschichte." *Deutsches Jahrbuch der Musikwissenschaft* 1 (1956): 76-110.

————, ed. *Die Ausbreitung des Historismus über die Musik. Studien zur Musikgeschichte des 19. Jahrhunderts* 14. Regensburg: Bosse, 1969.

Wolf, Johannes. *Geschichte der Mensural-Notation von 1250–1460*. 3 vols. Leipzig: Breitkopf & Härtel, 1904 (Reprint, Hildesheim: Olds, 1963).

————. *Handbuch der Notationskunde*. 2 vols. Leipzig: Breitkopf & Härtel, 1913/19.

————, ed. *Musica Practica Bartolomei Rami de Pareia* [1482]. *Beiheft der internationalen Musikgesellschaft* 2. Leipzig: Breitkopf & Härtel, 1901.

Yudkin, Jeremy. *The Music Treatise of Anonymous IV: A New Translation*. *Musicological Studies and Documents* 41. Neuhausen-Stuttgart: American Institute of Musicology/Hänssler Verlag, 1985.

Zaminer, Frieder. *Der Vatikanische Organum Traktat, Ottobibliothek lat. 3025: Organum–Praxis der frühen Notre Dame–Schule und ihrer Vorstufen*. *Münchner Veröffentlichungen zur Musikwissenschaft* 2, ed. Thrasybulos Georgiades. Tutzing: Schneider, 1959.

GENERAL INDEX

This index does not include every mention of ubiquitous terms or figures (e.g., "tenor" or "Dufay"), but it does attempt to account for the running subjects, as well as names of individuals, places, musical compositions, sources, and theory treatises. It should be noted, however, that the variegated shades of meaning associated with certain technical terms cannot adequately be reflected here (for a full account of these difficulties, see the editor's introduction, Part II, sections B–D, in conjunction with the appendix). Excluded entirely from the index are the following: 1) German terms used without accompanying English equivalents (this affects the editor's introduction only); 2) material in footnotes of a strictly documentary nature; and 3) all prefatory material, including the editor's prefaces introducing the numbered essays. In the indexing of contemporary manuscripts, compositions, and theoretical writings, every effort has been made to incorporate the most recent research on sources and attributions; to this end I have updated the entries wherever it proved practicable to do so. Hence, *RISM* sigla often augment manuscript identifications as originally given by the author, and many citations of works and sources have been considerably expanded. It is almost inevitable, however, that some entries will convey information that is anachronistic in light of current usage. Note also that entries of personal names are standardized according to modern format; thus, Jacques de Liège is listed as "Liège, Jacques de," rather than by his first name, as is done in the bibliography above.

COPYRIGHT PERMISSION

Foreword: Göllner, Theodor (newly written for this volume, 1996).

1   Besseler, Heinrich. "Dufay Schöpfer des Fauxbourdons." *Acta Musicologica* 20 (1948): 26-45.

2   Ficker, Rudolf von. "Zur Schöpfungsgeschichte des Fauxbourdon." *Acta Musicologica* 23 (1951): 93-123.

3   Besseler, Heinrich. "Tonalharmonik und Vollklang: Eine Antwort an Rudolf von Ficker." *Acta Musicologica* 24 (1952): 131-46.

4   Meier, Bernhard. "Die Harmonik im cantus-firmus-haltigen Satz des 15. Jahrhunderts." *Archiv für Musikwissenschaft* 9 (1952): 27-44.

5   Apfel, Ernst. "Der klangliche Satz und der freie Diskantsatz im 15. Jahrhundert." *Archiv für Musikwissenschaft* 12 (1955): 297-313.

6   Schmidt, Günther. "Zur Frage des Cantus firmus im 14. und beginnenden 15. Jahrhundert." *Archiv für Musikwissenschaft* 15 (1958): 230-50.

7   Apfel, Ernst. "Zur Entstehung des realen vierstimmigen Satzes in England." *Archiv für Musikwissenschaft* 17 (1960): 81-99.

8   Apfel, Ernst. "Über den vierstimmigen Satz im 14. und 15. Jahrhunderts." *Archiv für Musikwissenschaft* 18 (1961): 34-51.

9   Apfel, Ernst. "Die klangliche Struktur der spätmittelalterlichen Musik als Grundlage der Dur-Moll Tonalität." *Die Musikforschung* 15 (1962): 212-27.

10   Apfel, Ernst. "Spätmittelalterliche Klangstruktur und Dur-Moll Tonalität," *Die Musikforschung* 16 (1963): 153-6.

11   Marggraf, Wolfgang. "Tonalität und Harmonik in der französischen Chanson zwischen Machaut und Dufay." *Archiv für Musikwissenschaft* 23 (1966): 11-31.

12   Sanders, Ernest H. "Die Rolle der englischen Mehrstimmigkeit des Mittelalters in der Entwicklung von Cantus-firmus-Satz und Tonalitätsstruktur." *Archiv für Musikwissenschaft* 24 (1967): 24-53.